SUMMER JOBS FOR STUDENTS 1998

FEB 1 0 1999

47th Edition

Peterson's

Princeton, New Jersey

Peterson's Career Focus Books: helping people make successful job choices, maximize career potential, and stay competitive in today's workplace.

Visit Peterson's Education Center and Summer Options sector on the Internet (World Wide Web) at www.petersons.com

Copyright © 1997 by Peterson's

Previous editions published under the title *The Summer Employment Directory* © 1951–1978 by National Directory Service, © 1979–1989 by Writer's Digest Books, and © 1991–1992 by Peterson's Guides, Inc.; and the title *Summer Jobs* © 1993–1995 by Peterson's Guides, Inc.; and under the title *Summer Jobs for Students* © 1996 by Peterson's Inc.

Production Editor: Diane Hepburn   Compositor: Linda Williams
Research Analyst: Dan Karleen   Programmer: Barbara Dedecker
Data Analyst: Dan Margolin

ISSN 1064–6701
ISBN 1-56079-836-X

Printed in the United States of America

10   9   8   7   6   5   4   3   2   1

399-9548

CONTENTS

HOW TO USE THIS BOOK

What are you going to do to make this summer special? You already have a good start. *Summer Jobs for Students 1998* is an indispensable catalog of interesting and enriching summer work experiences for students, teachers, or anyone looking for summer employment. You'll find detailed, up-to-date information on more than 25,000 positions offered across the country—from counselors, instructors, and lifeguards to theater stagehands, wilderness guides, and office clerical workers. The list is long, and many of these jobs require little or no previous experience.

SEARCH BY YOUR INTERESTS

There are many different ways you can use *Summer Jobs for Students 1998* to find the right work opportunity:

- If your primary consideration is the geographic location of a job (if, for instance, you'd like to spend the summer working near your hometown or in a particular area of the country), you can turn directly to the **State-By-State Listings**, where employers are listed alphabetically by state.

- The section of **Canadian Listings** features summer employment opportunities in Canada. The section, which begins on page 311, profiles more than twenty employers offering hundreds of summer jobs to young adults.

- If you're interested in working at a U.S. national park, turn to the special section beginning on page 21 that tells you all about job opportunities for U.S. citizens at National Park Service sites in regions throughout the country.

Another way you can put *Summer Jobs for Students 1998* to work for you is by looking for jobs according to the services they provide. The opportunities featured in this book are divided into 25 main areas, which are listed in the **Category Index** at the back of the book (beginning on page 321). If you know, for instance, that you want to work at a summer camp that specializes in programs for persons with physical disabilities, turn to the **Category Index** for a listing of all such camps that are featured in the book. Use the following list of categories as your guide:

- Academic Programs
- Ballet Programs
- Camps—academic, horsemanship, outdoor adventure and travel, performing and fine arts, religious, special needs, sports, general activities, and special focus camps serving those with behavioral disabilities, developmental disabilities, learning disabilities, physical disabilities, and visual impairments
- Conference Centers
- Conservation and Environmental Programs
- Employment Clearinghouses
- Expeditions, Guide Trips, and Tours

- Government Agencies
- Ranches
- Resorts
- Sports Touring Programs
- State and National Parks
- Theaters/Summer Theaters
- Theme and Amusement Parks/Attractions
- Volunteer Programs
- Yacht Clubs

Of course, if you already know the name of the employer you want to contact, you can simply turn to the **Employer Index** for a page reference to the description of that employer's job opportunities.

If you're interested in knowing what kinds of jobs are most readily available, turn to the **Job Titles Index**. It lists the most frequently cited job titles in the book and the facilities that offer them.

READ THE EMPLOYER PROFILES

Once you have found an employer that interests you, you can read about the opportunities they provide. The **General Information** section of each profile provides details about the location, size, focus, and special features of the facility. You can check the **Profile of Summer Employees** to get an idea of who your coworkers might be. **Employment Information** includes descriptions of available jobs as well as important details about when positions are available, salaries, and special requirements. Any **Benefits** of the workplace, such as gratuities, laundry facilities, health insurance, or the possibility of college credit, are also noted. The **Contact** paragraph provides you with information on how the employer wants you to apply for a position and the application deadline. Finally, most of the employers have chosen to write an additional narrative description of the kinds of employees they are looking for; you can get a good feel for many of the facilities in these **From the Employer** statements.

International applicants for any of the positions found in this guide should pay special attention to valuable information found in both the **Employment Information** and **Contact** sections. If international students are encouraged to apply for available positions, a sentence stating such will appear at the end of the Employment Information section. The Contact section may list any special application procedures required of international applicants, such as referral through an agency designed to handle these applications. Additional information at the end of a profile may also describe restrictions or requirements for international applications.

The data in this book were collected in the spring and summer of 1997 from employers anxious to fill staff vacancies with high-quality, motivated workers. A representative of each employer completed a questionnaire to describe the job opportunities to be offered in the summer of 1998. Although Peterson's does not assume responsibility for the hiring policies or actions of these employers, we believe that the information listed is accurate and up-to-date. But you should always check with the employer first. A phone call to the contact person listed in the profile or a visit to their Web site (address is in the **Contact** section) will provide you with even more information about the employer and the type of employment that is available.

LEARN HOW TO APPLY

Summer Jobs for Students 1998 features four essays that will provide additional help in your search for a summer job. If you are just learning how to apply for a summer job, be sure to read "Looking for a Summer Job?" beginning on page 8. International job hunters are strongly urged to read "International Applications for Summer Employment and Training" beginning on page 14. "Working for the National Park Service" gives you all the information you'll need if you're a U.S. citizen considering a summer job at a U.S. National Park Service site; this article, which begins on page 21, tells you about the positions offered, job requirements, participating sites, and application contacts. "Do You Want to Work Temporarily in Canada . . ." tells you the steps you need to take before you begin a summer job in Canada; the article, which begins on page 34, outlines procedures you and your Canadian employer must follow for you to receive employment authorization.

Remember, all the employers listed in this book are actively looking for your help—they are waiting for your application! We hope that this book will help make your summer a fun, interesting—and profitable—experience.

ABBREVIATION CHART

The following are abbreviations commonly used in this book:

ACA	American Camping Association
AHSE	Association for Horsemanship Safety and Education
ALS	Advanced Life Saving
ARC	American Red Cross
BUNAC	British University North American Club
CAA	Camp Archery Association
CIT	Counselor-in-training
CPR	Cardiopulmonary Resuscitation
EMR	Educationally Mentally Retarded
EMT	Emergency Medical Technician
EOE	Equal Opportunity Employer
HSA	Horsemanship Safety Association
ICCP	International Camp Counselors Program
IDC	Instructor Development Center
LD	Learning Disabled
LPN	Licensed Practical Nurse
NAUI	National Association of Underwater Instructors
NRA	National Rifle Association
PADI	Professional Association of Diving Instructors
RN	Registered Nurse
SASE	Self-addressed, stamped envelope
SCI	Small Craft Instructor
SLS	Senior Life Saving
WSI	Water Safety Instructor

LOOKING FOR A SUMMER JOB?

by Shirley J. Longshore

As an older teenager or young adult concerned about your present and future, working at a job—for pay or not—is an important, if not mandatory, summer undertaking. If you've never done it, looking for a job may seem intimidating—but it's not. Hundreds of thousands of young people *do* find interesting and rewarding jobs every summer.

Many young adults turn to summer employment not only to pay for college expenses but also to earn spending money or even to help out their families. Competition for these jobs can be stiff, but keep in mind that summer employment can provide the background you'll need to compete aggressively both with other college-bound students when applying to schools *and* with other job seekers when looking for a full-time job. Guidance counselors, admissions officers, and corporate human-resource managers look for college and job applications that display outside activities, work experiences, and additional credentials. A good summer job record is a plus that colleges and employers now routinely expect to see.

"Strong academics are not enough any more," says a college admissions officer at a small university in Georgia. "We're looking very hard at what else students are doing, how they use their time, what other skills they are acquiring. Even the less competitive colleges are becoming much more demanding in evaluating prospective students." If you don't need to earn money, working as a volunteer will also give you a competitive edge.

GET STARTED NOW

Landing the summer job that will add to the bottom line in your bank book and bolster your resume is harder than it used to be. "The summer job market has dried up a lot. There are fewer jobs listed than ever," says a high school guidance counselor in New Jersey. And the competition can be tough, but you can overcome these obstacles. To increase your chance for success, you must be willing to work at mounting an organized, targeted job search; the sooner you get started, the better!

"The key is to start early," emphasizes the personnel director of a large state park that employs many young people each summer. "You can't wait until May and then see what's around, because there truly won't be anything left. I see this over and over. We have all of our hiring done, and then we get call after call and letter after letter from panicked, although qualified, students who are just applying much too late." A job seeker fortunate enough to get his or her application in early and who is hired also has the opportunity to ensure a somewhat more secure summer job situation throughout the rest of high school or college; those who prove themselves valuable will likely have first crack at getting the job back the following summer. To help you with your search,

Shirley J. Longshore is a writer, editor, and communications consultant. Her articles about business, work, and education have appeared in national publications.

this book lists more than 550 U.S. and Canadian employers who are looking for qualified, hard-working people to fill specific openings on their staffs.

Prepare Your Resume and Cover Letter

Your resume should be limited to one page and must communicate your strong points by detailing relevant experience and describing your background. It should present you in a way that will interest an employer enough to arrange an interview.

"I had a student this year who said he didn't have to be convinced that a summer job was important, but he didn't have a clue how to begin looking for one," says a guidance counselor at a large public high school in Florida. "High school students look at me like I'm from outer space when I tell them that, first, they should write a resume. They say things like: 'What would I put on it? I have no real skills; I've never done much of anything. A resume is for older people looking for real jobs.' But when we look at the clubs they have participated in, after-school activities, volunteer work, and baby-sitting jobs, we can often work up quite a list together. It gives young people an idea of what they have to offer an employer."

Everyone has the makings of a resume in their background—even those just starting out. You simply have to look at your past thoroughly. Don't overlook any activities that could enhance your credentials. Don't forget the computer knowledge you gained in school. Do you teach Sunday school? Have you worked in your town's recreation program? Do you assist in a shelter for the homeless or collect newspapers for recycling? All of these activities require skills that can be translated into proven experience for an employer. At the very least, participating in these kinds of activities will show that you are focused, well-rounded, community-minded, responsible, and trustworthy.

A resume should also list people who will give you good recommendations. (Before listing anyone as a reference, check to make sure he or she is willing to be listed.) To prepare a reference list, create a separate page with your name, address, and phone number followed by the names, addresses, and phone numbers of 2 to 4 people who will verify your skills and testify to the qualities that will convince the employer to hire you.

You may want to tailor your resume to appeal to a particular employer—using a computer makes this easy. Perhaps you are intrigued by a counselor's job at an academic-oriented camp. The resume for that position should contain an item that mentions that you put the skill you show in math to good use tutoring a third-grader after school. Phrase the item: "Demonstrated maturity and responsibility tutoring third-grade student in math in after-school sessions." With this entry on your resume, you are showcasing both a skill at an academic subject and experience working with a younger person. If you're using a computer, this item can easily be deleted from the resume you'll send in application to a job that doesn't involve academics or supervising children.

Your resume should also include items mentioning any athletics training you have had, such as swimming lessons, ballet classes, and team memberships. These activities demand those qualities employers look for—self-discipline, high energy, dedication, and desire for self-improvement.

A college student from Massachusetts didn't think his experience as head cook for the school's international club's dinners was very important. "I just did it for fun," the student admitted. "But then I saw an opening for an assistant chef at a lodge for the summer between my junior and senior years, and I realized I could parlay that experience into a job. It worked."

The best resume is one that is straightforward and clearly presented. If you're composing one for the first time, you should take advantage of the knowledge of older siblings or friends—talk with them and ask to see their resume. Remember, it must state relevant information about you and your skills.

This is where a strong cover letter comes into play. A cover letter serves as your introduction to a potential employer and, hopefully, will interest him or her enough to want to read your resume. A cover letter should draw the reader's attention to those experiences that best relate to the qualifications required for a particular job. For example, if a camp is looking for counselors to lead activities, your letter should mention your involvement in school plays (an item on your resume) and suggest that this experience would enable you to confidently instruct campers in drama or in a stage production. Although a cover letter should be brief and to the point, it doesn't hurt to help the resume reader along by flagging pertinent information. Sell yourself!

MY RESUME IS READY—NOW WHAT?

After you've identified your skills and written your resume, you need to consider what you want to get out of your summer job. Ask yourself: What do I enjoy doing? What am I really good at? What would I like to learn more about? What work experience would enhance my chances at future opportunities? Do I love to be outdoors in the summer, or do I really prefer the air-conditioned comfort of an office? Is this the time to go far away from home, or would I rather stay close by? Do I need to make money? Keep in mind that some jobs may be too costly for you. If you need to earn money to cover college expenses, for instance, you may not want your pay to be eaten away by transportation and room-and-board costs.

After answering the questions above, turn to the **Category Index** to zero in on the kinds of opportunities that make sense for you. The listings in *Summer Jobs for Students 1998* go beyond what you'll find in your local community through the usual pavement-pounding, want-ad-answering, asking-around methods. The jobs in this guide are located all over North America. Some may be in your geographic area, and others may be hundreds or thousands of miles away. Included are camps, resorts, summer theaters, conservation and environmental programs, lodges, ranches, conference and training centers, national parks, and amusement and theme parks that normally hire many young people for each busy summer season. The possibilities are endless, so you don't have to worry about ending up in a job in which you have little interest.

Keep in mind that many summer employers provide on-site training in the particular skills needed for their jobs, so don't be discouraged if your skills don't match exactly. These people are generally looking for qualities other than direct experience— motivation, interest, and the desire to learn. When you read about a position, *read between the lines* to see what kind of employee is really being sought.

WINNING INTERVIEWS

Once you have contacted the employers you'd like to work for, think about how you'll present yourself at interviews. An interview may take place over the phone or in a face-to-face meeting. In either case, it's an opportunity for you and the employer to get a better sense of each other.

Remember, an interview goes both ways. It is also an opportunity for you to ask any questions and to decide whether you really want the job. You may want to ask about the specific duties, hours, pay, what benefits are provided (such as room and board), and when hiring decisions will be made. Always write a brief, sincere thank-you note to follow up an interview, even if it was very short or conducted by telephone.

It's important to dress appropriately for an in-person interview. Bring with you any credentials that are required (i.e., working papers, birth certificate, school records, or Social Security card). If you don't have a Social Security card, you can—and should— get one right away. You can start the process by calling 800-772-1213, the nationwide toll-free number for Social Security information.

Finding a good summer job opportunity is not an impossible task. There are jobs out there. You have a good shot at landing one if you prepare your resume, start going after the jobs you know about early, and present yourself both on paper and in person in the best possible light.

SAMPLE COVER LETTER

ANNE MEREDITH

421 South Street
Apartment 2C
City Line, NJ 07685
821-663-4121

218 Tower Hall
State University
Brighton, PA 62451
580-341-6840

January 4, 1998

Name of person in charge, title
Name of camp or resort
Street address
Town, state, zip code

Dear Mr. or Ms. (last name):

I saw the listing describing your summer program in Summer Jobs for Students 1998. It states that you hire a Waterfront Director, a summer position for which I would like to apply.

As you will see from the attached resume, I am very qualified for such a position. I taught swimming, was a lifeguard, coached a swim team, and swam on my high school team for four years. I have been named to the Junior Varsity Swim Team at State University in both my freshman and sophomore years.

I am experienced at supervising and teaching both adults and children in swimming and waterfront safety. I enjoy working with people and sharing my expertise with them. Your summer program sounds like one in which my skills would be fully utilized.

I would appreciate the opportunity to explore this position with you further. I would be happy to talk with you by telephone or to arrange a personal interview during my winter break, which is until the end of this month.

Thank you for your consideration. I look forward to hearing from you soon. You can reach me at my home number in City Line until January 27th.

Sincerely,

Anne Meredith

SAMPLE RESUME

ANNE MEREDITH

421 South Street   218 Tower Hall
Apartment 2C   State University
City Line, NJ 07685   Brighton, PA 62451
821-663-4121   580-341-6840

EDUCATION: State University, Brighton, PA
                  Expected date of graduation, 1999
                  Major: Biology GPA: 3.4 Degree track: B.S.

HONORS: Dean's List, first semester, State University
                  Science Scholar Award, City Line High School, 1995
                  State Merit Scholarship Winner

EXPERIENCE: Head Lifeguard/Swimming Coach
                  River Edge Athletic Club, Edgeton, NJ
                  Summer 1996 and 1997
                      Responsibilities included scheduling and overseeing the
                      summer staff of ten lifeguards and serving as one of two
                      coaches for the club's competitive children's swim team (35
                      members). I also gave private swimming lessons to club
                      members.

                  Lifeguard
                  YWCA, City Line, NJ; Winter 1995–96

                  Swimming Instructor/Lifeguard
                  River Edge Athletic Club; Summer 1995 and 1994

                  Assistant Swimming Instructor (3- to 5-year-olds)
                  YWCA, City Line, NJ; Summer 1993

                  Day Camp Helper (9- and 10-year-olds)
                  YWCA, City Line, NJ; Summer 1992

ACTIVITIES: Swim Team, Junior Varsity, State University, 1996–97
                  Glee Club, State University, 1996–97
                  Swim Team, YWCA, City Line, NJ, 1994–95
                      Captain, 1994–95
                  Junior, Senior Chorus, City Line High School, 1993–95
                  Youth Group, St. John's Church, 1993–96
                      President, 1996
                  Springvale Nursing Home, volunteer visitor, 1995–96

SKILLS: Red Cross Certification, Lifesaving
                  Fluency in Spanish
                  Teaching experience with children and adults
                  Computer skills: MS-DOS, WordPerfect

WORDS OF ADVICE

by Rob Kyff

Just as a soup stain on your tie or blouse during a job interview can cost you an offer, even a seemingly "tiny" grammar or usage error also can land you in the soup.

Which verbal soup stains are most fatal? These 10 mistakes are guaranteed to make most interviewers wince:

"Irregardless"—Irrespective of what anyone tells you, and regardless of what your Uncle Elbert says, don't use "irregardless." It's not a word. Wince factor: 5 (on a scale of 1–5).

"Myself" for "me"—Don't use "myself" when a simple "me" will do, as in, "If you'd like more details about my 200-page thesis on cheese bacteria in 14th-century Luxembourg, just contact my professor or myself." Wince factor: 3.

"Graduate college"—Interviewers will hear fingernails scratching on blackboards if you say "I graduated college." Say, "I was graduated from college," or "I graduated from college," and they'll believe you did. Wince factor:4.

"Less" for "fewer"—Saying, "I have less F's on my transcript than it seems," can be less than impressive. Use "fewer" for countable items ("fewer F's"). Wince factor: 2.

"Between you and I"—Just between you and me, don't use "I" where the objective case "me" is required. Wince factor:4.

Corporatespeak—Unless you want to end up Dilberting a cubicle at a brain-dead corporation, junk bureaucratic jargon such as "empowerment," "access," "planful," "actualize," "proactive," "facilitate," "interface," "paradigm," and "parameter." Wince factor: 3.

Hopefully—Many people still bristle at the use of the sentence-modifying adverb "hopefully" to mean "it is to be hoped." Hopefully, the snobby prejudice against this handy usage is ending, but beware. Wince factor: 1.

Like—Like, don't use, like, this word to, like, fill gaps in your, like, sentences. Wince factor: 5. And don't use "like" as a conjunction, either. Remember, do "as I say," not "like I say." Wince factor: 2.

Very unique—Describe your rare collection of celebrities' used chewing gum as "unique," not "very unique." "Unique" already means "incomparable" or "one of a kind," and can't be intensified. Wince factor: 2.

Sweaty palms—While it's perfectly OK to have sweaty palms during a job interview, don't mention them. (And if you must, remember it's "pahms," not "palms.") Wince factor: 1.

Rob Kyff is a teacher and writer in West Hartford, Connecticut.

INTERNATIONAL APPLICATIONS FOR SUMMER EMPLOYMENT AND TRAINING

by Robert M. Sprinkle and Elizabeth Chazottes

In an effort to provide the most accurate guidance possible for students from outside the United States, Peterson's has asked each employer listed in *Summer Jobs for Students 1998* if applications will be accepted from international students who want to come to the United States for the summer. Peterson's has also asked if the employer is willing to undertake the necessary steps—either directly with the U.S. Immigration and Naturalization Service (INS) or through an educational exchange organization—to make it possible for the student to secure a proper U.S. visa that will allow legal employment while in the United States. **International applicants should read each profile carefully for this information before applying.**

There are significant penalties for employers who hire foreign nationals illegally. Foreign nationals can be deported and barred from returning to the United States for violating their visa status. If an employer in the United States offers you an internship, make certain that both you *and* the employer know and follow the requirements of U.S. law *before* you leave home.

PASSPORTS

In order to secure a U.S. visa that permits summer employment/training, you must have a valid passport from your own country. Your passport must be valid for six months beyond the date on which you expect to leave the United States. A number of countries have special "passport validity" agreements with the United States under which a passport is considered to be valid for six months beyond the expiration date stated in the passport. In order to avoid last-minute problems, you should contact U.S. consular officials as early as possible to determine the exact requirement for your country.

VISAS

Unlike many countries, the United States does not control the activities of noncitizens by the use of work permits, residence permits, police registration, or other documents.

Robert M. Sprinkle is the former Executive Director, Emeritus, Association for International Practical Training and has written numerous articles on international practical training, overseas employment, and student travel.

Elizabeth Chazottes is the Executive Director and CEO of the Association for International Practical Training.

Instead, what an individual may or may not do while in the United States depends entirely on the specific type of visa granted. As a result, the United States has the world's most complex visa system—there are currently forty-five different kinds of nonimmigrant visas! (Although an individual may be a full-time student in his/her own country, a "student" visa for admission to the United States applies *only* to people attending an American school for full-time study. Thus, the three kinds of student visas cannot be used by a student coming to the United States for summer work or internship experience.)

As a general rule, there are only four U.S. visas that are likely to be suitable for students coming to the United States for summer employment or training:

H-2B "TEMPORARY WORKER"

The procedures for this visa require a two-step process to be followed by the employer. First, a "temporary labor" certification must be secured through the state employment service of the area where the individual will work. Following rules established by the U.S. Department of Labor, the employer must submit evidence to demonstrate that: (a) a real job exists (i.e., not a job made up to suit the background of the foreign national); (b) substantial efforts have been made to fill the job with a U.S. citizen; (c) no qualified U.S. citizens can be found for the job; and (d) the job to be filled is of a one-time, seasonal, peak-load, or intermittent nature. Once the "labor certification" has been granted, the employer must then file an application with the U.S. Immigration and Naturalization Service District Office covering the area where the person will work.

H-3 "TRAINEE"

This visa does not require a "labor certification." The employer must submit the H-3 application to the Immigration Service District Office covering the area where the person will work. The application must include a detailed training plan to show what the trainee will do in the United States, including how much time will be spent in "classroom and other instruction" and how much time will be devoted to "on-the-job" work. The application must also provide information on the position or duties outside the United States for which the individual is being trained and show why the individual cannot receive suitable or similar training in his or her own country.

Q "INTERNATIONAL CULTURAL EXCHANGE VISITOR"

This visa allows the employer to apply to INS for permission to hire a person from another country who is over 18 years of age for a period of not more than fifteen months to undertake prearranged employment or training *and* to share or demonstrate his or her own culture with Americans. A frequently cited example of a major "Q" employer is the EPCOT Center at Walt Disney World in Florida. Another example would be a museum or a department of a museum devoted to the art and culture of the student's home country.

The "cultural component" must be an integral part of the employment or training offered. The employer must demonstrate that the individual to be hired is fully able to communicate with Americans about his or her culture as well as being fully qualified for the work aspects of the position. Substantial documentation is required as part of the employer's application.

J-1 "EXCHANGE VISITOR"

Special Note: Unlike all other U.S. visa categories administered by the Immigration Service, the U.S. Information Agency (USIA) has primary responsibility for the regulations governing the use of the J-1 "Exchange Visitor" visa. While the information contained in this article is accurate as of the publication date, you should seek updated and current information from U.S. consular officials overseas and/or from individual J-1 sponsoring organizations.

The J-1 visa may be used only by individuals who are participants in educational programs that have been specifically approved by the U.S. Information Agency. There are eleven different J-1 categories, each with its own specific rules and regulations. Approved "Exchange Visitor Programs" are granted only to U.S. sponsoring organizations such as government agencies, schools, hospitals, companies, and private educational exchange organizations. Each sponsor is granted a specific "program description"—a short statement that specifically mentions those activities permitted for participants in the sponsor's specific program.

Of the eleven J-1 categories, only the "trainee" category is suitable for international students coming to the United States for paid practical training. The number of sponsors having J-1 programs that permit practical training employment is extremely limited. The International Association of Students in Economics and Business Management and the International Association for the Exchange of Students for Technical Experience (IAESTE) Trainee Program are the two principal trainee exchange organizations for students. The maximum length of practical training time permitted any one person (regardless of the number of sponsors or employers) is eighteen months.

A small number of sponsoring organizations have been granted J-1 authorizations for "summer travel/work" programs. These programs permit bona fide university students to work at any job they may find during the summer months (November to February for students from the Southern hemisphere). No extensions of visas are permitted, nor are changes to either another J-1 sponsor or to some other type of visa. Students sponsored on such programs must have a prearranged job before they come to the United States, firm appointments with prospective employers, or have sufficient personal funds so as to be financially independent if not employed. If students have preplacements for jobs, they may begin their program at any time. Travel for students who have not been preplaced should take place after June 15. Employment as servants, mother's helpers, or au pairs or in domestic positions in private homes is not authorized.

A third type of J-1 authorization covers placement in summer camps for camp-counselor experience. Participants must be at least 18 years old. Such placements are limited to a maximum of four months and must be for genuine camp counseling/teaching assignments. Placements in office, kitchen, or custodial jobs are not permitted.

In some cases, an individual coming to the United States on the J-1 visa may be subject to the "two-year foreign residence requirement" as the result of a "skills list" that the person's home country has asked USIA to establish for its citizens. If the person's field is included on the "skills list" for his/her country, it will generally be necessary for the individual to return to his/her country for a minimum of two years before coming back to the United States on most of the nonimmigrant visas or as a "permanent resident." Most European countries do not have skills lists, but many other countries do, and, if return to the United States within a two-year period is of concern, specific information should be sought from U.S. consular officials.

J-1 PROGRAM SPONSORS

TRAINEE EXCHANGE PROGRAMS:

AIESEC/US
135 West 50th Street, 17th Floor
New York, New York 10020
212-757-3774
Fax: 212-757-4062
E-mail: aiesec@us.aiesec.org
World Wide Web: http://www.aiesec.org/us

AMERICAN-SCANDINAVIAN FOUNDATION
725 Park Avenue
New York, New York 10021
212-879-9779
Fax: 212-249-3444
E-mail: training@amscan.org
World Wide Web: http://www.amscan.org

CDS INTERNATIONAL
330 Seventh Avenue
New York, New York 10001
212-497-3500
E-mail: webmaster@cdsintl.org
World Wide Web: http://www.cdsintl.org

COUNCIL ON INTERNATIONAL EDUCATIONAL EXCHANGE
205 East 42nd Street
New York, New York 10017
212-822-2600
Fax: 212-822-2699
E-mail: info@ciee.org
World Wide Web: http://www.ciee.org

IAESTE TRAINEE PROGRAM
Association for International Practical Training
10400 Little Patuxent Parkway, Suite 250
Columbia, Maryland 21044-3510
410-997-3069
Fax: 410-992-3924
E-mail: aipt@aipt.org
World Wide Web: http://www.aipt.org

INTEREXCHANGE, INC.
161 Sixth Avenue
New York, New York 10013
212-924-0446
Fax: 212-924-0575
E-mail: interex@earthlink.net

MAST INTERNATIONAL
University of Minnesota
1954 Buford Avenue, Room 240
St. Paul, Minnesota 55108-6197
612-624-3740
Fax: 612-624-7031
E-mail: mast@coal.agoff.umn.edu
World Wide Web: http://www.mast.agri.umn.edu

OHIO INTERNATIONAL AGRICULTURAL AND HORTICULTURAL INTERN PROGRAM
113 Agricultural Administration Building
The Ohio State University
2120 Fyffe Road
Columbus, Ohio 43210-1067
614-292-7720
Fax: 614-292-2757
E-mail: mchrisma@pop.service.ohio-state.edu

SISTER CITIES INTERNATIONAL
120 South Payne Street
Alexandria, Virginia 22314
703-836-3535
Fax: 703-836-4815
E-mail: info@sister-cities.org
World Wide Web: http://www.sister-cities.org

SUMMER TRAVEL/WORK PROGRAMS:

COUNCIL ON INTERNATIONAL EDUCATIONAL EXCHANGE
see address under 'Trainee' listings

INTEREXCHANGE
see address under 'Trainee' listings

YMCA INTERNATIONAL PROGRAM SERVICES
71 West 23rd Street, Suite 1904
New York, New York 10010
212-727-3800
212-IPS-YMCA
Fax: 212-727-8814
E-mail: ips@ymcanyc.org

CAMP COUNSELOR PROGRAMS AND CLEARINGHOUSES:

BUNAC (BUNACAMP/WORK AMERICA/ WORK CANADA)
16 Bowling Green Lane
London EC1R 0BD
United Kingdom
011-44-171-251-34722

CAMP AMERICA
37A Queen's Gate
London SW7 5HR
United Kingdom
011-44-171-581-7373

CAMP COUNSELORS USA
420 Florence Street
Palo Alto, California 94301
415-617-8390

800-999-CAMP (toll-free)
Fax: 415-321-3261

INTEREXCHANGE
see address under 'Trainee' listings

YMCA INTERNATIONAL PROGRAM SERVICES
see address under 'Trainee' listings

Visa Procedures

If an employer's applications for an H-2B, H-3, or Q visa are successful, the District Office of the Immigration and Naturalization Service will advise the U.S. Embassy in the student's country. The student can then secure the visa and travel to the United States. In the case of the J-1 visa, the sponsoring organization that has agreed to include the student issues a U.S. government document called an IAP-66 (a "Certificate of Eligibility"). The IAP-66 is sent to the student to use to apply for the J-1 visa in his or her country.

Upon entering the United States, the admitting Immigration Inspector issues a Form I-94 (Arrival/Departure Record), on which is noted the specific visa granted and the date when the "Permit-to-Stay" expires. Admission to the United States in the H-2B, H-3, or trainee category of the J-1 visa with such status being noted on the Form I-94 is the only documentation needed for the student to proceed to the workplace and take up the assignment.

Employment Eligibility Verification

U.S. law requires all employers to examine documentation proving that persons hired are either citizens of the United States or noncitizens legally authorized for employment during their stay in the United States.

Essentially, the law requires that within three business days after a person is hired, the employer must *physically examine* documentation that (a) establishes proof of the new employee's identity and (b) establishes that the person is either a U.S. citizen or is a noncitizen who has the legal right to be employed in the United States. The law and the related regulations, administered by INS, require that a record of the verification process be maintained in the employer's files for a period of three years after the date of hiring. For this purpose, the INS has developed the I-9 Form.

Virtually all kinds of employment are covered, from a full-time job with a large employer such as IBM to mowing grass on a regular basis for your next door neighbor. Certainly, all of the jobs listed in *Summer Jobs for Students 1998* will require you and your employer to complete the I-9 form. The I-9 form is in two parts. You must fill out the top half. You then present the form, together with your documentation, to your employer, who will complete the bottom half of the form.

INCOME TAX

As a general rule, individuals coming to the United States on any of the visas discussed in this article will be subject to U.S. income tax (and possibly state and local income tax) on the money they earn while in the country. If you leave the country before the end of the current calendar year, you will need to secure a "Certificate of Compliance" (often called a "sailing permit") from the Internal Revenue Service (IRS). You will need to provide documentation that all applicable tax has been paid—income tax will usually be withheld from your pay by the U.S. employer. Between January 1 and April 15 of the year following your employment, you will have to submit an income tax "return" (a form 1040NR) to the IRS. If you have remained in the country from one year to the next, you will also be required to submit a Form 8843 to verify your nonresident status. Tax regulations and procedures are not simple, and you should seek help from your employer and/or your sponsoring organization if you are participating in a J-1 program. You may also wish to secure a copy of IRS Publication 519—"U.S. Tax Guide for Aliens"—which is available free of charge from the Internal Revenue Service.

SOCIAL SECURITY NUMBER

In most cases, you will find it necessary to secure a Social Security number, which is widely used in the United States as a basic identification number—it is used in most automated payroll systems, in university enrollment systems, and for transactions such as opening a bank account.

Individuals entering the United States on the J-1 visa will usually be exempt from the U.S. Social Security Tax, but those entering on other visas (F-1, M-1, H-2B, H-3, and Q) can expect to have the tax withheld from their pay.

While it is possible to apply for a Social Security number at an American Embassy or Consulate General, it is often four to six months before the individual receives the number. Since Social Security regulations require an in-person application, it is usually better to take care of this matter after arrival in the United States. Normally, numbers are issued within four to six weeks after the application has been submitted to a local Social Security office.

It will be important for you to provide full documentation that clearly shows that you have a visa that permits employment. The Social Security official to whom you submit your application will want to see your passport, your I-94 form, visa documents (such as the triplicate copy of the IAP-66), and any documents related to your work placement. If you do not present the proper documentation, a Social Security card marked "Not Valid for Employment" will be issued.

FULL-TIME STUDENTS AT U.S. SCHOOLS

Individuals enrolled at U.S. colleges and universities for full-time academic study are usually admitted on the basis of the F-1 (student), M-1 (student), or student category of the J-1 visa. In each case, internship employment may be possible before graduation, after graduation, or both. When such employment may take place, the length of time allowed and what the employment is called (practical training, curricular practical training, academic training) depend on the specific visa and circumstances of the individual student.

A number of schools in the United States offer academic courses—usually known as cooperative education programs—that combine periods of study with periods of practical training employment. Under certain conditions, students from other countries who are enrolled as regular full-time students in a cooperative education program are allowed to undertake the practical training assignments (usually paid) in the same manner as American students. For information on enrollment in cooperative education programs and American colleges and universities that offer these opportunities, contact:

Cooperative Education Association
8640 Guilford Road, Suite 215
Columbia, Maryland 21046 USA
410-290-3666
Fax: 410-290-7084
E-mail: jleim@aol.com
World Wide Web: http://www.ceainc.org

Whether enrolled in a cooperative education program before or after graduation and regardless of the type of visa (M-1, F-1, or J-1), the student remains under the legal sponsorship of their college, university, or (in the case of some J-1 students) Exchange Visitor Program sponsor. Thus, assistance with proper arrangements for periods of practical training (including summer employment) must be sought from the international student adviser of the student's school.

Since fall 1996, important changes to U.S. immigration laws have taken effect and more changes are ahead. All international visitors, trainees, and temporary work visa holders will be affected by these laws. It is extremely important that you know exactly what you are permitted to do on the type of visa you have been granted and how long you are permitted to remain in the United States. If you have any questions about this, please check with your program sponsor, employer, or the INS. If your program ends early, you are not permitted to remain in the United States. You must either return home upon completion of your internship or work program or take the steps necessary to legally remain in the United States. Recent changes in immigration laws have been passed with severe penalties for foreign nationals who overstay their visas or who violate their status. You could be barred from returning to the U.S. for ten years or longer if you violate your visa status, even unintentionally.

In Conclusion

Most countries of the world have very strict regulations regarding employment for noncitizens in order to protect job opportunities for their own citizens. The United States is no different from other countries, especially in periods of high unemployment. What is different, however, is the U.S. system of visas and the rules and regulations that apply to each type (and subtype) of visa. The process of securing a proper visa takes a good deal of time (sometimes as long as four to six months) and can often be frustrating. Thus, it is wise to contact prospective employers as early as possible so that the employer has sufficient time to undertake the paperwork involved. If you have applied to or have been accepted by an organization such as AIESEC or IAESTE, make that fact known to the employer as each sponsoring organization has its own internal procedures that must be followed. With careful advance preparation, however, most people will be able to cope with the complexities of the U.S. legal system.

WORKING FOR THE NATIONAL PARK SERVICE

Since its inception in 1916, the National Park Service has been dedicated to the preservation and management of this country's outstanding natural, historical, and recreational areas. Today the National Park Service encompasses more than 360 sites across the United States and in Guam, Puerto Rico, and the Virgin Islands. There are parks of great natural beauty and grandeur, such as the Grand Canyon and Yellowstone; parks that preserve the nation's cultural and historical treasures, such as Mesa Verde, the Statue of Liberty, and Gettysburg Battlefield; parks of significant recreational value along seashores, lakeshores, and riverways that provide opportunities for outdoor activities and relaxation, such as Assateague Island and Lake Mead. The National Park Service is a bureau of the U.S. Department of the Interior; it should not be confused with the U.S. Forest Service of the Department of Agriculture.

Every year, millions of people from the United States and abroad visit our national park areas. To protect park resources and to serve the public, the National Park Service employs a permanent workforce and an essential seasonal workforce. Seasonals are hired every year to help permanent staff at many National Park Service parks and offices. The variety of positions available may surprise you: campground rangers, fee collectors, tour guides, naturalists, landscape architects, firefighters, laborers, law enforcement rangers, lifeguards, carpenters, clerks, historians; persons are hired for these seasonal jobs and more. Whatever the job, seasonal employees have the opportunity to learn more about the National Park Service and its mission.

Competition for seasonal jobs is keen. The number of applicants far outnumbers the positions available every year, particularly at larger, well-known parks. Some positions are filled by experienced seasonal employees who have worked previously for the National Park Service. And, Office of Personnel Management regulations require that veterans of the United States Armed Forces may be given preference among applicants. In the summer season, when most seasonal employees are hired, employment opportunities are extremely competitive.

ABOUT SEASONAL JOBS

PAY: Most seasonal positions require irregular hours of work, including weekends, holidays, and evenings. Entry-level grades for National Park Service seasonal positions generally range from the GS-3 to GS-7. GS levels indicate the rate of pay for most federal government positions. For current salary information for these grades, check with any federal agency or the Office of Personnel Management in that geographic

Information in this article is supplied by the National Park Service. Many thanks to Maureen Foster, Program Specialist for the National Park Service Office in Washington, D.C., for her cooperation in updating this information every year.

area where you desire employment. Prevailing local wages govern certain positions, such as laborer, maintenance, and skilled trades and crafts. WG levels indicate the rate of pay: the higher the WG number, the higher the wage. WG wages are paid on an hourly basis with a standard work week of 40 hours. Overtime may be required; additional compensation is provided for extra hours worked. GS levels and WG levels are not equivalent.

UNIFORMS: Most seasonal park rangers and maintenance personnel are required to wear the official Park Service uniform; specific requirements and ordering information are contained in the employment package forwarded to successful applicants. For those positions requiring a uniform, an allowance is allotted which partially covers its cost.

HOUSING: Address specific questions about housing, area living conditions, and similar matters to the park or office where you desire employment. Seasonal employee housing may or may not be available.

EQUAL EMPLOYMENT OPPORTUNITY: The National Park Service is an Equal Opportunity employer. Selection for positions will be made solely on the basis of merit, fitness, and qualifications, without regard to race, sex, color, creed, age, marital status, national origin, sexual orientation, non-disqualifying handicap conditions, or any other non-merit factors.

GENERAL INFORMATION ON APPLYING

The NPS has a centralized recruitment program for seasonal hiring. In addition, some parks may choose to hire directly. For information on these and other seasonal job opportunities, visit the Office of Personnel Management's Web page: www.usajobs. opm.gov. Information can also be accessed through the NPS Web page on the Internet (www.nps.gov and go to InfoZone for employment information).

CENTRALIZED SEASONAL RECRUITMENT: For information, including the list of parks hiring through the centralized recruitment program for a particular season, contact the National Park Service's Seasonal Employment Program office. The address is: Seasonal Employment Program, Human Resources Office, National Park Service, 1849 C Street, NW, Mail Stop 2225, Washington, DC 20240; telephone: 202-208-5074. A packet that includes the necessary forms will be sent to you when your letter or telephone inquiry is received. All applicants must complete the required computerized forms and file them during the specified filing period. The filing period for winter employment is June 1 through (postmarked by) July 15. The filing period for summer employment is November 15 through (postmarked by) January 15. Information can also be accessed through the NPS Web page on the Internet (www.nps.gov and go to InfoZone for employment information).

SEASONAL POSITIONS

PARK RANGER

Grades: GS-3, GS-4, GS-5, GS-7

Duties

Duties vary greatly from position to position and may include providing visitor services; interpreting a park's natural, historic, or archeological features through talks, guided walks, and demonstrations; working at an information desk; planning and implementing resource management programs, including fire control; performing search-and-rescue activities; providing for the public's safety through law enforcement; collecting fees; firefighting; lifeguarding; and radio dispatching.

Qualifications

GS-3: 6 months of general experience and 3 months of specialized experience that demonstrates the knowledge, skills, and abilities necessary to perform the job duties **or** 1 year of college (30 semester hours with 6 semester hours of natural sciences, social sciences, park and recreation management, and other disciplines related to management and protection of park resources, both natural and cultural).

GS-4: 6 months of general experience and 6 months of specialized experience that demonstrates the knowledge, skills, and abilities necessary to perform the job duties **or** 2 years of college (60 semester hours with 12 semester hours of natural sciences, social sciences, park and recreation management, and other disciplines related to management and protection of park resources, both natural and cultural).

GS-5: 1 year of specialized experience equivalent to the GS-4 level **or** 4 years of college leading to a bachelor's degree (120 semester hours with 24 semester hours of natural sciences, social sciences, park and recreation management, and other disciplines related to management and protection of park resources, both natural and cultural).

GS-7: 1 year of specialized experience equivalent to the GS-5 or GS-6 level **or** 1 full academic year of graduate education related to the management and protection of park resources or superior academic achievement.

How to Apply: For centralized recruitment: complete an Application for Seasonal Employment (Form 10-139), available from the Seasonal Employment Program; the summer seasonal recruitment period is November 15 through January 15; winter seasonal recruitment period is June 1 through July 15. For information on other seasonal job opportunities: contact the personnel office in the geographic area in which you want to work, or visit the Office of Personnel Management's Web page (www.usajobs.opm.gov) or NPS Web page (www.nps.gov and go to InfoZone for employment information).

GUIDE

Grades: GS-3 through GS-5

Duties

Provides guided tours, gives formal talks on natural and historic features, answers questions, and provides miscellaneous services to visitors.

Requirements

GS-3: 6 months general experience **or** 1 year of college (30 semester hours with 6 semester hours in American history, science, and public speaking).

GS-4: 6 months of general experience and 6 months of specialized experience **or** 1 year as a Guide, GS-3 **or** 2 years of college (60 semester hours with 12 semester hours in American history, science, and public speaking).

GS-5: 1 year of specialized experience **or** 1 year as a Guide, GS-4 **or** 4 years of college leading to a bachelor's degree (120 semester hours with 24 semester hours in American history, science, and public speaking).

How to Apply

For centralized recruitment: complete an Application for Seasonal Employment (Form 10-139), available from the Seasonal Employment Program; the summer seasonal recruitment period is November 15 through January 15; winter seasonal recruitment period is June 1 through July 15. For information on other seasonal job opportunities:

contact the personnel office in the geographic area in which you want to work, or visit the Office of Personnel Management's Web page (www.usajobs.opm.gov) or NPS Web page (www.nps.gov and go to InfoZone for employment information).

VISITOR USE ASSISTANT

Grades: GS-4, GS-5

Duties

Collects and accounts for fees and provides miscellaneous services and information to visitors.

Requirements

GS-4: 1 year of general experience **or** 1 year as a Visitor Use Assistant, GS-3 **or** 2 years of college (60 semester hours).

GS-5: 1 year of specialized experience **or** 1 year as a Visitor Use Assistant, GS-4 **or** 4 years of college (120 semester hours).

How to Apply

For centralized recruitment: Complete an Application for Seasonal Employment (Form 10-139), available from the Seasonal Employment Program; the summer seasonal recruitment period is November 15 through January 15; winter seasonal recruitment period is June 1 through July 15. For information on other seasonal job opportunities: contact the personnel office in the geographic area in which you want to work, or visit the Office of Personnel Management's Web page (www.usajobs.opm.gov) or NPS Web page (www.nps.gov and go to InfoZone for employment information).

RECREATIONAL AID/ASSISTANT

Grades: GS-3 through GS-6

Duties

Guards and manages beach and swimming areas and performs lifesaving and rescue work as needed for persons in rivers, lakes, and oceans. Positions are located at national recreation areas, seashores, and lakeshores.

Qualifications

GS-3: 6 months of general experience **or** 1 year of college.

GS-4: 6 months of general experience and 6 months specialized experience **or** 2 years of college (60 semester hours with 12 semester hours of courses related to recreation).

GS-5: 1 year of specialized experience equivalent to the GS-4 level **or** 4 years of college leading to a bachelor's degree (120 semester hours with 24 semester hours or a degree in recreation or physical education).

GS-6: 1 year of specialized experience equivalent to the GS-5 level.

How to Apply

Contact the personnel office in the geographic area in which you want to work, or visit the Office of Personnel Management's Web page (www.usajobs.opm.gov) or NPS Web page (www.nps.gov and go to InfoZone for employment information).

BIOLOGICAL TECHNICIAN

Grades: GS-4, GS-5

Duties

Assists researchers and management staff in collecting and analyzing data on flora and fauna in parks.

Qualifications

GS-4: 6 months of general experience and 6 months specialized experience **or** 2 years of college (60 semester hours with 12 semester hours in biology, chemistry, statistics, entomology, animal husbandry, botany, physics, agriculture, and mathematics with 6 of those directly related to the position to be filled).

GS-5: 1 year of specialized experience equivalent to the GS-4 level **or** 4 years of college leading to a bachelor's degree (120 semester hours with 24 semester hours or a degree in biology, chemistry, statistics, entomology, animal husbandry, botany, physics, agriculture, or mathematics with 6 of those directly related to the position to be filled).

How to Apply

Contact the personnel office in the geographic area in which you want to work, or visit the Office of Personnel Management's Web page (www.usajobs.opm.gov) or NPS Web page (www.nps.gov and go to InfoZone for employment information).

FORESTRY TECHNICIAN

Grades: GS-4, GS-5

Duties

Assists in fire control, prevention, and suppression work on park lands.

Qualifications

GS-4: 6 months of general experience and 6 months of specialized experience **or** 4 seasons of specialized experience **or** 2 years of college (60 semester hours with 12 semester hours in forestry, agriculture, crop or plant science, range management or conservation, wildlife management, and other related fields).

GS-5: 1 year of specialized experience equivalent to the GS-4 level **or** 4 years of college leading to a bachelor's degree (120 semester hours with 24 semester hours or a degree in forestry, agriculture, crop or plant science, range management or conservation, wildlife management, or other related field).

How to Apply

Contact the personnel office in the geographic area in which you want to work, or visit the Office of Personnel Management's Web page (www.usajobs.opm.gov) or NPS Web page (www.nps.gov and go to InfoZone for employment information).

ARCHITECTURE AND LANDSCAPE ARCHITECTURE

Grades: GS-4 and above

Duties

Produces drawings of structures of historical, architectural, landscape, engineering industrials, and maritime significance; prepares field notes; develops and edits measured drawings.

Qualifications

GS-4: 2 years of study (60 semester hours with 12 semester hours in architecture and landscape architecture).

GS-5: 4 years of study leading to a bachelor's degree, with major study or 24 semester hours in architecture or landscape architecture.

GS-7 and above: currently working toward a master's or doctoral degree in architecture or landscape architecture.

How to Apply

Contact Summer Program Administrator, HABS/HAER, National Park Service, 1849 C Street, NW, Washington, DC 20240. Submit a personal qualifications statement (resume, SF-171, or OF-612), letter of recommendation from a faculty member or employer familiar with your work, and samples indicating drafting ability (copies of sketches, lettering, and precision drafting).

HISTORIAN

Grades: GS-5, GS-7, and above

Duties

Conducts research using primary and secondary sources to produce inventories and reports on specific sites, structures, or technical processes.

Qualifications

A graduate degree in architectural history, landscape architecture, history of technology, American civilization, historic preservation, or a related field is preferred; a B.A. is required.

How to Apply

Contact Summer Program Administrator, HABS/HAER, National Park Service, 1849 C Street, NW, Washington, DC 20240. Submit a personal qualifications statement (resume, SF-171, or OF-612), letter of recommendation from a faculty member or employer familiar with your work, and (a) a paper demonstrating primary research in architectural history, landscape architecture, or history of technology or (b) a paper focusing on an aspect of the built environment.

CLERICAL

Grades: GS-1 through GS-4

Duties

Performs duties of receptionist, administrative clerk, clerk-typist, and data entry. The number of jobs available is limited.

Qualifications

GS-1: no education or experience required.

GS-2: 3 months of experience **or** high school graduate.

GS-3: 6 months of experience **or** 1 year of college (30 semester hours).

GS-4: 1 year of experience **or** 2 years of college (60 semester hours).

For typing positions, must be able to type 40 words per minute.

How to Apply

Contact the personnel office in the geographic area in which you want to work, or visit the Office of Personnel Management's Web page (www.usajobs.opm.gov) or NPS Web page (www.nps.gov and go to InfoZone for employment information).

LABORER

Grades: WG-2 through WG-4

Duties

Performs manual outdoor work on trails and for forestry programs; other park maintenance activities, such as cleaning campgrounds; and similar work in which physical labor must be performed.

Qualifications

Ability to perform the job duties, including necessary physical requirements.

How to Apply

Contact the personnel office in the geographic area in which you want to work, or visit the Office of Personnel Management's Web page (www.usajobs.opm.gov) or NPS Web page (www.nps.gov and go to InfoZone for employment information).

MAINTENANCE, TRADES, AND CRAFTS

Grades: WG-4 and above

Duties

Performs skilled and semi-skilled trades work: carpenter, mechanic, sawyer (woodsworker), trail maintenance worker, motor vehicle operation, and other similar positions.

Qualifications

Helper- to journeyman-level proficiency usually required.

How to Apply

Contact the personnel office in the geographic area in which you want to work, or visit the Office of Personnel Management's Web page (www.usajobs.opm.gov) or NPS Web page (www.nps.gov and go to InfoZone for employment information).

OTHER EMPLOYMENT OPPORTUNITIES

Other types of positions may be available in National Park Service parks and offices. Contact the park or office where you are interested in working for information. In addition, hotels, lodges, restaurants, stores, transportation services, marinas, and many other visitor facilities in National Parks may have positions available. These facilities are operated by private companies and individuals called park concessioners who recruit and hire their own employees. These are not federal government positions. Concessioners usually pay the minimum wage set by the state in which their operation is located. Although some pay a small bonus at the end of the season, they do not pay or make arrangements for travel to and from the parks. The National Park Service Regional Office for the geographic region in which you want to work, or the park itself, can provide names and addresses of concessioners. Contact the concessioner for applications and information about concession jobs, salaries, and working and living conditions.

NATIONAL PARK SERVICE REGIONAL OFFICES AND SITES

ALASKA REGION

Alagnak Wild River
Aniakchak National Monument and
    Preserve
Bering Land Bridge National Preserve
Cape Krusenstern National Monument
Denali National Park and Preserve
Gates of Arctic National Park and Preserve
Glacier Bay National Park and Preserve
Katmai National Park and Preserve
Kenai Fjords National Park

Klondike Gold Rush National Historical
    Park
Kobuk Valley National Park
Lake Clark National Park and Preserve
Noatak National Preserve
Sitka National Historical Park
Wrangell-St. Elias National Park and
    Preserve
Yukon-Charley Rivers National Preserve

For information about seasonal employment opportunities in this region, contact:
National Park Service, 2525 Gambell Street, Anchorage, Alaska 99503; telephone:
907-257-2526.

INTERMOUNTAIN REGION

COLORADO PLATEAU CLUSTER
Arches National Park
Aztec Ruins National Monument
Bryce Canyon National Park
California National Historical Trail (Salt
    Lake City)
Canyon de Chelly National Monument
Canyonlands National Park
Capitol Reef National Park
Cedar Breaks National Monument
Chaco Culture National Historical Park
Colorado National Monument
Dinosaur National Monument
El Malpais National Monument
El Morro National Monument
Fossil Butte National Monument
Glen Canyon National Recreation Area
Golden Spike National Historic Site
Grand Canyon National Park
Grand Staircase-Escalante National
    Monument
Hovenweep National Monument
Hubbell Trading Post National Historic Site
Mesa Verde National Park
Mormon Pioneer National Historical Trail
    (Salt Lake City)
Oregon National Historical Trail (Salt Lake
    City)
Pony Express National Historical Trail
    (Salt Lake City)
Natural Bridges National Monument

Navajo National Monument
Petrified Forest National Park
Pipe Spring National Monument
Rainbow Bridge National Monument
Sunset Crater Volcano National Monument
Timpanogos Cave National Monument
Walnut Canyon National Monument
Wupatki National Monument
Yucca House National Monument
Zion National Park

ROCKY MOUNTAIN CLUSTER
Bent's Old Fort National Historic Site
Bighorn Canyon National Recreation Area
Black Canyon of the Gunnison National
    Monument
Curecanti National Recreation Area
Devils Tower National Monument
Florissant Fossil Beds National Monument
Fort Laramie National Historic Site
Glacier National Park
Grand Teton National Park
Grant-Kohrs Ranch National Historic Site
Great Sand Dunes National Monument
John D. Rockefeller, Jr. Memorial Parkway
Little Bighorn Battlefield National
    Monument
Rocky Mountain National Park
Yellowstone National Park

SOUTHWEST CLUSTER

Alibates Flint Quarrie National Monument
Amistad National Recreation Area
Bandelier National Monument
Big Bend National Park
Big Thicket National Preserve
Capulin Volcano National Monument
Carlsbad Cavern National Park
Casa Grande Ruins National Monument
Chamizal National Monument
Chickasaw National Recreation Area
Chiricahua National Monument
Coronado National Monument
Fort Bowie National Historic Site
Fort Union National Monument
Fort Davis National Historic Site
Gila Cliff Dwellings National Monument
Glorieta Battlefield
Guadalupe Mountains National Park
Hohokam Pima National Monument
Lake Meredith National Recreation Area
Lyndon B. Johnson National Historical
  Park

Montezuma Castle National Monument
Organ Pipe Cactus National Monument
Padre Island National Seashore
Palo Alto Battlefield National Historic Site
Pecos National Historical Park
Petroglyph National Monument
Rio Grand Wild and Scenic River
Saguaro National Park
Salinas Pueblo Missions National
  Monument
San Antonio Missions National Historical
  Park
Sante Fe National Historical Trail
  (Santa Fe)
Trail of Tears National Historic Trail
  (Santa Fe)
Tonto National Monument
Tumacacori National Historical Park
Tuzigoot National Monument
White Sands National Monument

For information about seasonal employment opportunities in this region, contact:
National Park Service, P.O. Box 25287, 12795 West Alameda Parkway, Denver,
Colorado, 80225-0287; telephone: 303-969-2020.

MIDWEST REGION

GREAT LAKES CLUSTER

Apostle Islands National Lakeshore
Cuyahoga Valley National Recreation Area
Dayton Aviation Heritage National
  Historical Park
George Rogers Clark National Historical
  Park
Grand Portage National Monument
Hopewell Culture National Historical Park
Ice Age National Scenic Trail
Indiana Dunes National Lakeshore
Isle Royale National Park
James A. Garfield National Historic Site
Keweenaw National Historical Park
Lewis & Clark National Historical Trail
Lincoln Boyhood National Monument
Lincoln Home National Historic Site
Mississippi National River and Recreation
  Area
North Country National Scenic Trail
Perry's Victory and International Peace
  Memorial
Pictured Rocks National Lakeshore
Sleeping Bear Dunes National Lakeshore

St. Croix/Lower St. Croix National Scenic
  Riverways
Voyageurs National Park
William Howard Taft National Historic Site

GREAT PLAINS CLUSTER

Agate Fossil Beds National Monument
Arkansas Post National Monument
Badlands National Park
Brown vs. Board of Education National
  Historic Site
Buffalo National River
Effigy Mounds National Monument
Fort Larned National Historic Site
Fort Smith National Historic Site
Fort Scott National Historic Site
Fort Union Trading Post National Historic
  Site
George Washington Carver National
  Monument
Harry S Truman National Historic Site
Herbert Hoover National Historic Site
Homestead National Monument of America
Hot Springs National Park

Jewel Cave National Monument
Jefferson National Expansion Memorial
Knife River Indian Villages National
   Historic Site
Missouri National Recreational River
Mount Rushmore National Monument
Niobrara National Scenic Riverway
Ozark National Scenic Riverways

Pea Ridge National Military Park
Pipestone National Monument
Scotts Bluff National Monument
Theodore Roosevelt National Park
Ulysses S. Grant National Historic Site
Wilson's Creek National Battlefield
Wind Cave National Park

For information about seasonal employment opportunities in this region, contact:
National Park Service,1709 Jackson Street, Omaha, Nebraska 68102; telephone: 402-221-3456.

NATIONAL CAPITAL FIELD AREA

NATIONAL CAPITAL CLUSTER
Antietam National Battlefield
Antietam National Cemetery
Arlington House, The Robert E. Lee
   Memorial
Baltimore-Washington Parkway
Battleground National Cemetery
Catoctin Mountain Park
Chesapeake and Ohio Canal National
   Historical Park
Clara Barton National Historic Site
Clara Barton Parkway
Constitution Gardens
Ford's Theatre National Historic Site
Fort Washington Park
Francis Scott Key Memorial
Franklin Delano Roosevelt Memorial Park
Frederick Douglass National Historic Site
George Washington Memorial Parkway
Greenbelt Park
Harpers Ferry National Historical Park
Kahlil Gibran Memorial Garden
Korean War Veterans Memorial
Lincoln Memorial
Lyndon Baines Johnson Memorial Grove
   on the Potomac

Manassas National Battlefield Park
Mary McLeod Bethune Memorial
Mary McLeod Bethune Council House
   National Historic Site
Monocacy National Battlefield
National Capital Parks
National Mall
National Law Enforcement Officers
   Memorial
Pennsylvania Avenue National Historic Site
Piscataway Park
Potomac Heritage National Scenic Trail
Prince William Forest Park
Rock Creek Park
Rock Creek Parkway
Suitland Parkway
Theodore Roosevelt Island
Thomas Jefferson Memorial
United States Navy Memorial
Vietnam Veterans Memorial
Vietnam Woman's Memorial
Washington Monument
White House
Wolf Trap Farm Park

For information about seasonal employment opportunities in this region, contact:
National Park Service,1100 Ohio Drive, SW, Washington, DC 20242; telelphone: 202-619-7256.

NORTHEAST REGION

ALLEGHENY AND CHESAPEAKE
   CLUSTER
Allegheny Portage Railroad National
   Historic Site
Appomattox Court House National
   Historical Park
Assateague Island National Seashore

Bluestone National Scenic River
Booker T. Washington National Monument
Colonial National Historical Park
Delaware & Lehigh Navigation Canal
   National Heritage Corridor Commission
Delaware Water Gap National Recreation
   Area

Edgar Allen Poe National Historic Site
Eisenhower National Historic Site
Fort McHenry National Monument and
  Historic Shrine
Fort Necessity National Battlefield
Fredericksburg and Spotsylvania County
  Battlefields Memorial National Military
  Park
Friendship Hill National Historic Site
Gauley River National Recreation Area
George Washington Birthplace National
  Monument
Gettysburg National Military Park
Gloria Dei National Historic Site
Great Egg Harbor National Scenic and
  Recreational River
Hampton National Historic Site
Hopewell Furnace National Historical Park

Independence National Historical Park
Johnstown Flood National Monument
Maggie Walker National Historic Site
New Jersey Coastal Heritage Trail Route
New River Gorge National River
Petersburg National Battlefield
Pinelands National Reserve
Richmond National Battlefield Park
Shenandoah National Park
Southwestern Pennsylvania Heritage
  Preservation Commission
Steamtown National Historic Site
Thaddeus Kosciuszko National Monument
Thomas Stone National Historic Site
Upper Delaware National Scenic and
  Recreational River
Valley Forge National Historical Park

For information about seasonal employment opportunities in this cluster of the region, contact: National Park Service, U.S. Custom House, 200 Chestnut Street, Philadelphia, Pennsylvania 19106; telephone: 215-597-4971.

NEW ENGLAND CLUSTER

Acadia National Park
Adams National Historic Site
Blackstone River Valley National Heritage
  Conservation Corridor
Boston African-American National Historic
  Site
Boston National Historical Park
Cape Cod National Seashore
Castle Clinton National Monument
Edison National Historic Site
Eleanor Roosevelt National Historic Site
Farmington Wild and Scenic River
Federal Hall National Monument
Fire Island National Seashore
Fort Stanwix National Monument
Frederick Law Olmsted National Historic
  Site
Gateway National Recreation Area
General Grant National Monument
Hamilton Grange National Monument
Home of Franklin D. Roosevelt National
  Historic Site
John F. Kennedy National Historic Site
Longfellow National Historic Site
Lowell National Historical Park
Maine Acadian Culture Preservation
  Commission

Marsh-Billings National Historical Park
Martin Van Buren National Historic Site
Minute Man National Historical Park
Morristown National Historical Park
Quinebaug-Shetucket National Heritage
  Corridor
Roger Williams National Monument
Roosevelt Campobello International Park
Sagamore Hill National Historic Site
Saint Paul's Church National Historic Site
Saint Croix Island International Historic
  Site
Saint-Gaudens National Historic Site
Salem Maritime National Historic Site
Saratoga National Historical Park
Saugus Iron Works National Historic Site
Springfield Armory National Historic Site
Statue of Liberty/Ellis Island National
  Monuments
Theodore Roosevelt Birthplace National
  Historic Site
Theodore Roosevelt Inaugural National
  Historic Site
Touro Synagogue National Historic Site
Vanderbilt Mansion National Historic Site
Weir Farm National Historic Site
Wildcat Brook Wild and Scenic River
Women's Rights National Historical Park

For information about seasonal employment opportunities in this cluster of the region, contact: National Park Service, 15 State Street, Boston, Massachusetts 02109; telephone: 617-223-5101.

PACIFIC WEST REGION

COLUMBIA CASCADES CLUSTER
Big Hole National Battlefield
City of Rocks National Reserve
Coulee Dam National Recreation Area
Crater Lake National Park
Craters of the Moon National Monument
Ebey's Landing National Reserve
Fort Vancouver National Historic Site
Fort Clatsop National Monument
Hagerman Fossil Beds National Monument
John Day Fossil Beds National Monument
Klondike Gold Rush National Historical
Park
Lake Chelan National Recreation Area
Mount Rainier National Park
Nez Perce National Historical Park
North Cascades National Park
Olympic National Park
Oregon Caves National Monument
Ross Lake National Recreation Area
San Juan Island National Historical Park
Whitman Mission National Historic Site

For information about seasonal employment opportunities in this cluster of the region, contact: National Park Service, 909 First Avenue, Seattle, Washington 98104-1060; telephone: 206-220-4053.

PACIFIC GREAT BASIN CLUSTER
Cabrillo National Monument
Channel Islands National Park
Death Valley National Park
Devils Postpile National Monument
Eugene O'Neill National Historic Site
Fort Point National Historic Site
Golden Gate National Recreation Area
Great Basin National Park
John Muir National Historic Site
Joshua Tree National Park
Juan Bautista De Anza National Heritage
Trail
Kings Canyon National Park
Lake Mead National Recreation Area
Lassen Volcanic National Park
Lava Beds National Monument
Manzanar National Historic Site
Mojave National Preserve
Muir Woods National Monument
Pinnacles National Monument
Point Reyes National Seashore
Redwood National and State Parks
San Francisco Maritime National Historical
Park
Santa Monica Mountains National
Recreation Area
Sequoia National Park
Whiskeytown-Shasta-Trinity National
Recreation Area
Yosemite National Park

For information about seasonal employment opportunities in this cluster of the region, contact: National Park Service, 600 Harrison Street, Suite 600, San Francisco, California 94107; telephone: 415-427-1300, option 2

PACIFIC ISLANDS CLUSTER
American Memorial Park
Haleakala National Park
Hawaii Volcanoes National Park
Kalaupapa National Historic Site
Kaloko-Honokohau National Historical
Park
Pu'uhonua O Honaunau National Historical
Park
Puukohola Heiau National Historic Site
The National Park of American Samoa
USS Arizona Memorial
War in the Pacific National Historical Park

For information about seasonal employment opportunities in this cluster of the region, contact: National Park Service, 300 Ala Moana Boulevard, Suite 6305, P.O. Box 50165, Honolulu, Hawaii 96850; telephone: 808-541-2693.

SOUTHEAST FIELD AREA

APPALACHIAN CLUSTER
Abraham Lincoln Birthplace National
Historic Site
Andrew Johnson National Historic Site
Big South Fork National River and
National Recreation Area

Blue Ridge Parkway
Carl Sandburg Home National Historic Site
Chickamauga & Chattanooga National
    Military Park
Cowpens National Battlefield
Cumberland Gap National Historical Park
Fort Donelson National Battlefield
Great Smoky Mountains National Park
Guilford Courthouse National Military Park
Kings Mountain National Military Park
Little River Canyon National Preserve
Mammoth Cave National Park
Ninety Six National Historic Site
Obed Wild and Scenic River
Overmountain Victory National Historic
    Trail
Russell Cave National Monument
Stones River National Battlefield

ATLANTIC COAST CLUSTER
Andersonville National Historic Site
Canaveral National Seashore
Cape Hatteras National Seashore
Cape Lookout National Seashore
Castillo de San Marcos National
    Monument
Charles Pinckney National Historic Site
Chattahoochee River National Recreation
    Area
Congaree Swamp National Monument
Cumberland Island National Seashore
Fort Caroline National Monument
Fort Frederica National Monument
Fort Mantanzas National Monument
Fort Pulaski National Monument
Fort Raleigh National Historic Site
Fort Sumter National Monument

Horseshoe Bend National Military Park
Jimmy Carter National Historic Site
Kennesaw Mountain National Battlefield
    Park
Martin Luther King, Jr. National Historic
    Site
Moores Creek National Battlefield
Ocmulgee National Monument
Timucuan Ecological and Historic Preserve
Tuskegee Institute National Historic Site
Wright Brothers National Monument

GULF COAST CLUSTER
Big Cypress National Preserve
Biscayne National Park
Brices Cross Roads National Battlefield
    Site
Buck Island Reef National Monument
Cane River Creole National Historical Park
    and Heritage Area
Christiansted National Historic Site
DeSoto National Monument
Dry Tortugas National Park
Everglades National Park
Gulf Islands National Seashore
Jean Lafitte National Historical Park and
    Preserve
Natchez National Historical Park
Natchez Trace Parkway
New Orleans Jazz National Historical Park
Poverty Point National Monument
Salt River Bay National Historical Park
San Juan National Historic Site
Shiloh National Military Park
Tupelo National Battlefield
Vicksburg National Military Park
Virgin Islands National Park

For information about seasonal employment opportunities in this field area, contact: National Park Service, Atlanta Federal Center, 1924 Building, 100 Alabama Street, SW, Atlanta, Georgia 30303; telephone: 404-562-3296.

DO YOU WANT TO WORK TEMPORARILY IN CANADA . . .

WHAT YOU NEED TO KNOW

If you wish to work temporarily in Canada, you will likely be required to have **employment authorization.** An employment authorization is issued by an immigration officer after a Canada Employment Centre (CEC) approves your job offer.

This article outlines what you and your employer must do *before* you arrive in Canada. For additional advice, contact the Canadian Embassy, High Commission, or Consulate General near you.

Additional procedures may be required if you wish to work in Quebec. For further information, contact the Canadian Embassy abroad or a Canada Immigration Centre in Canada.

WHAT YOUR EMPLOYER MUST DO

Your employer must give details of your job offer to a Canada Employment Centre. An employment counselor will check to determine if your offer of employment meets the prevailing wages and working conditions for the occupation concerned. A check will also be made to see if the job cannot be filled by a suitably qualified and available Canadian or permanent resident. If these conditions are met, the CEC will approve your job offer. They will then issue a confirmation of offer of employment and send this to the Canadian Embassy, High Commission, or Consulate in your country.

The employer will be provided with a copy of the confirmation of offer of employment, to be forwarded to you. Your employer is responsible for arranging your worker's compensation and medical coverage when you arrive in Canada.

Some jobs may be exempt from CEC approval, and either the CEC or a visa office at a Canadian embassy or consulate can advise you on this.

WHAT YOU MUST DO

The Canadian visa office near you will contact you upon receipt of your confirmation of offer of employment. You may be asked to go to an interview or to send some information by mail. You may also be asked to have a medical checkup, which you will have to pay for yourself. If you qualify and have all the necessary documents, you will receive an employment authorization and will possibly have a separate visitor visa placed in your passport.

Produced by Public Affairs Citizenship and Immigration Canada. Reproduced with the permission of Citizenship and Immigration Canada and Supply and Services Canada, 1996. To obtain more copies, contact: Public Enquiries Centre, Citizenship and Immigration, Ottawa, Ontario, K1A 1L1, Canada; 613-954-9019; fax: 613-954-2221.

The employment authorization will state that you can work at a specific job for a specific period of time for a specific employer. You will need to produce the authorization when you arrive in Canada, as well as your passport, visa (if issued), and airline tickets.

There is a processing fee when you submit an application for an employment authorization. There are no refunds if your application is refused. Please request the Public Enquiries Centre's brochure on immigration fees or ask an immigration officer for fee information.

Different procedures exist for citizens or permanent residents of the United States. You should seek clarification from the nearest Canadian embassy or consulate; general procedures are stated later in this article.

An employment authorization will not be issued to you to come to Canada to look for work. *It is valid only for the specific job, the specific amount of time, and the employer stated on the form.*

WHEN YOU ARRIVE IN CANADA

When you arrive at the port of entry to Canada, show your confirmation of offer of employment, your employment authorization, and other papers to an immigration officer. You will be given forms to fill out so that you can get a Social Insurance Number (SIN). These forms and proper identification, such as a birth certificate, should be taken to a counselor at a CEC, who can help you if you have trouble filling them out. When you receive your SIN card, you will have to give your number to your employer.

Your employment authorization is not a contract. Your job can be ended by you or your employer at any time. However, if your duties change or the job is to be extended, you must contact a Canada Immigration Centre right away, before the expiry date of your current authorization.

SOME WORKERS CAN APPLY AT A PORT OF ENTRY

Most foreign workers must apply for employment authorization outside of Canada, but if you are a resident of the United States, Greenland, or St. Pierre and Miquelon, you can apply for an employment authorization when you arrive at a port of entry to Canada. To apply this way, you must produce your confirmation of offer of employment and other papers when you arrive at the port of entry. Remember that you must find out what papers you will need *before* arriving in Canada. Check with the Canadian Embassy, High Commission, or Consulate General.

REMEMBER

- There is a nonrefundable fee to process a request for an employment authorization.

- Most foreign workers must get their employment authorizations before arriving in Canada. Visitors *cannot* obtain employment authorization while in Canada.

- You must follow the terms of your employment authorization while in Canada. If you do not, you may be asked to leave the country.

- CEC staff in Canada and Canadian government representatives in your home country cannot help you find a job.

- If you want to work temporarily or if you have further questions about working in Canada, contact the nearest Canadian Embassy, High Commission, or Consulate.

- This is not a legal document. For precise, legal information consult the Immigration Act and Regulations.

STATE-BY-STATE LISTINGS

ALABAMA

CAMP SKYLINE
MENTONE, ALABAMA 35984

General Information Residential camp located on top of Lookout Mountain serving 275–315 girls. Established in 1947. Owned by Cash Summer Camps. Affiliated with American Camping Association, Christian Camping International. 80-acre facility located 45 miles southwest of Chattanooga, Tennessee. Features: 1 Western and 3 English riding rings; river with slide, rope swing, and "blob"; private freshwater lake and swimming pool; Riverside historical hotel for teenagers; beach volleyball court; outdoor basketball court; 4 tennis courts; softball fields; ropes course; climbing tower; open-air gymnasium; fine arts building; lodge.

Profile of Summer Employees Total number: 100; average age: 19; 5% male, 95% female; 10% high school students; 90% college students; 2% international; 5% local residents; 1% teachers. Nonsmokers only.

Employment Information Openings are from June 3 to August 10. Jobs available: ► 2 *sports instructors* (archery, tennis, swimming, diving, horseback riding, and gymnastics); ► *lifeguards and swimming instructors* with WSI certification; ► *fine and performing arts instructors* (music, dance, arts and crafts, and drama); ► *riflery instructors;* ► *cheerleading/flag twirling/baton twirling instructors;* ► *computer instructors;* ► *ropes course instructors for climbing tower;* ► *nature specialists;* ► *canoeing instructors;* ► *Christian leadership instructors.* All positions offered at $900–$1200 per season.

Benefits On-the-job training, on-site room and board at no charge, incentive bonus. Preemployment training of 10 days is required and includes safety and accident prevention, group interaction, first-aid, CPR, leadership. Orientation is paid.

Contact Personnel Director, Camp Skyline, Department SJ, PO Box 287, Mentone, Alabama 35984; 205-634-4001, Fax 205-634-3018. Application deadline: March 1.

ALASKA

ALASKA STATE PARKS VOLUNTEER PROGRAM
3601 C STREET, SUITE 1200
ANCHORAGE, ALASKA 99503-5921

General Information Program offering volunteer positions in state parks throughout the state of Alaska. Established in 1970. Owned by State of Alaska.

Profile of Summer Employees Total number: 70.

Employment Information Openings are from May 15 to September 15. Jobs available: ▶ 24 *ranger assistants* with outdoor experience and some college education in natural resources; ▶ 10 *trail crews* with outdoor experience and knowledge of hand and power tools; ▶ 15 *natural history interpreter* with outdoor experience, good people skills, and some education in natural resources; ▶ 20 *various positions*.

Benefits College credit, on-the-job training, on-site room and board (cost varies with position).

Contact Kathryn Reid, Volunteer Coordinator, Alaska State Parks Volunteer Program, 3601 C Street, Suite 1200, Anchorage, Alaska 99503-5921; 907-269-8708, Fax 907-269-8907, E-mail volunteer@dnr.state.ak.us. Application deadline: April 1.

AMERICA & PACIFIC TOURS, INC. (A&P)
WEST FIFTH AVENUE AND K STREET, SUITE 434
ANCHORAGE, ALASKA 99510

General Information Japanese land operator for Japanese tourists providing planned, individualized, and special guided trips of Alaska. Established in 1970. Owned by Keizo Sugimoto. Affiliated with Alaska Visitors' Association, Anchorage Convention and Visitors' Bureau, Alaska Sportfishing Association. Features: King and Silver Salmon fishing (late May to middle of September); coastal trail for walking, rollerblading, running, and cycling year-round; hiking trails for summer; cross-country skiing trails in winter.

Profile of Summer Employees Total number: 20; average age: 23; 50% male, 50% female; 90% college students; 50% international; 50% local residents.

Employment Information Openings are from June 1 to September 15. Spring break, Christmas break, year-round positions also offered. Jobs available: ▶ 20 *tour guides and office workers* with current driver's license and fluency in Japanese (salary depends upon experience as guide) at $600–$2800 per month. International students encouraged to apply; must apply through recognized agency.

Benefits College credit, on-the-job training, on-site room and board at $180 per month, laundry facilities, one-way travel reimbursement for second-year employees, round-trip travel reimbursement for third-year or longer employees. Preemployment orientation is optional and includes information for guiding Alaska. Orientation is paid.

Contact Keizo Sugimoto, President, America & Pacific Tours, Inc. (A&P), PO Box 10-1068, Anchorage, Alaska 99510; 907-272-9401, Fax 907-272-0251. Application deadline: March 31.

BRISTOL BAY LODGE
PO BOX 1509
DILLINGHAM, ALASKA 99576

General Information Wilderness sportfishing lodge catering to 20 anglers per week. Established in 1972. Owned by Ron and Maggie McMillan. Affiliated with Trout Unlimited, Federation of Fly Fishermen, Audubon Society, Nature Conservancy. 5-acre facility located 350 miles west of Anchorage. Features: remote location (accessible by float plane); scenic area (mountain, lakes, rivers); wilderness lodge; great sport fishing; hot tub and sauna; game room and library.

Profile of Summer Employees Total number: 20; average age: 21; 75% male, 25% female; 50% college students.

Employment Information Openings are from June 5 to September 20. Jobs available: ▶ 1 *chef* with experience at $2000–$2400 per month; ▶ 4 *household workers* with CPR and standard first aid at $900 per month; ▶ 2 *pilots* with communication, instrumentation, and seaplane ratings (over 1,500 hours); ▶ 1 *pilot/mechanic* with communication, instrumentation, and seaplane ratings (P or A and I); ▶ 10 *fishing guides* with CPR and standard first aid certification at $800–$1200 per month.

Benefits On-the-job training, on-site room and board at no charge, laundry facilities, travel reimbursement, sharing of gratuities.

Contact Ron McMillan, President/General Manager, Bristol Bay Lodge, 2422 Hunter Road, Ellensburg, Washington 98926; 509-964-2094, Fax 509-964-2269. Application deadline: February 1.

CAMP TOGOWOODS
HC 30, BOX 5400
WASILLA, ALASKA 99654

General Information Residential program of traditional camping activities for girls ages 7–15. Established in 1958. Owned by Girl Scouts Susitna Council. Affiliated with American Camping Association. 260-acre facility located 58 miles north of Anchorage. Features: freshwater lake frontage; location 3 hours from Mt. McKinley (tallest peak in North America); wood-fired lakeside sauna; platform tents; rustic log lodges.

Profile of Summer Employees Total number: 21; average age: 22; 100% female; 24% minorities; 95% college students; 38% local residents. Nonsmokers preferred.

Employment Information Openings are from May 31 to August 6. Jobs available: ▶ 10 *counselors* at $1700–$1850 per season; ▶ 1 *waterfront director* with WSI certification, lifeguard training, and waterfront lifeguarding at $2500–$2700 per season; ▶ 2 *lifeguards* with lifeguard certification (waterfront lifeguarding preferred) at $1900–$2025 per season; ▶ 2 *cooks* at $2000–$2050 per season; ▶ 1 *food service manager* at $2400–$2800 per season; ▶ 1 *assistant director* at $2400–$2700 per season; ▶ 1 *health supervisor* with RN license (Alaska) or EMT and current CPR certification at $2800–$3000 per season; ▶ 1 *business manager* at $1800–$1900 per season; ▶ *creative arts specialist/counselor* at $1900–$2300 per season; ▶ *environmental specialist/counselor* at $1900–$2300 per season.

Benefits On-the-job training, on-site room and board at no charge, health insurance. Preemployment training of 6 to 7 days is required and includes safety and accident prevention, group interaction, first-aid, CPR, leadership. Orientation is paid.

Contact Helen Bartholomy, Camp Director, Girl Scouts Susitna Council, Camp Togowoods, 3911 Turnagain Street, Anchorage, Alaska 99517; 907-248-2250, Fax 907-243-4819, E-mail susitna@alaska.net. Application deadline: April 15.

LONGACRE EXPEDITIONS
SITKA, ALASKA

General Information Adventure travel program emphasizing group living skills and physical challenges. Using base camp as a staging area, 2–3 staffers and 10–14 campers participate in advanced expeditions on which they engage in human-powered sports. Established in 1981. Owned by Longacre Expeditions. Affiliated with American Camping Association.

Profile of Summer Employees Total number: 10; average age: 25; 50% male, 50% female; 10% minorities; 40% college students; 30% local residents. Nonsmokers only.

Employment Information Openings are from June 14 to July 31. Jobs available: ▶ 1 *mountaineering instructor* (minimum age 21) with advanced first aid or advanced wilderness first aid, CPR, and completion of water safety course at $300–$400 per week; ▶ 3 *support and logistics staff members* (minimum age 21) at $150–$175 per week; ▶ 8 *assistant trip leaders* (minimum age 21) at $150–$175 per week.

Benefits On-the-job training, on-site room and board at no charge, Pro-Deal package. Preemployment training of 9 days is required and includes safety and accident prevention, group interaction, first-aid, CPR, leadership, camper-counselor relations. Orientation is unpaid.

Contact Roger Smith, Longacre Expeditions, RD 3, Box 106, Newport, Pennsylvania 17074; 717-567-6790, Fax 717-567-3955, E-mail longacre@pa.net, URL http://www.longex.com.

RAINBOW KING LODGE
PO BOX 106
ILIAMNA, ALASKA 99606

General Information Luxury sportfishing lodge offering weekly guest packages for the upper-income market. Established in 1971. Owned by Tom Robinson. Affiliated with Aircraft Owners and Pilots Association, International Game Fish Association, Alaska Professional Sportfishing Association. 4-acre facility located 190 miles southwest of Anchorage. Features: remote Alaskan surroundings; world-class fishing; 4 private aircraft fly-outs for crew; mountain-bike trails; rustic lodge setting; wildlife, including bear, moose, and caribou.

Profile of Summer Employees Total number: 36; average age: 25; 65% male, 35% female; 80% college students; 5% retirees; 5% local residents.

Employment Information Openings are from June 1 to October 1. Jobs available: ▶ 14 *fishing guides* with first aid/CPR certification and fly-fishing and boating experience at $1050–$1850 per month; ▶ 10 *lodge workers, experienced preferred,* at $1050–$1700 per month; ▶ 4 *maintenance personnel, experience preferred,* at $1050–$1850 per month.

Benefits On-the-job training, on-site room and board at no charge, laundry facilities.

Contact Craig Augustynovich, Manager, Rainbow King Lodge, 333 South State Street, Suite 126, Lake Oswego, Oregon 97034; 800-458-6539, Fax 503-635-3079, URL http://www. rainbowking.com. Application deadline: April 1.

ARIZONA

ARAMARK LEISURE SERVICES
PO BOX 1597
PAGE, ARIZONA 86040

General Information Concessionaire at Glen Canyon Recreation Area operating all guest services at five marina locations on Lake Powell with hotel, restaurant, retail, and marina operations. Established in 1972. Owned by National Park Service and ARAMARK Leisure Services. Located 127 miles north of Flagstaff. Features: location on Lake Powell which is 200 miles long with 2000 miles of shoreline; 2 resort locations offering hotel and restaurant facilities; employee recreation program; proximity to Grand Canyon, Zion National Park, Bryce National Park, and Monument Valley; Colorado River rafting operation.

Profile of Summer Employees Total number: 800; average age: 20; 50% male, 50% female; 40% minorities; 20% high school students; 30% college students; 20% retirees; 5% international; 50% local residents.

Employment Information Openings are from April 1 to November 1. Year-round positions also offered. Jobs available: ▶ 30 *boat cleaners* at $5 per hour; ▶ 40 *cashiers* at $5 per hour; ▶ 30 *kitchen help* at $5 per hour; ▶ 20 *front desk staff* at $5 per hour; ▶ 60 *boat rental agents* at $5 per hour; ▶ 20 *fuel attendants* at $5 per hour; ▶ 20 *deckhands* at $5 per hour. International students encouraged to apply; must obtain own visa and working papers prior to employment; must apply through recognized agency.

Benefits College credit, on-the-job training, on-site room and board at $200 per month, laundry facilities, discounts on boat rentals and water toys, $.25 per hour completion bonus, week's houseboat vacation (some restrictions apply). Preemployment training of 1 day is required and includes safety and accident prevention, group interaction, camper-counselor relations, customer service. Orientation is paid.

Contact Inta Bingham, Staffing and Placement Specialist, ARAMARK Leisure Services, Department SJ, PO Box 1597, Page, Arizona 86040; 520-645-1081, Fax 520-645-1016, E-mail lprmhr@ page.az.net, URL http://www.coolworks.com/showme/kpowell/.

GRAND CANYON NATIONAL PARK LODGES
PO BOX 699
GRAND CANYON, ARIZONA 86023

General Information National park concessioner providing all hotel, restaurant, retail, and transportation services on the south rim of the Grand Canyon. Established in 1901. Owned by

AMFAC Resorts, Inc. Affiliated with American Hotel and Motel Association, Arizona Hotel and Motel Association. Located 80 miles north of Flagstaff. Features: location within south rim of Grand Canyon National Park; hotels including 135-room Moqui Lodge; 5 restaurants and cafeterias; 7 retail shops; tour bus operation.

Profile of Summer Employees Total number: 1,200; average age: 28; 50% male, 50% female; 30% minorities; 20% college students; 20% retirees; 30% local residents.

Employment Information Year-round positions offered. Jobs available: ▶ *guest room attendants* at $5.15–$7 per hour; ▶ *kitchen/utility personnel* at $5.15–$7 per hour; ▶ *retail clerks* at $5.15–$7 per hour; ▶ *cashiers/accounting personnel* at $6–$8 per hour; ▶ *buspersons/lineservers* at $5.15–$7 per hour; ▶ *hosts/hostesses* at $5.25–$7 per hour; ▶ *cooks-I,II,III* at $6–$10 per hour; ▶ *cooks' helpers* at $5.35–$7 per hour; ▶ *tour bus drivers* at $7–$10 per hour. International students encouraged to apply; must obtain own visa and working papers prior to employment; must apply through recognized agency.

Benefits College credit, on-the-job training, on-site room and board at $16 per week, laundry facilities, health insurance, 50% discount on food in cafeterias, 20% retail discount on most gifts and hand-crafted items.

Contact Grand Canyon National Park Lodges, Personnel Department, Grand Canyon National Park Lodges, Department SJ, PO Box 699, Grand Canyon, Arizona 86023; 520-638-2812, Fax 520-638-2361, URL http://www.coolworks.com/showme/thecanyon/index.html.

ORME SUMMER CAMP
HC 63, BOX 3040
MAYER, ARIZONA 86333-9799

General Information Residential coed camp serving up to 200 campers with a wide variety of indoor and outdoor activities, including mountain biking. Established in 1929. Owned by The Orme School. Affiliated with American Camping Association, Western Association of Independent Camps. 40,000-acre facility located 60 miles north of Phoenix. Features: 4 tennis courts; fully equipped gymnasium; 4 athletic fields; 1 regulation, lighted rodeo arena; Olympic-size pool; 20,000 volume library.

Profile of Summer Employees Total number: 35; average age: 25; 50% male, 50% female; 2% minorities; 80% college students; 1% retirees; 18% international; 10% local residents. Nonsmokers preferred.

Employment Information Openings are from June 10 to August 13. Jobs available: ▶ *outdoor adventure/survival instructor* with Outward Bound or NOLS completion or equivalent at $1000–$1300 per season; ▶ *senior counselors* at $750–$1100 per season; ▶ *horsemanship staff* at $850–$1100 per season. International students encouraged to apply; must apply through recognized agency.

Benefits On-the-job training, on-site room and board at no charge, laundry facilities, travel reimbursement. Preemployment training of 8 days is required and includes safety and accident prevention, group interaction, first-aid, CPR, leadership, camper-counselor relations, CHA horsemanship training. Orientation is unpaid.

Contact Benjamin W. Powers, Director, Orme Summer Camp, Department SJ, The Orme Summer Camp, Mayer, Arizona 86333; 520-632-7601, Fax 520-632-7605, E-mail bpowers@orme.k12.az.us. Application deadline: February 1.

ARKANSAS

NOARK GIRL SCOUT CAMP
ROUTE 3, BOX 22
HUNTSVILLE, ARKANSAS 72740

General Information Residential Girl Scout camp serving approximately 100 girls ages 8–17 weekly. Program includes a balance of traditional and innovative activities. Established in 1967. Owned by Noark Girl Scout Council. 1,039-acre facility located 40 miles east of Fayetteville. Features: location in Ozark Mountains; primitive outdoor living; tennis/sports court; 25-acre multipurpose meadow; hiking trail system; craft house.

Profile of Summer Employees Total number: 25; average age: 20; 5% male, 95% female; 5% minorities; 95% college students; 15% international; 85% local residents; 5% teachers. Nonsmokers preferred.

Employment Information Openings are from May 31 to August 8. Jobs available: ▶ 4 *unit leaders* (minimum age 21) with maturity and recreation/physical education degree (preferred) at $160 per week; ▶ 12 *unit counselors* (minimum age 18) at $140 per week; ▶ 1 *waterfront director* (minimum age 21) with WSI and lifeguard certification and ability to teach children, supervise instructors, keep records, and organize large groups at $160–$200 per week; ▶ 1 *health supervisor* (minimum age 21) with RN, LPN, or paramedic license at $250 per week; ▶ *wrangler* with Western riding instruction and horse experience at $140 per week; ▶ *business manager* (minimum age 21) with experience in business methods, record keeping, buying, and inventory control at $160 per week; ▶ *assistant camp director* with Girl Scouts and residential camp experience at $180 per week. International students encouraged to apply; must apply through recognized agency.

Benefits College credit, on-the-job training, formal ongoing training, on-site room and board at no charge, laundry facilities, health insurance, staff shirt, partial reimbursement for physical examination. Preemployment training of 7 days is required and includes safety and accident prevention, group interaction, first-aid, CPR, leadership, camper-counselor relations, lifeguard training. Orientation is paid.

Contact Camp Director, Noark Girl Scout Camp, Department SJ, PO Box 1004, Harrison, Arkansas 72602; 501-750-2442, Fax 501-750-4699, E-mail kampjk@aol.com(noark). Application deadline: April 15.

CALIFORNIA

ADVENTURE CONNECTION, INC.
986 LOTUS ROAD
LOTUS, CALIFORNIA 95651

General Information River trips for children and adults ages 7 and up. Established in 1984. Owned by Nate and Wendy Rangel. Affiliated with America Outdoors, California Outdoors. 5-acre facility located 45 miles east of Sacramento. Features: volleyball court; badminton court; hot shower facilities; hot tub; location on American River.

Profile of Summer Employees Total number: 25; 50% male, 50% female; 20% minorities;

35% college students; 15% retirees; 10% international; 50% local residents; 25% teachers.
Employment Information Openings are from May 1 to September 30. Spring break positions also offered. Jobs available: ▶ 25 *river guides* with experience guiding or completion of guide school. International students encouraged to apply; must obtain own visa and working papers prior to employment.
Benefits On-the-job training, formal ongoing training, on-site room and board at $50 per month. Preemployment training of 2 days is required and includes safety and accident prevention, group interaction, first-aid, CPR, leadership, camper-counselor relations. Orientation is paid.
Contact Nate Rangel, President, Adventure Connection, Inc., Department SJ, PO Box 475, Coloma, California 95613; 800-556-6060, Fax 916-626-9268, URL http://www.adventure-connection.com. Application deadline: March 1.

AMERICAN ADVENTURES
6762A CENTINELA AVENUE
CULVER CITY, CALIFORNIA 90230

General Information Adventure camping and hostelling tours for international passengers (ages 18–35) throughout the USA, Canada, and Mexico. Established in 1981. Owned by AmeriCan Adventures. Affiliated with Federation of International Youth Travel Organizations, Travel Industry Association of America, Alliance of Canadian Travel Associations. Features: custom-made tents and camping equipment; fleet of customized 15-passenger vans; bases in Los Angeles, New York, and Seattle/Vancouver.
Profile of Summer Employees Total number: 80; average age: 26; 50% male, 50% female; 20% minorities; 50% college students; 5% international; 5% local residents; 10% teachers. Nonsmokers preferred.
Employment Information Openings are from May 1 to October 31. Spring break, winter break, Christmas break, year-round positions also offered. Jobs available: ▶ 75 *tour leaders/ drivers* (minimum age 21) with strong leadership and driving skills and knowledge of history/ culture and current events of North America (foreign language and first aid skills helpful) at $210–$330 per week. International students encouraged to apply; must obtain own visa and working papers prior to employment; must apply through recognized agency.
Benefits College credit, on-the-job training, formal ongoing training, on-site room and board at no charge, travel reimbursement, end-of-season bonus, tips and commissions. Preemployment training of 7 to 14 days is required and includes safety and accident prevention, group interaction, leadership, camper-counselor relations, driving instruction. Orientation is unpaid.
Contact Rhonda Anisman, Operations Manager, AmeriCan Adventures, 6762 A Centinela Avenue, Culver City, California 90230; 310-390-7495, Fax 310-390-1446, E-mail amadlax@attmail. com.

AMERICAN RIVER TOURING ASSOCIATION
24000 CASA LOMA ROAD
GROVELAND, CALIFORNIA 95321

General Information Guided whitewater rafting trips throughout the western United States. Established in 1963. Affiliated with America Outdoors, Idaho Outfitters and Guides, Oregon Outdoors. Features: 5–12 day Idaho-Selway, Main Salmon, and M.F. Salmon River expeditions; 3–5 day Oregon-Rogue, Illinois, and Umpqua River expeditions; 4–7 day Utah-Green and Yampa River expeditions; 1–3 day California-Merced, Tuolumne, American, and Klamath River expeditions.
Profile of Summer Employees Total number: 50; average age: 25; 70% male, 30% female; 5% minorities; 50% college students; 20% local residents; 10% teachers. Nonsmokers only.
Employment Information Openings are from June 1 to September 15. Jobs available: ▶ 10 *river guides* with first aid and CPR certification at $420–$700 per week.
Benefits On-site room and board at no charge.
Contact Steve Welch, General Manager, American River Touring Association, 24000 Casa

Loma Road, Groveland, California 95321; 209-962-7873, Fax 209-962-4819, E-mail arta-info@ arta.org, URL http://www.arta.org. Application deadline: January 3.

BAR 717 RANCH
STAR ROUTE, BOX 150
HAYFORK, CALIFORNIA 96041

General Information Coed ranch offering horsemanship, swimming, hiking, crafts, animal care, ranch work projects, pottery, and the teaching of responsibility. Established in 1930. Affiliated with Western Association of Independent Camps, American Camping Association. 450-acre facility located 80 miles west of Redding. Features: horsemanship program; river swimming; overnight backpacking in surrounding forest; barn with small animals; vegetable gardens; pottery kiln.

Profile of Summer Employees Total number: 35; average age: 21; 50% male, 50% female; 10% minorities; 5% high school students; 90% college students; 5% retirees; 10% international; 10% local residents; 5% teachers. Nonsmokers only.

Employment Information Openings are from June 20 to September 1. Jobs available: ▶ *junior counselors* (minimum age 18) at $165 per week; ▶ *counselors* with 2 years of college at $190&–$250 per week; ▶ *kitchen staff members* (minimum age 17) at $165 per week. International students encouraged to apply; must obtain own visa and working papers prior to employment.

Benefits On-the-job training, on-site room and board, laundry facilities.

Contact Phil Fisher, Director, Bar 717 Ranch, Department SJ, Star Route, Box 150, Hayfork, California 96041; 916-628-5992, Fax 916-628-5992, E-mail bar717@aol.com, URL http://camping. org/bar717.htm. Application deadline: March 15.

BASSETT-MARTIN TENNIS CAMP
PO BOX 64335
LOS ANGELES, CALIFORNIA 90064

General Information Tennis camp for boys and girls ages 8–18 of all different ability levels. Established in 1972. Owned by William W. Martin. Affiliated with The Thacher School. 100-acre facility located 80 miles northwest of Los Angeles. Features: 10 outdoor tennis courts; soccer field and surrounding track; gymnasium; pool; game room; baseball field.

Profile of Summer Employees Total number: 15; average age: 21; 65% male, 35% female; 50% minorities; 85% college students; 10% international; 75% local residents. Nonsmokers only.

Employment Information Openings are from June 20 to August 30. Christmas break positions also offered. Jobs available: ▶ 10 *tennis camp counselors* with CPR certification, tennis teaching experience, and good swimming skills at $250 per week. International students encouraged to apply.

Benefits On-the-job training, on-site room and board at no charge, laundry facilities. Preemployment training of 2 days is required and includes safety and accident prevention, group interaction, first-aid, leadership, camper-counselor relations. Orientation is unpaid.

Contact Bill Martin, Director, Bassett-Martin Tennis Camp, Department SJ, PO Box 64335, Los Angeles, California 90064; 310-475-5853, Fax 310-475-5853. Application deadline: June 1.

CAMP HARMON
BOULDER CREEK, CALIFORNIA 95006

General Information Residential camp serving physically and developmentally disabled children and adults. Work involves people with a wide range of disabilities, including the severely disabled. Established in 1969. Operated by Easter Seal Society of Central California. Affiliated with American Camping Association. 23-acre facility located 25 miles north of Santa Cruz. Features: wheelchair-accessible swimming pool; boating and fishing area; arts and crafts area;

completely accessible facilities; one-half hour from Pacific Ocean; one hour south of San Francisco.

Profile of Summer Employees Total number: 60; average age: 20; 48% male, 52% female; 10% minorities; 2% high school students; 98% college students; 10% international; 30% local residents. Nonsmokers preferred.

Employment Information Openings are from June 4 to August 24. Spring break, year-round positions also offered. Jobs available: ▶ *cabin counselors* at $175 per week; ▶ *program specialists* at $200 per week. International students encouraged to apply; must apply through recognized agency.

Benefits On-the-job training, on-site room and board at no charge, laundry facilities. Preemployment training of 4 days is required and includes safety and accident prevention, group interaction, first-aid, CPR, leadership, camper-counselor relations, orientation to special needs, types of disabilities, and required skills. Orientation is paid.

Contact Jane Carr, Camp Director, Camp Harmon, Department SJ, 430 West Grant Street, Healdsburg, California 95448; 707-433-3530. Application deadline: June 1.

CAMP JCA SHOLOM
34342 MULHOLLAND HIGHWAY
MALIBU, CALIFORNIA 90265

General Information Residential Jewish camp offering a warm, supportive atmosphere for campers ages 7–17. Established in 1951. Owned by Jewish Community Centers. Affiliated with American Camping Association, United Way, Jewish Community Centers, North America. 135-acre facility located 25 miles north of Los Angeles. Features: Olympic-size swimming pool; expanded ropes course; location in Malibu Mountains; proximity to Pacific Ocean (5 miles); 15 miles of hiking trails.

Profile of Summer Employees Total number: 75; average age: 20; 50% male, 50% female; 10% minorities; 20% high school students; 78% college students; 10% international; 70% local residents. Nonsmokers preferred.

Employment Information Openings are from June 17 to August 22. Winter break positions also offered. Jobs available: ▶ 40 *counselors* with high school senior status; ▶ 8 *swimming and water safety instructors* with CPR, ALS, and WSI certifications; ▶ 1 *ropes course leader* with ability to lead groups through high and low elements; ▶ 1 *song leader* with ability to lead camp-wide singing of American and Hebrew folk songs, highly spirited nature, and guitar-playing skills; ▶ 1 *Jewish education instructor* with knowledge of Jewish traditions, culture, history, and entertainment, as well as the ability to develop and lead camp-wide programs, including all-day Shabbat programs; ▶ 3 *unit heads* with college degree, three years of camping experience, and good Jewish program skills (graduate training or social work experience helpful); ▶ 2 *teen travel leaders* (minimum age 21) with college degree, knowledge of outdoors (experience with children essential), and current first aid and CPR certification; ▶ 1 *experienced registered nurse* with ability to run the infirmary, supervise nurse's aide, and interact well with parents; ▶ 1 *bus driver* with current Class II California driver's license and a clean driving record (knowledge of mountain driving extremely helpful). All positions offered at $1000–$3000 per season.

Benefits On-the-job training, on-site room and board at no charge, laundry facilities.

Contact Tami Gelb, Assistant Director, Camp JCA Sholom, Department SJ, 34342 Mulholland Highway, Malibu, California 90265; 818-889-5500, Fax 818-889-5132. Application deadline: March 31.

CAMP LA JOLLA
10050 NORTH TORREY PINES ROAD
LA JOLLA, CALIFORNIA 92037

General Information Weight-loss/fitness camp for ages 8 and older serving separate age and gender groups in fitness, sports, nutrition, behavior modification, field trips, beach visits, theater arts and arts and crafts; emphasis on healthy lifestyle. Established in 1979. Owned by Nancy Lenhart. Affiliated with American Camping Association, Western Association of Independent Camps. 50-acre facility located 8 miles north of San Diego. Features: gymnasium and university facilities; suite-style residences with private baths and lounges; exclusive indoor/outdoor dining; volleyball and tennis courts; university-size swimming pool, indoor pool, and Jacuzzi; 35-million-dollar fitness sports complex; hiking and biking trails; one mile from the beach.

Profile of Summer Employees Total number: 35; average age: 22; 20% male, 80% female; 25% minorities; 5% high school students; 95% college students; 30% local residents. Nonsmokers preferred.

Employment Information Openings are from June 12 to August 20. Jobs available: ▶ 10 *exercise specialists* with WSI and lifeguard certification at $600–$1600 per season; ▶ 15 *counselors* at $600–$1600 per season; ▶ 3 *nutritionists* at $600–$1600 per season; ▶ 3 *behavior modification specialists* at $600–$1600 per season; ▶ 2 *nurses* with RN, EMT, or LPN license at $1800–$2600 per season; ▶ *aerobics instructors* at $600–$1600 per season; ▶ *tennis instructors* at $600–$1600 per season.

Benefits College credit, on-the-job training, on-site room and board at no charge, laundry facilities, health insurance, all field trips, special outings, and cultural events paid for by camp. Preemployment training is required and includes safety and accident prevention, group interaction, first-aid, leadership, camper-counselor relations. Orientation is paid.

Contact Nancy Lenhart, Director, Camp La Jolla, 753 B Avenue, Coronado, California 92118; 800-825-8746, Fax 619-435-8188, URL http://camplajolla.com. Application deadline: April 15.

CAMP LAKOTA
11220 DOROTHY LANE
FRAZIER PARK, CALIFORNIA 93225

General Information Residential camp serving 140 girls ages 7–17 weekly and emphasizing traditional activities, horsemanship, and Girl Scout programs. Established in 1949. Owned by San Fernando Valley Girl Scout Council. Affiliated with Girl Scouts of the United States of America, American Camping Association. 54-acre facility located 75 miles north of Los Angeles. Features: proximity to mountains and Los Padres National Forest; swimming pool; horse center.

Profile of Summer Employees Total number: 45; average age: 20; 5% male, 95% female; 30% minorities; 5% high school students; 95% college students; 20% international; 2% local residents. Nonsmokers preferred.

Employment Information Openings are from June 14 to August 26. Jobs available: ▶ 1 *head cook* at $200–$230 per week; ▶ 1 *program director* at $150–$190 per week; ▶ 1 *health supervisor* (nurse) with RN license (preferred) at $200–$285 per week; ▶ 1 *riding director* with AHA certification or equivalent (preferred) at $170–$200 per week; ▶ 2 *wranglers* with horse experience at $150–$190 per week; ▶ 1 *pool director* with standard first aid, WSI, CPR, and lifeguarding certification at $170–$200 per week; ▶ 15 *unit counselors* at $145–$175 per week; ▶ 1 *maintenance person* at $145–$175 per week; ▶ 7 *unit leaders* at $150–$190 per week; ▶ 3 *kitchen staff members* at $120–$175 per week; ▶ 1 *assistant pool director* with lifeguard, CPR, and standard first aid certification at $145–$175 per week. International students encouraged to apply; must apply through recognized agency.

Benefits On-the-job training, on-site room and board at no charge, laundry facilities, health insurance. Preemployment training of 10 days is required and includes safety and accident prevention, group interaction, first-aid, CPR, leadership, camper-counselor relations. Orientation is paid.

Contact Karen Morrow, Outdoor Program/Property Manager, Camp Lakota, Department SJ, 9421 Winnetka Avenue, Chatsworth, California 91311; 818-886-1801 Ext. 31, Fax 818-407-4840, E-mail sfvgsc@earthlink.com. Application deadline: May 31.

CAMP SCHERMAN
MOUNTAIN CENTER, CALIFORNIA 92561

General Information Residential Girl Scout camp serving over 2,500 girls per season. Established in 1968. Owned by Girl Scout Council of Orange County. Affiliated with Girl Scouts of the United States of America, American Camping Association. 700-acre facility located 50 miles west of Palm Springs. Features: high desert chaparral; 2 lakes; pool; miles of trails; modern cabins and facilities.

Profile of Summer Employees Total number: 90; average age: 21; 5% male, 95% female; 13% minorities; 90% college students; 5% international; 5% local residents. Nonsmokers preferred.

Employment Information Openings are from June 12 to August 25. Jobs available: ► 30 *unit staff members* at $1798 per season; ► 10 *staff supervisors* at $2046 per season; ► 1 *counselor-in-training director* at $2108 per season; ► 1 *counselor-in-training assistant director* at $1860 per season; ► 1 *boating director* with lifeguard training, first aid, and CPR for professional certification waterfront module at $2170 per season; ► 1 *waterfront director* with lifeguard training, first aid, and CPR for professional certification waterfront module at $2170 per season; ► 5 *waterfront staff members* with lifeguard training, first aid, and CPR for professional certification waterfront module at $1922 per season; ► 5 *boating staff members* with lifeguard training, first aid, and CPR for professional certification waterfront module at $1922 per season; ► 5 *program assistants* with skills in nature, arts and crafts, archery, and rock climbing at $1798 per season; ► 5 *experienced riding assistants* at $1860 per season; ► 4 *program directors* with skills and experience in nature, arts and crafts or archery at $2046 per season; ► 2 *awareness aide staff members* with experience working with campers with disabilities at $1798 per season; ► 5 *kitchen staff members* at $2430 per season; ► 2 *pack-out cooks* at $2130 per season; ► *rock climbing director* with experience in rock climbing and teaching rock climbing (certification preferred) at $2046 per season. International students encouraged to apply; must apply through recognized agency.

Benefits On-the-job training, on-site room and board at no charge. Preemployment training of 7 to 9 days is required and includes safety and accident prevention, group interaction, first-aid, CPR, leadership, camper-counselor relations, Girl Scouting, policies and procedures. Orientation is paid.

Contact Margie Haupt, Camp Director, Camp Scherman, Department SJ, PO Box 3739, Costa Mesa, California 92628-3739; 714-979-7900 Ext. 353, Fax 714-850-1299. Application deadline: May 15.

CAMP WASEWAGAN
42121 SEVEN OAKS ROAD
ANGELUS OAKS, CALIFORNIA 92305

General Information Residential camp serving weekly 150 campers from southern California. Established in 1937. Owned by Camp Fire Council of the Foothills. Affiliated with Camp Fire Boys and Girls, Inc., American Camping Association. 50-acre facility located 45 miles northeast of Riverside. Features: 1 outdoor swimming pool; proximity to Jenks Lake; river flowing on edge of camp; heavily wooded location with tall pines; camp store; spacious unit buildings.

Profile of Summer Employees Total number: 30; average age: 22; 50% male, 50% female; 35% minorities; 80% college students; 2% retirees; 25% international; 75% local residents; 10% teachers. Nonsmokers preferred.

Employment Information Openings are from June 20 to August 14. Jobs available: ► *unit director* (minimum age 21) at $950–$1000 per season; ► *general counselors* (minimum age 18) at $900 per season; ► *waterfront director* (minimum age 21) with WSI, senior lifesaving, first aid, and CPR certification at $1500 per season; ► *waterfront assistant* (minimum age 18) with senior lifesaving, first aid, and CPR certification at $975 per season; ► *assistant cook* at $1050 per season. International students encouraged to apply; must obtain own visa and working papers prior to employment.

Benefits On-the-job training, formal ongoing training, on-site room and board at no charge, laundry facilities, close friendly atmosphere, work with children of all age groups, secondary accident insurance.

Contact Carol Eckert, Director of Marketing, Camp Fire Council of the Foothills, Camp Wasewagan, 136 West Lime Avenue, Monrovia, California 91016; 818-305-1200, Fax 818-305-1205. Application deadline: May 31.

CEDAR LAKE EDUCATION CENTER AMERICAN YOUTH FOUNDATION
PO BOX 1568, 1100 MILL CREEK ROAD
BIG BEAR LAKE, CALIFORNIA 92315-1568

General Information Coed residential camp for 60 campers ages 9-17 offers rock climbing, mountain biking, and backpacking. Established in 1955. Owned by First Congregational Church of Los Angeles. Affiliated with American Camping Association.

Profile of Summer Employees Nonsmokers only.

Employment Information Jobs available: ▶ 1 *waterfront director* with lifeguard certification at $180–$200 per week; ▶ *general counselors* with CPR and first aid certification at $125–$200 per week. International students encouraged to apply; must obtain own visa and working papers prior to employment.

Benefits On-the-job training, formal ongoing training, on-site room and board at no charge, laundry facilities, travel reimbursement, workmen's compensation. Preemployment training is required.

Contact John Ryan, Director, Cedar Lake Education Center American Youth Foundation, Department SJ, PO Box 1568, Big Bear Lake, California 92315; 909-866-5724, Fax 909-866-5715.

DOUGLAS RANCH CAMPS
33200 EAST CARMEL VALLEY ROAD
CARMEL VALLEY, CALIFORNIA 93924

General Information Private, traditional, residential summer camp for 100 children ages 7–14. Structured program in horseback riding, swimming, archery, tennis, riflery, and crafts. Focuses on improving social skills, self-esteem, and confidence in a positive and nurturing environment. Established in 1925. Owned by Carole Ehrhardt. Affiliated with American Camping Association, Western Association of Independent Camps, National Archery Association, National Rifle Association. 120-acre facility located 15 miles east of Carmel. Features: large outdoor riding ring; 4 outdoor tennis courts; swimming pool; private trails for hikes and rides; 2 archery ranges; 1 large ball field.

Profile of Summer Employees Total number: 40; average age: 21; 40% male, 60% female; 20% minorities; 70% college students; 5% retirees; 35% international; 50% local residents; 15% teachers. Nonsmokers only.

Employment Information Openings are from June 12 to August 24. Jobs available: ▶ *swimming instructors* with WSI and/or lifeguard certification at $2000–$2200 per season; ▶ *riding instructors* with experience giving riding lessons, teaching children, riding, saddling, and in general horse care at $2000–$2300 per season; ▶ *tennis instructors* with experience on tennis team or in teaching at $2000–$2200 per season; ▶ *archery instructors* with camp, school, or archery team experience at $2000–$2200 per season; ▶ *riflery instructors* with camp, school, or riflery team experience at $2000–$2200 per season; ▶ *general counselors* with experience working with children, general experience in at least 2 activities (riding, swimming, tennis, archery, riflery, crafts) at $2000–$2200 per season; ▶ *kitchen assistants* with experience in general food preparation and dishwashing at $2000–$2200 per season. International students encouraged to apply; must apply through recognized agency.

Benefits On-the-job training, on-site room and board at no charge, small camp with family atmosphere, constant contact, feedback, and input from camp directors. Preemployment training of 7 days is required and includes safety and accident prevention, group interaction, first-aid, CPR, leadership, camper-counselor relations, training in activities. Orientation is paid.

Contact Kristen Smith, Assistant Director, Douglas Ranch Camps, 8 Pala Avenue, Piedmont, California 94611; 510-547-3925, Fax 510-653-5036, E-mail director@doulgascamp.com, URL http://www.douglascamp.com. Application deadline: May 1.

DRAKESBAD GUEST RANCH
END OF WARNER VALLEY ROAD
CHESTER, CALIFORNIA 96020

General Information Rustic guest ranch in the heart of Lassen National Park. Established in 1900. Owned by National Park Service. Operated by California Guest Service. Located 115 miles northwest of Reno, Nevada. Features: 180 miles of hiking trails; hot spring swimming pool; 80 miles of trail rides; stream fishing; freshwater lake; hot springs and steam vent for geothermal activities.

Profile of Summer Employees Total number: 22; average age: 26; 15% male, 85% female; 10% minorities; 5% high school students; 80% college students; 10% international; 20% local residents. Nonsmokers preferred.

Employment Information Openings are from June 1 to October 15. Jobs available: ► *wrangler* with first aid and CPR certification at $6 per hour; ► *wait person* at $5.15 per hour; ► *kitchen help/food prep person* at $5.15 per hour; ► *kitchen maintenance* at $5.15 per hour; ► *maintenance/ groundskeeper* with technical skills at $6 per hour. International students encouraged to apply; must apply through recognized agency.

Benefits On-the-job training, on-site room and board at $55 per week, laundry facilities, job safety bonus, company-sponsored employee activities. Preemployment training of 1 day is required and includes safety and accident prevention, group interaction, CPR, customer relations, sanitation, fire suppression. Orientation is paid.

Contact Ed Fiebiger, Ranch Host, Drakesbad Guest Ranch, 2150 North Main Street, Red Bluff, California 96080; 916-529-9820, Fax 916-529-4511, E-mail calguest@mci.com. Application deadline: March 31.

EMANDAL–A FARM ON A RIVER
16500 HEARST ROAD
WILLITS, CALIFORNIA 95490

General Information Coeducational residential camp for 50 youngsters ages 6–16 for the first half of the summer; a family vacation farm for 45–55 people of all ages for the second half. Established in 1908. Owned by Clive and Tamara Adams. Affiliated with American Camping Association, Western Association of Independent Camps. 1,000-acre facility located 140 miles north of San Francisco. Features: location adjacent to a river and national forest; organic farm and garden; proximity to town (16 miles); spring water; hiking trails; farm animals.

Profile of Summer Employees Total number: 20; average age: 22; 50% male, 50% female; 1% minorities; 15% high school students; 50% college students; 1% retirees; 10% international; 20% local residents. Nonsmokers only.

Employment Information Openings are from February 1 to November 30. Year-round positions also offered. Jobs available: ► 15 *camp counselors* (June-July) at $975 per season; ► 8 *family camp workers* (July-August) at $180 per week; ► 2 *gardeners* (entire summer) at $180 per week; ► 1 *pickle maker* (August–October) at $180 per week; ► 2 *farm workers* (until Thanksgiving) at $180 per week; ► *gardener's apprentice* (volunteer from April–November); ► *environmental education naturalists (March-June)* at $190 per week.

Benefits College credit, on-the-job training, on-site room and board at no charge, laundry facilities, health insurance. Preemployment training of 2 to 8 days is required and includes safety and accident prevention, group interaction, first-aid, CPR, leadership, camper-counselor relations, conflict mediation. Orientation is unpaid.

Contact Tamara Adams, Director, Emandal–A Farm on a River, Department SJ, 16500 Hearst Road, Willits, California 95490; 707-459-5439, Fax 707-459-1808, E-mail emandal@pacific.net, URL http://wwwpacific.net:80/~emandal/.

FURNACE CREEK INN AND RANCH
PO BOX 187
DEATH VALLEY, CALIFORNIA 92328

General Information Resort in Death Valley National Park. Established in 1931. Owned by Amfac Parks and Resorts. Affiliated with American Hotel and Motel Association. 10-acre facility located 140 miles west of Las Vegas, Nevada. Features: desert location; unusual geological formations; hiking; elevation below sea level.

Profile of Summer Employees Total number: 300; average age: 28; 75% male, 25% female; 10% minorities; 25% college students; 25% retirees; 10% international; 25% local residents; 5% teachers.

Employment Information Year-round positions offered. Jobs available: ▶ *housekeeping staff members* at $5 per hour; ▶ *dishwashing staff members* at $5 per hour; ▶ *desk clerks* at $5.50 per hour; ▶ *bus persons* at $5 per hour; ▶ *cooks* at $5 per hour; ▶ *retail clerks* at $5.50 per hour. International students encouraged to apply; must obtain own visa and working papers prior to employment; must apply through recognized agency.

Benefits College credit, on-the-job training, formal ongoing training, on-site room and board, laundry facilities, health insurance, tuition reimbursement, free golf, tennis, and swimming, breakfast and lunch are free, dinner costs $2.00, meals are free for desk clerks.

Contact Robin Copeland, Human Resources Recruiter, Furnace Creek Inn and Ranch, Department SJ, PO Box 187, Death Valley, California 92328; 760-786-2311, Fax 760-786-2396.

GOLD ARROW CAMP
HUNTINGTON LAKE, CALIFORNIA 93634

General Information Private residential camp for boys and girls ages 6–14. Established in 1933. Affiliated with American Camping Association, Western Association of Independent Camps, Association of Independent Camps. 25-acre facility located 65 miles northeast of Fresno. Features: location on 6-mile long Huntington Lake; location in Sierra National Forest and 30 miles south of Yosemite National Park.

Profile of Summer Employees Total number: 100; average age: 21; 55% male, 45% female; 10% minorities; 80% college students; 5% retirees; 8% international; 15% local residents; 10% teachers. Nonsmokers only.

Employment Information Openings are from June 16 to August 17. Year-round positions also offered. Jobs available: ▶ *group counselor* at $141 per week; ▶ *activity counselor* with training or certification depending on activity at $141 per week; ▶ *maintenance staff/driver* with class B driver's license at $175–$200 per week; ▶ *kitchen staff* at $150–$200 per week. International students encouraged to apply; must obtain own visa and working papers prior to employment; must apply through recognized agency.

Benefits College credit, on-site room and board at $62 per week, laundry facilities, travel reimbursement, room/board expense is already taken out of salary. Preemployment training of 7 days is required and includes safety and accident prevention, group interaction, first-aid, leadership, camper-counselor relations. Orientation is paid.

Contact Steven Monke, Director, Gold Arrow Camp, 260 Newport Center Drive, Suite 400, Newport Beach, California 92660; 714-759-9292, Fax 714-721-8318, E-mail mail@goldarrowcamp. com. Application deadline: April 30.

HUNEWILL GUEST RANCH
TWIN LAKES ROAD
BRIDGEPORT, CALIFORNIA 93517

General Information Guest ranch accommodating 45–55 guests weekly. Established in 1861. Owned by Hunewill family. Operated by Hunewill Land and Livestock. Affiliated with Dude Ranchers' Association. 4,800-acre facility located 120 miles south of Reno, Nevada. Features: lush meadows; working cattle ranch; view of Sierra Nevada Mountains; individual cottages; Victorian ranch house with kitchen and dining room; 100 horses for riding.

Profile of Summer Employees Total number: 19; average age: 21; 25% male, 75% female; 5% high school students; 85% college students; 10% local residents. Nonsmokers preferred.

Employment Information Openings are from May 15 to October 3. Jobs available: ▶ 4 *experienced waiters/waitresses* at $260–$300 per week; ▶ 3 *cabin staff members* with ability to work quickly and eye for neatness at $260 per week; ▶ 1 *maintenance person* with general plumbing, electrical, and carpentry ability including fence building and some work with livestock at $260 per week; ▶ 1 *cook* with previous cooking experience or cooking school certification at $1400–$1700 per month; ▶ 1 *breakfast/pastry chef* with experience baking for groups at $1400 per month; ▶ 3 *wranglers* with extensive horse experience and good people skills at $900–$1000 per month.

Benefits On-the-job training, on-site room and board at $170 per month, laundry facilities, free horseback riding during time off, tips that range from $70–$130 weekly. Off-site boarding costs are $600 per month.

Contact Betsy Hunewill Elliott, Assistant Manager, Hunewill Guest Ranch, Department SJ, 205 Hunewill Lane, Wellington, Nevada 89444; 702-465-2238. Application deadline: February 1.

JAMESON RANCH CAMP
GLENNVILLE, CALIFORNIA 93226

General Information Jameson Ranch Camp connects children to a self-sufficient ranch lifestyle where campers grow some of the food and help with the farm animals. Established in 1934. Owned by Ross and Debby Jameson. Affiliated with American Camping Association, Western Association of Independent Camps. 520-acre facility located 40 miles east of Bakersfield. Features: elevation of 4,600 feet; property bordered on two sides by Sequoia National Forest; status as self-sufficient ranch; lake for boating and fishing; farm animals; noncompetitive environment; nestled in rolling hills and oaks with majestic pines.

Profile of Summer Employees Total number: 25; average age: 21; 50% male, 50% female; 20% minorities; 90% college students; 5% retirees; 10% international; 5% local residents. Nonsmokers only.

Employment Information Openings are from June 21 to September 6. Year-round positions also offered. Jobs available: ▶ 2 *swimming instructors* with WSI certification at $2100 per season; ▶ 4 *lifeguards* with ALS certification at $2100 per season; ▶ 1 *rock climbing instructor* at $2100 per season; ▶ 2 *horse instructors* at $2100 per season; ▶ 2 *crafts instructors* at $2100 per season; ▶ 1 *mountain biking instructor* at $2100 per season; ▶ 1 *drama instructor* at $2100 per season; ▶ 1 *horse-vaulting instructor* at $2100 per season; ▶ 1 *archery instructor* at $2100 per season; ▶ 1 *riflery instructor* at $2100 per season; ▶ 2 *kitchen persons* at $2100 per season; ▶ 1 *head cook* at $3100 per season; ▶ 1 *photography instructor* at $2100 per season. International students encouraged to apply; must obtain own visa and working papers prior to employment; must apply through recognized agency.

Benefits College credit, on-the-job training, formal ongoing training, on-site room and board at no charge, laundry facilities, workmen's compensation insurance. Preemployment training of 6 days is required and includes safety and accident prevention, group interaction, leadership, camper-counselor relations. Orientation is paid.

Contact Mr. Ross Jameson, Owner/Director, Jameson Ranch Camp, Department SJ, PO Box 459, Glennville, California 93226; 805-536-8888. Application deadline: May 30.

LOS ANGELES DESIGNERS' THEATRE
BOX 1883
STUDIO CITY, CALIFORNIA 91614-0883

General Information Summer theater that produces stage productions and teaches theatrical producing, including the legal aspects of production. Established in 1970. Owned by Los Angeles Designers' Theatre. Features: over 100 lighting instruments and a computerized dimmer board; 16 channels of sound in theater; proximity to CBS studio center, Warner Brothers studios, Universal Studios, Disney studios, ABC and NBC studios; proximity to Sony studios, Paramount studios and approximately 500 live theaters; proximity to CBS Television City and dozens of recording studios; contact with hundreds in entertainment industry; proximity to University of Southern California, University of California-Los Angeles, CalTech, Cal Arts, and other universities and colleges.

Profile of Summer Employees Total number: 100; average age: 30; 50% male, 50% female; 20% minorities; 15% high school students; 30% college students; 2% retirees; 35% local residents. Nonsmokers only.

Employment Information Openings are from January 1 to December 31. Year-round positions also offered. Jobs available: ▶ 6 *directors;* ▶ *actors and actresses;* ▶ *singers and dancers;* ▶ 6 *set designers;* ▶ 6 *lighting designers;* ▶ 6 *property designers;* ▶ 6 *sound designers;* ▶ 6 *costume designers;* ▶ 1 *program/graphics designer;* ▶ 4 *crew members;* ▶ 2 *cutters/drapers* (first hands); ▶ 2 *electricians;* ▶ 3 *carpenters;* ▶ 1 *musical director;* ▶ 1 *choreographer;* ▶ 1 *box office/ house manager;* ▶ *production assistants.*

Benefits College credit, on-the-job training, networking opportunities in the entertainment capital of the world. Off-site boarding costs are $500 per month.

Contact Richard Niederberg, Artistic Director, Los Angeles Designers' Theatre, PO Box 1883 Department P98, Studio City, California 91614-0883; 213-650-9600, Fax 818-985-9200, TDD 818-769-9000.

MOUNT HERMON ASSOCIATION
PO BOX 413
MOUNT HERMON, CALIFORNIA 95041

General Information Mount Hermon comprises three facilities: the Conference Center is a residential center for families; Redwood Camp is a residential camp for primary school through junior high school students; and Ponderosa Lodge is a residential camp for high school students. Established in 1906. Owned by Mount Hermon Association. Affiliated with American Camping Association, Christian Camping International/USA. 500-acre facility located 20 miles south of San Jose. Features: 3 outdoor tennis courts; 3 large sport fields; high and low ropes course; 3 swimming pools, 1 diving pool; 2 climbing towers.

Profile of Summer Employees Total number: 220; average age: 20; 50% male, 50% female; 10% minorities; 5% high school students; 95% college students; 5% international. Nonsmokers only.

Employment Information Openings are from June 9 to September 1. Jobs available: ▶ 66 *experienced counseling staff members* (various positions) with lifeguard certification at $110–$160 per week; ▶ 84 *experienced operational staff* (various positions) at $110–$145 per week; ▶ 65 *experienced program staff* (various positions) at $125–$160 per week. International students encouraged to apply; must apply through recognized agency.

Benefits College credit, on-the-job training, on-site room and board at no charge, laundry facilities, workmen's compensation.

Contact Bob Russell, Personnel Manager, Mount Hermon Association, Department SJ, PO Box 413, Mount Hermon, California 95041; 408-335-4466, Fax 408-335-9218, E-mail mhbob@aol. com, URL http://www.mounthermon.org.

RESORT AT SQUAW CREEK
PO BOX 3333
OLYMPIC VALLEY, CALIFORNIA 96146

General Information 405 room luxury resort and conference center with 5 restaurants, 33,000 square feet of conference space, and championship 18-hole golf course located on scenic Lake Tahoe. Established in 1990. Owned by HCV Partners. 400-acre facility located 42 miles west of Reno, Nevada. Features: 18-hole championship golf course; 5 gourmet restaurants; 3 swimming pools and 4 Jacuzzis; executive fitness and spa; 5 miles from Lake Tahoe; 2 tennis courts.

Profile of Summer Employees Total number: 100; average age: 25; 50% male, 50% female; 5% minorities; 30% college students; 5% retirees; 10% local residents; 1% teachers.

Employment Information Openings are from May 1 to October 1. Jobs available: ▶ *front desk agent* at $8 per hour; ▶ *reservations agent* at $8 per hour; ▶ *telephone operator* at $7 per hour; ▶ *shuttle driver* at $7 per hour; ▶ *room attendant* at $7.25 per hour; ▶ *security officer* at $8 per hour; ▶ *line cook* at $8 per hour; ▶ *pantry cook* at $7.25 per hour; ▶ *steward* at $6.50 per hour; ▶ *banquet server* at $5 per hour; ▶ *busser* at $5 per hour; ▶ *food server* at $5 per hour; ▶ *lifeguard* at $7 per hour; ▶ *mountain buddies attendant* at $7 per hour; ▶ *greeter* at $6.75 per hour; ▶ *bartender* at $6.25 per hour; ▶ *room service server* at $5 per hour; ▶ *honor bar attendant* at $6 per hour; ▶ *deli attendant* at $6.75 per hour; ▶ *pool food runner* at $6.75 per hour; ▶ *pool bartender* at $6.25 per hour; ▶ *pool server* at $5 per hour; ▶ *retail sales associates* at $6.75 per hour; ▶ *greenskeeper* at $7 per hour; ▶ *landscaper* at $7 per hour; ▶ *bike and tennis attendant* at $6.75 per hour; ▶ *assistant golf professional* at $7 per hour; ▶ *golf cart beverage server* at $6.25 per hour.

Benefits College credit, on-the-job training, one free meal per shift in employee cafe. Off-site boarding costs are $700 per month.

Contact Ms. Kim Kelsey, Human Resources Manager, Resort at Squaw Creek, PO Box 3333, Olympic Valley, California 96146; 916-581-6642, Fax 916-581-6648.

SANTA CATALINA SCHOOL SUMMER CAMP
1500 MARK THOMAS DRIVE
MONTEREY, CALIFORNIA 93940

General Information Residential and day camp for girls ages 8–14 with an emphasis on performing and fine arts and athletics. Established in 1953. Owned by Santa Catalina School. 35-acre facility located 75 miles south of San Jose. Features: location on Monterey Bay near Carmel; campus with gardens and Spanish architecture; gymnasium and heated pool; 500-seat theater; modern dormitories (single and double rooms); 6 tennis courts.

Profile of Summer Employees Total number: 40; average age: 22; 20% male, 80% female; 5% minorities; 40% college students; 60% local residents; 60% teachers. Nonsmokers preferred.

Employment Information Openings are from June 16 to July 26. Jobs available: ▶ 14 *counselors* with one year of college completed at $900–$1000 per season; ▶ 6 *experienced head counselors* with two years of college completed at $1050–$1150 per season.

Benefits On-the-job training, on-site room and board at no charge, laundry facilities. Preemployment training of 4 days is required and includes safety and accident prevention, group interaction, first-aid, CPR, leadership, camper-counselor relations. Orientation is paid.

Contact Dr. Nancy Diamonti, Director of Summer Programs, Santa Catalina School Summer Camp, 1500 Mark Thomas Drive, Monterey, California 93940; 408-655-9386, Fax 408-649-3056. Application deadline: April 1.

SKY MOUNTAIN CHRISTIAN CAMP
PO BOX 179
EMIGRANT GAP, CALIFORNIA 95715

General Information Camp conference center serving nondenominational church groups. Established in 1976. Affiliated with American Camping Association, Christian Camping International/USA. 40-acre facility located 65 miles east of Sacramento. Features: location on the shore of Lake Valley Reservoir in Tahoe National Forest; proximity to ski resorts; proximity to Lake Tahoe (40 miles); elevation of 6,000 feet; new gymnasium; newly remodeled cabins with full bathrooms.

Profile of Summer Employees Total number: 15; average age: 20; 50% male, 50% female; 10% high school students; 90% college students; 20% local residents. Nonsmokers only.

Employment Information Openings are from June 15 to August 25. Jobs available: ▶ 3 *experienced kitchen assistants* (minimum age 18) at $125–$175 per week; ▶ 4 *dishwashers* (minimum age 18) at $125–$150 per week; ▶ 4 *laborers* (minimum age 18) at $125–$150 per week; ▶ 2 *lifeguards* (minimum age 18) with senior lifeguard certification at $125–$150 per week; ▶ 1 *waterfront coordinator* (minimum age 21) with senior lifeguard certification at $150–$175 per week.

Benefits On-site room and board at no charge, laundry facilities. Preemployment training of 1 day is required and includes safety and accident prevention, group interaction, CPR. Orientation is paid.

Contact Dezra Saunders, Camp Coordinator, Sky Mountain Christian Camp, PO Box 179, Emigrant Gap, California 95715; 916-389-2118. Application deadline: April 30.

SUPERCAMP
PITZER COLLEGE
CLAREMONT, CALIFORNIA 91711

General Information Residential program for teens that includes life skills and academic courses designed to build self-confidence and lifelong learning skills. Established in 1981. Owned by Bobbi DePorter. Affiliated with American Camping Association, Oceanside Chamber of Commerce, International Alliance for Learning. Located 60 miles northeast of Los Angeles. Features: dormitory rooms; dining hall; swimming pool; ropes course; 6 different sites; location on college campuses.

Profile of Summer Employees Total number: 200; average age: 22; 50% male, 50% female; 80% college students. Nonsmokers only.

Employment Information Openings are from June 20 to August 20. Jobs available: ▶ 20 *facilitators* with presentation skills, college degree, and teaching credential preferred at $1500–$6000 per season; ▶ 10 *counselors* with college degree plus PPS credential or master's degree in counseling or MFCC license at $1000–$4000 per season; ▶ 3 *nurses* with RN license at $1000–$3000 per season; ▶ 76 *team leaders* (peer counselors, ages 18–25) with high school diploma at $500–$1000 per season; ▶ 1 *office manager* with high school diploma at $1000–$2000 per season; ▶ 3 *paramedics* with national or state registration at $700–$2100 per season.

Benefits On-the-job training, on-site room and board at no charge, laundry facilities, internships, experience working with teens in an educational and self-esteem building program, excellent experience for education and psychology majors. Preemployment training of 4 days is required and includes safety and accident prevention, group interaction, leadership, camper-counselor relations. Orientation is unpaid.

Contact Elisabeth Talmon, Human Resources Coordinator, SuperCamp, Department SJ, 1725 South Coast Highway, Oceanside, California 92054; 800-527-5321, Fax 760-722-3507, E-mail supercamp@aol.com, URL http://www.supercamp.com. Application deadline: May 1.

SUPERCAMP
STANFORD UNIVERSITY
STANFORD, CALIFORNIA 94305

General Information Residential program for teens designed to build self-confidence and lifelong learning skills through accelerated learning techniques. Established in 1981. Owned by Bobbi DePorter. Affiliated with American Camping Association, International Alliance for Learning. 8,200-acre facility located 30 miles south of San Francisco. Features: ropes course; swimming pools; volleyball courts; dormitory rooms.

Profile of Summer Employees Total number: 200; average age: 21; 50% male, 50% female; 80% college students. Nonsmokers only.

Employment Information Openings are from July 1 to August 20. Jobs available: ▶ *team leaders* with high school diploma at $500–$1000 per season; ▶ *office managers* with high school diploma at $500–$2000 per season; ▶ *nurse/paramedic* with national or state registration at $1000–$4000 per season; ▶ *EMT* with national or state registration at $700–$2800 per season.

Benefits On-the-job training, on-site room and board at no charge, laundry facilities, internships, experience working with teens in an educational and self-esteem building environment, excellent experience for education and psychology majors. Preemployment training of 4 days is required and includes safety and accident prevention, group interaction, leadership, camper-counselor relations. Orientation is unpaid.

Contact Elisabeth Talmon, Human Resources Coordinator, SuperCamp, Department SJ, 1725

South Coast Highway, Oceanside, California 92054; 800-527-5321, Fax 619-722-3507, E-mail supercamp@aol.com. Application deadline: May 1.

TUMBLEWEED COTTONWOOD DAY CAMP
1024 HANLEY AVENUE
BRENTWOOD, CALIFORNIA 90049

General Information Traditional day camp serving approximately 400 children per day in Los Angeles; helps children learn new activities, meet new people, and develop self-confidence. Established in 1954. Owned by Tumbleweed Educational Enterprises, Inc. Affiliated with American Camping Association, Western Association of Independent Camps, Association of Independent Camps. Situated on 100 acres. Features: 100 wooded acres in Santa Monica canyon; 2 outdoor heated pools; 3 sports fields; hiking and horseback riding trails; 2 archery courses; 2 nature study areas with farm animals.

Profile of Summer Employees Total number: 80; average age: 20; 40% male, 60% female; 20% minorities; 25% high school students; 65% college students; 5% international; 90% local residents; 10% teachers. Nonsmokers only.

Employment Information Openings are from June 22 to August 28. Spring break, Christmas break, year-round positions also offered. Jobs available: ▶ 30 *counselors/van drivers* with good driving record, 1 year of college or more, and experience with children at $235–$265 per week; ▶ 5 *counselors* with 1 year of college or more and experience with children at $205–$235 per week; ▶ 6 *counselors/bus drivers* (minimum age 21) with good driving record, 1 year of college or more, and experience with children at $250–$280 per week; ▶ 2 *specialists* with 1 year of college or more, experience with children, and experience in arts and crafts, creative play/video, gymnastics, or nature/science at $220–$250 per week; ▶ 4 *swim instructors/lifeguards* with LGT and WSI certification, Red Cross first aid, and CPR for the professional rescuer at $265–$295 per week; ▶ 4 *horseback riding instructors* with 2 years horseback riding experience and experience with children at $230–$275 per week; ▶ 2 *horseback riding wranglers* with experience with horses and with children at $205–$235 per week.

Benefits On-the-job training, formal ongoing training, bonus for completing contract, good/safe driver incentives. Off-site boarding costs are $500 per month. Preemployment training of 4 to 5 days is required and includes safety and accident prevention, group interaction, first-aid, CPR, leadership, camper-counselor relations, lifeguard training, drivers training for Class B license. Orientation is paid.

Contact Teri Naftulin, Human Resources Director, Tumbleweed Cottonwood Day Camp, PO Box 49291, Los Angeles, California 90049; 310-472-7474, Fax 310-476-7788. Application deadline: June 1.

UCLA BRUIN TENNIS CAMP
UCLA CAMPUS
LOS ANGELES, CALIFORNIA 90024

General Information Tennis camp for boys and girls ages 8–18 of all different ability levels. Established in 1994. Owned by Bill Martin. Affiliated with University of California Los Angeles. Situated on 30 acres. Features: 11 outdoor lighted tennis courts; swimming pool; game room; track; weight room; 2 large sports fields.

Profile of Summer Employees Total number: 10; average age: 21; 60% male, 40% female; 40% minorities; 90% college students; 10% international; 80% local residents. Nonsmokers only.

Employment Information Openings are from June 20 to August 30. Christmas break positions also offered. Jobs available: ▶ 8 *tennis camp counselors* with CPR certification, tennis instruction experience, and good swimming skills at $250 per week. International students encouraged to apply.

Benefits On-the-job training, on-site room and board at no charge, laundry facilities. Preemployment training of 2 days is required and includes safety and accident prevention, group interaction, first-aid, leadership, camper-counselor relations. Orientation is unpaid.

Contact Bill Martin, UCLA Bruin Tennis Camp, PO Box 64335, Los Angeles, California 90064; 310-475-5853, Fax 310-475-5853. Application deadline: June 1.

WHITEWATER EXPEDITIONS AND TOURS (W.E.T.)
PO BOX 160024
SACRAMENTO, CALIFORNIA 95816

General Information Whitewater rafting on Class III to Class V rivers throughout the western United States with majority in California, Oregon, and Arizona. Program emphasizes adventure sports. Established in 1978. Owned by Stephen P. Liles. Affiliated with Friends of the River, California Outdoors. Features: hot springs; camping on the river.

Profile of Summer Employees Total number: 19; average age: 25; 90% male, 10% female; 5% minorities; 1% high school students; 99% college students; 80% local residents; 50% teachers. Nonsmokers preferred.

Employment Information Openings are from March 1 to October 1. Spring break positions also offered. Jobs available: ▶ *whitewater guides* with CPR, first aid, EMT, and mountain medicine certification at $300–$2000 per month; ▶ *bus drivers* with driver's license, DMV records class B, medical release, and auto mechanic experience at $300–$2000 per month; ▶ *experienced office staff* at $800 per month. International students encouraged to apply; must obtain own visa and working papers prior to employment.

Benefits On-the-job training, college credit for recreation-based majors.

Contact Betty Lopez, Promotional Director, Whitewater Expeditions and Tours (W.E.T.), Department SJ, PO Box 160024, Sacramento, California 95816; 916-451-3241, Fax 916-455-8620.

YMCA CAMP OAKES
PO BOX 452
BIG BEAR CITY, CALIFORNIA 92314

General Information Residential summer camp serving children from around the world in a traditional camp program. Established in 1905. Owned by YMCA of Greater Long Beach. Affiliated with American Camping Association. 230-acre facility located 110 miles east of Los Angeles. Features: fully equipped observatory; elevation of 7,300 feet in the San Bernardino Mountains; sailing on Big Bear Lake; extensive equestrian program; canoeing and kayaking on on-site lake; high and low challenge courses.

Profile of Summer Employees Total number: 60; average age: 23; 50% male, 50% female; 10% minorities; 5% high school students; 95% college students; 10% international; 80% local residents. Nonsmokers only.

Employment Information Openings are from June 16 to September 3. Spring break, Christmas break positions also offered. Jobs available: ▶ *3 program directors* (minimum age 21) with three years of experience at $190&–$250 per week; ▶ *4 certified lifeguards* (minimum age 18) at $150–$170 per week; ▶ *8 cabin counselors* (minimum age 18) with one year of college completed at $150–$170 per week; ▶ *8 junior counselors* (minimum age 18) at $110–$130 per week; ▶ *7 program specialists* (minimum age 18) with experience in riflery, crafts, wrangling, nature, archery, ropes-challenge course, or astronomy at $150–$170 per week; ▶ *1 health care coordinator* (minimum age 21) with RN or EMT training at $175–$250 per week; ▶ *4 experienced cooks* (minimum age 18) at $120–$225 per week. International students encouraged to apply; must apply through recognized agency.

Benefits On-the-job training, on-site room and board at no charge, laundry facilities, spiritual growth, clean air in natural setting. Preemployment training of 5 days is required and includes safety and accident prevention, group interaction, CPR, leadership, program area operation. Orientation is paid.

Contact Michael McGinnis, Program Director, YMCA Camp Oakes, Department SJ, PO Box 90995, Long Beach, California 90809-0995; 562-496-2756, Fax 562-425-1169. Application deadline: May 31.

YMCA CAMP SURF
106 CARNATION AVENUE
IMPERIAL BEACH, CALIFORNIA 91932

General Information Residential oceanside camp serving groups and individuals for summer camp, outdoor education, teen leadership, youth retreats, and beach tent camping. Established in 1970. Operated by YMCA of San Diego County. Affiliated with Surf Riders Foundation, American Camping Association. 43-acre facility located 10 miles south of San Diego. Features: location on Pacific oceanfront in southern California; outdoor dining deck overlooking ocean; proximity to major attractions in southern California; 10 acres of marshland; miles of pristine undeveloped beach.

Profile of Summer Employees Total number: 50; average age: 21; 50% male, 50% female; 25% minorities; 15% high school students; 84% college students; 1% retirees; 30% international; 40% local residents; 5% teachers. Nonsmokers only.

Employment Information Openings are from May 1 to September 30. Year-round positions also offered. Jobs available: ▶ *camp counselors* with first aid and CPR certification at $135–$150 per week; ▶ *unit leader* with first aid and CPR certification at $175 per week; ▶ *cook* with food handler's certification at $6 per hour; ▶ *ocean lifeguard* with lifeguarding and Basic Life Support certification at $135–$150 per week; ▶ *health services coordinator* with first aid, CPR, BLS, and EMT certification at $175 per week; ▶ *kitchen assistant* at $5.25 per hour. International students encouraged to apply; must apply through recognized agency.

Benefits College credit, on-the-job training, on-site room and board at no charge, certification available in American Red Cross first aid and CPR, development in wide range of aquatic skills, gaining knowledge of environmental education. Preemployment training of 6 days is required and includes safety and accident prevention, group interaction, leadership, camper-counselor relations, activity. Orientation is paid.

Contact Brad Russell, Program Director, YMCA Camp Surf, 106 Carnation Avenue, Imperial Beach, California 91932; 619-423-5850, Fax 619-423-4141, URL http://wwwymca.org/.

YOSEMITE CONCESSION SERVICES CORPORATION
PO BOX 578
YOSEMITE NATIONAL PARK, CALIFORNIA 95389

General Information Main concessionaire for Yosemite National Park, providing all aspects of guest services. Owned by Delaware North Companies. Located 280 miles east of San Francisco. Features: location in the great outdoors; waterfalls; high mountains and granite peaks; scenic views; hiking and rock-climbing.

Profile of Summer Employees Total number: 1,100; average age: 33.

Employment Information Openings are from April 1 to September 5. Year-round positions also offered. Jobs available: ▶ 50 *food service persons* at $5.49 per hour; ▶ 50 *roomkeepers* at $5.52 per hour; ▶ 50 *custodians* at $5.52 per hour; ▶ 50 *fast food attendants* with cash handling experience at $5.49 per hour; ▶ 50 *sales clerks* with cash handling experience at $5.54 per hour; ▶ 50 *front desk personnel* with computer experience at $5.62 per hour; ▶ 50 *hosts/hostesses* with restaurant experience at $5.56 per hour; ▶ 50 *experienced cooks* at $5.56–$6.53 per hour.

Benefits On-the-job training, on-site room and board at $51 per week, laundry facilities, health insurance, recreation discounts, retail discounts, restaurant discounts.

Contact Marty Livingston, Manager of Employee Relations and Placement, Yosemite Concession Services Corporation, Department SJ, PO Box 578, Yosemite National Park, California 95389; 209-372-1236, Fax 209-372-1050.

COLORADO

ANDERSON WESTERN COLORADO CAMPS, LTD.
7177 COLORADO RIVER ROAD
GYPSUM, COLORADO 81637

General Information Residential coed camp serving 125 campers per session. Established in 1962. Owned by Scott Stuart. Affiliated with American Camping Association, Western Association of Independent Camps. Situated on 200 acres. Features: daily white-water rafting on Colorado River; heated swimming pool; 36-foot climbing wall; 4–5 day extended trips (rafting, horseback riding, caving, etc.); low ropes challenge course; many miles of horseback riding trails.

Profile of Summer Employees Total number: 40; average age: 25; 50% male, 50% female; 3% high school students; 60% college students. Nonsmokers only.

Employment Information Openings are from May 15 to August 29. Jobs available: ▶ 20 *camp counselors* at $975–$1200 per season; ▶ 3 *wranglers* at $975–$1200 per season; ▶ 1 *riding instructor* at $1200–$1500 per season; ▶ 2 *cooks* at $2500–$7000 per week; ▶ 4 *lodge/grounds staff members* at $975–$1200 per season; ▶ *nurse* at $200–$400 per week. International students encouraged to apply; must obtain own visa and working papers prior to employment; must apply through recognized agency.

Benefits On-the-job training, formal ongoing training, on-site room and board at no charge, laundry facilities, travel reimbursement.

Contact Christopher Porter, Director, Anderson Western Colorado Camps, Ltd., 7177 Colorado River Road, Gypsum, Colorado 81637; 970-524-7766, Fax 970-524-7107, E-mail andecamp@rof.net. Application deadline: March 30.

THE ASPEN LODGE AND RESORT
6120 HIGHWAY 7
ESTES PARK, COLORADO 80517

General Information Resort, conference center, and ranch providing lodging, entertainment, and meals. Established in 1940. Owned by Tom and Jill Hall. Affiliated with Colorado Dude and Guest Ranch Association, Automobile Association of America, Denver Metro Convention and Visitors' Bureau. 85-acre facility located 65 miles north of Denver. Features: 2 tennis courts; horseback riding trail; swimming pool; restaurant.

Profile of Summer Employees Total number: 30; average age: 20; 50% male, 50% female. Nonsmokers preferred.

Employment Information Openings are from May 1 to October 31. Spring break, winter break, Christmas break, year-round positions also offered. Jobs available: ▶ *recreation staff* at $5 per hour; ▶ *livery staff* at $5 per hour; ▶ *waitstaff* at $5 per hour; ▶ *children's counselors* at $5 per hour; ▶ *various positions.*

Benefits On-the-job training, formal ongoing training, laundry facilities, travel reimbursement, health insurance, female employees provided with on-site room/board for $150/month, male employees provided with off-site room/board for $150/month.

Contact Personnel Department, The Aspen Lodge and Resort, Department SJ, 6120 Highway 7, Estes Park, Colorado 80517; 970-586-8133, Fax 970-586-8133.

BAR LAZY J GUEST RANCH
447 COUNTY ROAD 3, BOX N
PARSHALL, COLORADO 80468

General Information Guest ranch with capacity for 40 people. Established in 1912. Owned by Jerry and Cheri Helmicki. Affiliated with Colorado Dude and Guest Ranch Association, Dude

Ranchers' Association, Granby Chamber of Commerce. 70-acre facility located 105 miles northwest of Denver. Features: horseback riding trails; Colorado River fishing; gold medal water (⅔ miles privately owned); trout pond (stocked yearly, no license needed); swimming pool and Jacuzzi.

Profile of Summer Employees Total number: 18; average age: 21; 50% male, 50% female; 82% college students; 18% retirees. Nonsmokers only.

Employment Information Openings are from May 1 to September 30. Jobs available: ▶ 1 *experienced head wrangler* at $800 per month; ▶ 5 *experienced wranglers* at $500 per month; ▶ 2 *counselors* with experience working with children at $450 per month; ▶ 2 *waitresses/ waiters* at $450 per month; ▶ 2 *housekeepers* at $450 per month; ▶ 1 *kitchen helper* at $450 per month; ▶ 1 *assistant cook* at $550 per month.

Benefits On-the-job training, formal ongoing training, on-site room and board at no charge, laundry facilities.

Contact Jerry Helmicki, Owner, Bar Lazy J Guest Ranch, Department SJ, Box N, Parshall, Colorado 80468; 970-725-3437, Fax 970-725-0121, E-mail barlazyj@rkymtnhi.com. Application deadline: May 1.

BAR NI RANCH
6614 HIGHWAY 12, STONEWALL GAP
WESTON, COLORADO 81091

General Information Private guest ranch with 15–35 guests per week. Features horseback riding, fishing, and hiking; lodge and ranch-style meals as well as gourmet health-conscious meals; and square dancing and cookouts. Established in 1950. 36,000-acre facility located 35 miles west of Trinidad. Features: 36,000 acre ranch; elevation from 8000 to 14000 feet; Sangro de Christo Mountains; conservation easement with The Nature Conservancy; 40–50 horses; extensive horseback trails.

Profile of Summer Employees Total number: 12; average age: 25; 50% male, 50% female; 20% minorities; 20% high school students; 25% college students; 10% local residents; 10% teachers. Nonsmokers preferred.

Employment Information Openings are from May 1 to October 31. Year-round positions also offered. Jobs available: ▶ 2 *experienced wranglers/general ranch help* with CPR and first aid certification preferred at $800 per month; ▶ 2 *mechanics/general ranch help* with large and small engine mechanical skills at $800 per month; ▶ 1 *chef* with cooking school certification at $1200 per month; ▶ 5 *cook's helpers/waitstaff/child care/lawn care* at $800 per month; ▶ 2 *housekeepers* at $800 per month.

Benefits On-the-job training, on-site room and board at no charge, laundry facilities, horseback riding, hiking, and fishing, gorgeous mountain living environment.

Contact Tom and Linda Perry, Ranch Managers, Bar NI Ranch, Department SJ, 6614 Highway 12, Weston, Colorado 81091; 719-868-3331, Fax 719-868-2708, E-mail barniranch@aol.com. Application deadline: April 1.

BLAZING PADDLES/SNOWMASS WHITEWATER, INC.
105 VILLAGE SQUARE
SNOWMASS VILLAGE, COLORADO 81615

General Information Outdoor adventure company providing guided raft, downhill mountain bike, 4-wheel drive, hiking, and scenic tours of the Colorado Rockies in the Aspen/Snowmass area. Established in 1969. Owned by Bob & Laurie Harris. Located 150 miles west of Denver. Features: Maroon Bells-two peaks over 14,000 feet high; White River National Forest; Colorado River, Roaring Fork River, Arkansas River for great white-water rafting; historical Aspen area; miles of bicycle trails; hiking trails for all abilities; Jeep roads in all directions; world-class fly fishing on several local rivers and lakes.

Profile of Summer Employees Total number: 65; average age: 30; 55% male, 45% female; 15% minorities; 5% college students; 80% local residents; 1% teachers. Nonsmokers preferred.

Employment Information Openings are from May 15 to September 6. Jobs available: ▶ *sales and marketing coordination interns* at $150 per week. International students encouraged to apply; must obtain own visa and working papers prior to employment.

Benefits College credit, on-the-job training. Off-site boarding costs are $400 per month. Preemployment training of 3 to 5 days is required and includes group interaction.

Contact Linda Blomquist, Sales and Marketing Manager, Blazing Paddles/Snowmass Whitewater, Inc., Department SJ, Box 5068, Snowmass Village, Colorado 81615; 970-923-4544, Fax 970-923-4994. Application deadline: February 1.

CENTRAL CITY OPERA
DENVER, COLORADO

General Information Opera house that produces three mainstage performances per summer between late June and early August. Established in 1932. Owned by Central City Opera House Association. Affiliated with Opera America. Located 40 miles west of Denver. Features: opera house.

Profile of Summer Employees Total number: 17; average age: 21; 50% male, 50% female; 20% minorities; 85% college students; 20% local residents.

Employment Information Openings are from June 1 to August 15. Jobs available: ▶ 1 *house manager* at $250–$300 per week; ▶ 1 *assistant house manager* at $180–$200 per week; ▶ 2 *office assistants* at $170–$180 per week; ▶ 2 *music librarians* at $170–$180 per week; ▶ 2 *production assistants* at $170–$180 per week; ▶ 2 *public relations assistants* at $170–$180 per week; ▶ 2 *gift shop managers* at $170–$180 per week; ▶ 2 *costume shop assistants* at $170–$180 per week; ▶ 2 *gardeners* at $170–$180 per week.

Benefits On-the-job training, on-site room and board at no charge, laundry facilities, partial travel reimbursement.

Contact Curt Hancock, Artistic Administrator, Central City Opera, Department SJ, 621 17th Street, Suite 1601, Denver, Colorado 80293; 303-292-6500. Application deadline: April 1.

CHELEY COLORADO CAMPS
PO BOX 1170
ESTES PARK, COLORADO 80517

General Information Residential camp serving 475 campers ages 9–17 for four-week sessions in a rigorous outdoor western adventure program. Established in 1921. Owned by Don and Carole Cheley. Affiliated with American Camping Association, Western Association of Independent Camps. 1,300-acre facility located 20 miles northwest of Boulder. Features: 14,000-foot snow-capped peaks; proximity to Rocky Mountain National Park; 500 miles of hiking trails; 8,000-foot elevation; 145 horses; log/stone lodges and cabins.

Profile of Summer Employees Total number: 180; average age: 21; 50% male, 50% female; 1% minorities; 90% college students; 10% retirees; 2% international; 1% local residents; 20% teachers. Nonsmokers only.

Employment Information Openings are from June 4 to August 12. Spring break positions also offered. Jobs available: ▶ *nurses* at $1750–$1800 per season; ▶ *cooks* at $1200–$1500 per season; ▶ *drivers* at $1150 per season; ▶ *counselors* at $1150–$1250 per season; ▶ *office staff members* at $1050–$1150 per season.

Benefits College credit, on-the-job training, formal ongoing training, on-site room and board at no charge, travel reimbursement, health insurance. Preemployment training of 8 days is required and includes safety and accident prevention, group interaction, first-aid, CPR, leadership, camper-counselor relations. Orientation is paid.

Contact Don and Carole Cheley, Directors, Cheley Colorado Camps, Department SJ, PO Box 6525, Denver, Colorado 80206; 303-377-3616, Fax 303-377-3605. Application deadline: February 15.

CHEROKEE PARK RANCH
PO BOX 97
LIVERMORE, COLORADO 80536

General Information Summer guest ranch providing fun outdoor activities for the entire family and specializing in Western hospitality. Established in 1880. Owned by Dickey and Christine Prince. Affiliated with Colorado Dude and Guest Ranch Association, Dude Ranchers' Association, Colorado Hotel and Lodging Association. 200-acre facility located 90 miles northwest of Denver. Features: heated outdoor swimming pool and hot tub; recreation hall with Ping-Pong and pool tables; location adjacent to a national forest; main lodge with 5 guest cabins and 7 staff cabins; outdoor volleyball, basketball, and horseshoes.

Profile of Summer Employees Total number: 22; average age: 20; 42% male, 58% female; 11% minorities; 90% college students; 12% local residents. Nonsmokers preferred.

Employment Information Openings are from May 16 to September 30. Jobs available: ▶ 5 *wranglers* with CPR certification (preferred) at $425 per month; ▶ 2 *children's counselors* with CPR/first aid and lifesaving certification at $425 per month; ▶ 5 *housekeepers/waitresses/waiters* at $425 per month; ▶ 1 *cook* at $550 per month; ▶ 1 *assistant cook/secretary* at $350–$450 per month.

Benefits On-the-job training, on-site room and board at no charge, laundry facilities.

Contact Director, Cherokee Park Ranch, Department SJ, PO Box 97, Livermore, Colorado 80536; 970-493-6522, Fax 970-493-5802. Application deadline: February 15.

COLORADO MOUNTAIN RANCH
PO BOX 711
BOULDER, COLORADO 80306

General Information Day camp serving approximately 100 boys and girls ages 6–16 and enjoyed by other clientele as a mountain retreat. Established in 1927. Owned by Walker family. Affiliated with American Camping Association, National Wildlife Federation. 200-acre facility located 10 miles west of Boulder. Features: location surrounded by Roosevelt National Forest with access to Indian Peaks Wilderness and Rocky Mountain National Park; heated swimming pool; elevation of 8,500 feet in the Colorado Rockies; challenge ropes course; lodge, cabins, old-style miner's tent, and tipi village.

Profile of Summer Employees Total number: 40; average age: 22; 40% male, 60% female; 5% minorities; 90% college students; 5% international. Nonsmokers only.

Employment Information Openings are from June 6 to August 19. Christmas break positions also offered. Jobs available: ▶ 4 *swimming instructors* with one required to have WSI certification and three required to have LGI certification at $900–$975 per season; ▶ 8 *wranglers* at $900–$975 per season; ▶ 1 *archery instructor* at $900–$975 per season; ▶ 1 *riflery instructor* at $900–$975 per season; ▶ 1 *arts and crafts instructor* at $900–$975 per season; ▶ 3 *gymnastics instructors* at $900–$975 per season; ▶ 1 *head cook/kitchen manager* at $1500 per season; ▶ 7 *kitchen workers* at $975 per season; ▶ 3 *maintenance persons* at $975 per season; ▶ 3 *bus drivers* at $1075 per season; ▶ 10 *day-camp counselors* at $975 per season; ▶ 1 *drama instructor* at $975 per season; ▶ 1 *Indian lore instructor* at $975 per season; ▶ 2 *office staff members* at $975 per season; ▶ 2 *backpacking instructors* at $975 per season; ▶ 2 *ropes course instructors* at $975 per season; ▶ 1 *nanny* at $975 per season; ▶ 2 *outcamp/hiking instructors* at $975 per season. International students encouraged to apply; must obtain own visa and working papers prior to employment.

Benefits On-the-job training, on-site room and board at no charge, workmen's compensation insurance, laundry service. Preemployment training of 6 days is required and includes safety and accident prevention, group interaction, first-aid, CPR, leadership, camper-counselor relations. Orientation is paid.

Contact The Walkers, Directors, Colorado Mountain Ranch, Department SJ, 10063 Gold Hill Road, Boulder, Colorado 80302; 303-442-4557. Application deadline: May 1.

COLVIG SILVER CAMPS
9665 FLORIDA ROAD
DURANGO, COLORADO 81301

General Information Outdoor adventure camp located in natural surroundings; mix of traditional summer camp activities and wilderness adventure. Established in 1969. Owned by Craig Colvig Trust. Affiliated with American Camping Association. 600-acre facility located 200 miles north of Albuquerque, New Mexico. Features: location in the mountains bordered by the San Juan National Forest; ropes course and climbing wall; 3 lakes; nearby desert areas with Anasazi Indian Ruins; 14,000-foot peaks; extensive hiking, riding, and biking trails in and around camp.

Profile of Summer Employees Total number: 45; average age: 22; 50% male, 50% female; 90% college students; 5% local residents. Nonsmokers preferred.

Employment Information Openings are from June 7 to August 17. Jobs available: ► 20 *counselors* with first aid and CPR certification and additional consideration for lifeguarding and wilderness first aid at $750–$1000 per season; ► 7 *assistant counselors* with first aid and CPR certification and additional consideration for lifeguarding and wilderness first aid at $700–$900 per season; ► 1 *nurse* with RN license at $2500–$3000 per season; ► 2 *wranglers* with first aid and CPR certification at $750–$900 per season; ► 1 *arts and crafts director* with first aid and CPR certification at $800–$900 per season; ► 1 *rock climbing specialist* with first aid and CPR certification at $1000–$1200 per season; ► 6 *program coordinators* with first aid and CPR certification and supervisory experience at $850–$1000 per season.

Benefits College credit, on-the-job training, on-site room and board at no charge, laundry facilities, health insurance. Preemployment training of 8 days is required and includes safety and accident prevention, group interaction, first-aid, CPR, leadership, camper-counselor relations, wilderness travel issues. Orientation is paid.

Contact Scott Kelley, Program Director, Colvig Silver Camps, 9665 Florida Road, Durango, Colorado 81301; 970-247-2564, Fax 970-247-2547, E-mail 76601.2705@compuserve.com, URL http://www.kidscamps.com/traditional/colvig-silver. Application deadline: March 30.

CROSS BAR X YOUTH RANCH
2111 COUNTY ROAD 222
DURANGO, COLORADO 81301

General Information Christian camp for low income and inner city youth. Established in 1977. Owned by Cross Bar X Youth Ranch, Inc. Affiliated with Christian Camping International/ USAA. 35-acre facility located 12 miles east of Durango. Features: a lake for swimming and fishing; proximity to Rocky Mountains; obstacle course; trails for horseback riding and mountain biking; log buildings and wildlife.

Profile of Summer Employees Total number: 9; average age: 22; 50% male, 50% female; 90% college students. Nonsmokers only.

Employment Information Openings are from June 1 to August 15. Jobs available: ► 8 *counselors* at $50–$100 per week; ► 1 *cook;* ► *activities coordinator* with experience in backpacking, mountain biking, and leadership.

Benefits College credit, on-the-job training, on-site room and board at no charge, laundry facilities. Preemployment training of 10 days is required and includes safety and accident prevention, group interaction, first-aid, leadership, camper-counselor relations. Orientation is paid.

Contact Nick Brothers, Director, Cross Bar X Youth Ranch, Department SJ, 2111 County Road 222, Durango, Colorado 81301; 970-259-2716, E-mail crossbar@frontier.net. Application deadline: May 1.

CURECANTI NATIONAL RECREATION AREA
102 ELK CREEK
GUNNISON, COLORADO 81230

General Information National recreation area with a focus on natural and cultural history interpretation and education serving 1.4 million visitors per year. Established in 1965. Owned by United States Department of the Interior, National Park Service. Affiliated with Southwest Parks and Monuments Association, National Association for Interpretation, Colorado Alliance for Environmental Education. 40,000-acre facility located 15 miles west of Gunnison. Features: location on Blue Mesa Lake (Colorado's largest body of water–20 miles long with 96 miles of shoreline); full-service marinas for boating/fishing; visitor center and ranger stations providing area information and sales items (mostly books); both developed and remote camping sites; expanse of semi-arid sage country surrounded by snow-capped mountains and many other geological features; remote inner canyons offering diverse ecosystems and solitude.

Profile of Summer Employees Total number: 14; average age: 23; 50% male, 50% female; 2% minorities; 50% college students; 25% retirees; 2% local residents; 1% teachers.

Employment Information Openings are from May 15 to August 15. Year-round positions also offered. Jobs available: ▶ *outreach education interns* with education or life science background; ▶ *interpretation interns* with education, life sciences, or history background. All positions offered at $35 per week.

Benefits College credit, on-the-job training, formal ongoing training, on-site room and board at no charge, laundry facilities, $7 per day stipend to offset food costs, workmen's compensation insurance. Preemployment training of 5 to 10 days is required and includes safety and accident prevention, group interaction, leadership. Orientation is paid.

Contact Bill Johnson, Education Specialist, Curecanti National Recreation Area, Department SJ, 102 Elk Creek, Gunnison, Colorado 81230; 970-641-2337 Ext. 204, Fax 970-641-3127, URL http://www.nps.gov/cure. Application deadline: January 15.

DON K RANCH
2677 SOUTH SILOAM ROAD
PUEBLO, COLORADO 81005

General Information Dude ranch serving up to 55 guests weekly in a Western atmosphere. Established in 1947. Owned by Smith family. Affiliated with Colorado Dude and Guest Ranch Association, Dude Ranchers' Association. 1,360-acre facility located 60 miles southwest of Colorado Springs. Features: ranch surrounded by 250,000 acres of the San Isabel National Forest; tennis court; hot tub and large heated swimming pool with diving board and slide; hiking trails; white-water rafting; brunch rides; gourmet meals and evening activities; setting in the hills; complete horseback riding program for guests with their own horse for the week; trail rides.

Profile of Summer Employees Total number: 22; average age: 22; 40% male, 60% female; 90% college students; 5% international. Nonsmokers preferred.

Employment Information Openings are from May 15 to September 30. Jobs available: ▶ 6 *experienced wranglers* with extensive riding experience and knowledge of horses at $350–$800 per month; ▶ 3 *children's counselors* with riding experience, ability to plan activities, lifesaving certification, and ability to work well with children at $350–$800 per month; ▶ 3 *waitstaff members* at $350–$800 per month; ▶ *dishwashing person* at $350–$800 per month; ▶ 1 *cook* at $800–$1200 per month; ▶ 1 *assistant cook* with baking skills at $450–$1000 per month; ▶ 3 *cabin housekeepers* at $350–$800 per month; ▶ 1 *outdoor maintenance person* at $350–$800 per month; ▶ 1 *experienced nanny* with ability to care for owner's children and perform light housekeeping at $350–$800 per month; ▶ 1 *office/store person* with ability to answer telephone, check in guests, assemble mailings, perform as store clerk, and stock and clean store at $350–$800 per month.

Benefits On-site room and board at no charge, laundry facilities, tips, use of facilities on days off, opportunity to meet people from around the world.

Contact Darlene, Mark, or Mary Smith, Don K Ranch, Department SJ, 2677 South Siloam Road, Pueblo, Colorado 81005; 719-784-6600. Application deadline: April 1.

DROWSY WATER RANCH
PO BOX 147 J
GRANBY, COLORADO 80446

General Information Mountain dude ranch serving 60 guests weekly. Established in 1929. Owned by Ken and Randy Sue Fosha. Affiliated with Colorado Dude and Guest Ranch Association, Dude Ranchers' Association, Colorado Hotel and Motel Association. 600-acre facility located 110 miles west of Denver. Features: swimming pool; location in Colorado mountains; spa; miles of hiking/riding trails; proximity to Rocky Mountain National Park; creek running through the ranch.

Profile of Summer Employees Total number: 26; average age: 21; 48% male, 52% female; 15% high school students; 75% college students; 5% local residents. Nonsmokers only.

Employment Information Openings are from May 15 to September 19. Jobs available: ▶ 7 *experienced horse wranglers/guides* with first aid certification at $1400 per month; ▶ 3 *maintenance staff members* at $1350 per month; ▶ 3 *assistant cooks, experience preferred* at $1350 per month; ▶ 1 *experienced head chef* at $1700 per month; ▶ 2 *dishwashers* at $1350 per month; ▶ 2 *experienced counselors* with first aid certification at $1350 per month; ▶ 6 *housekeeping staff members/wait persons* at $1350 per month; ▶ 1 *experienced office person* at $1350 per month.

Benefits College credit, on-the-job training, on-site room and board at no charge, laundry facilities, tips, use of all facilities, horseback riding. Preemployment training of 1 day is optional and includes safety and accident prevention, group interaction, leadership, guest relations. Orientation is paid.

Contact Randy Sue Fosha, Owner, Drowsy Water Ranch, Department SJ, PO Box 147 J, Granby, Colorado 80446; 970-725-3456, Fax 970-725-3611, E-mail dwrken@aol.com, URL http://www.dude-ranch.com/drowsy_water.html.

DVORAK'S KAYAKING AND RAFTING EXPEDITIONS
17921 HIGHWAY 285
NATHROP, COLORADO 81236

General Information Outfitters offering whitewater rafting and kayaking expeditions on 10 rivers and in 29 canyons in 5 states of the Southwest. Established in 1969. Owned by Bill and Jaci Dvorak. Affiliated with America Outdoors, Colorado River Outfitters' Association, Arkansas River Outfitters' Association. 10-acre facility located 160 miles northeast of Denver. Features: 10 different rivers with 29 canyons in 5 states; kayak and swiftwater rescue instructional programs; combination trips including mountain biking, hiking, 4WD, and horseback riding; custom fly fishing trips.

Profile of Summer Employees Total number: 30; average age: 25; 60% male, 40% female; 60% college students; 10% international; 30% local residents; 10% teachers. Nonsmokers preferred.

Employment Information Openings are from May 1 to October 1. Spring break, year-round positions also offered. Jobs available: ▶ 10 *river guides* (multi-day) with advanced first aid/CPR valid to year-end at $550 per month; ▶ 2 *reservations/office staff members* with computer and telephone skills and outdoor background for sales and customer service at $800 per month; ▶ 1 *logistics manager* with computer skills and ordering and packing experience at $1200 per month; ▶ 3 *instructors* (multi-day, kayaking, rafting) with instruction skills and guide experience at $550 per month; ▶ 1 *transportation manager/mechanic* with CDL license/driver and mechanic skills on buses/vans/trucks at $900 per month. International students encouraged to apply; must obtain own visa and working papers prior to employment.

Benefits On-the-job training, on-site room and board at no charge, travel reimbursement, Pro Deals on equipment and related clothing, additional instruction and training courses.

Preemployment training of 14 days is required and includes safety and accident prevention, group interaction, leadership, guide training. Orientation is unpaid.

Contact Bill or Jaci Dvorak, President, Dvorak's Kayaking and Rafting Expeditions, Department SJ, 17921 Highway 285, Nathrop, Colorado 81236; 719-539-6851, Fax 719-539-3378, E-mail dvorakex@rmii.com, URL http://www.vtinet.com/dvorak. Application deadline: March 31.

ECHO CANYON RIVER EXPEDITIONS
54000 U.S. HIGHWAY 50 WEST
CANON CITY, COLORADO 81212

General Information Professional white-water river outfitter offering guided river trips ranging from mild to wild to more than 20,000 guests per year. Established in 1978. Owned by David and Kim Burch. Affiliated with Colorado River Outfitters Association, Arkansas River Outfitters Association, Pikes Peak Country Attractions Association, Better Business Bureau–Colorado Springs, Tourism Industry Action Committee. 4-acre facility located 8 miles west of Canon City. Features: location near Royal Gorge; proximity to Colorado Springs; 60 miles from Continental Divide; close to Arkansas River; nearby camping and hiking.

Profile of Summer Employees Total number: 75; average age: 24; 60% male, 40% female; 10% minorities; 2% high school students; 65% college students; 4% retirees; 20% local residents; 10% teachers. Nonsmokers preferred.

Employment Information Openings are from May 1 to September 30. Jobs available: ▶ 40 *river guides* with standard first aid and CPR certification and river guide experience or completion of our training program (fee charged) at $200–$800 per week; ▶ 10 *bus drivers* with CDL license for Colorado, pre-employment drug/alcohol test, and physical at $200–$400 per week; ▶ 10 *customer service representatives* with guest service experience (preferred) at $200–$400 per week; ▶ 2 *equipment maintenance staff* with experience in raft and boating equipment repair at $200–$600 per week; ▶ 2 *vehicle mechanics* with CDL (preferred) at $300–$500 per week. International students encouraged to apply; must obtain own visa and working papers prior to employment.

Benefits On-the-job training, on-site room and board at no charge.

Contact David and Kim Burch, Owners, Echo Canyon River Expeditions, PO Box 1002, Colorado Springs, Colorado 80901; 719-576-1234. Application deadline: May 30.

ELK MOUNTAIN RANCH
BUENA VISTA, COLORADO 81211

General Information Guest ranch serving 35 guests a true western vacation experience on a weekly basis from June through the end of September. Established in 1981. Owned by C. LaRue and Susan Boyd. Operated by Thomas K. and Sue L. Murphy, Ranch Managers. Affiliated with Colorado Dude and Guest Ranch Association, Dude Ranchers' Association, Colorado Hotel and Lodging Association. 5-acre facility located 90 miles west of Colorado Springs. Features: wilderness setting; elevation of 9,600 feet; true mountain getaway surrounded by the San Isabel National Forest; whitewater rafting, trapshooting, hayrides, square dancing, and horseback riding; exceptional terrain and panoramic vistas; intimate size.

Profile of Summer Employees Total number: 13; average age: 21; 50% male, 50% female; 100% college students. Nonsmokers only.

Employment Information Openings are from May 11 to October 1. Jobs available: ▶ 1 *cook* with high-quality service and love of great food at $700 per month; ▶ 6 *wranglers* with experience riding and/or instructing horsemanship and basic knowledge of horses (care, feeding, and grooming) and good people skills at $475 per month; ▶ 1 *experienced children's counselor* with love of children ages 4–7 and familiarity with horses preferred at $475 per month; ▶ 5 *waitstaff/ housekeeping personnel/dishwashers* with service- and quality-oriented personality at $475 per month; ▶ 1 *assistant cook* with service-and quality-oriented personality at $525 per month; ▶ 1 *general maintenance person* with knowledge of minor repairs, groundskeeping, and vehicle maintenance at $475 per month.

Benefits College credit, on-the-job training, on-site room and board at no charge, laundry facilities, able to participate in activities on day off, tips that average $900 per person per month of employment.

Contact Sue Murphy, Manager, Elk Mountain Ranch, Department SJ, PO Box 910, Buena Vista, Colorado 81211; 719-539-4430, Fax 719-539-4430, E-mail murphs1@sni.net. Application deadline: April 15.

FLYING G RANCH, TOMAHAWK RANCH
400 SOUTH BROADWAY
DENVER, COLORADO 80209

General Information Residential camps serving approximately 1,500 girls ages 6–17 throughout the summer. Established in 1945. Owned by Girl Scouts–Mile-Hi Council. Affiliated with American Camping Association, Association for Horsemanship Safety and Education. 320-acre facility located 65 miles southwest of Denver. Features: proximity to Pike National Forest; hiking and backpacking in the Colorado Rocky Mountains; ropes adventure course; small working farm; archery range; horseback riding.

Profile of Summer Employees Total number: 70; average age: 20; 1% male, 99% female; 15% minorities; 1% high school students; 90% college students; 1% retirees; 17% international; 50% local residents. Nonsmokers preferred.

Employment Information Openings are from June 8 to August 12. Jobs available: ▶ 2 *assistant camp directors/program directors* at $150–$250 per week; ▶ 2 *health supervisors* with RN or LPN license at $300 per week; ▶ 12 *troop leaders* with supervisory skills and experience working with children at $135–$175 per week; ▶ 36 *assistant troop leaders* with experience working with children at $115–$130 per week; ▶ 1 *horseback riding director* with ability to teach, train, and supervise campers and staff in horsemanship at $135–$180 per week; ▶ 6 *horseback riding counselors* with training in Western riding at $115–$130 per week; ▶ 2 *arts and crafts specialists* with ability to teach craft activities to a variety of age levels at $115–$155 per week; ▶ 2 *nature specialists* at $115–$155 per week; ▶ 1 *sports/archery instructor* with ability to teach games and non-competitive sports and certification in archery instruction at $115–$155 per week; ▶ 1 *farm specialist* with ability to care for small farm animals and teach programs at $115–$155 per week; ▶ 1 *ropes course instructor* with training in different levels of ropes course at $115–$155 per week; ▶ 1 *arts/drama specialist* with ability to teach music, dance, puppetry, or theater to groups of children at $115–$155 per week; ▶ 2 *campcraft specialists* with knowledge of hiking, backpacking, compass use, and cooking at $115–$155 per week; ▶ 2 *administrative assistants* with skill in several program areas and business experience at $115–$150 per week. International students encouraged to apply; must obtain own visa and working papers prior to employment; must apply through recognized agency.

Benefits On-the-job training, on-site room and board at no charge, laundry facilities, health insurance, time off during camp. Preemployment training of 7 days is required and includes safety and accident prevention, group interaction, leadership, camper-counselor relations. Orientation is paid.

Contact Debora A. Speicher, Camp Administrator, Flying G Ranch, Tomahawk Ranch, Department SJ, PO Box 9407, Denver, Colorado 80209-0407; 303-778-8774, Fax 303-733-6345, E-mail debbies@gsmhc.org. Application deadline: May 1.

HARMEL'S RANCH RESORT
6748 COUNTY ROAD 742
ALMONT, COLORADO 81210

General Information Family-oriented guest ranch with 38 lodging units, stables, dining room, lounge, heated pool, and general store. Established in 1959. Owned by Bill and Jody Roberts. Affiliated with Colorado Dude and Guest Ranch Association. 300-acre facility located 150 miles west of Colorado Springs. Features: horseback riding; heated swimming pool; river rafting; mountain biking; 2 trout streams on premises; nearby rock climbing.

Profile of Summer Employees Total number: 50; average age: 21; 50% male, 50% female; 80% college students; 20% local residents. Nonsmokers preferred.

Employment Information Openings are from May 15 to September 30. Jobs available: ▶ 7 *wranglers* with first aid and CPR certification at $525 per month; ▶ 15 *housekeepers/waitpersons* at $475 per month; ▶ 2 *children's program personnel* with elementary education degree (preferred) and first aid and CPR certification at $475 per month; ▶ 3 *store and office personnel* at $475 per month; ▶ 3 *ranch hands* at $475 per month; ▶ 3 *kitchen workers* at $475 per month. International students encouraged to apply; must obtain own visa and working papers prior to employment.

Benefits College credit, on-the-job training, on-site room and board at no charge, laundry facilities, free use of ranch amenities, uniforms (shirts), end-of-season tip pool.

Contact Brad Milner, Manager, Harmel's Ranch Resort, PO Box 399, Almont, Colorado 81210; 970-641-1740, Fax 970-641-1944, E-mail harmels@gunnison.com, URL http://www.coloradovaction. com/duderanch/harmels. Application deadline: March 15.

HOLIDAY INN OF ESTES PARK
101 SOUTH SAINT VRAIN AVENUE PO BOX 1468
ESTES PARK, COLORADO 80517

General Information Hotel offering guests 150 rooms in an exceptional setting. Established in 1968. Owned by Forever Living Resorts. 2-acre facility located 65 miles northwest of Denver. Features: new conference center; location surrounding high mountain valley at an elevation of 7,500 feet; proximity to downtown shopping area; proximity to Rocky Mountain National Park; game and fitness rooms with an indoor pool and hot tub; restaurant, lounge, and banquet facilities.

Profile of Summer Employees Total number: 40; average age: 23; 50% male, 50% female; 80% college students; 10% retirees; 10% international.

Employment Information Openings are from May 10 to October 15. Year-round positions also offered. Jobs available: ▶ 4 *buspersons; per hour* ▶ 10 *waitstaff members* at $2.50 per hour; ▶ 4 *hosts* at $6.50 per hour; ▶ 4 *cooks* at $7–$8 per hour; ▶ 4 *kitchen help* (pantry, dishwashing) at $6–$7 per hour; ▶ 2 *housepeople* with ability to perform custodial duties, luggage handling, and conference set-ups at $6.50–$7 per hour; ▶ 15 *room attendants* (housekeeping) at $6–$6.50 per hour; ▶ 4 *front desk personnel; per hour* ▶ 20 *banquet staff members* at $2.50 per hour. International students encouraged to apply; must obtain own visa and working papers prior to employment.

Benefits College credit, on-the-job training, formal ongoing training, on-site room at $35 per week, discounted employee menu, gratuities for some positions.

Contact Paula Dunfee, Human Resource Director, Holiday Inn of Estes Park, Department SJ, PO Box 1468, Estes Park, Colorado 80517; 970-586-2332, Fax 970-586-2332 Ext. 299. Application deadline: April 1.

THE HOME RANCH
54880 ROUTT COUNTY ROAD 129
CLARK, COLORADO 80428

General Information Ranch resort accommodating 42 guests per week. Established in 1978. Owned by L. Kendrick Jones. Affiliated with Relais et Chateaux, Mobil Travel Guide, Dude Ranchers' Association. 1,500-acre facility located 172 miles west of Denver. Features: Rocky Mountain setting; wilderness hiking trails; horseback-riding trails; fly fishing in the Elk River.

Profile of Summer Employees Total number: 34; average age: 30; 50% male, 50% female; 5% minorities; 5% high school students; 50% college students; 5% retirees; 5% international; 30% local residents. Nonsmokers preferred.

Employment Information Openings are from May 20 to October 15. Winter break, Christmas break positions also offered. Jobs available: ▶ 3 *children's counselors* with first aid certification at $800–$1000 per month; ▶ 2 *prep cook;* ▶ 6 *waiters/waitresses;* ▶ 6 *housekeepers;* ▶ 4 *maintenance personnel;* ▶ 2 *hiking guides* with first aid certification; ▶ 6 *wranglers* with first aid certification; ▶ 2 *dishwashers;* ▶ 3 *cooks;* ▶ *fly fishing guide.*

Benefits On-the-job training, on-site room and board at no charge, laundry facilities. Preemployment training of 1 day is required and includes ranch-specific training. Orientation is paid.

Contact Ms. Ann C. Forajob, Manager, The Home Ranch, Department SJ, Box 822, Clark, Colorado 80428; 970-879-1780, Fax 970-879-1795. Application deadline: April 30.

LONGACRE EXPEDITIONS
TAYLOR PARK, COLORADO

General Information Adventure travel program emphasizing group living skills and physical challenges. Using base camp as a staging area, 2–3 staffers and 10–16 campers participate in intermediate and advanced expeditions on which they engage in human-powered sports. Established in 1981. Owned by Longacre Expeditions. Affiliated with American Camping Association. 60-acre facility located 30 miles east of Crested Butte. Features: ropes and initiatives course; wood-heated sauna and hot tub.

Profile of Summer Employees Total number: 20; average age: 25; 50% male, 50% female; 10% minorities; 40% college students; 30% local residents. Nonsmokers only.

Employment Information Openings are from June 14 to July 31. Jobs available: ▶ 8 *assistant trip leaders* (minimum age 21) with advanced first aid or advanced wilderness first aid, CPR, and completion of watersafety course at $150–$175 per week; ▶ 1 *mountaineering instructor* (minimum age 21) at $300–$400 per week; ▶ 1 *rock climbing instructor* (minimum age 21) at $300–$400 per week; ▶ 3 *support and logistics staff members* (minimum age 21) at $150–$175 per week.

Benefits On-the-job training, on-site room and board at no charge, Pro-Deal package. Preemployment training of 9 days is required and includes safety and accident prevention, group interaction, first-aid, CPR, leadership, camper-counselor relations. Orientation is unpaid.

Contact Roger Smith, Longacre Expeditions, RD 3, Box 106, Newport, Pennsylvania 17074; 717-567-6790, Fax 717-567-3955, E-mail longacre@pa.net, URL http://www.longex.com.

THE NAVIGATORS EAGLE LAKE CAMP
3820 NORTH 30TH STREET
COLORADO SPRINGS, COLORADO 80904

General Information Five camps including wilderness adventure, horsemanship, mountain and road biking, residential experiences, rock climbing and karate. Serves nearly 2000 campers ages 8–18 each summer. Bike camps accept persons up to age 28. Established in 1957. Owned by The Navigators. 320-acre facility located 9 miles west of Colorado Springs. Features: 10-acre lake; location surrounded by Pike National Forest; quarter of a mile long zip-line; several beach toys; flight simulator.

Profile of Summer Employees Total number: 125; average age: 21; 45% male, 55% female; 10% minorities; 90% college students; 10% local residents. Nonsmokers only.

Employment Information Openings are from May 20 to August 20. Jobs available: ▶ 65 *counselors* with one year of college and CPR/SFA certification; ▶ 2 *office administration staff members;* ▶ 2 *food service staff members;* ▶ 2 *emergency medical technicians* with EMT basic training; ▶ 2 *registered nurses;* ▶ 3 *lifeguards* with WSI certification; ▶ 5 *experienced maintenance staff members.* All positions offered at $1000 per season. International students encouraged to apply; must obtain own visa and working papers prior to employment.

Benefits On-the-job training, on-site room and board at no charge, health insurance, discipleship and ministry training. Preemployment training of 8 days is required and includes safety and accident prevention, group interaction, leadership, camper-counselor relations. Orientation is paid.

Contact Craig Dunham, Director of Communications, The Navigators Eagle Lake Camp, PO Box 6000, Colorado Springs, Colorado 80934; 719-472-1260, Fax 719-472-1208, E-mail craigd@navyouth.org. Application deadline: February 15.

NORTH FORK GUEST RANCH
55395 HIGHWAY 285, PO BOX B
SHAWNEE, COLORADO 80475

General Information Small ranch offering a weekly family-oriented vacation. All-inclusive package (meals, activities, and lodging) with lots of personal attention and western fun. Established in 1985. Owned by Dean and Karen May. Affiliated with Colorado Dude and Guest Ranch Association, Dude Ranchers' Association, Colorado Hotel and Motel Association. 520-acre facility located 50 miles southwest of Denver. Features: outdoor heated swimming pool; indoor hot tub; beautiful mountains for trail riding; river and pond fishing; hikes above timberline; overnight pack trips, lunch rides, and cookouts; white-water rafting trips.

Profile of Summer Employees Total number: 20; average age: 20; 40% male, 60% female; 90% college students; 10% local residents. Nonsmokers only.

Employment Information Openings are from April 1 to November 1. Jobs available: ► 3 *cooks* at $450–$550 per month; ► 6 *waitresses/waiters and cabin staff members* at $400–$500 per month; ► 8 *experienced wranglers* with CPR and first aid training at $400–$500 per month; ► 3 *kids' counselors* with WSI and lifeguard certification and CPR and first aid training preferred at $400–$500 per month; ► 3 *maintenance persons* at $400–$500 per month.

Benefits College credit, on-the-job training, on-site room and board at no charge, laundry facilities, one 24-hour period off per week, gratuity pool, opportunity to take part in all activities offered. Orientation is paid.

Contact Dean and Karen May, Owners/Managers, North Fork Guest Ranch, Department SJ, PO Box B, Shawnee, Colorado 80475; 800-843-7895, Fax 303-838-1549. Application deadline: May 15.

PEACEFUL VALLEY LODGE AND GUEST RANCH
475 PEACEFUL VALLEY ROAD
LYONS, COLORADO 80540

General Information Dude ranch serving 80–130 people in week long programs that include horseback lessons and rides, 4-wheel drive trips, fishing, hiking, swimming, a children's program, entertainment, 3 meals per day, cabins, and rooms. Established in 1953. Owned by Boehm Family. Affiliated with Colorado Dude and Guest Ranch Association, Dude Ranchers' Association, American Automobile Association. 320-acre facility located 60 miles northwest of Denver. Features: swimming pool; tennis court; location bordered by national forest; fishing pond and stream; playground; horseback riding in the Rocky Mountains.

Profile of Summer Employees Total number: 55; average age: 21; 50% male, 50% female. Nonsmokers preferred.

Employment Information Openings are from May 1 to October 31. Year-round positions also offered. Jobs available: ► 8 *waiters/waitresses; per hour* ► 3 *dishwashers; per hour* ► 4 *assistant cooks; per hour* ► 12 *wranglers* with first aid certification per hour; ► 4 *counselors* with first aid and water safety certification per hour; ► 7 *housekeepers; per hour* ► 2 *drivers/mechanical personnel* (minimum age 21) with a copy of driver's license and record per hour; ► 2 *gardeners/ grounds crew; per hour* ► 4 *skilled maintenance staff members* with mechanical aptitude per hour; ► 1 *office person* with typing ability per hour. International students encouraged to apply; must obtain own visa and working papers prior to employment.

Benefits On-the-job training, on-site room and board at no charge, laundry facilities, use of facilities during time off, opportunities for staff to use their talents (church choir, evening programs, talent show, and melodrama).

Contact Personnel Director, Peaceful Valley Lodge and Guest Ranch, Department SJ, 475 Peaceful Valley Road, Lyons, Colorado 80540; 303-747-2881, Fax 303-747-2167, E-mail peacefulvalley@juno.com, URL http://www.peacefulvalley.com. Application deadline: March 1.

THE PEAKS AT TELLURIDE RESORT
PO BOX 2702
TELLURIDE, COLORADO 81435

General Information Luxury resort and spa located in the southwest section of Colorado in Telluride Mountain Village and surrounded by 14,000-foot peaks of the San Juan Mountain Range. Established in 1992. Owned by Carefree Resorts. Affiliated with Small Luxury Hotels of the World, Colorado Hotel and Lodging Association. 6-acre facility located 65 miles southwest of Montrose. Features: 177 rooms and suites; 42,000-square-foot spa which includes 44 treatment rooms; 3 pools; full free weight and cardiovascular gym; golf-in/golf-out and ski-in/ski-out pro grams; kids spa and kids programs.

Profile of Summer Employees Total number: 30; 50% male, 50% female; 30% minorities; 25% high school students; 75% college students; 10% international; 20% local residents.

Employment Information Openings are from May 23 to September 2. Winter break, year-round positions also offered. Jobs available: ▶ *kids spa counselors* with neat appearance and pleasant demeanor; ▶ *bell staff* with valid driver's license and good driving record, neat appearance and pleasant demeanor; ▶ *food/beverage staff* with neat appearance and pleasant demeanor; ▶ *kitchen staff* with neat appearance and pleasant demeanor; ▶ *housekeeping staff* with neat appearance and pleasant demeanor; ▶ *spa staff* with neat appearance and pleasant demeanor. International students encouraged to apply; must obtain own visa and working papers prior to employment.

Benefits On-the-job training, health insurance. Off-site boarding costs are $390 per month.

Contact Human Resources, The Peaks at Telluride Resort, Department SJ, PO Box 2702, Telluride, Colorado 81435; 970-728-6800, Fax 920-728-4765. Application deadline: April 30.

POULTER COLORADO CAMPS
PO BOX 772947-P
STEAMBOAT SPRINGS, COLORADO 80477

General Information Residential camp serving 80 campers (ages 8–18) per session with group dynamics and outdoor education emphasis. There are frequent wilderness excursions. Established in 1957. Owned by The Whiteman School, Inc. Affiliated with American Camping Association. 180-acre facility located 150 miles northwest of Denver. Features: well-equipped gymnasium with climbing wall; athletics field; outdoor sand volleyball court; riding trails through the woods; spacious dormitory cabins; easy access to private hot springs.

Profile of Summer Employees Total number: 35; average age: 21; 43% male, 57% female; 10% minorities; 14% high school students; 71% college students; 5% international. Nonsmokers only.

Employment Information Openings are from June 6 to August 20. Winter break positions also offered. Jobs available: ▶ 1 *nurse* with RN license at $2000–$3000 per season; ▶ 3 *experienced cooks* at $1000–$2500 per season; ▶ 3 *wranglers* with strong horsemanship and teaching skills at $1000–$1500 per season; ▶ 1 *experienced office manager* with strong organizational and leadership skills (camp experience preferred) and administrative/secretarial experience at $1800–$2000 per season; ▶ 4 *experienced wilderness instructors* (minimum age 21) with technical skills and teaching experience at $1100–$2000 per season; ▶ 1 *arts and crafts counselor* with strong arts/crafts skills and teaching experience at $900–$1100 per season; ▶ 13 *experienced senior counselors* with first aid certification and lifeguard training (preferred) and experience working with youth at $1000–$1200 per season; ▶ 6 *assistant counselors* at $700 per season. International students encouraged to apply; must obtain own visa and working papers prior to employment.

Benefits On-the-job training, on-site room and board at no charge, local discounts. Preemployment training of 8 to 15 days is required and includes safety and accident prevention, group interaction, first-aid, leadership, camper-counselor relations, skills training. Orientation is unpaid.

Contact Jay B. Poulter, Director, Poulter Colorado Camps, PO Box 772947-P, Steamboat Springs, Colorado 80477; 970-879-4816, Fax 970-879-1307.

ROCKY MOUNTAIN OUTDOOR CENTER
10281 HIGHWAY 50
HOWARD, COLORADO 81233

General Information White-water rafting, kayaking, and canoeing instruction on the Arkansas and Dolores Rivers. Established in 1982. Owned by Colorado Corporation, Andy Waldbart. Affiliated with America Outdoors, Colorado River Outfitters Association, Arkansas River Outfitters Association. 4-acre facility located 100 miles southwest of Colorado Springs. Features: riverfront area; location at the base of Sangre de Cristo Mountains (13,000 feet); volleyball court; kayak rolling pool; remodeled changing rooms and bathroom facilities; easy access to 100 miles of variously difficult white water.

Profile of Summer Employees Total number: 35; average age: 23; 50% male, 50% female; 5% high school students; 50% college students; 5% local residents; 10% teachers. Nonsmokers preferred.

Employment Information Openings are from May 1 to September 1. Jobs available: ▶ 5 *raft guides* with experience and formal training per month; ▶ 5 *kayak and canoe instructors* with experience, formal training, and ACA certifications per month; ▶ *food preparation staff* with some experience at $4.25–$7 per hour; ▶ *dishwashers* at $4.25–$4.50 per hour. International students encouraged to apply; must obtain own visa and working papers prior to employment.

Benefits On-the-job training, formal ongoing training, on-site room and board, Pro-Deal discounts on outdoor equipment. Preemployment training of 2 to 3 days is required and includes safety and accident prevention, first-aid, CPR, river rescue, ACA kayak teacher certification. Orientation is unpaid.

Contact Andy Waldbart, President, Rocky Mountain Outdoor Center, Department SJ, 10281 Highway 50, Howard, Colorado 81233; 719-942-3214, Fax 719-942-3215, E-mail 73354.2030@ compuserv.com, URL http://www.rmoc.com. Application deadline: February 1.

ROCKY MOUNTAIN PARK COMPANY (THE TRAIL RIDGE STORE)
ROCKY MOUNTAIN NATIONAL PARK
ESTES PARK, COLORADO 80517

General Information Facility providing high-quality gifts and food service to national park visitors. Established in 1937. Owned by Forever Resorts. Affiliated with Tourist Industry Retail Merchants' Association, Indian Arts and Crafts Association, National Parks Conference of Concessioners. 1-acre facility located 22 miles west of Estes Park. Features: 71 peaks over 12,000 feet high; location in area above timberline in Alpine tundra; 355 miles of hiking trails; location at 12,000-foot elevation.

Profile of Summer Employees Total number: 55; average age: 23; 40% male, 60% female; 4% minorities; 75% college students; 25% retirees; 5% international; 2% local residents. Nonsmokers preferred.

Employment Information Openings are from May 31 to October 15. Jobs available: ▶ 20 *gift shop sales clerks* with outgoing and energetic personality at $800–$900 per month; ▶ 14 *snack bar assistants* with outgoing and energetic personality at $800–$900 per month; ▶ 4 *stockroom assistants* with ability to perform heavy lifting at $800–$900 per month; ▶ 4 *parking attendants* with outgoing and patient personality at $800–$900 per month; ▶ 3 *experienced sales supervisors* at $900–$1100 per month; ▶ 2 *experienced food supervisors* at $900–$1100 per month; ▶ 3 *experienced merchandising assistants* with three months of merchandising experience or six credit hours in color and design at $800–$1000 per month. International students encouraged to apply; must apply through recognized agency.

Benefits College credit, on-the-job training, on-site room and board at $63 per week, transportation to and from work each day, subsidized activities program, personalized employee meal program.

Contact Walt Poole, General Manager, Rocky Mountain Park Company (The Trail Ridge

Store), Department SJ, PO Box 2680, Estes Park, Colorado 80517; 970-586-9307, Fax 970-586-8590.

ROCKY MOUNTAIN VILLAGE
2644 ALVARADO ROAD
EMPIRE, COLORADO 80438

General Information Residential camp serving physically and developmentally disabled children and adults. Established in 1951. Owned by Colorado Easter Seal Society. Affiliated with American Camping Association. 95-acre facility located 40 miles west of Denver. Features: location in front range of the Rocky Mountains with Continental Divide visible from site; large trout ponds; mountain trails for biking and hiking; tennis court; computers; ropes course and climbing tower.

Profile of Summer Employees Total number: 45; average age: 21; 45% male, 55% female; 20% high school students; 75% college students; 5% local residents. Nonsmokers preferred.

Employment Information Openings are from May 15 to August 20. Year-round positions also offered. Jobs available: ▶ 1 *nature specialist* at $1300 per season; ▶ 1 *assistant cook* at $2000–$2100 per season; ▶ 1 *trip specialist* (minimum age 21) with outdoor camping experience at $1200–$1500 per season; ▶ 1 *arts and crafts instructor* (minimum age 21) at $1200–$1400 per season; ▶ 1 *computer specialist* (minimum age 21) at $1200–$1400 per season; ▶ 1 *horseback specialist* (minimum age 21) at $1200–$1400 per season; ▶ 1 *pool specialist* (minimum age 21) with WSI/lifesaving certification at $1200–$1400 per season; ▶ 1 *athletics specialist* (minimum age 18) at $1200–$1400 per season; ▶ 8 *girls counselors* (minimum age 18) at $1300 per season; ▶ 8 *boys counselors* (minimum age 18) at $1300 per season; ▶ 3 *maintenance helpers* (minimum age 16) at $1300 per season; ▶ 3 *kitchen helpers* (minimum age 16) at $1300 per season; ▶ 1 *secretary* (minimum age 16) at $1300 per season. International students encouraged to apply; must obtain own visa and working papers prior to employment; must apply through recognized agency.

Benefits College credit, on-the-job training, formal ongoing training, on-site room and board at no charge, laundry facilities, chance to gain experience working with people who have various types of disabilities.

Contact Christine Newell, Director, Rocky Mountain Village, Department SJ, PO Box 115, Empire, Colorado 80438; 303-892-6063, Fax 303-825-5004, E-mail campinfo@cess.org. Application deadline: April 1.

SANBORN WESTERN CAMPS
FLORISSANT, COLORADO 80816

General Information Boys and girls camps serving ages 7–17 in 2 five-week sessions. Established in 1948. Owned by Sanborn Western Camps. Affiliated with American Camping Association. 6,000-acre facility located 35 miles west of Colorado Springs. Features: 6,000 acres of private land; mountain climbing/backpacking; natural sciences programs; water sports.

Profile of Summer Employees Total number: 120; average age: 21; 50% male, 50% female; 20% minorities; 100% college students; 5% international. Nonsmokers preferred.

Employment Information Openings are from June 5 to August 20. Jobs available: ▶ 8 *riding instructors* at $1200 per season; ▶ 8 *canoeing instructors* at $1200 per season; ▶ 8 *rock climbing instructors* at $1200 per season; ▶ 20 *backpacking instructors* at $1200 per season; ▶ 10 *ecology instructors* at $1200 per season; ▶ 8 *tennis instructors* at $1200 per season; ▶ 4 *drama instructors* at $1200 per season; ▶ 4 *geology instructors* at $1200 per season; ▶ 8 *swimming instructors* with lifeguard training at $1200 per season; ▶ 8 *arts and crafts instructors* at $1200 per season; ▶ 8 *campcraft instructors* at $1200 per season; ▶ 8 *rafting instructors* at $1200 per season; ▶ 8 *sports instructors* at $1200 per season; ▶ 8 *caving instructors* at $1200 per season; ▶ 10 *mountaineering instructors* at $1200 per season; ▶ *cooks* at $1800–$2000 per season; ▶ 4 *nurses* at $2200–$2500 per season; ▶ *interpreters* at $1200 per season.

Benefits College credit, on-the-job training, on-site room and board at no charge, laundry facilities, health insurance. Preemployment training of 7 days is required and includes safety and accident prevention, group interaction, leadership, camper-counselor relations. Orientation is paid.

Contact Rick and Jane Sanborn, Directors, Sanborn Western Camps, Department SJ, Florissant, Colorado 80816; 719-748-3341, Fax 719-748-3259, E-mail interbarn@aol.com, URL http://www.usa.net/sanborn/sanborn.htm. Application deadline: May 10.

SHERATON STEAMBOAT RESORT AND CONFERENCE CENTER
2200 VILLAGE INN COURT BOX 774808
STEAMBOAT SPRINGS, COLORADO 80477

General Information Luxury resort hotel located at base of ski mountain. Owned by Ski Times Square Enterprises. Affiliated with Steamboat Springs Chamber Resort Association. Located 150 miles northwest of Denver. Features: river rafting, biking, hiking, fishing, golf, tennis, pro rodeo; 2 restaurants; 2 lounges; 18 hole golf course; 16 meeting rooms.

Profile of Summer Employees Total number: 200; average age: 25; 55% male, 45% female; 10% minorities; 5% high school students; 40% college students; 5% retirees; 95% local residents.

Employment Information Openings are from May 30 to October 15. Winter break, Christmas break, year-round positions also offered. Jobs available: ▶ 10 *room attendants* at $6.25 per hour; ▶ 5 *cooks* at $6.50–$7 per hour; ▶ 2 *front desk attendants* at $6.50 per hour; ▶ 5 *golf maintenance staff* at $6.25 per hour; ▶ 5 *stewards* at $6.50 per hour; ▶ 3 *utility staff* at $6 per hour; ▶ 5 *banquet housemen* at $5.40 per hour. International students encouraged to apply; must obtain own visa and working papers prior to employment.

Benefits On-the-job training, formal ongoing training, on-site room and board at $232 per month, health insurance, tuition reimbursement, free golf, $2.00 meals, holiday pay; uniforms cleaned at no charge; piece rate and tips for some jobs. Off-site boarding costs are $500 per month. Preemployment training of 1 day is required and includes safety and accident prevention, group interaction, Sheraton Guest Satisfaction System. Orientation is paid.

Contact Human Resources Office, Sheraton Steamboat Resort and Conference Center, Department SJ, PO Box 774808, Steamboat Springs, Colorado 80477; 970-879-2232, Fax 970-879-4684.

SUPERCAMP
COLORADO COLLEGE
COLORADO SPRINGS, COLORADO 80903

General Information Residential program for teens designed to build self-confidence and lifelong learning skills through accelerated learning techniques. Established in 1981. Owned by Bobbi DePorter. Affiliated with American Camping Association, International Alliance for Learning. Situated on 1,227 acres. Features: dormitory rooms; ropes course; swimming pool.

Profile of Summer Employees Total number: 200; average age: 20; 50% male, 50% female; 80% college students. Nonsmokers only.

Employment Information Openings are from July 1 to August 20. Jobs available: ▶ 15 *team leaders* with high school diploma at $500–$1000 per season; ▶ 1 *office manager* with high school diploma; ▶ 1 *nurse/paramedic* with national or state registration at $1000–$4000 per season; ▶ 1 *EMT* with national or state registration at $700–$2800 per season.

Benefits On-the-job training, on-site room and board at no charge, laundry facilities, internships, experience working with teens in an educational and self esteem-building environment, excellent experience for education and psychology majors. Preemployment training of 4 days is required and includes safety and accident prevention, group interaction, leadership, camper-counselor relations. Orientation is unpaid.

Contact Elisabeth Talmon, Human Resources Coordinator, SuperCamp, Department SJ, 1725 South Coast Highway, Oceanside, California 92054; 800-527-5321, Fax 619-722-3507, E-mail supercamp@aol.com, URL http://www.supercamp.com. Application deadline: May 1.

TUMBLING RIVER RANCH
PO BOX 30
GRANT, COLORADO 80448

General Information Guest ranch serving families. Established in 1940. Owned by Jim and Mary Dale Gordon. Affiliated with Colorado Dude and Guest Ranch Association, Dude Ranchers' Association. 200-acre facility located 62 miles southwest of Denver. Features: log cabins (all rooms have fireplaces); two rock lodges.

Profile of Summer Employees Total number: 30; average age: 20; 50% male, 50% female. Nonsmokers preferred.

Employment Information Openings are from May 15 to October 1. Winter break positions also offered. Jobs available: ▶ *waitresses/waiters;* ▶ *cabin staff members;* ▶ *cooks;* ▶ *assistant cooks;* ▶ *secretary;* ▶ *children's counselors* with first aid certification; ▶ *drivers;* ▶ *mechanics;* ▶ *wranglers* with first aid certification; ▶ *general maintenance personnel;* ▶ *groundskeepers.*

Benefits College credit, on-the-job training, formal ongoing training, on-site room and board at no charge, laundry facilities, end-of-summer bonus.

Contact Mary Dale Gordon, Owner, Tumbling River Ranch, PO Box 30, Grant, Colorado 80448; 303-838-5981. Application deadline: April 1.

VAIL ASSOCIATES, INC.
PO BOX 7
VAIL, COLORADO 81658

General Information Owners and operators of Vail, Beaver Creek, and Arrowhead ski resorts. Established in 1962. Owned by Vail Resorts, Inc. Affiliated with Colorado Ski Country USA. Located 100 miles west of Denver. Features: location in the heart of the Rocky Mountains; year-round recreation facilities; family-oriented resort area.

Profile of Summer Employees Total number: 500; average age: 27; 50% male, 50% female.

Employment Information Openings are from May 31 to September 1. Spring break, winter break, Christmas break, year-round positions also offered. Jobs available: ▶ *hospitality positions* at $8 per hour; ▶ *food service personnel* at $7.50–$8 per hour; ▶ *golf course staff members* at $6–$8 per hour; ▶ *grounds/maintenance persons* at $7.50–$8 per hour; ▶ *childcare staff members* at $7.50–$8 per hour; ▶ *day camp attendants* at $7.50 per hour; ▶ *lift-operations personnel* at $7.50–$8 per hour; ▶ *wranglers* at $7.50–$8 per hour. International students encouraged to apply; must obtain own visa and working papers prior to employment.

Benefits On-the-job training, formal ongoing training, on-site room and board at $300 per month, laundry facilities, health insurance, free season ski pass (winter employees), employee day care, retail and food discounts.

Contact Personnel Office, Vail Associates, Inc., PO Box 7, Vail, Colorado 81658; 970-845-2460, Fax 970-845-2465, E-mail lisan@seasons.vailassoc.com, URL http://www.vail.net.

VILLAGE AT BRECKENRIDGE RESORT
655 PARK STREET, PO BOX 8329
BRECKENRIDGE, COLORADO 80424

General Information Mountain resort hosting individuals, families, groups, and conventions in 6 hotel/lodge buildings with over 350 condos and rooms. Established in 1988. Operated by Nashville Country Club; Wyndham Resort. Affiliated with Colorado Restaurant Association, Breckenridge Resort Chamber, Summit County Chamber of Commerce. 20-acre facility located 80 miles west of Denver. Features: location at the base of mountains in a town listed on the National Register of Historic Places; health club facilities with hot tub and pools; 6 on-site restaurants; hiking and biking trails; pond for fishing and paddle boating; mall and plaza for convenient shopping; summer weekend concerts; location close to chair lifts, Alpine Slide, a human maze, horseback riding, and white-water rafting.

Profile of Summer Employees Total number: 150; average age: 22; 50% male, 50% female;

10% minorities; 40% college students; 5% international; 45% local residents. Nonsmokers preferred.

Employment Information Openings are from May 30 to September 30. Spring break, winter break, Christmas break, year-round positions also offered. Jobs available: ▶ *front desk clerks* with congenial personality and computer skills at $7.50 per hour; ▶ *reservationists* with excellent phone, computer, and selling skills at $7.50 per hour; ▶ *PBX operators* with excellent phone skills at $6.75 per hour; ▶ *experienced cooks* (all types) with knife, cooking, and prep skills at $7.50–$10 per hour; ▶ *kitchen stewards* at $6.50–$7.50 per hour; ▶ *waitstaff members* with pleasant, service-oriented attitude at $2.13 per hour; ▶ *buspersons* with pleasant, service-oriented attitude at $4.50–$6 per hour; ▶ *experienced cashiers/hosts/hostesses* with pleasant and detail-oriented personality at $6.50 per hour; ▶ *room attendants* with friendly, thorough, and efficient work habits at $8–$12 per hour; ▶ *laundry personnel* at $6.75 per hour; ▶ *grounds staff members* at $7.50 per hour; ▶ *health club attendants* with friendly personality at $7 per hour; ▶ *activities rangers* with ability to plan and lead activities at $6.75 per hour. International students encouraged to apply; must obtain own visa and working papers prior to employment.

Benefits On-the-job training, free employee meal per shift worked when working in food and beverage, uniforms (if required), 25 percent employee discount in restaurants, and on-site housing available at various costs. Off-site boarding costs are $500 per month.

Contact Sherilyn Gourly, Human Resources Manager, Village at Breckenridge Resort, Department SJ, PO Box 8329, Breckenridge, Colorado 80424; 303-453-3120, Fax 303-453-1878.

WILDERNESS TRAILS RANCH
23486 COUNTY ROAD 501
BAYFIELD, COLORADO 81122

General Information American plan ranch accommodating 48 guests weekly. Established in 1950. Owned by Gene and Jan Roberts. Affiliated with Mobil Travel Guide, American Automobile Association, Colorado Dude and Guest Ranch Association. 160-acre facility located 230 miles north of Albuquerque, New Mexico. Features: 72-foot heated pool and hot tub; secluded wilderness location; variety of horse trails; log cabin buildings; fishing pond; playground.

Profile of Summer Employees Total number: 30; average age: 21; 50% male, 50% female; 87% college students; 7% international; 7% local residents. Nonsmokers only.

Employment Information Openings are from May 1 to October 1. Jobs available: ▶ 10 *experienced wranglers* with first aid certification at $765–$1200 per month; ▶ 8 *cabin/kitchen staff members* at $825 per month; ▶ 3 *children's counselors* with first aid certification at $850 per month; ▶ 2 *office/clerical persons* with clerical and computer experience at $825 per month; ▶ 1 *grounds/maintenance person* with electrical and woodworking experience at $825–$1000 per month; ▶ 1 *kitchen aide* with organizational skills and cooking experience at $825 per month. International students encouraged to apply; must obtain own visa and working papers prior to employment.

Benefits College credit, on-the-job training, on-site room and board at no charge, laundry facilities, use of recreational/ranch facilities, bonus available for June, July, and August if contract is fulfilled and staff guidelines and stipulations are met. Preemployment training of 14 days is required and includes safety and accident prevention. Orientation is paid.

Contact Jan Roberts, Owner, Wilderness Trails Ranch, 1766 County Road 302, Durango, Colorado 81301; 970-247-0722, Fax 970-247-1006, E-mail wtr@sprynet.com, URL http://www.sprynet.com/sprynet/wtr. Application deadline: April 1.

WINTER PARK RESORT
PO BOX 36
WINTER PARK, COLORADO 80482

General Information Resort offering an alpine slide, scenic chairlift ride, mountain biking, hiking, mountain theme 18-hole mini golf course, and an outside ski museum. Established in 1940. Owned by City and County of Denver. Affiliated with National Ski Areas Association,

Colorado Ski Country, USA, Winter Park Chamber of Commerce. 1,413-acre facility located 70 miles north of Denver. Features: alpine slide; miniature golf course; mountain biking and racing; scenic chairlift ride; outdoor museum; jazz and American festival and outdoor music concerts.

Profile of Summer Employees Total number: 100; average age: 28; 60% male, 40% female.

Employment Information Openings are from June 1 to January 1. Spring break, winter break, Christmas break, year-round positions also offered. Jobs available: ▶ 25 *summer program attendant* with GED/high school diploma at $6.20–$8 per hour; ▶ *summer program crew leader* with GED/high school diploma at $6.45 per hour; ▶ *food and beverage assistants* with GED/high school diploma at $6.20 per hour. International students encouraged to apply; must obtain own visa and working papers prior to employment; must apply through recognized agency.

Benefits On-the-job training, laundry facilities, health insurance, discounts on food, Alpine slide rides, mini-golf, and mountain biking, free employee shuttle; on-site room/board costs $210–$290 per month, sports science fitness program. Preemployment training of 3 days is required. Orientation is paid.

Contact Gretchen Geckley, Winter Park Resort, Department SJ, Box 36, Winter Park, Colorado 80482; 970-726-1794, Fax 303-892-5823.

YMCA CAMP SHADY BROOK
8716 SOUTH Y-CAMP ROAD
SEDALIA, COLORADO 80135

General Information Residential facility serving campers ages 7–18 in 1- or 2-week sessions. Camp houses 182 campers and about 50 staff members. Activities include horsemanship, environmental arts and crafts, wilderness trips, canoeing, kayaking, nature trips, archery, riflery, and music. Established in 1948. Owned by YMCA of the Pikes Peak Region. Affiliated with American Camping Association, Association for Horsemanship Safety and Education, Association for Experiential Education. 150-acre facility located 50 miles northwest of Colorado Springs. Features: location with an elevation of 7000 feet; lake for swimming and boating; location surrounded on three sides by the Pike National Forest.

Profile of Summer Employees Total number: 50; average age: 20; 45% male, 55% female; 5% minorities; 5% high school students; 85% college students; 2% international; 60% local residents; 2% teachers. Nonsmokers only.

Employment Information Openings are from June 1 to August 23. Jobs available: ▶ 20 *counselors* (minimum age 18) with first aid, CPR certification, lifeguarding and wilderness camping experience (preferred) at $115–$135 per week; ▶ 2 *kitchen assistants* (minimum age 17) with first aid and CPR certification at $100–$115 per week; ▶ *registered nurse* with current license; ▶ 1 *waterfront assistant* (minimum age 18) with lifeguard, first aid, and CPR certification at $115–$125 per week; ▶ 1 *head wrangler* (minimum age 21) with Camp Horsemanship Association, first aid, and CPR certification at $130–$145 per week; ▶ 1 *wrangler* (minimum age 17) with first aid, CPR certification, and desire to learn more about riding and instruction at $75–$100 per week; ▶ 1 *waterfront supervisor* (minimum age 21) with WSI, first aid, lifeguarding, and CPR certification at $125–$135 per week; ▶ 4 *sectional leaders* (minimum age 19) with first aid, CPR certification, and counseling experience at $145–$160 per week; ▶ 10 *tripping assistants* (minimum age 17) with first aid, CPR certification, and lifeguarding at $100–$115 per week; ▶ 1 *trips coordinator* (minimum age 19) with first aid, CPR certification, wilderness camping experience, and management skills at $140–$160 per week; ▶ 1 *assistant trips coordinator* (minimum age 18) with first aid, CPR certification, and wilderness camping experience at $125–$135 per week; ▶ 1 *trips apprentice* (minimum age 17) with first aid and CPR certification at $75–$100 per week; ▶ 1 *assistant wrangler* (minimum age 18) with first aid, CPR certification, and experience riding and working with horses at $100–$115 per week; ▶ 1 *lifeguard* (minimum age 18) with first aid, CPR, and lifeguarding certification at $115–$120 per week; ▶ 1 *canoe/kayak instructor* (minimum age 18) with first aid, CPR certification, and experience in canoeing, kayaking, and boat maintenance at $120–$135 per week; ▶ 1 *arts and crafts instructor* (minimum age 18) with first aid, CPR certification, and experience and/or education in art-related field or area at $120–$135 per week; ▶ 1 *naturalist* (minimum age 18) with first aid, CPR certification, and experience and/or education in natural sciences at $120–$135 per week; ▶ 1 *music instructor* (minimum age 18) with first aid, CPR certification, experience playing a wide variety of musical instruments, and ability to lead songs at $120–$135 per week; ▶ 1 *archery instructor* (minimum age 18) with first aid, CPR certification, and experience and/or education in archery at $120–$135 per week; ▶ 1 *riflery instructor* (minimum age 18) with first aid, CPR certification, and experience and/or education in riflery at $120–$135 per week; ▶ 1 *recreation/ropes course instructor* (minimum age 18) with first aid, CPR, and low challenge course facilitator certification at $120–$135 per week; ▶ 1 *office assistant/store manager* (minimum age 19) with first aid, CPR certification, and general clerical skills at $130–$140 per week. International students encouraged to apply; must apply through recognized agency.

Benefits On-the-job training, formal ongoing training, on-site room and board at no charge, staff pass to Colorado Springs YMCA, internships available.

Contact Johnny Mclaughlin, Program Coordinator YMCA Camp Shady Brook, Department P98, YMCA Camp Shady Brook, 2380 Montebello Drive West, Colorado Springs, Colorado 80918; 303-647-2313, Fax 303-647-0513.

YMCA OF THE ROCKIES–CAMP CHIEF OURAY
PO BOX 648
GRANBY, COLORADO 80446-0648

General Information Residential camp dedicated to helping children grow in spirit, mind, and body. Programs for teens include backpacking and leadership training. Established in 1907. Owned by YMCA of the Rockies. Affiliated with American Camping Association, Christian Camping International/USA. 4,950-acre facility located 80 miles northwest of Denver. Features: 4,950 acres of trails, fields, and natural areas; 2 riding rings and many miles of riding trails.

Profile of Summer Employees Total number: 75; average age: 21; 50% male, 50% female; 1% minorities; 1% high school students; 98% college students; 1% retirees; 1% international; 1% teachers. Nonsmokers preferred.

Employment Information Openings are from May 28 to August 20. Jobs available: ▶ 46 *cabin counselors* with CPR and first aid certification at $100–$120 per week; ▶ 5 *riding staff members* at $115–$200 per week; ▶ 30 *support staff members* at $125–$175 per week; ▶ *nurses* with RN preferred at $400–$600 per week; ▶ *backpacking staff* at $125–$200 per week. International students encouraged to apply; must apply through recognized agency.

Benefits On-the-job training, on-site room and board at no charge, laundry facilities, health insurance. Preemployment training of 10 to 14 days is required and includes safety and accident prevention, group interaction, first-aid, CPR, leadership, camper-counselor relations. Orientation is paid.

Contact Trueman Hoffmeister, Camp Director, YMCA of the Rockies–Camp Chief Ouray, PO Box 648, Granby, Colorado 80446-0648; 970-887-2152 Ext. 4174, Fax 303-449-6781, E-mail chiefouray@aol.com. Application deadline: May 1.

YMCA OF THE ROCKIES, ESTES PARK CENTER
ESTES PARK, COLORADO 80511-2550

General Information Large Christian-oriented family resort and conference center offering a day camp and serving an average of 3,500 family and conference guests daily during the summer months. Established in 1907. Owned by YMCA of the Rockies. 750-acre facility located 70 miles west of Denver. Features: location bordered on 3 sides by Rocky Mountain National Park; indoor pool; gymnasium; Nautilus weight room; horseback riding into Rocky Mountain National Park; extensive hiking programs.

Profile of Summer Employees Total number: 370; average age: 21; 40% male, 60% female; 8% minorities; 60% college students; 30% retirees; 14% international; 2% local residents. Nonsmokers preferred.

Employment Information Openings are from April 1 to October 31. Spring break, winter break, Christmas break, year-round positions also offered. Jobs available: ▶ 12 *front desk clerks* with computer and public relations skills at $140 per week; ▶ 2 *telephone operators* with computer and public relations skills at $140 per week; ▶ 105 *food service personnel* at $140 per week; ▶ 80 *housekeeping staff members* at $140 per week; ▶ 12 *maintenance workers* with good driving record at $140 per week; ▶ 12 *craft shop staff members* with artistic talent and/or experience with arts and crafts at $140 per week; ▶ 5 *general store salespeople* at $140 per week; ▶ 11 *pool guards* with lifeguard certification (Red Cross or YMCA) at $140 per week; ▶ 60 *day camp/adventure camp counselors* with training and/or practical experience in education/ day camp work at $140 per week; ▶ 2 *miniature golf and roller skating rink attendants* at $140 per week; ▶ *experienced environmental education counselor* with background in environmental sciences at $140 per week. International students encouraged to apply; must apply through recognized agency.

Benefits   On-the-job training, on-site room and board at no charge, laundry facilities, shared gratuity for those who complete their employment successfully, affordable health insurance. Preemployment training of 1 day is required and includes safety and accident prevention, group interaction, leadership, camper-counselor relations. Orientation is paid.

Contact   Patrice A. Flauné, Human Resources Director, YMCA of the Rockies, Estes Park Center, Estes Park, Colorado 80511-2550; 303-586-3341 Ext. 1032, Fax 303-586-6078. Application deadline: April 30.

YMCA OF THE ROCKIES, SNOW MOUNTAIN RANCH
PO BOX 169
WINTER PARK, COLORADO 80482

General Information   A year-round YMCA conference center and family resort accommodating up to 2,100 guests per day. Established in 1969. Operated by YMCA of the Rockies. Affiliated with Colorado Visitors Bureau, Winter Park/Fraser Valley Chamber of Commerce, Denver Convention and Visitors Bureau, Ski Country USA. 5,000-acre facility located 70 miles northwest of Denver. Features: location near Winter Park ski resort and Rocky Mountain National Park; hiking, horseback riding, mountain biking and low and high elements ropes courses available on site; free use of roller skating rink, indoor pool, basketball and volleyball courts, and indoor climbing wall; 70 kilometers of groomed cross-country ski trails.

Profile of Summer Employees   Total number: 170; average age: 20; 40% male, 60% female; 10% minorities; 2% high school students; 75% college students; 10% retirees; 25% international; 3% local residents. Nonsmokers preferred.

Employment Information   Openings are from May 15 to September 10. Spring break, winter break, Christmas break, year-round positions also offered. Jobs available: ▶ 1 *human resources associate* with valid driver's license issued by a U.S. state's Department of Motor Vehicle at $120 per week; ▶ 12 *lifeguards* with American Red Cross lifeguard, first aid, and CPR certification or equivalent at $130 per week; ▶ 4 *crafts shop instructors* at $120 per week; ▶ 7 *conference services staff members* with valid driver's license issued by a U.S. state's Department of Motor Vehicles at $120 per week; ▶ 1 *chaplain's assistant* with valid driver's license issued by a U.S. state's Department of Motor Vehicles at $120 per week; ▶ 11 *youth program and early childhood counselors* with CPR and first aid certification at $120 per week; ▶ 46 *housekeeping personnel* at $120 per week; ▶ 42 *food service personnel* at $120 per week; ▶ 7 *maintenance personnel* with valid driver's license issued by a U.S. state's Department of Motor Vehicles at $120 per week; ▶ 3 *retail sales personnel* at $120 per week; ▶ 10 *front desk clerks* at $120 per week; ▶ 35 *resident-camp counselors* at $110 per week; ▶ 2 *family programs assistants* with first aid and CPR certification at $120 per week; ▶ 2 *recreation attendants* with first aid and CPR certification at $120 per week. International students encouraged to apply; must obtain own visa and working papers prior to employment; must apply through recognized agency.

Benefits   College credit, on-the-job training, formal ongoing training, on-site room and board at no charge, laundry facilities, internships, free use of recreation facilities and discount in gift shop, planned Christian activities for staff during time off. Preemployment training of 1 day is required and includes safety and accident prevention. Orientation is paid.

Contact Julie Watkins, Human Resources Director, YMCA of the Rockies, Snow Mountain Ranch, PO Box 169, Winter Park, Colorado 80482; 970-887-2152, Fax 303-449-6781.

CONNECTICUT

AWOSTING AND CHINQUEKA CAMPS
LITCHFIELD, CONNECTICUT 06750

General Information Residential camps serving 140 boys and 125 girls in programs of two to eight weeks. There are two separate campuses 4 miles apart that have daily coed programs as well as coed evening activities. Established in 1900. Owned by Ebner Camps, Inc. Affiliated with American Camping Association, Connecticut Camping Association. 200-acre facility located 10 miles south of Torrington. Features: location in the foothills of the Berkshires; Bantam Lake (3½ miles long); cabins with facilities for lodging nestled next to mountainside lakes; proximity to New York City and Boston (2½ hours).

Profile of Summer Employees Total number: 80; average age: 22; 50% male, 50% female; 10% minorities; 80% college students; 5% retirees; 30% international; 5% local residents. Nonsmokers only.

Employment Information Openings are from June 23 to August 23. Jobs available: ▶ 6 *swimming instructors* with WSI, LGT, or LGTI certification (clinic available) at $1200–$1600 per season; ▶ 6 *small craft instructors* with certification in one or more of the following: canoeing, sailing, kayaking, or boating (clinic available) at $1200–$1400 per season; ▶ 3 *waterskiing instructors* with LGT and CPR certification and teaching experience at $1200–$1400 per season; ▶ 6 *sports instructors* with background in one or more of the following: softball, soccer, tennis, golf at $1000–$1300 per season; ▶ 2 *archery instructors* with certification (clinic available) at $1000–$1300 per season; ▶ 2 *ceramics/clay instructors* with pottery wheel and kiln firing knowledge at $1200–$1400 per season; ▶ 2 *go-cart/minibike personnel* with knowledge of equipment and racing at $1000–$1300 per season; ▶ 4 *black-and-white photography/video/ filming instructors* with knowledge of equipment at $1000–$1300 per season; ▶ 3 *experienced gymnastics instructors* with coach certification at $1000–$1300 per season; ▶ 3 *dance/theater/ music instructors* with some stage and music background at $1000–$1300 per season; ▶ 4 *experienced computers and journalism staff members* with ability to operate Apple and IBM PC computers at $1000–$1300 per season; ▶ 2 *laundry workers* at $1400 per season; ▶ 2 *nurses or first aid persons* with RN, LPN, EMT, or standard first aid and CPR certification at $1600–$2200 per season; ▶ 2 *maintenance personnel* with background in painting, carpentry, and grounds maintenance at $1400–$1600 per season; ▶ 6 *experienced kitchen aides* at $1500 per season; ▶ 3 *arts and crafts instructors* at $1200–$1400 per season; ▶ 2 *experienced outdoor camping and hiking staff members* (minimum age 21) at $1200–$1400 per season; ▶ 2 *woodworking instructors* at $1200–$1400 per season; ▶ 2 *experienced fencing instructors* with some coaching background at $1200–$1400 per season; ▶ 2 *golf instructors* with experience at $1200–$1400 per season; ▶ 2 *mountain biking instructors* with off-road biking experience at $1200–$1400 per season.

Benefits College credit, on-the-job training, on-site room and board at no charge, laundry facilities, travel reimbursement, certification clinics, end-of-season bonus, tips. Preemployment training of 5 days is required and includes safety and accident prevention, group interaction, first-aid, CPR, leadership, camper-counselor relations, program planning. Orientation is paid.

Contact Oscar Ebner, Director, Awosting and Chinqueka Camps, Department SJ, 4 Breezy Hill, Harwinton, Connecticut 06791; 860-485-9566, Fax 860-868-0081, E-mail camps@netrax.net, URL http://www.awosting.com. Application deadline: May 15.

BUCK'S ROCK CAMP
59 BUCK'S ROCK ROAD
NEW MILFORD, CONNECTICUT 06776

General Information Creative arts camp primarily devoted to the development of talents and the potential of boys and girls ages 11–16. Established in 1942. Owned by Mickey and Laura Morris. Affiliated with American Camping Association, Connecticut Camping Association. 165-acre facility located 75 miles northeast of New York, New York. Features: facilities for theater, dance, and music; horses; large sporting fields; extensive horseback-riding trails; Olympic-size swimming pool.

Profile of Summer Employees Total number: 240; average age: 28; 50% male, 50% female; 10% minorities; 76% college students; 10% international; 5% local residents. Nonsmokers preferred.

Employment Information Openings are from June 23 to August 23. Jobs available: ▶ *fine arts instructor* at $1300–$1750 per season; ▶ *woodworking instructor* at $1300–$1750 per season; ▶ *weaving instructor* at $1250–$1650 per season; ▶ *photography instructor* at $1350–$1750 per season; ▶ *ceramics instructor* at $1350–$1750 per season; ▶ *sewing instructor* at $1300–$1650 per season; ▶ *silversmithing instructor* at $1350–$1750 per season; ▶ *creative writing instructor* at $1350–$1750 per season; ▶ *commercial art instructor* at $1350–$1650 per season; ▶ *printing instructor* at $1350–$1600 per season; ▶ *stage design and construction personnel* at $1350–$1700 per season; ▶ *music instructor* at $1250–$1750 per season; ▶ *videotaping instructor* at $1350–$1750 per season; ▶ *sports instructor* at $1350–$1650 per season; ▶ *farming instructor* at $1250–$1600 per season; ▶ *waterfront staff members* at $1350–$1850 per season; ▶ *computer science instructor* at $1350–$1750 per season; ▶ *kitchen staff members* at $1250–$1700 per season; ▶ *dining room staff members* at $1250–$1600 per season; ▶ *maintenance staff members* at $1250–$1600 per season; ▶ *guidance counselors* at $1250–$1700 per season; ▶ *registered nurses* at $1500–$2200 per season; ▶ *swimming instructors* with WSI certification at $800–$1000 per month. International students encouraged to apply.

Benefits On-the-job training, formal ongoing training, on-site room and board at no charge, laundry facilities, travel reimbursement, health insurance.

Contact Mickey and Laura Morris, Buck's Rock Camp, Department SJ, 29 Painter Hill Road, Roxury, Connecticut 06783; 860-350-5972, Fax 860-350-5973, E-mail buckrock@ix.netcom.com. Application deadline: December 1.

CAMP JEWELL YMCA
PROCK HILL ROAD
COLEBROOK, CONNECTICUT 06021

General Information Full-featured coeducational residential camp with teen adventure trips, year-round environmental education, and team building. Established in 1901. Owned by YMCA of Metro Hartford. Affiliated with American Camping Association. 500-acre facility located 35 miles northwest of Hartford. Features: location in the foothills of the Berkshires; 50-acre private lake; cabins with fireplaces and bathrooms/showers; 3 ropes courses and rope swing at waterfront; dynamic treehouse cabins.

Profile of Summer Employees Total number: 150; average age: 21; 50% male, 50% female; 10% minorities; 15% high school students; 65% college students; 1% retirees; 10% international; 25% local residents. Nonsmokers only.

Employment Information Openings are from June 19 to August 22. Year-round positions also offered. Jobs available: ▶ 2 *experienced ropes course directors* at $1750–$2000 per season; ▶ 1 *experienced waterfront director* with lifeguard/WSI certification at $1700–$3000 per season; ▶ 15 *teen trip leaders* (minimum age 21) at $1700–$1900 per season; ▶ 6 *experienced village directors* at $1800–$2000 per season; ▶ 3 *crafts program specialists* at $1600–$2000 per season; ▶ 2 *sailing program specialists* at $1600–$1800 per season; ▶ 2 *tennis program specialists* at $1600–$1700 per season; ▶ 4 *aquatic program specialists* at $1600–$1800 per season; ▶ 1 *drama program specialist* at $1600–$1700 per season; ▶ 2 *naturalists* at $1600–$2000 per season; ► 2 *leader-in-training directors* at $1800–$2000 per season; ► 30 *cabin counselors* at $1600–$1700 per season.

Benefits On-site room and board at no charge, laundry facilities, health insurance. Preemployment training of 9 days is required and includes safety and accident prevention, group interaction, first-aid, CPR, leadership, camper-counselor relations, programming skills, ropes course training. Orientation is paid.

Contact Paul Kamin, Camp Director, Camp Jewell YMCA, Department SJ, Prock Hill Road, Colebrook, Connecticut 06021; 203-379-2782, Fax 203-379-2782. Application deadline: June 1.

CAMP WASHINGTON
190 KENYON ROAD
LAKESIDE, CONNECTICUT 06758

General Information Coeducational summer resident and day camp serving a diverse popula-tion of campers from Connecticut. Traditional and specialty programs available: tripping program with backpacking, canoeing/kayaking, mountain biking; theater week; choir camp; inner-city day camp; family camps. Established in 1917. Operated by Episcopal Diocese of Connecticut. Affiliated with Connecticut Camping Association, American Camping Association, International Association for Conference Center Administrators. 300-acre facility located 25 miles south of Hartford. Features: year-round camp and conference center; 8 winterized cabins; rural location in foothills of New England's Berkshire Mountains; 300 acres of woodlands and trails; Adirondack shelter for backcountry camping; private swimming and canoeing pond.

Profile of Summer Employees Total number: 50; average age: 20; 50% male, 50% female; 30% minorities; 20% high school students; 80% college students; 20% international; 60% local residents; 5% teachers. Nonsmokers only.

Employment Information Openings are from June 10 to August 18. Jobs available: ► 7 *waterfront staff* with WSI certification and lifeguard training at $1300–$1500 per season; ► 16 *general counselors* with experience working with children at $1000–$1500 per season; ► 6 *program coordinators* with ability to teach a specific activity at $1300–$1500 per season; ► 1 *nurse* with RN or LPN license at $1500–$3000 per season; ► 2 *head counselors* with ability to work with staff, campers, and community in a conflict management position at $1500–$1900 per season; ► *counselor-in-training coordinator* with experience facilitating young people in leader-ship positions at $1500–$2000 per season; ► *office personnel* with familiarity with computers, phones, and running an office at $1100–$1500 per season. International students encouraged to apply; must apply through recognized agency.

Benefits On-the-job training, formal ongoing training, on-site room and board at no charge, laundry facilities, travel reimbursement, accident insurance. Preemployment training of 5 to 7 days is required and includes safety and accident prevention, group interaction, leadership, camper-counselor relations. Orientation is paid.

Contact Elia Vecchitto, Camp Director, Camp Washington, Department SJ, 190 Kenyon Road, Lakeside, Connecticut 06758; 203-567-9623, Fax 203-567-3037. Application deadline: June 1.

CHANNEL 3 COUNTRY CAMP
73 TIMES FARM ROAD
ANDOVER, CONNECTICUT 06232

General Information Camp for underprivileged children. Established in 1910. Owned by Almada Lodge Times Farm Camp Corporation Board of Directors. Operated by WFSB-TV 3. 365-acre facility located 20 miles east of Hartford. Features: stocked trout-fishing stream; Olympic-size swimming pool; playing fields; hardwood forest and trails; beach volleyball area.

Profile of Summer Employees Total number: 43; average age: 25; 50% male, 50% female; 35% minorities; 75% college students; 15% international; 60% local residents. Nonsmokers preferred.

Employment Information Openings are from June 23 to August 23. Jobs available: ► 8 *counselors* with two years of organizational camp experience and college junior or senior status at $1000–$2000 per season; ▶ 1 *swimming director* with lifeguard training and WSI, American Red Cross BLS, and CPR certification at $1300–$2300 per season; ▶ 1 *creative crafts instructor* with child-handicraft experience and college junior or senior status at $1100–$2100 per season; ▶ 1 *environmental education instructor* with interest and experience in nature and college junior or senior status at $1100–$2100 per season; ▶ 1 *archery instructor* (minimum age 18) with archery safety course certification at $1100–$2100 per season; ▶ 1 *health care director* (minimum age 21) with American Red Cross first aid, BLS, and CPR certification at $1800–$3000 per season; ▶ 2 *swimming instructors* (minimum age 19) with WSI and American Red Cross ALS certification *(preferred)* at $1100–$2100 per season; ▶ 2 *athletics instructors* at $1100–$2100 per season.

Benefits On-the-job training, on-site room and board at no charge, laundry facilities, health insurance, 48-hour period off with entire staff every 2 weeks, unique opportunity to work with underprivileged inner-city youth. Preemployment training of 6 days is required and includes safety and accident prevention, group interaction, first-aid, CPR, leadership, camper-counselor relations. Orientation is paid.

Contact Director, Channel 3 Country Camp, 73 Times Farm Road, Andover, Connecticut 06232; 860-742-2267, Fax 860-742-3298. Application deadline: May 15.

CHOATE ROSEMARY HALL
333 CHRISTIAN STREET
WALLINGFORD, CONNECTICUT 06492

General Information Five-week residential boarding experience for teaching interns who work with senior teachers in 2 different classes, serve as house advisors, and coaches. The summer program attracts over 500 students from 38 states and 35 countries. Established in 1916. Owned by Choate Rosemary Hall. Affiliated with National Association of Independent Schools. 400-acre facility located 100 miles northeast of New York. Features: air-conditioned science center; air-conditioned humanities and dining hall; pool; fieldhouse and squash courts; 30 tennis courts and numerous playing fields; state-of-the art language learning lab.

Profile of Summer Employees Total number: 32; average age: 22; 50% male, 50% female; 100% college students. Nonsmokers preferred.

Employment Information Openings are from June 29 to August 1. Year-round positions also offered. Jobs available: ▶ 35 *teaching interns* at $330–$360 per week. International students encouraged to apply; must obtain own visa and working papers prior to employment.

Benefits On-the-job training, on-site room and board at no charge, free use of all athletic facilities and library.

Contact Jim Irzyk, Director of Summer Program, Choate Rosemary Hall, 333 Christian Street, Wallingford, Connecticut 06492; 203-697-2365, Fax 203-697-2519, E-mail jirzyk@choate.edu, URL http://www.choate.edu/summer. Application deadline: February 1.

LAUREL RESIDENT CAMP
LEBANON, CONNECTICUT 06247

General Information Residential camp with an informal outdoor educational program serving 700 girls ages 6–17. Established in 1955. Owned by Connecticut Trails Girl Scout Council. Affiliated with American Camping Association, Association for Horsemanship Safety and Education, American Red Cross, National Wildlife Federation. 350-acre facility located 20 miles south of Hartford. Features: large private lake with extensive aquatic programs; horseback riding in 2 lighted rings and on trails; live-in cabins and tents; farm animals and garden; high/low ropes course; modern facilities such as program center for gymnastics, cheerleading, and photography.

Profile of Summer Employees Total number: 60; average age: 20; 5% male, 95% female; 10% minorities; 2% high school students; 50% college students; 10% international; 20% local residents. Nonsmokers preferred.

Employment Information Openings are from June 21 to August 20. Year-round positions also offered. Jobs available: ▶ 2 *experienced program directors* at $2200–$2800 per season; ▶ 1 *experienced assistant camp director* at $2200–$2800 per season; ► 1 *business manager* with business training and driver's license at $1200–$1500 per season; ► 2 *health directors* with nurse, LPN, or EMT license at $2000–$2800 per season; ► 2 *waterfront directors* (minimum age 21) with lifeguard, CPR, and FA certification at $1500–$1900 per season; ► 6 *waterfront assistants* with lifeguard, CPR, FA, or WSI certification at $1000–$1300 per season; ► 8 *unit leaders* with experience supervising children at $1300–$1600 per season; ► 24 *unit assistants* with experience camping and working with children at $1000–$1200 per season; ► 1 *experienced food supervisor* at $2500–$2800 per season; ► 2 *experienced assistant cooks* at $1600–$1900 per season; ► 4 *kitchen assistants* at $750–$900 per season; ► 1 *horseback riding director* with ability to develop and supervise equestrian programs at $1500–$2000 per season; ► 5 *experienced horseback riding staff members* at $750–$1600 per season; ► 1 *experienced arts and crafts director* at $1200–$1600 per season; ► 1 *experienced ropes course director* at $1200–$1600 per season; ► 1 *experienced naturalist* at $1200–$1600 per season; ► 1 *experienced farm life director* at $1200–$1600 per season; ► 1 *experienced archery director* at $1200–$1600 per season; ► 1 *experienced trip leader* at $1200–$1600 per season; ► 2 *maintenance assistants* with ability to lift and to work outdoors at $800–$1200 per season; ► 2 *experienced boating instructors* at $1000–$1300 per season. International students encouraged to apply; must apply through recognized agency.

Benefits College credit, on-the-job training, on-site room and board at no charge, laundry facilities, travel reimbursement, health insurance, cultural exchange, recruitment bonus. Preemployment training of 7 days is required and includes safety and accident prevention, group interaction, first-aid, CPR, leadership, camper-counselor relations, Girl Scout programming.

Contact Bridget Erin Healy, Outdoor Program/Property Director, Camping Department, Laurel Resident Camp, Department SJ, 20 Washington Avenue, North Haven, Connecticut 06473; 203-239-2922. Application deadline: June 10.

SHADYBROOK CAMP AND LEARNING CENTER
PO BOX 365
MOODUS, CONNECTICUT 06469

General Information Individualized programs serving at least 100 special needs campers blending traditional residential coed summer camp with educational, recreational, vocational, and clinical components in a therapeutic setting. Established in 1971. Owned by SLC II, Inc. Affiliated with American Camping Association, New England Association of Independent Camps, Connecticut Camping Association. 20-acre facility located 35 miles southeast of Hartford. Features: large, lighted sports fields for softball, volleyball, and soccer; large swimming pool designed especially for children with disabilities; large, lighted basketball courts; wooded campsite with lean-to near babbling brook; fishing pond; outdoor tennis court; separate indoor recreation halls for pre-teens and teens.

Profile of Summer Employees Total number: 80; average age: 21; 40% male, 60% female; 10% minorities; 20% high school students; 80% college students; 15% international; 15% local residents; 20% teachers. Nonsmokers preferred.

Employment Information Openings are from June 22 to August 16. Jobs available: ► *waterfront supervisor* with WSI certification at $2000–$2200 per season; ► *adaptive sports, athletics, and recreation specialist* at $1600–$1800 per season; ► *creative arts and media specialist* at $1800–$2000 per season; ► *counselor* at $800–$1200 per season; ► *behavior management specialist* at $2400–$2600 per season; ► *speech coordinator* with SLP/CCC at $2400–$2600 per season; ► *special events coordinator* at $1700–$1900 per season; ► *academics coordinator* with Special Education certification at $2400–$2600 per season; ► *dining hall supervisors* at $1300–$1500 per season; ► *nurses, CRN-LPN-EMT* with certification at $1400–$2800 per season. International students encouraged to apply; must apply through recognized agency.

Benefits College credit, on-the-job training, on-site room and board at no charge, laundry facilities, travel reimbursement. Preemployment training of 5 days is required and includes safety and accident prevention, group interaction, leadership, camper-counselor relations, dealing with special needs children. Orientation is paid.

Contact Kirk Zellers, Director, Shadybrook Camp and Learning Center, Department SJ, PO Box 365, Moodus, Connecticut 06469; 860-873-8800, Fax 860-873-1849, URL http://www.shadybrook.com/learningcenter. Application deadline: March 15.

SJ RANCH, INC.
130 SANDY BEACH ROAD
ELLINGTON, CONNECTICUT 06029

General Information Residential camp offering extensive riding and horse care programs for 40 girls ages 7–15. Established in 1956. Owned by Mary E. Haines. Affiliated with American Camping Association, Association for Horsemanship Safety and Education, Connecticut Camping Association. 100-acre facility located 22 miles north of Hartford. Features: 30 horses (camp-owned); tennis court; basketball court; 5-acre lake on property; 3 riding rings; riding trails and cross-country jumps.

Profile of Summer Employees Total number: 12; average age: 20; 1% male, 99% female; 10% high school students; 90% college students; 5% international; 10% local residents. Nonsmokers preferred.

Employment Information Openings are from June 25 to August 25. Jobs available: ▶ 4 *riding counselors* with one year of college completed at $1000–$1500 per season; ▶ *swimming counselor* (minimum age 20) with lifeguard training and BLS/CPR certification at $1200–$1400 per season; ▶ *crafts, kitchen, general, and sports staff members* at $1000–$1200 per season; ▶ 2 *swimming instructors* with WSI certification at $1000–$1200 per season. International students encouraged to apply; must obtain own visa and working papers prior to employment; must apply through recognized agency.

Benefits College credit, on-the-job training, on-site room and board at no charge, opportunity to gain experience and learn to ride. Preemployment training of 5 days is required and includes safety and accident prevention, group interaction, leadership, camper-counselor relations. Orientation is unpaid.

Contact Pat Haines, Director, SJ Ranch, Inc., 130 Sandy Beach Road, Ellington, Connecticut 06029; 860-872-4742, Fax 860-870-4914, E-mail sjranch@erols.com, URL http://www.kidscamps.com/specialty/sports/sjranch/.

SUNRISE RESORT
ROUTE 151, PO BOX 415
MOODUS, CONNECTICUT 06469

General Information Summer resort catering to families, day outing groups, music festivals, and weddings. Established in 1917. Owned by Bob Johnson. Affiliated with Connecticut River Valley and Shoreline Visitors' Council, Chamber of Commerce, Economic Development Commission. 140-acre facility located 20 miles southeast of Hartford. Features: 50' x 100' pool; 4 tennis courts; boating on the Salmon River; mountain biking on miles of trails; basketball and volleyball; horseback riding.

Profile of Summer Employees Total number: 150; average age: 21; 40% male, 60% female; 5% minorities; 40% high school students; 40% college students; 5% retirees; 8% international; 75% local residents.

Employment Information Openings are from May 15 to October 15. Jobs available: ▶ 4 *lifeguards* with ALS or WSI certification at $3000–$4000 per season; ▶ 25 *waiters/waitresses* at $2500–$4000 per season; ▶ 2 *swimming instructors* with WSI certification at $3000–$4000 per season; ▶ 4 *office personnel* with typing ability at $2500–$4000 per season; ▶ *tennis instructor* at $2000–$3500 per season.

Benefits College credit, on-the-job training, on-site room and board at $40 per week, laundry facilities, use of facilities. Preemployment training of 2 days is optional and includes job training. Orientation is paid.

Contact Jim Johnson, Director, Sunrise Resort, Department SJ, PO Box 415, Moodus, Connecticut 06469; 860-873-8681, Fax 860-873-8681. Application deadline: April 1.

TENNIS: EUROPE
146 COLD SPRING ROAD, #13
STAMFORD, CONNECTICUT 06905

General Information TENNIS: EUROPE takes teams of junior players to USTA and international tennis tournaments, allowing them to gain valuable experience in match play and providing them with intercultural educational experiences. There is one team in North America and nine in Europe. Established in 1973. Owned by Dr. Martin Vinokur. Affiliated with United States Professional Tennis Association, United States Tennis Association. Features: tennis clubs range from 3 courts to 55 courts, usually have a clubhouse, swimming pool, and other country club amenities.

Profile of Summer Employees Total number: 25; average age: 26; 50% male, 50% female; 5% minorities; 33% college students; 5% international; 10% teachers. Nonsmokers preferred.

Employment Information Openings are from June 24 to August 10. Jobs available: ▶ 22 *tennis coaches* (21 and older) with ability to coach tennis at high school varsity or rank player levels and must serve as chaperone to students during travel; all positions require extensive travel and no positions are in Connecticut–2 positions for California/Hawaii itinerary and 20 positions for European itineraries at $300–$500 per season. International students encouraged to apply; must obtain own visa and working papers prior to employment.

Benefits On-the-job training, on-site room and board at no charge, staff receives a free trip worth the equivalent of about $1000 per week for the 3 ½ to 5 week tours, travel from New York to Europe or New York to California/Hawaii. Preemployment training of 2 days is required and includes safety and accident prevention, group interaction, leadership, player-coach relations, conducting tennis practices. Orientation is unpaid.

Contact Dr. Martin Vinokur, Director, Tennis: Europe, Department SJ, 146 Cold Spring Road, #13, Stamford, Connecticut 06905; 203-964-1939, Fax 203-967-9499. Application deadline: April 1.

UNITED CEREBRAL PALSY ASSOCIATION OF GREATER HARTFORD
301 GREAT NECK ROAD
WATERFORD, CONNECTICUT 06385

General Information Residential camping program serving the physically disabled, ages 8–adult, during an eight-week summer program. Established in 1973. Owned by State of Connecticut. Operated by United Cerebral Palsy. Affiliated with Connecticut Recreation and Parks Association, National Recreation and Parks Association. Located 5 miles south of New London. Features: waterfront for boating and swimming on Long Island Sound; fully accessible location; heated cabins with full bathroom facilities; proximity to tourist attractions; fully accessible riding program; mansion and gardens within walking distance.

Profile of Summer Employees Total number: 23; average age: 25; 50% male, 50% female; 20% minorities; 85% college students; 1% international; 55% local residents. Nonsmokers preferred.

Employment Information Openings are from June 17 to August 16. Year-round positions also offered. Jobs available: ▶ 1 *program director* with ability to interact with disabled individuals as well as program and supervisory experience at $3000–$5000 per season; ▶ *assistant director* at $3000–$4500 per season; ▶ 2 *head counselors* with experience in personal care and working in a camp or residential setting at $2300–$2700 per season; ▶ 3 *activity leaders* with experience in skill area and ability to work with others at $2000–$2300 per season; ▶ 14 *general counselors* (minimum age 18) with dedication and maturity, willingness to learn, and experience working with disabled persons (preferred) at $1825–$2200 per season; ▶ *nurse* with LPN, RN certification and experience caring for individuals with disabilities at $4000–$5000 per season. International students encouraged to apply; must apply through recognized agency.

Benefits On-the-job training, on-site room and board at no charge, laundry facilities, expense-paid field trips. Preemployment training of 6 days is required and includes safety and accident prevention, group interaction, first-aid, CPR, leadership, camper-counselor relations. Orientation is paid.

Contact Camp Coordinator, United Cerebral Palsy Association of Greater Hartford, 80 Whitney Street, Hartford, Connecticut 06105; 860-236-6201, Fax 860-236-6205. Application deadline: May 15.

WESTPORT COUNTRY PLAYHOUSE
25 POWERS COURT
WESTPORT, CONNECTICUT 06880

General Information Professional summer theater producing six plays each year. Established in 1931. Owned by Playhouse Limited Partnership. Operated by Connecticut Theater Foundation. Affiliated with Actors' Equity Association, Council of Stock Theaters. 3-acre facility located 47 miles north of New York, New York. Features: historic site; red barn atmosphere; 700-seat theater; location near the beach; proximity to New York City.

Profile of Summer Employees Total number: 50; average age: 28; 50% male, 50% female; 10% high school students; 40% college students; 50% local residents. Nonsmokers preferred.

Employment Information Openings are from May 18 to August 29. Jobs available: ▶ 8 *technical interns* at $80 per week; ▶ 2 *administrative/press interns* at $125 per week; ▶ 6 *box office staff members* at $200 per week; ▶ 3 *production staff members* at $200–$400 per week.

Benefits College credit, on-the-job training, eligibility for points in the Actors' Equity Association membership candidate program. Off-site boarding costs are $400 per month.

Contact Julie Monahan, General Manager, Westport Country Playhouse, Department SJ, PO Box 629, Westport, Connecticut 06881; 203-227-5137, Fax 203-221-7482. Application deadline: May 1.

DELAWARE

CHESAPEAKE BAY GIRL SCOUT COUNCIL
501 SOUTH COLLEGE AVENUE
NEWARK, DELAWARE 19713

General Information Residential and day camps serving girls ages 5–17 during June, July, and August. Established in 1912. Owned by Chesapeake Bay Girl Scouts, Inc. Affiliated with American Camping Association, Girl Scouts of the United States of America. 265-acre facility located 40 miles south of Philadelphia, Pennsylvania. Features: location on Chesapeake Bay; environmental surroundings for nature study (forest, meadows, wetlands, and the beach); sailing, windsurfing, and canoeing; location close to Baltimore, Philadelphia, and Washington, DC; swimming pool; tennis courts.

Profile of Summer Employees Total number: 35; average age: 20; 5% male, 95% female; 10% minorities; 80% college students; 20% international; 50% local residents. Nonsmokers preferred.

Employment Information Openings are from June 20 to August 17. Jobs available: ▶ 1 *assistant director* with CPR certification, first aid training, driver's license, and bachelor's degree at $1800–$2000 per season; ▶ 1 *program director* with first aid certification and bachelor's degree at $1600–$1800 per season; ▶ 12 *unit counselors (minimum age 18)* with children/camp experience preferred at $1100–$1300 per season; ▶ 1 *beach director* (minimum age 21) with first aid, ARC waterfront module, CPR, and motor boat driving and/or windsurfing and sailing experience at $1600–$1800 per season; ▶ 1 *pool director* (minimum age 21) with WSI (preferred), Red Cross Advanced Lifesaving, first aid, and CPR certification at $1500–$1650 per season; ▶ 7 *aquatics assistants* with certification in advanced lifesaving or WSI, first aid, CPR, and windsurfing/sailing/canoeing experience preferred (one or all) at $1200–$1350 per season; ▶ 6 *experienced unit leaders* (minimum age 21) with training in Girl Scout program or camp counseling at $1300–$1500 per season. International students encouraged to apply; must apply through recognized agency.

Benefits On-the-job training, on-site room and board at no charge, laundry facilities.

Contact Dawn Mars, Director of Camp Programs, Chesapeake Bay Girl Scout Council, Department SJ, 501 South College Avenue, Newark, Delaware 19713; 302-456-7150, Fax 302-456-7188, E-mail dawn@hq.cbgsc.org, URL http://www.cbgsc.org. Application deadline: May 15.

FUNLAND
6 DELAWARE AVENUE
REHOBOTH BEACH, DELAWARE 19971

General Information Amusement park providing family entertainment. Established in 1962. 2-acre facility located 40 miles south of Dover. Features: 17 rides designed for both children and adults; 17 chance games; arcade.

Profile of Summer Employees Total number: 80; average age: 17; 50% male, 50% female; 5% minorities; 40% high school students; 60% college students; 5% international; 50% local residents. Nonsmokers preferred.

Employment Information Openings are from May 10 to September 7. Jobs available: ▶ 80 *ride and game attendants* at $6 per hour. International students encouraged to apply; must obtain own visa and working papers prior to employment.

Benefits On-the-job training, formal ongoing training, on-site room and board at no charge, laundry facilities, limited availability of sublet apartments at $900 per season, performance bonus paid at the end of summer, dormitory (men only). Preemployment training of 2 days is required and includes safety and accident prevention, group interaction. Orientation is paid.

Contact Steve Hendricks, Vice President/Personnel Manager, Funland, 6 Delaware Avenue, Rehoboth Beach, Delaware 19971; 302-227-2785, Fax 302-227-8276. Application deadline: June 15.

DISTRICT OF COLUMBIA

ST. ALBANS SUMMER PROGRAMS
MT. ST. ALBAN
WASHINGTON, D.C. 20016

General Information Summer programs at private school offering academic classes, sports camps, and a day camp. Established in 1968. Owned by St. Albans School. Situated on 200 acres. Features: 10 outdoor tennis courts; indoor pool; 2 gymnasiums; 1 large athletic field; location next to the Washington National Cathedral and gardens.

Profile of Summer Employees Total number: 200; average age: 30; 50% male, 50% female; 30% minorities; 10% high school students; 45% college students; 1% retirees; 10% international; 95% local residents; 45% teachers. Nonsmokers preferred.

Employment Information Openings are from June 24 to August 2. Jobs available: ▶ *counselors in various sports programs* (basketball, tennis, lacrosse, baseball, soccer, and a general sport camp) at $5.25–$10 per hour; ▶ *tutors* at $15–$27 per hour; ▶ *teachers;* ▶ *day camp counselors* at $1000–$2000 per season. International students encouraged to apply; must obtain own visa and working papers prior to employment.

Benefits On-the-job training.

Contact Ms. Kim Lau, St. Albans Summer Programs, Department SJ, Washington, D.C. 20016-5095; 202-537-6450, Fax 202-537-5613. Application deadline: March 15.

FLORIDA

ACTIONQUEST PROGRAMS
PO BOX 5507
SARASOTA, FLORIDA 34277

General Information On-board program serving an average of 300 teenagers in twelve three-week sessions. Intensive sailing, dive training, and other water sports emphasized. Established in 1970. Owned by James Stoll. Affiliated with American Sailing Association, American Waterskiing Association, Professional Association of Diving Instructors (Gold Palm Resort Facility), United States Windsurfing Association, United States Sailing Association. Features: 50-foot sailing yachts.

Profile of Summer Employees Total number: 30; average age: 28; 60% male, 40% female; 50% college students; 10% international. Nonsmokers only.

Employment Information Openings are from June 15 to August 25. Jobs available: ▶ 12 *United States Coast Guard licensed sailing teachers or British Yachtmasters* at $3000 per season; ▶ 12 *diving instructors* with PADI instructor-level certification and/or USCG license at $2200 per season; ▶ *U.S. Sailing certified windsurfing instructors* at $1000 per season; ▶ *marine science instructors* with PADI scuba instructor-level certification at $2200 per season. International students encouraged to apply.

Benefits On-site room and board at no charge, travel reimbursement, all expenses paid, opportunity to travel in British Virgin Islands. Preemployment training of 5 days is required and includes safety and accident prevention, group interaction, first-aid, CPR, leadership, camper-counselor relations. Orientation is paid.

Contact Mr. James Stoll, Director, Actionquest Programs, Department SJ, PO Box 5507, Sarasota, Florida 34277; 941-924-2115, Fax 941-924-6075, E-mail actionquest@msn.com, URL http://www.actionguest.com.

BLUEWATER BAY RESORT
1950 BLUEWATER BOULEVARD
NICEVILLE, FLORIDA 32578

General Information Resort offering facilities for golf, tennis, boating, and swimming. Established in 1992. Affiliated with American Hotel and Motel Association, Florida Hotel and Motel Association. 2,000-acre facility located 60 miles east of Pensacola. Features: 36 holes of golf; 19 tennis courts; 4 swimming pools; 120-slip full-service marina; biking and hiking trails; playground areas.

Profile of Summer Employees Total number: 17; average age: 20. Nonsmokers preferred.

Employment Information Openings are from May 30 to September 15. Year-round positions also offered. Jobs available: ▶ 6 *lifeguards* with lifeguard certification at $5.15 per hour; ▶ 5 *golf cart attendants* at $5.15 per hour; ▶ 6 *water safety instructors* with WSI certification at $6.50 per hour; ▶ 3 *recreation interns* with junior or senior in recreation program at $50 per week; ▶ *pool maintenance staff* at $5.50 per hour. International students encouraged to apply; must obtain own visa and working papers prior to employment.

Contact Pat Coleman, Human Resource Coordinator, Bluewater Bay Resort, Department SJ, 1950 Bluewater Boulevard, Niceville, Florida 32578; 904-897-3614, EXT 1140, Fax 904-897-2424. Application deadline: May 1.

CAMP BLUE RIDGE
BOX 2888
MIAMI, FLORIDA 33140

General Information Residential camp with an average of 200 campers providing athletics, waterfront, arts and crafts, rappelling, horseback riding, and waterskiing activities. Established in 1970. Owned by Sheila and Morris Waldman and J.I. Montgomery. Affiliated with American Camping Association. Situated on 212 acres. Features: 3 large sports fields; 2 large lakes and a swimming pool; gym; tennis courts; auditorium; science and zoology building; arts and crafts building.

Profile of Summer Employees Total number: 75; average age: 22; 50% male, 50% female; 80% college students; 50% international; 50% local residents. Nonsmokers only.

Employment Information Openings are from June 22 to August 16. Jobs available: ▶ 3 *rappelling instructors* at $1000–$1500 per season; ▶ 4 *arts and crafts instructors* at $1000–$1200 per season; ▶ 1 *martial arts instructor* at $1000–$1200 per season; ▶ 10 *athletics instructors* at $1000–$1200 per season; ▶ 6 *dance and drama instructors* at $1000–$1200 per season; ▶ 12 *swimming, boating, all-waterfront, and skiing instructors* at $1000–$1500 per season. International students encouraged to apply; must apply through recognized agency.

Benefits On-site room and board at no charge, laundry facilities.

Contact Camp Blue Ridge, Camp Blue Ridge, PO Box 2888, Miami, Florida 33140; 305-538-3434, Fax 305-532-3152.

CAMP THUNDERBIRD
909 EAST WELCH ROAD
APOPKA, FLORIDA 32712

General Information Residential camp designed exclusively to benefit children and adults who have a developmental disability. Campers participate in traditional camping activities which help increase the camper's level of independence and self-esteem. Established in 1985. Owned by Florida Foundation for Special Children. Affiliated with American Camping Association, Florida Association for Retarded Citizens, American Canoeing Association. 20-acre facility located 20 miles northwest of Orlando. Features: location on Wekiwa Springs State Park property; Florida pine and oak sand hill; swimming pool and lake; 6 cabins with ceiling fans/air conditioning; sports court; campfire area and amphitheater.

Profile of Summer Employees Total number: 60; average age: 25; 25% male, 75% female; 17% minorities; 60% college students; 50% international; 35% local residents. Nonsmokers preferred.

Employment Information Openings are from June 1 to August 20. Year-round positions also offered. Jobs available: ▶ 30 *cabin counselors* with experience working with the mentally retarded at $1100–$1800 per season; ▶ 5 *swimming pool staff members* with WSI and lifeguard certification at $1400–$1600 per season; ▶ 3 *experienced kitchen staff members* at $4.50–$6 per hour; ▶ 2 *camp nurses* with Florida nursing license at $650–$800 per week; ▶ *activity leaders* with experience leading a specific activity at $1300–$1800 per season; ▶ *head counselor* with experience working at summer camps at $1300–$1800 per season. International students encouraged to apply; must obtain own visa and working papers prior to employment; must apply through recognized agency.

Benefits College credit, on-the-job training, on-site room and board at no charge, laundry facilities, travel reimbursement. Preemployment training of 6 days is required and includes safety and accident prevention, group interaction, first-aid, CPR, leadership, camper-counselor relations. Orientation is paid.

Contact Nancy Johnson, Camp Director, Camp Thunderbird, Department SJ, 909 East Welch Road, Apopka, Florida 32712; 407-889-8088, Fax 407-889-8072, E-mail campthun@aol.com. Application deadline: May 31.

CAMP UNIVERSE
LAKE MIONA
WILDWOOD, FLORIDA 34785

General Information Residential camp for 200 active children. Established in 1958. Owned by Camp Universe, Inc. 110-acre facility located 50 miles north of Orlando. Features: horse trails; 3-mile freshwater lake; 20-acre athletic field; 300-seat professional theater; circus pavilion, including trapeze, highwire, stilts, and clown school; 4 tennis courts (2 lighted) adjoining an 18-hole golf course).

Profile of Summer Employees Total number: 70; average age: 25; 50% male, 50% female; 10% minorities; 4% high school students; 50% college students; 30% international; 10% local residents; 6% teachers. Nonsmokers preferred.

Employment Information Openings are from June 11 to August 23. Jobs available: ▶ 60 *skilled counselors* with ability to teach their specialty–canoeing, arts and crafts, archery, waterskiing, tennis, sailing, and more at $600–$1800 per season; ▶ *camp nurses* with RN license or equivalent; ▶ 2 *pianists* with ability to accompany shows, play by ear, and transpose at $1000 per season; ▶ 2 *lead singers* with ability to play guitar well and know camp-type and rock songs by heart at $900 per season; ▶ *drama staff members* at $900 per season; ▶ *horseback riding staff members* at $900 per season; ▶ *circus staff members* at $900 per season. International students encouraged to apply.

Benefits On-the-job training, formal ongoing training, on-site room and board at no charge, laundry facilities.

Contact Diana Mermell, Director, Camp Universe, Department SJ, 5875 SW 129 Terrace, Miami, Florida 33156; 305-666-6346, URL http://www.kidscamps.com/traditional/campuniverse. com. Application deadline: June 1.

CORKSCREW SWAMP SANCTUARY
375 SANCTUARY ROAD
NAPLES, FLORIDA 34120

General Information National Audubon Society sanctuary in Florida wilderness. Management goals are preservation of natural ecosystem and public education through extensive visitor programs. Established in 1954. Owned by National Audubon Society. 10,560-acre facility located 15 miles northeast of Naples. Features: North America's largest nesting colony of endangered wood storks; 2-mile boardwalk trail for visitors; visitor center with gift shop; largest remaining ancient subtropical bald cypress forest in the world.

Profile of Summer Employees Total number: 4; average age: 20; 50% male, 50% female; 100% college students. Nonsmokers preferred.

Employment Information Openings are from May 15 to September 1. Year-round positions also offered. Jobs available: ▶ 2 *seasonal naturalists* with some background in resource management and environmental education at $100 per week.

Benefits On-the-job training, formal ongoing training, laundry facilities, $50 uniform allowance, free housing.

Contact Andrew Mackie, Assistant Manager, Corkscrew Swamp Sanctuary, Department SJ, 375 Sanctuary Road, Naples, Florida 34120; 941-657-3771, Fax 941-657-6869, E-mail amackie@ audubon.org. Application deadline: March 15.

KAMPUS KAMPERS
3601 NORTH MILITARY TRAIL
BOCA RATON, FLORIDA 33431

General Information Residential camp serving 200 campers from the end of June to mid-August in three-week sessions. Camp provides computer, performing arts, circus, sports, and traditional programs. Established in 1991. Owned by Donald E. Ross. Affiliated with American Camping Association. 123-acre facility located 5 miles west of Boca Raton. Features: 6 tennis courts (2 lighted); 7 lakes and nature trails; 3 large sports fields; 4 basketball courts (2 lighted); large gymnasium; swimming pool.

Profile of Summer Employees Total number: 100; average age: 23; 50% male, 50% female; 10% minorities; 80% college students; 30% international; 40% local residents; 20% teachers. Nonsmokers preferred.

Employment Information Openings are from June 9 to August 18. Jobs available: ▶ *counselors* at $230–$260 per week; ▶ *experienced activity coordinators* with college degree at $265–$340 per week. International students encouraged to apply; must obtain own visa and working papers prior to employment; must apply through recognized agency.

Benefits College credit, on-the-job training, formal ongoing training, on-site room and board at no charge, laundry facilities. Preemployment training of 5 days is required and includes safety and accident prevention, group interaction, first-aid, CPR, leadership, camper-counselor relations. Orientation is paid.

Contact Sue Merrill, Kampus Kampers, Department SJ, 3601 North Military Trail, Boca Raton, Florida 33431; 561-994-2267, Fax 561-994-6662. Application deadline: April 1.

PINE TREE CAMPS AT LYNN UNIVERSITY
BOCA RATON, FLORIDA 33431

General Information Day camp serving campers ages 3–15. Established in 1978. Affiliated with Lynn University. 123-acre facility located 20 miles south of West Palm Beach. Features: 4 large sports fields; swimming pool; 6 tennis courts; gymnasium; 5 man-made lakes for fishing and boating; go-cart track.

Profile of Summer Employees Total number: 125; average age: 21; 40% male, 60% female; 10% minorities; 20% high school students; 59% college students; 1% retirees; 15% international; 100% local residents; 20% teachers. Nonsmokers preferred.

Employment Information Openings are from June 17 to August 16. Jobs available: ▶ *general counselors* at $120–$130 per week; ▶ *computer instructors* at $160–$180 per week; ▶ *preschool teachers* with Health and Rehabilitative Services clearance at $150–$170 per week; ▶ *swim instructors* with WSI certification at $140–$150 per week. International students encouraged to apply; must apply through recognized agency.

Benefits On-the-job training, laundry facilities. Off-site boarding costs are $500 per month.

Contact Diane DiCerbo, Director, Pine Tree Camps at Lynn University, 3601 North Military Terrace, Boca Raton, Florida 33431; 561-994-2267, Fax 561-994-6662. Application deadline: May 1.

SABIN-MULLOY-GARRISON TENNIS CAMP
11550 LASTCHANCE ROAD
CLERMONT, FLORIDA 34711

General Information Residential camp for boys and girls who have an interest in competitive tennis. Established in 1961. Owned by Dickey W. Garrison. Affiliated with United States Tennis Association. 5-acre facility located 40 miles west of Orlando. Features: lake for water sports; 4 clay tennis courts and 1 hard surface tennis court; attractions to visit in Orlando vicinity; tournaments outside camp program.

Profile of Summer Employees Total number: 4; average age: 20; 50% male, 50% female; 25% minorities; 75% college students; 25% international; 25% local residents. Nonsmokers only.

Employment Information Openings are from June 20 to August 10. Jobs available: ▶ *cook* at $700–$800 per season; ▶ *tennis instructors.* International students encouraged to apply; must obtain own visa and working papers prior to employment.

Benefits On-site room and board at no charge.

Contact Dickey W. Garrison, Owner, Sabin-Mulloy-Garrison Tennis Camp, 11550 Lastchance Road, Clermont, Florida 34711; 352-394-3543, Fax 352-394-3543. Application deadline: April 1.

SEA WORLD OF FLORIDA
7007 SEA WORLD DRIVE
ORLANDO, FLORIDA 32821

General Information Marine life theme park, open year-round, designed to entertain and educate guests. Established in 1973. Owned by Anheuser-Busch Entertainment Corporation. Situated on 195 acres. Features: restaurants and gift shops; shows; exhibits.

Profile of Summer Employees Total number: 300.

Employment Information Openings are from May 1 to September 1. Spring break, Christmas break, year-round positions also offered. Jobs available: ▶ *counter persons* at $5 per hour; ▶ *kitchen staff; per hour* ▶ *buspersons; per hour* ▶ *waiters/waitresses; per hour* ▶ *warehouse personnel; per hour* ▶ *prep cooks; per hour* ▶ *dishwashers; per hour* ▶ *gift shop personnel* with ability to operate cash register, assist guests, and stock shelves per hour; ▶ *operations, crowd and traffic control personnel* with desire to maintain park cleanliness and assist at information center per hour; ▶ *landscape personnel* with ability to work with a wide variety of plant material and design beds, plus maintain drainage and irrigation (some experience preferred) per hour; ▶ *ticket sellers; per hour* ▶ *tour guides* with ability to narrate at animal exhibits throughout the park and conduct educational tours per hour.

Benefits Employee lounge on premises for lunch and breaks, competitive salary, uniforms, complimentary tickets, employee discounts, free lunches for food service employees, end-of-season party. Preemployment training of 1 to 2 days is required and includes safety and accident prevention, group interaction. Orientation is paid.

Contact Human Resources Department, Sea World of Florida, Department SJ, 7007 Sea World Drive, Orlando, Florida 32821; 407-351-3600.

GEORGIA

CAMP BARNEY MEDINTZ
4165 HIGHWAY 129 NORTH
CLEVELAND, GEORGIA 30528-2309

General Information Residential camp serving 900 campers ages 8–16 during two 4-week sessions. Camp also offers Wonder Weeks, serving second, third, and fourth graders during four 2-week sessions, and Chalutzim, serving children ages 9–16 with special needs during a four-week session. Established in 1963. Owned by Atlanta Jewish Community Center. Affiliated with Atlanta Jewish Federation/Jewish Community Centers Association, United Way, American Camping Association. 500-acre facility located 75 miles north of Atlanta. Features: Olympic-size swimming pool; sports fields; tennis complex; 30-horse stable with miles of riding trails; open-air gymnasium with an indoor and outdoor stage; 2 self-contained lakes for canoeing, sailing, windsurfing, and waterskiing; view of Blue Ridge Mountains; cultural arts facility with theater, dance, photography, videography, arts and crafts, and pottery.

Profile of Summer Employees Total number: 200; average age: 19; 50% male, 50% female; 5% minorities; 28% high school students; 66% college students; 20% international; 65% local residents.

Employment Information Openings are from June 5 to August 15. Jobs available: ▶ 40 *counselors* (minimum age 18) at $750–$1500 per season; ▶ 10 *waterfront staff members* (minimum age 18) with LGT, WSI, CPR, and first aid certification at $750–$2200 per season; ▶ 10 *nature crafts staff members* with CPR and first aid certification at $750–$2200 per season; ▶ 2 *songleaders* at $1200–$2000 per season; ▶ 8 *horseback staff members* at $750–$2000 per season; ▶ 2 *theater directors* at $1200–$1800 per season; ▶ 10 *special-needs staff members* at $1200–$1800 per season.

Benefits College credit, on-the-job training, formal ongoing training, on-site room and board at no charge, laundry facilities.

Contact Mark Balser, Assistant Director, Camp Barney Medintz, Department SJ, 5342 Tilly Mill Road, Atlanta, Georgia 30338-4499; 770-396-3250, Fax 770-481-0101, E-mail summer@campbarney.org, URL http://www.campbarney.org. Application deadline: March 1.

CAMP WOODMONT FOR BOYS AND GIRLS ON LOOKOUT MOUNTAIN
1339 YANKEE ROAD
CLOUDLAND, GEORGIA 30731

General Information Residential camp serving up to 80 boys and girls ages 6–14 for one- to two-week sessions. Established in 1981. Owned by Jane and Jim Bennett. Affiliated with American Camping Association. 160-acre facility located 28 miles south of Chattanooga, Tennessee. Features: lake for canoeing and fishing; proximity to Cloudland Canyon State Park and other scenic areas; numerous riding trails for Western trail riding; well-built facilities, roomy cabins, and nice bathhouses.

Profile of Summer Employees Total number: 12; average age: 21; 50% male, 50% female; 100% college students. Nonsmokers only.

Employment Information Openings are from June 15 to August 15. Jobs available: ▶ 10 *counselors* with CPR/FA certification at $500–$800 per month; ▶ 2 *swimming instructors* with WSI certification at $600–$800 per month. International students encouraged to apply; must obtain own visa and working papers prior to employment.

Benefits On-the-job training, on-site room and board at no charge. Preemployment training of 5 days is required and includes safety and accident prevention, group interaction, leadership, camper-counselor relations. Orientation is paid.

Contact Jane and Jim Bennett, Camp Directors, Camp Woodmont for Boys and Girls on Lookout Mountain, Department SJ, 2339 Welton Place, Dunwoody, Georgia 30338; 770-457-0862. Application deadline: May 1.

SIX FLAGS OVER GEORGIA
7561 SIX FLAGS PARKWAY
AUSTELL, GEORGIA 30001

General Information Theme park offering more than 100 rides, shows, and attractions. Established in 1967. Owned by Warner Brothers. 300-acre facility located 10 miles west of Atlanta. Features: 7 major rollercoasters; softball and volleyball leagues; live musical shows.

Profile of Summer Employees Total number: 4,000; average age: 23.

Employment Information Openings are from May 1 to September 30. Spring break positions also offered. Jobs available: ▶ *hosts and hostesses* at $5.50–$6.75 per hour; ▶ *interns* at $6–$6.50 per hour. International students encouraged to apply; must obtain own visa and working papers prior to employment; must apply through recognized agency.

Benefits College credit, on-the-job training, formal ongoing training, scholarship program. Preemployment training of 1 day is required and includes safety and accident prevention, group interaction, first-aid, CPR, leadership. Orientation is paid.

Contact Melanie Walters Graham, Human Resources Generalist, Six Flags Over Georgia, Department SJ, PO Box 43187, Atlanta, Georgia 30378; 770-739-3411, Fax 770-948-4378. Application deadline: May 31.

SOUTHERN TENNIS ACADEMY
BERRY COLLEGE
ROME, GEORGIA 30149

General Information Residential or day camp teaching tennis to youngsters ages 9–16 weekly. Established in 1976. Owned by M.B. Chafin. Operated by Southern Tennis Academy. 10,000-acre facility located 2 miles north of Rome. Features: 22 tennis courts; housing in college dorms; fully equipped gymnasium; indoor pool; large playing fields; evening program.

Profile of Summer Employees Total number: 20; average age: 21; 40% male, 60% female; 5% minorities; 95% college students; 5% international; 80% local residents; 10% teachers. Nonsmokers preferred.

Employment Information Openings are from June 1 to August 1. Jobs available: ▶ 15 *tennis counselors (live-in)* at $175–$275 per week; ▶ 1 *office assistant* at $150–$250 per week. International students encouraged to apply; must obtain own visa and working papers prior to employment.

Benefits College credit, on-the-job training, on-site room and board at no charge, laundry facilities. Preemployment training of 2 days is required and includes safety and accident prevention, group interaction, first-aid, CPR, leadership, camper-counselor relations. Orientation is unpaid.

Contact M. B. Chafin, Director, Southern Tennis Academy, PO Box 14401, Gainesville, Florida 32604; 352-392-0581 Ext. 234, Fax 352-392-3404, E-mail mchafin@hhp.ufl.edu. Application deadline: June 1.

HAWAII

CAMP MOKULEIA
68-729 FARRINGTON HIGHWAY
WAIALUA, HAWAII 96791

General Information Residential coeducational camp serving 92 campers ages 7–15 weekly for six-week season. Established in 1947. Owned by The Episcopal Church in Hawaii. Affiliated with American Camping Association. 31-acre facility located 37 miles northwest of Honolulu. Features: Hawaii beachfront location; beach and reef for exploration; mountain and beachfront hiking trails nearby; ropes course; basketball court; ocean swimming, snorkeling, and outrigger canoeing.

Profile of Summer Employees Total number: 25; average age: 21; 50% male, 50% female; 35% minorities; 17% high school students; 35% college students; 5% retirees; 3% international; 50% local residents. Nonsmokers preferred.

Employment Information Openings are from June 29 to August 17. Winter break positions also offered. Jobs available: ▶ 1 *experienced waterfront director* with WSI, lifeguard, CPR, and AFA certification at $1000 per season; ▶ 14 *counselors* with camping experience and CPR and AFA certification at $700–$1000 per season; ▶ 7 *aides* (volunteer) with CPR and AFA certification.

Benefits On-the-job training, formal ongoing training, on-site room and board at no charge, laundry facilities, health insurance, accident insurance, workmen's compensation insurance. Preemployment training of 5 days is required and includes safety and accident prevention, group interaction, first-aid, CPR, leadership, camper-counselor relations, ropes training. Orientation is unpaid.

Contact Verta Betancourt, S.C. Programs Department, Camp Mokuleia, Department SJ, 68-729

Farrington Highway, Waialua, Hawaii 96791; 808-637-6241, Fax 808-637-5505. Application deadline: March 1.

IDAHO

EPLEY'S WHITEWATER ADVENTURES
BOX 987
MCCALL, IDAHO 83638

General Information River rafting on Salmon River offering adventures to groups of up to 100 people on short trips. Also offers overnight trips for 2–24 people. Established in 1962. Owned by Ted and Karen Epley. Affiliated with Idaho Outfitters and Guides Association, America Outdoors, Chamber of Commerce. 1-acre facility located 150 miles north of Boise. Features: location along Salmon River; bunkhouse facilities for employees; volleyball net, basketball hoop, and VCR/TV videos.

Profile of Summer Employees Total number: 15; average age: 22; 80% male, 20% female; 75% college students; 25% local residents; 5% teachers. Nonsmokers only.

Employment Information Openings are from May 15 to September 15. Jobs available: ▶ 12 *river guides* with Red Cross, first aid, and CPR at $700 per month; ▶ 4 *food service, laundry and office staff, and shuttle driver* with Red Cross, first aid, and CPR at $700 per month; ▶ *hunting guide* at $800–$1000 per month; ▶ *summer horse guide* at $700–$1200 per month.

Benefits On-the-job training, formal ongoing training, on-site room and board at no charge, laundry facilities.

Contact Ted Epley, Owner, Epley's Whitewater Adventures, Department SJ, Box 987, McCall, Idaho 83638; 208-634-5173, Fax 208-634-5270. Application deadline: January 1.

HIDDEN CREEK RANCH
7600 EAST BLUE LAKE ROAD
HARRISON, IDAHO 83833

General Information Guest ranch conducting six-day programs with daily scheduled activities such as horseback riding, hayrides, barrel racing rodeo, mountain biking, pond fishing, trap shooting, archery, campfires, hiking, boat tours, and Native American skill work and activities. Established in 1992. Owned by Iris Behr and John Muir. Affiliated with Dude Ranchers' Association, Idaho Guest and Dude Ranch Association, Idaho Outfitters and Guides Association, National Audubon Society, Nature Conservancy of Idaho, Sierra Club, National Wildlife Federation. 570-acre facility located 40 miles south of Coeur d'Alene. Features: 75 riding horses and 40 mountain bikes; mountain horseback riding trails overlooking the Coeur d'Alene chain of lakes; 3-acre fishing and swimming pond; 2 hot tubs; 7,000-square foot lodge with 6 guest cabins; many activities based on Native American philosophy; tipi village and 2 sweat lodges.

Profile of Summer Employees Total number: 20; average age: 23; 50% male, 50% female; 85% college students; 5% local residents. Nonsmokers preferred.

Employment Information Openings are from April 1 to October 31. Year-round positions also offered. Jobs available: ▶ 1 *head chef* with standard first aid/CPR certification at $700–$1000 per month; ▶ 1 *assistant cook* with standard first aid/CPR certification at $500–$600 per month; ▶ 5 *wranglers* with standard first aid/CPR certification and horse background at $500 per month; ▶ 2 *children's wranglers* with standard first aid/CPR certification, child care or camp experience, and horse background at $500 per month; ▶ 6 *housekeeping/waitstaff members* with standard first aid/CPR certification at $400 per month; ▶ 2 *maintenance/waitstaff members* with standard first aid/CPR certification and construction and mechanical background at $500 per month; ▶ 1 *kitchen assistant* (prep/dishwasher) with standard first aid/CPR certification at $400 per month; ▶ 1 *groundskeeping/waitstaff member* with standard first aid/CPR certification and experience in organic gardening and biological controls at $500 per month; ▶ 2 *children's counselors* with standard first aid/CPR certification and child care or camp experience at $500 per month; ▶ 1 *host/head housekeeper* with standard first aid/CPR certification and housekeeping experience at $600 per month. International students encouraged to apply; must obtain own visa and working papers prior to employment.

Benefits College credit, on-the-job training, on-site room and board at no charge, laundry facilities, participation with guests in activities and meals, seasonal employee housing with large recreation area and satellite TV, bonus at end of employment term. Preemployment training of 3 to 5 days is required and includes safety and accident prevention, group interaction, departmental training, specific activity training. Orientation is paid.

Contact Iris Behr, Owner, Hidden Creek Ranch, Department SJ, 7600 East Blue Lake Road, Harrison, Idaho 83833; 208-689-3209, Fax 208-689-9115, E-mail hiddencreek@hiddencreek.com, URL http://www.nidlink.com/~hiddencreek. Application deadline: April 31.

MYSTIC SADDLE RANCH
STATE HIGHWAY 75
STANLEY, IDAHO 83278

General Information Program offering pack trips, trail rides, and fall hunting trips. Established in 1969. Owned by Deb and Jeff Bitton. Affiliated with Stanley Chamber of Commerce, Idaho Outfitters and Guides Association, America Outdoors. Located 130 miles northeast of Boise. Features: 300 lakes; 180 miles of trails; wilderness setting.

Profile of Summer Employees Total number: 17; average age: 22; 80% male, 20% female; 60% college students; 10% teachers. Nonsmokers only.

Employment Information Openings are from June 1 to November 15. Year-round positions also offered. Jobs available: ▶ *trail ride guides* (minimum age 18) with no Fish and Game violations; ▶ *horse packers* (minimum age 18) with no Fish and Game violations; ▶ *corral manager* (minimum age 18) with no Fish and Game violations; ▶ *cook/house help* (minimum age 18); ▶ *fall hunting guides* (minimum age 18) with no Fish and Game violations. All positions offered at $900–$1400 per month.

Benefits On-the-job training, on-site room and board at $300 per month, laundry facilities. Preemployment training of 2 to 3 days is required and includes safety and accident prevention, group interaction. Orientation is paid.

Contact Deb Bitton, Owner, Mystic Saddle Ranch, Mystic Saddle Ranch, Stanley, Idaho 83278; 208-774-3591, Fax 208-774-3455, E-mail packid@cyberhighway.net.

REDFISH LAKE LODGE
BOX 9
STANLEY, IDAHO 83278

General Information Family-oriented rustic lodge on a lake in the Sawtooth Mountains with restaurant, marina, and general store. Established in 1929. Affiliated with National Restaurant Association, National Federation of Independent Businesses, Stanley and Sawtooth Chambers of Commerce. 20-acre facility located 160 miles northeast of Boise. Features: location on Redfish Lake; proximity to Sawtooth Mountains for hiking and camping; Salmon River fishing and rafting; white sand beaches; mountain bike trails; volleyball.

Profile of Summer Employees Total number: 50; average age: 21; 50% male, 50% female; 1% minorities; 1% high school students; 98% college students; 1% retirees; 50% local residents.

Employment Information Openings are from May 1 to October 5. Jobs available: ▶ 6 *cooks* with one year of restaurant line experience at $750–$1000 per month; ▶ 7 *waitresses/waiters* at $570 per month; ▶ 4 *buspersons* at $682 per month; ▶ 3 *dishwashers* at $700 per month; ▶ 8 *housekeepers* at $682 per month; ▶ 3 *service station personnel* at $682 per month; ▶ 5 *marina personnel* at $682–$900 per month; ▶ 1 *bartender* at $700–$900 per month; ▶ 4 *store personnel* at $682–$900 per month; ▶ 2 *front desk personnel* at $682–$900 per month; ▶ 3 *maintenance personnel* at $682–$900 per month.

Benefits College credit, on-the-job training, on-site room and board at no charge, laundry facilities, cash bonus for work through Labor Day, flexible scheduling, use of boats.

Contact Jack See, Manager, Redfish Lake Lodge, Department SJ, Box 9, Stanley, Idaho 83278; 208-774-3536. Application deadline: May 15.

ILLINOIS

CAMP CEDAR POINT
1327 CAMP CEDAR POINT LANE
MAKANDA, ILLINOIS 62958

General Information Girl Scout residential camp serving 150 girls weekly for both Girl Scouts and nonmembers ages 6–17. Established in 1953. Owned by U.S. Department of Interior: Crab Orchard National Wildlife Refuge. Operated by Shagbark Girl Scout Council. Affiliated with American Camping Association. 250-acre facility located 110 miles south of St. Louis, Missouri. Features: location in Crab Orchard National Wildlife Refuge; extensive freshwater lake for swimming and boating; rolling hills, woods, and open meadows; 8 living units of platform tents and hogans; location 12 miles from a university community.

Profile of Summer Employees Total number: 40; average age: 21; 5% male, 95% female; 10% minorities; 90% college students; 5% international; 40% local residents. Nonsmokers only.

Employment Information Openings are from June 1 to August 6. Jobs available: ▶ 1 *program coordinator* with experience at $200–$235 per week; ▶ 1 *waterfront director* (minimum age 21) with WSI and lifeguarding certification at $195&–$230 per week; ▶ 1 *assistant waterfront staff member* (minimum age 21) with WSI and lifeguarding certification at $190&–$205 per week; ▶ 5 *waterfront instructors* (minimum age 18) with lifeguarding and WSI certification (preferred) at $160–$180 per week; ▶ 1 *sailing instructor* (minimum age 18) with sailing, lifeguarding, and WSI certification (preferred) at $165–$190 per week; ▶ 8 *unit leaders/counselors* (minimum age 21), *experience preferred,* at $170–$185 per week; ▶ 15 *assistant unit leaders/counselors* (minimum age 18) at $155–$165 per week; ▶ 1 *environmentalist* (minimum age 18), *experience preferred,* at $155–$180 per week; ▶ 1 *arts/crafts instructor* (minimum age 18), *experience preferred,* at $155–$180 per week; ▶ 1 *nurse* with RN license at $375–$400 per week. International students encouraged to apply; must apply through recognized agency.

Benefits College credit, on-the-job training, on-site room and board at no charge, laundry facilities, health insurance, preemployment training including certification in American Red Cross community first aid/CPR and Project Wild instruction. Preemployment training of 6 to 7 days is required and includes safety and accident prevention, group interaction, first-aid, CPR, leadership, camper-counselor relations, child abuse, mandated reporter legislation. Orientation is paid.

Contact Janet Ridenour, Camp Director, Shagbark Girl Scout Council, Camp Cedar Point, Department SJ, PO Box 549, Herrin, Illinois 62948; 618-942-3164, Fax 618-942-7153. Application deadline: May 15.

CAMP TAPAWINGO
ROUTE 5, BOX 15
METAMORA, ILLINOIS 61548

General Information Residential camp serving 120 Girl Scouts and non–Girl Scouts per week. Established in 1957. Owned by Kickapoo Council of Girl Scouts. Affiliated with American

Camping Association. 640-acre facility located 20 miles east of Peoria. Features: pool; fitness course; teams course; small lake.

Profile of Summer Employees Total number: 25; average age: 20; 100% female; 1% minorities; 98% college students; 15% local residents. Nonsmokers preferred.

Employment Information Openings are from May 27 to August 8. Jobs available: ▶ 1 *assistant director* (minimum age 21) at $187–$205 per week; ▶ 1 *program director* (minimum age 21) at $170–$185 per week; ▶ 1 *business manager* (minimum age 21) at $170–$185 per week; ▶ 1 *health supervisor* (minimum age 21) with RN, LPN, or EMT license at $187–$205 per week; ▶ 1 *waterfront director* (minimum age 21) with WSI certification at $170–$185 per week; ▶ 1 *lakefront director* with lifeguard certification and canoeing background at $170–$185 per week; ▶ 2 *waterfront assistants* with lifeguard certification at $147–$163 per week; ▶ 1 *teams course/ campcraft instructor* (minimum age 21) at $170–$185 per week; ▶ 1 *riding instructor* (minimum age 21) with experience in teaching beginning/intermediate Western riding and accredited horsemanship instructor certification at $170–$185 per week; ▶ 5 *unit leaders* (minimum age 21) at $153–$168 per week; ▶ 12 *unit assistants* (minimum age 18) at $143–$158 per week. International students encouraged to apply; must apply through recognized agency.

Benefits On-the-job training, on-site room and board at no charge, health insurance, first aid/CPR class. Preemployment training of 7 days is required and includes safety and accident prevention, group interaction, first-aid, CPR, leadership. Orientation is paid.

Contact Beth Stalker, Director of Program and Properties, Camp Tapawingo, Department SJ, 1103 West Lake, Peoria, Illinois 61614; 309-688-8671, Fax 309-688-7358. Application deadline: May 15.

PEACOCK CAMP
38685 NORTH DEEP LAKE ROAD
LAKE VILLA, ILLINOIS 60046

General Information Residential camp offered every two weeks for 36 children ages 7–17 with physical disabilities. Established in 1935. Owned by Peacock Camp. Affiliated with American Camping Association. 22-acre facility located 40 miles north of Chicago. Features: outdoor heated pool with ramp; nature trail with wheelchair fitness course; lake and pontoon boat; arts and crafts cabin; recreation pavilion; lodge.

Profile of Summer Employees Total number: 23; average age: 21; 5% high school students; 70% college students; 5% international; 5% local residents. Nonsmokers preferred.

Employment Information Openings are from June 10 to August 15. Jobs available: ▶ 5 *counselors/aquatics instructors* with lifeguard experience (preferred) at $1425 per season; ▶ 1 *counselor/aquatics team leader* with WSI certification and lifeguard training at $1600 per season; ▶ 1 *counselor/arts and crafts team leader* at $1600 per season; ▶ 5 *counselors/arts and crafts instructors* at $1425 per season; ▶ 1 *counselor/recreation team leader* at $1600 per season; ▶ 5 *counselors/recreation personnel* at $1425 per season; ▶ 1 *head counselor* at $1900 per season; ▶ 1 *nurse* with RN license at $4800 per season; ▶ 2 *cooks* at $2000 per season; ▶ 1 *night attendant* at $2000 per season; ▶ 1 *maintenance person* at $1500 per season. International students encouraged to apply; must apply through recognized agency.

Benefits College credit, on-the-job training, on-site room and board at no charge, laundry facilities, free certification in CPR, first aid, and lifeguard training. Preemployment training of 6 days is required and includes safety and accident prevention, group interaction, first-aid, CPR, leadership, camper-counselor relations, lifeguard training, body mechanics for lifting, transferring, and feeding. Orientation is paid.

Contact Dave and Peggy Bogenschutz, Camp Directors, Peacock Camp, Department SJ, 38685 North Deep Lake Road, Lake Villa, Illinois 60046; 847-356-5201, Fax 847-356-7206, E-mail pbogenschutz@kiwi.dep.anl.gov.

THE ROAD LESS TRAVELED
2053 NORTH MAGNOLIA AVENUE
CHICAGO, ILLINOIS 60614

General Information Western and Pacific Northwest adventure activities, wilderness exploration, and cultural exposure. Two 3-week programs for campers ages 13–14 and three 4-week and one 6-week program that features hiking, rafting, rock climbing, mountaineering, kayaking, backpacking, and a leadership program. Established in 1991. Owned by Jim and Donna Stein. Affiliated with American Camping Association. Features: backcountry hiking in Montana, Wyoming, Idaho, Colorado, Utah, and Washington; rafting and kayaking on the Green, Salmon, and Arkansas Rivers; mountaineering and climbing on Mt. Rainier, Mt.Baker, and the Tetons.

Profile of Summer Employees Total number: 20; average age: 28; 50% male, 50% female; 40% teachers. Nonsmokers only.

Employment Information Openings are from June 1 to August 1. Jobs available: ▶ 16 *general staff members* (minimum age 21 or college grad) with First aid, CPR and lifeguard training, experience working with teens and in wilderness; ▶ 8 *trip leaders* (minimum age 21 or college grad) with First aid, CPR and lifeguard training, experience working with teens and in leading wilderness trips and advanced certification in Wilderness First Responder or by Stonehearth Open Learning Opportunities. International students encouraged to apply; must obtain own visa and working papers prior to employment.

Benefits On-the-job training, on-site room and board at no charge, laundry facilities, workmen's compensation.

Contact Jim Stein, Director, The Road Less Traveled, Department SJ, 2053 North Magnolia Avenue, Chicago, Illinois 60614; 773-348-4100, Fax 773-348-4399, E-mail rltiroad@aol.com. Application deadline: April 1.

INDIANA

CULVER SUMMER CAMPS
BOX 138 CEF
CULVER, INDIANA 46511

General Information Six-week all-activity program followed by a two-week session of ten specialty camps. Established in 1902. Owned by Culver Educational Foundation. Affiliated with American Camping Association, North Central Association of Colleges and Schools, Independent Schools Association of the Central States. 1,800-acre facility located 35 miles south of South Bend. Features: location on second largest natural lake in Indiana; 15 outdoor tennis courts; indoor riding and polo arena; fully equipped gymnasium with indoor track and swimming pool; indoor ice arena for skating and hockey; new library and academic buildings.

Profile of Summer Employees Total number: 250; average age: 35; 60% male, 40% female; 5% minorities; 20% college students; 5% retirees; 1% international; 10% local residents. Nonsmokers preferred.

Employment Information Openings are from June 20 to August 15. Jobs available: ▶ 4 *swimming instructors* with lifeguard and WSI certification at $1200–$1400 per season; ▶ *tennis instructors* at $1200–$1400 per season; ▶ 35 *counselors* with at least one year of college and experience working with children at $1300–$1500 per season; ▶ *soccer instructors* at $1200–$1400 per season; ▶ *sailing instructors;* ▶ *music instructors.*

Benefits On-the-job training, on-site room and board at no charge, laundry facilities, free use of golf course, tennis courts, sailboats, and other facilities, tuition reduction for employees' children.

Preemployment training of 7 days is required and includes safety and accident prevention, group interaction, first-aid, CPR, leadership, camper-counselor relations, values education. Orientation is paid.

Contact Bruce Holaday, Director, Culver Summer Camps, Department SJ, Box 138 CEF, Culver, Indiana 46511; 800-221-2020, Fax 219-842-8462. Application deadline: December 15.

DUDLEY GALLAHUE VALLEY CAMPS
MORGANTOWN, INDIANA 46160

General Information Residential camp serving 128–140 campers weekly and biweekly. Established in 1961. Owned by Girl Scouts of Hoosier Capital Council, Inc. 800-acre facility located 50 miles south of Indianapolis. Features: wooded area; 45-acre man-made lake; location in hills of scenic Brown County.

Profile of Summer Employees Total number: 30; average age: 23; 2% male, 98% female; 5% minorities; 5% high school students; 80% college students; 10% local residents. Nonsmokers preferred.

Employment Information Openings are from June 8 to August 12. Jobs available: ▶ 1 *experienced director* with successful completion of Girl Scout, American Camping Association, or college camp director training course; experience in planning and implementing outdoor living experiences; ability to select, train, and supervise staff; and college degree or equivalent; ▶ 1 *experienced assistant director* with successful completion of Girl Scout, American Camping Association, or college camp director training course; experience in planning and implementing outdoor activities in camps; ability to select, train, and supervise staff; and college degree or equivalent; ▶ 1 *business manager* with business training (typing, bookkeeping, and office practice), sound judgment in purchasing supplies, and experience coordinating business activities; ▶ 1 *health supervisor* with state license or registration as a physician, physician's assistant, RN, LPN, paramedic, camp health director, or EMT; advanced first aid and/or CPR certification; emotional stability to meet emergencies; and knowledge of medicine and pesticide storage and use; ▶ 1 *experienced food supervisor* with minimum of two years of training in institutional management specializing in food service; ▶ 4 *cooks* with ability to provide records of necessary health exams required by Department of Health; ▶ 4 *experienced unit leaders* with first aid and lifesaving training, training in Girl Scout program, and management and organizational skills; ▶ 12 *experienced assistant unit leaders* with completion of group leadership, counselor-in-training, or leader-in-training course; ▶ *waterfront unit leader, canoeing/sailing trip leader, smallcraft instructor* with current American Red Cross WSI, ALS, and CPR training certification; YMCA Aquatic Leader Examiner; or Boy Scouts of America National Aquatic Instructor certification; ▶ *waterfront assistant, canoe/sailing assistant* with current basic swimming instructor certification issued by the American Red Cross or equivalent from the YMCA or Boy Scouts of America; ▶ *trip unit leader* with leadership, outdoor, and program specialty training and work experience as a teacher or counselor of children; ▶ *experienced horseback unit leader* with leadership, outdoor, and program specialty training. All positions offered at $1000 per season.

Benefits College credit, on-the-job training, formal ongoing training, on-site room and board at no charge, laundry facilities.

Contact Bonnie Closey, Outdoor Program Specialist, c/o Hoosier Capital Girl Scout Council, Dudley Gallahue Valley Camps, Department SJ, 1800 North Meridian Street, Indianapolis, Indiana 46202-1433; 317-924-3450, Fax 317-924-2976, E-mail scouts@in-motion. Application deadline: June 1.

HAPPY HOLLOW CHILDREN'S CAMP, INC.
3049 HAPPY HOLLOW ROAD
NASHVILLE, INDIANA 47448

General Information Residential camp with separate programs for diabetic, asthmatic, and inner-city children; serving 110 youths per week. Established in 1951. Owned by Happy Hollow Camp, Inc. Operated by United Way. Affiliated with American Camping Association. 776-acre facility located 62 miles south of Indianapolis. Features: lake for swimming, boating. and canoeing; horseback riding program; athletics fields; hiking trails; farm program; ropes course.

Profile of Summer Employees Total number: 35; average age: 20; 50% male, 50% female; 20% minorities; 10% high school students; 90% college students; 2% international; 20% local residents; 15% teachers. Nonsmokers only.

Employment Information Openings are from June 1 to August 9. Jobs available: ▶ 20 *general counselors* at $130–$175 per week; ▶ 10 *program instructors* with certification in related area at $130–$175 per week; ▶ *swimming instructors* with WSI certification at $140–$180 per week. International students encouraged to apply; must apply through recognized agency.

Benefits On-the-job training, on-site room and board at no charge, laundry facilities, health insurance. Preemployment training of 13 days is required and includes safety and accident prevention, group interaction, first-aid, CPR, leadership, camper-counselor relations, campcrafts, program instruction. Orientation is paid.

Contact Bernie Schrader, Director, Happy Hollow Children's Camp, Inc., Department SJ, 3049 Happy Hollow Road, Nashville, Indiana 47448; 812-988-4900, Fax 812-988-7505, E-mail hhcdir@ aol.com. Application deadline: April 1.

HOLIDAY WORLD & SPLASHIN' SAFARI
JUNCTION HIGHWAYS 162 AND 245
SANTA CLAUS, INDIANA 47579

General Information Theme park, water park, golf course, and campground. Established in 1946. Owned by William A. Koch and family (Koch Development Corporation). Affiliated with International Association of Amusement Parks and Attractions, American Coaster Enthusiasts, World Waterpark Association. 100-acre facility located 60 miles west of Louisville, Kentucky. Features: The Raven: wooden roller coaster; The Watubee: 6-story white-water raft slide; The Wave: wave pool; Raging Rapids: white-water raft ride; 5 different shows with live entertainment, including a high dive show; adjacent campground.

Profile of Summer Employees Total number: 750; average age: 18; 40% male, 60% female; 1% minorities; 50% high school students; 31% college students; 7% retirees; 99% local residents; 1% teachers. Nonsmokers preferred.

Employment Information Openings are from May 1 to October 15. Jobs available: ▶ 100 *ride operators* with some age requirements for using equipment at $4.75–$6.30 per hour; ▶ 175 *food service staff* at $4.99–$6.50 per hour; ▶ 100 *lifeguards* with must pass minimal swim requirements at $4.75–$6.30 per hour; ▶ 100 *games staff* at $4.75–$6.30 per hour; ▶ 55 *facilities maintenance staff* with some age requirements for using equipment at $4.75–$6.30 per hour; ▶ 25 *entertainment staff* with audition at $200–$300 per week; ▶ 20 *admissions staff* at $4.75–$6.30 per hour; ▶ 15 *office and security staff* at $4.75–$6.30 per hour; ▶ 65 *gift shop clerks* at $4.75–$6.30 per hour. International students encouraged to apply; must obtain own visa and working papers prior to employment.

Benefits On-the-job training, formal ongoing training, season pass and 15 one-day passes, employee discounts, parties, prizes ($5000 value), and fall attendance rewards (bonus). Off-site boarding costs are $25 per week. Preemployment training of 1 day is required and includes safety and accident prevention, group interaction, first-aid, hospitality. Orientation is unpaid.

Contact Natalie Koch, Human Resources, Holiday World & Splashin' Safari, Department SJ, PO Box 179, Santa Claus, Indiana 47579; 812-937-4401 Ext. 292, Fax 812-937-4405, E-mail nkoch@holidayworld.com, URL http://www.holidayworld.com.

HOWE MILITARY SCHOOL SUMMER CAMP
PO BOX 191
HOWE, INDIANA 46746

General Information A residential camp serving boys ages 8–16, in a modified military setting, emphasizing leadership, sports and academics. Established in 1896. Owned by Howe Military School. Affiliated with American Camping Association, Midwest Association of Independent

Camps. 50-acre facility located 45 miles east of South Bend. Features: freshwater lake frontage; high ropes course in wooded acreage; modern cabins sleep 18; access to boarding school's athletic facilities; new bath house.

Profile of Summer Employees Total number: 25; average age: 22; 80% male, 20% female; 15% minorities; 75% high school students; 25% college students; 10% local residents; 20% teachers. Nonsmokers preferred.

Employment Information Openings are from June 20 to August 7. Jobs available: ▶ 6 *cabin counselors* with one year of college completed at $1200 per season; ▶ 3 *waterfront staff members* with WSI and lifeguard certifications at $1000–$1200 per season; ▶ 2 *math instructors* with a major in teaching at $1000–$1200 per season; ▶ 2 *English instructors* with a major in teaching at $1000–$1200 per season; ▶ 1 *licensed nurse* with minimum LPN at $1200–$1800 per season; ▶ 2 *certified high ropes course instructors* at $1000–$1200 per season; ▶ *activities director* at $1000 per season.

Benefits On-the-job training, on-site room and board at no charge, laundry facilities. Preemployment training of 4 days is required and includes safety and accident prevention, group interaction, first-aid, CPR, leadership, camper-counselor relations, military leadership. Orientation is paid.

Contact Duane Van Orden, Camp Director, Howe Military School Summer Camp, Department SJ, Howe Military School, Howe, Indiana 46746; 219-562-2131 Ext. 235, Fax 219-562-3678, E-mail howemil@aol.com. Application deadline: May 15.

LIMBERLOST GIRL SCOUT COUNCIL
2135 SPY RUN AVENUE
FORT WAYNE, INDIANA 46805

General Information Residential camp serving 60 girls ages 7–17 weekly. Established in 1928. Owned by Girl Scouts of Limberlost Council. Affiliated with Girl Scouts of the United States of America, American Camping Association. 200-acre facility located 50 miles northwest of Fort Wayne. Features: freshwater lake frontage; waterskiing; windsurfing and sailing; platform tent housing.

Profile of Summer Employees Total number: 20; average age: 21; 100% female; 5% minorities; 10% high school students; 75% college students; 5% international; 50% local residents; 5% teachers. Nonsmokers preferred.

Employment Information Openings are from June 3 to August 9. Jobs available: ▶ 3 *unit leaders* at $1200–$1300 per season; ▶ 7 *assistant unit leaders* at $900–$1100 per season; ▶ 3 *lifeguards* with lifeguard training and CPR/first aid certification at $1100–$1200 per season; ▶ 1 *waterfront director* with lifeguard training and CPR/first aid and WSI certification at $1700–$1800 per season; ▶ 1 *program director* with bachelor's degree at $1800–$2500 per season; ▶ 1 *C.I.T. director* at $1300–$1400 per season; ▶ 1 *registered nurse* at $1800–$2000 per season; ▶ 2 *cooks* at $1500–$1700 per season. International students encouraged to apply; must apply through recognized agency.

Benefits On-site room and board at no charge, laundry facilities, health insurance. Preemployment training of 7 days is required and includes safety and accident prevention, group interaction, first-aid, CPR, leadership, camper-counselor relations, Girl Scout program. Orientation is paid.

Contact Melissa Schneider, Camp Director, Limberlost Girl Scout Council, 2135 Spy Run Avenue, Fort Wayne, Indiana 46816; 219-422-3417, Fax 219-422-0084, E-mail mschneider@ctlnet.com. Application deadline: March 15.

IOWA

CAMP COURAGEOUS OF IOWA
12007 190TH STREET, PO BOX 418
MONTICELLO, IOWA 52310-0418

General Information Year-round residential and respite care facility for children and adults with disabilities offering traditional activities such as swimming, canoeing, and nature studies, adventure activities such as rock climbing, rappelling and caving. Established in 1972. Owned by Camp Courageous of Iowa. Affiliated with American Camping Association. 70-acre facility located 35 miles east of Cedar Rapids. Features: indoor swimming pool; gymnasium; 100' x 100' lodge with storm shelter; 3 modern winterized camper cabins and nature center; high and low ropes course; limestone bluffs for rock climbing, rappelling, and caving.

Profile of Summer Employees Total number: 50; average age: 23; 30% male, 70% female; 3% minorities; 70% college students; 1% retirees; 10% international; 5% local residents. Nonsmokers only.

Employment Information Openings are from May 18 to August 15. Year-round positions also offered. Jobs available: ► 15 *camp counselors* with a sincere desire to work with people with disabilities at $550–$900 per month; ► 1 *canoeing specialist* with current lifeguard training certification at $550–$900 per month; ► 1 *swimming specialist* with current lifeguard training certification at $550–$900 per month; ► 1 *nature specialist* with experience leading nature activities and working with small farm animals at $550–$900 per month; ► 1 *recreation specialist* with experience with recreational activities for people with disabilities at $550–$900 per month; ► 1 *outdoor living skills specialist* with experience teaching outdoor living skills for people with disabilities at $550–$900 per month; ► 1 *crafts specialist* with experience with projects for people with disabilities at $550–$900 per month. International students encouraged to apply; must obtain own visa and working papers prior to employment.

Benefits College credit, on-the-job training, formal ongoing training, on-site room and board at no charge, laundry facilities, health insurance, opportunity to work with a wide variety of people with disabilities, opportunity to experience a wide variety of adventure activities. Preemployment training of 6 days is required and includes safety and accident prevention, group interaction, first-aid, CPR, leadership, camper-counselor relations, abuse awareness, behavior management. Orientation is paid.

Contact Jeanne Muellerleile, Camp Director, Camp Courageous of Iowa, Department SJ, 12007 190th Street PO Box 418, Monticello, Iowa 52310-0418; 319-465-5916, Fax 319-465-5919. Application deadline: May 15.

CAMP HANTESA
1450 ORIOLE ROAD
BOONE, IOWA 50036

General Information Residential and day camp serving boys and girls ages 5–18. Established in 1919. Operated by Camp Fire Boys and Girls. Affiliated with American Camping Association. 144-acre facility located 4 miles south of Boone. Features: swimming pool; river canoeing; sailing; horseback riding; campcraft; trips; rappelling; low ropes; high ropes.

Profile of Summer Employees Total number: 40; average age: 20; 30% male, 70% female; 1% minorities; 99% college students; 80% local residents. Nonsmokers preferred.

Employment Information Openings are from June 1 to August 20. Spring break, winter break, Christmas break, year-round positions also offered. Jobs available: ► 20 *general counselors* with interest in children; ► 1 *swimming instructor* with WSI certification; ► 1 *swimming guard* with lifeguard training; ► 6 *unit directors* with management skills; ► 1 *arts and crafts instruc-*

tor; ▶ 5 *cooks;* ▶ 3 *riding instructors* with riding skills (English or Western style). All positions offered at $1200 per season. International students encouraged to apply; must apply through recognized agency.

Benefits College credit, on-the-job training, on-site room and board at no charge, laundry facilities, health insurance. Preemployment training of 14 to 20 days is required and includes safety and accident prevention, group interaction, first-aid, CPR, leadership, camper-counselor relations, lifeguard, high ropes, riding instructing. Orientation is paid.

Contact Suz Welch, Director, Camp Hantesa, Department SJ, 1450 Oriole Road, Boone, Iowa 50036; 515-432-1417, Fax 515-432-1294, E-mail hantesa@opencominc.com. Application deadline: March 31.

CAMP HITAGA
5551 HITAGA ROAD
WALKER, IOWA 52352

General Information Day camp serving boys and girls from kindergarten through fifth grade. Residential camp serving boys and girls from first to ninth grade. Conference center serving community groups. Established in 1931. Owned by Iowana Council of Camp Fire. Affiliated with Camp Fire Boys and Girls, American Camping Association, United Way. 240-acre facility located 20 miles north of Cedar Rapids. Features: swimming pool; 4 miles of riding trails; river bordering camp for canoeing; extensive hiking and nature trails; rustic-style dining lodge with fireplace; sleeping units with cabins, tents, covered wagons, and treehouses.

Profile of Summer Employees Total number: 18; average age: 20; 25% male, 75% female; 100% college students; 25% local residents; 10% teachers. Nonsmokers preferred.

Employment Information Openings are from June 8 to August 2. Jobs available: ▶ *riding and aquatic staff heads* at $1000–$1250 per season; ▶ *general counselors* at $750–$1000 per season; ▶ *assistant director* at $1200–$1500 per season. International students encouraged to apply; must obtain own visa and working papers prior to employment; must apply through recognized agency.

Benefits On-the-job training, on-site room and board at no charge, laundry facilities. Preemployment training of 5 days is required and includes safety and accident prevention, group interaction, first-aid, CPR, leadership, camper-counselor relations, program area training. Orientation is paid.

Contact Halane Cummings, Camp Director, Camp Hitaga, Department SJ, 226 29th Street Drive, SE, Suite E-2, Cedar Rapids, Iowa 52403; 319-362-8268, Fax 319-362-7963. Application deadline: April 15.

GIRL SCOUT CAMP TANGLEFOOT
14948 DOGWOOD AVENUE
CLEAR LAKE, IOWA 50428

General Information Residential summer camp serving 116 Girl Scouts weekly. Established in 1947. Operated by North Iowa Girl Scout Council. Affiliated with American Camping Association. 50-acre facility located 5 miles west of Clear Lake. Features: freshwater lake frontage; challenge/ropes course; restored wetland and prairie recreation area; fully equipped sailing and canoeing center; crafts building; forested living areas.

Profile of Summer Employees Total number: 30; average age: 21; 5% male, 95% female; 1% minorities; 70% college students; 90% local residents. Nonsmokers preferred.

Employment Information Openings are from June 1 to July 1. Jobs available: ▶ 1 *program director* at $1400–$1600 per season; ▶ 1 *business manager* at $1200–$1300 per season; ▶ 3 *food service staff members* at $1400–$1600 per season; ▶ 10 *program counselors* at $1100–$1200 per season; ▶ 1 *waterfront director* with Red Cross lifeguard training and WSI certification at $1300–$1400 per season; ▶ 5 *waterfront staff members* with Red Cross lifeguard training and WSI certification at $1200–$1300 per season; ▶ 1 *arts director* at $1100–$1300 per season. International students encouraged to apply; must apply through recognized agency.

Benefits College credit, on-the-job training, on-site room and board at no charge, health insurance, skill certification, personal and professional growth, workmen's compensation.

Contact Camp Director, Girl Scout Camp Tanglefoot, 14948 Dogwood Avenue, Clear Lake, Iowa 50428; 515-357-2481, URL http://www.willowtree.com/~nigsc. Application deadline: May 15.

LUTHERAN LAKESIDE CAMP
2491 170TH STREET
SPIRIT LAKE, IOWA 51360

General Information Residential Christian education camp. Established in 1960. Owned by Lutheran Lakeside Camp Association. Affiliated with Evangelical Lutheran Church of America. 130-acre facility located 140 miles east of Sioux Falls, South Dakota. Features: ½ mile of shoreline; boating activities; challenge course; hiking trails; swimming pool; extensive natural surroundings.

Profile of Summer Employees Total number: 30; average age: 21; 50% male, 50% female; 15% minorities; 5% high school students; 95% college students; 10% international. Nonsmokers only.

Employment Information Openings are from May 24 to August 16. Jobs available: ► 2 *maintenance personnel, experience preferred,* at $1500–$1600 per season; ► 18 *counselors, experienced preferred,* at $1500–$1600 per season; ► 3 *lifeguards* with first aid/CPR and lifeguard certification at $1650–$1800 per season; ► 1 *waterfront director* with first aid/CPR, lifeguard certification and sailing experience at $1650–$1800 per season; ► 1 *canteen staff member* at $1500–$1600 per season; ► 1 *program director* at $2000–$2500 per season. International students encouraged to apply; must obtain own visa and working papers prior to employment.

Benefits College credit, on-the-job training, formal ongoing training, on-site room and board at no charge, laundry facilities.

Contact Judy Engh, Director, Lutheran Lakeside Camp, Department SJ, 2491 170th Street, Spirit Lake, Iowa 51360; 712-336-2109, Fax 712-336-0638.

KENTUCKY

CAMP WOODMEN OF THE WORLD
93 SCHWARTZ ROAD
MURRAY, KENTUCKY 42071

General Information Residential camp serving Woodmen of the World members ages 8–15; also a senior program serving adults ages 60 and over with a general camp program that provides transportation Monday and Friday. Established in 1983. Owned by West Kentucky Woodmen of the World Youth Camp and Resort, Inc. Affiliated with American Camping Association, National Arbor Day Foundation, National Rifle Association, Starlight Outdoor Education, Inc. 14-acre facility located 4 miles north of Murray. Features: junior-size Olympic swimming pool; 2 tennis courts; low challenge course; high ropes course; basketball courts; 18-hole miniature golf course; NRA-approved rifle and archery ranges.

Profile of Summer Employees Total number: 24; average age: 20; 50% male, 50% female; 2% minorities; 30% high school students; 70% college students; 2% international; 40% local residents.

Employment Information Openings are from June 1 to August 8. Jobs available: ► *experienced or certified archery instructor* (minimum age 18); ► *experienced arts and crafts instructor* (minimum age 18); ► *experienced general counselors* (minimum age 18); ► *rifle instructor* (minimum age 18) with experience or NRA certification; ► *water safety instructor/pool manager* (minimum age 18) with WSI certification. All positions offered at $700–$1100 per season. International students encouraged to apply; must obtain own visa and working papers prior to employment.

Benefits On-the-job training, on-site room and board at no charge, laundry facilities, health insurance, lifeguard certification, Red Cross CPR and first aid certification.

Contact Colleen Anderson, Camp Director, Camp Woodmen of the World, 401-A Maple Street, Murray, Kentucky 42071; 502-753-4382, Fax 502-753-4396, E-mail campwow@idd.net.

LIFE ADVENTURE CAMP
ESTILL COUNTY, KENTUCKY

General Information Primitive wilderness camp with weekly programs that serve 32–40 campers per session (ages 9–18) who are either emotionally or behaviorally challenged, or who are in need of enhanced self-esteem, cooperation, and team-building skills. Established in 1976. Operated by Life Adventure Camp, Inc. Affiliated with American Camping Association, United Way. 500-acre facility located 65 miles east of Lexington. Features: 6 caves; 2 creeks; 500 acres of hiking trails; nature trail; group challenge course.

Profile of Summer Employees Total number: 16; average age: 21; 31% male, 69% female; 6% high school students; 94% college students; 50% local residents. Nonsmokers preferred.

Employment Information Openings are from May 9 to August 20. Jobs available: ▶ 12 *counselors* (beginning May 27) with first aid/CPR certification, one year of college or related work experience, some camping or outdoor experience, ability to live and work comfortably in a primitive outdoor setting, and some experience in a leadership role with children, preferably with children who have emotional and/or behavioral problems at $1000–$1300 per season; ▶ 1 *food director* (beginning May 9) with experience with food management and valid driver's license at $900–$1000 per season; ▶ 1 *health supervisor* (beginning May 16) with first aid/CPR certification and valid driver's license at $1200–$1400 per season. International students encouraged to apply; must obtain own visa and working papers prior to employment.

Benefits College credit, on-the-job training, formal ongoing training, on-site room and board, first aid/CPR training, free room (board not included on days off).

Contact Kathleen Reese, Program Director, Life Adventure Camp, Department SJ, 1122 Oak Hill Drive, Lexington, Kentucky 40505; 606-252-4733. Application deadline: May 1.

NATIONAL PARK CONCESSIONS
MAMMOTH CAVE HOTEL
MAMMOTH CAVE NATIONAL PARK, KENTUCKY 42259

General Information Provides services to national park visitors in five national park areas, including Mammoth Cave, such as food service, lodging, stores, and transportation. Established in 1941. Owned by National Park Concessions, Inc. Affiliated with National Tour Association, American Bus Association, Kentucky Travel Council, National Park Hospitality Association, National Restaurant Association, Kentucky Hotel and Motel Association, Kentucky Restaurant Association. 52,830-acre facility located 85 miles southwest of Louisville. Features: longest cave system in world with over 350 miles of explored and mapped passages; 31 miles of river within the park (no fishing license required); 69 miles of hiking and equestrian trails within the park; Mammoth Cave Hotel and facilities located close to natural cave entrance and park visitor center; three food service facilities, craft shop, and gift shop; cottages, motel, hotel, service station, camper store, laundry, and showers.

Profile of Summer Employees Total number: 100; average age: 25; 50% male, 50% female; 10% minorities; 5% high school students; 15% college students; 5% retirees; 75% local residents.

Employment Information Openings are from April 1 to October 31. Spring break positions also offered. Jobs available: ▶ 15 *cooks/cooks' helpers/general kitchen staff* with experience preferred at $4.75 per hour; ▶ 8 *desk clerks* at $4.75 per hour; ▶ 10 *gift shop/store clerks* at $4.75 per hour; ▶ 12 *room attendants* at $4.75 per hour; ▶ *bus drivers* with commercial driver's license at $4.50 per hour; ▶ *dining room service staff* at $4.15–$4.75 per hour; ▶ *maintenance/yard workers* at $4.75 per hour.

Benefits College credit, on-the-job training, on-site room and board at $265 per month, laundry facilities. Preemployment training of 1 day is required. Orientation is paid.

Contact Garner B. Hanson, Chairman and President, National Park Concessions, Department SJ, National Park Concessions, Inc., Mammoth Cave, Kentucky 42259-0027; 502-773-2191, Fax 502-773-5120. Application deadline: March 1.

LOUISIANA

CAMP FIRE CAMP WI-TA-WENTIN
2126 OAK PARK BOULEVARD
LAKE CHARLES, LOUISIANA 70601

General Information Three-week day camp and two-week resident camp. Established in 1955. Owned by Camp Fire Council of Sowela. 96-acre facility located 13 miles north of Lake Charles. Features: location on Burnett's Bay; large swimming pool; screened cabins with ceiling fans; large kitchen/dining lodge.

Profile of Summer Employees Total number: 18; average age: 21; 50% male, 50% female; 5% minorities; 20% high school students; 80% college students; 85% local residents. Nonsmokers preferred.

Employment Information Openings are from June 1 to July 15. Jobs available: ▶ *lifeguards* at $600–$675 per season; ▶ *general counselors* at $700–$800 per season; ▶ *canoeing instructor* at $700–$800 per season; ▶ *sports director* at $725–$825 per season; ▶ *program director* at $725–$825 per season; ▶ *water safety instructor* at $900 per season.

Benefits On-site room and board at no charge, laundry facilities, preemployment training.

Contact Joe Hill, Director, Camp Fire Camp Wi-Ta-Wentin, Department SJ, 2126 Oak Park Boulevard, Lake Charles, Louisiana 70601; 318-478-6550, Fax 318-478-6551, E-mail jdhill@ iamerica.net. Application deadline: May 1.

MARYDALE RESIDENT CAMP
10317 MARYDALE ROAD
ST. FRANCISVILLE, LOUISIANA 70775

General Information Residential camp serving girls ages 8–17 with a general outdoor program and specialty programs in horseback riding and swimming. Established in 1948. Owned by Audubon Girl Scout Council. Affiliated with Girl Scouts of the United States of America, American Camping Association, Association for Horsemanship Safety and Education. 400-acre facility located 35 miles north of Baton Rouge. Features: miles of riding/hiking trails; location 2 hours from New Orleans in the heart of plantation country; Olympic-size pool; lake for canoeing; equestrian unit/barn, bunkhouse, and 2 arenas.

Profile of Summer Employees Total number: 40; average age: 20; 1% male, 99% female; 25% minorities; 5% high school students; 95% college students; 90% local residents. Nonsmokers preferred.

Employment Information Openings are from May 31 to July 27. Jobs available: ▶ 5 *unit leaders* (minimum age 21) with camp and documented leadership experience at $115–$125 per week; ▶ 16 *counselors* (minimum age 18) with leadership experience at $100–$112 per week; ▶ 1 *waterfront director* (minimum age 21) with American Red Cross and WSI certification (possible nine-week contract) at $130–$137 per week; ▶ 1 *riding director* (minimum age 21) with CHA certification or documented experience (possible nine-week contract) at $130–$137 per week; ▶ 2 *health supervisors* (minimum age 21) with RN and EMT at $200–$225 per week; ▶ 1 *program director* (minimum age 21) with camp experience, preferably in Girl Scout programming, documented experience in leadership and activity organization, and recreation background at $145–$160 per week; ► 1 *business manager* (minimum age 25) with some type of accounting or bookkeeping experience at $120–$125 per week; ► 1 *naturalist* (minimum age 21) with experience in wildlife education at $120–$135 per week; ► 4 *lifeguards* (minimum age 18) with American Red Cross certification at $115–$122 per week; ► 4 *riding instructors* (minimum age 18) with Camp Horsemanship Association certification or documented experience at $115–$122 per week; ► 1 *arts and crafts director* (minimum age 18) at $120–$130 per week.

Benefits   College credit, on-the-job training, on-site room and board at no charge, laundry facilities, time to explore own interests, partial uniform.

Contact   Lydia Martin, Program Specialist, Marydale Resident Camp, Department SJ, 545 Colonial Drive, Baton Rouge, Louisiana 70806-6520; 800-852-8421, Fax 504-927-8402. Application deadline: May 1.

MAINE

ACADIA CORPORATION
85 MAIN STREET, BOX 24
BAR HARBOR, MAINE 04609

General Information   National park concessioner operating a restaurant and three gift shops in Acadia National Park and several shops in the town of Bar Harbor. Established in 1932. Owned by David Woodside, President. Affiliated with National Park Hospitality Association. Located 20 miles southeast of Ellsworth. Features: national park setting; proximity to busy resort community; natural beauty of Maine and Mt. Desert Island; more than 50 miles of gravel carriage roads for hiking and biking in Acadia National Park; more than 50 miles of foot trails in the park; abundant cultural, recreational, and sightseeing opportunities in surrounding villages.

Profile of Summer Employees   Total number: 125; average age: 21; 44% male, 56% female; 4% minorities; 1% high school students; 89% college students; 10% retirees; 2% international; 20% local residents. Nonsmokers preferred.

Employment Information   Openings are from May 15 to October 31. Jobs available: ► 36 *waiters/waitresses* with pleasant personality, and calm demeanor and ability to lift and carry more than 25 pounds up to 100 times per day at $2.38 per hour; ► 5 *buspersons* with ability to lift and carry more than 25 pounds up to 100 times per day at $5 per hour; ► 15 *kitchen workers* with ability to run cold food line and bakery and to perform food prep work, dishwashing, cleaning and lifting and carrying more that 25 pounds up to 100 times per day at $5.50 per hour; ► 3 *lead cooks* with strong creative cooking skills, including saute and sauces, and two years of supervisory experience or equivalent at $7 per hour; ► 3 *bartenders* with ability to operate service bar and cash register at $5 per hour; ► 2 *cashiers* with ability to operate cash register, count money, and prepare bank accounts (must have valid driver's license) at $5 per hour; ► 6 *hosts* with pleasant personality and calm demeanor to greet and seat customers and take reservations at $5 per hour; ► 32 *shop clerks* with ability to perform various duties, including operating cash register, assisting with purchases, stocking and ordering merchandise, and orienting park visitors at $5 per hour; ► 1 *housekeeper* with willingness to clean housing, offices, and restrooms at $5.50 per hour; ► 6 *building and grounds personnel* with ability to perform a variety of tasks (indoors and outdoors) and to interact well with park visitors at $5 per hour; ► 3 *office clerks* with ability to perform work accurately, pay attention to detail, and type (must have valid driver's license) at $5 per hour; ► 4 *warehouse clerks* with ability to maintain accurate records, pay attention to detail; good driving record, valid driver's license; ability to frequently lift and carry up to 50 pounds at $5 per hour; ► 1 *dormitory cook* with ability to perform institutional cafeteria cooking for up to 60 people, plan menus, and prepare food (must have valid driver's license) at $6 per hour. International students encouraged to apply; must obtain own visa and working papers prior to employment; must apply through recognized agency.

Benefits On-the-job training, on-site room and board at $70 per week, laundry facilities, possible end-of-season bonus. Preemployment training of 1 day is required and includes safety and accident prevention, camper-counselor relations, customer service. Orientation is paid.

Contact Rebecca Ghelli, Personnel, Acadia Corporation, PO Box 24, Bar Harbor, Maine 04609; 207-288-5592, Fax 207-288-2420, E-mail acadia@acadia.net.

ALFORD LAKE CAMP, INC.
RR 3
UNION, MAINE 04862

General Information Residential camp for girls offering a multiactivity program for 175 girls ages 8–15. Extensive trip programs for girls and/or boys on the Appalachian Trail and in Great Britain offered, as well as exchange programs in Mexico, Russia, Japan, and Lithuania. Established in 1907. Owned by the McMullan family. Affiliated with American Camping Association, Maine Youth Camping Association, American Camping Foundation Scholarship Program. 416-acre facility located 10 miles west of Camden. Features: clear, protected, 550-acre lake; location 2½ hours from Acadia National Park; proximity to rivers, mountains, forests, and fields; woods, fields, hills, and tree farm.

Profile of Summer Employees Total number: 90; average age: 21; 2% male, 98% female. Nonsmokers only.

Employment Information Openings are from June 16 to August 16. Jobs available: ▶ *swimming instructors* with WSI and American Red Cross lifeguard certification; ▶ *sailing instructors* with Red Cross lifeguard training and sailing experience; ▶ *nature counselor* with background in nature, environmental studies, and related fields; ▶ *tennis counselor* with teaching experience; ▶ *certified gymnastics instructor* with teaching experience and certification or documentation; ▶ *drama instructor* with teaching and production experience; ▶ *sailboarding instructor* with sailboarding experience documentation and ALS certification (minimum); ▶ *campcraft instructor* with Maine trip-leading certification; ▶ *canoeing instructor* with Red Cross canoeing (or equivalent) and ALS certification (minimum); ▶ *riding instructor* with British Horse Society or Pony Club certification or equivalent; ▶ *office person* with knowledge of computers and attention to detail. All positions offered at $900–$1500 per season. International students encouraged to apply; must apply through recognized agency.

Benefits On-the-job training, formal ongoing training, on-site room and board at no charge, laundry service, camp clothing provided on a loan basis.

Contact Sue McMullan, Director, Alford Lake Camp, Inc., Department SJ, 17 Pilot Point Road, Cape Elizabeth, Maine 04107; 207-799-3005, Fax 207-799-5004. Application deadline: May 1.

BOOTHBAY HARBOR YACHT CLUB
WEST BOOTHBAY HARBOR, MAINE 04538

General Information Yacht club with a junior activities program. Established in 1951. Situated on 4 acres. Features: waterfront with 10 one-design sailboats and 12 turnabouts (beginners' sailboats); 2 tennis courts.

Profile of Summer Employees Total number: 7; average age: 19; 50% male, 50% female; 40% high school students; 60% college students. Nonsmokers preferred.

Employment Information Openings are from June 19 to August 21. Jobs available: ▶ *director of sailing program* at $6000–$10000 per season; ▶ *sailing instructor* at $2500–$3500 per season; ▶ *tennis instructor* at $2000–$3500 per season.

Benefits Housing possibly available.

Contact Marianne Reynolds, Boothbay Harbor Yacht Club, Boothbay Harbor Yacht Club 34 Pin Oak Road, Skillman, New Jersey 08558; 609-466-0894. Application deadline: February 1.

CAMP AGAWAM
CRESCENT LAKE 54 AGAWAM ROAD
RAYMOND, MAINE 04071

General Information Residential camp serving 125 boys ages 8–15 in a single 7-week session. There is also a 1-week session for 85 disadvantaged boys. Established in 1919. Owned by Agawam Council. Affiliated with American Camping Association, Maine Youth Camping Association, Association of Independent Camps. 90-acre facility located 25 miles northwest of Portland. Features: 4 tennis courts; 40 acres of open fields, 50 acres of woods; newly constructed dining room, kitchen, and indoor recreation space; extensive freshwater lake for swimming, fishing, and boating; low and high element ropes/initiative course.

Profile of Summer Employees Total number: 50; average age: 20; 90% male, 10% female; 10% minorities; 20% high school students; 80% college students; 10% international; 10% local residents; 10% teachers. Nonsmokers only.

Employment Information Openings are from June 10 to August 13. Jobs available: ▶ 15 *counselors/sports instructors/coaches* at $1000–$1500 per season; ▶ 4 *counselors/water sports instructors* with CPR, first aid, and WSI or LGT certification at $1000–$1750 per season; ▶ 4 *counselors/campcraft and trip leaders* with LGT, CPR/first aid, and Maine Trip Leader certification at $1000–$1500 per season; ▶ 1 *counselor/dramatics instructor* at $1000–$1500 per season; ▶ 1 *counselor/woodworking instructor* at $1000–$2000 per season; ▶ 2 *counselors/archery and riflery instructors* with NAA or NRA certification or equivalent at $1000–$1750 per season; ▶ 1 *counselor/crafts instructor* at $1000–$1500 per season. International students encouraged to apply; must apply through recognized agency.

Benefits On-the-job training, on-site room and board at no charge, laundry facilities. Preemployment training of 7 days is required and includes safety and accident prevention, group interaction, first-aid, CPR, leadership, camper-counselor relations. Orientation is paid.

Contact Garth Nelson, Director, Camp Agawam, Department SJ, 30 Fieldstone Lane, Hanover, Massachusetts 02339; 617-826-5913, Fax 617-826-5913, E-mail 75463.306@compuserve.com. Application deadline: April 1.

CAMP ANDROSCOGGIN
WAYNE, MAINE 04284

General Information Private residential camp serving 220 boys from the United States and abroad in one 8-week session. Established in 1907. Owned by Peter Hirsch. Affiliated with American Camping Association, Maine Youth Camping Association. 125-acre facility located 50 miles north of Portland. Features: waterfront location with 1,900 feet of shoreline; 4 sports fields; 12 tennis courts; extensive arts and camping programs; ropes course; climbing wall; central location with easy access to coast, mountains, and state parks.

Profile of Summer Employees Total number: 80; average age: 21; 90% male, 10% female; 80% college students; 10% international; 10% local residents. Nonsmokers preferred.

Employment Information Openings are from June 20 to August 20. Jobs available: ▶ 10 *swimming instructors* with WSI certification or lifeguard training at $1000–$1250 per season; ▶ 3 *sailing instructors* at $1000–$1250 per season; ▶ 2 *canoeing instructors* at $1000–$1250 per season; ▶ 4 *waterskiing instructors* at $1000–$1250 per season; ▶ 4 *baseball instructors* at $1000–$1250 per season; ▶ 4 *basketball instructors* at $1000–$1250 per season; ▶ 4 *soccer instructors* at $1000–$1250 per season; ▶ 10 *tennis instructors* at $1000–$1250 per season; ▶ 2 *lacrosse instructors* at $1000–$1250 per season; ▶ 2 *drama instructors* at $1000–$1250 per season; ▶ 1 *woodworking instructor* at $1000–$1250 per season; ▶ 1 *photography instructor* at $1000–$1250 per season; ▶ 1 *campcraft instructor* at $1000–$1250 per season; ▶ 2 *nurses* at $2500–$3500 per season; ▶ 1 *archery instructor* at $1000–$1250 per season; ▶ 1 *riflery instructor* at $1000–$1250 per season; ▶ 1 *windsurfing instructor* at $1000–$1250 per season; ▶ 1 *radio broadcasting instructor* at $1000–$1250 per season; ▶ 1 *bicycling instructor* at $1000–$1250 per season; ▶ 1 *kayaking instructor* at $1000–$1250 per season; ▶ 1 *animation/video instructor* at $1000–$1250 per season; ▶ 4 *trip and ropes course instructors* at $1000–$1250 per season; ▶ 1 *ceramics instructor* at $1000–$1250 per season; ▶ 1 *crafts instructor* at $1000–$1250 per season.

Benefits College credit, on-the-job training, on-site room and board at no charge, laundry facilities, travel reimbursement. Preemployment training of 6 days is required and includes safety and accident prevention, group interaction, leadership, camper-counselor relations. Orientation is paid.

Contact Peter Hirsch, Director, Camp Androscoggin, 601 West Street, Harrison, New York 10528; 914-835-5800, Fax 914-777-2718, E-mail campandro@aol.com. Application deadline: May 1.

CAMP ARCADIA
ROUTE 121
CASCO, MAINE 04015

General Information Residential camp for girls serving 140 campers for part of the season or seven full weeks concentrating on individual camper growth and development in a warm, family atmosphere. Established in 1916. Owned by Anne H. Fritts and Louise L. Henderson. Affiliated with American Camping Association, Maine Youth Camping Association, Audubon Society, Camp Archery Association. 365-acre facility located 35 miles northwest of Portland. Features: extensive freshwater lake frontage on Pleasant Lake with two natural sandy beaches; sunny fields and pine woods; 4 outdoor tennis courts; screened-in summer lodges; proximity to mountains and ocean; riding ring and stables at the edge of a 10-acre field with riding trails.

Profile of Summer Employees Total number: 58; average age: 21; 10% male, 90% female; 5% minorities; 75% college students; 10% international. Nonsmokers preferred.

Employment Information Openings are from June 16 to August 14. Jobs available: ▶ 3 *swimming instructors* with WSI and lifeguard training certification at $1000–$1500 per season; ▶ 1 *archery instructor* at $1000–$1100 per season; ▶ 3 *canoeing instructors* with lifeguard training certification at $1000–$1500 per season; ▶ 3 *tennis instructors* with tennis team background at $1000–$1500 per season; ▶ 1 *music instructor* with piano playing and camp song leadership ability at $1000–$1200 per season; ▶ 3 *sailing instructors* with lifeguard training and knowledge of racing at $1000–$1300 per season; ▶ 2 *weaving instructors* with knowledge of floor, table, and hand looms at $1000–$1200 per season; ▶ 2 *riding instructors* with English balance seat-riding and stable management ability at $1000–$1400 per season; ▶ 2 *arts and crafts instructors* with silk-screening, block-printing, batik, drawing, and painting experience at $1000–$1200 per season; ▶ 1 *ceramics instructor* with electric kiln and potter's wheel experience at $1000–$1200 per season; ▶ 2 *drama instructors* with experience in children's drama, directing, lighting, and sets at $900–$1500 per season; ▶ 3 *trip instructors* (minimum age 21) with driver's license at $1000–$1500 per season; ▶ 1 *environmental* (nature) *instructor* at $900–$1200 per season; ▶ 2 *office workers* with 50 wpm typing and knowledge of computers at $1000–$1200 per season; ▶ 1 *photography instructor* with black-and-white darkroom experience at $1000–$1200 per season. International students encouraged to apply; must apply through recognized agency.

Benefits College credit, on-the-job training, formal ongoing training, on-site room and board at no charge, laundry facilities, travel reimbursement, health insurance. Preemployment training of 7 days is required and includes safety and accident prevention, group interaction, first-aid, CPR, leadership. Orientation is paid.

Contact Anne H. Fritts, Director, Camp Arcadia, Department SJ, Pleasantville Road, New Vernon, New Jersey 07976; 201-538-5409. Application deadline: May 1.

CAMP CEDAR
PO BOX 240
CASCO, MAINE 04015-0240

General Information Residential private camp for 250 boys offering one 8-week session including land sports, water sports, adventure activities and creative arts in a warm, nurturing environment. Established in 1954. Owned by Jeff Hacker and Susan Hacker-Wolf. Affiliated with American Camping Association, New England Camping Association, Maine Youth Camping Association. 80-acre facility located 30 miles north of Portland. Features: location on Maine lake; indoor gym; 9 tennis courts; 2 street/roller hockey rinks; climbing wall, ropes course, and indoor climbing gym; regulation soccer, lacrosse, and baseball fields.

Profile of Summer Employees Total number: 100; average age: 21; 80% male, 20% female; 10% minorities; 5% high school students; 80% college students; 10% international; 5% local residents. Nonsmokers preferred.

Employment Information Openings are from June 20 to August 20. Jobs available: ▶ 75 *counselors* with ability to teach an activity; ▶ 10 *swimming instructors* with WSI certification; ▶ 10 *tennis instructors* with high school or college varsity experience; ▶ 5 *experienced rock climbers* with background in technical rock climbing, top roping, and belaying. All positions offered at $1000–$1500 per season.

Benefits College credit, on-the-job training, formal ongoing training, on-site room and board at no charge, laundry facilities, travel reimbursement, health insurance. Preemployment training of 7 days is required and includes safety and accident prevention, group interaction, first-aid, CPR, leadership, camper-counselor relations, activity planning; selected certifications. Orientation is paid.

Contact Jeff Hacker, Director, Camp Cedar, Department SJ, 1758 Beacon Street, Brookline, Massachusetts 02146; 617-277-8080, Fax 617-277-1488, E-mail ccedarme@aol.com, URL http://www.campcedar.com/cedar.

CAMP COBBOSSEE
RFD 1, ROUTE 135
WINTHROP, MAINE 04364

General Information Residential competitive and instructionally-oriented sports camp serving 200 boys. Established in 1902. Owned by Steven and Nancy Rubin. Affiliated with American Camping Association. 150-acre facility located 15 miles west of Augusta. Features: location on lake that is 11 miles long by 6 miles wide with extensive waterfront area; 9 tennis courts (5 clay and 4 all-weather); ball fields and courts; climbing wall, zip line and ropes course.

Profile of Summer Employees Total number: 80; average age: 22; 90% male, 10% female; 15% minorities; 85% college students; 10% international; 10% teachers. Nonsmokers only.

Employment Information Openings are from June 15 to August 20. Jobs available: ▶ *swimming instructors* with LGT and WSI certification at $1000–$1500 per season; ▶ *team sports staff members* with experience in coaching or working with children at $1000–$1750 per season; ▶ *tennis staff members* with high school and/or college varsity or tournament competition experience at $1000–$1750 per season; ▶ *waterfront staff members* with sailing, waterskiing, or scuba experience at $1000–$1500 per season; ▶ *hiking/camping/rock climbing staff members* with experience in working with children at $1000–$1750 per season; ▶ *activity heads* with teaching and/or coaching experience (preference for high school or college coaches or teachers) at $1500–$4500 per season. International students encouraged to apply; must obtain own visa and working papers prior to employment; must apply through recognized agency.

Benefits College credit, on-the-job training, on-site room and board at no charge, laundry facilities, travel reimbursement.

Contact Steven Rubin, Owner, Camp Cobbossee, 10 Silvermine Drive, South Salem, New York 10590; 914-533-6104, Fax 914-533-6069, E-mail cobbachief@aol.com. Application deadline: June 1.

CAMP ENCORE-CODA FOR A GREAT SUMMER OF MUSIC, SPORTS, AND FRIENDS
STEARNS POND
SWEDEN, MAINE 04040

General Information Residential, private, coed camp for musical youths. Established in 1950. Owned by Saltman Family. Affiliated with Maine Youth Camping Association, American Camping Association. 80-acre facility located 50 miles west of Portland. Features: private pond; 2 tennis courts; several playing fields; 60 buildings; 32 music studios; dining hall; 2 concert halls.

Profile of Summer Employees Total number: 65; average age: 25; 50% male, 50% female; 5% minorities; 10% high school students; 70% college students; 5% international; 5% local residents; 15% teachers. Nonsmokers only.

Employment Information Openings are from June 23 to August 21. Jobs available: ► *swimming instructors* with LGT certification at $700–$1300 per season; ► *waterfront director* with LGT/WSI certification at $2000–$2500 per season; ► *land sports counselor* at $600–$1200 per season; ► *arts and crafts counselor* at $700–$1000 per season; ► *head counselor* with camp leadership experience and good organizational skills at $2000–$3000 per season; ► *assistant head counselor* with camp leadership experience and good organizational skills at $1500–$2000 per season; ► *tennis counselor* at $700–$1200 per season; ► *sailing counselor* with LGT certification at $700–$1200 per season; ► *boating counselor* with LGT certification at $700–$1200 per season. International students encouraged to apply; must apply through recognized agency.

Benefits On-the-job training, on-site room and board at no charge. Preemployment training of 3 to 7 days is required and includes safety and accident prevention, group interaction, leadership, camper-counselor relations. Orientation is paid.

Contact Ellen Donohue-Saltman, Director, Camp Encore-Coda for a Great Summer of Music, Sports, and Friends, Department SJ, 32 Grassmere Road, Brookline, Massachusetts 02167; 617-325-1541, Fax 617-325-7278, E-mail ellen@encore-coda.com.

CAMP HAWTHORNE
PLUMMER ROAD, PANTHER POND
RAYMOND, MAINE 04071

General Information Coed residential camp with visual and performing arts programs and noncompetitive sports. Established in 1919. Owned by Ronald Furst. Affiliated with Maine Camping Association. 140-acre facility located 26 miles west of Portland. Features: 2 miles of shorefront; 10 sailboats; large fields; rustic setting; theater.

Profile of Summer Employees Total number: 30; average age: 21; 50% male, 50% female; 15% minorities; 5% high school students; 80% college students; 5% international; 20% teachers. Nonsmokers preferred.

Employment Information Openings are from June 26 to August 21. Jobs available: ► 5 *swimming instructors* with lifeguard training or WSI certification at $1000–$1400 per season; ► 6 *sports instructors;* ► 4 *creative arts teachers;* ► 2 *archery/riflery instructors;* ► 6 *sailing instructors;* ► 2 *canoeing/boating instructors;* ► 2 *drama instructors.*

Benefits On-the-job training, on-site room and board at no charge, laundry facilities, travel reimbursement, professional reference.

Contact Ronald Furst, Owner, Camp Hawthorne, Department SJ, 10 Scotland Bridge Road, York, Maine 03909; 207-363-1773, Fax 207-363-1773. Application deadline: May 15.

CAMP KOHUT
151 KOHUT ROAD
OXFORD, MAINE 04270

General Information Residential camp serving 75 girls and 75 boys with traditional activities in four- or eight-week sessions. Focuses on single-gender classes at one campus facility. Established in 1907. Owned by Lisa Tripler. Affiliated with American Camping Association, Maine Youth Camping Association, Association of Independent Camps. 115-acre facility located 50 miles north of Portland. Features: 1-mile lakefront; wide-open fields and woods; 6 outdoor tennis courts; screened cabins and indoor plumbing; large theater and recreation halls; 2 basketball courts, 2 large sports fields, and 2 baseball diamonds; location 1 hour from ocean and 1 hour from the White Mountains.

Profile of Summer Employees Total number: 50; average age: 21; 50% male, 50% female; 1% minorities; 73% college students; 2% retirees; 25% international; 5% local residents. Nonsmokers preferred.

Employment Information Openings are from June 13 to August 16. Jobs available: ▶ *activity specialists* (minimum age 19 or completing first year of college) with enthusiasm, friendliness, energy, and reliability at $900–$3000 per season; ▶ *office staff* with enthusiasm, friendliness, energy, reliability, and computer literacy (Macintosh) at $1000–$1500 per season. International students encouraged to apply; must apply through recognized agency.

Benefits College credit, on-the-job training, formal ongoing training, on-site room and board at no charge, travel reimbursement, health insurance, laundry service, competitive salaries, regular time off. Preemployment training of 6 days is required and includes safety and accident prevention, group interaction, leadership, camper-counselor relations. Orientation is paid.

Contact Lisa Tripler, Director, Camp Kohut, Department SJ, Two Tall Pine Road, Cape Elizabeth, Maine 04107; 207-767-2406, Fax 207-767-0604, E-mail kampkohut@aol.com. Application deadline: June 1.

CAMP LAUREL
READFIELD, MAINE 04355

General Information Camp welcoming 400 boys and girls ages 8–16 from all over the United States as well as several other countries. Established in 1949. Owned by Keith Klein. Affiliated with American Camping Association, American Red Cross, National Waterski Association. 150-acre facility located 17 miles west of Augusta. Features: location on 4-mile spring-fed lake in south central Maine; 15 tennis courts, 3 baseball/softball fields; fitness center; soccer and lacrosse fields; gymnastics facility; large performing and fine arts complex; 18-horse riding stable and program.

Profile of Summer Employees Total number: 190; average age: 23; 50% male, 50% female; 75% college students; 3% international; 3% local residents; 20% teachers. Nonsmokers only.

Employment Information Openings are from June 20 to August 20. Jobs available: ▶ *athletics counselors;* ▶ *tennis counselors;* ▶ *swimming counselors;* ▶ *waterskiing counselors;* ▶ *windsurfing counselors;* ▶ *sailing counselors;* ▶ *fitness counselors;* ▶ *riding (English) counselors;* ▶ *lacrosse counselors;* ▶ *rollerblading counselors;* ▶ *roller hockey counselors;* ▶ *arts and crafts instructor;* ▶ *ceramics instructor;* ▶ *gymnastics instructor;* ▶ *archery instructor;* ▶ *piano/music instructor;* ▶ *photography instructor;* ▶ *AM radio personality;* ▶ *nature instructor;* ▶ *nurses;* ▶ *ice hockey counselors;* ▶ *dance counselors.*

Benefits College credit, on-the-job training, formal ongoing training, on-site room and board at no charge, laundry facilities, travel reimbursement, excellent facilities for use during time off (when available), staff lounge and snack bar, fitness facility.

Contact Keith M. Klein, Camp Director, Camp Laurel, Department SJ, Box 661, Alpine, New Jersey 07620; 800-327-3509, Fax 201-750-0665, E-mail summer@camplaurel.com.

CAMP MATOAKA FOR GIRLS
RR 1 BOX 1288
SMITHFIELD, MAINE 04978-1288

General Information Residential camp serving 225 girls with a variety of activities. Established in 1951. Owned by Mike, Paula, and Sue Nathanson. Affiliated with American Camping Association, World Waterpark Association, Maine Youth Camping Association, Private Independent Camps. 150-acre facility located 9 miles west of Waterville. Features: 1½ miles of shore frontage with 4 water-ski boats; largest recreation hall in New England; gym and dance complex; island on lake for overnight camping; 5 lighted tennis courts; 25-meter heated swimming pool with 3 water slides.

Profile of Summer Employees Total number: 120; average age: 23; 20% male, 80% female; 3% minorities; 10% high school students; 45% college students; 2% retirees; 30% international; 10% local residents. Nonsmokers only.

Employment Information Openings are from June 15 to August 17. Jobs available: ▶ *6 swimming instructors* with WSI certification at $1100–$1300 per season; ▶ *6 arts and crafts instructors* with a major in fine arts at $1000–$1200 per season; ▶ *2 sewing instructors* with a major in home economics at $1200 per season; ▶ 6 *tennis instructors* with college team experience at $1000–$1400 per season; ▶ 3 *gymnastics instructors* with college team experience at $1200–$1400 per season; ▶ 6 *ski instructors* with high skill level at $1100–$1500 per season; ▶ 3 *drama/music instructors* with a major in theater/drama at $1100–$1300 per season; ▶ 4 *experienced trip instructors (minimum age 21)* with valid driver's license at $1200–$1400 per season; ▶ 4 *land sports instructors* with a major in physical education or health/recreation at $1000–$1300 per season; ▶ 2 *ropes course instructors* with Project Adventure or Outward Bound certification at $1500 per season; ▶ 3 *English equitation instructors* with high skill level and horsemanship certification at $1100–$1300 per season; ▶ 6 *small craft instructors* with Red Cross, CPR, and lifeguard certification at $1200–$1400 per season; ▶ 1 *pianist/accompanist* with ability to sight read at $1100 per season; ▶ 2 *dance instructors* with a major in dance/movement and aerobics instructor experience at $1100–$1200 per season; ▶ 2 *photographers* with a major in photography at $1100–$1300 per season; ▶ 7 *video/radio personnel* with a major in video/radio/communication at $1150–$1400 per season.

Benefits College credit, on-site room and board at no charge, laundry facilities, travel reimbursement, camp facilities, including fitness equipment, available during free time.

Contact Michael Nathanson, Director/Owner, Camp Matoaka for Girls, 8751 Horseshoe Lane, Boca Raton, Florida 33496; 800-MATOAKA, Fax 407-488-6386. Application deadline: May 1.

CAMP MODIN
RR 2, BOX 3445
BELGRADE, MAINE 04917

General Information Privately owned Jewish camp in New England serving 250 international campers. Established in 1922. Owned by Howard Salzberg. Affiliated with American Camping Association, Maine Youth Camping Association. 50-acre facility located 175 miles north of Boston, Massachusetts. Features: 8 lit clay tennis courts; 75 boats, including ski, canoes, kayaks, sailboats, and windsurfers; 3 extensive craft studios; 5 large sports fields; 3-mile virtually private lake; modern and spacious living quarters.

Profile of Summer Employees Total number: 90; average age: 21; 50% male, 50% female; 100% college students; 20% international; 3% teachers. Nonsmokers only.

Employment Information Openings are from June 21 to August 23. Jobs available: ▶ *experienced general counselors* at $1100–$1500 per season; ▶ 3 *tennis instructors* with coaching experience at $1250–$1750 per season; ▶ 4 *experienced swimming instructors* with WSI certification at $1250–$2000 per season; ▶ 2 *arts and crafts instructors* with teaching experience in numerous areas at $1250–$2000 per season; ▶ 3 *experienced music, theater, and dance instructors* at $1500–$2000 per season; ▶ 1 *experienced photography instructor* at $1250–$1500 per season; ▶ 4 *experienced waterskiing/sailing instructors* at $1250–$1750 per season; ▶ 5 *tripping/ropes/outdoor pursuits instructors* with certification and/or experience at $1500–$2000 per season; ▶ 2 *registered nurses* with certification at $2000–$3000 per season; ▶ *experienced athletics instructors* at $1250–$1750 per season. International students encouraged to apply; must obtain own visa and working papers prior to employment; must apply through recognized agency.

Benefits On-the-job training, formal ongoing training, on-site room and board at no charge, laundry facilities, travel reimbursement. Preemployment training of 7 days is required and includes safety and accident prevention, group interaction, leadership, camper-counselor relations. Orientation is unpaid.

Contact Howard Salzberg, Director, Camp Modin, Department SJ, 401 East 80th Street, Suite 31B, New York, New York 10021; 212-570-1600, Fax 212-570-1677, E-mail staffsearch@modin.com, URL http://www.modin.com.

CAMP NASHOBA NORTH
RAYMOND HILL ROAD
RAYMOND, MAINE 04071

General Information International camp community of 180 boys and girls offering high-quality instruction in horsemanship, arts, sports, aquatics, theater, hiking, and dance. Established in 1933. Owned by Janet Seaward and Sarah Seaward. Affiliated with American Camping Association, Maine Youth Camping Association, American Horse Show Association, National Archery Association, New England Horse Show Association, Maine Audubon Society, National Audubon Society. 70-acre facility located 30 miles northwest of Portland. Features: location on beautiful Crescent Lake in the Sebago Lakes and Mountain area of southern Maine; large modern cabins with running water; 20-stall riding stable; numerous craft centers; spacious dining hall; wide variety of boats.

Profile of Summer Employees Total number: 40; average age: 21; 40% male, 60% female; 10% minorities; 90% college students; 30% international; 10% teachers. Nonsmokers only.

Employment Information Openings are from June 15 to August 16. Jobs available: ▶ 3 *swimming instructors* with LGT and WSI certifications at $1000–$1700 per season; ▶ 2 *sailing instructors* with LGT certification at $1000–$1700 per season; ▶ 2 *windsurfing instructors* with LGT certification at $1000–$1700 per season; ▶ 1 *boat driver/waterskiing instructor* with LGT certification at $1000–$1700 per season; ▶ 1 *canoeing instructor* with LGT certification at $1000–$1700 per season; ▶ 4 *riding instructors* with Pony Club, eventing, or showing experience at $1000–$1700 per season; ▶ 2 *experienced tennis instructors* at $1000–$1700 per season; ▶ 1 *ceramics/pottery instructor* at $1000–$1700 per season; ▶ 1 *photography instructor* at $1000–$1700 per season; ▶ 2 *dance instructors* at $1000–$1700 per season; ▶ 2 *theater instructors* at $1000–$1700 per season; ▶ 1 *certified archery instructor* at $1000–$1700 per season; ▶ 1 *music instructor* with ability to play guitar and piano at $1000–$1700 per season; ▶ 2 *trip instructors* at $1000–$1700 per season; ▶ 4 *kitchen helpers* at $1000–$1700 per season; ▶ 1 *chef* at $3000–$4000 per season; ▶ 2 *nurses* with RN license at $2600 per season. International students encouraged to apply; must apply through recognized agency.

Benefits College credit, on-the-job training, formal ongoing training, on-site room and board at no charge, laundry facilities, travel reimbursement, health insurance, one day off each week, healthful cuisine, precamp training and certification opportunities. Preemployment training of 8 days is required and includes safety and accident prevention, group interaction, first-aid, CPR, leadership. Orientation is unpaid.

Contact Sarah Seaward, Director, Camp Nashoba North, 140 Nashoba Road, Littleton, Massachusetts 01460; 508-486-8236, Fax 508-952-2442, E-mail seaward@ma.ultranet.com, URL http://www.campnashoba.com. Application deadline: June 1.

CAMP PINECLIFFE
HARRISON, MAINE 04040

General Information Traditional residential camp offering high-quality instruction at all levels. Established in 1917. Owned by Susan Lifter. Affiliated with American Camping Association, Maine Youth Camping Association. 75-acre facility located 40 miles northwest of Portland. Features: access to the ocean (1 hour) and the White Mountains (under 1 hour); extensive freshwater lake with separate waterski area; wooded environment with shaded paths and riding trails; 6 clay tennis courts (2 lit for night play); large sports fields; recreation hall, theater, and dance studio.

Profile of Summer Employees Total number: 85; average age: 25; 25% male, 75% female; 10% minorities; 60% college students; 25% international; 15% local residents; 40% teachers. Nonsmokers only.

Employment Information Openings are from June 15 to August 20. Jobs available: ▶ *swimming instructors* with WSI certification; ▶ *highly skilled waterskiing instructors* with lifesaving certification; ▶ *boating/sailing instructors* with Red Cross lifesaving certification; ▶ 1 *experienced drama instructor;* ▶ 1 *dance instructor;* ▶ 1 *music instructor* with ability to play piano by ear;

▶ *highly skilled arts and crafts instructors;* ▶ 1 *silversmithing instructor;* ▶ 1 *ceramics instructor;* ▶ *tennis instructors* with high school or college team experience; ▶ *riding instructor* with Pony Club experience; ▶ *land sports instructors;* ▶ 1 *archery instructor;* ▶ 1 *highly skilled gymnastics instructor;* ▶ *trip leaders.* All positions offered at $1200–$2000 per season. International students encouraged to apply; must obtain own visa and working papers prior to employment; must apply through recognized agency.

Benefits Formal ongoing training, on-site room and board at no charge, laundry facilities, travel reimbursement, tuition reimbursement. Preemployment training of 7 days is required and includes safety and accident prevention, group interaction, first-aid, CPR, leadership, camper-counselor relations. Orientation is unpaid.

Contact Susan R. Lifter, Director, Camp Pinecliffe, Department SJ, 277 South Cassingham Road, Columbus, Ohio 43209; 614-236-5698, Fax 614-235-2267. Application deadline: May 1.

CAMP PONDICHERRY
RR 2, BOX 588
BRIDGTON, MAINE 04009

General Information Residential camp serving 155 girls ages 7–17 per session; season includes three 2-week sessions and one 1-week session plus a week of pre-camp. Established in 1970. Owned by Kennebec Girl Scout Council, Inc. Affiliated with Girl Scouts of the United States of America, American Camping Association, Maine Youth Camping Association. 700-acre facility located 40 miles northwest of Portland. Features: location in the foothills of the White Mountains; miles of hiking trails; lake for swimming and boating; modern dining hall; shaded camp sites and platform tents with wooden roofs; unsurpassed views of woods, lake, and mountains.

Profile of Summer Employees Total number: 45; average age: 22; 1% male, 99% female; 5% minorities; 1% high school students; 90% college students; 30% international; 50% local residents; 40% teachers. Nonsmokers preferred.

Employment Information Openings are from June 20 to August 16. Jobs available: ▶ 1 *health supervisor* with RN, LPN, or EMT license at $310 per week; ▶ 1 *waterfront director* with certification in first aid, CPR, and lifeguard training at $300 per week; ▶ 6 *waterfront assistants* with lifeguard, first aid, and CPR certification at $190 per week; ▶ 1 *small craft instructor* with lifeguard training and canoeing instructor certification or documented experience at $220 per week; ▶ 1 *assistant camp director* with degree and administrative experience at $320 per week; ▶ 1 *business manager* with skills in money management at $190 per week; ▶ 1 *program consultant* with experience in dance or arts and crafts at $230 per week; ▶ *kitchen supervisor* with ability to supervise kitchen helpers and packout at $210 per week; ▶ 1 *counselor-in-training director* with experience working with older girls at $210 per week; ▶ 6 *unit leaders* at $210 per week; ▶ 6 *assistant unit leaders* at $180 per week; ▶ 1 *junior Maine guide leader* with strong background in camping and campcraft skills at $210 per week; ▶ 3 *kitchen helpers* at $140 per week; ▶ 1 *handy person* with valid driver's license at $140 per week; ▶ 1 *pack-out person* at $150 per week. International students encouraged to apply; must apply through recognized agency.

Benefits College credit, on-the-job training, formal ongoing training, on-site room and board at no charge, laundry facilities, travel reimbursement, health insurance. Preemployment training of 7 to 8 days is required and includes safety and accident prevention, group interaction, first-aid, CPR, leadership, camper-counselor relations, behavior management, programming. Orientation is paid.

Contact Jean M. Schroeder, Program Manager Kennebec Girl Scout Council, Inc., Camp Pondicherry, Department SJ, PO Box 9421, South Portland, Maine 04116-9421; 207-772-1177, Fax 207-874-2646.

CAMP RUNOIA FOR GIRLS
PO BOX 450
BELGRADE LAKES, MAINE 04918

General Information Residential camp for girls ages 7–17. Traditional program offering waterfront, riding, outdoor living skills, and more. Established in 1907. Owned by Cobb Family. Affiliated with American Camping Association, Maine Youth Camping Association, International Paper- Tree Farm. 88-acre facility located 15 miles north of Augusta. Features: cabins with running water and electricity; nearly a mile of freshwater lake shoreline; protected cove with sand beach; riding stables, pasture, and ring on property; campground on property; forest with hemlock, pine, birch, oak, and spruce.

Profile of Summer Employees Total number: 30; average age: 24; 5% male, 95% female; 5% minorities; 65% college students; 5% retirees; 15% international; 25% local residents; 10% teachers. Nonsmokers only.

Employment Information Openings are from June 15 to August 15. Jobs available: ► 1 *director of waterfront* with WSI certification, lifeguard, first aid, and CPR training at $1200–$1500 per season; ► 2 *sailing instructors* with lifeguard (or equivalent), first aid, CPR, and/or small watercraft certification at $1000–$1400 per season; ► 1 *canoeing instructor* with lifeguard (or equivalent), first aid, CPR, and/or small watercraft certification at $1000–$1400 per season; ► 1 *arts and crafts teacher* with documented experience at $1000–$1400 per season; ► 2 *riding instructors* with documented experience at $1100–$1500 per season; ► 1 *tennis instructor* with documented experience at $1000–$1400 per season; ► 2 *target sports* (archery and riflery) *instructors* with American Archery Association and National Riflery Association certification (or equivalent) at $1000–$1400 per season. International students encouraged to apply; must obtain own visa and working papers prior to employment; must apply through recognized agency.

Benefits On-the-job training, formal ongoing training, on-site room and board at no charge, college internships available for college credit, laundry is sent out of camp free of charge, opportunity for first aid (American Red Cross) and CPR certification. Preemployment training of 7 days is required and includes safety and accident prevention, group interaction, first-aid, CPR, leadership, camper-counselor relations. Orientation is paid.

Contact Pamela N. Cobb, Camp Runoia for Girls, Department SJ, 56 Jackson Street, Cambridge, Massachusetts 02140; 617-547-4676, Fax 617-661-1964, E-mail runoia@citysource.com, URL http://www.runoia.com. Application deadline: April 15.

CAMP SKYLEMAR
ROUTE 114
NAPLES, MAINE 04055

General Information Sports-oriented seven-week program for boys ages 8–16. Established in 1949. Owned by Lee Horowitz and Herb Blumenfeld. Affiliated with American Camping Association, Maine Youth Camping Association, Private Independent Camps. 200-acre facility located 30 miles east of Portland. Features: spring-fed lake; lakeside setting near White Mountains in an area with many tourist attractions; golf course on premises; 3 basketball courts (indoor and outdoor); 8 tennis courts; numerous athletics fields.

Profile of Summer Employees Total number: 40; average age: 20; 90% college students; 5% international; 5% local residents. Nonsmokers preferred.

Employment Information Openings are from June 23 to August 16. Winter break positions also offered. Jobs available: ► 4 *swimming instructors* with WSI certification at $1200–$1500 per season; ► 15 *experienced general sports counselors* at $1100–$2000 per season; ► 2 *experienced arts and crafts instructors* at $1100–$2000 per season; ► 2 *boating and skiing instructors* with small craft certification at $1100–$2000 per season; ► 3 *certified lifeguards* at $1300–$2000 per season; ► 1 *riflery instructor* with NRA instructor certification at $1100–$1400 per season; ► 2 *experienced trip counselors* at $1100–$2000 per season.

Benefits College credit, on-the-job training, formal ongoing training, on-site room and board at no charge, laundry facilities, travel reimbursement, use of all facilities and transportation to town every night.

Contact Lee Horowitz, Director, Camp Skylemar, Department SJ, 7900 Stevenson Road, Baltimore, Maryland 21208; 410-653-2480, Fax 410-653-1271. Application deadline: April 20.

CAMP TAKAJO
NAPLES, MAINE 04055

General Information Residential boys camp offering an eight-week session to 395 campers ages 7–16. Established in 1947. Owned by Jeffrey A. Konigsberg. Affiliated with American Camping Association, Maine Youth Camping Association. 75-acre facility located 30 miles west of Portland. Features: picturesque lakefront location; one hour from both the ocean and the mountains; 17 tennis courts (6 with lights); indoor fieldhouse and weight-training gymnasium.

Profile of Summer Employees Total number: 150; average age: 24; 95% male, 5% female; 5% minorities; 1% high school students; 90% college students; 1% retirees; 25% international; 1% local residents. Nonsmokers only.

Employment Information Openings are from June 22 to August 23. Jobs available: ▶ 15 *swimming instructors* with WSI certification (training provided); ▶ 6 *baseball instructors* with playing experience in high school or college; ▶ 6 *basketball instructors* with playing experience in high school or college; ▶ 20 *tennis instructors* with playing experience in high school or college; ▶ 6 *soccer instructors* with playing experience in high school or college; ▶ 2 *archery instructors;* ▶ 2 *riflery instructors;* ▶ 1 *journalism instructor;* ▶ 1 *photography instructor;* ▶ 2 *nature study instructors;* ▶ 15 *pioneering/trip instructors* with Boy Scout, Eagle Scout, Outward Bound, or similar experience; ▶ 8 *sailing instructors* with Red Cross certification; ▶ 6 *arts and crafts instructors* with appropriate schooling; ▶ 4 *waterskiing instructors;* ▶ 6 *general counselors.* All positions offered at $800–$1500 per season.

Benefits College credit, on-the-job training, on-site room and board at no charge, laundry facilities, travel reimbursement, medical insurance.

Contact Michael Sherbun, Staffing Coordinator Camp Takajo, Camp Takajo, Bares Run Drive, Loveland, Ohio 45140; 800-250-8252, Fax 513-697-0221. Application deadline: June 1.

CAMP TAPAWINGO
ROUTE 93
SWEDEN, MAINE 04040

General Information Residential private girls camp offering an eight-week program to 160 campers with a focus on developing self-confidence and independence in a caring environment. Established in 1919. Owned by Jane Lichtman. Affiliated with American Camping Association, Appalachian Mountain Club, Maine Youth Camping Association, United States Lawn Tennis Association. 200-acre facility located 50 miles northwest of Portland. Features: 22 cabins with electricity and running water; 8 tennis courts (6 Har-Tru, 2 all-weather); crystal-clear lake close to the mountains with swim lanes and boating areas; soccer/field hockey and softball fields; 2 basketball courts; high and low ropes course; 2 riding rings, extensive trails, and stables.

Profile of Summer Employees Total number: 60; average age: 24; 10% male, 90% female; 1% minorities; 80% college students; 8% international; 1% local residents; 20% teachers. Nonsmokers only.

Employment Information Openings are from June 21 to August 21. Jobs available: ▶ 2 *art instructors* at $900–$1100 per season; ▶ 1 *stained glass instructor* at $900–$1100 per season; ▶ *ceramics instructor* at $900–$1100 per season; ▶ 2 *experienced gymnastics instructors* at $900–$1100 per season; ▶ 1 *piano accompanist* with sight-reading and transposing ability at $900–$1100 per season; ▶ 5 *tennis instructors* at $900–$1100 per season; ▶ 2 *sailboard/sailing instructors* with lifeguard certification and instructor rating at $900–$1100 per season; ▶ 2 *canoeing instructors* with lifeguard certification and instructor rating at $900–$1100 per season; ▶ 4 *waterskiing instructors* with lifeguard certification and instructor rating at $900–$1100 per season; ▶ 8 *swimming instructors* with WSI and lifeguard certification at $900–$1100 per season; ▶ 2 *nurses* with RN license at $2000 per season; ▶ 1 *photography instructor* with knowledge of black-and-white photography and developing at $900–$1100 per season; ▶ 6 *trip leaders* (minimum age 21) with lifeguard, first aid, and CPR certification at $900–$1100 per season; ▶ 2 *dramatics instructors* at $900–$1100 per season; ▶ 2 *ropes instructors* with first aid, CPR, and instructor certification at $900–$1100 per season. International students encouraged to apply; must apply through recognized agency.

Benefits College credit, on-the-job training, on-site room and board at no charge, laundry facilities, travel reimbursement, use of facilities during free time. Preemployment training of 7 days is required and includes safety and accident prevention, group interaction, leadership, camper-counselor relations, child development. Orientation is unpaid.

Contact Becky Schumacher, Assistant Director, Camp Tapawingo, Department SJ, PO Box 1353, Scarborough, Maine 04070-1353; 207-885-0799.

CAMP WAWENOCK
33 CAMP WAWENOCK ROAD
RAYMOND, MAINE 04071-6824

General Information Residential camp serving 110 campers ages 8–16, all of whom attend for the full 7-week season. Features traditional camp experience with emphasis on human relationships and personal development. Leadership Training Program offered for 10th and 11th graders; counselor-in-training programs offered to 12th graders. Established in 1910. Owned by June W. Gray, Lillian K. Ussher. Affiliated with Maine Youth Camp Directors, New England Section of American Camping Association, American Camping Association. 80-acre facility located 26 miles north of Portland. Features: stables, riding ring, and paddock; Lake Sebago frontage, sandy beach; 4 all-weather tennis courts; craft shop; theater; lodge for younger campers; cabins that are shuttered and screened.

Profile of Summer Employees Total number: 50; average age: 20; 5% male, 95% female; 3% minorities; 5% high school students; 95% college students; 1% retirees; 10% international; 3% local residents; 5% teachers. Nonsmokers only.

Employment Information Openings are from June 22 to August 15. Jobs available: ▶ 2 *swimming instructors* with WSI certification at $900–$1300 per season; ▶ 1 *riding instructor* with certification or documented experience at $1000–$1400 per season; ▶ 1 *riflery instructor* with instructor certification at $1000–$1400 per season. International students encouraged to apply; must apply through recognized agency.

Benefits On-the-job training, on-site room and board at no charge, laundry facilities, travel reimbursement. Preemployment training of 6 days is required and includes safety and accident prevention, group interaction, first-aid, CPR, leadership, camper-counselor relations. Orientation is paid.

Contact June W. Gray, Director, Camp Wawenock, 33 Camp Wawenock Road, Raymond, Maine 04071-6824; 207-655-4657. Application deadline: March 15.

CAMP WAZIYATAH
RR 2, BOX 465
WATERFORD, MAINE 04088

General Information Traditional residential camp serving 220 campers in two-, three-, four-, and eight-week sessions featuring junior and teen programs. Established in 1922. Owned by Penny and Peter Kerns. Affiliated with American Camping Association, Maine Youth Camping Association, Association of Independent Camps. 150-acre facility located 40 miles northwest of Portland. Features: 3½-mile lake; old farm house with arts media theater, dance room, studio, photo lab, and video facilities; 10 tennis courts, 3 basketball courts, 2 volleyball courts, 2 soccer fields, and baseball and softball fields; riding stables, ring, and trails; rifle range, archery range, fencing court, and indoor/outdoor theater; gymnasium.

Profile of Summer Employees Total number: 100; average age: 23; 55% male, 45% female; 2% minorities; 70% college students; 3% retirees; 45% international; 2% local residents; 15% teachers. Nonsmokers only.

Employment Information Openings are from June 13 to August 23. Jobs available: ▶ 6 *swimming instructors* with WSI certification at $800–$1500 per season; ▶ 1 *sailing instructor* with Red Cross sailing certification at $800–$1500 per season; ▶ 1 *windsurfing instructor* with Red Cross sailing certification at $800–$1500 per season; ▶ 4 *waterskiing instructors* with experience as a boat driver/ski instructor at $800–$1500 per season; ▶ 1 *certified canoe instructor* at $800–$1500 per season; ▶ 2 *rifle instructors* with certification at $800–$1500 per season; ▶ 1 *archery instructor* with certification at $800–$1500 per season; ▶ 2 *trip leaders* with CPR, first aid, lifeguard certification, and experience at $800–$1500 per season; ▶ 1 *experienced baseball/ softball instructor* at $800–$1400 per season; ▶ 3 *experienced arts and crafts instructors* at $800–$1400 per season; ▶ 2 *experienced theater personnel* at $800–$1400 per season; ▶ *experienced song leader;* ▶ 6 *tennis instructors* at $800–$1400 per season; ▶ 3 *English riding instructors* with certification at $800–$1400 per season; ▶ 1 *video instructor* with professional training and experience at $800–$1500 per season; ▶ 1 *photo instructor* with professional training and experience at $800–$1500 per season. International students encouraged to apply; must apply through recognized agency.

Benefits On-the-job training, on-site room and board at no charge, laundry facilities, transportation on days off, staff lounge. Preemployment training of 5 to 6 days is required. Orientation is paid.

Contact Penny and Peter Kerns, Directors, Camp Waziyatah, Department SJ, 19 Rose Lane, East Walpole, Massachusetts 02032; 800-732-0223, Fax 813-391-7119, E-mail peterotter@aol. com. Application deadline: April 15.

CAMP WEKEELA
RFD 1, BOX 275, ROUTE 219
CANTON, MAINE 04221

General Information Residential traditional coeducational camp serving 270 campers with an emphasis on sports, water sports, and arts. Established in 1922. Owned by Eric and Lauren Scoblionko. Affiliated with American Camping Association, United States Tennis Association, Maine Youth Camping Association. 150-acre facility located 10 miles southeast of Lewiston. Features: lakeside setting at mountain base; proximity to Portland (1 hour) and Boston (3 hours); ocean and mountains nearby; 12 tennis courts (6 lit).

Profile of Summer Employees Total number: 110; average age: 21; 50% male, 50% female; 85% college students; 10% international; 5% local residents. Nonsmokers only.

Employment Information Openings are from June 15 to August 24. Jobs available: ▶ *ropes instructors* at $900–$1100 per season; ▶ *pioneering staff members* at $900–$1100 per season; ▶ *tennis staff members* at $900–$1500 per season; ▶ *gymnastics staff members* at $900–$1400 per season; ▶ *folksingers* at $900–$1300 per season; ▶ *piano/music staff members* at $900– $1300 per season; ▶ *land sports staff members* at $900–$2000 per season; ▶ *creative arts staff members* at $900–$1300 per season; ▶ *woodworking staff members* at $1100–$1500 per season; ▶ *ceramics staff members* at $900–$1100 per season; ▶ *theatrical arts staff members* at $900– $1500 per season; ▶ *radio staff members* at $900–$1200 per season; ▶ *video/photo staff members* at $900–$1200 per season; ▶ *waterfront staff members* at $900–$1600 per season; ▶ *waterskiing staff members* at $900–$1500 per season.

Benefits College credit, on-the-job training, formal ongoing training, on-site room and board at no charge, laundry facilities, travel reimbursement, use of all facilities in free time. Preemployment training of 7 days is required and includes safety and accident prevention, group interaction, first-aid, CPR, leadership, camper-counselor relations. Orientation is paid.

Contact Eric Scoblionko, Director, Camp Wekeela, Department SJ, 2807 C Delmar Drive, Columbus, Ohio 43209; 614-253-3177, Fax 614-253-3661, E-mail wekeela1@aol.com. Application deadline: May 1.

CAMP WINNEBAGO
ROUTE 17
KENTS HILL, MAINE 20190

General Information   Residential camp serving 140 boys for four- and eight-week sessions. Established in 1919. Owned by Philip Lilienthal. Affiliated with American Camping Association, Maine Youth Camping Association, American Independent Camps. 350-acre facility located 17 miles west of Augusta. Features: 7 Har-Tru tennis courts; 2 miles of lake frontage on 1,100-acre Echo Lake; towering pines; cabins surrounded by trees and streams; baseball and soccer fields; hockey rink; beach and regular volleyball; 6 basketball courts.

Profile of Summer Employees   Total number: 65; average age: 25; 90% male, 10% female; 10% minorities; 60% college students; 13% international; 15% local residents. Nonsmokers only.

Employment Information   Openings are from June 21 to August 20. Jobs available: ▶ 4 *swimming instructors* with WSI or lifeguard certification at $1100–$2000 per season; ▶ 4 *athletics instructors;* ▶ 4 *tennis instructors;* ▶ 2 *arts and crafts instructors;* ▶ 2 *theater instructors;* ▶ 2 *experienced photography instructors;* ▶ 2 *certified riflery instructors;* ▶ 2 *certified archery instructors;* ▶ 1 *piano accompanist* with knowledge of show music; ▶ 1 *newspaper instructor;* ▶ 1 *radio instructor;* ▶ 1 *videography instructor;* ▶ 3 *camping skills instructors.*

Benefits   On-site room and board at no charge, laundry facilities, travel reimbursement. Preemployment training of 6 days is required and includes safety and accident prevention, group interaction, first-aid, leadership, camper-counselor relations. Orientation is unpaid.

Contact   Philip Lilienthal, Director, Camp Winnebago, Department SJ, 1606 Washington Plaza, Reston, Virginia 20190; 703-437-0808, Fax 703-437-8620, E-mail philcwhv@aol.com.

FOREST ACRES CAMP FOR GIRLS
RURAL ROUTE 1, BOX 48
FRYEBURG, MAINE 04037

General Information   Residential camp for 125 girls ages 6 to 16 for seven weeks. Established in 1924. Owned by Sandra and Richard Krasker. Affiliated with Maine Youth Camping Association, American Camping Association, New England Camping Association. 100-acre facility located 150 miles north of Boston, Massachusetts. Features: 6 tennis courts; indoor gym for basketball and gymnastics; heated Olympic-size swimming pool; 10 acres on lake for skiing and sailing; softball and soccer fields; indoor theater.

Profile of Summer Employees   Total number: 60; average age: 24; 2% male, 98% female; 50% college students; 2% retirees; 10% international; 10% local residents; 50% teachers. Nonsmokers preferred.

Employment Information   Openings are from June 17 to August 17. Jobs available: ▶ *WSI-certified swimming instructors* at $800–$1200 per season; ▶ *sailing and waterskiing instructors* at $800–$1200 per season; ▶ *tennis instructors* at $800–$1200 per season; ▶ *arts and crafts instructors* at $800–$1200 per season; ▶ *gymnastics instructors* at $800–$1200 per season; ▶ *unit leaders/administrators* at $1200–$1500 per season. International students encouraged to apply; must obtain own visa and working papers prior to employment; must apply through recognized agency.

Benefits   On-the-job training, formal ongoing training, on-site room and board at no charge, laundry facilities. Preemployment training of 5 to 7 days is required and includes safety and accident prevention, group interaction, leadership, camper-counselor relations. Orientation is paid.

Contact   Sandra and Richard Krasker, Directors, Forest Acres Camp for Girls, Department SJ, 95 Woodchester Drive, Chestnut Hill, Massachusetts 02167; 617-969-5242.

HIDDEN VALLEY CAMP
HIDDEN VALLEY CAMP ROAD
FREEDOM, MAINE 04941

General Information Residential, international, noncompetitive camp offering two 4-week sessions to 230 campers. Established in 1947. Owned by Peter and Meg Kassen. Affiliated with American Camping Association, Maine Youth Camping Association. 300-acre facility located 85 miles east of Portland. Features: farm-like environment; fields and forest; location near Atlantic Ocean; llama herd; lake and pool.

Profile of Summer Employees Total number: 90; average age: 24; 40% male, 60% female; 10% minorities; 5% high school students; 40% college students; 3% retirees; 20% international; 10% local residents. Nonsmokers only.

Employment Information Openings are from June 15 to August 20. Jobs available: ▶ 3 *swimming instructors* with WSI/lifeguard certification; ▶ 3 *experienced ropes instructors;* ▶ 3 *experienced dance instructors;* ▶ 5 *experienced English riding instructors;* ▶ 2 *soccer instructors;* ▶ 3 *stained glass instructors;* ▶ 2 *pottery instructors;* ▶ *experienced animal care person;* ▶ *gymnastics instructor.* All positions offered at $1000–$1400 per season.

Benefits College credit, on-the-job training, formal ongoing training, on-site room and board at no charge, laundry facilities, internships, vegetarian diet.

Contact Peter and Meg Kassen, Directors/Owners, Hidden Valley Camp, Department SJ, RR 1, Box 2360, Freedom, Maine 04941; 207-342-5177, Fax 207-342-5685, E-mail hvc@hiddenvalleycamp.com, URL http://www.hiddenvalleycamp.com. Application deadline: March 31.

IDLEASE AND SHORELANDS GUEST RESORT
ROUTE 9, PO BOX 3035
KENNEBUNK, MAINE 04043

General Information Resort serving visitors to scenic Kennebunkport. Established in 1950. Owned by Sonja Haag-Ducharme. Affiliated with Kennebunk Chamber of Commerce, Maine Innkeepers' Association. 4-acre facility located 2 miles west of Kennebunkport. Features: proximity to the seacoast village of Kennebunkport; restaurants, art galleries, antique shops, marinas, craft stores, and deep-sea fishing/whale-watching boat trips; proximity to beaches; country atmosphere, swimming pool, and outdoor barbecues; bicycle trails; nature preserves; historic homes, including the home of former President George Bush; boat dock and playground.

Profile of Summer Employees Total number: 4; average age: 22; 20% male, 80% female; 30% high school students; 60% college students; 50% international; 50% local residents. Nonsmokers preferred.

Employment Information Openings are from June 1 to October 1. Jobs available: ▶ 1 *assistant manager/housekeeper* with ability to perform general duties, desk work, scheduling, and supervise hourly help (must be a French-speaking college student or college teacher and be able to work from May to September) at $175–$200 per week; ▶ 4 *housekeeping associates* with ability to stay from June to October (should be college or high school student or teacher) at $150–$200 per week. International students encouraged to apply; must obtain own visa and working papers prior to employment.

Benefits On-site room and board, laundry facilities, free shared room and kitchen privileges.

Contact Sonja Haag-Ducharme, Owner, Idlease and Shorelands Guest Resort, Department SJ, PO Box 3035, Kennebunk, Maine 04043; 207-985-4460, E-mail idlease@mail.vrmedia.com, URL http://www.vrmedia.com/idlease/. Application deadline: March 1.

INDIAN ACRES CAMP FOR BOYS
RURAL ROUTE 1, BOX 48
FRYEBURG, MAINE 04037

General Information Residential camp for 125 boys ages 6–16. Established in 1924. Owned by Sandra and Richard Krasker. Affiliated with Maine Youth Camping Association, American

Camping Association, New England Camping Association. 100-acre facility located 50 miles northwest of Boston, Massachusetts. Features: baseball and soccer fields; heated Olympic-size swimming pool; indoor basketball gym, weight training rooms, and Nautilus equipment; six all-weather tennis courts; street hockey court; rifle and archery ranges.

Profile of Summer Employees Total number: 60; average age: 24; 98% male, 2% female; 50% college students; 2% retirees; 10% international; 10% local residents; 50% teachers. Nonsmokers preferred.

Employment Information Openings are from June 17 to August 17. Jobs available: ▶ *WSI-certified swimming instructors* at $800–$1200 per season; ▶ *sailing and skiing instructors and lifeguards* at $800–$1200 per season; ▶ *tennis instructors* at $800–$1200 per season; ▶ *basketball, baseball, hockey, and soccer instructors* at $800–$1200 per season; ▶ *archery and riflery instructors* at $800–$1200 per season; ▶ *unit leaders, administrators, and teachers* at $1200–$1500 per season. International students encouraged to apply; must obtain own visa and working papers prior to employment; must apply through recognized agency.

Benefits On-the-job training, formal ongoing training, on-site room and board at no charge, laundry facilities. Preemployment training of 5 to 7 days is required and includes safety and accident prevention, group interaction, leadership, camper-counselor relations. Orientation is paid.

Contact Sandra and Richard Krasker, Directors, Indian Acres Camp for Boys, Department SJ, 95 Woodchester Drive, Chestnut Hill, Massachusetts 02167; 617-969-5242.

KIPPEWA FOR GIRLS
1 KIPPEWA DRIVE
MONMOUTH, MAINE 04259-6700

General Information Residential camp serving 140 girls for one- and two-month enrollments. Established in 1957. Affiliated with American Camping Association, Maine Youth Camping Association. 100-acre facility located 12 miles west of Augusta. Features: lakeside cabins; 10-mile lake; 75 boats; 56 buildings; 20-acre on-site horse farm; location near coast, mountains, and rivers.

Profile of Summer Employees Total number: 85; 5% male, 95% female; 10% minorities; 65% college students; 1% retirees; 40% international; 5% local residents; 15% teachers. Nonsmokers only.

Employment Information Openings are from June 20 to August 30. Jobs available: ▶ *instructors for horseback riding (English), gymnasium, field, team sports, martial arts, and tennis* with certification (preferred) where relevant; ▶ *arts and crafts, dance, and theater staff members;* ▶ *kitchen staff members;* ▶ *laundry staff members;* ▶ *office staff members;* ▶ *drivers* with valid driver's license; ▶ *instructors for swimming, sailing, canoeing, kayaking, and water skiing;* ▶ *wilderness trip leaders.* International students encouraged to apply.

Benefits College credit, formal ongoing training, on-site room and board at no charge, laundry facilities, travel reimbursement, individualized guidance, small, manageable cabins and classes help employees succeed, teach your specialties and be trained in new skills.

Contact Martin Silverman or Jon Silverman, Directors, Kippewa For Girls, PO Box 307, Westwood, Massachusetts 02090-0307; 617-762-8291, Fax 617-255-7167, E-mail kippewa@tiac. net, URL http://www.kippewa.com/fun.

LONGACRE EXPEDITIONS
WASHINGTON, MAINE 04574

General Information Adventure travel program emphasizing group living skills and physical challenges. Using base camp as a staging area 2–3 staffers and 10–16 campers participate in intermediate-level expeditions on which they engage in human-powered sports. Established in 1981. Owned by Longacre Expeditions. Affiliated with American Camping Association. 240-acre facility located 20 miles north of Camden. Features: extensive freshwater lake frontage.

Profile of Summer Employees Total number: 30; average age: 25; 50% male, 50% female;

10% minorities; 40% college students; 10% local residents. Nonsmokers only.

Employment Information Openings are from June 1 to August 15. Jobs available: ▶ 16 *assistant trip leaders* (minimum age 21) with first aid, CPR, and completion of water safety course at $150–$175 per week; ▶ 1 *rock climbing instructor* (minimum age 21) at $360–$450 per week; ▶ 4 *support and logistics staff members* (minimum age 21) at $150–$175 per week.

Benefits On-the-job training, on-site room and board at no charge, Pro-Deal package. Preemployment training of 9 days is required and includes safety and accident prevention, group interaction, first-aid, CPR, leadership, camper-counselor relations. Orientation is unpaid.

Contact Roger Smith, Longacre Expeditions, RD 3, Box 106, Newport, Pennsylvania 17074; 717-567-6790, Fax 717-567-3955, E-mail longacre@pa.net, URL http://www/longex.com.

MAINE TEEN CAMP
RR 1, BOX 39
KEZAR FALLS, MAINE 04047

General Information Residential coed camp for teenagers offering two sessions with 230 campers participating in each session. Established in 1984. Owned by Bob Briskin. Affiliated with American Camping Association, Maine Youth Camping Association. 50-acre facility located 35 miles west of Portland. Features: 2 lakes; 5 tennis courts, ropes course, basketball courts, and volleyball court; learning center, theater, and music recording studio; modern lodge in a secluded setting; 2 large athletic fields.

Profile of Summer Employees Total number: 70; average age: 25; 47% male, 53% female; 10% minorities; 50% college students; 2% retirees; 30% international; 2% local residents; 40% teachers. Nonsmokers preferred.

Employment Information Openings are from June 19 to August 22. Year-round positions also offered. Jobs available: ▶ *drum instructor* at $1000–$3000 per season; ▶ *keyboard instructor* at $1000–$3000 per season; ▶ *guitar instructor* at $1000–$3000 per season; ▶ *MIDI instructor* at $1000–$3000 per season; ▶ *tennis instructor* at $1000–$3000 per season; ▶ *swimming instructor* at $1000–$3000 per season; ▶ *jewelry-crafting instructor* at $1000–$3000 per season; ▶ *dance instructor* at $1000–$3000 per season; ▶ *theater instructor* at $1000–$3000 per season; ▶ *sailing/windsurfing instructor* at $1000–$3000 per season; ▶ *waterskiing instructor* at $1000–$3000 per season; ▶ *arts instructor* at $1000–$3000 per season; ▶ *land sports instructor* at $1000–$3000 per season; ▶ *ropes instructor* at $1000–$3000 per season; ▶ *waterfront director* at $2500–$3000 per season; ▶ *trip leaders* at $1000–$3000 per season. All applicants must have experience and/or certification. International students encouraged to apply; must obtain own visa and working papers prior to employment; must apply through recognized agency.

Benefits On-the-job training, formal ongoing training, on-site room and board at no charge. Preemployment training of 10 days is required and includes safety and accident prevention, group interaction, first-aid, CPR, leadership, camper-counselor relations. Orientation is paid.

Contact Bob Briskin and Rich Jenkins, Director/Assistant Director, Maine Teen Camp, Department SJ, 180 Upper Gulph Road, Radnor, Pennsylvania 19087; 610-527-6759, Fax 610-520-0182, E-mail teencamp@ix.netcom.com.

NEW ENGLAND CAMPING ADVENTURES
PANTHER POND, PO BOX 160
RAYMOND, MAINE 04071

General Information Coed wilderness rafting and sailing programs that include backpacking, white-water canoe trips, rock climbing, ocean kayaking, mountain biking, and ocean sailing. Established in 1919. Owned by Ronald Furst. Affiliated with Maine Camping Association, National Camp Association. 140-acre facility located 30 miles west of Portland. Features: 2 miles of shorefront on lake; white-water canoe trips on Allagash waterway; backpacking trips in White Mountains of New Hampshire; rock climbing in North Conway, New Hampshire; lake and ocean sailing and racing program; ocean kayaking trips.

Profile of Summer Employees 50% male, 50% female; 15% minorities; 5% high school students; 80% college students; 5% international; 20% local residents; 20% teachers. Nonsmokers preferred.

Employment Information Openings are from June 25 to August 18. Jobs available: ▶ 5 *canoe trip leaders;* ▶ 4 *backpacking leaders;* ▶ 2 *rock climbing leaders;* ▶ 6 *sailing instructors.* All positions offered at $1100–$1400 per season. International students encouraged to apply.

Benefits On-the-job training, formal ongoing training, on-site room and board at no charge, laundry facilities, travel reimbursement, professional references upon job completion.

Contact Ronald Furst, Owner, New England Camping Adventures, 10 Scotland Bridge Road, York, Maine 03909; 207-363-1773, Fax 207-363-1773. Application deadline: May 1.

OAKLAND HOUSE
HERRICK ROAD
BROOKSVILLE, MAINE 04617

General Information Rural low-key family vacation resort and adults-only inn accommodating a combined total of approximately 75 guests. Established in 1889. Owned by Sally and Jim Littlefield. Affiliated with Maine Innkeepers Association, New England Business Association, State of Maine Publicity Bureau, Maine Restaurant Association, East Penobscot Bay Resort Association. 50-acre facility located 50 miles south of Bangor. Features: lake with beach and rowboats; hiking trails to high lookouts and views of the bay and distant islands and hills; lawn games; recreation hall with piano, fireplace, and video screen; 1½ mile of ocean frontage with dock, rowboats, and beach; proximity to Acadia National Park (1 hour).

Profile of Summer Employees Total number: 22; average age: 24; 46% male, 54% female; 5% minorities; 8% high school students; 45% college students; 8% international; 36% local residents. Nonsmokers preferred.

Employment Information Openings are from June 15 to September 7. Jobs available: ▶ 1 *office receptionist* at $209–$249 per week; ▶ 3 *housekeepers* at $170–$400 per week; ▶ 4 *kitchen staff members* at $209–$249 per week; ▶ 2 *maintenance and grounds staff members* at $209–$264 per week; ▶ 1 *cabin service staff member* at $170–$300 per week; ▶ 5 *waiters/ waitresses* at $170–$400 per week; ▶ *host/hostess.* International students encouraged to apply; must apply through recognized agency.

Benefits On-the-job training, on-site room and board at $50 per week, laundry facilities, use of recreational facilities in rural setting, additional merit bonus when employees finish season, friendly, high-grade clientele. Preemployment training of 2 days is required and includes first-aid. Orientation is paid.

Contact Mr. James Littlefield, Owner, Oakland House, Department SJ, RR 1, Box 400, Brooksville, Maine 04617; 207-359-8521. Application deadline: June 1.

QUISISANA RESORT
CENTER LOVELL, MAINE 04016

General Information Summer resort for families, couples, and individuals. Established in 1947. Owned by Jane Orans. 55-acre facility located 75 miles west of Portland. Features: 2 sandy beaches on lake; 3 tennis courts; hiking trails.

Profile of Summer Employees Total number: 75; average age: 21; 50% male, 50% female; 90% college students. Nonsmokers preferred.

Employment Information Openings are from June 1 to September 1. Jobs available: ▶ *waitstaff members;* ▶ *beach staff members;* ▶ *office staff members;* ▶ *kitchen staff members;* ▶ *maintenance persons;* ▶ *chamber staff members.*

Benefits On-the-job training, on-site room and board at no charge.

Contact Jane Orans, Owner, Quisisana Resort, PO Box 142, Larchmont, New York 10538; 914-833-0293. Application deadline: May 15.

WOHELO-LUTHER GULICK CAMPS
PO BOX 39
SOUTH CASCO, MAINE 04077

General Information Residential camp for girls on Sebago Lake emphasizing lifelong activities and personal growth. Established in 1907. Affiliated with American Camping Association, Maine Youth Camping Association. 250-acre facility located 25 miles west of Portland. Features: 1-mile of shorefront on Sebago Lake; 25 sailboats; 6 outdoor tennis courts.

Profile of Summer Employees 5% male, 95% female. Nonsmokers preferred.

Employment Information Openings are from June 20 to August 14. Jobs available: ▶ 2 *dramatics instructors;* ▶ 1 *pottery instructor;* ▶ *sailing instructor;* ▶ *canoeing instructor;* ▶ *tennis instructor;* ▶ 2 *nature/ecology instructors;* ▶ 2 *swimming instructors* with WSI or LG certification. All positions offered at $950–$1350 per season. International students encouraged to apply; must obtain own visa and working papers prior to employment; must apply through recognized agency.

Benefits On-the-job training, on-site room and board at no charge, laundry facilities. Preemployment training of 4 days is required and includes safety and accident prevention, group interaction, leadership, camper-counselor relations. Orientation is paid.

Contact W. Davis Van Winkle, Director, Wohelo-Luther Gulick Camps, PO Box 39, South Casco, Maine 04077; 207-655-4739, Fax 207-655-2292, E-mail wohelo@compuserve.com.

WYONEGONIC CAMPS
RR 1, BOX 186
DENMARK, MAINE 04022

General Information Residential girls camp for 181 girls for 3½ or 7 weeks. Established in 1902. Owned by Carol Sudduth. Affiliated with American Camping Association, Maine Youth Camping Association, Association of Independent Camps. 300-acre facility located 40 miles west of Portland. Features: freshwater lake; access to mountains and hiking; rustic setting in pine forest; canoe trips on river and lakes; 6 clay tennis courts; horses, barn, and trails on property.

Profile of Summer Employees Total number: 70; average age: 21; 12% male, 88% female; 1% minorities; 75% college students; 15% international; 5% local residents; 5% teachers. Nonsmokers only.

Employment Information Openings are from June 8 to August 28. Jobs available: ▶ *swimming instructor* with WSI and LGT certification at $1000–$1800 per season; ▶ *sailing instructor* with LGT certification at $1000–$1800 per season; ▶ *sailboarding instructor* with LGT certification at $1000–$1800 per season; ▶ *waterskiing instructor* with LGT certification and boat driving experience at $1000–$1800 per season; ▶ *tennis instructor* at $1000–$1800 per season; ▶ *riding instructor* at $1000–$1800 per season; ▶ *pottery instructor* at $1000–$1800 per season; ▶ *arts and crafts instructor* at $1000–$1800 per season; ▶ *canoe trips instructor/ trip leader* (minimum age 21) with SFA/LGT certification at $1000–$1800 per season; ▶ *hiking instructor/trip leader* (minimum age 21) with SFA/LGT certification/Maine trip leader experience at $1000–$1800 per season; ▶ *archery instructor* with Maine State certification at $1000–$1800 per season; ▶ *riflery instructor* with NRA certification at $1000–$1800 per season; ▶ *dramatics instructor* at $1000–$1800 per season; ▶ *nurses* with RN license at $2000 per season; ▶ *kitchen workers* at $1200–$1800 per season; ▶ *maintenance staff members* at $250 per week. International students encouraged to apply; must apply through recognized agency.

Benefits College credit, on-the-job training, formal ongoing training, on-site room and board at no charge, laundry facilities, travel reimbursement, certification training. Preemployment training of 6 days is required and includes safety and accident prevention, group interaction, first-aid, CPR, leadership, camper-counselor relations, certification in WSI, LGT, CPR, tennis, archery, canoe. Orientation is paid.

Contact Carol S. Sudduth, Director, Wyonegonic Camps, RR 1, Box 186, Denmark, Maine 04022; 207-452-2051, Fax 207-452-2611. Application deadline: April 1.

MARYLAND

CAMPS AIRY AND LOUISE
MARYLAND

General Information Residential camps serving boys and girls. Established in 1922. Owned by Aaron and Lilie Straus Foundation. Affiliated with American Camping Association, Maryland Youth Camps. Located 60 miles north of Washington, DC. Features: open-air theaters; proximity to the Appalachian Trail and the Blue Ridge Summit; numerous athletics fields; large swimming pools; state-of-the-art health centers.

Profile of Summer Employees Total number: 285; average age: 25; 2% minorities; 95% college students; 3% retirees; 3% international; 10% local residents.

Employment Information Openings are from June 18 to August 18. Jobs available: ▶ 30 *general counselors* at $850–$1300 per season; ▶ 15 *swimming instructors* with WSI or lifeguard certification; ▶ 10 *outdoor living instructors* at $1000–$1600 per season; ▶ 10 *music instructors;* ▶ 8 *drama instructors;* ▶ 30 *athletics instructors;* ▶ 4 *karate instructors;* ▶ 2 *riflery instructors* with NRA instructor certification (preferred); ▶ 2 *nature instructors;* ▶ 6 *arts and crafts instructors;* ▶ 3 *ceramics instructors;* ▶ 6 *dance instructors;* ▶ 4 *archery instructors* with NAA instructor certification (preferred); ▶ *photography instructors;* ▶ *fencing instructors.* International students encouraged to apply; must apply through recognized agency.

Benefits On-the-job training, on-site room and board at no charge, laundry facilities, travel reimbursement, catered food service and medical staff available at each facility, one 24-hour day off and one night off from 5 p.m. to 7 a.m. per week, 2 staff members per cabin with private counselor rooms.

Contact Ed Cohen, Executive Director, Camps Airy and Louise, Department SJ, 5750 Park Heights Avenue, Baltimore, Maryland 21215; 410-466-9010, Fax 410-466-0560, E-mail airlou@ airylouise.org, URL http://www.airylouise.org.

ECHO HILL CAMP
13655 BLOOMINGNECK ROAD
WORTON, MARYLAND 21678

General Information Coeducational residential camp serving 140 campers per session in two-, four-, and eight-week sessions along with one-week postcamp sail and ski and fishing and crabbing camps; Labor Day weekend family camp. Established in 1944. Owned by Peter P. Rice, Jr. Affiliated with American Camping Association. 350-acre facility located 90 miles northeast of Washington, DC. Features: proximity to Chesapeake Bay; 1 mile of sandy beachfront; rustic environment; living quarters on platform tents; extensive waterfront activities.

Profile of Summer Employees Total number: 45; average age: 20; 55% male, 45% female; 2% minorities; 10% high school students; 70% college students; 10% international; 2% local residents.

Employment Information Openings are from June 15 to August 24. Jobs available: ▶ *counselors;* ▶ 2 *swimming instructors* with WSI and American Red Cross lifeguard certification at $600 per month. International students encouraged to apply; must apply through recognized agency.

Benefits On-the-job training, formal ongoing training, on-site room and board at no charge, laundry facilities.

Contact Peter Rice, Director, Echo Hill Camp, Department SJ, Echo Hill Camp, Worton, Maryland 21678; 410-348-5303, Fax 410-348-2010. Application deadline: May 31.

THE INSTITUTE FOR THE ACADEMIC ADVANCEMENT OF YOUTH/THE JOHNS HOPKINS UNIVERSITY
34TH AND CHARLES STREETS
BALTIMORE, MARYLAND 21218

General Information Residential and commuter camps for academically talented youth serving second through sixth graders and seventh graders through 16½-year-olds. Concentration on accelerated academic courses and recreational activities. Established in 1980. Owned by The Johns Hopkins University. Features: amenities of a modern university campus; large sports fields; swimming pools; excellent classroom space; computer labs.

Profile of Summer Employees Total number: 850; average age: 30; 50% male, 50% female; 10% minorities; 60% college students; 10% local residents; 20% teachers.

Employment Information Openings are from June 20 to August 7. Jobs available: ▶ 6 *site directors* with master's degree preferred, teaching and administrative background, and leadership in an educational environment at $6600 per season; ▶ *deans of residential life* with master's degree preferred, 2 years' residential administrative experience in a school or college, and counseling experience at $4600–$5000 per season; ▶ 130 *instructors* with BA or BS *(master's degree preferred)*, experience with students in this age group, and leadership skills at $1500–$2000 per season; ▶ 130 *teaching/laboratory assistants* with GPA of 3.2 or higher, strong interest in teaching, and experience with young people at $1600 per season; ▶ 150 *resident advisers* with experience as a college RA or as a camp counselor, GPA of 3.2 or higher, and experience in events planning at $1800 per season; ▶ 12 *office/general assistants* with office experience, at least one year of college, and 3.2 GPA at $1800 per season; ▶ 6 *academic counselors* with graduate training in counseling with 2 years counseling experience, familiarity with Attention Deficit Disorder, and experience in a boarding school or residential camp environment at $4000 per season; ▶ *academic deans* with graduate training in an academic discipline and teaching experience at $4600–$5000 per season. International students encouraged to apply; must obtain own visa and working papers prior to employment.

Benefits On-the-job training, on-site room and board at no charge, laundry facilities, opportunity to work with highly-motivated students, opportunity to meet dynamic colleagues from around the country. Preemployment training of 3 days is required and includes safety and accident prevention, group interaction, camper-counselor relations. Orientation is paid.

Contact Ms. Kimberly Theobald, Coordinator for Academic Programs, The Institute for the Academic Advancement of Youth/The Johns Hopkins University, Department SJ, 3400 North Charles Street The Johns Hopkins University/IAAY, Baltimore, Maryland 21218; 410-516-0053, Fax 410-516-0804, E-mail academic@jhunix.hcf.jhu.edu, URL http://www.jhu.edu/~gifted/cty. html. Application deadline: January 31.

MANIDOKAN OUTDOOR MINISTRY CENTER
1620 HARPERS FERRY ROAD
KNOXVILLE, MARYLAND 21758

General Information Residential camp with a variety of accommodations and programs for all ages. Established in 1949. Owned by Baltimore-Washington Conference of the United Methodist Church. 426-acre facility located 70 miles west of Washington, DC. Features: extensive ropes and initiatives course; canoe and raft programs; swimming pool; large athletics field; location near the Chesapeake and Ohio Canal, Harpers Ferry, and Antietam Battlefield.

Profile of Summer Employees Total number: 14; average age: 20; 50% male, 50% female; 7% minorities; 7% high school students; 73% college students; 20% retirees; 35% local residents. Nonsmokers preferred.

Employment Information Openings are from June 7 to August 22. Jobs available: ▶ 4 *program resource personnel* with lifeguard training (preferred) at $150–$200 per week; ▶ 1 *lifeguard* with WSI certification (preferred) at $150–$200 per week; ▶ 1 *canoe instructor* with Red Cross canoe instructor certification at $175–$225 per week; ▶ 2 *cooks* at $200–$300 per week; ▶ 3 *kitchen aides* at $130–$150 per week; ▶ 1 *maintenance person* at $130–$150 per week; ▶ 1 *nurse* at $250–$350 per week.

Benefits On-the-job training, on-site room and board at no charge, laundry facilities, health insurance.

Contact Carl Zenkert, Manager, Manidokan Outdoor Ministry Center, 1620 Harpers Ferry Road, Knoxville, Maryland 21758; 301-834-7244, Fax 301-834-7244. Application deadline: January 1.

WEST RIVER UNITED METHODIST CENTER
CHALK POINT ROAD, PO BOX 429
CHURCHTON, MARYLAND 20733

General Information Residential camp on a mile-long waterfront near the Chesapeake Bay. Established in 1951. Owned by Baltimore-Washington Conference of the United Methodist Church. Affiliated with National Camp Leaders of the United Methodist Church. 45-acre facility located 15 miles south of Annapolis. Features: wetlands and shoreline nature study areas; swimming pool and athletics fields; comfortable lodges and retreat center; waterfront activities, including canoeing, rowing, and sailing.

Profile of Summer Employees Total number: 16; average age: 20; 40% male, 60% female; 18% minorities; 12% high school students; 62% college students; 37% local residents. Nonsmokers preferred.

Employment Information Openings are from June 7 to August 22. Year-round positions also offered. Jobs available: ▶ 3 *lifeguards* with Red Cross lifeguard training at $175–$200 per week; ▶ 1 *head lifeguard* with WSI certification at $200–$250 per week; ▶ 1 *sailing instructor* with Red Cross sailing instructor certification at $175–$225 per week; ▶ 2 *cooks* at $300–$400 per week; ▶ 4 *kitchen aides* at $150–$200 per week; ▶ 2 *maintenance personnel* at $150–$200 per week; ▶ 2 *program resource persons* with lifesaving training (preferred) at $175–$225 per week; ▶ 1 *nurse* at $250–$350 per week. International students encouraged to apply; must obtain own visa and working papers prior to employment; must apply through recognized agency.

Benefits On-the-job training, on-site room and board at no charge, laundry facilities. Preemployment training of 5 to 10 days is required and includes safety and accident prevention, group interaction, leadership, camper-counselor relations. Orientation is paid.

Contact Andrew Thornton, West River United Methodist Center, PO Box 429, Churchton, Maryland 20733; 410-867-0991, Fax 410-867-3741. Application deadline: January 1.

YMCA CAMP LETTS
4003 CAMP LETTS ROAD, PO BOX 208
EDGEWATER, MARYLAND 21037

General Information Residential camp serving 300 campers during four 2-week sessions. Character development through sailing, horsemanship, low and high ropes programs, and fun. Established in 1906. Owned by YMCA of Metropolitan Washington. Affiliated with American Camping Association, Annapolis Chamber of Commerce, YMCA. 219-acre facility located 25 miles east of Washington, DC. Features: location on 219-acre peninsula on Rhode River off the Chesapeake Bay; 25-meter freshwater swimming pool; large stables with 28 horses, two riding rings, and miles of wooded trails; land activities area with tennis courts, basketball courts, and large playing fields; well-developed sailing and waterskiing center with Lasers, Optimist, and Flying Scotts; ropes initiative course with high-wire bridge, zip line, and 7 new high events.

Profile of Summer Employees Total number: 100; average age: 21; 50% male, 50% female; 20% minorities; 10% high school students; 80% college students; 10% international; 5% local residents. Nonsmokers only.

Employment Information Openings are from June 17 to August 17. Spring break positions also offered. Jobs available: ▶ 5 *crew skippers* (minimum age 21) at $1800–$2100 per season; ▶ 30 *counselors* (minimum age 19) with first year of college completed at $1400–$1800 per season; ▶ 30 *assistant counselors* (minimum age 18) with high school diploma at $100–$1400 per season; ▶ 1 *experienced photographer/editor* with resume at $1300–$1800 per season; ▶ 1 *program director* with college upperclassman or graduate status and managerial skills at $1800–$2300 per season; ▶ 1 *horsemanship director* with college upperclassman or graduate status and Pony Club background *(preferred)* at $1800–$2300 per season; ▶ 1 *land activities director* with college upperclassman or graduate status, background in physical fitness, and CPR and first aid training at $1800–$2300 per season; ▶ 1 *small craft director* with college upperclassman or graduate status, WSI and AWSA certification (preferred), and lifeguarding and CPR certification at $1800–$2300 per season; ▶ 1 *sailing director* with lifeguarding and CPR certification and USYRU certification or USCG captain's license (preferred) at $1800–$2300 per season. International students encouraged to apply; must apply through recognized agency.

Benefits College credit, on-the-job training, on-site room and board at no charge, laundry facilities. Preemployment training of 2 to 7 days is required and includes safety and accident prevention, group interaction, first-aid, CPR, leadership, camper-counselor relations, instructor level-certification in a variety of sports. Orientation is paid.

Contact Patrick Butcher, Executive Director, YMCA Camp Letts, Department SJ, PO Box 208, Edgewater, Maryland 21037; 301-261-4286, Fax 301-261-7336.

MASSACHUSETTS

BELVOIR TERRACE
LENOX, MASSACHUSETTS 01240

General Information Residential camp serving 180 girls with a focus on fine and performing arts. The program provides specific services for the academically talented and the gifted. Established in 1954. Owned by Nancy S. Goldberg. Affiliated with American Camping Association. Situated on 48 acres. Features: proximity to Tanglewood, Jacob's Pillow, and Williamstown Theater; 18 estate-quality buildings; Olympic gymnasium; 6 tennis courts; 3 theaters.

Profile of Summer Employees Total number: 80; average age: 28; 10% male, 90% female; 5% minorities; 10% college students; 5% international; 90% teachers. Nonsmokers only.

Employment Information Openings are from June 16 to August 20. Jobs available: ▶ 2 *swimming counselors* (graduate students only) with lifeguard training and WSI certification at $700 per month; ▶ 1 *tennis counselor* (graduate student only) with tennis team playing ability and teaching experience at $600–$1000 per month; ▶ *musicians* (graduate students only) with expertise in an instrument or in voice at $600–$800 per month.

Benefits College credit, on-the-job training, on-site room and board at no charge, laundry facilities, travel reimbursement. Preemployment training of 5 days is required and includes safety and accident prevention, group interaction, first-aid, CPR, leadership, camper-counselor relations. Orientation is paid.

Contact Nancy S. Goldberg, Director, Belvoir Terrace, Department SJ, 145 Central Park West, New York, New York 10023; 212-580-3398, Fax 212-579-7282, E-mail belvoirt@aol.com.

BONNIE CASTLE RIDING CAMP
STONELEIGH–BURNHAM SCHOOL
GREENFIELD, MASSACHUSETTS 01301

General Information Residential camp for girls ages 10–15½ with two 3-week sessions. Established in 1979. Owned by Stoneleigh-Burnham School. Affiliated with New England Association of Schools and Colleges, Independent Schools Association of Massachusetts, National

Association of Independent Schools. 100-acre facility located 60 miles north of Hartford, Connecticut. Features: 60 horse stables; 2 indoor riding rings; riding trails; event course; outdoor pool; arts programs, including dance, ceramics, and photography.

Profile of Summer Employees Total number: 12; average age: 22; 100% female; 10% minorities; 70% college students; 60% local residents; 30% teachers. Nonsmokers preferred.

Employment Information Openings are from July 1 to August 13. Jobs available: ▶ 6 *riding instructors* (minimum age 18) at $1100–$1800 per season; ▶ 2 *arts/photography instructors* (minimum age 18) at $1100–$1800 per season; ▶ 1 *drama instructor* (minimum age 18) at $1100–$1800 per season; ▶ 1 *swimming instructor* with WSI and CPR certification at $1100–$1800 per season; ▶ 1 *dance instructor* at $1100–$1800 per season; ▶ 1 *camp nurse* with RN license and current CPR certification at $2700 per season.

Benefits On-site room and board at no charge, laundry facilities.

Contact Bonnie Castle Riding Camp, Director, Bonnie Castle Riding Camp, Department SJ, Stoneleigh-Burnham School, Greenfield, Massachusetts 01301; 413-774-2711, Fax 413-772-2602. Application deadline: March 30.

CAMP EMERSON
212 LONGVIEW AVENUE
HINSDALE, MASSACHUSETTS 01235

General Information Residential camp serving 220 boys and girls ages 7–15½. Established in 1968. Owned by Marv, Addie, and Sue Lein and Kevin McDonough. Affiliated with American Camping Association, Massachusetts Camping Association, Western Massachusetts Camping Association. 143-acre facility located 150 miles northeast of New York, New York. Features: heated pool and 2 lakes; roller hockey/skating rink; proximity to cultural centers of the Berkshires; facilities for all land and water sports, including 6 tennis courts; proximity to Boston and New York City (approximately 3 hours); theater, art, and gymnastics centers.

Profile of Summer Employees Total number: 100; average age: 24; 50% male, 50% female; 70% college students; 30% teachers. Nonsmokers only.

Employment Information Openings are from June 15 to August 22. Jobs available: ▶ *creative arts instructors* with experience in fine arts/drawing and painting, ceramics, sculpting, batik, leather, jewelry, model rocketry, woodworking, photography, yearbook, newspaper/creative writing, video, and computers at $1300 per season; ▶ *performing arts instructors* with experience in dramatics/directing, stagecraft, costuming/sewing, skits and stunts, storytelling, music (all instruments), piano (play by ear and/or play for shows and transpose), dance (jazz/aerobic/ballet/modern), choreography, guitar (play, sing, teach), and puppetry at $1300 per season; ▶ *land sports instructors* with experience in archery, basketball, fencing, golf, gymnastics, hockey, judo, karate, soccer, softball, tennis, track, volleyball, fitness, baseball, and lacrosse at $1300 per season; ▶ *water sports instructors* with experience in sailing, canoeing, kayaking, water polo, windsurfing, waterskiing, motorboat driving, lifeguarding, competitive swimming (WSI certification), and water aerobics at $1300 per season; ▶ *wilderness instructor* with experience in campcraft, fire building, outdoor cooking, overnight trips, forestry, nature, hiking, fishing, and ropes at $1300 per season; ▶ *nurses* with RN license; ▶ *administrative program assistant* with word processing and additional computer skills (such as desktop publishing) at $1300 per season; ▶ *key staff members* with experience in directing waterfront, aquatics, theater, sports, tennis, art, programming, and wilderness programs; ▶ *chefs/cooks.* International students encouraged to apply; must apply through recognized agency.

Benefits College credit, on-the-job training, on-site room and board at no charge, laundry facilities, health insurance, highly skilled peer group, healthy menu including salad bar and vegetarian fare, staff lounge and after-hours activities. Preemployment training of 7 days is required and includes safety and accident prevention, group interaction, first-aid, leadership, camper-counselor relations. Orientation is paid.

Contact Sue Lein, Camp Director, Camp Emerson, Department SJ, 78 Deerfield Road, Sharon, Massachusetts 02067; 800-782-3395, Fax 617-784-2094, E-mail cmpemerson@aol.com. Application deadline: June 1.

CAMP GOOD NEWS
ROUTE 130
FORESTDALE, MASSACHUSETTS 02644

General Information Coeducational residential and day camp serving 220 children ages 6–16. Established in 1935. Owned by Society for Christian Activities. Affiliated with American Camping Association, Pioneers of Camping Club, Cape Cod Canal Region Chamber of Commerce. 214-acre facility located 13 miles east of Hyannis. Features: location in wooded area; extensive shorefront on freshwater pond; location 6 miles from ocean on Cape Cod; sandy beach.

Profile of Summer Employees Total number: 80; average age: 23; 45% male, 55% female; 3% minorities; 1% high school students; 58% college students; 1% retirees; 2% international; 5% local residents. Nonsmokers only.

Employment Information Openings are from June 17 to August 15. Jobs available: ▶ 35 *counselors* with college student status at $1100–$1200 per season; ▶ 10 *kitchen staff members* (minimum age 18) at $1000 per season; ▶ 2 *experienced arts and crafts instructors* at $1200 per season; ▶ 2 *nurses* at $1500 per season; ▶ 1 *store manager* at $1000–$1200 per season; ▶ *sports experts* with boating certification at $1000–$1200 per season.

Benefits On-the-job training, on-site room and board at no charge, laundry facilities, tuition reimbursement. Preemployment training of 10 days is required and includes group interaction, first-aid, CPR, WST training, lifeguard training. Orientation is unpaid.

Contact Faith Willard, Director, Camp Good News, Department SJ, PO Box 95, Forestdale, Massachusetts 02644; 508-477-9731, Fax 508-477-8016. Application deadline: May 30.

CAMP PEMBROKE
PEMBROKE, MASSACHUSETTS 02359

General Information Residential Jewish cultural camp serving 275 girls. Established in 1936. Operated by Cohen Foundation. Affiliated with American Camping Association, Massachusetts Camping Association, Association of Independent Camps. 68-acre facility located 30 miles south of Boston. Features: Olympic-size pool; modern plant; proximity to Cape Cod and Boston.

Profile of Summer Employees Total number: 85; average age: 19; 18% high school students; 80% college students; 2% international. Nonsmokers preferred.

Employment Information Openings are from June 17 to August 24. Jobs available: ▶ 3 *arts and crafts instructors* at $1350–$1800 per season; ▶ 1 *arts director* at $2000–$2500 per season; ▶ 1 *music instructor* at $2000–$2500 per season; ▶ 2 *canoeing instructors* at $1350–$2000 per season; ▶ 2 *sailing instructors* at $1350–$2000 per season; ▶ 3 *swimming instructors* at $1350–$2000 per season; ▶ 1 *swimming director* at $2000–$2500 per season; ▶ 1 *athletics director* at $2000–$2500 per season; ▶ 1 *waterskiing director* at $1500–$1900 per season; ▶ 1 *archery instructor* at $1500–$1900 per season. International students encouraged to apply; must apply through recognized agency.

Benefits College credit, on-the-job training, formal ongoing training, on-site room and board at no charge, laundry facilities, gratuities. Preemployment training of 5 days is required and includes safety and accident prevention, group interaction, first-aid, CPR, leadership, camper-counselor relations, WSI & lifeguard. Orientation is paid.

Contact Leslie Brenner, Director, Camp Pembroke, Department SJ, 42 McAdams Road, Framingham, Massachusetts 01701; 508-788-6968, Fax 508-881-1006, E-mail cpembrokebren@juno.com. Application deadline: April 1.

CAMP TACONIC
770 NEW WINDSOR ROAD
HINSDALE, MASSACHUSETTS 01235

General Information Residential 8-week coed camp for 280 children offering top instruction in a wide range of program areas. Established in 1931. Owned by Bob and Barbara Ezrol. Affiliated with American Camping Association, Western Massachusetts Camp Directors' Association, Association of Independent Camps. 250-acre facility located 10 miles east of Pittsfield.

Features: 8 tennis courts with lighting for night play; 2 swimming pools; lake with full waterfront facility; full theater and arts facilities; stables and riding trails; playing fields.

Profile of Summer Employees Total number: 100; average age: 21; 50% male, 50% female; 85% college students; 15% teachers. Nonsmokers only.

Employment Information Openings are from June 18 to August 20. Jobs available: ▶ 16 *aquatics staff members* (swimming, sailing, waterskiing, and boating) with WSI certification for swimming; ▶ 14 *athletics staff members* (team and individual sports); ▶ 12 *theater arts staff members* (dance, costume making, musical theater, and stagecraft); ▶ 5 *outdoor adventure staff members* (pioneering, climbing wall, and ropes course); ▶ 10 *arts and crafts staff members* (fine arts, ceramics, crafts, and silver jewelry); ▶ 6 *media arts staff members* (newspaper, photography, and video); ▶ 12 *tennis staff members;* ▶ 12 *general counselors for 7–10 year olds.* All positions offered at $1200–$2000 per season.

Benefits College credit, on-the-job training, formal ongoing training, on-site room and board at no charge, laundry facilities, travel reimbursement, competitive salary, workmen's compensation. Preemployment training of 7 days is required and includes safety and accident prevention, group interaction, leadership, camper-counselor relations. Orientation is paid.

Contact Bob and Barbara Ezrol, Directors, Camp Taconic, 66 Chestnut Hill Lane, Briarcliff Manor, New York 10510; 914-762-2820, Fax 914-762-4437, E-mail ctaconic@aol.com.

CAMP WATITOH
CENTER LAKE
BECKET, MASSACHUSETTS 01223

General Information Residential summer camp serving 200 children with a wide variety of land and water sports activities, including drama, nature, and trips to all Berkshire area attractions. Established in 1937. Owned by Sandy, William, and Suzanne Hoch. Affiliated with American Camping Association, Massachusetts Camping Association, Western Massachusetts Camp Directors' Association. 85-acre facility located 150 miles north of New York, New York. Features: mountaintop location; lake setting; 2 shops for creative arts.

Profile of Summer Employees Total number: 65; average age: 20; 50% male, 50% female; 85% college students; 10% international. Nonsmokers preferred.

Employment Information Openings are from June 25 to August 22. Jobs available: ▶ 6 *swimming instructors* with WSI certification at $1200–$1400 per season; ▶ 2 *sailing instructors* at $1200–$1400 per season; ▶ 2 *waterskiing instructors* at $1200–$1400 per season; ▶ 3 *arts and crafts instructors, experience preferred,* at $1500–$2500 per season; ▶ *general sports instructor* at $1100–$1600 per season. International students encouraged to apply; must apply through recognized agency.

Benefits College credit, on-the-job training, on-site room and board at no charge, travel reimbursement, health insurance. Preemployment training of 3 days is required and includes safety and accident prevention, group interaction, leadership, camper-counselor relations. Orientation is paid.

Contact William Hoch, Director, Camp Watitoh, 28 Sammis Lane, White Plains, New York 10605; 914-428-1894, Fax 914-428-1648, E-mail bihoc@aol.com. Application deadline: June 1.

CAPE COD SEA CAMPS
PO BOX 1880
BREWSTER, MASSACHUSETTS 02631

General Information Residential camp serving 350 campers for 3½ or 7 weeks and a day camp serving 240 campers weekly. Established in 1922. Owned by Mrs. Berry D. Richardson. Affiliated with American Camping Association, Cape Cod Association of Children's Camps. 125-acre facility located 90 miles southeast of Boston. Features: 3 waterfronts (saltwater, lake, pool); location on Cape Cod Bay with a 1,000-foot beach; 9 tennis courts, 15 acres of playing fields; easy access to all of Cape Cod; location close to Cape Cod bike trail.

Profile of Summer Employees Total number: 120; average age: 21; 50% male, 50% female;

5% minorities; 80% college students; 5% international; 10% local residents; 10% teachers. Nonsmokers preferred.

Employment Information Openings are from June 20 to August 16. Jobs available: ▶ 3 *activity department heads* with teaching certification at $1900–$2500 per season; ▶ 10 *general counselors* with documented experience in camp activities at $1000–$1500 per season; ▶ 5 *sailing staff members* with instruction and racing experience at $1100–$2000 per season; ▶ 2 *swimming instructors* with WSI certification at $1000–$1600 per season. International students encouraged to apply; must apply through recognized agency.

Benefits On-the-job training, on-site room and board at no charge, laundry facilities, internship for college credit. Preemployment training of 6 days is required and includes safety and accident prevention, group interaction, first-aid, CPR, leadership, camper-counselor relations, activity clinics. Orientation is paid.

Contact Sherry Mernick, Associate Director, Cape Cod Sea Camps, Department SJ, PO Box 1880, Brewster, Massachusetts 02631; 508-896-3451, Fax 508-896-8272, URL http://www. kidscamps.com/traditional.capecodsea. Application deadline: April 15.

CHIMNEY CORNERS CAMP FOR GIRLS
748 HAMILTON ROAD
BECKET, MASSACHUSETTS 01223

General Information Residential YMCA camp serving 240 girls in each four-week session. Camp is international, and it promotes character development and personal growth. Established in 1931. Owned by Becket Chimney Corners YMCA. Affiliated with YMCA, American Camping Association. 1,200-acre facility located 120 miles west of Boston. Features: lake; playing fields and 6 tennis courts; 2 riding rings and stables; 1200 acres of conservation land; Environmental Learning Center (nature building); performing arts stage and creative arts studios.

Profile of Summer Employees Total number: 150; average age: 20; 10% male, 90% female; 5% minorities; 100% college students; 20% international; 1% local residents. Nonsmokers preferred.

Employment Information Openings are from June 20 to August 21. Year-round positions also offered. Jobs available: ▶ *counselors* at $1400–$1600 per season; ▶ *lifeguards/swimming instructors* at $1400–$2000 per season; ▶ *horseback riding instructors* at $1400–$2000 per season; ▶ *performing and creative arts staff* at $1400–$2200 per season; ▶ *food service assistants* at $1400–$1600 per season; ▶ *sports instructors* at $1200–$1400 per season; ▶ *tennis coach* at $1400–$2000 per season. International students encouraged to apply; must apply through recognized agency.

Benefits On-site room and board at no charge, laundry facilities. Preemployment training of 7 days is required and includes safety and accident prevention, group interaction, first-aid, CPR, leadership, camper-counselor relations. Orientation is paid.

Contact Shannon Donovan-Moati, Chimney Corners Camp Director, Chimney Corners Camp for Girls, Department SJ, 748 Hamilton Road, Becket, Massachusetts 01223; 413-623-8991, Fax 413-623-5890. Application deadline: May 1.

COLLEGE LIGHT OPERA COMPANY
HIGHFIELD THEATRE, PO DRAWER F
FALMOUTH, MASSACHUSETTS 02541

General Information Residential summer-stock music theater for training undergraduate and graduate students. Established in 1969. Owned by College Light Opera Company Board of Trustees. 6-acre facility located 70 miles south of Boston. Features: full pit orchestra; location on the beach on Cape Cod.

Profile of Summer Employees Total number: 85; average age: 21; 50% male, 50% female; 5% minorities; 2% high school students; 80% college students; 13% teachers. Nonsmokers preferred.

Employment Information Openings are from June 9 to August 29. Jobs available: ▶ 32 *experienced vocalists* (salary is room and board); ▶ 18 *experienced orchestra staff* at $500 per season; ► 6 *experienced stage crew* at $1000 per season; ► 5 *experienced costume crew* at $1000 per season; ► 2 *box office treasurers* with outgoing, friendly personality at $1200 per season; ► 1 *experienced assistant business manager* with word processing skills at $1200 per season; ► 1 *experienced publicity director* with word processing skills and car at $1200 per season; ► 1 *experienced choreographer* at $1400 per season; ► 2 *experienced chorus masters* with piano experience at $1200 per season; ► 2 *experienced piano accompanists* at $1000 per season; ► 1 *experienced costume designer* at $2200 per season; ► 1 *experienced set designer/ technical director* at $2200 per season; ► 1 *experienced co-op work director* at $2200 per season; ► 1 *experienced cook* at $2500 per season.

Benefits College credit, on-the-job training, on-site room and board at no charge.

Contact Ursula P. Haslun, Producer, College Light Opera Company, 162 South Cedar Street, Oberlin, Ohio 44074; 216-774-8485, Fax 216-775-8642, E-mail ursula_haslun@qmgate.cc.oberlin. edu. Application deadline: March 15.

CRANE LAKE CAMP
STATE LINE ROAD
WEST STOCKBRIDGE, MASSACHUSETTS 01266

General Information Coeducational camp serving children ages 6–15 with traditional sports and a full cultural program. Established in 1922. Owned by Ed and Barbara Ulanoff. Affiliated with American Camping Association. 120-acre facility located 12 miles south of Pittsfield. Features: private spring-fed lake; heated swimming pool; 3 baseball fields; 2 soccer fields; location 3 miles from Tanglewood Music Festival (close to New York City and Boston in the Berkshire Mountains); 10 tennis courts; 4 indoor courts; modern cabins; gymnastics pavilion; 2 arts and crafts studios.

Profile of Summer Employees Total number: 125; average age: 21; 52% male, 48% female; 75% college students; 15% teachers. Nonsmokers only.

Employment Information Openings are from June 20 to August 21. Jobs available: ► 10 *athletics counselors* with a major in physical education or varsity athletics experience at $900–$1200 per season; ► 6 *waterfront instructors* with small crafts certification and waterskiing, sailing, or canoeing experience at $900–$1200 per season; ► 4 *experienced gymnastics instructors* at $900–$1200 per season; ► 2 *arts and crafts instructors* at $900–$1200 per season; ► *nurse* with RN license at $1600 per season; ► *nature instructor* at $900–$1200 per season; ► *horseback riding instructor* at $900–$1200 per season; ► *tennis instructor* with college playing experience at $1200–$1500 per season; ► *pioneering/hiking instructor* at $900–$1200 per season; ► *painting/sketching instructor* at $900–$1200 per season; ► *guitar instructor* at $900–$1200 per season; ► *piano instructor* with ability to play by ear at $900–$1200 per season; ► *dance staff* at $900–$1200 per season.

Benefits College credit, on-the-job training, formal ongoing training, on-site room and board at no charge, laundry facilities, travel reimbursement, health insurance, tuition reimbursement, car available on days and evenings off, facilities available during time off. Preemployment training of 5 days is required and includes safety and accident prevention, group interaction, first-aid, CPR, leadership. Orientation is paid.

Contact Ed Ulanoff, Director, Crane Lake Camp, Department SJ, 10 West 66th Street, New York, New York 10023; 800-227-2660, Fax 212-724-2960, URL http://www.kidscamps.com/ traditional/crane-lake/. Application deadline: May 1.

4–H FARLEY OUTDOOR EDUCATION CENTER
615 ROUTE 130
MASHPEE, MASSACHUSETTS 02649

General Information Camp emphasizing overnight and day programs for boys and girls ages 7–14. There is limited mainstreaming of special needs children. Activities include nature,, agriculture, outdoor living skills, arts, canoeing, kayaking, horseback riding, and a ropes course. Established in 1934. Owned by Cape Cod 4-H Camp Corporation. Affiliated with University of

Massachusetts Extension, United States Department of Agriculture. 32-acre facility located 80 miles south of Boston. Features: freshwater lake (largest on Cape Cod); adjacent woodland areas; location close to ocean; small farm with animals; auditorium/outside amphitheater; nature classroom with native and domestic small animals.

Profile of Summer Employees Total number: 48; average age: 22; 25% male, 75% female; 10% minorities; 20% high school students; 60% college students; 10% international; 10% local residents. Nonsmokers preferred.

Employment Information Openings are from July 5 to August 27. Jobs available: ▶ 3 *waterfront directors* (minimum age 21) with WSI certification at $230–$270 per week; ▶ 8 *lifeguards* with LGT certification or equivalent at $160–$200 per week; ▶ 30 *counselors* with specialized program skills and camping experience at $100–$200 per week; ▶ 1 *child care coordinator* with background in youth development at $250–$300 per week; ▶ 1 *health-care provider* with EMT, RN, or LPN license or special training in first aid at $300–$350 per week; ▶ 3 *kitchen staff members* at $200–$300 per week; ▶ *experienced canoeing instructors* with documented experience or certification at $200–$230 per week; ▶ *archery instructors* with documented experience or certification at $200–$230 per week; ▶ *ropes instructor* with documented experience or certification at $200–$230 per week. International students encouraged to apply.

Benefits On-the-job training, formal ongoing training, on-site room and board at no charge, laundry facilities, health insurance, weekends off.

Contact Michael Campbell, Executive Director, 4–H Farley Outdoor Education Center, Department SJ, 615 Route 130, Mashpee, Massachusetts 02649; 508-477-0181, Fax 508-539-0080.

HORIZONS FOR YOUTH
121 LAKEVIEW STREET
SHARON, MASSACHUSETTS 02067

General Information A general residential camping program including arts and crafts, drama, nature, sports, and swimming for inner-city youths ages 7–14. Established in 1938. Owned by Horizons For Youth, Inc. Affiliated with American Camping Association, Massachusetts Camping Association, Association of Experiential Education. 150-acre facility located 20 miles south of Boston. Features: freshwater lakefront; sports field; 150 acres of woods, fields, and swamps; extensive trail network.

Profile of Summer Employees Total number: 70; average age: 21; 50% male, 50% female; 20% minorities; 85% college students; 1% retirees; 20% international; 20% local residents; 10% teachers. Nonsmokers preferred.

Employment Information Openings are from June 9 to August 21. Jobs available: ▶ 2 *waterfront directors* (minimum age 21) with CPR, LGT, WSI, and first aid certification at $1200–$1500 per season; ▶ 4 *unit leaders* (minimum age 21) with supervisory and extensive experience with children; first aid/CPR certification preferred at $1500–$1800 per season; ▶ 36 *counselors* (minimum age 21) with experience working with children; first aid/CPR certification preferred at $860–$1000 per season; ▶ 5 *activity specialists* (minimum age 18) with experience with children and in activity area; first aid/CPR certification preferred at $1000–$1200 per season; ▶ 1 *CIT director* (minimum age 21) with significant experience in working with teens; first aid/CPR certification preferred at $1000–$1200 per season; ▶ 3 *kitchen staff* (minimum age 18) with experience preferred in general kitchen skills; first aid/CPR certification preferred at $1100–$1600 per season; ▶ 2 *maintenance staff members* (minimum age 18) with general skills including carpentry, painting, and landscaping; first aid/CPR certification preferred at $1100–$1400 per season. International students encouraged to apply; must obtain own visa and working papers prior to employment; must apply through recognized agency.

Benefits College credit, on-the-job training, formal ongoing training, on-site room and board at no charge, laundry facilities, performance reviews and staff evaluations. Preemployment training of 14 days is required and includes safety and accident prevention, group interaction, leadership, camper-counselor relations. Orientation is paid.

Contact Cindy Gallagher, Summer Program Director, Horizons for Youth, Department SJ, 121

Lakeview Street, Sharon, Massachusetts 02067; 617-828-7550, Fax 617-784-1287, E-mail camp@ horizons.tiac.net. Application deadline: June 1.

NORTH SHORE MUSIC THEATRE
DUNHAM ROAD, PO BOX 62
BEVERLY, MASSACHUSETTS 01915–0062

General Information Musical theater with a six-show season of Broadway musicals as well as children's shows, concerts, and special events. Established in 1955. Owned by North Shore Community Arts Foundation, Inc. Affiliated with National Alliance of Musical Theater Producers, Council of Stock Theaters, Actors' Equity Association. Located 25 miles north of Boston. Features: 1,800-seat arena theater; computerized lighting; state-of-the-art sound system; modern production facility; location in the woods on landscaped grounds; full production shops and rehearsal halls.

Profile of Summer Employees Total number: 65; average age: 21; 40% male, 60% female; 10% minorities; 10% high school students; 70% college students; 75% local residents. Nonsmokers preferred.

Employment Information Openings are from March 15 to December 23. Year-round positions also offered. Jobs available: ▶ 20 *technical theater interns, experience preferred,* at $150–$200 per week; ▶ 20 *technical theater staff members, experience preferred,* at $275–$425 per week.

Benefits College credit, on-the-job training at $80 per week.

Contact Assistant Production Manager, North Shore Music Theatre, Department SJ, PO Box 62, Beverly, Massachusetts 01915–0062; 508-922-8500 Ext. 261, Fax 508-921-0793. Application deadline: April 15.

OFFENSE-DEFENSE GOLF CAMP, MASSACHUSETTS
THE WINCHENDON SCHOOL AND GOLF FACILITY
WINCHENDON, MASSACHUSETTS 01475

General Information Residential and day camp teaching golf to boys and girls ages 10–18. Established in 1993. Owned by Winchendon School and Golf Facility. Operated by Offense-Defense Golf Camp. Affiliated with New England Camping Association, United States Tennis Association, Professional Golfers Association. 1,000-acre facility located 25 miles north of Boston. Features: prep school dorms and cafeteria; 18-hole regulation golf course; putting green; golf range; outdoor swimming pool and gymnasium; 4 tennis courts.

Profile of Summer Employees Total number: 25; average age: 28; 80% male, 20% female; 10% minorities; 25% college students; 25% retirees; 10% local residents; 50% teachers. Nonsmokers preferred.

Employment Information Openings are from June 21 to August 10. Jobs available: ▶ 1 *bus driver* (minimum age 21) with license to drive yellow school bus and CDL at $150–$300 per week; ▶ 10 *golf instructors* with college varsity, college coaching, or PGA Pro (very low handicap players) status at $250–$400 per week; ▶ 10 *general* (non-golf) *counselors* (minimum age 20) at $125–$150 per week; ▶ *swimming counselors* with WSI certification at $200–$250 per week. International students encouraged to apply; must obtain own visa and working papers prior to employment.

Benefits College credit, on-the-job training, formal ongoing training, on-site room and board at no charge, laundry facilities, play golf, teach golf, non-golf counselors have free trips an d excursions to Boston.

Contact Mike Meshken, President, Offense-Defense Golf Camp, Massachusetts, Department SJ, PO Box 6, Easton, Connecticut 06612; 800-824-7336, Fax 203-255-5666. Application deadline: May 10.

OFFENSE-DEFENSE TENNIS CAMP
CURRY COLLEGE
MILTON, MASSACHUSETTS 02186

General Information Tennis camp for boys and girls ages 10–18. Accommodates all levels from beginners to tournament players. Established in 1972. Owned by Mike and Judy Meshken. Operated by Offense-Defense Tennis Camp. Affiliated with New England Lawn Tennis Association, New England Camping Association, United States Tennis Association. 150-acre facility located 9 miles south of Boston. Features: college dorms; gymnasium; cafeteria; game room; wooded campus; proximity to scenic and historical sites in and near Boston.

Profile of Summer Employees Total number: 70; average age: 23; 60% male, 40% female; 85% college students; 10% local residents; 15% teachers. Nonsmokers preferred.

Employment Information Openings are from June 20 to August 15. Jobs available: ▶ 16 *general counselors* (ages 19–28) at $880–$1000 per season; ▶ 2 *licensed bus drivers* with CDL at $1200–$1800 per season; ▶ 24 *tennis instructors* with tennis instructor certification or varsity college playing and teaching experience at $800–$1200 per season.

Benefits College credit, on-the-job training, formal ongoing training, on-site room and board at no charge, laundry facilities, travel reimbursement, trips to Boston, full day off each week, use of weight room, swimming pool, and gym.

Contact Mehdi Belhassan, Director, Offense-Defense Tennis Camp, Department SJ, PO Box 280136, Tampa, Florida 33682; 800-836-6473, Fax 813-972-3302, E-mail mbtennis@aol.com. Application deadline: May 15.

RIVERSIDE PARK
PO BOX 307
AGAWAM, MASSACHUSETTS 01001

General Information Theme park featuring more than 100 rides, shows, major concerts, games, and restaurants. Established in 1939. Owned by Premier Parks, Inc. 150-acre facility located 6 miles west of Springfield. Features: seven roller coasters including 2 kiddie coasters; water rides; classic 1909 carousel; largest Ferris wheel in the Northeast.

Profile of Summer Employees Total number: 1,500; average age: 20; 55% male, 45% female; 25% minorities; 25% high school students; 45% college students; 30% retirees; 10% international; 50% local residents.

Employment Information Openings are from April 1 to October 1. Jobs available: ▶ 350 *ride operators* at $4.50–$5.25 per hour; ▶ 50 *park security staff members;* ▶ 200 *food service attendants;* ▶ 100 *games attendants;* ▶ 20 *first aid staff members;* ▶ 30 *cash control staff members;* ▶ 60 *merchandise sales staff members.* International students encouraged to apply; must apply through recognized agency.

Benefits College scholarships, wardrobe furnished, employee cafeteria. Preemployment training is required and includes safety and accident prevention, group interaction, guest service/relations. Orientation is paid.

Contact Jason Freeman, Director of Operations, Riverside Park, Department SJ, PO Box 307, Agawan, Massachusetts 01001; 413-786-9300, Fax 413-789-4585.

SOUTH SHORE YMCA CAMPS
75 STOWE ROAD
SANDWICH, MASSACHUSETTS 02563

General Information Brother/sister residential camp on Cape Cod. Established in 1928. Owned by South Shore YMCA. Affiliated with American Camping Association, YMCA. 400-acre facility located 60 miles south of Boston. Features: 3 freshwater ponds; athletic fields; tennis courts; bathroom facilities with hot showers and flush toilets; high and low ropes courses; horseback riding.

Profile of Summer Employees Total number: 120; average age: 22; 50% male, 50% female;

2% minorities; 20% high school students; 80% college students; 30% international; 5% local residents.

Employment Information Openings are from April 1 to October 31. Year-round positions also offered. Jobs available: ▶ 60 *cabin counselors* with one year of college completed at $120–$130 per week; ▶ *unit leaders* with leadership qualities at $130–$150 per week; ▶ *specialists* with any appropriate specialized skills and WSI, CPR, and first aid certification at $130–$150 per week; ▶ *support staff* (in kitchen, maintenance, and bathroom) at $120–$130 per week; ▶ *nurse* at $300–$350 per week; ▶ *cooks* at $300–$400 per week. International students encouraged to apply; must apply through recognized agency.

Benefits On-the-job training, formal ongoing training, on-site room and board at no charge, travel reimbursement. Preemployment training of 7 days is required and includes safety and accident prevention, group interaction, first-aid, leadership, camper-counselor relations. Orientation is paid.

Contact Gareth Thomas, Executive Director, South Shore YMCA Camps, Department SJ, 75 Stowe Road, Sandwich, Massachusetts 02563; 508-428-2571, Fax 508-420-3545, E-mail ssymca@ capecod.net. Application deadline: June 1.

SUMMER THEATER AT MOUNT HOLYOKE COLLEGE
SOUTH HADLEY, MASSACHUSETTS 01075

General Information Professional summer-stock company producing eight mainstage plays and three plays for children in one-week stock. Established in 1970. Owned by Production Arts, Limited. Affiliated with New England Theater Conference, East Central Theater Conference, Southeast Theater Conference, Theater Communications Group. 20-acre facility located 10 miles north of Springfield. Features: facility at nation's oldest women's college; proximity to Hartford, Boston, and New York City; access to all gyms, libraries, and pools of Mount Holyoke College.

Profile of Summer Employees Total number: 75; average age: 25; 50% male, 50% female; 5% minorities; 7% high school students; 30% college students; 2% international; 16% local residents.

Employment Information Openings are from May 30 to August 25. Jobs available: ▶ 12 *actors* (non-Equity) at $200 per season; ▶ 3 *carpenters* at $750–$1000 per season; ▶ 3 *prop artisans* at $750–$1000 per season; ▶ 2 *stitchers* at $750–$1000 per season; ▶ 1 *wardrobe staff member* at $850–$1000 per season; ▶ 1 *technical director* at $1200–$1800 per season; ▶ 3 *stage managers* (non-Equity) at $200–$900 per season; ▶ 1 *prop master* at $1000 per season; ▶ 1 *box office manager* at $750–$1000 per season; ▶ 1 *publicity assistant* at $750–$1000 per season; ▶ 1 *sound designer* at $1000 per season; ▶ 1 *costume designer* at $1800 per season; ▶ 1 *master electrician* at $1000–$1500 per season.

Benefits On-the-job training, formal ongoing training, on-site room and board at no charge, laundry facilities, travel reimbursement, Equity membership candidate points.

Contact John Grassilli, Producing Director, Summer Theater at Mount Holyoke College, Department SJ, South Hadley, Massachusetts 01075; 413-538-2632, Fax 413-538-3036. Application deadline: March 1.

SUPERCAMP
HAMPSHIRE COLLEGE
AMHERST, MASSACHUSETTS 01002

General Information Residential program for teens designed to build self-confidence and lifelong learning skills through accelerated learning techniques. Established in 1981. Owned by Bobbi DePorter. Affiliated with American Camping Association, International Alliance for Learning. North of Hartford, Connecticut. Features: location on college campus; dormitory rooms; swimming pool; ropes course.

Profile of Summer Employees Total number: 200; average age: 22; 50% male, 50% female; 80% college students. Nonsmokers only.

Employment Information Openings are from June 20 to August 20. Jobs available: ▶ 24 *team leaders* at $500–$1000 per season; ▶ 1 *office manager* at $1000–$2000 per season; ▶ 1 *licensed* *paramedic* with national or state registration at $700–$2800 per season; ► 1 *nurse* with national or state registration at $1000–$4000 per season.

Benefits On-the-job training, on-site room and board at no charge, laundry facilities, internships, experience working with teens in an educational and self-esteem building program, excellent experience for education and psychology majors. Preemployment training of 4 days is required and includes safety and accident prevention, group interaction, leadership, camper-counselor relations. Orientation is unpaid.

Contact Elisabeth Talmon, Human Resources Coordinator, SuperCamp, Department SJ, 1725 South Coast Highway, Oceanside, California 92054; 800-527-5321, Fax 619-722-3507, E-mail supercamp@aol.com, URL http://www.supercamp.com. Application deadline: May 1.

WILDERNESS EXPERIENCES UNLIMITED
499 LOOMIS STREET
WESTFIELD, MASSACHUSETTS 01085

General Information Residential program which ranges from five days to two weeks. It serves approximately 30–40 campers ages 8–17 per week, and it offers general outdoor activities through high adventure. Established in 1982. Owned by Wilderness Experiences Unlimited. 75-acre facility located 15 miles west of Springfield. Features: ropes course; swimming pool; small pond; miles of hiking/biking trails; primitive setting.

Profile of Summer Employees Total number: 10; average age: 22; 70% male, 30% female; 50% high school students; 50% college students. Nonsmokers only.

Employment Information Openings are from June 25 to August 25. Jobs available: ► *senior counselors* with first aid/CPR certification and LGT at $150–$200 per week; ► *trip leaders* with outdoor and leadership skills, first aid/CPR certification, and LGT at $150–$200 per week. International students encouraged to apply; must obtain own visa and working papers prior to employment.

Benefits On-the-job training, on-site room and board at no charge. Preemployment training of 5 days is required and includes safety and accident prevention, group interaction, first-aid, CPR, leadership. Orientation is unpaid.

Contact T. Scott Cook, Executive Director, Wilderness Experiences Unlimited, Department SJ, 499 Loomis Street, Westfield, Massachusetts 01085; 413-562-7431, Fax 413-569-1287, URL http://www.weu.com. Application deadline: February 15.

WILLIAMSTOWN THEATER FESTIVAL
WILLIAMSTOWN, MASSACHUSETTS 01267

General Information Professional summer theater performing 10 full-scale productions in 10 weeks. Established in 1954. Operated by Williamstown Theater Foundation. Affiliated with Theater Communications Group. Located 50 miles east of Albany, New York. Features: location in a northwestern Massachusetts small college town in the Berkshire Hills; proximity to Clark Art Institute and Williams College Museum of Art; proximity to Tanglewood, Jacob's Pillow, and the Appalachian Trail.

Profile of Summer Employees Total number: 300; average age: 25; 50% male, 50% female; 10% minorities; 1% high school students; 30% college students; 1% retirees; 1% international; 5% local residents.

Employment Information Openings are from June 2 to August 31. Jobs available: ► 60 *staff members* at $50–$400 per week; ► 85 *apprentices;* ► 60 *Equity actors;* ► 50 *interns;* ► 25 *non-Equity actors.* International students encouraged to apply; must obtain own visa and working papers prior to employment.

Benefits College credit, on-the-job training, on-site room and board at no charge, summer room/board free for staff, $450/month for interns and apprentices, location in a region noted for cultural vitality and natural beauty, use of college recreational facilities, opportunity to work with professional designers, directors, and actors.

Contact Anne Lowrie, Company Manager, Williamstown Theater Festival, 100 East 17th Street,

3rd Floor, New York, New York 10003; 212-228-2286, Fax 212-228-9091. Application deadline: May 1.

YMCA CAMP LYNDON
117 STOWE ROAD
SANDWICH, MASSACHUSETTS 02563

General Information Day camp serving 400 children. Established in 1912. Owned by YMCA Cape Cod. Affiliated with YMCA. 80-acre facility located 60 miles south of Boston. Features: location on Cape Cod; proximity to beaches; availability of 30 campsites, tents, and RV's; lakefront property.

Profile of Summer Employees Total number: 100; average age: 20; 40% male, 60% female; 2% minorities; 35% high school students; 55% college students; 10% international; 65% local residents. Nonsmokers preferred.

Employment Information Openings are from June 19 to September 1. Spring break, winter break, Christmas break positions also offered. Jobs available: ▶ 60 *counselors* with youth experience at $140–$175 per week; ▶ 2 *experienced certified archery specialists* with leadership experience in an archery program at $180–$250 per week; ▶ 10 *experienced boating instructors* with small craft or equivalent certification and sailing and canoeing experience at $140–$175 per week; ▶ 3 *experienced nature specialists* with degree in related subject at $180–$240 per week; ▶ 2 *waterfront directors* with WSI and LGT certifications at $200–$275 per week; ▶ 3 *experienced arts and crafts specialists* with teaching certification at $180–$240 per week; ▶ 12 *swimming instructors* with LGT certification (minimum) at $150–$190 per week; ▶ 3 *horseback riding directors* with Massachusetts riding license, must live on property at $180–$250 per week; ▶ 2 *experienced ropes/initiative specialists* with completion of course at $200–$250 per week; ▶ *experienced dramatic arts specialist* with formal training at $150–$190 per week; ▶ *horseback-riding instructors* with teaching experience at $150–$170 per week; ▶ *age-specific unit directors* with certification or related experience with specific age group at $180–$250 per week; ▶ *special populations director* with Massachusetts resident familiar with ADA laws at $200–$250 per week. International students encouraged to apply; must obtain own visa and working papers prior to employment; must apply through recognized agency.

Benefits College credit, on-the-job training, formal ongoing training, 36-hour work week, YMCA summer membership. Off-site boarding costs are $800 per month.

Contact Doreen Murphy, Youth and Camping Services Director, YMCA Camp Lyndon, Department SJ, 117 Stowe Road, Sandwich, Massachusetts 02563; 508-428-9251, Fax 508-362-5379. Application deadline: May 15.

MICHIGAN

AMERICAN YOUTH FOUNDATION–CAMP
MINIWANCA
8845 WEST GARFIELD ROAD
SHELBY, MICHIGAN 49455

General Information Camp focusing on developing the leadership capacities of young people by helping them achieve their personal best, lead balanced lives, and serve others. Established in 1924. Owned by American Youth Foundation. Affiliated with American Camping Association, Association for Experiential Education. 360-acre facility located 70 miles northwest of Grand Rapids. Features: 1 mile of Lake Michigan beach; sand dunes; wooded hills; retreat/conference facility; 2 waterfronts (Lake Michigan and Stony Lake); extensive boating area.

Profile of Summer Employees Total number: 200; average age: 21; 40% male, 60% female; 3% minorities; 10% high school students; 55% college students; 5% retirees; 8% international; 10% local residents; 5% teachers. Nonsmokers preferred.

Employment Information Openings are from June 1 to August 31. Year-round positions also offered. Jobs available: ▶ 90 *leaders* with college student or teacher status at $125–$200 per week; ▶ 26 *central summer staff members* with teacher status at $200–$300 per week; ▶ 20 *kitchen personnel* with high school student or retired person status at $125–$175 per week; ▶ 6 *camp cleaning personnel* with college student or retired person status at $125–$175 per week; ▶ 5 *building/grounds personnel* with some skill with tools and power equipment at $175–$250 per week; ▶ 5 *interns* with junior/senior status in college or college degree at $120 per week; ▶ 2 *wood shop staff* with college student or retired person status at $125–$200 per week; ▶ 5 *office staff* with college student or retired person status at $150–$175 per week; ▶ 4 *camp store staff* with college student or retired person status at $125–$175 per week; ▶ 4 *craft house staff* with college student or retired person status at $125–$175 per week; ▶ 2 *resident hall supervisors* at $150–$200 per week; ▶ 4 *drivers* with CDL license and at least 21 years old at $8 per hour; ▶ 2 *security personnel* at $150–$200 per week; ▶ 4 *waterfront staff* with WSI and sailing and canoeing experience at $150–$250; ▶ 10 *kitchen/dining hall workers* at $125–$175 per week; ▶ 4 *health center staff* with EMT, RN, LPN or 2nd year RN students at $175–$250 per week. International students encouraged to apply; must apply through recognized agency.

Benefits College credit, on-the-job training, formal ongoing training, on-site room and board at no charge, laundry facilities, travel reimbursement, leadership development. Preemployment training of 8 days is required and includes safety and accident prevention, group interaction, first-aid, CPR, leadership, camper-counselor relations. Orientation is paid.

Contact David C. Jones, Site Director, American Youth Foundation–Camp Miniwanca, Department SJ, 8845 West Garfield Road, Shelby, Michigan 49455; 616-861-2262, Fax 616-861-5244, E-mail wancadave@oceana.net, URL http://www.ayf.com. Application deadline: April 1.

BAY CLIFF HEALTH CAMP
BIG BAY, MICHIGAN 49808

General Information Residential therapy camp serving 200 handicapped children ages 3–17 during one 8-week session. Established in 1933. Owned by Bay Cliff Health Camp. 170-acre facility located 300 miles north of Milwaukee, Wisconsin. Features: natural area; location on Lake Superior; indoor heated swimming pool and sauna; sand beach; proximity to state and national parks; farm atmosphere.

Profile of Summer Employees Total number: 135; average age: 25; 30% male, 70% female; 5% minorities; 10% high school students; 50% college students; 2% retirees; 15% local residents; 3% teachers. Nonsmokers only.

Employment Information Openings are from June 14 to August 9. Jobs available: ▶ 5 *unit leaders* with teaching experience and special education degree (preferred) at $2000 per season; ▶ 50 *counselors* (minimum age 18) with one year of college completed (preferably in the study of special education, therapy, nursing, or human services) at $1300 per season; ▶ 8 *roving counselors* (minimum age 18) with one year of college completed (preferably in the study of special education, therapy, nursing, or human services) at $1300 per season; ▶ 3 *instructors for hearing impaired* at $2200 per season; ▶ 1 *certified music therapist* at $2000 per season; ▶ 5 *certified occupational therapists* at $2500 per season; ▶ 5 *certified physical therapists* at $2500 per season; ▶ 10 *certified speech therapists* at $2000–$2500 per season; ▶ 6 *student therapists* with formal school affiliation and ability to work with a supervising therapist at $600 per season; ▶ 3 *nurses* with RN or LPN license at $1800–$2500 per season; ▶ *arts and crafts aide* at $1000 per season; ▶ 1 *licensed dentist* at $3000 per season; ▶ 1 *licensed dental assistant* at $1300 per season; ▶ 1 *licensed dental hygienist* at $1800 per season; ▶ 1 *arts and crafts instructor, experience preferred,* with ability to plan and implement classes for all camp units at $1800 per season; ▶ 1 *nature instructor, experience preferred,* with ability to plan and implement classes for all camp units at $1800 per season; ▶ 1 *recreation instructor, experience preferred,* with ability to plan and implement classes for all camp units at $1800 per season; ▶ 4 *waterfront staff members* with WSI or lifeguard certification at $1200 per season; ▶ 2 *instructors for visually impaired* at $2000 per season; ▶ 1 *experienced head cook* at $250–$300 per week; ▶ 1 *experienced assistant cook* at $200–$250 per week; ▶ 1 *baker* at $1500 per season; ▶ 12 *dining room aides* (minimum age 16) at $900 per season; ▶ 3 *laundry/housekeeping personnel* at $1000 per season; ▶ 2 *linen room personnel* at $1000 per season; ▶ 4 *experienced maintenance personnel* (minimum age 18) at $1200 per season; ▶ 2 *secretaries* with good clerical skills and a pleasant, enthusiastic personality at $1200 per season; ▶ *waterfront/pool supervisor* at $1800 per season.

Benefits College credit, on-site room and board at no charge, laundry facilities, travel reimbursement, opportunity to work with handicapped children. Preemployment training of 5 days is required and includes safety and accident prevention, group interaction, first-aid, camper-counselor relations. Orientation is paid.

Contact Tim Bennett, Camp Director, Bay Cliff Health Camp, 310 West Washington Street, Suite 300, Marquette, Michigan 49855; 906-228-5770, Fax 906-228-5769, E-mail baycliffhc@aol.com. Application deadline: May 15.

BLACK RIVER FARM AND RANCH
5040 SHERIDAN LINE
CROSWELL, MICHIGAN 48422

General Information Residential camp serving 125 girls ages 7–15 in one- and two-week sessions with Western riding and vaulting program. Established in 1962. Owned by John Donovan. Affiliated with CHA-The Association for Horsemanship Safety and Education, American Vaulting Association. 150-acre facility located 60 miles north of Detroit. Features: 65 horses; 2 indoor riding arenas; 7 riding rings; 5 miles of trails.

Profile of Summer Employees Total number: 45; 100% female. Nonsmokers preferred.

Employment Information Openings are from June 15 to August 22. Jobs available: ▶ *riding instructors/cabin counselors* with teaching experience (preferred) at $2000 per season; ▶ *vaulting instructors/cabin counselors* at $2000 per season; ▶ *lifeguards/cabin counselors* with LGT certification at $2000 per season; ▶ *kitchen staff*. International students encouraged to apply; must apply through recognized agency.

Benefits College credit, on-the-job training, formal ongoing training, on-site room and board at no charge, possible internships. Preemployment training of 5 to 7 days is required and includes safety and accident prevention, group interaction, CPR, leadership, camper-counselor relations. Orientation is paid.

Contact Meg Graham, Director, Black River Farm and Ranch, Department SJ, 5040 Sheridan Line, Croswell, Michigan 48422; 810-679-2505, Fax 810-679-3188, E-mail brranch@greatlakes.net.

BLUE LAKE FINE ARTS CAMP
ROUTE 2
TWIN LAKE, MICHIGAN 49457

General Information Summer school of the arts serving nearly 4,000 campers over eight-week season. Established in 1966. Operated by William F. Stansell. 1,200-acre facility located 40 miles northwest of Grand Rapids. Features: extensive freshwater lake frontage (2 lakes); large outdoor performance facility which seats 5,000; three swimming pools; three large sports fields; large basketball facility; rustic, heavily wooded campus located in the Manistee National Forest of Michigan; over 350 cabins, rehearsal facilities, performance facilities, and other camp buildings; on-site public radio station.

Profile of Summer Employees Total number: 300; average age: 23; 45% male, 55% female; 20% minorities; 60% college students; 1% retirees; 5% international; 5% local residents; 50% teachers. Nonsmokers preferred.

Employment Information Openings are from June 1 to August 30. Year-round positions also offered. Jobs available: ▶ 96 *counselors* (minimum age 18) with one year of college and interest and/or experience in the fine arts at $850–$1350 per season; ▶ 10 *health lodge staff members* with Red Cross Response to Emergencies, EMT, or First Responder certification at $1000–$2000 per season; ▶ 5 *camp nurses* with RN or LPN license at $450 per week; ▶ 1 *waterfront director* with WSI or LGI certification and managerial experience at $2000–$3000 per season; ▶ 1 *assistant waterfront director* with WSI certification at $1200–$1500 per season; ▶ 1 *health lodge director* with Red Cross First Responder certification and managerial/administrative experience at $2000–$3000 per season; ▶ 4 *music library staff members* with office experience and knowledge of music at $5 per hour. International students encouraged to apply; must obtain own visa and working papers prior to employment.

Benefits On-the-job training, on-site room and board at no charge, laundry facilities, extensive performance opportunities for college students (musicians), limited teaching experience for those who qualify, work with professional faculty from across the country. Preemployment training of 9 days is required and includes safety and accident prevention, group interaction, first-aid, CPR, leadership, camper-counselor relations. Orientation is paid.

Contact Heidi Stansell, Staff Director, Blue Lake Fine Arts Camp, Route 2, Blue Lake Fine Arts Camp, Twin Lake, Michigan 49457; 616-894-1966, Fax 616-893-5120. Application deadline: June 15.

BOYNE U.S.A. RESORTS, INC.
PO BOX 19, 1 BOYNE MOUNTAIN ROAD
BOYNE FALLS, MICHIGAN 49713

General Information Resorts offering an escape from the big city; with over 56 ski runs, a wealth of world class golf courses, and conference and tennis centers. Established in 1948. Owned by Everett Kircher. Situated on 15,000 acres. Features: 8 world class golf courses; tennis center; miles of hiking and biking trails; heated outdoor and indoor pools, whirlpools, and saunas; meeting and conference centers; over 56 ski runs plus the Midwest's most extensive chairlift and snowmaking and grooming systems.

Profile of Summer Employees Total number: 700.

Employment Information Openings are from May 1 to September 7. Winter break, Christmas break positions also offered. Jobs available: ▶ 60 *housekeepers* at $5.50 per hour; ▶ 20 *dishwashers* at $5.50 per hour; ▶ 20 *waitstaff* at $3.50 per hour; ▶ 15 *maintenance staff* at $5.25–$7 per hour; ▶ 5 *front desk/reservations staff* at $5.50–$6 per hour; ▶ 15 *bus staff* at $5–$5.50 per hour; ▶ 10 *line cooks* at $6–$7.50 per hour. International students encouraged to apply; must obtain own visa and working papers prior to employment.

Benefits On-the-job training, formal ongoing training, 40% off meals, 20–30% off retail purchases at ski and pro shops, discounts on golf and ski packages. Off-site boarding costs are $450 per month.

Contact Tania Schripsema, Recruitment Administrator, Boyne U.S.A. Resorts Inc., Department SJ, PO Box 19, Boyne Falls, Michigan 49713; 616-549-6048, Fax 616-549-6896.

CAMP FOWLER AT THE FOWLER CENTER
2315 HARMON LAKE ROAD
MAYVILLE, MICHIGAN 48744-9737

General Information Accessible outdoor recreation camp for children and adults with developmental disabilities promoting personal growth in those with special needs. Established in 1957. Owned by The Fowler Center. Affiliated with American Camping Association, Metropolitan Camp Council of Detroit, Michigan Residential Care Association. 202-acre facility located 90 miles north of Detroit. Features: spring-fed lake and beach area; horse stable; organic garden and small animal barn; 4 miles of nature trails; sports fields and courts; creative arts facility.

Profile of Summer Employees Total number: 55; average age: 22; 45% male, 55% female; 12% minorities; 3% high school students; 85% college students; 5% retirees; 5% international; 15% local residents; 8% teachers. Nonsmokers only.

Employment Information Openings are from June 9 to August 15. Spring break, winter break, Christmas break, year-round positions also offered. Jobs available: ▶ *counselors;* ▶ *waterfront staff members* with lifeguard and WSI certification; ▶ *horseback riding instructors* with CHA or equivalent certification; ▶ *outdoor education instructor;* ▶ *organic garden and barn instructor;* ▶ *sports and recreation instructor;* ▶ *creative arts instructor.* All positions offered at $1700–$2300 per season. International students encouraged to apply; must obtain own visa and working papers prior to employment; must apply through recognized agency.

Benefits College credit, on-the-job training, formal ongoing training, on-site room and board at no charge, laundry facilities, health insurance, life-shaping experience, health club membership. Preemployment training of 7 days is required and includes safety and accident prevention, group interaction, first-aid, CPR, leadership, camper-counselor relations, disability awareness. Orientation is paid.

Contact Stephen B. Greene, Executive Director, Camp Fowler at The Fowler Center, 2315 Harmon Lake Road, Mayville, Michigan 48744-9737; 517-673-2050, Fax 517-673-6355, E-mail greenes@msen.com.

CAMP MAAS
4361 PERRYVILLE ROAD
ORTONVILLE, MICHIGAN 48462

General Information Residential camp and outdoor travel program to Alaska and western United States. Established in 1902. Operated by Jewish Community of Metropolitan Detroit. 1,500-acre facility located 50 miles north of Detroit. Features: 8 tennis courts; 2 lakes; 3 ballfields; horseback riding; 6 campsites; full waterfront activities.

Profile of Summer Employees Total number: 350; average age: 21; 50% male, 50% female; 80% college students; 20% international; 50% local residents. Nonsmokers preferred.

Employment Information Openings are from June 15 to August 19. Spring break, winter break, Christmas break positions also offered. Jobs available: ▶ *counselors* at $1000–$1500 per season; ▶ *specialists in all areas* at $1000–$1500 per season; ▶ *supervisors in all areas* at $2000–$3500 per season; ▶ *head nurse* at $3000–$5000 per season; ▶ *song leader* at $2000–$3000 per season. International students encouraged to apply; must apply through recognized agency.

Benefits On-site room and board at no charge, laundry facilities.

Contact Harvey Finkelberg, Executive Director, Camp Maas, Department SJ, 6600 West Maple Road, West Bloomfield, Michigan 48322; 248-661-0600, Fax 248-661-1725.

CAMP MAPLEHURST
12055 WARING ROAD
KEWADIN, MICHIGAN 49648

General Information Residential camp serving 100 campers per session. Wide variety of activities offered. Community spirit and development of decision-making abilities is encouraged among campers. Established in 1955. Owned by TSC Associates. Affiliated with American Camping Association, Midwest Association of Independent Camps. 400-acre facility located 18 miles north of Traverse City. Features: 80-acre private lake; access to a second waterfront on Torch Lake (42 miles of shoreline); 3 tennis courts; horse stables and miles of trails; fields for softball, golf, and soccer; complete arts and crafts facility.

Profile of Summer Employees Total number: 40; average age: 20; 50% male, 50% female; 5% high school students; 70% college students; 5% retirees; 10% international; 10% teachers. Nonsmokers only.

Employment Information Openings are from June 15 to August 20. Jobs available: ▶ 2 *swimming instructors* with WSI and lifeguard certification at $1000–$1600 per season; ▶ 1 *sailing instructor* at $900–$1500 per season; ▶ 1 *tennis instructor* at $900–$1500 per season; ▶ 1 *scuba instructor* at $1000–$1600 per season; ▶ 4 *sports instructors* at $900–$1500 per season; ▶ 2 *cooks* at $150–$350 per week; ▶ 1 *nurse* at $150–$300 per week. International students encouraged to apply; must obtain own visa and working papers prior to employment; must apply through recognized agency.

Benefits College credit, on-the-job training, formal ongoing training, on-site room and board at no charge.

Contact Laurence Cohn, Director, Camp Maplehurst, Department SJ, 1455 Quarton Road, Birmingham, Michigan 48009; 248-647-2646, Fax 248-647-6716, E-mail campmaple@aol.com. Application deadline: June 15.

CAMP WALDEN
5607 SOUTH RIVER ROAD
CHEBOYGAN, MICHIGAN 49721

General Information Coed residential camp serving children ages 7–16 that emphasizes riding, sailing, kayaking, waterskiing, windsurfing, theater, tennis, soccer, gymnastics, photography, fine arts and crafts, computers, wilderness camping, canoeing, and mountain bike trips. Two-, four-, and eight-week sessions available. Established in 1959. Owned by Larry Stevens and Ina Stevens. Affiliated with American Camping Association, Private Independent Camps, Association for Horsemanship Safety and Education. 160-acre facility located 8 miles west of Cheboygan. Features: proximity to Mackinaw Island and Bridge to Michigan's upper peninsula and location of many nature conservancy areas; canoeing, biking, and backpacking in the Great Lakes area; 8 outdoor tennis courts and 2 large athletics fields; wooded camp environment and lake for sailing, skiing, windsurfing, kayaking, and canoeing; 25 horses with English and Western programs; fine arts and crafts facilities for jewelry, ceramics, weaving, silk-screening, painting, and sculpting.

Profile of Summer Employees Total number: 100; average age: 23; 50% male, 50% female; 90% college students; 40% international; 10% teachers. Nonsmokers only.

Employment Information Openings are from June 15 to August 25. Jobs available: ▶ 6 *riding instructors* with CHA certification or equivalent experience; ▶ 2 *certified windsurfing instructors;* ▶ 2 *certified sailing instructors;* ▶ 2 *certified kayaking instructors;* ▶ 2 *certified waterskiing instructors;* ▶ 3 *experienced tennis instructors;* ▶ 1 *certified archery instructor;* ▶ 2 *experienced gymnastics instructors;* ▶ 3 *theater instructors* with training, acting, and directing experience; ▶ 2 *experienced dance instructors;* ▶ 2 *experienced fencing instructors;* ▶ 4 *experienced arts and crafts instructors;* ▶ 2 *experienced natural science instructors;* ▶ 2 *experienced mountain biking instructors;* ▶ 3 *experienced backpack/canoe/trip instructors;* ▶ 4 *swimming instructors* with lifeguard and/or WSI certification. All positions offered at $1500–$2250 per season. International students encouraged to apply; must apply through recognized agency.

Benefits College credit, on-the-job training, formal ongoing training, on-site room and board at no charge, travel reimbursement. Preemployment training of 7 days is required and includes safety and accident prevention, group interaction, first-aid, CPR, leadership, camper-counselor relations. Orientation is paid.

Contact Larry Stevens, Director, Camp Walden, Department SJ, 31070 Applewood Lane, Farmington Hills, Michigan 48331; 810-661-1890, Fax 810-661-1891.

CAMP WESTMINSTER
116 WESTMINSTER DRIVE
ROSCOMMON, MICHIGAN 48653

General Information Residential camp offering a unique combination of activities designed to promote a sense of responsibility and self-worth in a Christian community. Established in 1925. Owned by Westminster Church of Detroit. Affiliated with American Camping Association, Presbyterian Church Camp and Conference Associates, Detroit Metropolitan Camp Council. Situated on 40 acres. Features: location on Higgins Lake; challenge course; sailing program; nature quest program; rustic cabins on beach.

Profile of Summer Employees Total number: 35; average age: 20; 50% male, 50% female; 30% minorities; 25% high school students; 70% college students; 5% retirees; 25% international; 5% teachers. Nonsmokers only.

Employment Information   Openings are from June 10 to August 23. Jobs available: ▶ 1 *waterfront director* with WSI certification at $150–$200 per week; ▶ 6 *lifeguards* with lifeguard training and CPR and First Aid certification at $125–$200 per week; ▶ 20 *counselors/program specialists* with specialized training at $125–$200 per week; ▶ 6 *ropes course facilitators* with certification at $10–$12 per hour; ▶ 1 *registered nurse* at $200–$400 per week; ▶ 1 *program director* at $150–$250 per week; ▶ *kitchen staff* at $125–$500 per week. International students encouraged to apply; must apply through recognized agency.

Benefits   On-the-job training, formal ongoing training, on-site room and board at no charge, laundry facilities.

Contact   Suzanne Getz Bates, Executive Director, Camp Westminster, Department SJ, 17567 Hubbell Avenue, Detroit, Michigan 48235; 313-341-2697 Ext. 204, Fax 313-341-1514, E-mail suzanne_bates@pcusa.org.

CEDAR LODGE
47138 52ND STREET
LAWRENCE, MICHIGAN 49064

General Information   Residential coeducational camp serving 60 campers in a relaxed, loosely structured program with a special emphasis on horsemanship from the beginner to the show jumper. Established in 1964. Owned by Cedar Lodge, Inc. Affiliated with American Camping Association, Association for Horsemanship Safety and Education. 160-acre facility located 105 miles east of Chicago, Illinois. Features: private lake; location in the heart of fruit country; rustic setting; screened wooden cabins; 5 miles of riding trails; 3 riding rings and large boxstall barn; indoor arena.

Profile of Summer Employees   Total number: 16; average age: 20; 25% male, 75% female; 95% college students; 5% retirees; 60% international; 5% local residents. Nonsmokers only.

Employment Information   Openings are from June 10 to August 20. Spring break positions also offered. Jobs available: ▶ 2 *swimming instructors* with swimming experience at $800–$1300 per season; ▶ 1 *riding instructor* with English riding experience at $800–$1300 per season; ▶ 1 *arts and crafts instructor* at $800–$1200 per season; ▶ 1 *music/dance/drama instructor* at $800–$1200 per season; ▶ 1 *biking/trip instructor* at $800–$1200 per season; ▶ *sports instructor* at $800–$1200 per season; ▶ 1 *kitchen assistant* at $800–$1400 per season. International students encouraged to apply; must obtain own visa and working papers prior to employment; must apply through recognized agency.

Benefits   College credit, on-the-job training, formal ongoing training, on-site room and board at no charge, laundry facilities, precamp certification for riding and swimming instructors. Preemployment training is required and includes first-aid, CPR, CHA horsemanship. Orientation is unpaid.

Contact   Amy Edwards, Program Director, Cedar Lodge, Department SJ, PO Box 218, Lawrence, Michigan 49064; 616-674-8071, Fax 616-674-3143, E-mail eddy@cedarlodge.com. Application deadline: June 5.

CIRCLE PINES CENTER SUMMER CAMP
8650 MULLEN ROAD
DELTON, MICHIGAN 49046

General Information   A small, coeducational, residential, multicultural camp for children ages 8–17 promoting peace, cooperation, and social justice. Established in 1938. Owned by Circle Pines Center. Affiliated with American Camping Association, Michigan Federation of Food Co-ops, Co-op America. 284-acre facility located 25 miles northeast of Kalamazoo. Features: spring-fed lake with sandy beach; rolling hills, meadows, and forests; location one hour from Lake Michigan; miles of hiking trails; proximity to 10,000 acres of state land; organic garden and orchard.

Profile of Summer Employees   Total number: 30; average age: 24; 45% male, 55% female; 15% minorities; 40% college students; 5% retirees; 5% international; 5% local residents. Nonsmokers preferred.

Employment Information Openings are from June 16 to August 18. Spring break, winter break, Christmas break, year-round positions also offered. Jobs available: ▶ 1 *waterfront director* (minimum age 21) with WSI, CPR, and lifeguard training/certification at $700–$1000 per season; ▶ 1 *waterfront assistant* with CPR certificate plus lifeguard and first aid training at $600–$800 per season; ▶ 1 *health officer* with RN, LPN, or EMT license (RN preferred) at $100–$125 per week; ▶ 14 *counselors* with experience with children, skills in leading activities at $500–$700 per season; ▶ 4 *cooks* with experience working with whole foods, large groups, and children at $500–$1000 per season; ▶ 2 *maintenance staff members* with ability to work with children and maintenance skills at $300–$500 per month; ▶ 1 *gardener* with organic gardening experience and ability to work with children at $200–$400 per month; ▶ 1 *office manager* with office experience at $600–$800 per season; ▶ 1 *housekeeper/recycling coordinator* with ability to work with children and knowledge of cleaning and recycling at $600–$800 per season. International students encouraged to apply; must obtain own visa and working papers prior to employment.

Benefits College credit, on-the-job training, on-site room and board at no charge, whole food, vegetarian, or meat meals, on-site medical care, nonviolent conflict resolution training. Preemployment training of 7 days is required and includes safety and accident prevention, group interaction, first-aid, CPR, leadership, camper-counselor relations, conflict resolution. Orientation is paid.

Contact Tim Dwyer, Camp Director, Circle Pines Center Summer Camp, Department SJ, 8650 Mullen Road, Delton, Michigan 49046; 616-623-5555, URL http://www.circlepinescenter.org. Application deadline: April 15.

CRYSTALAIRE CAMP
2768 SOUTH SHORE ROAD EAST
FRANKFORT, MICHIGAN 49635

General Information Small, coeducational, loosely-structured residential camp that is noncompetitive and nonsectarian, emphasizing individual growth. Established in 1921. Owned by David B. Reid. Affiliated with American Camping Association. 145-acre facility located 35 miles west of Traverse City. Features: location on Crystal Lake; proximity to Sleeping Bear National Lake shore; rustic setting; extensive use of Lake Michigan Wilderness beaches; Crystalaire at Lookout fronts Lake Michigan and lower Herring Lakes.

Profile of Summer Employees Total number: 30; average age: 22; 50% male, 50% female; 5% minorities; 20% high school students; 65% college students; 5% retirees; 10% international; 5% local residents. Nonsmokers only.

Employment Information Openings are from June 15 to August 18. Jobs available: ▶ 14 *counselors* with lifesaving training and art, sailing, trip, and sports skills at $900–$1500 per season; ▶ 1 *experienced riding instructor* with ability to manage Western-style riding program at $950–$1600 per season; ▶ 3 *experienced sailing/windsurfing instructors* with lifesaving training at $950–$1600 per season; ▶ 1 *art specialist* with ability to organize art program (teacher preferred) at $1000–$2000 per season; ▶ 1 *nurse* with RN, LPN, or EMT license at $1200–$2200 per season; ▶ 1 *trip coordinator* with ability to organize wilderness camping trips, train staff, and maintain bicycles, tents, and camping equipment at $950–$2000 per season; ▶ 2 *experienced cooks* at $1200–$2500 per season; ▶ 1 *experienced waterfront director* with WSI certification at $1200–$2400 per season; ▶ 1 *stable helper* at $60–$150 per week; ▶ 5 *junior counselors* (high school students) at $500–$700 per season; ▶ *sports specialist* with experience in competitive and noncompetitive sports and games at $1000–$1500 per season; ▶ *experienced assistant director/program director* with ability to conduct programs for small and large groups at $1500–$2500 per season. International students encouraged to apply; must obtain own visa and working papers prior to employment; must apply through recognized agency.

Benefits College credit, formal ongoing training, on-site room and board at no charge, CPR/first aid training, vegetarian menu options. Preemployment training of 6 days is required and includes safety and accident prevention, group interaction, first-aid, CPR, leadership, camper-counselor relations. Orientation is paid.

Contact David B. Reid, Director, Crystalaire Camp, 2768 South Shore Road East, Frankfort, Michigan 49635; 616-352-7589, Fax 616-352-6609, E-mail khouston@manistee-isd.k12.mi.us.

CYO BOYS CAMP
1295 LAKESHORE ROAD
CARSONVILLE, MICHIGAN 48419

General Information CYO summer camps are open to boys ages 7½–16. The Pioneer Program is especially designed to meet the needs of experienced campers ages 14–16. Special programs for developmentally disabled youth are also available. Established in 1946. Owned by Catholic Youth Organization- Archdiocese of Detroit. Affiliated with American Camping Association. 30-acre facility located 90 miles northwest of Detroit. Features: location on Lake Huron; sandy beaches; acres of woods and nature trails; off-camp canoe trips and camping; outdoor challenge course; swimming, archery, baseball, soccer, and volleyball.

Profile of Summer Employees Total number: 40; 90% male, 10% female; 25% minorities; 45% high school students; 50% college students; 5% retirees; 10% teachers. Nonsmokers preferred.

Employment Information Openings are from June 18 to August 5. Year-round positions also offered. Jobs available: ▶ *waterfront director/assistant* with WSI certification at $1000–$1200 per season; ▶ *archery director* at $800–$1000 per season; ▶ *arts and crafts director* at $800–$1000 per season; ▶ *group counselors/assistants* at $800–$1000 per season; ▶ *nurse or health officer* with RN, LPN, or EMT with CPR training at $1000–$1400 per season; ▶ *counselor-in-training* at $650 per season; ▶ *business manager* at $800–$1000 per season. International students encouraged to apply; must obtain own visa and working papers prior to employment; must apply through recognized agency.

Benefits On-the-job training, on-site room and board at no charge, health insurance, multi-cultural staff.

Contact Ebony Padgett, Office Manager, CYO Boys Camp, 305 Michigan Avenue, 9th Floor, Detroit, Michigan 48266; 313-963-9758, Fax 313-963-7179.

CYO GIRLS CAMP
1564 LAKESHORE ROAD
PORT SANILAC, MICHIGAN 48462

General Information CYO summer camps are open to girls ages 7½–16. The Pioneer Program is especially designed to meet the needs of experienced campers ages 14–16. Special programs for developmentally disabled youth are also available. Established in 1946. Owned by Catholic Youth Organization Archdiocese of Detroit. Affiliated with American Camping Association. 30-acre facility located 90 miles north of Detroit. Features: location on the shores of Lake Huron, with long sandy beaches; acres of woods and nature trails; off-camp canoe trips; outdoor challenge course (ropes course); volleyball, softball, soccer, swimming, and archery facilities.

Profile of Summer Employees Total number: 40; 10% male, 90% female; 25% minorities; 40% high school students; 50% college students; 10% retirees; 15% teachers. Nonsmokers preferred.

Employment Information Openings are from June 18 to August 5. Year-round positions also offered. Jobs available: ▶ 2 *waterfront director/assistant* with WSI certification at $1000–$1200 per season; ▶ 1 *archery director* at $800–$1000 per season; ▶ *arts and crafts director* at $800–$900 per season; ▶ *group counselors/assistants* at $800–$1400 per season; ▶ *nurse or health officer* with RN, LPN, EMT, or advanced first aid with CPR at $1000–$1200 per season; ▶ *counselor-in-training* at $650 per season; ▶ *business manager* at $800–$1000 per season. International students encouraged to apply; must obtain own visa and working papers prior to employment; must apply through recognized agency.

Benefits On-the-job training, on-site room and board at no charge, health insurance, multi-cultural staff.

Contact Ebony Padgett, Office Manager, CYO Girls Camp, 305 Michigan Avenue, 9th Floor, Detroit, Michigan 48226; 313-963-9758, Fax 313-963-7179.

DOUBLE JJ RESORT RANCH
PO BOX 94
ROTHBURY, MICHIGAN 49452

General Information Resort ranch for adults. Golf club open to the public. Established in 1937. Owned by Joan and Bob Lipsitz. Affiliated with Circle Michigan, West Michigan Tourist Association, White Lake, Muskegon, Grand Rapids Chamber of Commerce. 1,000-acre facility located 20 miles north of Muskegon. Features: heated pool and spa; private lake; wooded acres; location near sand dunes of Lake Michigan; 18-hole championship golf course; horseback riding.

Profile of Summer Employees Total number: 200; average age: 25; 50% male, 50% female; 2% minorities; 5% high school students; 50% college students; 5% retirees; 8% international; 30% local residents.

Employment Information Openings are from May 1 to November 1. Year-round positions also offered. Jobs available: ▶ 9 *talented entertainers* (guitarists and singers) with outgoing personality at $150–$200 per week; ▶ 6 *waiters/waitresses* at $130 per week; ▶ 5 *experienced prep cooks/bakers* at $150–$200 per week; ▶ 20 *lawn maintenance personnel* at $130–$200 per week; ▶ 1 *experienced disc jockey* at $150–$200 per week; ▶ 6 *housekeepers* at $150–$200 per week; ▶ 8 *experienced wranglers* at $150–$220 per week; ▶ 6 *snack bar/bar staff members* (minimum age 21) at $130 per week; ▶ 2 *dishwashers* at $150 per week; ▶ 1 *dining room manager* with waiter/waitressing experience at $150–$220 per week; ▶ 6 *office staff members* with computer experience and ability to answer phones and make reservations at $150 per week; ▶ 6 *pro shop/gift shop staff members* at $150 per week; ▶ 10 *golf course personnel* at $150 per week; ▶ 10 *golf course groundskeepers* at $150 per week. International students encouraged to apply; must apply through recognized agency.

Benefits College credit, on-the-job training, on-site room and board at no charge, laundry facilities, use of all facilities.

Contact Joan Lipsitz, Owner, Double JJ Resort Ranch, Department SJ, PO Box 94, Rothbury, Michigan 49452; 616-894-4444, Fax 616-893-5355.

EL RANCHO STEVENS
2332 EAST DIXON LAKE ROAD
GAYLORD, MICHIGAN 49735

General Information Family resort serving 80 people weekly, specializing in horses, waterskiing, and children's programs. Established in 1947. Owned by Steven S. Stevens. Affiliated with West Michigan Tourist Association, Gaylord Chamber of Commerce, Michigan Lodging Association. 1,000-acre facility located 3 miles southeast of Gaylord. Features: heated pool; indoor recreation room; lake (DNR stocked); tennis court and archery range; dining room; 500 acres of riding trails.

Profile of Summer Employees Total number: 25; average age: 25; 20% male, 80% female; 10% minorities; 10% high school students; 75% college students; 10% retirees; 25% local residents. Nonsmokers preferred.

Employment Information Openings are from May 29 to September 5. Jobs available: ▶ 5 *waitresses/waiters* at $150–$180 per week; ▶ 2 *experienced cooks* at $150–$200 per week; ▶ 2 *kitchen helpers* at $150–$180 per week; ▶ 3 *housekeepers* at $150–$180 per week; ▶ 1 *waterskiing instructor/boat driver* (minimum age 18) with knowledge of water safety rules at $150–$180 per week; ▶ 2 *experienced riding instructors/trail guides* (minimum age 18) at $150–$180 per week; ▶ 3 *children's counselors* at $150–$180 per week; ▶ 1 *recreational director* with ability to work with people of all ages at $150–$180 per week; ▶ 2 *bartenders/barmaids* (minimum age 18) at $150–$180 per week; ▶ 2 *office personnel* with good phone, typing, and bookkeeping skills at $150–$180 per week.

Benefits College credit, on-the-job training, on-site room and board at no charge. Preemployment training of 1 day is required and includes safety and accident prevention, group interaction, basic ranch operation. Orientation is paid.

Contact Personnel Department, El Rancho Stevens, PO Box 495, Gaylord, Michigan 49735; 517-732-5090. Application deadline: May 15.

LAKE OF THE WOODS AND GREENWOODS CAMPS
DECATUR, MICHIGAN 49045

General Information Private residential summer camp for children with a program that runs 4 to 8 weeks. Established in 1935. Owned by Marc Seeger. Affiliated with American Camping Association, Midwest Association of Private Camps. 50-acre facility located 20 miles southwest of Kalamazoo. Features: modern spacious cabins; location in southwestern Michigan on ¼-mile private lake frontage; recreational facilities; 4 outdoor tennis courts; driving range and 6-hole modified golf course; modern riding stables, 2 corrals and riding trails located on camp grounds.

Profile of Summer Employees Total number: 65; average age: 21; 50% male, 50% female; 2% minorities; 90% college students; 10% international. Nonsmokers preferred.

Employment Information Openings are from June 16 to August 19. Year-round positions also offered. Jobs available: ▶ 8 *swimming instructors* with lifeguard training and WSI certification at $1500 per season; ▶ 3 *sailing instructors* at $1300 per season; ▶ 3 *riding instructors* at $1500 per season; ▶ 1 *computer instructor* with Basic, Logo, and PASCAL experience (preferred) at $1300 per season; ▶ 7 *waterskiing instructors* with boat driving experience at $1300 per season; ▶ 2 *tennis instructors* at $1300 per season; ▶ 1 *golf instructor* at $1300 per season; ▶ 1 *gymnastics instructor* at $1300 per season; ▶ 2 *arts and crafts instructors* at $1300 per season; ▶ 1 *dramatics instructor* at $1300 per season; ▶ 1 *dance/aerobics instructor* at $1300 per season; ▶ 2 *sports coaches* at $1300 per season; ▶ 2 *nurses* with RN license (preferred) at $2800 per season; ▶ 2 *experienced office persons* at $1300 per season; ▶ *kitchen personnel* (cooks and assistants) at $175–$500 per week; ▶ *riflery instructor* (minimum age 19) at $1300 per season; ▶ *archery instructor* (minimum age 19) at $1300 per season; ▶ *rowing/canoe instructor* (minimum age 19) at $1300 per season; ▶ *model rocketry instructor* (minimum age 19) at $1300 per season; ▶ *ceramics instructor* (minimum age 19) at $1300 per season. International students encouraged to apply; must apply through recognized agency.

Benefits College credit, on-site room and board at no charge, travel reimbursement, free copy of video yearbook, subsidized laundry. Preemployment training of 7 days is required and includes safety and accident prevention, group interaction, first-aid, CPR, leadership, camper-counselor relations, activity training. Orientation is paid.

Contact Marc Seeger, Owner/Director, Lake of the Woods and Greenwoods Camps, Department SJ, 1765 Maple Street, Northfield, Illinois 60093; 847-446-2444, Fax 847-446-2454, E-mail lwcgwc@aol.com. Application deadline: June 15.

MICHIGAN TECHNOLOGICAL UNIVERSITY SUMMER YOUTH PROGRAM
1400 TOWNSEND DRIVE
HOUGHTON, MICHIGAN 49931

General Information Summer program for students ages 12–18 in 57 explorations designed to introduce students to careers and knowledge (theater, engineering, pottery, and more). Established in 1885. Operated by Michigan Technological University. Located 470 miles north of Detroit. Features: campus located on the Portage Canal; access to Student Development Complex (pool, racquetball, weight room, tennis, and gym); location in the scenic Copper Country.

Profile of Summer Employees Total number: 100; average age: 20; 50% male, 50% female; 20% minorities; 97% college students; 1% retirees; 10% local residents; 25% teachers. Nonsmokers preferred.

Employment Information Openings are from June 8 to August 10. Year-round positions also offered. Jobs available: ▶ *counselors* at $195 per week; ▶ *teaching assistants* at $175 per week. International students encouraged to apply; must obtain own visa and working papers prior to employment.

Benefits On-the-job training, on-site room and board at no charge, laundry facilities.

Contact Beth Balcom, Youth Programs Secretary, Michigan Technological University Summer Youth Program, Department SJ, Michigan Technological University 1400 Townsend Drive, Houghton, Michigan 49931; 906-487-2219, Fax 906-487-3101, E-mail edopp@mtu.edu, URL http://www.yth.mtu.edu/syp/syp.html.

MICHILLINDA BEACH LODGE
5207 SCENIC DRIVE
WHITEHALL, MICHIGAN 49461

General Information Modified American-plan resort with 50 guest units overlooking Lake Michigan. Established in 1928. Owned by Donald E. Eilers. Affiliated with West Michigan Tourist Association, Michigan Lodging Association, American Hotel Association. 22-acre facility located 25 miles north of Muskegon. Features: location on Lake Michigan Beach; tennis courts; swimming and wading pools; miniature golf.

Profile of Summer Employees Total number: 35; average age: 18; 33% male, 67% female; 50% high school students; 50% college students; 90% local residents. Nonsmokers preferred.

Employment Information Openings are from June 12 to September 6. Spring break positions also offered. Jobs available: ▶ 10 *housekeeping staff members;* ▶ 6 *kitchen staff members;* ▶ 5 *bellpersons;* ▶ 3 *grounds maintenance staff members;* ▶ 9 *dining room staff members.*

Benefits College credit, on-the-job training, laundry facilities, bonus in place of tips, on-site rooms are available for $30 a month (for women only), on-site meals available for $4 per day.

Contact Don Eilers, Manager, Michillinda Beach Lodge, Department SJ, 5207 Scenic Drive, Whitehall, Michigan 49461; 616-893-1895, Fax 616-893-1805. Application deadline: April 1.

MCGAW YMCA CAMP ECHO AND THE OUTDOOR DISCOVERY CENTER
2000 WEST 32ND STREET
FREMONT, MICHIGAN 49412

General Information Residential coeducational camp serving 250 youngsters in two-week sessions. Emphasis is on building self-esteem through YMCA principles. Outdoor education center operates during nonsummer months for Michigan schools and interest groups. Established in 1899. Owned by YMCA Camp Echo. Operated by McGaw YMCA. 460-acre facility located 40 miles north of Grand Rapids. Features: location on scenic peninsula; cabins with porches overlooking lake; forest and field areas; nature trail; extended horse and bike trails; separate beaches for sailing, canoeing, waterskiing, and swimming instruction; low and high elements ropes courses.

Profile of Summer Employees Total number: 75; average age: 22; 50% male, 50% female; 10% minorities; 25% high school students; 75% college students; 5% international; 75% local residents. Nonsmokers only.

Employment Information Openings are from April 19 to October 3. Jobs available: ▶ 15 *senior counselors* with standard first aid and CPR certification at $110–$120 per week; ▶ 1 *aquatic director* with first aid, CPR, and Lifeguard Instructor certification at $125–$150 per week; ▶ 1 *arts and crafts director* with standard first aid and CPR certification at $110–$125 per week; ▶ 1 *office manager* with first aid and CPR certification at $125–$150 per week; ▶ 10 *adventure trip leaders* with lifeguard, wilderness, first aid, and CPR certification at $150–$200 per week; ▶ 2 *wilderness site leaders* with lifeguard, first aid, and CPR certification at $130–$150 per week; ▶ 1 *wrangler* with CHA training and first aid and CPR certification at $130–$150 per week; ▶ 1 *assistant wrangler* with standard first aid and CPR certification at $120–$140 per week; ▶ 5 *health officers* with RN license and CPR and standard first aid certification at $250–$265 per week; ▶ 1 *van driver* with standard first aid and CPR certification at $100–$125 per week; ▶ 3 *cooks* with CPR certification and experience with large groups at $100–$300 per week; ▶ 3 *sailing/canoeing/waterskiing directors* with standard first aid, CPR, and lifeguard certification at $110–$130 per week; ▶ 12 *outdoor education staff members* at $110 per week. International students encouraged to apply; must apply through recognized agency.

Benefits College credit, on-the-job training, on-site room and board at no charge, use of facility, YMCA membership.
Contact Robert Guy, Director, McGaw YMCA Camp Echo and the Outdoor Discovery Center, Department SJ, 1000 Grove Street, Evanston, Illinois 60201; 847-475-7400, Fax 847-475-7959.

MINNESOTA

AUDUBON CENTER OF THE NORTHWOODS
PO BOX 530
SANDSTONE, MINNESOTA 55072

General Information Residential environmental learning center with ecology tours for adults, a multilevel youth ecology camp (North Woods Wilderness School), and a raptor rehabilitation center. Established in 1971. Owned by Northwoods Audubon Center, Inc. Affiliated with Association of Nature Center Administrators, National Audubon Society. 535-acre facility located 75 miles southwest of Duluth. Features: 500-acre lake with extensive frontage; proximity to extensive state wildlands and rivers; Northern Raptor Rehabilitation Center.

Profile of Summer Employees Total number: 6; average age: 22; 50% male, 50% female; 10% minorities; 90% college students; 20% international; 10% local residents; 10% teachers. Nonsmokers preferred.

Employment Information Openings are from June 1 to August 31. Year-round positions also offered. Jobs available: ▶ 1 *raptor rehabilitation/education staff member;* ▶ 4 *environmental education staff members* with WSI and first aid certification; ▶ 1 *administrative staff member;* ▶ 1 *land management staff member.* All positions offered at $200 per month. International students encouraged to apply; must obtain own visa and working papers prior to employment.

Benefits On-the-job training, on-site room and board at no charge, variety of environmental experiences, variety of clientele. Preemployment training of 3 to 5 days is required and includes safety and accident prevention, group interaction, first-aid, leadership, camper-counselor relations. Orientation is paid.

Contact Kate Crowley, Intern Coordinator, Audubon Center of the Northwoods, Department SJ, PO Box 530, Sandstone, Minnesota 55072; 320-245-2148, Fax 320-245-5272, E-mail hn3329@ handsnet.org. Application deadline: March 15.

CAMP BUCKSKIN
BOX 389
ELY, MINNESOTA 55731

General Information Residential camp offering two 32-day sessions for youths with academic and/or social skills difficulties (learning disabilities, Attention Deficit Disorder, and related difficulties). Established in 1959. Owned by Mr. and Mrs. R. S. Bauer. Affiliated with American Camping Association. 165-acre facility located 80 miles northeast of Duluth. Features: location in the scenic Superior National Forest; extensive lakeshore for swimming and canoeing activities; separate canoe trip program in Boundary Waters Canoe Area wilderness; variety of environments for nature program (lakeshore, river, pond, marsh, woodlands, and meadows); well-equipped library for program and staff use; several large sports fields.

Profile of Summer Employees Total number: 75; average age: 22; 50% male, 50% female; 5% minorities; 12% high school students; 70% college students; 10% international; 10% local residents. Nonsmokers only.

Employment Information Openings are from June 3 to August 22. Jobs available: ▶ 8 *counselors/swimming instructors* with WSI certification, lifeguard training, standard first aid, and CPR (preferred) at $1200–$1700 per season; ▶ 10 *counselors/canoeing instructors* with lifeguard training, standard first aid, and CPR (preferred) at $1200–$1700 per season; ▶ 6 *experienced counselors/nature and environment instructors* with certification in programs such as NOLS and Nature Quest (preferred) at $1200–$1700 per season; ▶ 6 *counselors/arts and crafts instructors* with creativity and ability to teach at $1200–$1700 per season; ▶ 3 *experienced counselors/archery instructors* with certification from such organizations as the National Archery Association at $1200–$1700 per season; ▶ 3 *counselors/riflery instructors* with gun and range safety training with the National Rifle Association, military, or similar agency (preferred) at $1200–$1700 per season; ▶ 8 *reading teachers* with license in elementary or secondary education or special education certification (preferred) at $1500–$2000 per season; ▶ 2 *office assistants* with good typing and phone skills (computer experience a plus) at $1200–$1700 per season; ▶ 5 *kitchen assistants* with positive attitude and ability to work with others at $1050–$1350 per season; ▶ 8 *trip counselors* with lifeguard, CPR, and standard first aid training at $1300–$1850 per season; ▶ 2 *nurses* with RN license (preferred), or LPN license.

Benefits College credit, on-the-job training, formal ongoing training, on-site room and board at no charge, possible internships, increased responsibilities and compensation for returning staff, travel stipend for returning staff. Preemployment training of 10 days is required and includes safety and accident prevention, group interaction, leadership, camper-counselor relations, behavior management. Orientation is paid.

Contact Thomas Bauer, Director, Camp Buckskin, Department SJ, 8700 West 36th Street, Suite 6W, St. Louis Park, Minnesota 55426-3936; 612-930-3544, Fax 612-938-6996, E-mail camp_buckskin@prodigy.com. Application deadline: May 30.

CAMP CHIPPEWA
CASS LAKE, MINNESOTA 56633

General Information Residential camp for 60 boys offering land and water activities including extensive Canadian fishing, canoe, and kayak tripping. Established in 1935. Operated by Camp Chippewa for Boys, Inc. Affiliated with American Camping Association, Midwest Association of Independent Camps. 88-acre facility located 250 miles north of Minneapolis. Features: location in the Chippewa National Forest; two lake fronts of ½ mile each and clear sand bottom lakes; fishing lodge on Canadian island in Rainy Lake (north campus); three tennis courts, athletic field; NRA range; target and field archery ranges.

Profile of Summer Employees Total number: 26; average age: 25; 95% male, 5% female; 5% minorities; 10% high school students; 60% college students; 10% international; 5% local residents; 10% teachers. Nonsmokers only.

Employment Information Openings are from June 10 to August 14. Jobs available: ▶ *NRA rifle instructor* with NRA certification at $1000–$1200 per season; ▶ *swimming instructor* with WSI certification at $1000–$1400 per season; ▶ *archery instructor* at $1000–$1200 per season; ▶ *general cabin counselors* at $1000–$1200 per season. International students encouraged to apply; must obtain own visa and working papers prior to employment; must apply through recognized agency.

Benefits On-the-job training, on-site room and board at no charge, laundry facilities, travel reimbursement, health insurance. Preemployment training of 7 days is required and includes safety and accident prevention, group interaction, leadership. Orientation is paid.

Contact John P. Endres, Director, Camp Chippewa, 11427 North Pinehurst Circle, Mequon, Wisconsin 53092; 414-241-5733, Fax 414-241-3893. Application deadline: March 1.

CAMP COURAGE
8046 83RD STREET, NW
MAPLE LAKE, MINNESOTA 55358

General Information Programs offered for physically disabled children and adults, including adventure camping for the deaf and speech therapy for speech/language-impaired children. Established in 1955. Owned by Courage Center. Affiliated with American Camping Association.

300-acre facility located 50 miles west of Minneapolis. Features: 2 lakes; extensive freshwater frontage; indoor heated, accessible pool; indoor gymnasium and recreation center; forest areas; accessible site for mobility-impaired individuals; horses; accessible riding ring and riding trails.

Profile of Summer Employees Total number: 100; average age: 22; 50% male, 50% female; 8% minorities; 10% high school students; 80% college students; 1% retirees; 8% international; 60% local residents; 9% teachers.

Employment Information Openings are from June 7 to September 1. Year-round positions also offered. Jobs available: ▶ 6 *waterfront personnel* with WSI/lifeguard certification at $145–$165 per week; ▶ 36 *counselors* at $145–$165 per week; ▶ 3 *nurses* with RN, LPN, or GN license at $330–$435 per week; ▶ 20 *program specialists* with appropriate certification for area at $150–$175 per week; ▶ 10 *speech clinicians* with M.S. in speech pathology/communications disorders at $335–$455 per week.

Benefits College credit, on-the-job training, formal ongoing training, on-site room and board at no charge, laundry facilities, health insurance, tuition reimbursement, scholarships. Preemployment training of 5 to 7 days is required and includes safety and accident prevention, group interaction, first-aid, CPR, leadership, camper-counselor relations, orientation to disability. Orientation is paid.

Contact Roger Upcraft, Program Manager, Camp Courage, Department SJ, 8046 83rd Street, NW, Maple Lake, Minnesota 55358; 320-963-3121, Fax 320-963-3698, E-mail camping@mtn. org, URL http://www.lkdllink.net/~courage. Application deadline: May 31.

CAMP LINCOLN FOR BOYS/CAMP LAKE HUBERT FOR GIRLS
BOX 308
LAKE HUBERT, MINNESOTA 56459

General Information Private residential camps for boys and girls ages 7–17 offering a variety of land and water sports. Established in 1909. Owned by Sam Cote. Affiliated with American Camping Association, Association of Independent Camps. 800-acre facility located 150 miles north of Minneapolis. Features: 2 miles of camp shoreline on spring-fed Lake Hubert; 800 acres of trails in birch and pine forests; archery, riflery, sailing, riding, tennis, sports, canoeing, kayaking, windsurfing, fishing, biking, ecology; log cabins.

Profile of Summer Employees Total number: 200; average age: 22; 50% male, 50% female; 5% minorities; 80% college students; 2% retirees; 15% international; 15% local residents; 5% teachers. Nonsmokers preferred.

Employment Information Openings are from June 1 to August 25. Jobs available: ▶ *counselors* at $1250–$1650 per season; ▶ *head counselors* at $1250–$1650 per season; ▶ *activity directors* at $1250–$1650 per season; ▶ *cooks, bakers* at $1700–$2200 per season; ▶ *general food service staff members* at $1700–$1900 per season; ▶ *drivers* at $1250–$1650 per season; ▶ *office staff members* at $1250–$1650 per season; ▶ *nurses* at $1500–$1900 per season. International students encouraged to apply; must obtain own visa and working papers prior to employment; must apply through recognized agency.

Benefits College credit, on-the-job training, formal ongoing training, on-site room and board at no charge, travel reimbursement. Preemployment training of 8 days is required and includes safety and accident prevention, group interaction, leadership, camper-counselor relations. Orientation is paid.

Contact Sam Cote/Bill Jones, Directors, Camp Lincoln for Boys/Camp Lake Hubert for Girls, 5201 Eden Circle, Suite 202, Minneapolis, Minnesota 55436; 800-242-1909, Fax 612-922-7149, E-mail clclh@uslink.net. Application deadline: April 1.

CAMP THUNDERBIRD FOR BOYS/CAMP THUNDERBIRD FOR GIRLS
ROUTE 2, BOX 225
BEMIDJI, MINNESOTA 56601

General Information Separate residential facilities serving 150 girls and 200 boys from forty U.S. cities and five other countries. Established in 1946. Owned by Camp Thunderbird, Inc. Affiliated with American Camping Association. 700-acre facility located 12 miles south of Bemidji. Features: pine and hardwood forest; 7-mile shoreline on serene, crystal-clear, sand-bottom lake; extensive riding and hiking trails; low ropes teams course with climbing/rappelling wall; 3 athletic fields; volleyball and basketball courts; 7 outdoor asphalt tennis courts.

Profile of Summer Employees Total number: 200; average age: 24; 55% male, 45% female; 5% minorities; 12% high school students; 60% college students; 1% retirees; 10% international; 1% local residents; 10% teachers. Nonsmokers preferred.

Employment Information Openings are from June 1 to August 12. Year-round positions also offered. Jobs available: ▶ 35 *cabin counselors* (minimum age 19) with freshman year of college completed, experience working with children, high-energy, caring attitude, ability to assist or teach in several camp activities, and outdoor orientation; ▶ 2 *certified riflery instructors* (minimum age 21) with teaching experience (required); ▶ 1 *arts and crafts specialist* (minimum age 21) with experience as an art teacher or student status preferred (completion of junior year required); ▶ 3 *experienced horseback specialists* (minimum age 21) with experience in Western and English Hunt Seat specialties, completion of junior year of college, and CHA or HSA certification preferred, but will send to clinic for certification; ▶ 1 *waterfront director* (minimum age 25) with WSI certification, college degree, and knowledge of various water sports; ▶ 10 *swimming instructors* (minimum age 22) with WSI certification and teaching experience (preferred); ▶ 4 *certified sailing instructors* (minimum age 21) with sailing and lifeguard certification; ▶ 2 *unit directors* (minimum age 22) with experience encompassing staff supervision and direct leadership of children in outdoor recreation/camp activities and college degree; ▶ 1 *program director* (minimum age 21) with experience encompassing staff supervision and direct leadership of children in outdoor recreation/camp activities and college degree; ▶ 1 *trip director* (minimum age 21) with experience in diverse kinds of wilderness trips and equipment use and college degree; ▶ 15 *wilderness and trip leaders* (minimum age 21) with certifications in CPR, lifeguard, and advanced first aid (must be comfortable and confident living in the wilderness); ▶ 3 *nurses* with RN or LPN license; ▶ 10 *kitchen personnel* (minimum age 19) with ability to assist with kitchen operations, food preparation, dishwashing, and cleanup and one year of college completed; ▶ 2 *office personnel* (minimum age 20) with bookkeeping and computer knowledge, ability to handle camper/staff cash accounts, sophomore year of college completed, and average or above-average typing skills. International students encouraged to apply; must apply through recognized agency.

Benefits College credit, on-the-job training, on-site room and board at no charge, laundry facilities, travel reimbursement, medical services, families accepted.

Contact Carol A. Sigoloff, Camp Thunderbird for Boys/Camp Thunderbird for Girls, Department SJ, 967 Gardenview Office Parkway, St. Louis, Missouri 63141; 314-567-3167, Fax 314-567-7218. Application deadline: April 30.

DEEP PORTAGE CONSERVATION RESERVE
ROUTE 1, BOX 129
HACKENSACK, MINNESOTA 56452

General Information Environmental education and resource management demonstration for school classes, in-house summer camps, families, tourists, natural resource professionals, and nature-related hobby groups. Established in 1973. Owned by Cass County. Operated by Deep Portage Conservation Foundation. Affiliated with Alliance for Environmental Education, National Audubon Society, Izaak Walton League. 6,107-acre facility located 50 miles north of Brainerd. Features: 6,107-acre demonstration working forest; resort area with over 400 lakes in a 35-mile radius; 30 miles of recreational trails; proximity to Chippewa National Forest (with largest breeding population of bald eagles in the lower 48 states); interpretive center with museum, wildflower garden, and bookstore; 27,000-square foot conference center with classrooms, theater, and overnight accommodations for 120 people.

Profile of Summer Employees Total number: 14; average age: 22; 50% male, 50% female; 10% minorities; 10% high school students; 70% college students; 10% international.

Employment Information Openings are from June 5 to August 25. Year-round positions also offered. Jobs available: ▶ 12 *instructors/naturalists* with college training in related fields at $125–$150 per week.

Benefits On-the-job training, formal ongoing training, on-site room and board at no charge, laundry facilities.

Contact Mr. Dale Yerger, Camp Director, Deep Portage Conservation Reserve, Department SJ, Rt. 1, Box 129, Hackensack, Minnesota 56452; 218-682-2325, Fax 218-682-3121, E-mail portage@uslink.net, URL http://www.deep-portage.org.

DRIFTWOOD FAMILY RESORT & GOLF
ROUTE 1, BOX 404
PINE RIVER, MINNESOTA 56474

General Information Resort specializing in family vacations with an emphasis on many different types of recreation. Established in 1902. Owned by Tim and Sue Leagjeld. Located 30 miles north of Brainerd. Features: 9-hole golf course; heated outdoor pool and indoor spa; 2 tennis courts, shuffleboard; canoes, kayaks, funbugs, row boats; museum; hiking trails.

Profile of Summer Employees Total number: 20; average age: 20; 50% male, 50% female. Nonsmokers preferred.

Employment Information Openings are from May 25 to September 20. Jobs available: ▶ 8 *waiters/waitresses;* ▶ 1 *dining room host/hostess;* ▶ 2 *cooks or cook's helpers;* ▶ 2 *cabin maids;* ▶ 2 *front desk/office staff members;* ▶ 1 *recreation director;* ▶ 2 *lawn/golf maintenance staff members/gardeners.* All positions offered at $800–$1000 per month.

Benefits On-site room and board at $300 per month, laundry facilities, use of all recreational facilities, end-of-season bonus to staff who stay to the end of their contract period, extra pay for those who participate in weekly staff and family musical show.

Contact Tim and Sue Leagjeld, Owners, Driftwood Family Resort & Golf, Route 1, Box 404, Pine River, Minnesota 56474; 218-568-4221, Fax 218-568-4222, URL http://www.driftwoodresort.com.

FRIENDSHIP VENTURES/CAMP FRIENDSHIP
10509 108TH STREET, NW
ANNANDALE, MINNESOTA 55302

General Information Residential camp serving children and adults with developmental disabilities. Established in 1964. Owned by Friendship Ventures. Affiliated with American Camping Association. 100-acre facility located 60 miles north of Minneapolis. Features: location on a large lake; 80 wooded acres; resort-style camping; challenge/adventure course; hayride and hiking trails; tent-camping sites, including an island.

Profile of Summer Employees Total number: 100; average age: 20; 25% male, 75% female; 5% minorities; 15% high school students; 85% college students; 10% international; 20% local residents; 5% teachers. Nonsmokers preferred.

Employment Information Openings are from June 1 to August 31. Winter break, Christmas break, year-round positions also offered. Jobs available: ▶ 2 *laundry/housekeeping staff members;* ▶ 60 *counselors* at $120–$155 per week; ▶ 1 *waterfront director* with WSI and lifeguard certification at $130–$160 per week; ▶ 3 *waterfront lifeguards* with lifeguard WSI and lifeguard certification (preferred) at $120–$155 per week; ▶ 1 *boating specialist* with knowledge of outboard motors, canoes, rowboats, and pontoon boats at $120–$155 per week; ▶ 1 *canteen/ camp store manager* with record-keeping skills at $120–$155 per week; ▶ 2 *office support staff* with computer, typing, phone, and filing experience at $120–$155 per week; ▶ 1 *adventure specialist* with ropes course experience and biking and canoeing skills at $120–$155 per week; ▶ 4 *nurses* with RN, LPN, or GN license or B.S.N. degree; ▶ 1 *dietary specialist* with experience in food service area with an emphasis on special diets; ▶ 3 *weekend counselors* with physical strength, mental alertness, and at least one year of college completed at $125–$130 per week; ▶ 12 *junior counselors* with physical and emotional strength, mental alertness, creativity, flexibility, and high school student status (successful volunteer experience may be substituted for the age requirement) at $90 per week; ▶ 2 *arts and crafts specialists* with current major in therapeutic recreation, occupational therapy, or art education/therapy or experience planning and implementing arts and crafts activities/projects at $120–$155 per week; ▶ 2 *music specialists* with current major in music, music therapy, or special education and experience planning and implementing activities at $120–$155 per week; ▶ 1 *outdoor specialist* with current major in an environmental, outdoor, or education field at $120–$155 per week; ▶ 1 *recreation specialist* with current major in recreation, physical education, or adaptive physical recreation and leadership skills involving group activities at $120–$155 per week; ▶ 1 *public relations assistant* with current major in journalism, photography, or related field and experience with a 35mm camera at $120–$155 per week; ▶ 2 *dining hall workers* with experience working in food service or dining hall areas; ▶ 1 *special interest session leader* with excellent organization skills and willingness to work with varied curriculum of program areas at $120–$155 per week; ▶ 1 *camping specialist* with tent camping and outdoor experience and environmental education knowledge at $120–$155 per week. International students encouraged to apply; must apply through recognized agency.

Benefits College credit, on-the-job training, formal ongoing training, on-site room and board at no charge, laundry facilities. Preemployment training of 3 to 6 days is required and includes safety and accident prevention, group interaction, first-aid, CPR, leadership, camper-counselor relations, disability awareness training. Orientation is paid.

Contact Joanne Fieldseth, Human Resources Director, Friendship Ventures/Camp Friendship, Department SJ, 10509 108th Street, NW, Annandale, Minnesota 55302; 320-274-8376, Fax 320-274-3238, E-mail friendl@spacestar.com. Application deadline: May 1.

FRIENDSHIP VENTURES/EDEN WOOD CAMP
6350 INDIAN CHIEF ROAD
EDEN PRAIRIE, MINNESOTA 55347

General Information Residential and day camp serving children and adults with developmental disabilities. Established in 1958. Owned by Friendship Ventures. Affiliated with American Camping Association. 12-acre facility located 5 miles west of Minneapolis. Features: location near large metropolitan area; wooded acres; resort-style camping; hiking trails; tent camping sites.

Profile of Summer Employees Total number: 40; average age: 20; 25% male, 75% female; 5% minorities; 15% high school students; 85% college students; 10% international; 20% local residents. Nonsmokers preferred.

Employment Information Openings are from June 1 to August 31. Year-round positions also offered. Jobs available: ▶ 2 *laundry/housekeeping staff members;* ▶ 30 *counselors* at $120–$155 per week; ▶ 2 *lifeguards* with lifeguard WSI and lifeguard certification (preferred) at $120–$155 per week; ▶ 6 *travel leaders* with leadership skills and valid driver's license at $120–$155 per week; ▶ 1 *office support staff* with computer, typing, phone, and filing experience at $145 per week; ▶ 2 *nurses* with RN, LPN, or GN license or B.S.N. degree; ▶ 4 *weekend counselors* with physical strength, mental alertness, and at least one year of college completed at $125–$130 per week; ▶ 6 *junior counselors* with physical and emotional strength, mental alertness, creativity, flexibility, and high school student status (successful volunteer experience may be substituted for the age requirement) at $90 per week; ▶ 1 *arts and crafts specialist* with current major in therapeutic recreation, occupational therapy, or art education/therapy or experience planning and implementing arts and crafts activities/projects at $120–$155 per week; ▶ 1 *music specialist* with current major in music, music therapy, or special education and experience planning and implementing activities at $120–$155 per week; ▶ 1 *outdoor specialist* with current major in environmental, outdoor, or education field at $120–$155 per week; ▶ 1 *recreation specialist* with current major in recreation, physical education, or adaptive physical recreation and leadership skills involving group activities at $120–$155 per week; ▶ 1 *dining hall staff worker* with experience in food service/dining hall area; ▶ 1 *creative movement/drama specialist* with experience in the performing arts field at $120–$155 per week. International students encouraged to apply; must apply through recognized agency.

Benefits College credit, on-the-job training, formal ongoing training, on-site room and board at no charge, laundry facilities. Preemployment training of 3 to 6 days is required and includes safety and accident prevention, group interaction, first-aid, CPR, leadership, camper-counselor relations, disability awareness. Orientation is paid.

Contact Joanne Fieldseth, Human Resources Director, Friendship Ventures/Eden Wood Camp, Department SJ, 10509 108th Street, NW, Annandale, Minnesota 55302; 320-274-8376, Fax 320-274-3238, E-mail friendl@spacestar.com. Application deadline: May 1.

GRAND VIEW LODGE GOLF AND TENNIS CLUB
SOUTH 134 NOKOMIS AVENUE
NISSWA, MINNESOTA 56468

General Information Resort that caters to families and business conventions and operates the most popular public golf courses in Minnesota. Established in 1919. Owned by ETOC Corporation. Affiliated with Minnesota Resort Association, Resort Commercial Recreation Association (RCRA), Minnesota Hotel/Motel Association. 1,300-acre facility located 140 miles north of Minneapolis. Features: historic main lodge and 60 cabins; full-service conference center; 1,500 feet of beach; 3 golf courses, 11 tennis courts, Jacuzzi, and indoor pool; great hiking and biking trails; lakes for swimming, boating, and fishing.

Profile of Summer Employees Total number: 300; average age: 21; 10% minorities; 20% high school students; 70% college students; 10% retirees; 20% international; 20% local residents.

Employment Information Openings are from April 20 to October 20. Jobs available: ▶ 25 *dining room personnel* at $190&–$220 per week; ▶ 5 *experienced bartenders* at $175–$195 per week; ▶ 5 *beach staff members* with knowledge of boats and motors at $165–$185 per week; ▶ 15 *housekeepers* at $195&–$220 per week; ▶ 3 *skilled desk clerks* at $185–$205 per week; ▶ 3 *children's program instructors* at $165–$185 per week. International students encouraged to apply; must obtain own visa and working papers prior to employment; must apply through recognized agency.

Benefits On-the-job training, formal ongoing training, on-site room and board at $175 per month, laundry facilities, partial room rebate if work contract is completed, use of resort facilities at little or no charge, interaction with people from around the world. Preemployment training of 1 day is required and includes safety and accident prevention, group interaction, leadership. Orientation is paid.

Contact Paul Welch, Operations Manager, Grand View Lodge Golf and Tennis Club, Department SJ, South 134 Nokomis Avenue, Nisswa, Minnesota 56468; 218-963-2234, Fax 218-963-2269, URL http://www.grandviewlodge.com. Application deadline: June 1.

GUNFLINT LODGE AND OUTFITTERS
750 GUNFLINT TRAIL
GRAND MARAIS, MINNESOTA 55604

General Information Family and fishing resort offering cabin accommodations with modified or full American plan packages; guide services, naturalist activities, and access to boundary Waters Canoe Area (B.W.C.A.). Established in 1928. Owned by Bruce and Sue Kerfoot. Affiliated with American Automobile Association, Minnesota Resort Association, National Association of Canoe Liveries and Outfitters. 100-acre facility located 43 miles northwest of Grand Marais. Features: location in the heart of Minnesota's Superior National Forest; location surrounded by Minnesota's Boundary Waters Canoe Area (BWCA); 25 cabins spread along the shoreline of Gunflint Lake; hiking and mountain biking trails; 60 miles of groomed cross country ski trails in winter; dog sledding in winter.

Profile of Summer Employees Total number: 45; average age: 55; 55% male, 45% female; 1% minorities; 5% high school students; 60% college students; 20% retirees; 8% international; 5% local residents; 1% teachers. Nonsmokers preferred.

Employment Information Openings are from April 15 to November 15. Year-round positions also offered. Jobs available: ▶ 3 *dishwashers* with must be at least 17 at $1000 per month; ▶ 3 *dock staff* with ability to lift and carry 75 pounds, knowledge of outboard motors, and clean valid driver's license at $1000 per month; ▶ 10 *waitresses/housekeepers (combined positions)* with experience preferred at $900 per month; ▶ 1 *baker* with experience or great desire to learn at $1000–$1300 per month; ▶ 6 *busters, haulers, and packers* with clean valid driver's license and ability to lift and carry 75 pounds at $1000 per month; ▶ 1 *breakfast and lunch cook* with experience or great desire to learn at $1000–$1300 per month; ▶ 1 *prep cook* with experience or great desire to learn at $1000–$1150 per month. International students encouraged to apply; must obtain own visa and working papers prior to employment; must apply through recognized agency.

Benefits On-the-job training, laundry facilities, use of camping and recreational equipment at minimal cost, bonus program for completed lodge contracts, on-site room costs $110 per month.

Contact Shari Baker, Assistant Manager, Gunflint Lodge and Outfitters, 143 South Gunflint Lake, Grand Marais, Minnesota 55604; 800-328-3325, Fax 218-388-9429, E-mail gunflint@gunflint.com.

GUNFLINT WILDERNESS CAMP
H.C. 64, BOX 948
GRAND MARAIS, MINNESOTA 55604

General Information Camp for 40 campers offering 29 off-site canoeing, backpacking, rock climbing, mountain biking, sea kayaking or fishing trips of 2 to 7 days. Established in 1969. Owned by Nancy Bredemus. Affiliated with Association of Independent Camps, American Camping Association. 40-acre facility located 180 miles north of Duluth. Features: main lodge; location bordering Superior National Forest; largest U.S. wilderness canoe park adjacent to camp; many rock climbing sites within a 70-mile radius of camp; remote campsite not accessible by vehicle.

Profile of Summer Employees Total number: 15; average age: 21; 80% male, 20% female; 100% college students. Nonsmokers only.

Employment Information Openings are from June 8 to August 13. Jobs available: ▶ 10 *canoe guides/counselors* with first aid, CPR, and LGT at $1200–$1300 per season; ▶ 3 *rock climbing instructors/ counselors* with first aid and CPR at $1200–$1300 per season; ▶ 2 *food service staff members* at $1000–$1300 per season; ▶ 1 *swimming instructor* with WSI certification/LGT at $1200–$1300 per season. International students encouraged to apply; must apply through recognized agency.

Benefits On-site room and board at no charge. Preemployment training of 7 days is required and includes safety and accident prevention, group interaction, leadership, camper-counselor relations, skills instruction. Orientation is paid.

Contact Jeff Wubbels, Director, Gunflint Wilderness Camp, Department SJ, PO Box 547, St. Cloud, Minnesota 56302; 800-451-5270, Fax 320-656-1029. Application deadline: May 7.

LAKE HUBERT TENNIS CAMP
BOX 308
LAKE HUBERT, MINNESOTA 56459

General Information Seven day tennis camps featuring five hours of court time instruction daily for all skill levels; 12 courts for 36 campers. Established in 1909. Operated by Camp Lincoln/Camp Lake Hubert. Affiliated with American Camping Association, Midwest Tennis Association, American International Camping. 750-acre facility located 12 miles north of Brainerd. Features: 12 courts; separate counseling and coaching staff; separate dining room.

Profile of Summer Employees 50% male, 50% female; 75% college students; 25% teachers. Nonsmokers preferred.

Employment Information Openings are from June 1 to August 25. Jobs available: ▶ 10 *tennis instructors* at $150–$250 per week; ▶ 6 *cabin counselors* at $125–$150 per week; ▶ 2 *waterfront staff* at $125–$200 per week. International students encouraged to apply; must apply through recognized agency.

Benefits On-site room and board at no charge, travel reimbursement.

Contact Sam Cote, Director, Lake Hubert Tennis Camp, 5201 Eden Circle, Minneapolis, Minnesota 55436; 800-242-1909, Fax 612-922-7149, E-mail clclh@uslink.net. Application deadline: May 1.

MENOGYN-YMCA WILDERNESS ADVENTURES
55 MENOGYN TRAIL
GRAND MARAIS, MINNESOTA 55604

General Information Wilderness camp specializing in canoeing, backpacking, and rock-climbing trips in wilderness areas of North America. Established in 1922. Owned by YMCA of Metropolitan Minneapolis. Affiliated with American Camping Association, YMCA. 80-acre facility located 32 miles north of Grand Marais. Features: location near Canada bordering the Boundary Waters Canoe Area Wilderness; rustic base camp facility with very limited modern conveniences; rock climbing programs along north shore of Lake Superior; extensive wilderness canoe trips in Northeast Minnesota, Ontario, and Manitoba; backpacking on Isle Royale, Superior Hiking Trail, the Rocky Mountains, and Alaska; fleet of 85 wood, aluminum, and plastic canoes.

Profile of Summer Employees Total number: 46; average age: 22; 50% male, 50% female; 5% minorities; 90% college students; 5% international; 75% local residents. Nonsmokers only.

Employment Information Openings are from June 1 to August 30. Spring break, winter break, Christmas break, year-round positions also offered. Jobs available: ▶ 24 *trail counselors* with CPR, first aid, and lifeguard training at $110–$150 per week; ▶ 1 *experienced cook* with references at $2000–$3000 per season; ▶ 1 *program director* with CPR, first aid, and lifeguard training at $120–$150 per week; ▶ 3 *in-camp staff members* with CPR, first aid, and lifeguard training at $110–$150 per week; ▶ 1 *nurse* with current license at $1200–$2000 per season; ▶ 1 *maintenance person* with CPR, first aid, and lifeguard training at $1200–$2000 per season.

Benefits On-the-job training, formal ongoing training, on-site room and board at no charge. Preemployment training of 10 days is required and includes safety and accident prevention, group interaction, first-aid, CPR, leadership, camper-counselor relations, wilderness skills. Orientation is paid.

Contact David L. Palmer, Executive Director, Menogyn-YMCA Wilderness Adventures, Department SJ, 4 West Rustic Lodge Avenue, Minneapolis, Minnesota 55409; 612-823-5282, Fax 612-823-2482. Application deadline: March 15.

NELSON'S RESORT
7632 NELSON ROAD
CRANE LAKE, MINNESOTA 55725

General Information Family resort with conventions in the fall. Established in 1931. Owned by Gloria N. Pohlman. Affiliated with Minnesota Resort Association, Minnesota Arrowhead, Northeastern Division of Minnesota Department of Tourism, Crane Lake Commercial Club. 84-acre facility located 75 miles north of Virginia. Features: 28 cabins with extensive freshwater lake frontage; dining room/cocktail lounge; gift shop; marina; proximity to Voyageur National Park and Boundary Waters Canoe Area; professional fishing guides with access to 60 miles of Canadian/United States border lakes; hiking trails.

Profile of Summer Employees Total number: 32; average age: 20; 44% male, 56% female; 25% college students; 2% retirees; 1% international; 6% local residents.

Employment Information Openings are from May 1 to October 15. Jobs available: ▶ 6 *waiters/waitresses* at $800–$900 per month; ▶ 5 *cabin staff members* at $800–$900 per month; ▶ 3 *dock attendants* at $800–$900 per month; ▶ 1 *bellperson* at $800–$900 per month; ▶ 3 *kitchen helpers* at $800–$900 per month; ▶ 1 *store clerk* at $800–$900 per month; ▶ 1 *bartender* at $800–$1000 per month.

Benefits On-the-job training, on-site room and board at $90 per month, laundry facilities, use of facilities, bonus, free housing; minimal charge for meals.

Contact Jacque Eggen, Owner, Nelson's Resort, Department SJ, 7632 Nelson Road, Crane Lake, Minnesota 55725; 218-993-2295, Fax 218-993-2242. Application deadline: April 30.

SINGING HILLS GIRL SCOUT CAMP AND CANNON VALLEY DAY CAMPS
PO BOX 69
WATERVILLE, MINNESOTA 56096

General Information Residential camp serving 64 girls (grades 4–12) weekly, and day camp serving 60–100 girls (grades 2–5) weekly; day camps held at several sites. Owned by Girl Scout Council of Cannon Valley. Affiliated with Girl Scouts of the United States of America, American Camping Association, American Canoeing Association. 160-acre facility located 30 miles south of Minneapolis/St. Paul. Features: small freshwater lake frontage; wooded sites with very old hardwood trees; Sunfish sailboats and canoes; fully-equipped program center and lodge facilities; waterfront view from all living quarters.

Profile of Summer Employees Total number: 27; average age: 20; 10% high school students; 70% college students; 10% retirees; 10% international; 90% local residents; 20% teachers. Nonsmokers preferred.

Employment Information Openings are from June 5 to August 23. Jobs available: ▶ 12 *general counselors* at $1500 per season; ▶ 1 *waterfront director (minimum age 21)* with lifeguard training at $1800 per season; ▶ *waterfront assistants* at $1500 per season; ▶ 2 *experienced administrative staff* at $2000 per season; ▶ 2 *cooks* with experience in group cooking and menu planning at $1750 per season; ▶ *unit leaders (minimum age 21)* at $1700 per season. International students encouraged to apply; must apply through recognized agency.

Benefits On-the-job training, formal ongoing training, on-site room and board at no charge, laundry facilities, health insurance.

Contact Tracy D. Christeson, Program Director, Cannon Valley Girl Scouts, Singing Hills Girl Scout Camp and Cannon Valley Day Camps, Department SJ, PO Box 61, Northfield, Minnesota 55057-0061; 507-645-6603. Application deadline: May 15.

STRAW HAT PLAYERS
CENTER FOR THE ARTS–MOORHEAD STATE UNIVERSITY
MOORHEAD, MINNESOTA 56563

General Information Summer stock theater producing four shows in a nine-week season. Established in 1963. Owned by Moorhead State University. Affiliated with American College Theater Festival, Communication and Theater Association of Minnesota, American Theater in Higher Education. 20-acre facility located 1 mile east of Fargo, North Dakota. Features: 900-seat proscenium theater; 350-seat thrust theater; scene shops, costume shops, and dance studio; access to university facilities: library, pool, and athletic center; largest metropolitan area between Minneapolis and Seattle.

Profile of Summer Employees Total number: 60; average age: 22; 40% male, 60% female; 5% minorities; 10% high school students; 80% college students; 40% local residents. Nonsmokers preferred.

Employment Information Openings are from May 27 to July 26. Jobs available: ▶ 40 *acting company members* at $100–$180 per week; ▶ 5 *theater technicians* at $100–$300 per week; ▶ 1 *musical director* with extensive professional experience at $200–$300 per week; ▶ 1 *choreographer* with M.F.A. or professional experience at $150–$250 per week; ▶ *guest designers* with M.F.A. or professional experience at $150–$250 per week; ▶ 1 *properties master* at $150–$250 per week; ▶ 3 *costume stitchers* at $100–$250 per week. International students encouraged to apply; must obtain own visa and working papers prior to employment; must apply through recognized agency.

Benefits College credit, on-the-job training, formal ongoing training, on-site room and board at $100 per month, laundry facilities, dormitory housing available.

Contact Director of Theater, Straw Hat Players, Department SJ, Moorhead State University, Moorhead, Minnesota 56563; 218-236-4613, Fax 218-236-2168. Application deadline: January 2.

TOM & WOODS' MOOSE LAKE WILDERNESS CANOE TRIPS
PO BOX 358
ELY, MINNESOTA 55731

General Information Wilderness canoe/fishing outfitter for trips into the Boundary Waters Canoe Area Wilderness and Quetico Parks. Established in 1966. Owned by Lyle Williams. Affiliated with Chamber of Commerce of Ely, NACLO, Ely Outfitters Association. 8-acre facility located 125 miles north of Duluth. Features: proximity to 1500 lakes; 1.3 million acres available for trips.

Profile of Summer Employees 50% male, 50% female; 10% high school students; 90% college students; 25% local residents. Nonsmokers preferred.

Employment Information Openings are from May 1 to September 31. Jobs available: ▶ *general staff members* at $1450–$1700 per month; ▶ *cook* at $10 per hour.

Benefits On-the-job training, on-site room and board at $325 per month, laundry facilities, use of boats and canoes on days and evenings off, 25 percent discount on items purchased in our store, 25 percent discount on trips taken by immediate family.

Contact Lyle Williams, Tom & Woods' Moose Lake Wilderness Canoe Trips, PO Box 358, Ely, Minnesota 55731; 218-365-5837, Fax 218-365-6393. Application deadline: December 1.

VALLEYFAIR FAMILY AMUSEMENT PARK
1 VALLEYFAIR DRIVE
SHAKOPEE, MINNESOTA 55379

General Information Family amusement park offering a variety of entertainment attractions. Established in 1976. Owned by Cedar Fair Limited Partnership. Affiliated with International Association of Amusement Parks and Attractions. 90-acre facility located 20 miles south of Minneapolis/St. Paul. Features: location along the Minnesota River; more than 60 rides and attractions; water park; "wild thing" hyper-coaster; live entertainment.

Profile of Summer Employees Total number: 1,400; average age: 18; 50% male, 50% female.

Employment Information Openings are from May 1 to September 30. Jobs available: ▶ 200 *ride hosts/hostesses* at $2500–$5000 per season; ▶ 270 *food hosts/hostesses;* ▶ 90 *merchandise attendants;* ▶ 140 *game attendants;* ▶ 30 *accounting clerks/tellers;* ▶ 1 *employee relations coordinator;* ▶ 1 *marketing assistant;* ▶ 25 *park-service attendants;* ▶ 28 *security officers/ EMT's* with Emergency Medical Technician certification for some positions; ▶ 40 *admissions cashiers;* ▶ 40 *ticket takers;* ▶ 20 *landscapers;* ▶ 2 *mechanic's assistants;* ▶ 4 *seasonal group-sales representatives;* ▶ 4 *human resource clerks;* ▶ 30 *lifeguards.* International students encouraged to apply; must obtain own visa and working papers prior to employment.

Benefits College credit, on-the-job training, on-site room and board at $30 per week, laundry facilities, free admission to the park with Valley Fair identification and passes for friends and relatives, weekly parties, dances, and other social events, rent subsidy program; possible internships for certain positions. Preemployment training of 1 to 2 days is required and includes safety and accident prevention, first-aid, CPR, leadership, disability awareness. Orientation is paid.

Contact Dawn Cooper, Human Resources Manager, Valleyfair Family Amusement Park, Department SJ, 1 Valleyfair Drive, Shakopee, Minnesota 55379; 612-445-7600, Fax 612-445-1539, URL http://www.valleyfair.com.

WIDJIWAGAN–YMCA WILDERNESS ADVENTURES
3788 NORTH ARM ROAD
ELY, MINNESOTA 55731

General Information Summer wilderness trips for teens as well as school-year wilderness environmental education. Established in 1929. Owned by YMCA of Greater St. Paul. Affiliated with American Camping Association, YMCA, Association for Experiential Education. 400-acre facility located 250 miles north of St. Paul. Features: location in the Superior National Forest; setting one-half mile from the Boundary Waters Canoe Area (a 700,000-acre wilderness on the Minnesota-Canada border); hand-hewn log cabin camper housing; wilderness lake and forest setting.

Profile of Summer Employees Total number: 70; average age: 23; 55% male, 45% female; 5% minorities; 70% college students; 2% international; 2% local residents. Nonsmokers only.

Employment Information Openings are from June 5 to August 31. Year-round positions also offered. Jobs available: ▶ 50 *wilderness trail leaders* with CPR, first aid, and lifeguard certification at $1200–$2000 per season. International students encouraged to apply; must apply through recognized agency.

Benefits On-the-job training, formal ongoing training, on-site room and board at no charge, laundry facilities, use of available camping gear (canoes/packs) for personal outings. Preemployment training of 10 to 15 days is required and includes safety and accident prevention, group interaction, first-aid, CPR, leadership, camper-counselor relations, "Leave No Trace" camping, specific backpack and canoe skills. Orientation is paid.

Contact Sara Mairs, Program Director, Widjiwagan–YMCA Wilderness Adventures, Department SJ, 1761 University Avenue West, St. Paul, Minnesota 55104-3599; 612-645-6605, Fax 612-646-5521. Application deadline: February 10.

YMCA CAMP IHDUHPI
BOX 37
LORETTO, MINNESOTA 55357

General Information Residential camp serving 150 boys and girls weekly, offering sailing and horsemanship as well as leadership program for campers ages 13-15. Established in 1930. Owned by YMCA of Metropolitan Minneapolis. 200-acre facility located 25 miles west of Minneapolis. Features: high adventure center, 7 high rope courses; horse program; extensive waterfront program; sailing program with 10 boats 12–28 feet in length; 7 windsurfers.

Profile of Summer Employees Total number: 60; average age: 21; 50% male, 50% female; 5% minorities; 30% high school students; 70% college students; 10% international; 50% local residents. Nonsmokers only.

Employment Information Openings are from June 2 to August 28. Year-round positions also offered. Jobs available: ▶ 1 *program director* at $1500–$1800 per season; ▶ 2 *unit directors* at $1400–$1700 per season; ▶ 1 *waterfront director* at $1400–$1700 per season; ▶ 1 *riding director* at $1350–$1600 per season; ▶ 1 *experienced ropes course director* at $1350–$1600 per season; ▶ 20 *counselors* at $1250–$1400 per season; ▶ 1 *nurse* at $1700–$2000 per season; ▶ 3 *cooks* at $1400–$1700 per season; ▶ *summer business manager* at $1300–$1500 per season; ▶ 1 *nature director* at $1300–$1450 per season; ▶ 1 *arts and crafts director* at $1250–$1450 per season; ▶ 1 *trip director* at $1250–$1500 per season.

Benefits College credit, on-the-job training, formal ongoing training, on-site room and board at no charge, laundry facilities, scholarships for college-enrolled staff. Preemployment training of 7 days is required and includes safety and accident prevention, group interaction, first-aid, CPR, leadership, camper-counselor relations. Orientation is paid.

Contact Paul Danicic, Camp Director, YMCA Camp Ihduhpi, Department SJ, Box 37, Loretto, Minnesota 55357; 612-479-1146, Fax 612-479-1333, E-mail ymca-ihd@mtn.org. Application deadline: May 1.

MISSOURI

SIX FLAGS–ST. LOUIS
PO BOX 60
EUREKA, MISSOURI 63025

General Information Theme park offering exciting thrill rides, shows, attractions, and family entertainment to people of all ages. Established in 1971. Owned by Boston Ventures. 200-acre facility located 30 miles west of St. Louis.

Profile of Summer Employees Total number: 3,000; average age: 17; 49% male, 51% female; 20% minorities; 41% high school students; 36% college students; 5% retirees; 100% local residents; 5% teachers.

Employment Information Openings are from March 1 to October 1. Spring break positions also offered. Jobs available: ▶ *food service hosts/hostesses* at $5.50 per hour; ▶ *operations hosts/hostesses* at $5.25 per hour; ▶ *admissions hosts/hostesses* at $5.25 per hour; ▶ *merchandise hosts/hostesses* at $5.25 per hour; ▶ *security officers* at $6.25 per hour; ▶ *entertainment hosts/ hostesses* at $5.25 per hour; ▶ *cash control agents* at $6.50 per hour. International students encouraged to apply; must obtain own visa and working papers prior to employment; must apply through recognized agency.

Benefits College credit, on-the-job training, formal ongoing training, laundry facilities. Off-site boarding costs are $450 per month.

Contact Human Resources, Six Flags–St. Louis, Department SJ, PO Box 60, Eureka, Missouri 63025; 314-938-5300, Fax 314-938-4964, URL http://www.sixflags.com.

WORLDS OF FUN/OCEANS OF FUN
4545 WOF AVENUE
KANSAS CITY, MISSOURI 64161

General Information Amusement park. Established in 1973. Owned by Cedar Fair, LP. 170-acre facility located 5 miles northeast of Kansas City. Features: ride park in Worlds of Fun; water park in Oceans of Fun.

Profile of Summer Employees Total number: 3,400; average age: 18; 40% male, 60% female; 70% high school students; 20% college students; 10% retirees.

Employment Information Openings are from April 15 to October 15. Jobs available: ▶ *food operations staff* at $6.25 per hour; ▶ *ride operations staff* at $6 per hour; ▶ *merchandise staff* at $6 per hour; ▶ *games staff* at $6 per hour; ▶ *lifeguards* at $6.25 per hour; ▶ *ticket sellers* at $6 per hour; ▶ *grounds personnel* at $6 per hour. International students encouraged to apply; must obtain own visa and working papers prior to employment.

Benefits On-the-job training. Preemployment training of 1 day is required and includes safety and accident prevention, group interaction, first-aid, leadership. Orientation is paid.

Contact Human Resources Department, Worlds of Fun/Oceans of Fun, 4545 WOF Avenue, Kansas City, Missouri 64161; 816-454-4545. Application deadline: June 1.

MONTANA

BEST WESTERN BUCKS T-4 LODGE OF BIG SKY
PO BOX 160279
BIG SKY, MONTANA 59716

General Information 75-unit Best Western Lodge serving skiers, outdoor enthusiasts, and visitors to Yellowstone National Park. Established in 1946. Owned by Mike Scholz. Located 45 miles south of Bozeman. Features: location 9 miles from Big Sky ski resort; 40 miles from Yellowstone National Park; 200 yards from Gallatin River; in Gallatin National Forest.

Profile of Summer Employees Total number: 65; average age: 20; 50% male, 50% female; 10% minorities; 5% high school students; 20% college students; 5% retirees; 80% local residents.

Employment Information Openings are from June 1 to October 1. Year-round positions also offered. Jobs available: ▶ 25 *waitstaff* at $4.75 per hour; ▶ 10 *housekeeping staff* at $6 per hour; ▶ 10 *cooks* at $5–$8 per hour; ▶ 5 *front desk staff* at $6 per hour; ▶ 8 *dishwashers* at $5.50 per hour. International students encouraged to apply; must obtain own visa and working papers prior to employment.

Benefits On-site room and board at $55 per week, laundry facilities, employee meal discount.

Contact Deb Dechert, Operations Manager, Best Western Bucks T-4 Lodge of Big Sky, PO Box 160279, Big Sky, Montana 59716; 406-995-4111, Fax 406-995-2191, E-mail buckst4@mcn.net, URL http://www.dmix.com/ami/sites/bigsky/bucks.html.

BIG SKY OF MONTANA SKI AND SUMMER RESORT
PO BOX 160001
BIG SKY, MONTANA 59716

General Information Winter and summer resort attracting both families and conventions. Established in 1974. Owned by John E. Kircher. Affiliated with Montana Innkeepers' Association, Montana Taverns' Association, Ski the Rockies. 10,000-acre facility located 45 miles south of Bozeman. Features: location 18 miles north of Yellowstone National Park; site in Rocky Mountains surrounded by millions of acres of national forest and wilderness; accommodations for over 3,000 guests; 15 restaurants and night spots.

Profile of Summer Employees Total number: 300; average age: 21; 50% male, 50% female; 5% minorities; 5% high school students; 80% college students; 5% local residents.

Employment Information Openings are from June 2 to October 15. Spring break, winter break, Christmas break positions also offered. Jobs available: ▶ 50 *housekeepers* at $170 per week; ▶ 75 *food and beverage positions, experience preferred,* at $160 per week; ▶ 10 *accountants, experience preferred,* at $200 per week; ▶ 2 *night auditors, experience preferred,* at $200 per week; ▶ 7 *front desk personnel, experience preferred,* at $180 per week; ▶ 5 *bellmen* at $180 per week; ▶ 15 *retail sales personnel* at $180 per week; ▶ 30 *golf course maintenance persons* at $190 per week; ▶ 3 *conference services personnel* at $190 per week; ▶ 3 *reservations staff, experience preferred,* at $200 per week; ▶ 3 *hotel maintenance personnel* at $200 per week.

Benefits On-the-job training, on-site room and board at $200 per month, laundry facilities, employee discounts on meals. Preemployment training of 1 day is required and includes CPR. Orientation is paid.

Contact Veda Barner, Human Resources, Big Sky of Montana Ski and Summer Resort, Department SJ, PO Box 160001, Big Sky, Montana 59716; 406-995-5820, Fax 406-995-5001. Application deadline: May 1.

HAMILTON STORES, INC.
PO BOX 250
WEST YELLOWSTONE, MONTANA 59758

General Information Fourteen general stores located throughout Yellowstone National Park with general offices and a warehouse in West Yellowstone, Montana. Established in 1915. Affiliated with National Park Conference of Concessioners. Located 90 miles south of Bozeman. Features: more than 65 named thermal features; 2 million acres of hiking and backpacking; dorm with family-style meals available at nominal charge; fly fishing in lake or stream.

Profile of Summer Employees Total number: 1,000; 49% male, 51% female; 40% college students; 60% retirees; 5% teachers.

Employment Information Openings are from March 15 to October 15. Jobs available: ▶ *sales clerks* at $4.75–$6.75 per hour; ▶ *grocery clerks* at $4.75–$6.75 per hour; ▶ *food service clerks* at $4.75–$6.75 per hour; ▶ 20 *employee dining room cooks* with experience in large volume food preparation at $5.05–$7.25 per hour; ▶ *dining room assistants* at $4.75–$5.25 per hour; ▶ *dishwashers* at $4.75–$5.25 per hour; ▶ *custodians* at $4.75–$5.25 per hour; ▶ 12 *dormitory managers* at $4.90–$5.50 per hour; ▶ 20 *auditors* with background in bookkeeping and money handling at $4.95–$5.75 per hour; ▶ 2 *maintenance workers* with general maintenance experience in plumbing, electrical work, etc. at $7–$10 per hour; ▶ *warehouse workers* at $4.75–$8 per hour; ▶ 5 *clerical personnel* at $4.75–$5.25 per hour; ▶ *fry cooks* at $4.90–$5.25 per hour. International students encouraged to apply; must apply through recognized agency.

Benefits On-the-job training, laundry facilities, employee discount, active employee recreation co-op, two consecutive days off, guaranteed 7–8-hour day, RV sites available, on site room/board cost $8.75/day and medical plan, $.58/day. Preemployment training of 1 day is required and includes safety and accident prevention. Orientation is paid.

Contact Human Resources Department, Hamilton Stores, Inc., Department SJ, 1709 West College, Bozeman, Montana 59715; 406-587-2208, Fax 406-587-3105, E-mail hamiltons@ montana.net. Application deadline: August 1.

LAZY K BAR RANCH
PO BOX 550
BIG TIMBER, MONTANA 59011

General Information One-hundred-seventeen-year-old operating cattle and horse ranch that has welcomed selected guests for seventy-four summers. Established in 1880. Owned by Van Cleve family. Affiliated with Dude Ranchers' Association, Montana Ranch Vacation Association. 22,000-acre facility located 100 miles west of Billings. Features: swimming pool; rural setting in an isolated, unspoiled mountain environment; authentic ranch; horses; fossil fields; local rodeos.

Profile of Summer Employees Total number: 19; average age: 20; 40% male, 60% female; 45% high school students; 40% college students; 5% retirees; 5% international; 5% local residents. Nonsmokers preferred.

Employment Information Openings are from June 10 to September 5. Jobs available: ▶ 1 *experienced head cook* with ability to cook for 55–60 people at $800 per month; ▶ 1 *second cook/baker* at $600 per month; ▶ 3 *waiters/waitresses* at $450 per month; ▶ 2 *housekeepers* at $450 per month; ▶ 1 *laundry worker* at $450 per month; ▶ 1 *split-shift worker* at $475 per month; ▶ 1 *storekeeper* at $425 per month; ▶ 1 *choreperson* with experience with milk cows at $450 per month; ▶ 3 *experienced wranglers* at $550 per month; ▶ 1 *experienced children's wrangler (female)* at $550 per month; ▶ 1 *dishwasher* at $450 per month; ▶ 1 *winter caretaker* with desire for solitude and experience with chainsaws and other tools (position available from September 12 to June 12) at $500 per month. International students encouraged to apply; must obtain own visa and working papers prior to employment; must apply through recognized agency.

Benefits College credit, on-the-job training, on-site room and board at no charge, laundry facilities, riding on days off, square dancing instruction, excellent tips.

Contact Lazy K Bar Ranch, Department SJ, PO Box 1181, Big Timber, Montana 59011;

406-537-4404, Fax 406-537-4593. Application deadline: March 1.

NINE QUARTER CIRCLE RANCH
5000 TAYLOR FORK ROAD
GALLATIN GATEWAY, MONTANA 59730

General Information Family-oriented dude ranch hosting 75 guests weekly. Established in 1946. Owned by Kim and Kelly Kelsey. Affiliated with Dude Ranchers' Association, State Chamber of Commerce, Montana Dude Ranch Association. 1,000-acre facility located 60 miles south of Bozeman. Features: mountain setting; log cabin buildings; isolated stream-side location; thousands of acres of national forest land surrounding ranch; vast countryside for horseback riding; view of Yellowstone Park.

Profile of Summer Employees Total number: 20; average age: 21; 40% male, 60% female; 90% college students; 10% retirees. Nonsmokers preferred.

Employment Information Openings are from June 1 to September 15. Jobs available: ▶ 4 *cabin cleaners/servers* at $700–$800 per month; ▶ 2 *kitchen helpers/dishwashers;* ▶ 2 *baby sitters* with first aid and adult, child, and infant CPR certification at $700–$800 per month; ▶ 1 *laundry worker* at $700 per month; ▶ 2 *second cooks* at $700–$800 per month; ▶ 2 *ranch hands* with first aid and adult, child, and infant CPR certification at $700–$800 per month; ▶ *maintenance workers* with ability to make minor repairs and knowledge of carpentry at $700–$800 per month.

Benefits College credit, on-the-job training, on-site room and board at no charge, laundry facilities, use of horses on days off, participation in ranch activities such as square dances, movies, and games.

Contact Kim and Kelly Kelsey, Nine Quarter Circle Ranch, Department SJ, 5000 Taylor Fork Road, Gallatin Gateway, Montana 59730; 406-995-4276, URL http://www.9quarter/index.htm. Application deadline: April 1.

ST. MARY LODGE & RESORT
GLACIER NATIONAL PARK
ST. MARY, MONTANA 59417

General Information One of Montana's noted full-service high country resorts. Established in 1932. Owned by Roscoe Black. 100-acre facility located 89 miles east of Kalispell. Features: location at the east entrance to Glacier National Park; 900 miles of hiking trails; internationally famous dining room; proximity to Canada.

Profile of Summer Employees Total number: 180; average age: 21; 40% male, 60% female; 5% high school students; 85% college students; 10% retirees; 20% local residents. Nonsmokers preferred.

Employment Information Openings are from May 1 to October 15. Year-round positions also offered. Jobs available: ▶ 26 *experienced waiters/waitresses* at $893 per month; ▶ 12 *pantry/fry cooks, experience preferred,* at $936–$953 per month; ▶ 5 *gas station attendants* at $910 per month; ▶ 15 *housekeepers* at $936 per month; ▶ 10 *gift shop clerks, experience preferred,* at $910 per month; ▶ 3 *sporting-goods clerks* at $910 per month; ▶ 6 *bartenders/cocktail servers, experience preferred,* at $893 per month; ▶ 4 *pizza parlor staff members* at $910–$936 per month; ▶ 9 *supermarket staff members* at $910 per month; ▶ 4 *front desk clerks* at $910 per month; ▶ 10 *maintenance personnel* at $910 per month; ▶ 14 *dishwashing/kitchen personnel* at $910 per month; ▶ 11 *deli cooks* at $910 per month; ▶ 4 *experienced accounting/secretarial staff members* at $910 per month; ▶ 5 *clerical staff members* at $910 per month; ▶ 6 *hosts/buspersons* at $893 per month. International students encouraged to apply; must obtain own visa and working papers prior to employment.

Benefits College credit, on-the-job training, on-site room and board at $265 per month, laundry facilities, guaranteed year-end bonuses, retail discount, internships.

Contact Rocky Black, Resort Manager, St. Mary Lodge & Resort, Department SJ, PO Box 1808, Sun Valley, Idaho 83353; 208-726-6279, Fax 208-726-6282, E-mail gluobs@magiclink. com, URL http://www.glcpark.com. Application deadline: April 10.

63 RANCH
PO BOX 979
LIVINGSTON, MONTANA 59047

General Information Working cattle and dude ranch operating from June through September with capacity for 30 guests. Ranch specializes in teaching horseback riding on all levels. Established in 1929. Owned by Sandra C. Cahill. Affiliated with Dude Ranchers' Association, Montana Ranch Vacation Association, Federation of Fly Fishermen, Montana Farm Bureau, Gallatin Outfitters Association, Trout Unlimited. 2,000-acre facility located 50 miles east of Bozeman. Features: location in Big Sky country bordering Gallatin National Forest and Absaroka-Beartooth wilderness; clean air and water in scenic Absaroka Mountains; proximity to Yellowstone National Park and blue-ribbon trout streams; location far from town; 100 miles of trails and open country; the first Crow Indian agency location–Mission Creek is located on our land.

Profile of Summer Employees Total number: 15; average age: 25; 47% male, 53% female; 5% high school students; 45% college students; 10% retirees; 10% local residents. Nonsmokers only.

Employment Information Openings are from June 1 to September 20. Jobs available: ▶ 1 *experienced head cook* with first aid, CPR, and ability to run a kitchen and cook for 50 people at $1000 per month; ▶ 1 *experienced second cook* with first aid and CPR at $800 per month; ▶ 1 *dishwasher* with first aid and CPR at $600 per month; ▶ 2 *waiters/waitresses* with first aid and CPR at $600 per month; ▶ 1 *kitchen helper* with first aid and CPR at $600 per month; ▶ 1 *experienced head housekeeper* with first aid and CPR at $800 per month; ▶ 2 *cabin cleaners* with first aid and CPR at $600 per month; ▶ 1 *chore person* with physical strength (lifting involved), first aid, and CPR at $600 per month. International students encouraged to apply; must obtain own visa and working papers prior to employment.

Benefits On-the-job training, on-site room and board at no charge, laundry facilities, workmen's compensation and possible end-of-season bonus, use of ranch facilities during time off, transportation to and from town and airport and parking. Preemployment training of 1 day is optional. Orientation is unpaid.

Contact Sandra C. Cahill, President, 63 Ranch, Department SJ, PO Box 979-P, Livingston, Montana 59047; 406-222-0570, Fax 406-222-9446, E-mail sixty3ranch@mcn.net, URL http://www.ranchweb.com.

SWEET GRASS RANCH
MELVILLE ROUTE, BOX 161
BIG TIMBER, MONTANA 59011

General Information Working cattle ranch that accepts 20 guests to live ranch life. Established in 1926. Owned by Bill and Shelly Carroccia. Affiliated with National Register of Historic Places, Dude Ranchers' Association, National Cattlemen's Association. 20,000-acre facility located 120 miles northwest of Billings. Features: unspoiled scenery; clear lake and streams for fishing; unlimited riding; garden.

Profile of Summer Employees Total number: 8; average age: 21; 50% male, 50% female; 100% college students; 25% local residents. Nonsmokers preferred.

Employment Information Openings are from June 1 to September 10. Jobs available: ▶ 2 *cooks* with experience or training as a baker and ability to work well with others at $600–$800 per month; ▶ 2 *cabin staff members* with organizational and interpersonal skills and attention to cleanliness at $500–$600 per month. International students encouraged to apply; must obtain own visa and working papers prior to employment.

Benefits On-the-job training, on-site room and board at no charge, laundry facilities, tips.

Contact Mrs. William Carroccia, Owner, Sweet Grass Ranch, Department SJ, HC 87 Box 2161, Big Timber, Montana 59011; 406-537-4497, Fax 406-537-4477. Application deadline: March 31.

NEBRASKA

CALVIN CREST CAMP, RETREAT, AND CONFERENCE CENTER
RURAL ROUTE 2, BOX 226
FREMONT, NEBRASKA 68025

General Information Church-affiliated camp and conference/retreat facility serving approximately 800 campers annually. Established in 1962. Owned by Homestead Presbytery. Operated by Presbyterian Church. Affiliated with Christian Camping International/USA, American Camping Association, Presbyterian Church of the United States of America. 255-acre facility located 2 miles southwest of Fremont. Features: outdoor swimming pool; 12 covered wagons, 5 A-frames/cabins (summer only), 8 cabins (year-round); wildlife–wild turkeys, whitetail deer, and foxes; dining facility (year-round); 6–8 conference rooms (30–175 capacity); motel-like lodging for 80 people.

Profile of Summer Employees Total number: 8; average age: 25; 50% male, 50% female; 20% high school students; 50% college students; 30% retirees; 80% local residents. Nonsmokers preferred.

Employment Information Openings are from May 15 to August 15. Year-round positions also offered. Jobs available: ▶ 3 *swimming instructors* with Red Cross lifeguard certification at $130–$150 per week; ▶ 2 *food service staff members;* ▶ 1 *housekeeping staff member.* International students encouraged to apply; must obtain own visa and working papers prior to employment; must apply through recognized agency.

Benefits On-the-job training, on-site room and board at no charge, laundry facilities. Preemployment training of 1 day is required and includes safety and accident prevention, group interaction, leadership, camper-counselor relations. Orientation is paid.

Contact Doug Morton, Administrator, Calvin Crest Camp, Retreat, and Conference Center, R.R. 2, Box 226, Fremont, Nebraska 68025; 402-628-6455, Fax 402-628-8255. Application deadline: April 15.

CAMP EASTER SEAL
2470 VAN DORN ROAD
MILFORD, NEBRASKA 68405

General Information Residential camp serving children and adults with physical and developmental disabilities. Established in 1968. Operated by Nebraska Easter Seal Society. Affiliated with American Camping Association, National Easter Seal Society. 70-acre facility located 20 miles west of Lincoln. Features: swimming pool; softball field and meadow; large activity lodge; location bordered by Big Blue River; 9 camper cabins (wheelchair accessible); ropes course.

Profile of Summer Employees Total number: 35; average age: 21; 33% male, 67% female; 5% minorities; 33% high school students; 50% college students; 25% local residents. Nonsmokers preferred.

Employment Information Openings are from May 24 to August 7. Jobs available: ▶ 9 *cabin leaders* at $175–$195 per week; ▶ 6 *program positions* at $175–$195 per week; ▶ 3 *kitchen assistants* at $120–$140 per week; ▶ 2 *nurses* with RN/LPN license (Nebraska) at $350–$450 per week; ▶ 1 *lifeguard* with WSI certification at $175–$275 per week; ▶ 1 *program director* at $250–$300 per week; ▶ 1 *head counselor* at $175–$200 per week.

Benefits College credit, on-site room and board at no charge, laundry facilities. Preemployment training of 6 days is required and includes safety and accident prevention, group interaction, first-aid, CPR, leadership, camper-counselor relations, disability awareness. Orientation is paid.

Contact Andi Reed, Director of Camping and Recreation, Camp Easter Seal, Department SJ, 2470 Van Dorn Road, Milford, Nebraska 68405; 402-761-2875, Fax 402-761-2282. Application deadline: May 1.

NEW HAMPSHIRE

BALSAMS GRAND RESORT HOTEL
ROUTE 26
DIXVILLE NOTCH, NEW HAMPSHIRE 03576

General Information Facility catering to vacationers (July, August, and winter) as well as convention groups (spring and fall). Established in 1873. Owned by Balsams Corporation. Affiliated with American Hospitality Association, American Culinary Federation, Chaines Des Rotisseurs. 15,000-acre facility located 300 miles north of Boston, MA. Features: location in the White Mountains of New Hampshire 13 miles south of Canada; panoramic golf courses; Lake Gloriette; hiking trails; tennis courts; swimming pool.

Profile of Summer Employees Total number: 450; average age: 21; 50% male, 50% female; 11% minorities; 4% high school students; 22% college students; 6% retirees; 6% international; 53% local residents.

Employment Information Openings are from May 22 to October 20. Winter break positions also offered. Jobs available: ▶ 3 *lifeguards* at $720 per month; ▶ 30 *dining room wait staff members* at $200–$400 per week; ▶ 10 *housekeeping staff members* at $200–$300 per week; ▶ 5 *beverage servers* at $200–$300 per week; ▶ 5 *bellpersons;* ▶ 5 *kitchen staff members;* ▶ 5 *laundry staff members.* International students encouraged to apply; must obtain own visa and working papers prior to employment.

Benefits On-the-job training, formal ongoing training, on-site room and board at $30 per week, laundry facilities, free use of lake, golf course, tennis courts, and hiking trails.

Contact Suzanne Ingram, Director of Personnel, Balsams Grand Resort Hotel, Department SJ, Route 26, Dixville Notch, New Hampshire 03576; 603-255-3400 Ext. 2666, Fax 603-255-4670. Application deadline: April 1.

BROOKWOODS FOR BOYS/DEER RUN FOR GIRLS
CHESTNUT COVE ROAD
ALTON, NEW HAMPSHIRE 03809

General Information Residential religious camps serving 250 campers in two-, four-, six-, and eight-week sessions. Established in 1944. Owned by Christian Camps and Conferences. Affiliated with Christian Camps and Conference, Inc., American Camping Association, Christian Camping International/USA. 250-acre facility located 100 miles north of Boston, Massachusetts. Features: frontage on Lake Winnipesaukee; rustic wilderness environment; lodge and recreation hall; location surrounded by wilderness area.

Profile of Summer Employees Total number: 100; average age: 28; 50% male, 50% female; 10% minorities; 10% high school students; 90% college students; 10% international; 20% local residents. Nonsmokers only.

Employment Information Openings are from June 15 to August 22. Spring break, winter break, Christmas break positions also offered. Jobs available: ▶ 4 *trip staff members* with CPR and first aid certification at $1000–$1200 per season; ▶ 10 *waterfront staff members* with WSI and LGT certification at $1000–$1200 per season; ▶ 10 *general counselors* at $1000–$1200 per season; ▶ 3 *riding instructors* (minimum age 21) with CHA certification at $1200–$1300 per season; ▶ 2 *riflery instructors* with NRA certification at $1100–$1200 per season; ▶ 2 *waterskiing* *instructors* with LGT certification at $1100–$1200 per season. International students encouraged to apply; must apply through recognized agency.

Benefits On-the-job training, formal ongoing training, on-site room and board at no charge, travel reimbursement. Preemployment training of 10 days is required and includes safety and accident prevention, first-aid, CPR, camper-counselor relations. Orientation is unpaid.

Contact Bob Strodel, Executive Director, Brookwoods for Boys/Deer Run for Girls, Chestnut Cove Road, Alton, New Hampshire 03809; 603-875-3600, Fax 603-875-4602, E-mail brook@worldpath.net, URL http://www.brookwoods.org. Application deadline: May 1.

CAMP DEERWOOD
HOLDERNESS, NEW HAMPSHIRE 03245

General Information Residential camp serving 120 boys for seven weeks. Established in 1945. Owned by Ferris Thomsen, Jr. Affiliated with New Hampshire Camping Association. 80-acre facility located 110 miles south of Boston, Massachusetts. Features: 1600 feet of shore frontage on Squam Lake; location in the foothills of the White Mountains; 4 tennis courts; 1 large athletic field.

Profile of Summer Employees Total number: 40; average age: 28; 100% male; 8% high school students; 30% college students. Nonsmokers only.

Employment Information Openings are from June 15 to August 15. Jobs available: ▶ 2 *swimming instructors* with WSI/lifeguard certification; ▶ *general counselors–crafts/outdoor camp skills/riflery/archery.* All positions offered at $1200–$2000 per season. International students encouraged to apply; must obtain own visa and working papers prior to employment; must apply through recognized agency.

Benefits On-the-job training, on-site room and board at no charge, laundry facilities. Preemployment training of 8 days is required and includes safety and accident prevention, group interaction, first-aid, CPR, leadership, camper-counselor relations. Orientation is paid.

Contact Tommy Thomsen, Director-Deerwood, Camp Deerwood, Box 188, Holderness, New Hampshire 03245; 603-279-4237. Application deadline: February 1.

CAMP MERRIMAC
ROUTE 2
CONTOOCOOK, NEW HAMPSHIRE 03229

General Information Residential camp serving over 200 highly motivated boys and girls. Established in 1919. Owned by Robert M. Martin. Affiliated with American Camping Association, New England Camping Association. 400-acre facility located 10 miles northwest of Concord, Massachusetts. Features: lake; location 72 miles from Boston; modern cabins; pine forest location; 4 large sports fields.

Profile of Summer Employees Total number: 100; average age: 21; 60% male, 40% female; 40% college students; 40% international. Nonsmokers only.

Employment Information Openings are from June 23 to August 23. Jobs available: ▶ 1 *experienced archery instructor* at $800–$1200 per season; ▶ 1 *experienced riflery instructor* at $800–$1200 per season; ▶ *swimming instructors;* ▶ 1 *canoeing instructor* at $800–$1200 per season; ▶ 2 *waterskiing instructors* at $800–$1200 per season; ▶ 1 *sailing instructor* at $800–$1200 per season; ▶ 1 *athletic director* at $800–$1400 per season; ▶ 1 *head of waterfront* with WSI certification at $800–$2000 per season; ▶ 2 *soccer instructors* at $800–$1200 per season; ▶ 2 *softball instructors* at $800–$1200 per season; ▶ 2 *basketball instructors* at $800–$1200 per season; ▶ 4 *group leaders* at $1200–$1600 per season; ▶ 1 *fine arts instructor* at $800–$1200 per season; ▶ 1 *crafts instructor* at $800–$1200 per season; ▶ 3 *science instructors* at $1200–$1400 per season; ▶ 6 *bus drivers* at $800–$1200 per season; ▶ *tennis instructors* at $800–$1200 per season. International students encouraged to apply; must apply through recognized agency.

Benefits College credit, on-site room and board at no charge, laundry facilities, workmen's compensation insurance. Preemployment training is required and includes safety and accident prevention, CPR, leadership. Orientation is paid.

Contact Robert M. Martin, President, Camp Merrimac, Department SJ, 260 Harrison Avenue, Harrison, New York 10528; 914-835-5012, Fax 914-835-4965. Application deadline: March 1.

CAMP MERROWVISTA
OSSIPEE, NEW HAMPSHIRE 03864

General Information Coed residential program for students ages 8–16. The focus is on leadership development and includes general program activities for students ages 8–12 and extended backpacking, canoeing, and cycling for students ages 13–16. Established in 1924. Owned by American Youth Foundation. Affiliated with American Camping Association (National and New England), Association of Experiential Education. 600-acre facility located 120 miles north of Boston, Massachusetts. Features: lakefront on Dan Hole Pond for swimming, sailing, and windsurfing; 600 acres in Ossipee Mountains for backpacking; high and low ropes courses and climbing tower; cycling and canoeing throughout New Hampshire, Vermont, Maine, and Southern Canada; backpacking trips in the White Mountains.

Profile of Summer Employees Total number: 60; average age: 24; 50% male, 50% female; 2% minorities; 10% high school students; 60% college students; 28% teachers. Nonsmokers only.

Employment Information Openings are from June 15 to August 24. Year-round positions also offered. Jobs available: ▶ 20 *village leaders* with WSI and lifeguard certification, CPR/first aid training preferred at $125–$190 per week; ▶ 12 *trip leaders* (minimum age 21) with experience leading trips, lifeguard and CPR/first aid training preferred at $160–$215 per week; ▶ 2 *waterfront staff members* with WSI and lifeguard certification required at $800–$2000 per season; ▶ 1 *sailing instructor* with experience sailing Laser I and Laser II boats, lifeguard certification at $800–$1000 per season; ▶ 1 *nurse* with RN eligibility for New Hampshire license; ▶ 1 *bike mechanic* with experience repairing and assembling touring bicycles, instruction of touring road safety, and bike maintenance at $800–$1000 per season; ▶ 1 *outcamping equipment coordinator* with repair, inventory, check-out/check-in of backpacking and canoeing equipment; some driving of passenger vans required at $800–$1000 per season; ▶ 1 *outcamping food coordinator* at $800–$1000 per season; ▶ 1 *arts and crafts coordinator* with crafts knowledge at $800–$1000 per season; ▶ *kitchen staff members* at $600–$2000 per season; ▶ *office staff members* with computer skills at $600–$1300 per season. International students encouraged to apply; must obtain own visa and working papers prior to employment.

Benefits College credit, on-site room and board at no charge, laundry facilities, travel reimbursement, workmen's compensation, wilderness first aid training. Preemployment training of 7 to 14 days is required and includes safety and accident prevention, group interaction, first-aid, leadership, camper-counselor relations. Orientation is paid.

Contact Heather R. Kiley, Director of Camp Programs, Camp Merrowvista, Department SJ, 147 Canaan Road, Ossipee, New Hampshire 03864; 603-539-6607, Fax 603-539-7504. Application deadline: April 15.

CAMP PEMIGEWASSETT
ROUTE 25A
WENTWORTH, NEW HAMPSHIRE 03282

General Information Traditional residential camp for 170 boys ages 8–15. We have a seven–week session and a broad range of activities including sports, hiking, nature study, dramatics, and art. Established in 1908. Owned by Alfred N. Fauver/Thomas L. Reed. Affiliated with American Camping Association- New England Section, New Hampshire Camp Directors Association, Association of Independent Camps. 600-acre facility located 70 miles north of Manchester. Features: location in lakes region of New Hampshire on the edge of the White Mountain National Forest; shore frontage surrounding a mile-long lake; sports facilities including 7 tennis courts, 2 soccer fields, and 3 baseball fields; waterfronts include 2 swimming areas with docks and diving floats; sailing equipment: 5 sunfish, 7 sailboards, 16 canoes, 7 kayaks, and 3 day sailers; extensively-equipped nature lodge and natural history library.

Profile of Summer Employees Total number: 70; average age: 24; 90% male, 10% female; 5%

minorities; 20% high school students; 40% college students; 8% retirees; 8% international; 10% local residents; 15% teachers. Nonsmokers only.

Employment Information Openings are from June 19 to August 16. Jobs available: ▶ *cabin counselors/instructors* (minimum of one year of college completed) with Red Cross first aid and CPR certification preferred at $1100–$1400 per season; ▶ *cabin counselors/swimming instructors* (minimum of one year of college completed) with Red Cross WSI certification at $1100–$1500 per season; ▶ *assistant counselors* (minimum age 17) with Red Cross CPR certification preferred at $900–$1000 per season; ▶ *kitchen workers* (minimum age 17) at $1000–$1300 per season. International students encouraged to apply; must apply through recognized agency.

Benefits On-the-job training, on-site room and board at no charge, laundry facilities, great staff morale and cameraderie.

Contact Robert Grabill, Director, Camp Pemigewassett, Department SJ, 25 Rayton Road, Hanover, New Hampshire 03755; 603-643-8055, Fax 603-643-9601, E-mail robertgraybill@valley.net.

CAMP ROBIN HOOD FOR BOYS AND GIRLS
FREEDOM, NEW HAMPSHIRE 03836

General Information Residential camp serving 240 boys and girls ages 7–16 for 4- and 8-week sessions. Established in 1927. Owned by John Klein and Drew Friedman. Affiliated with American Camping Association, New Hampshire Camp Directors Association. 210-acre facility located 125 miles northwest of Boston, Massachusetts. Features: ½ mile of shoreline on Broad Bay of Lake Ossipee; 6 lighted outdoor tennis courts; 4 extensive, level sports fields; 12-horse stable with trails, riding and jumping rings; state-of-the-art theater; 140 acres of woods.

Profile of Summer Employees Total number: 115; average age: 22; 60% male, 40% female; 3% minorities; 20% high school students; 70% college students; 20% international; 10% teachers. Nonsmokers preferred.

Employment Information Openings are from June 20 to August 20. Jobs available: ▶ 4 *swimming instructors* with WSI certification, lifeguard training, or Bronze Medallion at $800–$1400 per season; ▶ 10 *general counselors* at $600–$800 per season; ▶ 8 *sports coaches* at $800–$1500 per season; ▶ 3 *riding instructors* with English riding teaching experience at $800–$1500 per season; ▶ 3 *sailing and canoeing instructors* with teaching experience at $700–$1200 per season; ▶ 1 *experienced archery instructor* at $700–$1400 per season; ▶ 1 *experienced gymnastics instructor* at $700–$1200 per season; ▶ 2 *nurses* with RN certification at $2000–$3000 per season; ▶ 3 *waterskiing instructors/boat drivers* at $800–$1400 per season; ▶ 1 *waterfront director* with Red Cross certification at $1800–$3000 per season; ▶ 5 *tennis instructors* with playing and/or teaching experience. at $800–$1500 per season; ▶ 1 *tennis director* at $1800–$3000 per season; ▶ 10 *kitchen/pantry staff* at $500–$1200 per season; ▶ 2 *secretary* at $500–$1200 per season; ▶ 2 *crafts instructors* at $800–$1200 per season; ▶ 1 *ceramics instructor* with experience with wheel and kiln at $800–$1200 per season. International students encouraged to apply; must obtain own visa and working papers prior to employment; must apply through recognized agency.

Benefits College credit, on-the-job training, formal ongoing training, on-site room and board at no charge, laundry facilities, experience working with children, leadership training. Preemployment training of 5 to 8 days is required and includes safety and accident prevention, group interaction, first-aid, CPR, leadership, camper-counselor relations.

Contact John Klein, Director, Camp Robin Hood for Boys and Girls, 344 Thistle Trail, Mayfield Heights, Ohio 44124; 216-646-1911, Fax 216-646-1972. Application deadline: May 1.

CAMP TEL NOAR
167 MAIN STREET
HAMPSTEAD, NEW HAMPSHIRE 03841

General Information Jewish coeducational cultural residential camp serving 265 children. Established in 1952. Operated by Cohen Foundation. Affiliated with American Camping Association, New Hampshire Camping Association, Association of Independent Camps. 60-acre facility located 50 miles north of Boston, Massachusetts. Features: unique housing; spring-fed lake; 8 tennis courts; multipurpose gym with stage.

Profile of Summer Employees Total number: 95; average age: 19; 50% male, 50% female; 16% high school students; 82% college students; 2% international. Nonsmokers preferred.

Employment Information Openings are from June 17 to August 17. Jobs available: ▶ *3 arts and crafts instructors* at $1350–$1800 per season; ▶ *kitchen workers* at $185–$205 per week; ▶ 1 *windsurf instructor* with lifeguard training certification at $1500–$1900 per season; ▶ *2 canoe instructors* with lifeguard training certification at $1350–$2000 per season; ▶ *2 sailing instructors* with lifeguard training certification at $1350–$2000 per season; ▶ *3 swimming instructors* with WSI and lifeguard training certification at $1350–$2000 per season; ▶ 1 *swimming program director* with WSI and lifeguard training certification at $2000–$2500 per season; ▶ *4 maintenance workers* at $185–$205 per week; ▶ 1 *archery instructor* at $1500–$1900 per season.

Benefits College credit, on-the-job training, formal ongoing training, on-site room and board at no charge, laundry facilities, gratuities. Preemployment training of 5 days is required and includes safety and accident prevention, group interaction, leadership, camper-counselor relations. Orientation is paid.

Contact Marty Wiadro, Director, Camp Tel Noar, Department SJ, 131 Victoria Road, Sudbury, Massachusetts 01776; 508-443-3655, Fax 508-881-1006, E-mail ctn.wiadro@juno.com. Application deadline: April 1.

CAMP TEVYA
BROOKLINE, NEW HAMPSHIRE 03033

General Information Jewish coeducational cultural camp serving 325 campers. Established in 1940. Operated by Cohen Foundation. Affiliated with American Camping Association, New Hampshire Camping Association, Association of Independent Camps. 650-acre facility located 65 miles north of Boston, Massachusetts. Features: waterfront area; 8 tennis courts; 2 theater stages; 3 ball fields; indoor gym.

Profile of Summer Employees Total number: 120; average age: 20; 50% male, 50% female; 16% high school students; 82% college students; 2% international. Nonsmokers preferred.

Employment Information Openings are from June 20 to August 20. Jobs available: ▶ *3 arts and crafts instructors* at $1350–$1800 per season; ▶ 1 *arts and crafts head* at $2000–$2500 per season; ▶ 1 *music head* at $2000–$2500 per season; ▶ *2 canoe instructors* at $1350–$2000 per season; ▶ *2 sailing instructors* at $1350–$2000 per season; ▶ *3 swimming instructors* at $1350–$2000 per season; ▶ 1 *swimming head* at $2000–$2500 per season; ▶ 1 *athletics head* at $2000–$2500 per season; ▶ 1 *waterskiing head* at $1500–$1900 per season; ▶ 1 *archery instructor* at $1500–$1900 per season; ▶ 1 *photography head* at $1350–$2000 per season; ▶ 1 *drama head* at $1500–$2000 per season.

Benefits College credit, on-the-job training, formal ongoing training, on-site room and board at no charge, laundry facilities, gratuities. Preemployment training of 5 days is required and includes safety and accident prevention, group interaction, CPR, leadership, camper-counselor relations. Orientation is paid.

Contact Pearl Lourie, Executive Director, Camp Tevya, Department SJ, 30 Main Street, Ashland, Massachusetts 01701; 508-881-1002, Fax 508-881-1006. Application deadline: April 1.

CAMP TOKHOMEUPOG
HC 63, BOX 40
EAST MADISON, NEW HAMPSHIRE 03849

General Information Residential camp accommodating 120 boys ages 6–16 and featuring sports, mountain and canoe camping trips, and adventure program including ropes course and rock climbing. Established in 1932. Owned by Hoyt Family. Affiliated with American Camping Association, American Red Cross, National Rifle Association. 1,000-acre facility located 110 miles north of Boston, Massachusetts. Features: private lake; 5 tennis courts; location near White Mountain National Forest; 2 large sports fields; ropes course with climbing wall; indoor basketball court.

Profile of Summer Employees   Total number: 35; average age: 22; 95% male, 5% female; 5% minorities; 10% high school students; 70% college students; 10% international; 85% local residents; 20% teachers. Nonsmokers preferred.

Employment Information   Openings are from June 26 to August 26. Christmas break positions also offered. Jobs available: ▶ 8 *cabin counselors* with CPR, lifeguard, and first aid training at $700–$1400 per season; ▶ 1 *rock climbing instructor* at $1200–$1800; ▶ 1 *waterfront WSI* at $2000–$2500 per season; ▶ 1 *tennis pro (part-time)* at $1000–$1400 per season; ▶ *kitchen helper* at $2000–$3000 per season; ▶ *mountain bike instructor* at $1200–$1800 per season. International students encouraged to apply; must obtain own visa and working papers prior to employment.

Benefits   On-the-job training, on-site room and board at no charge, laundry facilities. Preemployment training of 4 to 9 days is required and includes safety and accident prevention, group interaction, first-aid, CPR, leadership, camper-counselor relations. Orientation is paid.

Contact   Ted Hoyt, Director, Camp Tokhomeupog, HC 63, Box 40, East Madison, New Hampshire 03849; 603-367-8896, Fax 603-367-8664.

CAMP WALT WHITMAN
PIKE, NEW HAMPSHIRE 03780

General Information   Coeducational residential camp serving 350 campers and offering a strong general program. Established in 1948. Owned by Jancy and Bill Dorfman. Affiliated with American Camping Association. 300-acre facility located 120 miles north of Boston, Massachusetts. Features: location in White Mountains on a lake; 11 clay tennis courts; playing fields; indoor facilities and modern cabins; natural environment; Olympic-size heated swimming pool.

Profile of Summer Employees   Total number: 170; average age: 21; 50% male, 50% female; 5% high school students; 65% college students; 2% retirees; 10% international; 15% teachers. Nonsmokers only.

Employment Information   Openings are from June 15 to August 18. Jobs available: ▶ 20 *experienced general counselors* at $900–$1400 per season; ▶ 6 *experienced sports coaches* at $1200–$2000 per season; ▶ 6 *experienced tennis instructors* at $1000–$1800 per season; ▶ 6 *swimming instructors* with WSI certification at $1000–$1800 per season; ▶ 3 *experienced hiking and camping specialists* at $1000–$1800 per season; ▶ 6 *experienced kitchen and maintenance personnel* at $1200–$2500 per season; ▶ 2 *experienced dance/gymnastics instructors* at $1200–$1800 per season; ▶ 3 *experienced art/woodshop instructors* at $1200–$2000 per season; ▶ 3 *experienced sailing, canoeing, and windsurfing instructors* at $1000–$1800 per season; ▶ 2 *experienced water skiing instructors* at $1200–$2000 per season.

Benefits   College credit, on-the-job training, formal ongoing training, on-site room and board at no charge, travel reimbursement, health insurance, staff recreation program, staff lounge and kitchen, accessibility to Boston, Montreal, and the Maine seacoast for days off. Preemployment training of 7 days is required and includes safety and accident prevention, group interaction, first-aid, CPR, leadership, camper-counselor relations. Orientation is paid.

Contact   Jancy Dorfman, Director, Camp Walt Whitman, Department SJ, PO Box 558, Armonk, New York 10504; 800-657-8282, Fax 914-273-6186, E-mail campwalt@aol.com.

CHENOA
BRIMSTONE CORNER ROAD
ANTRIM, NEW HAMPSHIRE 03440

General Information   Girl Scout residential camp serving 115 girls ages 6–16 in one- and two-week sessions, emphasizing girl decision-making and leadership development. Established in 1994. Owned by Swift Water Girl Scout Council. Affiliated with American Camping Association, New Hampshire Camp Directors Association. 250-acre facility located 80 miles north of Boston, Massachusetts. Features: frontage on 200-acre Gregg Lake; Southwest New Hampshire Monadnock Region location; forests, rock ledges, and beaver pond; new cabins built with campers' help.

Profile of Summer Employees Total number: 40; average age: 21; 1% male, 99% female; 2% minorities; 50% college students; 15% international; 15% local residents. Nonsmokers preferred.

Employment Information Openings are from June 15 to August 20. Jobs available: ▶ *waterfront director* with WSI, LGT certification at $2000–$2700 per season; ▶ *waterfront assistant* with WSI, LGT at $1250–$2000 per season; ▶ *art specialist* with experience teaching groups of children at $1250–$2000 per season; ▶ *nurse* with RN, LPN or EMT at $2000–$3800 per season; ▶ *unit counselors* with experience working with groups of children at $1250–$2100 per season. International students encouraged to apply; must obtain own visa and working papers prior to employment; must apply through recognized agency.

Benefits On-the-job training, formal ongoing training, on-site room and board at no charge, health insurance. Preemployment training of 7 days is required and includes safety and accident prevention, group interaction, first-aid, CPR, leadership, camper-counselor relations. Orientation is paid.

Contact Nancy Frankel, Director of Outdoor Education, Chenoa, Department SJ, 88 Harvey Road, Manchester, New Hampshire 03103; 603-627-4158, Fax 603-627-4169, E-mail camping@ swgirlscouts.org, URL http://www.swgirlscouts.org.

CRAGGED MOUNTAIN FARM
FREEDOM, NEW HAMPSHIRE 03836

General Information Residential coed camp serving 75 campers with traditional program emphasizing tripping in Maine and New Hampshire. Established in 1927. Affiliated with American Camping Association. Features: scenic location on the side of Cragged Mountain.

Profile of Summer Employees Total number: 14; 50% male, 50% female.

Employment Information Jobs available: ▶ 14 *cabin counselors (minimum age 16)* with lifeguard training (preferred) and experience/interest in athletics and crafts at $400–$1000 per season; ▶ 6 *trip leaders* with CPR, basic first aid, and ability to qualify for Maine and New Hampshire trip leaders permit at $1200–$1400 per season; ▶ 6 *kitchen staff (minimum age 15)* at $300 per season; ▶ 2 *maintenance staff (minimum age 15)* at $300 per season; ▶ 1 *waterfront director* with WSI at $1000–$1200 per season; ▶ 1 *registered nurse* at $400 per week. International students encouraged to apply; must obtain own visa and working papers prior to employment.

Benefits On-the-job training, formal ongoing training, on-site room and board at no charge, laundry facilities, health insurance, workmen's comp. Preemployment training is required.

Contact Jim and Elizabeth Scully, Directors, Cragged Mountain Farm, Department SJ, 1551 Commodore Road, Lyndhurst, Ohio 44124; 216-605-1434.

GENEVA POINT CENTER
MOULTONBORO, NEW HAMPSHIRE 03254

General Information Ecumenical conference center hosting groups and Elderhostel. Established in 1921. Owned by Geneva Point Center, Inc. Affiliated with American Camping Association, International Association of Conference Center Administrators. 200-acre facility located 40 miles north of Concord. Features: location on Lake Winnipesaukee in central New Hampshire; 3 beaches; proximity to the White Mountains.

Profile of Summer Employees Total number: 40; average age: 19; 50% male, 50% female; 5% minorities; 70% college students; 25% retirees; 5% international; 5% local residents. Nonsmokers only.

Employment Information Openings are from May 1 to October 1. Jobs available: ▶ 5 *lifeguards* at $200–$220 per week; ▶ *general kitchen staff* at $170 per week; ▶ 4 *dining room staff* at $170 per week; ▶ 3 *housekeepers* at $170 per week. International students encouraged to apply; must obtain own visa and working papers prior to employment; must apply through recognized agency.

Benefits   On-the-job training, on-site room and board at no charge, laundry facilities. Preemployment training of 1 day is required and includes safety and accident prevention, group interaction, customer service. Orientation is paid.

Contact   Tom MacKay, Operations Manager, Geneva Point Center, HCR 62, Box 469, Center Harbor, New Hampshire 03226; 603-253-4366, Fax 603-253-4883, E-mail geneva@lr.net, URL http://www.genevapoint.org. Application deadline: February 1.

INTERLOCKEN INTERNATIONAL SUMMER CAMP
RURAL ROUTE 2, BOX 165
HILLSBORO, NEW HAMPSHIRE 03244

General Information   Creative, noncompetitive international summer camp offering a wide range of activities to 160 campers from the United States and around the world. Established in 1961. Owned by Richard Herman. Affiliated with Association for Experiential Education, American Camping Association. 500-acre facility located 75 miles northwest of Boston, Massachusetts. Features: wilderness area; full ropes course; lakefront with blueberry island; extensive mountain biking trails; architect-designed dining hall and dance pavilion.

Profile of Summer Employees   Total number: 50; average age: 26; 50% male, 50% female; 20% minorities; 50% college students; 20% international. Nonsmokers only.

Employment Information   Openings are from June 15 to August 20. Jobs available: ▶ 4 *experienced sports staff members;* ▶ 6 *experienced wilderness staff members;* ▶ 4 *experienced performing arts staff members;* ▶ 4 *experienced applied arts staff members;* ▶ 4 *experienced music staff members;* ▶ 2 *experienced dance instructors;* ▶ 2 *experienced environmental education staff members.* International students encouraged to apply; must apply through recognized agency.

Benefits   On-the-job training, on-site room and board at no charge, laundry facilities. Preemployment training of 10 days is required and includes safety and accident prevention, group interaction, first-aid, CPR, leadership, camper-counselor relations. Orientation is paid.

Contact   Judi Wisch, Staffing Coordinator, Interlocken International Summer Camp, Department SJ, RR 2, Box 165, Hillsboro, New Hampshire 03244; 603-478-3166, Fax 603-478-5260, E-mail mail@interlocken.org, URL http://www.interlocken.org. Application deadline: April 1.

INTERLOCKEN TRAVEL PROGRAMS
RR 2, BOX 165
HILLSBORO, NEW HAMPSHIRE 03244

General Information   Experientially-based domestic and international small group travel programs that focus on performing arts, adventure/wilderness, commmunity service, language, and environment. Our travel programs are an outgrowth of the Interlocken International Summer Camp. Established in 1961. Owned by Richard Herman. Affiliated with Association for Experiential Education, American Camping Association. 500-acre facility located 75 miles northwest of Boston, Massachusetts.

Profile of Summer Employees   Total number: 45; average age: 28; 50% male, 50% female; 20% minorities; 20% international. Nonsmokers only.

Employment Information   Openings are from June 15 to August 25. Jobs available: ▶ 2 *experienced cycling leaders* with experience working with high school age students as well as expertise in program focus and geographic location at $200 per week; ▶ 12 *experienced adventure/ wilderness leaders;* ▶ 4 *experienced performing arts leaders;* ▶ 35 *experienced travel leaders* with experience working with high school age students as well as expertise in program focus and geographic location at $200 per week; ▶ 4 *experienced language leaders;* ▶ 4 *experienced environmental study leaders;* ▶ 4 *experienced leadership training leaders.* International students encouraged to apply; must obtain own visa and working papers prior to employment.

Benefits   On-site room and board at no charge, laundry facilities, travel expenses to program location, opportunity to implement creative experiential education ideas. Preemployment training of 10 days is required and includes safety and accident prevention, group interaction, first-aid, CPR, leadership, camper-counselor relations. Orientation is paid.

Contact Judi Wisch, Staffing Coordinator, Interlocken Travel Programs, Department SJ, RR 2, Box 165, Hillsboro, New Hampshire 03244; 603-478-3166, Fax 603-478-5260, URL http://www. interlocken.org. Application deadline: March 1.

KINYON/JONES TENNIS CAMP AT DARTMOUTH COLLEGE
6083 ALUMNI GYM
HANOVER, NEW HAMPSHIRE 03755-3512

General Information Tennis camp for boys and girls age 10–17. Established in 1988. Owned by Chuck Kinyon and David Jones. Located 120 miles northwest of Boston, Massachusetts. Features: 9 outdoor hard court tennis courts; 4 indoor tennis courts; use of college facilities; indoor Olympic-size swimming pool; 10 squash courts.

Profile of Summer Employees Total number: 12; average age: 23; 50% male, 50% female; 90% college students; 10% teachers. Nonsmokers only.

Employment Information Openings are from June 10 to July 20. Jobs available: ▶ 8 *tennis instructors* at $235 per week.

Benefits On-the-job training, on-site room and board at no charge, laundry facilities.

Contact David Jones, Co-Director, Kinyon/Jones Tennis Camp at Dartmouth College, Department SJ, 6083 Alumni Gym, Hanover, New Hampshire 03755-3512; 603-646-3819, Fax 603-646-3348, E-mail chuck.kinyon@dartmouth.edu, URL http://www.xmission.com/~gastown/tennis/kjtc.htm.

NEW HAMPSHIRE TENNIS AND GOLF CAMP
ROUTE 2
CONTOOCOOK, NEW HAMPSHIRE 03229

General Information Residential camp specializing in tennis (rain or shine) and golf; also offering other land and water sports. Established in 1975. Affiliated with American Camping Association, New Hampshire Camp Directors Association. 175-acre facility located 12 miles east of Concord. Features: 4 outdoor tennis courts; 4 indoor tennis courts; golf driving range; miniature golf course; 9-hole golf course.

Profile of Summer Employees 60% male, 40% female; 100% college students. Nonsmokers only.

Employment Information Openings are from June 25 to August 23. Jobs available: ▶ 5 *tennis instructors;* ▶ 5 *golf instructors.* International students encouraged to apply; must apply through recognized agency.

Benefits On-site room and board at no charge, laundry facilities.

Contact Mr. Werner Rothschild, Director, New Hampshire Tennis and Golf Camp, Department SJ, Route 2, Contoocook, New Hampshire 03229; 516-364-8050, Fax 516-364-8099.

ROAD'S END FARM HORSEMANSHIP CAMP
JACKSON HILL ROAD
CHESTERFIELD, NEW HAMPSHIRE 03443-0197

General Information Residential camp program serving 60 girls ages 8–16 who love horses, English pleasure riding, and the noncompetitive atmosphere of a family-owned horse farm at the end of a quiet dirt road. Sessions vary from 2 to 8 weeks in length. Established in 1958. Owned by Thomas E. Woodman. 430-acre facility located 90 miles west of Boston, Massachusetts. Features: three tree-rimmed riding rings; twenty miles of private and scenic bridle paths; one quarter mile track; nearby private beach with two deep water rafts on spring-fed lake; adjacent to the 13,000-acre Pisgah Wilderness Area; nearby frontage on the Connecticut River.

Profile of Summer Employees Total number: 12; average age: 20; 100% female; 10% minorities; 80% college students; 10% international; 20% local residents. Nonsmokers only.

Employment Information Openings are from June 15 to August 20. Christmas break positions also offered. Jobs available: ▶ 4 *riding instructors* with Pony Club, CHA, or BHS credentials or some very good experience at $2000–$2500 per season; ▶ 3 *experienced swimming instructors* with WSI certification at $2000–$2500 per season; ▶ 4 *experienced lifeguards* with Red Cross credentials at $2000–$2500 per season; ▶ 1 *experienced canoeing instructor* with Red Cross credentials at $2000–$2500 per season; ▶ 1 *cook* at $4000–$5000 per season; ▶ 1 *prep cook* at $3000–$4000 per season. International students encouraged to apply; must obtain own visa and working papers prior to employment; must apply through recognized agency.

Benefits On-the-job training, on-site room and board at no charge, laundry facilities, congenial working environment, plenty of responsibility and freedom of choice, varied daily activities. Preemployment training of 3 days is required and includes safety and accident prevention, group interaction, leadership, camper-counselor relations. Orientation is paid.

Contact Tom Woodman, Director, Road's End Farm Horsemanship Camp, PO Box 197, Chesterfield, New Hampshire 03443-0197; 603-363-4900, Fax 603-363-4949, URL http://www. roadsendfarm.com. Application deadline: April 30.

ROCKYWOLD–DEEPHAVEN CAMPS, INC. (RDC)
PINEHURST ROAD, PO BOX B
HOLDERNESS, NEW HAMPSHIRE 03245

General Information Family vacation camp providing guests with a unique family living experience offering rustic simplicity, high-quality services, and a natural setting. Established in 1897. Owned by Rockywold–Deephaven Camps, Inc. Affiliated with American Camping Association, Squam Lake Association, Science Center of New Hampshire. 115-acre facility located 45 miles north of Concord. Features: location at the southern edge of the White Mountains on Squam Lake; 8 tennis courts, basketball court, and sports field; unlimited miles of hiking trails; 1½ miles of shore front, with a large fleet of canoes, kayaks, rowboats, and sailboats.

Profile of Summer Employees Total number: 80; average age: 23; 50% male, 50% female; 5% minorities; 70% college students; 5% retirees; 5% international; 10% local residents. Nonsmokers only.

Employment Information Openings are from May 20 to October 15. Jobs available: ▶ 22 *housekeeping personnel* with a positive and flexible attitude and high work standards at $176–$280 per week; ▶ 20 *food service personnel* with a positive and flexible attitude and high work standards at $176–$360 per week; ▶ 10 *grounds/maintenance personnel* with experience in soft-surface tennis court maintenance and carpentry at $176–$280 per week; ▶ 5 *recreation staff members* with experience in tennis, water sports, and working with various age groups at $200–$250 per week; ▶ 6 *office staff members* with word-processing and money handling skills and experience working with the public at $184–$280 per week. International students encouraged to apply; must apply through recognized agency.

Benefits On-the-job training, on-site room and board at no charge, laundry facilities, possible end-of-season bonus, limited use of recreational facilities and equipment.

Contact John Jurczynski, General Manager, Rockywold–Deephaven Camps, Inc. (RDC), Department SJ, PO Box B, Holderness, New Hampshire 03245; 603-968-3313, Fax 603-968-3438. Application deadline: March 15.

STUDENT CONSERVATION ASSOCIATION (SCA)
PO BOX 550
CHARLESTOWN, NEW HAMPSHIRE 03603

General Information Non-profit conservation organization that places volunteers in natural resource management positions in national wilderness areas. Established in 1957. Owned by Student Conservation Association. Features: access to national parks, forests, and wildlife refuges across America (including Alaska, Hawaii, and Scotland.

Profile of Summer Employees Total number: 1,600; average age: 22; 50% male, 50% female; 35% high school students; 65% college students.

Employment Information Openings are from May 1 to September 1. Year-round positions also offered. Jobs available: ▶ 1100 *resource assistants* (minimum age 18) with high school diploma at $50 per week; ▶ 450 *high school trail crew members* (ages 16–19); ▶ *high school crew leaders* with experience with high school students at $800 per season.

Benefits College credit, on-the-job training, formal ongoing training, on-site room and board at no charge, opportunity to live in a beautiful wilderness area, internship opportunities.

Contact Mel Tuck, Recruitment Director, Student Conservation Association (SCA), PO Box 550, Charlestown, New Hampshire 03603; 603-543-1700, Fax 603-543-1828.

NEW JERSEY

APPEL FARM ARTS AND MUSIC CENTER
ELMER-SHIRLEY ROAD
ELMER, NEW JERSEY 08318

General Information Residential camp offering instruction in the fine and performing arts. Established in 1960. Owned by Appel Farm Arts and Music Center. Affiliated with American Camping Association, National Guild of Community Schools, Southern New Jersey Development Council. 176-acre facility located 30 miles south of Philadelphia, Pennsylvania. Features: extensive visual arts studios, including video, fine arts, and photography facilities; rural area with playing fields; air-conditioned 300-seat theater; 2-acre organic garden; Olympic-size swimming pool; more than a dozen air-conditioned rehearsal and practice studios.

Profile of Summer Employees Total number: 80; average age: 26; 40% male, 60% female; 20% minorities; 15% college students; 20% international; 10% local residents; 40% teachers. Nonsmokers only.

Employment Information Openings are from June 15 to August 18. Jobs available: ▶ 3 *experienced dance instructors* with expert knowledge of modern, jazz, and ballet dancing at $1100–$1400 per season; ▶ 10 *music instructors* with extensive experience in woodwinds, piano, strings, percussion, voice, brass, electronic music, and rock at $1100–$1400 per season; ▶ 5 *experienced photography instructors* at $1100–$1400 per season; ▶ 3 *experienced video instructors* at $1100–$1400 per season; ▶ 2 *registered nurses* with RN license, NJ certification preferred,; ▶ 10 *experienced theater instructors* with directing experience at $1100–$1400 per season; ▶ 3 *technical theater personnel* with experience in stage craft, set design, costumes, and lighting at $1100–$1400 per season; ▶ 10 *art instructors* with extensive experience in painting, drawing, printmaking, sculpture, weaving, and ceramics at $1100–$1400 per season; ▶ 4 *swimming instructors* with lifeguard training or WSI certification at $1100–$1400 per season; ▶ 3 *sports staff members* with experience in tennis and noncompetitive sports at $1100–$1400 per season; ▶ 1 *community-outreach coordinator* with organizational ability and office work experience at $1100–$1400 per season. International students encouraged to apply; must apply through recognized agency.

Benefits On-site room and board at no charge, laundry facilities, opportunity to work in a community of artists, rehearsal/studio space. Preemployment training is required.

Contact Rena Levitt, Camp Director, Appel Farm Arts and Music Center, PO Box 888, Elmer, New Jersey 08318; 609-358-2472, Fax 609-358-6513, E-mail appelcamp@aol.com.

CAMP MERRY HEART/EASTER SEALS
21 O'BRIEN ROAD
HACKETTSTOWN, NEW JERSEY 07840

General Information Residential camp for persons with a disability ages 5–60, day camp for nondisabled children ages 5–12, and Travel Recreation Experiences in Camping (TREC) program for persons with a disability. Established in 1949. Operated by Easter Seal Society of New Jersey. Affiliated with American Camping Association. 121-acre facility located 60 miles west of New York, New York. Features: pool; lake for boating and fishing; cabins; paths and walkways accessible for persons with disabilities; nature/hiking trails.

Profile of Summer Employees Total number: 55; average age: 21; 50% male, 50% female; 25% minorities; 10% high school students; 75% college students; 25% international; 10% local residents. Nonsmokers only.

Employment Information Openings are from June 8 to August 30. Spring break, winter break, Christmas break positions also offered. Jobs available: ▶ 1 *swimming instructor* with lifeguard certification, experience, and teaching ability at $1200–$1300 per season; ▶ 1 *nature specialist* with ecology background at $1200–$1300 per season; ▶ 1 *recreation specialist* with therapeutic background at $1200–$1300 per season; ▶ 1 *boating specialist* with small craft certification at $1110–$1300 per season; ▶ 20 *counselors* (female) with college student status and special education background at $1100–$1200 per season; ▶ 20 *counselors* (male) with college student status and special education background at $1100–$1200 per season; ▶ 2 *cooks* with knowledge of cooking for groups at $3600–$4800 per season; ▶ 1 *experienced program specialist* at $1600–$2500 per season; ▶ 2 *nurses* with RN license, first aid, and CPR certification at $3600–$4800 per season. International students encouraged to apply; must apply through recognized agency.

Benefits College credit, formal ongoing training, on-site room and board at no charge, laundry facilities. Preemployment training of 14 days is required and includes safety and accident prevention, group interaction, leadership, camper-counselor relations. Orientation is paid.

Contact Mary Ellen Ross, Director of Camping, Camp Merry Heart/Easter Seals, Department SJ, 21 O'Brien Road, Hackettstown, New Jersey 07840; 908-852-3896, Fax 908-852-9263. Application deadline: May 15.

COLLEGE GIFTED PROGRAMS
120 LITTLETON ROAD, SUITE 201
PARSIPPANY, NEW JERSEY 07054-1803

General Information Residential educational academic summer camp for gifted and talented students in grades 4-11. Located at five sites, program blends academics with recreational and cultural activities. Established in 1984. Owned by College Gifted Programs. Operated by Drew University (Madison, NJ); Bryn Mawr College (Bryn Mawr, PA); Vassar College (Poughkeepsie, NY); George School (Newtown, PA); Oberlin College (Oberlin, OH); Pacific Lutheran University (Tacoma, WA). Features: outdoor tennis courts; swimming pools; playing fields.

Profile of Summer Employees Total number: 200; average age: 25; 50% male, 50% female; 30% minorities; 50% college students; 10% retirees; 10% international; 25% local residents; 30% teachers. Nonsmokers preferred.

Employment Information Openings are from June 25 to August 22. Jobs available: ▶ 100 *counselors* with two years of undergraduate college at $1500–$2200 per season; ▶ 30 *housemasters/instructors* (residential) with master's degree at $2500–$4250 per season; ▶ 70 *instructors* (non-residential) with master's degree at $1000–$2500 per season. International students encouraged to apply; must apply through recognized agency.

Benefits On-site room and board at no charge, laundry facilities. Preemployment training of 2 days is required and includes safety and accident prevention, group interaction, leadership, camper-counselor relations, gifted and talented education. Orientation is paid.

Contact Mrs. Margaret Solitario, Executive Director, College Gifted Programs, Department SJ,

120 Littleton Road, Suite 201, Parsippany, New Jersey 07054-1803; 201-334-6991, Fax 201-334-9756. Application deadline: April 30.

FAIRVIEW LAKE ENVIRONMENTAL TRIP
1035 FAIRVIEW LAKE ROAD
NEWTON, NEW JERSEY 07860

General Information Facility offering discovery and challenge trips to enhance an appreciation of the natural environment while fostering skills in communication, cooperation, and trust through physical challenges. Established in 1915. Owned by YMCA. Affiliated with American Camping Association. 600-acre facility located 64 miles west of New York City. Features: mile-long lake; location adjoining the Delaware Water Gap National Recreation Area; hockey rink; 600 acres of varying ecosystems; 10 miles of trails; location ½ mile from Appalachian Trail.

Profile of Summer Employees Total number: 7; average age: 25; 50% male, 50% female; 50% college students; 50% teachers. Nonsmokers only.

Employment Information Openings are from June 15 to August 20. Year-round positions also offered. Jobs available: ▶ 3 *trip leaders* with lifeguard training, first aid, and CPR certification at $200–$250 per week; ▶ 3 *trip counselors* with lifeguard training, first aid, and CPR certification at $180–$200 per week.

Benefits College credit, on-site room and board at no charge, laundry facilities.

Contact Christina Henriksen, Fairview Lake Environmental Trip, Department SJ, Fairview Lake YMCA, 1035 Fairview Lake Road, Newton, New Jersey 07860; 973-383-9282, Fax 973-383-6386. Application deadline: March 1.

FAIRVIEW LAKE YMCA CAMP
1035 FAIRVIEW LAKE ROAD
NEWTON, NEW JERSEY 07860

General Information Coed residential camp serving 200 campers. Emphasis is on improving self-esteem through creativity and/or physical challenges. Large sports, drama, and communications programs offered. Established in 1915. Owned by YMCA. Affiliated with American Camping Association, Young Men's Christian Association of the United States of America. 600-acre facility located 64 miles west of New York City. Features: mile-long freshwater lake; hockey rink; location adjoining Delaware Water Gap Recreation Area; ½ mile from Appalachian Trail; 10 miles of trails.

Profile of Summer Employees Total number: 65; average age: 22; 50% male, 50% female; 25% minorities; 15% high school students; 80% college students; 5% retirees; 25% international; 5% local residents; 10% teachers. Nonsmokers only.

Employment Information Openings are from June 18 to August 12. Spring break positions also offered. Jobs available: ▶ *junior counselors* (minimum age 17) at $500 per season; ▶ *counselors* with lifeguard certification at $1000–$1300 per season; ▶ *waterfront director* (minimum age 21) with WSI certification at $1800–$2500 per season; ▶ *riding director* (minimum age 21) with a minimum of 3 years of experience at $1800–$2500 per season; ▶ *unit leaders* at $1200–$1800 per season; ▶ *nurses* with RN and state license at $300–$450 per week. International students encouraged to apply; must obtain own visa and working papers prior to employment; must apply through recognized agency.

Benefits College credit, on-site room and board at no charge, laundry facilities.

Contact Mike Bordonaro, Summer Camp Director, Fairview Lake YMCA Camp, Department SJ, 1035 Fairview Lake Road, Newton, New Jersey 07860; 973-383-9282, Fax 973-383-6386. Application deadline: April 1.

FELLOWSHIP DEACONRY, INC. (DAY CAMP SUNSHINE & FELLOWSHIP CONFERENCE CENTER)
3575 VALLEY ROAD PO BOX 204
LIBERTY CORNER, NEW JERSEY 07938-0204

General Information Day camp and conference center that provides a well-balanced program to meet the spiritual and physical needs of all participants by providing rest, recreation, and the study of God's word. Established in 1933. Owned by Fellowship Deaconry, Inc. Affiliated with Christian Camping International/USA. 60-acre facility located 40 miles southwest of New York City. Features: location surrounded by Watchung Mountains; well-stocked Christian bookstore/ gift shop; 2 swimming pools and a pond for canoeing; historic area with sight-seeing attractions; miniature golf course; tennis court; athletic fields for baseball and soccer.

Profile of Summer Employees Nonsmokers only.

Employment Information Openings are from June 1 to September 30. Jobs available: ▶ 20 *counselors* at $95–$180 per week; ▶ 10 *counselors-in-training* at $65–$90 per week; ▶ 4 *kitchen crew* (day camp) at $65–$120 per week; ▶ 4 *housekeeping staff* at $65–$200 per week; ▶ 5 *waitresses* at $85–$200 per week; ▶ 1 *pantry person* at $85–$200 per week; ▶ 6 *lifeguards* with Red Cross advanced lifesaving certification at $120–$200 per week.

Benefits On-the-job training, on-site room and board, laundry facilities, Christian fellowship and bible studies.

Contact Rita Krohn, Directing Deaconess, Fellowship Deaconry, Inc. (Day Camp Sunshine & Fellowship Conference Center), Department SJ, PO Box 204, Liberty Corner, New Jersey 07938-0204; 908-647-1777, Fax 908-647-4117. Application deadline: June 1.

NEW JERSEY 4-H CAMPS
50 NIELSON ROAD
SUSSEX, NEW JERSEY 07461

General Information Two residential camp facilities with a total weekly capacity of 300 campers ages 7–13. Established in 1951. Owned by Rutgers University. Operated by Rutgers Cooperative Extension System. 700-acre facility located 70 miles northwest of New York, New York. Features: 6-acre lake; farm animals (working farm); proximity to Stokes State Forest, High Point State Park, and the Delaware River; access to the Appalachian Trail for hiking trips.

Profile of Summer Employees Total number: 30; average age: 19; 40% male, 60% female; 10% minorities; 35% high school students; 35% college students; 10% international; 10% local residents. Nonsmokers preferred.

Employment Information Openings are from June 27 to August 20. Jobs available: ▶ 2 *waterfront supervisors* (minimum age 18) with lifeguard certification at $230–$250 per week; ▶ 4 *certified lifeguards* at $180–$210 per week; ▶ 2 *experienced boating/canoeing instructors* (minimum age 18) with lifeguard certification at $180–$210 per week; ▶ 2 *chefs* with kitchen, ordering, and supervisory experience at $230–$260 per week; ▶ 2 *experienced cooks* at $180–$200 per week; ▶ 2 *experienced assistant cooks* at $170–$180 per week; ▶ 4 *health directors* (minimum age 18) with Red Cross advanced first aid and CPR certification (as a minimum) at $270–$370 per week; ▶ 2 *experienced horseback riding instructors* (minimum age 18) at $200–$230 per week; ▶ 2 *animal science instructors* (minimum age 18) with experience working with farm animals at $200–$230 per week; ▶ 2 *nature instructors* (minimum age 18) at $200–$230 per week; ▶ 1 *hiking/camping instructor* (minimum age 18) with Red Cross standard first aid and CPR certification at $200–$230 per week; ▶ 1 *fishing instructor* (minimum age 18) at $200–$230 per week; ▶ 2 *crafts shop managers* (minimum age 18) with experience maintaining inventories at $200–$230 per week; ▶ 1 *experienced horse-care person* at $170–$180 per week; ▶ *counselors* at $170–$220 per week. International students encouraged to apply; must apply through recognized agency.

Benefits College credit, on-the-job training, formal ongoing training, on-site room and board at no charge, laundry facilities, health insurance, first aid training, 1½ days off each week, possible end-of-season bonus. Preemployment training of 5 days is required and includes safety and

accident prevention, group interaction, first-aid, CPR, leadership. Orientation is paid.
Contact Kevin Mitchell, Director, 4-H Outdoor Education Centers, New Jersey 4-H Camps, Department SJ, 50 Nielson Road, Sussex, New Jersey 07461; 201-875-4715, Fax 201-875-1289, E-mail 4hcamp@aesop.rutgers.edu. Application deadline: June 15.

NEW JERSEY SUMMER ARTS INSTITUTE
MARIE KATZENBACH SCHOOL
EWING, NEW JERSEY 08648

General Information Residential 5-week school of the arts serving 125–150 artistically talented students entering grades 8 through freshman year in college. Established in 1981. Owned by Institute for Arts and Humanities Education. Affiliated with International Network Performing and Visual Arts Schools, National Guild Community Schools of the Arts, Alliance for Arts Education/New Jersey. 100-acre facility located 6 miles southwest of Princeton.
Profile of Summer Employees Total number: 85; average age: 30; 33% male, 67% female; 16% minorities; 10% college students; 25% teachers. Nonsmokers preferred.
Employment Information Openings are from June 27 to August 6. Jobs available: ▶ 3 *residence supervisors* with at least a masters level education, preferably in the arts at $1500–$1800 per season; ▶ 12 *residence advisors* with at least completing sophomore year, preferably in an arts or social sciences at $900–$1200 per season; ▶ 8 *teaching assistants* with at least completion of sophomore year and experience in the arts at $1000–$1200 per season; ▶ 1 *residence life coordinator* with experience in a college setting or comparable training at $2000–$2800 per season; ▶ 1 *social worker* with MSW and an interest in the arts at $2500–$3500 per season; ▶ 1 *administrative assistant* with computer literacy, good writing skills, and ability to work under pressure at $2000–$3500 per season. International students encouraged to apply; must obtain own visa and working papers prior to employment.
Benefits On-the-job training, on-site room and board at no charge, laundry facilities, travel reimbursement, opportunity to study/work with professional artists, opportunity to work in studios on off hours. Preemployment training is required and includes group interaction, CPR, leadership, camper-counselor relations, community service guidelines.
Contact Rina Shere, Executive Director, New Jersey Summer Arts Institute, 100 Jersey Avenue, Suite B-104, New Brunswick, New Jersey 08901; 908-220-1600, Fax 908-220-1515.

NEW JERSEY YMHA-YWHA CAMPS
21 PLYMOUTH STREET
FAIRFIELD, NEW JERSEY 07004

General Information Five Jewish residential camps: Nah-Jee-Wah–coed for 1st–6th grades (350 campers); Cedar Lakes–coed for 7–9th grades (500 campers); Teen-Age Camp–coed for 10th-11th grades (150 campers); Round Lake–coed for children with ADHD or learning disabilities (180 campers); Nesher–coed orthodox for grades 3-9 (200 campers). Established in 1921. Operated by New Jersey Federation of YMHA & YWHA's. 2,400-acre facility located 150 miles north of New York, New York. Features: 2 Olympic-size pools; full lake programs with sailing and boating; miles of hiking trails and natural wooded areas; full athletic facility with 12 tennis courts, 4 softball fields, archery range, 3 soccer pitches, and 4 basketball courts; regulation-size rollerblading pavilion.
Profile of Summer Employees Total number: 500; average age: 21; 40% male, 60% female; 10% high school students; 75% college students; 2% retirees; 40% international; 60% local residents; 13% teachers. Nonsmokers preferred.
Employment Information Openings are from June 10 to August 22. Jobs available: ▶ *counselors* with camp experience or course study in early childhood education, psychology, sociology, recreation, or special needs at $1000–$1500 per season; ▶ *waterfront–boating and pool staff members* with WSI, canoeing, and sailing certification at $1100–$1600 per season; ▶ *athletics staff members–all sports plus archery and gymnastics* with coaching experience at $1000–$1500 per season; ▶ *specialists–radio, computers, art, photo, cooking, and nature* with teaching experi-

ence in area at $1000–$1500 per season; ▶ *division heads* with supervisory experience (must be a graduate student with camp experience) at $1800–$2500 per season. International students encouraged to apply; must apply through recognized agency.

Benefits On-the-job training, formal ongoing training, on-site room and board at no charge, laundry facilities, travel reimbursement, certification by national associations in certain areas such as waterfront, tennis, ropes, and archery. Preemployment training of 5 days is required and includes safety and accident prevention, group interaction, first-aid, CPR, leadership. Orientation is paid.

Contact Anne Tursky, Assistant Director, New Jersey YMHA-YWHA Camps, Department SJ, 21 Plymouth Street, Fairfield, New Jersey 07004; 201-575-4268 Ext. 25, Fax 201-575-4188, E-mail njw@njycamps.org.

PALISADES INTERSTATE PARK COMMISSION
PO BOX 155
ALPINE, NEW JERSEY 07620

General Information State park serving the cultural, historical, environmental, and recreational needs of the general public. Established in 1900. Owned by Palisades Interstate Park Commission. Affiliated with New Jersey Recreation and Park Association. 2,500-acre facility located 2 miles west of New York, New York. Features: over 30 miles of hiking/cross-country skiing trails and 20 miles of scenic roads; 4 major picnic areas; 2 boat basins and 1 boat launching ramp; 2 historic sites; 2 refreshment stands; bookstore/gift shop; 11-mile frontage along the Hudson River and Palisades Cliffs.

Profile of Summer Employees Total number: 20; average age: 20; 60% male, 40% female; 20% minorities; 49% high school students; 50% college students; 1% retirees; 100% local residents. Nonsmokers preferred.

Employment Information Openings are from April 1 to November 30. Jobs available: ▶ 3 *boat basin stewards* with knowledge of the Hudson River at $7.50–$8 per hour; ▶ 2 *assistant boat stewards* with knowledge of the Hudson River at $7–$8 per hour; ▶ 12 *fee collectors/ parking attendants* at $5.25–$6.50 per hour; ▶ *concession stand operators* at $6–$7 per hour; ▶ 2 *historic site assistants* with strong interest in history, research, giving tours, and related activities at $5.25–$6.50 per hour; ▶ 10 *maintenance workers* with interest in learning grounds maintenance, recycling, and trail maintenance at $5.50–$6.50 per hour.

Benefits College credit, on-the-job training, opportunity to meet many interesting people. Off-site boarding costs are $500 per month.

Contact Jennifer A. March, Administrative Assistant, Palisades Interstate Park Commission, Department SJ, PO Box 155, Alpine, New Jersey 07620; 201-768-1360, Fax 201-767-3842.

SOMERSET COUNTY PARK COMMISSION
ENVIRONMENTAL EDUCATION CENTER
190 LORD STIRLING ROAD
BASKING RIDGE, NEW JERSEY 07920

General Information Environmental education programs for children, adults, and families, including nature day camps during the summer. Established in 1970. Owned by Somerset County Park Commission. Affiliated with National Association for Interpretation, Alliance for New Jersey Environmental Education. 430-acre facility located 35 miles west of New York, New York. Features: location within the Great Swamp Basin; 8½ miles of trails and boardwalk; 18,000-square-foot education building.

Profile of Summer Employees Total number: 5; average age: 20; 50% male, 50% female; 100% college students; 80% local residents. Nonsmokers preferred.

Employment Information Openings are from June 1 to August 31. Jobs available: ▶ 5 *seasonal naturalists* with college degree or upperclassman status at $240 per week.

Benefits On-the-job training. Off-site boarding costs are $900 per month.

Contact Ross A. Zito, Manager of Environmental Science Somerset County Park Commission,

Somerset County Park Commission Environmental Education Center, Department SJ, 190 Lord Stirling Road, Basking Ridge, New Jersey 07920; 908-766-2489. Application deadline: March 1.

STONY BROOK-MILLSTONE WATERSHEDS ASSOCIATION-ENVIRONMENT EDUCATION DAY CAMP
31 TITUS MILL ROAD
PENNINGTON, NEW JERSEY 08534

General Information Environmental education day camp conducting one- and two-week programs. Established in 1952. Owned by Stony Brook-Millstone Watershed Association. 585-acre facility located 10 miles north of Trenton. Features: nature center; 4-acre pond; 8 miles of trails; 585 acres of fields and forest; organic farm.

Profile of Summer Employees Total number: 10; average age: 24; 40% male, 60% female; 10% minorities; 10% high school students; 50% college students; 100% local residents; 20% teachers.

Employment Information Openings are from July 6 to August 14. Jobs available: ▶ 2 *camp group leaders* with experience in camp setting, teaching, and ecology at $2400 per season; ▶ 2 *camp naturalists* with extensive knowledge of local ecology at $1800 per season; ▶ 4 *camp interns* with experience or interest in camps, teaching, and ecology at $1400 per season; ▶ 1 *teacher/naturalist* with experience in nature center or environmental education at $2000 per season.

Contact Jeff Hoagland, Education Director, Stony Brook-Millstone Watersheds Association-Environment Education Day Camp, 31 Titus Mill Road, Pennington, New Jersey 08534; 609-737-7592, Fax 609-737-3075. Application deadline: April 20.

TRAIL BLAZER CAMPS
210 DECKERTOWN TURNPIKE
MONTAGUE, NEW JERSEY 07827

General Information Residential camp serving disadvantaged campers in a primitive setting. Established in 1887. Owned by Trail Blazers. Affiliated with American Camping Association. 1,000-acre facility located 60 miles northwest of New York, New York. Features: location surrounded by 30,000 acres of state park and forest; 55-acre lake; backpacking and camping.

Profile of Summer Employees Total number: 70; average age: 21; 40% male, 60% female; 3% minorities; 60% college students; 5% retirees; 25% international; 10% local residents; 15% teachers. Nonsmokers preferred.

Employment Information Openings are from June 12 to August 22. Jobs available: ▶ 45 *counselors* with one year of college completed at $900–$1000 per season; ▶ 5 *waterfront staff members* with WSI, ALS, and lifeguard certification at $850–$1100 per season; ▶ 1 *maintenance staff member* at $850–$1100 per season; ▶ 3 *infirmary staff members* with RN, EMT, or LPN license at $1500–$3500 per season; ▶ 8 *kitchen staff members* at $850–$1200 per season; ▶ 1 *secretary* at $1000 per season; ▶ *waterfront director* with WSI and lifeguard certification at $1500 per season; ▶ 2 *head cooks* at $1500–$2500 per season.

Benefits College credit, on-the-job training, formal ongoing training, on-site room and board at no charge, travel reimbursement, tuition reimbursement, potential scholarships for returning staff, 50% of roundtrip transportation provided (up to $200).

Contact Phillip Hatchett, Camp Director, Trail Blazer Camps, 45 East 20th Street, 9th Floor, New York, New York 10003; 212-529-5113, Fax 212-529-2704. Application deadline: May 1.

NEW MEXICO

BRUSH RANCH CAMPS FOR GIRLS AND BOYS
HC 73, BOX 32
TERERRO, NEW MEXICO 87573

General Information Residential camp serving 80 girls ages 8–16 and 50 boys ages 8–14 with camp programs in a noncompetitive atmosphere. Also, high adventure and family camp. Established in 1957. Owned by Scott and Kay Rice. Affiliated with American Camping Association, Western Association of Independent Camps, Association for Horsemanship Safety and Education. 290-acre facility located 35 miles east of Santa Fe. Features: high mountain camp surrounded by Santa Fe National Forest; well-maintained camp and grounds; log cabins and buildings in the mountains; heated swimming pool; 4 tennis courts; 2 miles of Pecos River.

Profile of Summer Employees Total number: 49; average age: 23; 50% male, 50% female; 1% high school students; 90% college students; 1% local residents. Nonsmokers preferred.

Employment Information Openings are from June 9 to August 10. Jobs available: ▶ 2 *dance instructors;* ▶ 2 *drama instructors;* ▶ 1 *music instructor* with piano playing experience; ▶ 3 *art instructors* with emphasis on ceramics experience; ▶ 3 *swimming instructors* with WSI certification and synchronized swimming experience; ▶ 2 *fencing instructors;* ▶ 2 *tennis instructors;* ▶ 2 *riding instructors* (English- and Western-style); ▶ 1 *nurse* with RN license; ▶ 1 *shooting instructor;* ▶ 3 *certified ropes challenge-course instructors* with a minimum of 40 hours training or 100 hours of leadership on ropes course in last 12 months; ▶ 2 *nature instructors;* ▶ 1 *archery instructor;* ▶ 2 *fishing instructors* with fly-fishing experience; ▶ *mountain biking instructor;* ▶ 2 *soccer instructors.* International students encouraged to apply; must obtain own visa and working papers prior to employment; must apply through recognized agency.

Benefits College credit, on-the-job training, on-site room and board at no charge, travel reimbursement, cost-sharing or full tuition for training courses after first summer. Preemployment training of 7 days is required and includes safety and accident prevention, group interaction, first-aid, CPR, leadership, camper-counselor relations. Orientation is paid.

Contact Scott Rice, Owner/Director, Brush Ranch Camps for Girls and Boys, Department SJ, PO Box 5759, Santa Fe, New Mexico 87502-5759; 800-722-2843, Fax 505-757-8822. Application deadline: May 10.

GLORIETA BAPTIST CONFERENCE CENTER
EXIT 299, I-25
GLORIETA, NEW MEXICO 87535

General Information Support facilities and services for approximately 28,000 guests attending summer conferences. Established in 1952. Owned by The Sunday School Board of the Southern Baptist Convention. Affiliated with Christian Camping International/USA, American Camping Association. 2,271-acre facility located 18 miles east of Santa Fe. Features: location in the Sangre de Cristo Mountains at 7,500-foot elevation; 37,530 square feet of conference space; tennis courts and recreation fields.

Profile of Summer Employees Total number: 175; average age: 20; 40% male, 60% female; 18% minorities; 35% high school students; 60% college students; 5% retirees; 2% international; 20% local residents.

Employment Information Openings are from May 20 to September 5. Year-round positions also offered. Jobs available: ▶ *front desk staff;* ▶ *sound and lighting technicians;* ▶ *day-camp workers;* ▶ *preschool workers;* ▶ *chuckwagon workers;* ▶ *food service workers;* ▶ *housekeepers;* ▶ *conference service workers;* ▶ *residence hall/campus ministry coordinators;* ▶ *maintenance/grounds workers.*

Benefits College credit, on-the-job training, on-site room and board at $50 per week, travel reimbursement for some positions, activities during off-duty hours include worship, discipleship opportunities, recreation, and campouts.

Contact Billie L. Koller, Administrative Coordinator, Glorieta Baptist Conference Center, Department SJ, PO Box 8, Glorieta, New Mexico 87535; 505-757-6161, Fax 505-757-6149. Application deadline: March 1.

PHILMONT SCOUT RANCH
CIMARRON, NEW MEXICO 87714

General Information Camp and family conference center offering mountain backpacking with a wide variety of outdoor and historical experiences. Established in 1938. Owned by Boy Scouts of America. Affiliated with American Camping Association, Boy Scouts of America. 137,493-acre facility located 200 miles northeast of Albuquerque. Features: mountain/high-country location with elevations of 6,500 to 12,441 feet; wilderness atmosphere for low-impact camping; conference facilities for the whole family; 32 staffed camps in the backcountry, each offering a program specialty ranging from archaeology to western lore; more than 300 miles of trails for ten-day mountain backpacking treks; large headquarters area, including museums, dining halls, trading post, supply issue, health lodge, and commissary.

Profile of Summer Employees Total number: 750; average age: 21; 75% male, 25% female; 2% high school students; 91% college students; 1% retirees; 3% local residents; 3% teachers. Nonsmokers preferred.

Employment Information Openings are from May 25 to August 25. Jobs available: ▶ *bookkeeping clerk and clerks/typists;* ▶ *food services staff members* (dining hall manager, backcountry cook, assistant dining hall manager, dining hall staff, and snack bar clerks); ▶ commissary staff members *(manager, backcountry manager, and clerks);* ▶ truck driver *(minimum age 21) with experience driving a two-ton truck over dirt roads;* ▶ trading post managers and clerks for headquarters, craft lodge, and backcountry; ▶ quartermaster staff members *(equipment and tent repair manager, tent repair helper, and warehouse clerk);* ▶ custodial staff members *(custodian, housekeeper, and lawn maintenance personnel);* ▶ seasonal registrars; ▶ security staff members; ▶ conservation staff members *(director of conservation, associate director of conservation, conservation crew foreman, trail crew foreman, assistant trail crew foreman, trail construction supervisor, and staff members);* ▶ logistic services manager, assistant manager, and staff members; ▶ transportation manager; ▶ headquarters activities manager and staff members; ▶ headquarters services manager, assistant manager, and staff members; ▶ postmaster; ▶ news and photo service members *(manager, assistant manager, photo lab manager, and photographers);* ▶ medical/ health lodge staff members *(administrator, medics, medical secretary, nurse, and health lodge drivers);* ▶ headquarters maintenance staff members; ▶ chief ranger, associate chief ranger, Rayado trek coordinator, mountain trek coordinator, training rangers, and approximately 160 rangers; ▶ backcountry manager; ▶ camp directors; ▶ program counselors *with knowledge of and experience in one or more of the following: adobe construction, archaeology, black powder weapons, blacksmithing, burro packing and racing, challenge events, environmental ecology and nature studies, fishing and fly tying, gold mining and panning, mountain technology, Indian ethnology, logging skills, mountain biking, mountain living and homesteading, no-trace camping, riflery, rock climbing, search and rescue, shotgun instruction, trapping, and Western lore;* ▶ museum shop clerks and guides; ▶ horse department staff members *(supervisors and wranglers);* ▶ training center office staff members; ▶ support services manager and staff members; ▶ tent city managers and assistant managers; ▶ family programs staff members *(manager, assistant manager, nursery leader, and leaders for activities for various age groups);* ▶ crafts lodge manager and staff members. *All positions offered at $520 per month.*

Benefits College credit, on-the-job training, formal ongoing training, on-site room and board at no charge, laundry facilities, health insurance, working with other people who have high values and service motivation, developing close friendships in a diverse group of people, opportunities for growth and inspiration, pay increase possible with greater job responsibility or supervisory capacity. Preemployment training of 7 to 10 days is required and includes safety and accident prevention, group interaction, first-aid, CPR, leadership, camper-counselor relations. Orientation is paid.

Contact Philmont Scout Ranch, Seasonal Personnel, Philmont Scout Ranch, Department SJ, Cimarron, New Mexico 87714; 505-376-2281, Fax 505-376-2281 Ext. 19. Application deadline: May 30.

NEW YORK

ADIRONDACK WOODCRAFT CAMPS
RONDAXE ROAD, PO BOX 219
OLD FORGE, NEW YORK 13420

General Information Residential coeducational camp and environmental education center offering teaching, learning, and outdoor activities. Established in 1925. Owned by The Leach family. 400-acre facility located 60 miles north of Utica. Features: 2 private wilderness lakes, 2 miles of riverfront; secluded location in the Adirondacks; location surrounded by hundreds of miles of hiking and canoeing routes; 4 separate waterfronts; basketball courts, tennis courts, large fields, and low ropes course.

Profile of Summer Employees Total number: 30; average age: 22; 65% male, 35% female; 10% minorities; 10% high school students; 55% college students; 5% retirees; 20% international; 15% local residents. Nonsmokers preferred.

Employment Information Openings are from May 3 to August 30. Jobs available: ▶ 16 *counselors* with experience working with children at $850–$1400 per season; ▶ 2 *kitchen assistants* at $110–$150 per week; ▶ 1 *office assistant* with typing, computer, and good communication skills at $120–$175 per week; ▶ 2 *experienced wilderness trip leaders* at $1000–$1500 per season; ▶ 4 *waterfront staff members* with WSI, lifeguard, and BLS certification at $900–$1600 per season. International students encouraged to apply; must apply through recognized agency.

Benefits On-the-job training, on-site room and board at no charge, laundry facilities, tuition reimbursement.

Contact Chris Clemans, Program Director, Adirondack Woodcraft Camps, Department SJ, PO Box 219, Old Forge, New York 13420; 315-369-6031, Fax 315-369-6032. Application deadline: May 1.

AMERICAN CAMPING ASSOCIATION
12 WEST 31ST STREET
NEW YORK, NEW YORK 10001

General Information Employment clearinghouse for camps that offers a free placement service for college students and faculty, teachers, and school administrators who desire a summer job outdoors.

Profile of Summer Employees 50% male, 50% female; 10% minorities; 90% college students; 2% retirees; 2% local residents; 1% teachers. Nonsmokers preferred.

Employment Information Openings are from June 15 to August 25. Spring break, winter break positions also offered. Jobs available: ▶ *drama staff members* with experience with children and current certification; ▶ *music staff members* with experience with children and current certification; ▶ *team sports staff members* with experience with children and current certification; ▶ *individual sports staff members* with experience with children and current certification; ▶ *kitchen staff members* with experience with children and current certification; ▶ *registered nurses* with experience with children and current certification; ▶ *medical doctors* with experience with children and current certification; ▶ *EMT staff members* with experience with children and current certification; ▶ *general counselors* with experience with children and current certification; ▶ *land and water sports staff members* with experience with children and current certification; ▶ *visual and performing arts staff members* with experience with children and current certification; ▶ *secretarial staff members* with computer skills and experience with children; ▶ *maintenance staff members* with experience with children; ▶ *swimming instructors* with WSI or lifeguard certification and experience with children at $1200 per season.

Benefits College credit, on-the-job training, formal ongoing training, on-site room and board, laundry facilities, travel reimbursement, end-of-season bonus possible.

Contact Ellen Reiner, Coordinator, American Camping Association, Department SJ, 12 West 31st Street, 12th Floor, New York, New York 10001; 800-777-2267, Fax 212-594-1684. Application deadline: June 1.

ANTONIO'S RESORT
DALE LANE
ELKA PARK, NEW YORK 12427

General Information Family resort providing a variety of activities for guests. Established in 1973. Owned by Nat Manzella. 7-acre facility located 40 miles south of Albany. Features: access to downhill and cross-country skiing; indoor/outdoor sports including basketball, racquetball, bocci, shuffleboard, volleyball, softball, and tennis; restaurant/lounge; indoor/outdoor pools, Jacuzzi, and steam showers.

Profile of Summer Employees Total number: 35; average age: 20; 50% male, 50% female; 25% college students; 75% international. Nonsmokers preferred.

Employment Information Openings are from May 15 to October 15. Spring break, winter break, Christmas break, year-round positions also offered. Jobs available: ▶ 2 *social directors* with knowledge of sports and social games at $170 per week; ▶ 2 *child counselors* with knowledge of sports and social games at $170 per week; ▶ 2 *pool attendants* with junior Red Cross certification at $228 per week; ▶ 3 *maintenance/grounds persons* at $228 per week; ▶ 2 *office personnel* at $228 per week; ▶ 4 *housekeepers* at $170 per week; ▶ 1 *laundry person/ floater* at $228 per week; ▶ 1 *cocktail waitress/waiter* at $140 per week; ▶ 6 *waiters/waitresses* at $140 per week; ▶ 2 *subwaitresses/subwaiters* at $140 per week; ▶ 5 *kitchen helpers* at $228 per week; ▶ 2 *dish and pot washers* at $228 per week; ▶ 1 *floater* at $228 per week; ▶ 1 *host/office person* at $228 per week. International students encouraged to apply; must obtain own visa and working papers prior to employment; must apply through recognized agency.

Benefits College credit, on-the-job training, on-site room and board at $80 per week, end-of-season bonus, possible gratuities for some jobs.

Contact Cathy Manzella, Personnel Receptionist, Antonio's Resort, Department SJ, Dale Lane, Elka Park, New York 12427; 518-589-5197, Fax 518-589-5278.

BRANT LAKE CAMP
ROUTE 8
BRANT LAKE, NEW YORK 12815

General Information Eight-week high-tuition private residential camp for boys ages 7–15 with a capacity of 330 campers. Also two- and three-week sessions for 41 teenage girls in dance, arts, and sports–particularly tennis. Established in 1917. Owned by Robert S. Gersten, Karen Gerstenzang-Meltzer, and Richard Gersten. Affiliated with American Camping Association, New York State Camp Directors Association. Located 80 miles north of Albany. Features: location on 5-mile-long lake; 16 tennis courts; 4 baseball fields; 5 basketball courts; 2 soccer fields; 3 art studios.

Profile of Summer Employees Total number: 150; average age: 23; 85% male, 15% female; 10% minorities; 5% high school students; 70% college students; 2% retirees; 20% international; 5% local residents. Nonsmokers preferred.

Employment Information Openings are from June 20 to August 20. Jobs available: ▶ 15

general staff members (college-age) at $900–$1400 per season; ▶ 9 *athletics specialists* (college-age) at $1000–$1600 per season; ▶ 6 *waterfront staff members* (college-age) with WSI certification/lifeguard training at $1100–$1600 per season; ▶ 2 *group heads/athletics directors* with experience teaching/coaching at $1800–$2500 per season; ▶ 2 *swimming instructors* with WSI certification at $1200–$1500 per season.

Benefits On-the-job training, on-site room and board at no charge, laundry facilities. Preemployment training is required and includes safety and accident prevention, group interaction, first-aid, CPR, leadership. Orientation is paid.

Contact Richard Gersten, Director, Brant Lake Camp, Department SJ, 1202 Lexington Avenue, Suite 342, New York, New York 10028; 212-734-6216, Fax 212-288-0937, E-mail brantlakec@ aol.com. Application deadline: May 1.

CAMP BACO FOR BOYS/CAMP CHE–NA–WAH FOR GIRLS
ROUTE 28N
MINERVA, NEW YORK 12851

General Information Residential camp serving 160 girls and 190 boys in a traditional eight-week program. Established in 1923. Owned by Baco/Che-Na-Wah Equities Corporation. Affiliated with American Camping Association, New York State Camp Directors Association, Gore Mountain Chamber of Commerce. 100-acre facility located 225 miles north of New York City. Features: location in the beautiful Adirondack Mountains with scenic views of the High Peaks; private lake; 14 tennis courts (8 at Baco and 6 at Che-Na-Wah); weight-training and gymnastics building; indoor and outdoor basketball courts and theaters; ropes climbing tower.

Profile of Summer Employees Total number: 110; average age: 20; 20% high school students; 80% college students. Nonsmokers preferred.

Employment Information Openings are from June 20 to August 20. Jobs available: ▶ 4 *swimming instructors* with WSI, LGT, and BLS certification at $1200–$2500 per season; ▶ 3 *tennis instructors* with college team playing or coaching experience at $1400–$2500 per season; ▶ 1 *experienced gymnastics instructor* with college team experience at $1400–$2500 per season; ▶ 2 *music instructors* with ability to accompany on the piano at $1400–$2500 per season; ▶ 2 *ceramics instructors* at $1400–$2500 per season; ▶ 2 *sailing/windsurfing instructors* with LGT, BLS, and American Red Cross small crafts instructor certification at $1400–$2500 per season; ▶ 2 *canoeing instructors* with LGT, BLS, and American Red Cross small crafts instructor certification at $1400–$2500 per season; ▶ *experienced basketball instructor* at $1400–$2500 per season; ▶ *soccer instructor* at $1400–$2500 per season; ▶ *baseball/softball instructor* at $1400–$2500 per season; ▶ *sports instructors* at $1400–$2500 per season; ▶ *hiking/pioneering instructor* with first aid or CPR certification at $1400–$2500 per season.

Benefits College credit, on-the-job training, formal ongoing training, on-site room and board at no charge, laundry facilities, transportation provided five evenings per week for off-duty counselors, transportation provided to public bus on counselors' days off. Preemployment training of 5 days is required and includes safety and accident prevention, group interaction, first-aid, CPR, leadership, camper-counselor relations. Orientation is paid.

Contact Bob Wortman, Director, Camp Baco for Boys/Camp Che–Na–Wah for Girls, Department SJ, 484 South Wood Road, Rockville Center, New York 11570; 516-867-3895, Fax 516-868-3819, E-mail campbaco@aol.com, URL http://www.campbaco.com/chenawah. Application deadline: May 30.

CAMP DUDLEY
RURAL ROUTE 1, BOX 1034
WESTPORT, NEW YORK 12993-9711

General Information All-around Christian residential camp offering all sports, hiking, canoeing, fine arts, drama, and music for boys ages 10 to 16. Established in 1885. Owned by Camp Dudley YMCA, Inc. Affiliated with American Camping Association, YMCA. 2,000-acre facility located 60 miles west of Burlington, VT. Features: 2 miles of shoreline on Lake Champlain; Adirondack Wilderness Park for hiking, canoeing, and rock climbing; 4 outdoor basketball courts, 4 baseball diamonds, and 4 soccer or lacrosse fields; 8 tennis courts; 450-seat theater; gymnasium; 4 lean-tos for overnights by roaring brook or lake.

Profile of Summer Employees Total number: 150; average age: 27; 86% male, 14% female; 10% minorities; 25% high school students; 50% college students; 5% international; 4% local residents; 25% teachers. Nonsmokers preferred.

Employment Information Openings are from June 16 to August 25. Jobs available: ▶ *6 general counselors* with American Red Cross Lifeguard, American Red Cross Response to Emergencies, CPR for Professional Rescuer certification, and athletic specialty to teach at $1200–$1800 per season; ▶ *drama tech staff members* with verifiable skills at $1700–$2000 per season; ▶ *outdoor/ hiking staff members* with American Red Cross certification in lifeguarding, Response to Emergencies, and CPR for Professional Rescuer and verifiable skills at $1700–$2000 per season; ▶ *3 arts and crafts instructors* at $1700–$2000 per season; ▶ *registered nurse* with New York State license at $2750–$3000 per season. International students encouraged to apply; must apply through recognized agency.

Benefits On-the-job training, on-site room and board at no charge, tuition reimbursement, staff children attend camp for free, day care for young children, one day off per week, most nights off. Preemployment training of 10 days is required and includes safety and accident prevention, group interaction, first-aid, CPR, leadership, camper-counselor relations. Orientation is paid.

Contact Wheaton I. Griffin, Director, Camp Dudley, Department SJ, RR 1, Box 1034, Westport, New York 12993-9711; 518-962-4720, Fax 518-962-4320. Application deadline: February 1.

CAMP HILLCROFT
BOX 5
BILLINGS, NEW YORK 12510

General Information Day camp serving 400 children ages 4–14 for 4–8 weeks. Established in 1950. Owned by Dennis and Judy Buttinger. Affiliated with American Camping Association, New York State Camp Directors Association, Southern Dutchess Chamber of Commerce. 185-acre facility located 11 miles east of Poughkeepsie. Features: 2 pools and a lake; studios for art, ceramics, wood, photography, graphics, weaving, enamelling, and metal sculpture; dance studio, theater, and gymnastics center; 3 large sport fields for soccer, softball, and games; courts for tennis, volleyball, and basketball; outdoor adventure course–climbing, zip line, obstacle, ropes, and orienteering course.

Profile of Summer Employees Total number: 120; average age: 22; 50% male, 50% female; 50% college students; 20% international. Nonsmokers preferred.

Employment Information Openings are from June 29 to August 21. Jobs available: ▶ *group leaders* with senior year of college completed and leadership experience with children at $1200–$1500 per season; ▶ *waterfront staff members/lifeguards/instructors* with current lifeguard and WSI certification at $1000–$1400 per season; ▶ *outdoor adventure instructors* with experience with ropes, climbing, and initiative games and compatibility with children at $1000–$1400 per season; ▶ *ceramics and wood instructors* with teaching experience at $1000–$1400 per season; ▶ *tennis and archery instructors* at $1000–$1400 per season. International students encouraged to apply; must apply through recognized agency.

Benefits On-the-job training, formal ongoing training, on-site room and board at no charge, laundry facilities, 5-day program; weekends off.

Contact Dennis Buttinger, Director, Camp Hillcroft, Department SJ, RR 2, Box 109A Verbank Club Road, Verbank, New York 15585; 914-223-5826, Fax 914-677-5562, E-mail chillcroft@idsi. net. Application deadline: May 1.

CAMP HILLTOP
HC 72, BOX 56
HANCOCK, NEW YORK 13783

General Information Traditional residential coed camp for campers ages 6–16. Established in 1924. Owned by Bill and Kathy Young. Affiliated with American Camping Association. 400-acre facility located 35 miles southeast of Binghamton. Features: private lake; swimming pool; 300 acres of horse trails; batting cage; go-cart track; 14-station challenge course.

Profile of Summer Employees Total number: 70; average age: 21; 50% male, 50% female; 5% minorities; 60% college students; 30% international; 5% teachers. Nonsmokers only.

Employment Information Openings are from June 18 to August 16. Jobs available: ▶ 7 *waterfront staff members* at $1300–$2000 per season; ▶ 3 *riflery and archery staff members* at $1000–$1500 per season; ▶ 5 *arts and crafts staff members* at $1000–$1500 per season; ▶ 4 *sports staff members* at $1000–$1500 per season; ▶ 2 *tennis staff members* at $1000–$1500 per season; ▶ 2 *computer staff members* at $1000–$1500 per season; ▶ 3 *horseback riding staff members* at $1000–$2000 per season; ▶ *lifeguards* with WSI certification at $1000–$2000 per season. International students encouraged to apply; must apply through recognized agency.

Benefits On-the-job training, on-site room and board at no charge, travel reimbursement. Preemployment training of 5 days is required and includes safety and accident prevention, group interaction, first-aid, CPR, leadership, camper-counselor relations. Orientation is paid.

Contact William H. Young, Director, Camp Hilltop, Department SJ, HC 72, Box 56, Hancock, New York 13783; 607-637-5201, Fax 607-637-2389. Application deadline: June 1.

CAMP JEANNE D'ARC
154 GADWAY ROAD
MERRILL, NEW YORK 12955

General Information Residential camp for 120 girls ages 6–17 focusing on individual activities and personal achievement. Established in 1922. Owned by Fran McIntyre. Affiliated with American Camping Association, New York State Camp Directors Association, Camp Directors' Roundtable. 230-acre facility located 30 miles west of Plattsburgh. Features: two-story Swiss chalet-type cabins with fireplace and living room; indoor plumbing and electricity; mile-long 28-station fitness trail; location on a 14-mile crystal-clear lake in Adirondack State Park, surrounded by miles of woodland and mountains.

Profile of Summer Employees Total number: 50; average age: 21; 5% male, 95% female; 10% minorities; 10% high school students; 75% college students; 20% international; 15% local residents; 5% teachers. Nonsmokers preferred.

Employment Information Openings are from June 20 to August 22. Jobs available: ▶ 3 *riding instructors* with CHA certification; ▶ 2 *waterskiing instructors;* ▶ 1 *riflery instructor* with NRA rifle instructor certification; ▶ 2 *tennis instructors;* ▶ 1 *canoeing instructor;* ▶ 1 *sailing instructor;* ▶ 1 *music/guitar instructor;* ▶ 1 *dance instructor;* ▶ 1 *drama instructor;* ▶ 2 *arts and crafts instructors;* ▶ 2 *outdoor camping counselors;* ▶ 2 *other land sports instructors;* ▶ 2 *other water sports instructors;* ▶ 3 *swimming instructors* with WSI and American Red Cross lifeguard certification. All positions offered at $1000–$2000 per season. International students encouraged to apply.

Benefits On-the-job training, on-site room and board at no charge, laundry facilities, travel reimbursement, reimbursement and payment of specialized training, i.e., for WSI or CHA instructor.

Contact Brian P. McIntyre, Assistant Director, Camp Jeanne D'Arc, 154 Gadway Road, Merrill, New York 12955; 518-425-3311, Fax 518-425-6673, E-mail funatcjda@aol.com. Application deadline: June 15.

CAMP LOYALTOWN-AHRC
GLEN AVENUE
HUNTER, NEW YORK 12442

General Information Summer residential recreational vacation camp for mentally retarded and developmentally disabled children and adults of all ages and functional levels. Established in 1974. Owned by Camp Loyaltown, Inc. Operated by Association for the Help of Retarded Children (Nassau County Chapter). Affiliated with United Way, Association for the Help of Retarded Children. 240-acre facility located 150 miles north of New York City. Features: location in the Catskill Mountains, adjacent to ski resorts; extensive and fully equipped recreation program; heated swimming pool; Special Olympics coaches' training; short walk to the village of Hunter, New York, and equally short walk into forest-covered mountains.

Profile of Summer Employees Total number: 160; average age: 20; 50% male, 50% female; 10% minorities; 3% high school students; 90% college students; 30% international; 5% teachers. Nonsmokers preferred.

Employment Information Openings are from June 19 to August 20. Jobs available: ▶ 1 *waterfront director* with WSI certification at $1900–$2200 per season; ▶ 4 *certified lifeguards* at $1400–$1600 per season; ▶ 80 *cabin counselors* with a major in special education or related field at $1100–$1500 per season; ▶ 2 *arts and crafts instructors* at $1400–$1600 per season; ▶ 6 *kitchen assistants* at $1200–$1500 per season; ▶ 4 *office staff members* with knowledge of office procedures and typing and clerical skills at $1200–$1600 per season; ▶ 4 *cooks* with experience in ordering, preparing, and serving meals; ▶ 1 *dance instructor* at $1400–$1600 per season; ▶ 1 *drama instructor* at $1400–$1600 per season; ▶ 1 *music instructor* at $1400–$1600 per season; ▶ 1 *nature instructor* at $1400–$1600 per season; ▶ 1 *cooking instructor* at $1400–$1600 per season; ▶ 1 *sewing instructor* at $1400–$1600 per season; ▶ 1 *athletics instructor* at $1400–$1600 per season; ▶ 1 *woodshop instructor* at $1400–$1600 per season; ▶ 1 *recreation instructor* at $1400–$1600 per season; ▶ 1 *ceramics instructor* at $1400–$1600 per season. International students encouraged to apply; must apply through recognized agency.

Benefits College credit, on-the-job training, formal ongoing training, on-site room and board at no charge, laundry facilities, workmen's compensation. Preemployment training of 5 to 6 days is required and includes safety and accident prevention, group interaction, leadership, camper-counselor relations. Orientation is paid.

Contact Mr. Paul H. Cullen, Director of Camping, Camp Loyaltown-AHRC, Department SJ, 189 Wheatley Road, Brookville, New York 11545; 516-626-1000 Ext. 1045, Fax 516-626-1510, E-mail admin.ahrc@psinet.com, URL http://www.ahrc.org. Application deadline: June 15.

CAMP MADISON
201 POWDER MILL BRIDGE ROAD
KINGSTON, NEW YORK 12401

General Information Residential camp for boys and girls who are members of the Madison Square Boys and Girls Club. Established in 1984. Owned by Madison Square Boys and Girls Club. Affiliated with American Camping Association. 118-acre facility located 100 miles north of New York City. Features: 2 outdoor tennis courts; softball field; theater; 2 lakes; computers; hiking trails.

Profile of Summer Employees Total number: 50; average age: 22; 50% male, 50% female; 60% minorities; 10% high school students; 90% college students; 30% international; 10% local residents. Nonsmokers preferred.

Employment Information Openings are from June 22 to August 30. Year-round positions also offered. Jobs available: ▶ 23 *general camp counselors* at $900–$1100 per season; ▶ 3 *lifeguards* with lifeguard, BLS, CPR, and first aid certifications at $1000–$1200 per season; ▶ 2 *nurses* with RN, LPN, EMT, or PA (New York state licensed) at $2500–$4000 per season; ▶ 1 *outdoor educator* at $1000–$1400 per season; ▶ 1 *computer instructor* at $1000–$1400 per season; ▶ *arts and crafts staff members* at $1000–$1400 per season. International students encouraged to apply; must apply through recognized agency.

Benefits On-the-job training, formal ongoing training, on-site room and board at no charge, laundry facilities. Preemployment training of 5 days is required and includes safety and accident prevention, group interaction, first-aid, leadership, camper-counselor relations. Orientation is paid.

Contact Jack Thomas, Camp Director, Camp Madison, Department SJ, 301 East 29th Street, New York, New York 10016; 212-532-5751, Fax 212-779-2169. Application deadline: April 15.

CAMP MICHIKAMAU
BEAR MOUNTAIN, NEW YORK 10911

General Information Coed residential YMCA camp in rustic setting serving 110 campers ages 8–15. Features traditional camping, waterfront activities, arts and crafts, and outdoor activities. Established in 1920. Owned by YMCA Greater Bergen County. Affiliated with YMCA. 20-acre facility located 30 miles north of New York City. Features: large lake and lakefront; low ropes course; basketball courts; hiking trails.

Profile of Summer Employees Total number: 30; average age: 21; 60% male, 40% female; 20% high school students; 80% college students; 10% international; 60% local residents; 2% teachers. Nonsmokers preferred.

Employment Information Openings are from June 20 to August 23. Jobs available: ▶ 20 *counselors* at $800–$1200 per season; ▶ 5 *lifeguards/counselors* with American Red Cross and lifeguard training at $900–$1400 per season; ▶ 1 *arts and crafts director* at $1000–$1200 per season; ▶ 2 *nurses* with LPN or RN at $1300–$2500 per season; ▶ *waterfront director* with WSI certification/lifeguard training at $1500–$2000 per season. International students encouraged to apply; must apply through recognized agency.

Benefits On-site room and board at no charge. Preemployment training of 5 days is required and includes safety and accident prevention, group interaction, first-aid, CPR, leadership, camper-counselor relations. Orientation is paid.

Contact Ken Riscinti, Camping Director, Camp Michikamau, Department SJ, 360 Main Street, Hackensack, New Jersey 07601; 201-487-6600, Fax 201-487-4539. Application deadline: June 10.

CAMP MONROE
PO BOX 475
MONROE, NEW YORK 10950

General Information A well-structured, coed camp meeting the needs and interests of today's youth in a traditional Jewish camp setting. Established in 1941. Owned by Camp Stan-Jack DBA Camp Monroe. Affiliated with American Camping Association. 192-acre facility located 40 miles north of New York City. Features: pool and lake; 2 indoor gyms; horseback riding stables on premises; computer center; outdoor hockey rink; tennis courts.

Profile of Summer Employees Total number: 120; average age: 25; 50% male, 50% female; 10% high school students; 60% college students; 1% retirees; 30% international; 10% local residents; 25% teachers. Nonsmokers preferred.

Employment Information Openings are from June 26 to August 20. Jobs available: ▶ *general counselors* at $450–$1200 per season; ▶ *arts and crafts instructors* at $450–$1200 per season; ▶ *swimming instructors* with LI/WSI certification at $450–$1200 per season; ▶ *gymnastics/ aerobics instructors* at $450 per season; ▶ *volleyball instructors* at $450 per season; ▶ *softball instructors* at $450 per season; ▶ *hockey instructors* at $450 per season. International students encouraged to apply; must apply through recognized agency.

Benefits On-the-job training, formal ongoing training, on-site room and board at no charge, laundry facilities. Preemployment training of 5 to 6 days is required and includes safety and accident prevention, group interaction, first-aid, leadership, camper-counselor relations. Orientation is unpaid.

Contact Stanley Felsinger, Director, Camp Monroe, Department SJ, PO Box 475, Monroe, New York 10950; 914-782-8695, Fax 914-782-2247. Application deadline: June 1.

CAMP OF THE WOODS
ROUTE 30
SPECULATOR, NEW YORK 12164

General Information Nondenominational Christian family camp serving over 750 people and Christian girls camp, Tapawingo, serving 72 girls ages 8–16 per week. Established in 1900. Owned by Gospel Volunteers, Inc. Affiliated with Christian Camping International/USA, American Camping Association. 120-acre facility located 90 miles north of Albany. Features: location in the Adirondack Mountains; lakefront with a quarter-mile natural sand beach; 1,500-seat auditorium; full recreational facilities and program.

Profile of Summer Employees Total number: 250; average age: 20; 45% male, 55% female; 5% minorities; 45% high school students; 55% college students; 2% retirees; 1% international; 1% local residents. Nonsmokers only.

Employment Information Openings are from May 10 to September 4. Year-round positions also offered. Jobs available: ▶ 50 *counselors/teachers* with ability to provide leadership and programming for children in preschool through high school at $500–$1200 per season; ▶ 10 *recreation leaders* with tennis, hiking, rafting, and team sports experience at $600–$1500 per season; ▶ 10 *waterfront staff members* with WSI certification (director), lifeguard training, and CPR training (staff) at $600–$1500 per season; ▶ 45 *musical performance staff members* (instrumental/vocal; double as waitstaff) at $600–$1500 per season; ▶ 45 *food service personnel* at $500–$2000 per season; ▶ 50 *operational personnel* (dishwashers, maintenance staff, and housekeepers) at $500–$1200 per season; ▶ 10 *office/clerical staff members* at $600–$1000 per season; ▶ 15 *supervisors* (all departments) at $1500–$2100 per season; ▶ 3 *nurses* with RN, LPN, or EMT license at $1500–$2100 per season.

Benefits College credit, on-the-job training, on-site room and board at no charge, laundry facilities.

Contact Scott Sonju, Personnel Director, Camp of the Woods, Department SJ, Route 30, Speculator, New York 12164; 518-548-4311, Fax 518-548-4324, URL http://www.camp-of-the-woods.org. Application deadline: March 15.

CAMP POK-O-MACCREADY
100 MOUNTAIN ROAD
WILLSBORO, NEW YORK 12996

General Information Traditional camp in the Adirondacks serving 230 boys and girls. Established in 1905. Owned by Jack Swan. Affiliated with American Camping Association. 450-acre facility located 20 miles southwest of Burlington, Vermont. Features: 2½ mile lake; 5 tennis courts; athletics fields; working farm from the 1830's; access to Adirondack wilderness by land and water; 32 horses.

Profile of Summer Employees Total number: 60; average age: 20; 51% male, 49% female; 2% high school students; 85% college students; 10% international.

Employment Information Openings are from June 20 to August 17. Year-round positions also offered. Jobs available: ▶ 1 *Indian crafts/dancing instructor* at $1000–$1500 per season; ▶ 2 *swimming instructors* with WSI and lifeguard certification at $1000–$1500 per season; ▶ 1 *lacrosse instructor* at $1000–$1500 per season; ▶ 1 *woodworking instructor* at $1100–$1600 per season; ▶ *rock climbing instructor* at $1100–$1600 per season; ▶ *theater director* at $1100–$1600 per season. International students encouraged to apply; must apply through recognized agency.

Benefits On-the-job training, on-site room and board at no charge, laundry facilities, travel reimbursement, additional work available May and June. Preemployment training of 7 days is required and includes safety and accident prevention, group interaction, first-aid, CPR, leadership, camper-counselor relations, wilderness trip leaders course. Orientation is unpaid.

Contact Jack Swan, Director, Camp Pok-O-MacCready, Department SJ, PO Box 5016, Brookfield, Connecticut 06804; 203-775-9865, Fax 203-740-7984, URL http://members.aol.com/pokomac/.

CAMP REGIS AND APPLEJACK
PO BOX 245
PAUL SMITHS, NEW YORK 12970

General Information Residential coed children's camp serving 300 campers ages 6–16. Established in 1946. Owned by Michael E. Humes. Affiliated with American Camping Association, New York State Camp Directors Association, American Water Ski Association. 100-acre facility located 18 miles east of Lake Placid. Features: location in Adirondack Park on 7½-mile long lake; camper cabins equipped with bedrooms, bathrooms, and rustic living room with fireplace; large athletic area with playing fields, basketball and volleyball courts, and 7 tennis courts; waterskiing, sailing, rowing, canoeing, and windsurfing (60-boat fleet); large indoor arts/crafts, dance, and drama complex; outdoor adventure program which includes mountain biking, hiking, and canoeing expeditions.

Profile of Summer Employees Total number: 100; average age: 20; 50% male, 50% female; 20% minorities; 70% college students; 5% international; 10% local residents; 30% teachers. Nonsmokers only.

Employment Information Openings are from June 20 to August 22. Jobs available: ▶ *athletics instructors* at $1100–$2000 per season; ▶ *tennis instructors* at $1100–$2000 per season; ▶ *sailing and windsurfing instructors* at $1100–$2000 per season; ▶ *waterskiing instructors* at $1100–$2000 per season; ▶ *arts and crafts instructors* at $1100–$2000 per season; ▶ *dramatics instructors* at $1100–$2000 per season; ▶ *dance instructor* at $1100 per season; ▶ *swimming instructors* at $1100–$2000 per season; ▶ *pioneering/trips instructors* at $1100–$2000 per season; ▶ *in-camp nature/ecology instructors* at $1100–$2000 per season; ▶ *gymnastics instructors* at $1100–$2000 per season; ▶ *mountain biking instructors* at $1100–$2000 per season; ▶ *health care workers* at $1000–$1400 per month; ▶ *office manager* at $1100–$2000 per season; ▶ *unit leaders/head counselors* at $1400–$2400 per season; ▶ *program directors* at $1500–$3000 per season; ▶ *cooks* at $1600–$3600 per season; ▶ *dishwashers* at $1000–$1300 per season; ▶ *laundry workers* at $1000–$1400 per season; ▶ *music instructor* at $1100–$2000 per season.

Benefits College credit, on-the-job training, formal ongoing training, on-site room and board at no charge, laundry facilities, travel reimbursement, tuition reimbursement, ability to participate in camp activities, family accommodations available, staff children welcomed into program. Preemployment training of 1 to 7 days is required and includes safety and accident prevention, group interaction, first-aid, CPR, leadership, camper-counselor relations. Orientation is unpaid.

Contact Michael Humes, Director, Camp Regis and Applejack, 107 Robinhood Road, White Plains, New York 10605; 914-997-7039, Fax 914-761-8228, E-mail campregis@aol.com.

CAMP SEVEN HILLS
OLEAN ROAD
HOLLAND, NEW YORK 14080

General Information Residential Girl Scout camp serving 150–200 girls ages 6–17 offering one-week, two-week and mini-sessions which include challenge courses. Established in 1927. Owned by Girl Scout Council of Buffalo/Erie. Affiliated with American Camping Association, Girl Scouts of the United States of America. 610-acre facility located 45 miles south of Buffalo. Features: large indoor riding arena equipped for English and Western riding programs; sports complex with tennis and basketball courts; 2 small lakes; Olympic-size swimming pool; proximity to Niagara Falls and Toronto, Canada; high and low ropes course; backpack trip programs.

Profile of Summer Employees Total number: 65; average age: 18; 2% male, 98% female; 5% minorities; 10% high school students; 90% college students; 5% international; 95% local residents. Nonsmokers preferred.

Employment Information Openings are from June 20 to August 21. Jobs available: ▶ 1 *program director* with Girl Scout and camping background and creativity at $2000–$2200 per season; ▶ 1 *health supervisor* with RN, LPN, or EMT level 4 physician's assistant at $2200–$3000 per season; ▶ 1 *waterfront director* (minimum age 21) with WSI and lifeguard certification at $1900–$2100 per season; ▶ 5 *lifeguards* (minimum age 17) with lifeguard certification, first aid, and CPR at $1200–$1600 per season; ▶ 7 *unit leaders* with camping and Girl Scout background and experience working with children at $1300–$1500 per season; ▶ 15 *assistant unit leaders* with experience working with children and camping and Girl Scout background at $1000–$1225 per season; ▶ 5 *riding instructors* with western and English riding ability and knowledge of simple horse medications at $1350–$1500 per season; ▶ 1 *experienced arts and crafts director* with knowledge in the field of the arts and experience working with children at $1400–$1600 per season; ▶ 5 *experienced ropes course specialists* with Project Adventure/ropes course certification and group dynamics experience at $1400–$1650 per season; ▶ 1 *counselor-in-training director* with extensive Girl Scout camp experience and experience teaching older adolescents at $1400–$1600 per season; ▶ 1 *head counselor* with camping experience, knowledge of Girl Scout program, and experience supervising and training staff at $1900–$2100 per season; ▶ 1 *stable manager* with knowledge of barn management and equine care, experience in English and western riding at $1250–$1350 per season; ▶ 1 *handyperson* with knowledge of basic machinery, and some maintenance skills at $1100–$1250 per season; ▶ 1 *boating director* with current lifeguard and CPR/BLS certification, certification in the fundamentals of canoeing and/or boating at $1500–$1800 per season; ▶ 1 *assistant waterfront director* with current lifeguard training and first aid and CPR certification at $1600–$1700 per season; ▶ 1 *archery director* with camping experience, knowledge of Girl Scout Program, certification in archery, and ability to teach adolescents at $1400–$1600 per season; ▶ 7 *junior counselors* (minimum age 17) with camp experience and successful completion of CIT program at $750–$850 per season; ▶ 5 *activity specialists* with specialization in sports/recreation, nature, arts and crafts, drama, and campcraft and ability to supervise adults and instruct classes at $1400–$1600 per season; ▶ 1 *riding director* with western and English riding ability, knowledge of horses, simple medications, and proper care, ability to manage horse program, and CHA certification preferred at $1500–$2100 per season; ▶ 1 *dining hall manager* with ability to supervise operation and procedures of dining hall at $1600–$1700 per season; ▶ 1 *assistant cook* with experience in food preparation for large groups and ability to meet deadlines at $1500–$1700 per season; ▶ 4 *kitchen aides* with ability to work under supervision and as a team player at $650–$750 per season; ▶ 1 *camp aide* with ability to work with limited supervision at $750–$850 per season; ▶ 4 *trip counselors* with experience in backpacking, canoeing, and outdoor living at $1500–$2000 per season; ▶ 1 *business manager* with knowledge of bookkeeping and budgeting and ability to manage tuck-shop operation at $1850–$2050 per season. International students encouraged to apply; must apply through recognized agency.

Benefits College credit, on-the-job training, on-site room and board at no charge, laundry facilities, health insurance, workmen's compensation, disability insurance, time off. Preemployment training of 6 to 7 days is required and includes safety and accident prevention, group interaction, first-aid, CPR, leadership, camper-counselor relations, risk management, Girl Scout program. Orientation is paid.

Contact Janet M. DePetrillo, Director of Outdoor Program, Camp Seven Hills, Department SJ, 70 Jewett Parkway, Buffalo, New York 14214; 716-837-6400, Fax 716-837-6407, E-mail janetp@localnet.com, URL http://www.bflogirlscouts.org. Application deadline: June 10.

CAMP SOMERHILL
HIGH STREET PO BOX 127
ATHOL, NEW YORK 12810

General Information Residential camp for 150 youngsters ages 7–17 interested in activities in the areas of water sports, land sports (individual and team), creative and performing arts, trips, science, and horses; leadership program for campers ages 15–17. Established in 1960. Owned by Larry Singer. Affiliated with American Camping Association, New York State Camp Directors Association. 102-acre facility located 200 miles north of New York City. Features: 2 pools and a lake; large field for soccer, softball, field hockey, or lacrosse; 10 different shop areas; 6 lighted tennis courts; outdoor theater; stable and riding trails.

Profile of Summer Employees Total number: 30; average age: 25; 50% male, 50% female;

15% minorities; 40% college students; 2% retirees; 5% international; 3% local residents; 45% teachers. Nonsmokers preferred.

Employment Information Openings are from June 23 to August 23. Jobs available: ▶ 3 *swimming/sailing/canoeing instructors* with certification; ▶ *horseback riding instructor;* ▶ *team sports* (soccer/softball/basketball/hockey) *instructors;* ▶ *individual sports* (weight training/fencing/ wrestling) *instructors;* ▶ *creative arts/music instructors;* ▶ *industrial arts instructor;* ▶ *fine arts instructor.* All positions offered at $1200–$2000 per season. International students encouraged to apply; must obtain own visa and working papers prior to employment; must apply through recognized agency.

Benefits On-the-job training, formal ongoing training, on-site room and board at no charge, laundry facilities, partial travel reimbursement.

Contact Larry Singer, Director, Camp Somerhill, 20 Huntley Road, Box 295, Eastchester, New York 10709-0295; 914-793-1303, Fax 914-793-1303, E-mail somerhil@ziplink.net.

CAMP TEL YEHUDAH
11 NYS ROUTE 97
BARRYVILLE, NEW YORK 12719

General Information Residential kosher Zionist camp serving teens ages 14–17. Established in 1948. Owned by Young Judaea, Inc. Affiliated with American Camping Association, Association of Jewish Sponsored Camps. 125-acre facility located 20 miles north of Port Jervis. Features: pool; tennis courts; basketball courts; softball field; soccer field; location on Delaware River.

Profile of Summer Employees Total number: 85; average age: 22. Nonsmokers preferred.

Employment Information Openings are from May 21 to August 31. Jobs available: ▶ *lifeguards* (minimum age 18) with BLS and WSI certification at $1050–$1500 per season; ▶ *general counselors* with experience working with teens and group leadership skills at $1050–$1500 per season; ▶ *hiking and outdoor specialists* with personal and group hiking experience at $1050– $1500 per season; ▶ *drama specialists* with experience in play directing and education background at $1050–$1500 per season; ▶ *arts and crafts specialists* with experience and skill with a variety of crafts at $1050–$1500 per season; ▶ *kitchen workers* at $1050–$1500 per season; ▶ *drivers* (minimum age 21) with CDL training and experience with 15-passenger vans at $1200–$1500 per season. International students encouraged to apply; must apply through recognized agency.

Benefits On-the-job training, on-site room and board at no charge, laundry facilities, travel reimbursement.

Contact Barry Finestone, Director, Camp Tel Yehudah, 50 West 58th Street, New York, New York 10019; 800-970-CAMP, Fax 212-303-4572, E-mail yjcamps@aol.com.

CAMP WENDY
151 SAINT ELMO ROAD
WALLKILL, NEW YORK 12589

General Information Combination three-week residential camp and three-week day camp. Activities offered cover badge work for the Girl Scouts. Well-rounded program of outdoor activities. Established in 1931. Owned by Ulster County Council of Girl Scouts. Affiliated with Girl Scouts of the United States of America, World Association of Girl Guides and Girl Scouts. 54-acre facility located 90 miles north of New York City. Features: freshwater lake; Olympic-size swimming pool; proximity to Catskill Mountains (off-site hiking location); nearby stables for horseback riding; location near the Hudson River.

Profile of Summer Employees Total number: 28; average age: 19; 2% male, 98% female; 20% minorities; 10% high school students; 35% college students; 10% international; 25% local residents. Nonsmokers preferred.

Employment Information Openings are from June 22 to August 16. Jobs available: ▶ 1 *health director* (minimum age 21) with RN or EMT with first aid and CPR certification at $1900– $2400 per season; ▶ 1 *waterfront director* (minimum age 21) with WSI, lifeguard, and CPR certification and 3 years camp experience at $1900–$2200 per season; ▶ 4 *unit directors* (minimum age 21) with desire to work with children in the out-of-doors at $1200–$1500 per season; ▶ 10 *unit counselors* (minimum age 18) with desire to work with children in the out-of-doors at $900–$1200 per season; ▶ 4 *waterfront staff* (minimum age 18) with lifeguard or small craft certification at $1200–$1400 per season; ▶ 1 *head cook* (minimum age 21) with experience in quantity cooking at $1300–$1600 per season; ▶ 2 *kitchen helpers* (minimum age 16) with interest in food preparation at $400–$500 per season. International students encouraged to apply; must apply through recognized agency.

Benefits On-the-job training, on-site room and board at no charge, laundry facilities. Preemployment training of 10 days is required and includes safety and accident prevention, group interaction, first-aid, CPR, leadership, camper-counselor relations, child abuse awareness. Orientation is paid.

Contact Fran Gallagher, Camp Director, Camp Wendy, 65 St. James Street, PO Box 3039, Kingston, New York 12402; 914-338-5367, Fax 914-338-6802. Application deadline: June 19.

CAROUSEL DAY SCHOOL
9 WEST AVENUE
HICKSVILLE, NEW YORK 11801

General Information Summer day camp for children ages 3–15. Established in 1956. Owned by Gene and Jane Formica. Affiliated with American Camping Association, Long Island Association of Private Schools and Day Camps. Located 30 miles east of New York City. Features: 2 pools; basketball court; gymnasium for nursery school children; 3 playgrounds; Kids Kourt; 6 sports fields.

Profile of Summer Employees Total number: 100; average age: 19; 90% college students. Nonsmokers preferred.

Employment Information Openings are from June 29 to August 21. Jobs available: ▶ 4 *swimming instructors and lifeguards* with WSI, Nassau County, and CPR/BLS certification at $1500–$1900 per season; ▶ 4 *sports instructors/counselors* with knowledge of basketball coaching and skills in soccer and baseball at $850–$1300 per season; ▶ 1 *nature instructor* with ability to develop a nature science program at $850–$1100 per season; ▶ 30 *general counselors* with ability to relate to children at $850–$1200 per season; ▶ 1 *director/instructor for crafts program* with ability to order, supervise, and implement crafts programs at $2500 per season; ▶ *archery instructor* with knowledge of archery and ability to teach at $1100–$1400 per season; ▶ *group leaders* at $1200 per season. International students encouraged to apply; must apply through recognized agency.

Benefits College credit, formal ongoing training. Preemployment training of 2 days is required and includes safety and accident prevention, group interaction, leadership, camper-counselor relations. Orientation is paid.

Contact Mike Epstein, Carousel Day School, Department SJ, 9 West Avenue, Hicksville, New York 11801; 516-938-1137, Fax 516-822-9269. Application deadline: May 31.

CENTRAL NEW YORK GIRL SCOUT CAMP NEAR WILDERNESS

General Information Residential Girl Scout camp offering general camp activities to 600 girls per summer. Established in 1961. Owned by Central New York Girl Scouts, Inc. 180-acre facility located 25 miles north of Syracuse. Features: large open field for sports/games; private lake; challenge course.

Profile of Summer Employees Total number: 32; average age: 22; 10% male, 90% female; 8% minorities; 2% high school students; 60% college students; 3% retirees; 15% international; 15% local residents.

Employment Information Openings are from June 29 to August 18. Jobs available: ▶ 5 *swimming instructors* with WSI certification or lifeguard training at $1100–$1500 per season; ▶ 1 *counselor-in-training director* with Girl Scout program knowledge at $1300–$1700 per season; ▶ 1 *health director* with RN, LPN, or EMT license at $2000–$2400 per season; ▶ *sports director* at $1200–$1600 per season; ▶ 1 *project-adventure director* with knowledge of challenge courses at $1200–$1600 per season; ▶ 1 *cook* at $2000–$2400 per season; ▶ 1 *assistant cook* at $1400–$1800 per season; ▶ 3 *kitchen aides* at $800–$1000 per season; ▶ 1 *maintenance person* at $800–$1000 per season; ▶ *waterfront director* with WSI certification at $1600–$2000 per season; ▶ *unit leader/assistant* with experience with children in groups at $1000–$1600 per season. International students encouraged to apply; must apply through recognized agency.

Benefits On-the-job training, on-site room and board at no charge, health insurance.

Contact Amy Posner, Camps Administrator, Central New York Girl Scout Camp Near Wilderness, Department SJ, PO Box 482, Syracuse, New York 13211; 315-437-6531, Fax 315-437-0559. Application deadline: April 15.

CHAUTAUQUA INSTITUTION SUMMER SCHOOLS
CHAUTAUQUA, NEW YORK 14722

General Information Residential summer school focusing on orchestra, piano, drama, and dance/ballet. Established in 1874. Owned by Chautauqua Institution. 175-acre facility located 90 miles south of Buffalo. Features: 17-mile-long freshwater lake; 5000-seat amphitheater; 150-seat black box theater; dance studio with 4 studios; 350-seat recital hall; practice shacks for instrumentalists.

Profile of Summer Employees Total number: 30; 70% male, 30% female; 100% teachers.

Employment Information Openings are from June 23 to August 25. Jobs available: ▶ *technical director* (theater) at $2000 per season; ▶ *scenic designers* (theater) at $2000 per season; ▶ *costume designers* (theater interns) at $1220 per season; ▶ *lighting designers* (theater) at $3200 per season; ▶ *stage managers* (theater) at $1220 per season; ▶ *lighting intern* at $1220 per season; ▶ *carpenter intern* at $1220 per season. International students encouraged to apply; must obtain own visa and working papers prior to employment.

Benefits On-site room and board, free admission to all concerts in amphitheater, interns receive free housing.

Contact Richard R. Redington, Vice President, Chautauqua Institution Summer Schools, Department SJ, PO Box 1098, Chautauqua, New York 14722; 716-357-6232, Fax 716-357-9014. Application deadline: March 1.

DARROW SCHOOL SUMMER PROGRAM: MOUNTAINSIDE LANGUAGE INSTITUTE
DARROW ROAD
NEW LEBANON, NEW YORK 12125

General Information Residential camp serving international students with intensive English and academic courses. Total enrollment of 20–25 students. Established in 1991. Owned by Darrow School. 365-acre facility located 9 miles west of Pittsfield, Massachusetts. Features: fully equipped gymnasium; 5 large sports fields; swimming pool; 2 outdoor tennis courts; hiking trails; rock climbing facilities.

Profile of Summer Employees Total number: 6; average age: 27; 50% male, 50% female; 15% minorities; 15% college students; 85% teachers. Nonsmokers only.

Employment Information Openings are from June 30 to August 20. Jobs available: ▶ 1 *teaching intern* with minimum of 3 years of college ESL completed at $800–$1000 per season; ▶ 1 *swimming instructor* with WSI certification. International students encouraged to apply; must apply through recognized agency.

Benefits On-the-job training, on-site room and board at no charge, laundry facilities, travel reimbursement.

Contact J. Kirk Russell III, Mountainside Language Institute Coordinator, Darrow School Summer Program: Mountainside Language Institute, Department SJ, 110 Darrow Road, New Lebanon, New York 12125; 518-794-6000, Fax 518-794-7065. Application deadline: May 30.

EASTERN EXCEL TENNIS
LONG ISLAND UNIVERSITY
BROOKVALE, NEW YORK 11545

General Information Camp which trains children in playing all aspects of tennis, including competition and match play. Established in 1990. Owned by Robbie Wagner. Located 15 miles east of New York City. Features: 40 tennis courts; 4 sports fields; 1 indoor gym; indoor tennis courts; swimming pool.

Profile of Summer Employees Total number: 20; average age: 24; 50% male, 50% female; 40% college students; 5% international. Nonsmokers only.

Employment Information Openings are from June 1 to August 1. Jobs available: ▶ 10 *tennis instructors* at $200–$500 per week; ▶ 1 *evening and weekend activities director* at $300–$500 per week. International students encouraged to apply; must obtain own visa and working papers prior to employment.

Benefits On-site room and board at no charge.

Contact Robbie Wagner, Owner, Eastern Excel Tennis, Eastern Excel Tennis, Department SJ, 81 Round Hill Road, East Hills, New York 11577; 516-625-1110, Fax 516-625-9618. Application deadline: January 1.

FIVE RIVERS CENTER
GAME FARM ROAD
DELMAR, NEW YORK 12054

General Information Environmental education center serving schools and families. Established in 1973. Owned by New York State Department of Environmental Conservation. 330-acre facility located 5 miles west of Albany. Features: 6 nature trails; classrooms; exhibit room; picnic area.

Profile of Summer Employees Total number: 2; average age: 27; 50% male, 50% female. Nonsmokers only.

Employment Information Openings are from June 21 to August 30. Year-round positions also offered. Jobs available: ▶ 2 *naturalist interns* at $100 per week.

Benefits College credit, on-the-job training, formal ongoing training, on-site room and board at no charge, travel reimbursement, employment recommendations.

Contact A. Sanchez, Five Rivers Center, Game Farm Road, Delmar, New York 12054; 518-475-0291. Application deadline: February 1.

FOREST LAKE CAMP
FOREST LAKE ROAD, BOX 67
WARRENSBURG, NEW YORK 12885

General Information Residential brother/sister camp for 100 boys and 85 girls with private lake. Features general program of sports, hobbies, waterfront activities, wilderness trips, and riding. Established in 1926. Owned by Gary Confer. Affiliated with American Camping Association, New York State Camp Directors Association. 400-acre facility located 60 miles north of Albany. Features: 3 large riding rings; private lake owned and exclusively used by camp; miles of woodlot trails on camp and surrounding property; 2 soccer fields, 2 baseball fields, and 5 tennis courts; well-appointed cabins with modern bathrooms.

Profile of Summer Employees Total number: 65; average age: 22; 50% male, 50% female; 10% minorities; 5% high school students; 75% college students; 10% international; 15% local residents; 15% teachers.

Employment Information Openings are from June 20 to August 20. Jobs available: ▶ 4 *swimming instructors* with lifeguard, first aid, and CPR training at $1100–$1600 per season; ▶ 2 *tennis coaches* with minimum high school varsity playing experience at $1200–$1600 per season; ▶ 1 *basketball coach* with minimum high school varsity playing experience at $1200–$1600 per season; ▶ 1 *baseball coach* with minimum high school varsity playing experience at

$1200–$1600 per season; ▶ *archery instructor* with competitive background at $1200–$1600 per season. International students encouraged to apply; must apply through recognized agency.

Benefits On-the-job training, on-site room and board at no charge, laundry facilities, travel reimbursement, tuition reimbursement.

Contact Gary Confer, Director, Forest Lake Camp, Department SJ, Box 648, Oldwick, New Jersey 08858; 908-534-9809, Fax 908-534-8474.

FORRESTEL FARM CAMP
11380 MAIN STREET
MEDINA, NEW YORK 14103

General Information Coed residential camp serving 60 children ages 7–15 for four 2-week sessions. Established in 1980. Owned by Mary V. Herbert. Affiliated with American Camping Association, New York State Camp Directors Association, American Independent Camps. 1,000-acre facility located 40 miles northeast of Buffalo. Features: 1000-acre working farm; 20 miles of trails with horseback riding overnight site; 1 tennis court; 7 riding arenas; 2-acre pond, 3 miles of Oak Orchard creek; 2 large sports fields.

Profile of Summer Employees Total number: 17; average age: 21; 100% college students; 80% international; 20% local residents; 1% teachers. Nonsmokers preferred.

Employment Information Openings are from June 20 to August 20. Spring break, winter break positions also offered. Jobs available: ▶ 4 *lifeguards* with Red Cross lifeguard or WSI certification at $800–$1100 per season; ▶ 8 *riding instructors* with CHA, Red Cross, CPR, Community First Aid and Safety, and Basic Life Support training at $800–$1100 per season; ▶ *athletic instructors* (soccer, volleyball, basketball, softball, lacrosse, archery, and riflery) with Red Cross, CPR, and Basic Life Support training and coaching and teaching experience at $800–$1100 per season; ▶ 2 *tennis instructors* with USTA coaching or teaching experience at $800–$1100 per season; ▶ 3 *experienced outdoor adventure instructors* (canoeing, hiking, mountain biking, and fishing) at $800–$1100 per season; ▶ 1 *experienced naturalist/conservationist* at $800–$1110 per season; ▶ 2 *experienced cooks*. International students encouraged to apply; must obtain own visa and working papers prior to employment.

Benefits College credit, on-the-job training, on-site room and board at no charge, travel reimbursement, salaries commensurate with experience. Preemployment training of 7 days is required and includes safety and accident prevention, group interaction, first-aid, CPR, leadership, camper-counselor relations. Orientation is unpaid.

Contact Mary Herbert, Camp Owner/Director, Forrestel Farm Camp, Department SJ, 4536 South Gravel Road, Medina, New York 14103; 716-798-0941. Application deadline: June 1.

THE FRESH AIR FUND
SHARPE RESERVATION, VAN WYCK LAKE ROAD
FISHKILL, NEW YORK 12524

General Information Five residential camps serving 2,900 inner-city children each summer. Established in 1947. Owned by The Fresh Air Fund. Affiliated with American Camping Association, New York State Outdoor Education Association, Child Welfare League of America. 3,000-acre facility located 65 miles north of New York City. Features: 2 lakes and a swimming pool; 14 miles of trails through wooded terrain; proximity to New York City; model farm, planetarium, and wildlife refuge; high and low ropes courses.

Profile of Summer Employees Total number: 300; average age: 20; 55% male, 45% female; 35% minorities; 3% high school students; 90% college students; 15% international; 30% local residents. Nonsmokers preferred.

Employment Information Openings are from June 20 to August 21. Jobs available: ▶ 200 *general counselors* (minimum age 18) with some college and experience with children at $1450–$1850 per season; ▶ 22 *experienced village leaders* at $1800–$2200 per season; ▶ 5 *waterfront directors* (minimum age 21) with WSI certification and three years of experience at $2200–$2800 per season; ▶ 20 *waterfront assistants* with lifeguard certification at $1600–$2000 per season; ▶ 35 *program specialists* (photography, video, music, sewing, pioneering, nature, and arts and crafts) with ability to teach specialty at $1600–$2000 per season; ▶ 9 *nurses* with RN license at $3800–$4200 per season. International students encouraged to apply; must apply through recognized agency.

Benefits College credit, on-the-job training, formal ongoing training, on-site room and board at no charge, laundry facilities, travel reimbursement, three-day breaks between twelve-day sessions, transportation to nearby town during free time. Preemployment training of 6 to 8 days is required and includes safety and accident prevention, group interaction, first-aid, CPR, leadership. Orientation is paid.

Contact Thomas S. Karger, Associate Executive Director, The Fresh Air Fund, 1040 Avenue of the Americas, New York, New York 10018; 800-367-0003, Fax 212-302-7875, E-mail freshair@ freshair.org, URL http://www.freshair.org. Application deadline: June 1.

FROST VALLEY YMCA CAMPS
2000 FROST VALLEY ROAD
CLARYVILLE, NEW YORK 12725

General Information Camp offering traditional activities. Established in 1886. Operated by The Frost Valley Association. Affiliated with American Camping Association, YMCA. 5,000-acre facility located 100 miles northwest of New York City. Features: diverse camper population; mountain environment; composting and recycling facility; adventure trips for teenagers; extensive high, low, and group ropes courses.

Profile of Summer Employees Total number: 200; average age: 23; 50% male, 50% female; 15% minorities; 15% high school students; 65% college students; 2% retirees; 15% international; 5% local residents. Nonsmokers preferred.

Employment Information Openings are from June 19 to August 26. Year-round positions also offered. Jobs available: ▶ 10 *experienced unit leaders* (minimum age 21) at $1600–$2000 per season; ▶ 40 *experienced counselors* (minimum age 19) at $900–$1500 per season; ▶ 5 *waterfront staff members* with lifeguard, CPR, and first aid certification at $1000–$1500 per season; ▶ 5 *riding staff members* with experience teaching Western riding at $1000–$1500 per season; ▶ 2 *licensed nurses* at $2500–$3500 per season; ▶ 3 *experienced art instructors* at $1000–$1500 per season; ▶ 10 *trip leaders* with experience in canoeing, biking, and hiking at $140–$180 per week; ▶ 3 *experienced sports staff members* at $1000–$1300 per season; ▶ 8 *program area directors* with ability to supervise staff and develop programs in various areas, including riding, waterfront, art, sports, and health at $1300–$2200 per season.

Benefits College credit, on-the-job training, on-site room and board at no charge, laundry facilities, travel reimbursement. Preemployment training of 7 days is required and includes safety and accident prevention, group interaction, first-aid, CPR, leadership, camper-counselor relations. Orientation is paid.

Contact Rob Lehman, Director of Camping, Frost Valley YMCA Camps, Department SJ, 2000 Frost Valley Road, Claryville, New York 12725; 914-985-2291, Fax 914-985-0056, E-mail camp4me@aol.com, URL http://frostvalley.com. Application deadline: June 1.

GOLDEN ACRES FARM AND RANCH RESORT
COUNTY ROAD 14
GILBOA, NEW YORK 12076

General Information Kosher family farm and ranch resort catering to young professional families with children. Established in 1950. Owned by Patricia and Jerry Gauthier. Affiliated with New York State Hospitality and Tourism Association, American Camping Association, Schoharie County Chamber of Commerce. 600-acre facility located 60 miles southwest of Albany. Features: dude ranch with indoor riding arena and extensive trails; location in central Catskill Mountains; indoor and outdoor pools and hot tubs; child care for children ages 3 months to 16 years; lake with rowboats and paddleboats.

Profile of Summer Employees Total number: 100; average age: 21; 40% male, 60% female;

5% minorities; 51% college students; 2% retirees; 30% international; 10% local residents; 3% teachers. Nonsmokers preferred.

Employment Information Openings are from June 15 to September 1. Jobs available: ► 13 *experienced counselors* at $195&–$225 per week; ► 3 *experienced nursery counselors* at $195&–$225 per week; ► 2 *swimming instructors* with American Red Cross lifesaving certification at $600 per month; ► 1 *social director* with driver's license at $200–$250 per week; ► 4 *front desk clerks* with computer, cash, and credit card experience at $200–$250 per week; ► 3 *bellhops/maintenance personnel* (minimum age 21) with driver's license and mechanical abilities at $200–$250 per week; ► 1 *head housekeeper* with supervisory skills at $250–$350 per week; ► 11 *chamber staff members* with clean and neat appearance at $200 per week; ► 1 *experienced bartender/barmaid* with cash-handling references at $200–$275 per week; ► 20 *experienced food service assistants* at $200–$250 per week; ► 1 *experienced baker* at $600–$700 per week; ► 8 *experienced wranglers* at $200–$300 per week. International students encouraged to apply; must obtain own visa and working papers prior to employment; must apply through recognized agency.

Benefits College credit, on-the-job training, on-site room and board at $67 per week, laundry facilities, use of resort facilities, opportunity to meet people from all over the world, staff outings. Preemployment training of 1 to 2 days is optional and includes safety and accident prevention, group interaction, first-aid. Orientation is paid.

Contact Patricia Gauthier, Golden Acres Farm and Ranch Resort, Department SJ, County Road 14, Gilboa, New York 12076; 607-588-7329, Fax 607-588-6911. Application deadline: May 1.

GORDON KENT'S NEW ENGLAND TENNIS CAMP AT TRINITY-PAWLING SCHOOL
300 ROUTE 22
PAWLING, NEW YORK 12564

General Information Tennis camp located at Trinity-Pawling School in Pawling, New York, for 80 campers ages 9–17. Established in 1965. Owned by Gordon Kent. Features: 16 outdoor tennis courts; modern dorms; athletic fields; lake nearby for swimming; gymnasium; weight room.

Profile of Summer Employees Total number: 20; average age: 20; 60% male, 40% female; 10% minorities; 5% high school students; 90% college students; 20% international. Nonsmokers only.

Employment Information Openings are from June 21 to August 14. Jobs available: ► *counselors/tennis instructors* with experience playing tennis (on school team), outgoing personality, and patience at $1250–$2000 per season. International students encouraged to apply; must obtain own visa and working papers prior to employment; must apply through recognized agency.

Benefits On-the-job training, on-site room and board at no charge, laundry facilities.

Contact Gordon Kent, Owner/Director, Gordon Kent's New England Tennis Camp at Trinity-Pawling School, PO Box 143, Riverdale, New York 10471; 800-528-2752, Fax 212-932-2462, E-mail netennis@aol.com.

GURNEY'S INN RESORT AND SPA
290 OLD MONTAUK HIGHWAY
MONTAUK, NEW YORK 11954

General Information International health and fitness timeshare resort, inn, and spa with oceanfront restaurant. Established in 1938. Affiliated with National Restaurant Association, American Hotel and Motel Association, Resorts International. Situated on 10 acres. Features: white, wide, private, sandy beach; indoor Olympic seawater pool; complete spa; state of the art weightroom; beauty salon; world class restaurant.

Profile of Summer Employees Total number: 50; average age: 25; 25% minorities; 5% high school students; 40% college students; 2% retirees; 30% international; 10% local residents; 5% teachers. Nonsmokers preferred.

Employment Information Openings are from April 15 to October 15. Spring break, winter break, Christmas break, year-round positions also offered. Jobs available: ▶ *lifeguards for pool and ocean* with all appropriate certifications at $7.50–$9.50 per hour; ▶ *beach attendants* at $6 per hour; ▶ *waitstaff/buspersons* with ability to carry trays on shoulder and some knowledge of food and wines at $3.25 per hour; ▶ *front desk/spa desk staff* with computer literacy at $7–$8 per hour; ▶ *cafe servers* at $6 per hour; ▶ *valets/bellpersons* with clean driver's license and ability to carry heavy bags at $4 per hour; ▶ *weight room attendants* with certification as personal trainer preferred at $6.50–$7.50 per hour. International students encouraged to apply; must obtain own visa and working papers prior to employment.

Benefits On-the-job training, on-site room and board at $50 per week, use of beach, discounted use of spa.

Contact Dan Rutan, Director of Human Resources, Gurney's Inn Resort and Spa, Department SJ, 290 Old Montauk Highway, Montauk, New York 11954; 516-668-2345, Fax 516-668-3576.

HILLSIDE OUTDOOR EDUCATION CENTER DAY, TRIPPING, AND HORSE CAMP
GAGE ROAD
BREWSTER, NEW YORK 10509

General Information Coed day, tripping, and residential horse camp serving approximately 150 children ages 5–15. Established in 1960. Owned by Green Chimneys School. Affiliated with American Camping Association. 100-acre facility located 60 miles north of New York City. Features: heated indoor pool; high ropes course; challenge course; climbing tower; farm; Native American area with teepee and wishing circle.

Profile of Summer Employees Total number: 35; average age: 24; 30% male, 70% female; 2% minorities; 1% high school students; 80% college students; 25% international; 25% local residents; 40% teachers. Nonsmokers only.

Employment Information Openings are from June 30 to August 31. Jobs available: ▶ 10 *general counselors* (minimum age 21) with experience teaching children at $175–$200 per week; ▶ 1 *archery instructor* (minimum age 21) with archery instructor certification at $250 per week; ▶ 2 *adventure specialists* with experience leading ropes courses, climbing tower, caving, and canoeing at $250 per week; ▶ 1 *experienced arts and crafts instructor* at $250 per week; ▶ 8 *horseback riding instructors* with experience teaching riding and children at $175–$250 per week; ▶ 2 *swimming instructors* (must be at least 21) with WSI certification and experience as pool director at $500–$650 per month. International students encouraged to apply; must obtain own visa and working papers prior to employment; must apply through recognized agency.

Benefits On-the-job training, on-site room and board, laundry facilities. Preemployment training of 5 days is required and includes safety and accident prevention, group interaction, first-aid, leadership, camper-counselor relations, adventure training, scheduling. Orientation is paid.

Contact Marty Newell, Director HOEC, Hillside Outdoor Education Center Day, Tripping, and Horse Camp, Department SJ, Gage Road, Brewster, New York 10509; 914-279-2996 Ext. 316, Fax 914-279-2714. Application deadline: April 1.

INTRODUCTION TO INDEPENDENCE
NEW YORK INSTITUTE OF TECHNOLOGY
CENTRAL ISLIP, NEW YORK 11722

General Information Residential pre-college/independent living experience serving 30–45 moderately to severely learning disabled young adults ages 16–20. Established in 1987. Affiliated with New York Institute of Technology. 600-acre facility located 50 miles east of New York City. Features: 2 outdoor tennis courts; 9-hole golf course; indoor swimming pool; bowling alley; fully equipped gymnasium; 2 full exercise rooms.

Profile of Summer Employees Total number: 16; average age: 35; 33% male, 67% female;

15% minorities; 15% college students; 75% teachers. Nonsmokers preferred.

Employment Information Openings are from July 5 to August 22. Year-round positions also offered. Jobs available: ▶ *resident advisors* with special education, psychology, or social work backgrounds (graduate students) at $1000 per season.

Benefits On-the-job training, on-site room and board at no charge, laundry facilities.

Contact David Finkelstein, Introduction to Independence, PO Box 465, Islip Terrace, New York 11752; 516-348-3354, Fax 516-348-0437. Application deadline: May 1.

JOHN DREW THEATER OF GUILD HALL
158 MAIN STREET
EAST HAMPTON, NEW YORK 11937

General Information Organization presenting the performing arts in a 387-seat theater. Established in 1931. Operated by Guild Hall of East Hampton, Inc. Affiliated with Association of Performing Arts Presenters, Actors' Equity Letter of Agreement. Located 80 miles east of New York City. Features: resort community and ocean beaches.

Profile of Summer Employees Total number: 12; average age: 22; 25% male, 75% female; 85% college students; 90% local residents.

Employment Information Openings are from May 23 to September 5. Jobs available: ▶ 3 *experienced box office staff members* at $7 per hour; ▶ 2 *experienced technical staff members* at $300–$400 per week; ▶ 3 *interns* with backstage experience required of technical interns (administrative and production interns should be outgoing and willing to work long hours) at $100 per week; ▶ *administrative staff members* at $300–$400 per week.

Benefits College credit, on-the-job training. Off-site boarding costs are $2000 per month.

Contact Brigitte Blachere, General Manager, John Drew Theater of Guild Hall, 158 Main Street, East Hampton, New York 11937; 516-324-4051, Fax 516-324-2722. Application deadline: March 30.

KUTSHER'S SPORTS ACADEMY
MONTICELLO, NEW YORK 12701

General Information Residential coeducational sports camp featuring an elective instructional sports program for 500 campers, as well as arts and crafts, woodworking, dance, drama, computers, and photography programs. Established in 1968. Owned by the Kutsher family. Affiliated with American Camping Association, Association of Independent Camps, New York State Camp Directors Association. 100-acre facility located 90 miles northwest of New York City. Features: fieldhouse with indoor tennis and basketball courts; large private lake; 20 lit outdoor tennis courts; 6 lit outdoor basketball courts; athletic facilities; location in Catskill Mountains.

Profile of Summer Employees Total number: 160; average age: 21; 69% male, 31% female; 20% minorities; 100% college students; 25% international. Nonsmokers only.

Employment Information Openings are from June 23 to August 20. Jobs available: ▶ *counselors* with a specialty in at least one sport or college/high school athletics experience at $900–$1300 per season; ▶ *experienced coaches* at $1800–$3000 per season; ▶ *nurses* at $2200–$2800 per season; ▶ *athletic trainer* with certification at $2000–$2300 per season.

Benefits College credit, on-the-job training, formal ongoing training, on-site room and board at no charge, laundry facilities, travel allowance. Preemployment training of 3 days is required and includes safety and accident prevention, group interaction, first-aid, leadership, camper-counselor relations. Orientation is unpaid.

Contact Robert Trupin, Executive Director, Kutsher's Sports Academy, Department SJ, 2 Snowflake Lane, Westport, Connecticut 06880; 203-454-4991.

MARTIN'S FANTASY ISLAND
2400 GRAND ISLAND BOULEVARD
GRAND ISLAND, NEW YORK 14072

General Information Amusement park offering rides, shows, waterpark, miniature golf, western shoot-out, pony rides, petting zoo, group outings, and school days. Owned by Martin DiPietro. Affiliated with International Association of Amusement Parks and Attractions, New York State Business Council, Grand Island Chamber of Commerce. 80-acre facility located 12 miles south of Buffalo. Features: wave pool; adult and kiddie waterslides; 18-hole miniature golf course; petting zoo; log flume ride; storytelling and puppet shows.

Profile of Summer Employees Total number: 250; average age: 17. Nonsmokers preferred.

Employment Information Openings are from May 15 to September 5. Jobs available: ▶ *food service/catering staff;* ▶ 25 *lifeguards* with Red Cross/lifesaving and CPR certification; ▶ *ride operators(minimum age 18);* ▶ *shops/retail staff;* ▶ *games staff;* ▶ *front gate staff/cashiers;* ▶ *grounds staff;* ▶ *restroom staff.*

Benefits College credit, on-the-job training. Off-site boarding costs are $400 per month.

Contact Martin Fantasy Island, Human Resources, Martin's Fantasy Island, Department SJ, 2400 Grand Island Boulevard, Grand Island, New York 14072; 716-773-7591, Fax 716-773-7043. Application deadline: April 15.

MUSIKER TOURS
1326 OLD NORTHERN BOULEVARD
ROSLYN, NEW YORK 11576

General Information Active tours and adventure travel for students ages 13–18. Travel through the United States, Canada, and Europe, staying in campgrounds, dormitories, and hotels. Established in 1966. Owned by The Musiker Family. Affiliated with American Camping Association, National Tour Association, American Society of Travel Agents.

Profile of Summer Employees Total number: 100; average age: 24; 50% male, 50% female; 10% minorities; 40% college students; 50% teachers. Nonsmokers only.

Employment Information Openings are from June 30 to August 5. Jobs available: ▶ 100 *summer counselors* with experience in summer camp and with junior and senior high school students at $50 per week.

Benefits On-site room and board at no charge, all excursion and entrance fees included, workmen's compensation. Preemployment training of 3 days is required and includes safety and accident prevention, group interaction, leadership, camper-counselor relations, good camping practice. Orientation is unpaid.

Contact Jen Strauss, Director, Musiker Tours, Department SJ, 1326 Old Northern Boulevard, Roslyn, New York 11576; 516-621-0718, Fax 516-625-3438, E-mail info@summerfun.com. Application deadline: May 31.

NEW YORK MILITARY ACADEMY–ACADEMIC
SUMMER SESSION
90 ACADEMY AVENUE
CORNWALL-ON-HUDSON, NEW YORK 12520

General Information A 2- to 6-week academic program for repeat or advanced-credit courses. Classes are from 8:00 a.m. to 1:00 p.m. daily with afternoon recreational activities including a large horsemanship program. Established in 1954. Owned by New York Military Academy. Affiliated with New York State Board of Regents, Middle States Association of Colleges and Schools. 325-acre facility located 62 miles north of New York City. Features: 3 swimming pools (2 indoor and 1 outdoor); large gymnasium with a weight training center; fully operational stable with 225 acres of riding trails; 3 soccer fields, 1 baseball diamond, 2 lacrosse fields; 3 tennis courts; 1 indoor rifle range.

Profile of Summer Employees Total number: 50; average age: 23; 50% male, 50% female; 9%

minorities; 10% high school students; 60% college students; 30% teachers. Nonsmokers only.

Employment Information Openings are from June 28 to August 9. Jobs available: ▶ *lifeguard/ swimming instructor* at $1500–$2000 per season; ▶ *dormitory heads* at $2000–$2500 per season; ▶ *dormitory counselors* at $1000–$1800 per season; ▶ *athletic coaches/heads* at $1500–$2500 per season; ▶ *academic teachers* at $1200–$2000 per season. International students encouraged to apply; must obtain own visa and working papers prior to employment.

Benefits On-the-job training, on-site room and board at no charge. Preemployment training of 3 to 4 days is required and includes safety and accident prevention, group interaction, leadership, camper-counselor relations. Orientation is paid.

Contact Peter C. Wicker, Deputy Superintendent, New York Military Academy–Academic Summer Session, Department SJ, NYMA, Cornwall-On-Hudson, New York 12520; 914-534-3710 Ext. 233, Fax 914-534-7121. Application deadline: May 1.

NORTH SHORE HOLIDAY HOUSE
74 HUNTINGTON ROAD
HUNTINGTON, NEW YORK 11743

General Information Residential camp serving girls from low-income homes. Established in 1914. Owned by North Shore Holiday House. Affiliated with Townwide Fund of Huntington. 5-acre facility located 25 miles east of New York City. Features: pool; gazebo for dances and rainy days; 2 ball fields; large main building.

Profile of Summer Employees Total number: 22; average age: 19; 100% female; 50% minorities; 80% college students; 33% international; 20% local residents. Nonsmokers preferred.

Employment Information Openings are from June 26 to August 23. Jobs available: ▶ 5 *bunk counselors* at $1000 per season; ▶ 1 *arts and crafts staff member* at $1000–$1500 per season; ▶ 1 *music staff member* at $1000–$1500 per season; ▶ 1 *dance staff member* at $1000–$1500 per season; ▶ 1 *swimming instructor* (minimum age 21) with WSI and lifeguard certification at $1500 per season; ▶ *computor instructor* at $1000–$1500 per season.

Benefits College credit, on-the-job training, formal ongoing training, on-site room and board at no charge, laundry facilities. Preemployment training is required and includes safety and accident prevention, group interaction, first-aid, CPR, leadership, camper-counselor relations. Orientation is unpaid.

Contact Marty Gordon, Director, North Shore Holiday House, Department SJ, 3 Marine Street, Huntington, New York 11743; 516-549-6892. Application deadline: May 1.

OFFENSE-DEFENSE FOOTBALL CAMP
HOFSTRA UNIVERSITY
HEMPSTEAD, NEW YORK 11550

General Information Residential and day camp offering instruction in full-gear contact football to boys ages 8–18; taught by 60 college coaches and 15 National Football League professionals. Established in 1969. Owned by Mike Meshken- Offense-Defense. Affiliated with New England Camping Association. 300-acre facility located 12 miles east of New York City. Features: location on college campus in country setting; pool; weight room; 4 basketball courts; gym; 5 sports fields.

Profile of Summer Employees Total number: 80; average age: 23; 88% male, 12% female; 20% college students; 3% retirees; 10% local residents; 25% teachers. Nonsmokers preferred.

Employment Information Openings are from June 20 to July 10. Jobs available: ▶ 2 *swimming instructors* with WSI certification at $150 per week; ▶ 15 *counselors* with ability to work well with children at $100–$150 per week; ▶ 20 *football coaches* with experience as a high school or college American football coach at $200–$300 per week; ▶ 3 *experienced student athletics trainers* with work toward certification at $150–$200 per week; ▶ 4 *certified athletics trainers* at $275–$400 per week; ▶ 1 *bus driver* with CDL at $200–$300 per week.

Benefits College credit, on-the-job training, formal ongoing training, on-site room and board, laundry facilities, chance to work out with other college players, visits to New York City.

Contact Rick Whittier, President, Offense-Defense Football Camp, Department SJ, PO Box 1056, Fairfield, Connecticut 06432; 800-243-4296, Fax 203-259-7959. Application deadline: May 15.

PECONIC DUNES CAMP
SOUNDVIEW AVENUE
PECONIC, NEW YORK 11958

General Information Residential and day camp emphasizing environmental and recreational activities including canoeing, archery, swimming, fishing, and arts and crafts. Established in 1931. Owned by Suffolk County Parks Department. Operated by Suffolk County Organization for the Promotion of Education (SCOPE). Affiliated with American Camping Association. 98-acre facility located 75 miles east of New York City. Features: private beach on Long Island Sound; mile-long spring-fed lake; biodiverse habitats.

Profile of Summer Employees Total number: 40; average age: 20; 50% male, 50% female; 15% minorities; 90% college students; 10% local residents. Nonsmokers preferred.

Employment Information Openings are from June 21 to August 24. Jobs available: ▶ 1 *waterfront director* with WSI certification at $400 per week; ▶ 4 *waterfront staff members* with lifesaving or WSI certification at $300–$350 per week; ▶ 2 *athletics director and assistant* at $300–$325 per week; ▶ 12 *experienced senior counselors* with college senior or graduate status at $285–$300 per week; ▶ 1 *nurse* with RN license at $600–$630 per week; ▶ 2 *maintenance personnel* with maturity and full knowledge of carpentry, plumbing, and electrical wiring at $150–$400 per week; ▶ 1 *head cook* with mature responsible personality (pay commensurate with experience) at $400–$425 per week; ▶ 3 *kitchen helpers* with high school student status and mature attitude at $125–$150 per week; ▶ 4 *environmental educators* at $400 per week; ▶ *assistant cook* at $250–$325 per week.

Benefits On-site room and board at no charge, laundry facilities. Preemployment training of 3 days is required and includes safety and accident prevention, group interaction, first-aid, CPR, leadership, camper-counselor relations. Orientation is unpaid.

Contact Peconic Dunes Camp, Peconic Dunes Camp, PO Box 204, Peconic, New York 11958; 516-765-5770, Fax 516-765-0017. Application deadline: April 15.

POINT O'PINES CAMP
7201 STATE ROUTE 8
BRANT LAKE, NEW YORK 12815-2236

General Information Eight-week traditional residential girls camp with professional sports instruction as well as arts, performing arts, and horsemanship for 290 campers; winter restaurant and wedding caterers. Established in 1957. Owned by James and Margaret Sue Himoff. Affiliated with American Camping Association, American Quarter Horse Association. 523-acre facility located 76 miles north of Albany. Features: extensive freshwater lake frontage; 1 indoor and 12 outdoor tennis courts (red clay and Har-Tru surfaces); indoor sports recreational building; indoor dance/gymnastics building; 3 outdoor sports fields; fitness center; 500-acre horse farm, 3 horseback riding rings, and extensive riding trails.

Profile of Summer Employees Total number: 145; average age: 22; 10% male, 90% female; 10% minorities; 80% college students; 10% international; 5% local residents. Nonsmokers only.

Employment Information Openings are from June 15 to August 23. Year-round positions also offered. Jobs available: ▶ 23 *waterfront staff members* with extensive water sports experience at $1100–$1400 per season; ▶ 14 *tennis staff members* with experience as college team player or professional instructor at $900–$1400 per season; ▶ 6 *athletics staff members* with experience as college team player or professional instructor at $1000–$1400 per season; ▶ 6 *gymnastics/dance staff members* with experience as college team player or instructor at $900–$1400 per season; ▶ 6 *arts and crafts staff members* with professional teaching experience and/or a major in art at $900–$1400 per season; ▶ 2 *video/radio instructors* with at least two years of experience in operating equipment at $900–$1400 per season; ▶ 4 *experienced English horseback* *riding instructors* with at least two years of teaching experience at $900–$1400 per season; ▶ 2 *photography staff members* with college or professional experience at $900–$1400 per season; ▶ 8 *experienced waterskiing instructors* at $900–$1400 per season; ▶ 3 *experienced sailing instructors* at $900–$1400 per season; ▶ 2 *experienced boating instructors* at $900–$1400 per season; ▶ 4 *experienced outdoor adventure staff members* with extensive training in safety at $900–$1400 per season; ▶ 1 *music director* with experience as piano accompanist for theater (must be able to transpose) at $900–$1400 per season; ▶ 1 *experienced drama director* at $900–$1400 per season; ▶ 1 *drama technical person* with at least two years of experience in college or community theater at $900–$1400 per season; ▶ *experienced fitness and conditioning instructor* with extensive training and certification at $900–$1400 per season; ▶ *experienced cleaning and kitchen help* with references; ▶ *drama-costume director* with must sew at $900–$1400 per season; ▶ 3 *nurses* with RN certification and clinical experience at $2500–$3000 per season; ▶ *year-round dining room manager for restaurant* with experience in restaurant work and organizational skills.

Benefits College credit, on-the-job training, formal ongoing training, on-site room and board at no charge, laundry facilities, travel reimbursement, separate staff laundry and lounge, weekly scheduled recreation programs for off-duty staff. Preemployment training of 7 to 10 days is required and includes safety and accident prevention, group interaction, first-aid, CPR, leadership, Red Cross 1st Responder, WSI course. Orientation is paid.

Contact Sue Himoff, Director, Point O'Pines Camp, Department SJ, 7201 State Route 8, Brant Lake, New York 12815-2236; 518-494-3213, Fax 518-494-3489. Application deadline: May 15.

REGIS-APPLEJACK
PO BOX 245
PAUL SMITH'S, NEW YORK 12970

General Information Nonsectarian friendly coed camps for children ages 6–12 (Regis) and ages 13–17 (Applejack Teen Camp). Established in 1946. Owned by Humes family. Affiliated with American Camping Association, National Waterski Association, National Archery Association. 100-acre facility located 20 miles west of Lake Placid. Features: location in Adirondack Mountain Park on the shore of 7½-mile long St. Regis Lake; large boating/sailing program with 55 boats; cabins have 3–4 bedrooms, rustic living rooms with fireplaces, and bathrooms; 7 all-weather tennis courts, and 2 large athletic fields; extensive arts center for dramatics, dance, arts and crafts, and photography.

Profile of Summer Employees Total number: 80; average age: 23; 50% male, 50% female; 10% minorities; 70% college students; 1% retirees; 10% international; 20% local residents; 25% teachers. Nonsmokers only.

Employment Information Openings are from June 23 to August 25. Jobs available: ▶ *counselors* (minimum age 19); ▶ *aquatic specialists* (minimum age 19) with lifeguard, WSI, first aid, BLS, and CPR certification; ▶ *boating department head;* ▶ *sailing instructors;* ▶ *waterski instructors;* ▶ *athletics staff;* ▶ *tennis counselors and head;* ▶ *arts & crafts instructors;* ▶ *drama instructors;* ▶ *wilderness trip leaders* (minimum age 19) with first aid, BLS, and CPR certification; ▶ *mountain biking counselors;* ▶ *office secretary/manager;* ▶ *nurses* with NY state license; ▶ *cooks;* ▶ *maintenance staff.* All positions offered at $900–$1500 per season.

Benefits College credit, on-the-job training, on-site room and board, laundry facilities, travel reimbursement, opportunity to meet campers and staff from all over the United States and the world, no cost for laundry facilities.

Contact Michael Humes, Regis-Applejack, 107 Robinhood Road, White Plains, New York 10605; 914-997-7039, Fax 914-761-8228.

SAIL CARIBBEAN
79 CHURCH STREET
NORTHPORT, NEW YORK 11768

General Information Summer sailing program in Caribbean for teens. Established in 1979. Owned by Michael D. Liese. Affiliated with US Sailing.

Profile of Summer Employees Total number: 45; average age: 22; 66% male, 34% female; 60% college students; 40% teachers. Nonsmokers only.

Employment Information Openings are from June 18 to August 24. Jobs available: ▶ 6 *skippers;* ▶ 6 *assistant skippers;* ▶ 2 *food supervisors;* ▶ 2 *ARC lifeguard instructors;* ▶ 4 *PADI scuba instructors;* ▶ 2 *French teachers;* ▶ 6 *marine biology teachers.*

Benefits On-the-job training, on-site room and board at no charge, laundry facilities, travel reimbursement. Preemployment training of 7 days is required and includes safety and accident prevention, group interaction, first-aid, CPR, leadership, camper-counselor relations. Orientation is paid.

Contact Michael D. Liese, Owner/Director, Sail Caribbean, 79 Church Street, Northport, New York 11768; 800-321-0994, Fax 516-754-3362, E-mail info@sailcaribbean.com, URL http://www.sailcaribbean.com. Application deadline: March 1.

STAGEDOOR MANOR THEATRE AND DANCE CAMP
KARMEL ROAD
LOCH SHELDRAKE, NEW YORK 12759

General Information Residential coeducational camp serving 240 campers in performing arts. Established in 1976. Owned by Stagedoor Enterprises, Inc. Affiliated with American Camping Association. 25-acre facility located 95 miles northwest of New York City. Features: proximity to town and health club; former resort hotel converted into a camp; indoor and outdoor pools; nearby lake for boating; 5 theater spaces, 3 television studios, and 5 dance studios; location in the Catskill Mountains just 2 hours from New York City.

Profile of Summer Employees Total number: 117; average age: 25; 40% male, 60% female; 50% college students; 25% international; 2% local residents. Nonsmokers preferred.

Employment Information Openings are from June 20 to August 26. Jobs available: ▶ 6 *experience theater directors* at $2000–$2500 per season; ▶ 6 *pianists* with excellent sight-reading ability and musical theater experience at $1800–$2500 per season; ▶ 3 *choreographers* with musical theater experience at $1800–$2200 per season; ▶ 10 *technicians* with theater experience at $1600–$2200 per season; ▶ 3 *designers* with theater experience at $1800–$2500 per season; ▶ 3 *swimming instructors/lifeguards* with American Red Cross certification at $1600–$2000 per season; ▶ 3 *nurses* with RN or LPN license at $1600–$3000 per season; ▶ 2 *office managers* with administrative experience with good people and phone skills at $1600–$2500 per season; ▶ 4 *group leaders* with camp management experience at $1800–$2500 per season; ▶ 2 *office assistants* with typing and bookkeeping skills at $1400–$2000 per season; ▶ 2 *groundspersons* with gardening, painting, and housekeeping skills at $1500–$1800 per season; ▶ 30 *counselors* with college student status and involvement in theater, sports, or other program areas (minimum age 21) at $1000–$1400 per season; ▶ 2 *tennis counselors* at $1000–$1500 per season. International students encouraged to apply.

Benefits College credit, on-the-job training, formal ongoing training, on-site room and board at no charge, laundry facilities, theater and dance classes offered during time off, recreational facilities available for use during off hours, including tennis and swimming. Preemployment training is required.

Contact Konnie Kittrell, Production Director, Stagedoor Manor Theatre and Dance Camp, Department SJ, 269 Moneymaker Circle, Gatlinburg, Tennessee 37738; 423-436-3030, Fax 423-436-3030. Application deadline: May 1.

SUMMER DISCOVERY AT UCLA, MICHIGAN, GEORGETOWN, VERMONT, AND CAMBRIDGE
1326 OLD NORTHERN BOULEVARD
ROSLYN, NEW YORK 11576

General Information Precollege enrichment program for high school students at University of Michigan, University of Vermont, Georgetown University, Cambridge University in England, and University of California, Los Angeles. Established in 1986. Owned by The Musiker Family.

Affiliated with National Tour Association, American Society of Travel Agents. Features: fully equipped recreation centers.

Profile of Summer Employees Total number: 100; average age: 23; 40% male, 60% female; 10% minorities; 40% college students; 50% teachers. Nonsmokers only.

Employment Information Openings are from June 20 to August 6. Jobs available: ▶ 120 *resident counselors* with experience working with students at $125–$400 per week.

Benefits On-the-job training, on-site room and board at no charge, laundry facilities, workmen's compensation, all excursions and entrance fees included. Preemployment training of 5 to 7 days is required and includes safety and accident prevention, group interaction, CPR, leadership. Orientation is paid.

Contact Lewis Biblowitz, Admissions Director, Summer Discovery at UCLA, Michigan, Georgetown, Vermont, and Cambridge, Department SJ, 1326 Old Northern Boulevard, Roslyn, New York 11576; 516-621-3939, Fax 516-625-3438, E-mail info@summerfun.com. Application deadline: June 1.

SUMMIT CAMP
339 NORTH BROADWAY
UPPER NYACK, NEW YORK 10960

General Information Traditional residential program modified to meet the special needs of our campers. Established in 1969. Owned by Mayer and Ninette Stiskin, Regina Skyer. Affiliated with American Camping Association. 100-acre facility located 20 miles east of Scranton, Pennsylvania. Features: lake setting for swimming and boating programs; paved go-cart and rollerblade track; computer labs and science labs; day/night tennis and basketball courts; staff lounge.

Profile of Summer Employees Total number: 175; average age: 22; 5% minorities; 100% college students; 90% international. Nonsmokers preferred.

Employment Information Openings are from June 18 to August 20. Jobs available: ▶ 80 *cabin counselors* at $1300–$1800 per season; ▶ 15 *activity specialists* at $1400–$1900 per season; ▶ 15 *water safety instructors* at $1400–$1900 per season; ▶ 3 *teachers* at $2000–$2500 per season; ▶ 2 *computer instructors* at $1500–$1900 per season. All applicants must have experience working with special needs populations. International students encouraged to apply; must apply through recognized agency.

Benefits On-the-job training, formal ongoing training, on-site room and board at no charge, laundry facilities, travel reimbursement.

Contact Ninette Stiskin, Director, Summit Camp, Department SJ, 339 North Broadway, Upper Nyack, New York 10960; 914-358-7772, Fax 914-358-5612, E-mail summitcamp@aol.com, URL http://www.castlepoint.com/summit.

TIMBER LAKE WEST
BURNT HILL ROAD
ROSCOE, NEW YORK 12776

General Information Residential camp serving 320 campers in a traditional four-week program. Established in 1987. Owned by Jay S. Jacobs. Affiliated with American Camping Association, New York State Camp Directors Association. 320-acre facility located 120 miles northwest of New York City. Features: 6 tennis courts; 2 heated pools; indoor gym; lake; roller hockey arena; lighted sports courts.

Profile of Summer Employees Total number: 150; average age: 20; 50% male, 50% female; 4% high school students; 75% college students; 15% international; 1% local residents; 5% teachers. Nonsmokers preferred.

Employment Information Openings are from June 23 to August 22. Jobs available: ▶ 6 *water safety instructors* with WSI, first aid, and CPR certification and lifeguard training at $1400–$1600 per season; ▶ 6 *tennis instructors* at $1400–$1600 per season; ▶ 15 *arts and crafts instructors* at $1400–$1600 per season; ▶ 3 *boating instructors* at $1400–$1600 per season;

▶ 70 *general counselors* at $1400–$1600 per season; ▶ 14 *kitchen staff members* at $1750 per season; ▶ 8 *housekeeping/maintenance staff members* at $1750 per season.

Benefits On-the-job training, on-site room and board at no charge, laundry facilities, travel reimbursement, use of facilities, organized day trips on day off, bonus for additional certifications in some jobs. Preemployment training of 5 days is required and includes first-aid, CPR, leadership, camper-counselor relations. Orientation is paid.

Contact Jennifer A. Quinn, Assistant Director, Timber Lake West, 144 Woodbury Road, #36, Woodbury, New York 11797; 516-367-6700, Fax 516-367-2737, E-mail west@camptlc.com, URL http://www.camptlc.com.

TIMBERLOCK VOYAGEURS
INDIAN LAKE, NEW YORK 12864

General Information Resident wilderness trip camp for nine boys and nine girls needing highly qualified leadership. Established in 1964. Owned by Timberlock Camp, Inc. 66-acre facility located 150 miles north of Albany. Features: ½ mile lakefront on Indian Lake; trails leading out from base; lakeside cabin for campers; fully equipped waterfront with docks, boats, canoes, and windsurfers.

Profile of Summer Employees Total number: 4; average age: 21; 50% male, 50% female; 100% college students. Nonsmokers preferred.

Employment Information Openings are from June 25 to August 20. Jobs available: ▶ *group leader* at $300–$400 per week.

Benefits On-the-job training, on-site room and board at no charge.

Contact Richard Catlin, Timberlock Voyageurs, Department SJ, RR1, Box 630, Woodstock, Vermont 05091; 802-457-1621. Application deadline: March 31.

TOP OF THE PINES
HARRIMAN STATE PARK
BEAR MOUNTAIN, NEW YORK 10911

General Information Residential camp serving 150 urban youths ages 6–14 in each of the four sessions. Established in 1991. Owned by Palisades Interstate Park Commission. Operated by Camp Vacamas Association of New York and New Jersey. Affiliated with American Camping Association. Located 50 miles north of New York City. Features: freshwater lake frontage; extensive hiking trails; use of entire Harriman State Park facility; Bear Mountain State Park.

Profile of Summer Employees Total number: 40; average age: 21; 40% male, 60% female; 30% minorities; 80% college students; 20% international; 1% local residents. Nonsmokers preferred.

Employment Information Openings are from June 15 to August 31. Year-round positions also offered. Jobs available: ▶ *general counselors* at $1100 per season; ▶ *waterfront specialists* with American Red Cross lifeguard or WSI certification at $1100–$1300 per season; ▶ *kitchen staff members* at $1100–$1800 per season; ▶ *nurse* with New York RN license at $2000–$3000 per season. International students encouraged to apply.

Benefits College credit, on-the-job training, on-site room and board at no charge. Preemployment training is required and includes safety and accident prevention, group interaction, first-aid, CPR, leadership.

Contact Michael H. Friedman, Executive Director, Top of the Pines, 250 West 57th Street, Room 1209, New York, New York 10019; 212-765-4420, Fax 201-838-7534. Application deadline: May 15.

TRAILMARK OUTDOOR ADVENTURES
16 SCHUYLER ROAD
NYACK, NEW YORK 10960

General Information Travel adventure program in New England, the northern Rockies, the Pacific Northwest, and southwest Colorado. Established in 1984. Owned by Rusty and Donna Pedersen.

Profile of Summer Employees Total number: 50; average age: 23; 50% male, 50% female; 20% college students; 80% teachers. Nonsmokers only.

Employment Information Openings are from June 15 to August 30. Jobs available: ▶ 30 *trip leaders* with knowledge of first aid and CPR at $100–$300 per week.

Benefits On-the-job training, on-site room and board at no charge, opportunity to participate in a variety of outdoor activities such as rock climbing, mountain biking, rafting, canoeing and backpacking. Preemployment training of 7 days is required and includes safety and accident prevention, group interaction, leadership, camper-counselor relations, driving. Orientation is paid.

Contact Rusty Pedersen, Director, Trailmark Outdoor Adventures, 16 Schuyler Road, Nyack, New York 10960; 800-229-0262, Fax 914-348-0437, E-mail rusty@trailmark.com, URL http://www.trailmark.com. Application deadline: June 15.

WEISSMAN TEEN TOURS
517 ALMENA AVENUE
ARDSLEY, NEW YORK 10502

General Information Owner-operated and escorted personalized student travel program in the United States, Western Canada, and Europe. Established in 1974. Owned by Ronee and Eugene Weissman. Affiliated with American Camping Association.

Profile of Summer Employees Total number: 9; average age: 23; 50% male, 50% female; 5% international; 50% local residents; 25% teachers. Nonsmokers only.

Employment Information Openings are from June 29 to August 11. Jobs available: ▶ 3 *tour leaders-U.S./Western Canada* (minimum age 21) with experience working with teenagers, CPR, and first aid at $100 per week; ▶ 3 *tour leaders-Europe* (minimum age 21) with fluency in French and/or Italian, experience working with teenagers, CPR, and first aid at $100 per week.

Benefits On-the-job training, formal ongoing training, on-site room and board at no charge, 4 and 5 star hotel accommodations, excellent restaurants–3 meals per day, all expenses paid. Preemployment training of 4 days is required and includes safety and accident prevention, group interaction, leadership, camper-counselor relations. Orientation is unpaid.

Contact Ms. Ronee Weissman, Owner/Director, Weissman Teen Tours, Department SJ, 517 Almena Avenue, Ardsley, New York 10502; 914-693-7575, Fax 914-693-4807, E-mail wtt@cloud. 9.net.

WESTCOAST CONNECTION TRAVEL CAMP
154 EAST BOSTON POST ROAD
MAMARONECK, NEW YORK 10543

General Information Exciting travel programs in the United States, western Canada, and Europe, for students ages 13–18, including active teen tours and outdoor adventure trips. Established in 1982. Affiliated with American Camping Association, Canadian Camping Association.

Profile of Summer Employees Total number: 90; average age: 23; 50% male, 50% female; 50% college students. Nonsmokers only.

Employment Information Openings are from June 15 to August 20. Year-round positions also offered. Jobs available: ▶ *tour staff members/leaders* with experience working with teens at $50–$400 per week. International students encouraged to apply; must obtain own visa and working papers prior to employment.

Benefits On-the-job training, on-site room and board at no charge, laundry facilities, chance to tour USA, Canada, or Europe, all group activities included.

Contact Mr. Mark Segal, Director, Westcoast Connection Travel Camp, Department SJ, 154 East Boston Post Road, Mamaroneck, New York 10543; 914-835-0699, Fax 914-835-0798, E-mail usa@westcoastconnection.com, URL http://www.westcoastconnection.com.

YMCA CAMP CHINGACHGOOK
PILOT KNOB ROAD
KATTSKILL BAY, NEW YORK 12844

General Information Coed residential camp serving 225 campers in one- and two-week sessions. Established in 1913. Owned by Capital District YMCA. Affiliated with American Camping Association. 200-acre facility located 60 miles north of Albany. Features: location in Adirondack Park on Lake George; extensive high ropes course; waterfront focus; access to thousands of acres of State Forest Preserve bordering camp.

Profile of Summer Employees Total number: 100; average age: 20; 55% male, 45% female; 5% minorities; 20% high school students; 75% college students; 15% international; 30% local residents. Nonsmokers preferred.

Employment Information Openings are from May 1 to November 1. Jobs available: ▶ 45 *general camp staff members* at $500–$4500 per season; ▶ 35 *counselors* at $900–$1500 per season; ▶ 6 *adventure trip leaders* at $1200–$2000 per season. International students encouraged to apply.

Benefits College credit, on-the-job training, formal ongoing training, on-site room and board at no charge, use of camp boats, camping gear, and climbing gear on days off.

Contact Matthew Kerchner, Summer Camp Director, YMCA Camp Chingachgook, Department SJ, Kattskill Bay, New York 12844; 518-656-9462, Fax 518-656-9362, E-mail chingacook@aol. com. Application deadline: March 15.

YMCA/YWCA CAMPING SERVICES–CAMPS GREENKILL/ MCALISTER/TALCOTT
BIG POND ROAD
HUGUENOT, NEW YORK 12746

General Information Residential camps serving general population. Camps are split into two age groups: 6–11 and 11–15. Established in 1906. Owned by YMCA of Greater New York. Affiliated with American Camping Association. 1,000-acre facility located 90 miles northwest of New York City. Features: 3 private lakes; easy access to Pocono and Catskill Mountains, rafting on the Delaware River, and New York City attractions; 1000 acres forested land; 3 separate camps 1 mile apart from each other; high ropes course.

Profile of Summer Employees Total number: 80; average age: 20; 50% male, 50% female; 30% minorities; 8% high school students; 60% college students; 35% international; 10% local residents. Nonsmokers preferred.

Employment Information Openings are from June 15 to August 28. Christmas break positions also offered. Jobs available: ▶ 30 *general counselors* at $110–$130 per week; ▶ 3 *aquatic directors* (minimum age 21) with WSI, LGT, CPR, Basic Life Support, and first aid certification at $170–$200 per week; ▶ *unit director* with leadership and camp experience at $150–$170 per week; ▶ 6 *swimming instructors* with WSI certification at $120–$140 per week; ▶ 10 *kitchen staff members* at $130–$160 per week; ▶ 2 *high ropes instructors* at $110–$130 per week; ▶ 2 *certified small craft instructors* at $110–$130 per week; ▶ *nurses* with RN or LPN certification at $275–$350 per week; ▶ *naturalist/counselor* (2 weeks only) at $160–$200 per week. International students encouraged to apply.

Benefits College credit, on-the-job training, formal ongoing training, on-site room and board at no charge, laundry facilities. Preemployment training of 7 days is required and includes safety and accident prevention, group interaction, first-aid, CPR, leadership, camper-counselor relations, YMCA lifeguard training. Orientation is paid.

Contact John Nystrom, Director of Camping, YMCA/YWCA Camping Services–Camps GreenKill/McAlister/Talcott, Department SJ, PO Box B, Huguenot, New York 12746; 914-858-2200, Fax 914-858-7823. Application deadline: June 1.

NORTH CAROLINA

BLUE STAR CAMPS
HENDERSONVILLE, NORTH CAROLINA 28793

General Information Private residential coed camp serving 750 children per four-week session. Established in 1948. Owned by Rodger and Candy Popkin. Affiliated with American Camping Association, American Canoe Association, Association for Horsemanship Safety and Education. 625-acre facility located 20 miles east of Asheville. Features: 12 outdoor tennis courts; 5 riding rings and 25 horses; 2 freshwater lakes and 1 swimming pool; high cables ropes course and challenge course; 3 outdoor and 4 indoor basketball courts; 60-foot climbing tower.

Profile of Summer Employees Total number: 320; average age: 19; 50% male, 50% female; 5% minorities; 34% college students; 34% international; 1% local residents; 10% teachers. Nonsmokers preferred.

Employment Information Openings are from June 1 to August 12. Jobs available: ▶ *cabin counselors* at $900–$1600 per season; ▶ *swimming instructor* with WSI certification and lifeguard training at $1200–$1600 per season; ▶ *horseback instructor* with teaching experience in English riding at $1500 per season; ▶ *tennis instructor* with teaching experience at $1750 per season; ▶ *nurse's aides;* ▶ *nurses.* International students encouraged to apply; must apply through recognized agency.

Benefits College credit, on-the-job training, on-site room and board at no charge, laundry facilities, travel reimbursement. Preemployment training of 7 days is optional and includes safety and accident prevention, group interaction, first-aid, CPR, leadership, camper-counselor relations. Orientation is paid.

Contact Rodger and Candy Popkin, Owners/Directors, Blue Star Camps, Department SJ, PO Box 1029, Crab Creek Road, Hendersonville, North Carolina 28793; 704-692-3591, Fax 704-692-7030, E-mail staff@bluestarcamps.com.

CAMP HIGH ROCKS
PO BOX 127-H
CEDAR MOUNTAIN, NORTH CAROLINA 28718

General Information Small residential boys camp focusing on development of skills in a non-competitive environment. There is a strong emphasis on outdoor adventure programming with many off-site trips. Established in 1958. Owned by Henry and Townsend Birdsong. Affiliated with Association for Experiential Education. 1,100-acre facility located 8 miles south of Brevard. Features: 12-acre lake; 15 miles of riding and hiking trails; 53-foot climbing tower; full gymnasium; barn facility with 5 instruction rings.

Profile of Summer Employees Total number: 60; average age: 24; 67% male, 33% female; 80% college students. Nonsmokers preferred.

Employment Information Openings are from June 8 to August 16. Jobs available: ▶ 7 *rock climbing instructors;* ▶ 8 *horseback riding instructors;* ▶ 23 *cabin counselor/skill instructors;* ▶ 7 *white-water canoeing instructors;* ▶ 4 *mountain biking instructors;* ▶ 6 *backpacking instructors;* ▶ 3 *crafts instructors;* ▶ 2 *athletics/tennis instructors;* ▶ 3 *ropes course facilitators;* ▶ 2 *pottery instructors;* ▶ 3 *swimming instructors* with WSI certification. All positions offered at $170–$230 per week.

Benefits On-site room and board at no charge, laundry facilities, American Canoeing Association instructor workshops, rock site instructor and rock rescue training, wilderness first aid training. Preemployment training of 6 days is required and includes safety and accident prevention, group interaction, leadership, camper-counselor relations. Orientation is unpaid.

Contact Henry Birdsong, Camp Director, Camp High Rocks, PO Box 127-H, Cedar Mountain, North Carolina 28718; 704-885-2153, Fax 704-884-4612, E-mail mail@highrocks.com, URL http://www.highrocks.com. Application deadline: April 1.

CAMP KANATA
13524 CAMP KANATA ROAD
WAKE FOREST, NORTH CAROLINA 27587

General Information Coeducational residential YMCA camp for children ages 6–15. Established in 1954. Operated by YMCA of Greater Durham. Affiliated with American Camping Association. 188-acre facility located 10 miles north of Raleigh. Features: 2 zip lines; 2 spring-fed lakes; seventeen cabins; 7,000-square-foot gymnasium; ropes course; 2 ball fields.

Profile of Summer Employees Total number: 42; average age: 20; 50% male, 50% female; 2% minorities; 30% high school students; 70% college students; 4% international; 35% local residents. Nonsmokers preferred.

Employment Information Openings are from June 5 to August 15. Jobs available: ▶ 37 *cabin counselors* with child work experience at $1300–$1500 per season; ▶ 2 *nature instructor* at $1300–$1500 per season; ▶ 1 *experienced arts and crafts director* at $1300 per season; ▶ 1 *program director* (minimum age 20) with creativity and camp experience at $2100–$2400 per season; ▶ 1 *staff-trainee director* (minimum age 20) with camp experience at $2200–$2400 per season; ▶ 1 *waterfront director* (minimum age 20) with camp experience and WSI, lifeguard instructor, or YMCA certification at $2000–$2200 per season; ▶ 1 *ropes course director* (minimum age 20) with camp experience and ropes course training at $1400 per season. International students encouraged to apply; must apply through recognized agency.

Benefits On-the-job training, on-site room and board at no charge, laundry facilities. Preemployment training of 8 days is required and includes safety and accident prevention, group interaction, first-aid, CPR, leadership, camper-counselor relations. Orientation is paid.

Contact Richard R. Hamilton, Director, Camp Kanata, Department SJ, 13524 Camp Kanata Road, Wake Forest, North Carolina 27587; 919-556-2661. Application deadline: May 15.

CAMP MERRIE-WOODE
100 MERRIE-WOODE ROAD
SAPPHIRE, NORTH CAROLINA 28774

General Information A residential girls summer camp dedicated to building self-esteem and confidence through traditional camp and high adventure activities. Established in 1919. Owned by Merrie-Woode Foundation, Inc. Affiliated with Association for Experiential Education, American Camping Association. 230-acre facility located 60 miles southwest of Asheville. Features: location on mile-long, privately owned lake with 3 docks; three tennis courts; gym equipped with a climbing wall; 4 riding rings (1 covered) and horse trails; state-of-the-art equipped canoeing and kayaking program; large sports field and archery field.

Profile of Summer Employees Total number: 80; average age: 20; 10% male, 90% female; 70% college students; 30% teachers. Nonsmokers only.

Employment Information Openings are from June 1 to August 18. Jobs available: ▶ *performing arts staff members* at $2000–$3000 per season; ▶ *land sports staff members;* ▶ *tennis staff members;* ▶ *archery staff members;* ▶ *nature staff members;* ▶ *riding staff members;* ▶ *arts/crafts staff members;* ▶ *woodworking staff members;* ▶ *weaving staff members;* ▶ *jewelry staff members;* ▶ *photography staff members;* ▶ *swimming staff members;* ▶ *canoeing and kayaking staff members;* ▶ *sailing staff members;* ▶ *mountaineering staff members;* ▶ *rock climbing staff members.*

Benefits College credit, on-site room and board at no charge, tuition reimbursement, CPR

training. Preemployment training of 4 days is required and includes safety and accident prevention, group interaction, first-aid, leadership, camper-counselor relations. Orientation is paid.
Contact Laurie Strayhorn, Director, Camp Merrie-Woode, 100 Merrie Woode Road, Sapphire, North Carolina 28774; 704-743-3300, Fax 704-743-5846, E-mail mwoode@aol.com.

CAMP MERRI-MAC
MONTREAT ROAD
BLACK MOUNTAIN, NORTH CAROLINA 28711
General Information Residential camp for girls. Established in 1950. Owned by Spencer Boyd. Affiliated with American Camping Association. 150-acre facility located 12 miles east of Asheville. Features: 3 tennis courts; private lake; fully equipped gymnasium; 17-stall barn; large playing field.
Profile of Summer Employees Total number: 60; average age: 20; 5% male, 95% female. Nonsmokers only.
Employment Information Openings are from June 4 to August 10. Jobs available: ▶ 35 *counselors* with strong expertise and requisite certification in activity at $1000–$1500 per season. International students encouraged to apply; must obtain own visa and working papers prior to employment.
Benefits On-the-job training, on-site room and board, laundry facilities. Preemployment training of 7 days is required and includes safety and accident prevention, group interaction, first-aid, CPR, leadership, camper-counselor relations. Orientation is unpaid.
Contact Adam Boyd, Director, Camp Merri-Mac, Camp Merri-Mac, Black Mountain, North Carolina 28711; 704-669-8766, Fax 704-669-6822. Application deadline: April 1.

CAMPS MONDAMIN AND GREEN COVE
TUXEDO, NORTH CAROLINA 28784
General Information Residential camps focusing on noncompetitive, lifetime, and outdoor skills with an emphasis on extended trips. Established in 1922. Owned by Bell family. 800-acre facility located 10 miles south of Hendersonville. Features: location close to the Blue Ridge Mountains, lakes, rivers, and national forests; rustic but comfortable facilities.
Profile of Summer Employees Total number: 100; average age: 25; 50% male, 50% female; 2% minorities; 60% college students; 5% retirees; 2% international; 5% local residents. Nonsmokers only.
Employment Information Openings are from May 31 to August 20. Jobs available: ▶ 2 *swimming instructors* with WSI certification; ▶ 2 *tennis instructors;* ▶ 2 *crafts and games instructors* with archery and riflery experience; ▶ 2 *sailing instructors* with small boat experience; ▶ 2 *mountain biking instructors* with camping experience and mechanical expertise; ▶ 2 *horseback riding instructors* with hunter-style riding and barn experience; ▶ 2 *mountaineering instructors* (hiking, rock climbing) with Outward Bound or NOLS experience helpful (other experience considered). All positions offered at $1200 per season. International students encouraged to apply; must apply through recognized agency.
Benefits On-the-job training, formal ongoing training, on-site room and board at no charge, laundry facilities. Preemployment training of 6 days is required and includes safety and accident prevention, group interaction, first-aid, CPR, leadership, camper-counselor relations. Orientation is paid.
Contact Frank or Nancy Bell, Directors, Camps Mondamin and Green Cove, Department SJ, Tuxedo, North Carolina 28784; 704-693-7446, Fax 704-696-8895, E-mail mondanin@ioa.com, URL http://www.modamin.com. Application deadline: March 31.

CAMP SKY RANCH
634 SKY RANCH ROAD
BLOWING ROCK, NORTH CAROLINA 28605-9738

General Information Coed private residential camp serving 114 mentally disabled children and adults in four 2-week sessions. Campers must be able to walk, dress, and feed themselves, as well as take care of their toilet needs. Established in 1948. Owned by Camp Sky Ranch, Inc. 175-acre facility located 100 miles northwest of Charlotte. Features: swimming pool *(heated)*; private freshwater lake; 6 creeks and streams; fully equipped infirmary; large meadow; hiking trails.

Profile of Summer Employees Total number: 30; average age: 20; 45% male, 55% female; 10% minorities; 10% high school students; 90% college students; 15% local residents. Nonsmokers preferred.

Employment Information Openings are from June 5 to August 10. Jobs available: ▶ 22 *counselors/activity leaders* at $120–$150 per week; ▶ 1 *waterfront director* with WSI certification at $130–$160 per week; ▶ 2 *lifeguards* with lifeguard training at $120–$160 per week.

Benefits On-site room and board at no charge, laundry facilities.

Contact Dan C. Norman, Director, Camp Sky Ranch, 634 Sky Ranch Road, Blowing Rock, North Carolina 28605-9738; 704-264-8600, Fax 704-265-2339.

CAMP TIMBERLAKE
BLACK MOUNTAIN, NORTH CAROLINA 28711

General Information A Christian camp for boys offering a traditional residential program with outstanding staff. Established in 1982. Owned by Spencer Boyd. Affiliated with American Camping Association. 150-acre facility located 12 miles east of Asheville. Features: 3 tennis courts; private lake; fully equipped gymnasium; 17-stall barn; large playing field; three climbing walls.

Profile of Summer Employees Total number: 60; average age: 20; 100% male; 90% college students. Nonsmokers only.

Employment Information Openings are from June 4 to August 10. Jobs available: ▶ 35 *counselors* with strong expertise and requisite certification in activity at $1000–$1500 per season. International students encouraged to apply; must obtain own visa and working papers prior to employment.

Benefits On-the-job training, on-site room and board, laundry facilities. Preemployment training of 7 days is required and includes safety and accident prevention, group interaction, first-aid, CPR, leadership, camper-counselor relations. Orientation is unpaid.

Contact Adam Boyd, Director, Camp Timberlake, Camp Timberlake, Black Mountain, North Carolina 28711; 704-669-8766, Fax 704-669-6822. Application deadline: April 1.

CAROWINDS
14523 CAROWINDS BOULEVARD
CHARLOTTE, NORTH CAROLINA 28273

General Information Theme park entertaining more than 1.7 million guests each season with thrilling rides, shows, concerts, food, and games. Seasonal operation March through October. Established in 1973. Owned by Paramount Parks. 360-acre facility located 10 miles south of Charlotte. Features: more than 40 state-of-the-art rides, shows, and movies; theme experiences for all ages; six roller coasters; drop zone stunt tower with 16-story 56 mile-per-hour free fall; 12-acre water park within the theme park.

Profile of Summer Employees Total number: 2,000; average age: 22; 49% male, 51% female.

Employment Information Openings are from January 15 to September 15. Jobs available: ▶ *ride operators and food and beverage associates* at $5.50–$6.50 per hour; ▶ *merchandise, games, and admissions associates* at $5.25–$6.25 per hour.

Benefits On-the-job training, free admission when off duty, complimentary tickets for Carowinds and other area attractions, discount movie tickets, park merchandise, and concert tickets, five

$1000 college scholarships each season. Off-site boarding costs are $500 per month. Preemployment training of 1 to 2 days is required and includes safety and accident prevention, group interaction, guest service, department-specific training. Orientation is paid.

Contact Jim Stubbs, Recruiter, Carowinds, Department SJ, PO Box 410289, Charlotte, North Carolina 28241-0289; 704-587-9002, Fax 704-587-9101. Application deadline: June 15.

DUKE TENNIS CAMP
DUKE UNIVERSITY WEST CAMPUS COURTS
DURHAM, NORTH CAROLINA 27715

General Information Camp teaching the fundamentals of tennis to residential, day, and half-day campers. Focus is on fun and learning including footwork, racquet work, timing, strokes, strategy, mental toughness, and match play. For the beginner through tournament player. Owned by Duke University. Operated by Jay Lapidus. Features: 16 laykold courts; location on Duke University campus; indoor acquatic center on campus; 30 minutes from RDU airport; 30 minutes from Chapel Hill and Raleigh; air conditioned dorms.

Profile of Summer Employees Total number: 14; average age: 22; 40% male, 60% female; 95% college students; 5% teachers. Nonsmokers only.

Employment Information Openings are from June 1 to July 31. Jobs available: ▶ 14 *tennis instructors/general counselors* at $175–$200 per week. International students encouraged to apply; must obtain own visa and working papers prior to employment.

Benefits On-the-job training, on-site room and board at no charge, laundry facilities.

Contact Stacey Flur, Administrative Director, Duke Tennis Camp, Department SJ, PO Box 2553, Durham, North Carolina 27715-2553; 919-479-0854, Fax 919-471-8268, URL http://www.duke.edu/sports. Application deadline: May 1.

DUKE YOUTH PROGRAMS–DUKE UNIVERSITY CONTINUING EDUCATION
203 BISHOP'S HOUSE BOX 90702
DURHAM, NORTH CAROLINA 27708

General Information Five summer enrichment programs serving 650 middle and high school students. Established in 1982. Owned by Duke University. Operated by Continuing Education and Summer Programs.

Profile of Summer Employees Total number: 21; average age: 20; 40% male, 60% female; 100% college students.

Employment Information Openings are from May 1 to August 15. Jobs available: ▶ 14 *residential counselors* at $1200–$2000 per season; ▶ 5 *teaching assistants* at $500–$1300 per season; ▶ *office assistants* at $6–$10 per hour.

Benefits On-the-job training, formal ongoing training, on-site room and board at no charge, laundry facilities. Preemployment training of 5 to 6 days is required and includes safety and accident prevention, group interaction, first-aid, CPR, camper-counselor relations. Orientation is paid.

Contact Kim Price, Program Coordinator, Duke Youth Programs– Duke University Continuing Education, Box 90702, Durham, North Carolina 27708; 919-684-2827, Fax 919-681-8235, E-mail kprice@mail.duke.edu. Application deadline: February 1.

EAGLE'S NEST CAMP
43 HART ROAD
PISGAH FOREST, NORTH CAROLINA 28768

General Information Residential camp serving 185 campers in three 3-week sessions. Experiential education for young people, promoting the natural world and the betterment of human character. Specializes in wilderness adventure and the arts. Established in 1945. Owned by Eagle's Nest Foundation, Inc. Affiliated with American Camping Association, Association for

Experiential Education. 40-acre facility located 30 miles southwest of Asheville. Features: location adjacent to Pisgah National Forest; freshwater swimming and canoeing lake; ropes course with high and low elements; 2 outdoor tennis courts; athletic field; arts arena.

Profile of Summer Employees Total number: 65; average age: 22; 50% male, 50% female; 1% minorities; 1% high school students; 80% college students; 3% international; 1% local residents; 3% teachers. Nonsmokers preferred.

Employment Information Openings are from June 1 to August 20. Year-round positions also offered. Jobs available: ▶ 4 *swimming instructors* with WSI, LGT, CPR, and basic first aid certification at $140–$250 per week; ▶ 4 *experienced horseback instructors* with CPR and basic first aid certification at $140–$230 per week; ▶ 10 *wilderness instructors* with wilderness first aid, CPR, and basic first aid certification at $160–$230 per week; ▶ 6 *canoeing instructors* with experience or American Canoe Association Instructor, CPR, and basic first aid certification at $140–$230 per week; ▶ 5 *arts instructors* with creativity, teaching experience, CPR, and basic first aid certification at $140–$230 per week; ▶ 6 *experienced rock climbing instructors* at $150–$250 per week; ▶ *kitchen staff* with experience in whole foods cooking at $150–$250 per week. International students encouraged to apply; must apply through recognized agency.

Benefits College credit, on-the-job training, on-site room and board at no charge, laundry facilities. Preemployment training of 6 days is required and includes safety and accident prevention, group interaction, leadership, camper-counselor relations, canoeing, rock climbing, ropes course. Orientation is unpaid.

Contact Noni Waite-Kucera, Summer Director, Eagle's Nest Camp, Department SJ, 633 Summit Street, Winston-Salem, North Carolina 27101; 910-761-1040, Fax 910-727-0030. Application deadline: January 15.

FALLING CREEK CAMP FOR BOYS
PO BOX 98
TUXEDO, NORTH CAROLINA 28784

General Information Privately owned camp in the western North Carolina mountains provides boys ages 7–16 with opportunity for growth and fun. Established in 1969. Owned by Charles W. McGrady. Affiliated with American Camping Association. 1,000-acre facility located 12 miles south of Hendersonville. Features: 2 horseback riding rings with barn and stable; 40-foot artificial climbing wall; high and low elements ropes course; miles of horseback riding, mountain biking, and hiking trails; lodge and dining hall; sailing and waterskiing facilities.

Profile of Summer Employees Total number: 90; average age: 24; 90% male, 10% female; 90% college students; 10% international; 10% teachers. Nonsmokers preferred.

Employment Information Openings are from May 30 to August 20. Jobs available: ▶ 5 *swimming instructors* with WSI and lifeguard certification at $1600–$1900 per season; ▶ 2 *experienced riflery instructors* at $1600–$1900 per season; ▶ 2 *experienced archery instructors* at $1600–$1900 per season; ▶ 3 *arts and crafts instructors* at $1600–$1900 per season; ▶ 4 *land sports counselors* at $1600–$1900 per season; ▶ 4 *experienced tennis instructors* at $1600–$1900 per season; ▶ 4 *camp nurses* with RN (North Carolina) at $1900–$2500 per season; ▶ 4 *mountaineering staff members* with experience in rock climbing and backpacking trips at $1600–$1900 per season; ▶ 4 *canoeing staff members* with experience in white water in closed and open boats at $1600–$1900 per season; ▶ 2 *horseback riding staff members* with experience in English-saddle instruction at $1600–$1900 per season; ▶ 2 *nature counselors* with background in biology, zoology, or ecology at $1600–$1900 per season; ▶ 2 *Indian lore counselors* with knowledge of Indian lore at $1600–$1900 per season. International students encouraged to apply; must apply through recognized agency.

Benefits College credit, on-the-job training, on-site room and board, optional laundry service. Preemployment training of 5 to 7 days is required and includes safety and accident prevention, group interaction, first-aid, CPR, leadership, camper-counselor relations. Orientation is paid.

Contact Donnie Bain, Director, Falling Creek Camp for Boys, Department SJ, PO Box 98, Tuxedo, North Carolina 28784; 704-692-0262, Fax 704-696-1616, E-mail fallingcrk@ioa.com, URL http://www.fallingcreek.com. Application deadline: March 1.

GWYNN VALLEY
1080 ISLAND FORD ROAD
BREVARD, NORTH CAROLINA 28712

General Information Noncompetitive, creative, residential camp for young boys and girls ages 5–12. Established in 1935. Owned by H. W. Boyd. Affiliated with American Camping Association, Nature Quest. 350-acre facility located 30 miles southeast of Asheville. Features: 50-acre integrated working farm; swimming pool; spring-fed lake and streams; 300 wooded acres for hiking and camping; turn-of-the-century operational Grist Mill; location in the heart of the Blue Ridge Mountains.

Profile of Summer Employees Total number: 120; average age: 27; 50% male, 50% female; 5% minorities; 5% high school students; 60% college students; 5% retirees; 30% international; 5% local residents; 5% teachers. Nonsmokers only.

Employment Information Openings are from June 1 to August 20. Jobs available: ▶ *cabin counselors* at $110–$200 per week; ▶ *swimming instructors;* ▶ *lifeguards;* ▶ *archery instructor;* ▶ *potter;* ▶ *ecology specialist;* ▶ *horseback riding (English) instructor;* ▶ *miller;* ▶ *drama specialist;* ▶ *weaver.*

Benefits College credit, on-the-job training, on-site room and board at no charge, laundry facilities, partial camper tuition waivers, housing for married couples, possible reimbursement of certification costs. Preemployment training of 7 days is required and includes safety and accident prevention, group interaction, first-aid, CPR, leadership, camper-counselor relations, risk management. Orientation is unpaid.

Contact Gwynn Powell, Assistant Director–Staff, Gwynn Valley, Department SJ, 1080 Island Ford Road, Brevard, North Carolina 28712; 704-885-2900, URL http://camppage.com/gwynnvalley. Application deadline: March 1.

KEYSTONE CAMP
CASHIERS VALLEY ROAD
BREVARD, NORTH CAROLINA 28712

General Information A camp for girls (ages 7–17) offering programs in horsemanship, daily horseback riding, tennis, land sports, water sports on two lakes, gymnastics, rock climbing, and hiking in Pisgah National Forest. Established in 1916. Owned by Page Ives Lemel. 80-acre facility located 30 miles north of Asheville. Features: 3 riding rings; 15 miles of riding and hiking trails; lakes for swimming and canoeing; 4 outdoor tennis courts; fully equipped gymnasium; located outside Pisgah National Forest.

Profile of Summer Employees Total number: 35; average age: 20; 10% male, 90% female; 20% minorities; 100% college students; 20% international. Nonsmokers preferred.

Employment Information Openings are from June 3 to August 15. Jobs available: ▶ 1 *aerobics instructor* at $1100–$1800 per season; ▶ 1 *archery instructor* at $1100–$1800 per season; ▶ 3 *art instructors* at $1100–$1800 per season; ▶ 1 *badminton instructor* at $1100–$1800 per season; ▶ 2 *canoeing instructors* with lifeguard certification at $1100–$1800 per season; ▶ 3 *hiking and camping instructors* at $1100–$1800 per season; ▶ 1 *dance instructor* at $1100–$1800 per season; ▶ *various sports instructors* at $1100–$1800 per season; ▶ *dramatics instructor* at $1100–$1800 per season; ▶ *nature instructor* at $1100–$1800 per season; ▶ *stable helper* at $1100–$1800 per season; ▶ *program director* at $1500–$2000 per season; ▶ *adventure program director* at $1500–$2000 per season; ▶ *head counselor* at $1500–$2000 per season; ▶ *riding instructor* at $1100–$1800 per season; ▶ *swimming instructor* with WSI and/or lifeguard certification at $1100–$1800 per season. International students encouraged to apply; must apply through recognized agency.

Benefits On-the-job training, formal ongoing training, on-site room and board at no charge, laundry facilities. Preemployment training of 5 days is required and includes safety and accident prevention, group interaction, first-aid, CPR, leadership, camper-counselor relations. Orientation is paid.

Contact Katherine C. Kaderabek, Associate Director, Keystone Camp, Department SJ, PO Box

829, Brevard, North Carolina 28712; 704-884-9125, Fax 704-883-8234. Application deadline: April 15.

NORTH BEACH SAILING/BARRIER ISLAND SAILING CENTER
BOX 8279
DUCK, NORTH CAROLINA 27949

General Information Sailing center specializing in rental and sale of windsurfing, sailing, and jet ski equipment and teaching proper use of this equipment. Offers a line of clothing for enthusiasts. Also offers parasailing and kayak eco-tours. Established in 1985. Owned by William H. Miles, Jr. Affiliated with American Windsurfing Industry Association, Outer Banks Chamber of Commerce, Windsurfing Instructors of America, American Sailing Association. Located 70 miles south of Virginia Beach, Virginia. Features: windsurfing and sailing instruction and rental; parasailing; waverunners; kayaks and canoes; 50 square miles of flat water sailing on Currituck Sound; unspoiled ocean beaches.

Profile of Summer Employees Total number: 30; average age: 23; 50% male, 50% female; 5% high school students; 70% college students; 10% international; 5% local residents; 5% teachers. Nonsmokers preferred.

Employment Information Openings are from May 1 to October 15. Jobs available: ▶ 8 *experienced windsurfing instructors* with ability to relate to students in a positive manner at $250–$350 per week; ▶ 4 *experienced sailing instructors* with ability to relate to students in a positive manner at $250–$350 per week; ▶ 8 *rental/desk persons* with knowledge of sailing and windsurfing at $200–$250 per week; ▶ 3 *experienced retail salespersons* with sailing/windsurfing experience at $200–$300 per week; ▶ 1 *parasailing instructor/captain* with Coast Guard captain's license at $550–$650 per week; ▶ 2 *experienced kayaking and canoeing instructors* (for teaching and renting duties and conducting eco-tours) at $200–$250 per week. International students encouraged to apply; must obtain own visa and working papers prior to employment.

Benefits College credit, on-the-job training, opportunity to learn to sail, windsurf, parasail, and jet ski, discounts on outdoor clothing, opportunity to learn the operation of professional water sports center. Off-site boarding costs are $350 per month.

Contact Bill Miles, President, North Beach Sailing/Barrier Island Sailing Center, Department SJ, Box 8279, Duck, North Carolina 27949; 919-261-6262, Fax 919-261-1494, E-mail nbsail@ interpath.com. Application deadline: May 1.

ROCKBROOK CAMP
HIGHWAY 276
BREVARD, NORTH CAROLINA 28712

General Information Residential camp serving girls ages 6–16, promoting independence in a non-competitive environment. Camp has two-, three-, and four-week sessions. Established in 1921. Owned by Jerry Stone. Affiliated with American Camping Association, Association for Experiential Education, Association for Independent Camps. 185-acre facility located 30 miles south of Asheville. Features: rustic mountain setting; freshwater lake; English forward seat riding facility; in-camp rock site for climbing; pottery studio and two other craft centers; gymnasium.

Profile of Summer Employees Total number: 50; average age: 21; 8% male, 92% female; 8% minorities; 3% high school students; 75% college students; 2% retirees; 8% international; 8% local residents; 8% teachers. Nonsmokers only.

Employment Information Openings are from June 2 to August 10. Jobs available: ▶ 50 *cabin counselors* (women only) at $150–$175 per week; ▶ 6 *registered nurses* (women only) at $450 per week; ▶ 2 *rock climbers* at $150–$200 per week; ▶ 2 *raft and canoeing guides* at $150–$200 per week; ▶ 2 *riding instructors* (women only) at $150–$175 per week. International students encouraged to apply; must apply through recognized agency.

Benefits On-the-job training, on-site room and board at no charge, laundry facilities.

Preemployment training is required and includes safety and accident prevention, group interaction, leadership, camper-counselor relations. Orientation is unpaid.

Contact Grant Bullard, General Manager, Rockbrook Camp, Department SJ, PO Box 792, Brevard, North Carolina 28712; 704-884-6151, Fax 704-884-6151.

RUBIN'S OSCEOLA LAKE INN
PO BOX 2258
HENDERSONVILLE, NORTH CAROLINA 28793

General Information Summer resort hotel with eighty rooms, serving three meals daily. Established in 1941. Owned by Stuart Rubin. Affiliated with Hendersonville Chamber of Commerce, Henderson County Travel and Tourism. 12-acre facility located 1 mile south of Hendersonville. Features: original inn and newer lodge rooms; lake and pool; scenic attractions; sports; state theater (playhouse); state forests and hiking trails.

Profile of Summer Employees Total number: 40; 50% male, 50% female. Nonsmokers preferred.

Employment Information Openings are from June 12 to September 30. Jobs available: ► 6 *waiters/waitresses;* ► 6 *buspersons;* ► 6 *housekeeping personnel;* ► 4 *desk clerks;* ► 3 *bellhops;* ► 1 *chauffeur;* ► 3 *kitchen aides.* International students encouraged to apply; must obtain own visa and working papers prior to employment.

Benefits On-the-job training, on-site room and board, bonus payable upon completion of contract.

Contact Stuart Rubin, Owner/Manager, Rubin's Osceola Lake Inn, Department SJ, 5005 Collins Avenue, PH7, Miami Beach, Florida 33140; 305-865-6015.

UNITED METHODIST CAMPS
1307 GLENWOOD AVENUE
RALEIGH, NORTH CAROLINA 27605

General Information Three campsites located in eastern North Carolina providing camping and outdoor experiences in an atmosphere of Christian faith. Established in 1949. Owned by United Methodist Church. Affiliated with American Camping Association. Features: horseback riding and rustic camp with tent cabins (featured at Chestnut Ridge Camp, located 15 miles west of Durham); tree houses and canoeing (featured at Rockfish Camp, located 15 miles south of Fayetteville on a lake); sailing (featured at Camp Don Lee, located 25 miles east of New Bern on Neuse River).

Profile of Summer Employees Total number: 150; average age: 19; 40% male, 60% female; 20% minorities; 10% high school students; 90% college students. Nonsmokers preferred.

Employment Information Openings are from June 1 to August 15. Jobs available: ► *cabin counselors* at $130–$165 per week; ► *nurses;* ► *lifeguards;* ► *sailing staff members/canoeing instructors;* ► *naturalists* at $130–$160 per week; ► *arts and crafts instructors.* International students encouraged to apply; must obtain own visa and working papers prior to employment.

Benefits On-the-job training, on-site room and board at no charge, laundry facilities, health insurance, accident insurance. Preemployment training of 10 days is required and includes safety and accident prevention, group interaction, first-aid, CPR, leadership, camper-counselor relations.

Contact Sue Ellen Nicholson, Director, Camping Ministries, United Methodist Camps, PO Box 10955, Raleigh, North Carolina 27605; 919-832-9560, Fax 919-834-7989. Application deadline: March 1.

YMCA BLUE RIDGE ASSEMBLY
84 BLUE RIDGE CIRCLE
BLACK MOUNTAIN, NORTH CAROLINA 28711

General Information Conference center serving families, teenagers, and adults. Established in 1906. Affiliated with YMCA. 1,200-acre facility located 17 miles east of Asheville. Features: location in the Appalachian woodlands of the Blue Ridge Mountains; athletics facilities, swimming pool, tennis courts, and hiking trails; alpine tower and climbing tower.

Profile of Summer Employees Total number: 120; average age: 20; 40% male, 60% female;

11% minorities; 5% high school students; 85% college students; 3% retirees; 14% international; 5% local residents; 2% teachers. Nonsmokers preferred.

Employment Information Openings are from June 1 to August 19. Jobs available: ▶ 85 *collegiate staff members* with at least 6 months of work or volunteer experience at $850–$1100 per season; ▶ 1 *pool director* with WSI, lifeguard, CPR, and first aid certification at $1000–$1200 per season; ▶ 1 *staff program director* with work or school experience in recreation with adults at $1000–$1200 per season; ▶ 30 *department supervisors* with at least one year work experience at $1000–$1200 per season; ▶ 1 *chaplain* with at least one year of divinity (seminary) school at $1500–$2000 per season. International students encouraged to apply; must apply through recognized agency.

Benefits College credit, on-the-job training, formal ongoing training, on-site room and board at no charge, laundry facilities, travel reimbursement, health insurance, tuition reimbursement, internships and programs, workmen's compensation insurance. Preemployment training of 3 days is required and includes safety and accident prevention, group interaction, leadership. Orientation is paid.

Contact Assistant Operations Director, YMCA Blue Ridge Assembly, Department SJ, 84 Blue Ridge Circle, Black Mountain, North Carolina 28711; 704-669-8422, Fax 704-669-8497, E-mail ymcabra@aol.com. Application deadline: April 20.

YMCA CAMP CHEERIO
CAMP CHEERIO ROAD
GLADE VALLEY, NORTH CAROLINA 28627

General Information Residential camp serving 200 campers in one- and two-week sessions. A high-adventure camp serving 50 campers per week is also offered, as well as a program for senior adults in the spring and fall. Established in 1960. Owned by High Point YMCA. Affiliated with American Camping Association, YMCA. 194-acre facility located 60 miles west of Winston-Salem. Features: 3-acre lake; swimming pool; 16 cabins with bathroom facilities; 23-room conference center; 4 tennis courts; 2 rappelling towers.

Profile of Summer Employees Total number: 90; average age: 20; 50% male, 50% female; 10% minorities; 40% high school students; 60% college students; 5% international; 10% local residents. Nonsmokers preferred.

Employment Information Openings are from June 1 to August 20. Year-round positions also offered. Jobs available: ▶ 16 *senior cabin counselors* with rising college sophomore status at $135–$155 per week; ▶ 16 *junior cabin counselors* with rising high school senior status at $100–$110 per week; ▶ 1 *aquatic director* (minimum age 21) with WSI certification at $170–$240 per week; ▶ 1 *rappelling director* (minimum age 21) at $170–$210 per week; ▶ *riding master* at $600 per month; ▶ *wilderness trip leaders* at $135–$155 per week. International students encouraged to apply; must obtain own visa and working papers prior to employment; must apply through recognized agency.

Benefits College credit, on-the-job training, on-site room and board at no charge, laundry facilities, health insurance. Preemployment training of 7 days is required and includes safety and accident prevention, group interaction, first-aid, CPR, leadership, camper-counselor relations. Orientation is unpaid.

Contact Michaux Crocker, Executive Director, YMCA Camp Cheerio, Department SJ, PO Box 6258, High Point, North Carolina 27262; 910-869-0195, Fax 910-869-0118, E-mail ymcaheerio@ aol.com. Application deadline: May 1.

YMCA CAMP HANES
KING, NORTH CAROLINA 27021

General Information Residential camp serving 150 campers weekly. Special programs for the physically disabled and diabetic. Established in 1927. Owned by YMCA of Greater Winston-Salem. Affiliated with YMCA United States of America, American Camping Association, National Rifle Association. 400-acre facility located 25 miles north of Winston-Salem. Features: 0roximity to Sauratown Mountain; two small freshwater lakes; four outdoor basketball courts; two large sports fields; archery and riflery range; four-mile horse riding trails.

Profile of Summer Employees Total number: 45; average age: 22; 50% male, 50% female; 10% minorities; 2% high school students; 90% college students; 25% international; 75% local residents; 10% teachers. Nonsmokers preferred.

Employment Information Openings are from June 1 to August 15. Spring break positions also offered. Jobs available: ▶ 25 *cabin counselors* at $100–$150 per week; ▶ *equestrian director* with riding experience at $125–$175 per week; ▶ *waterfront director* with WSI certification at $125–$175 per week; ▶ *program director* at $150–$200 per week; ▶ *registered nurse* with RN degree at $250–$300 per week; ▶ *counselor-in-training director* with at least one year of college at $120–$175 per week; ▶ *wrangler director* at $150–$200 per week. International students encouraged to apply; must apply through recognized agency.

Benefits On-the-job training, on-site room and board at no charge, laundry facilities.

Contact Neil Rosenbaum, Executive Director, YMCA Camp Hanes, Department SJ, Route 5, Box 99, King, North Carolina 27021; 910-983-3131, Fax 910-983-4624, URL http://www.camphanes.org. Application deadline: April 15.

NORTH DAKOTA

INTERNATIONAL MUSIC CAMP
INTERNATIONAL PEACE GARDEN
DUNSEITH, NORTH DAKOTA 58329

General Information Residential camp serving 500 students per week in 24 different arts programs. Established in 1956. Owned by International Music Camp, Inc. Affiliated with American Camping Association, Canadian Music Educational Conference, U.S. Music Educational National Conference, Canadian and U.S. Band Associations. 120-acre facility located 117 miles north of Minot. Features: 2,000-seat concert hall; 500-seat performing arts center; 3 rehearsal halls; 3 dance studios; percussive arts center; 70 studios and classrooms.

Profile of Summer Employees Total number: 200; average age: 35; 50% male, 50% female; 5% minorities; 35% college students; 5% retirees; 1% international; 20% local residents. Nonsmokers preferred.

Employment Information Openings are from June 1 to July 31. Jobs available: ▶ 4 *dishwashers* at $175 per week; ▶ 6 *cooks* at $200–$250 per week; ▶ 20 *deans/counselors* with college degree or college senior status at $200–$250 per week; ▶ 6 *secretaries* with ability to type 50 wpm and knowledge of computers at $175–$200 per week; ▶ 4 *music librarians* with instrumental knowledge at $175–$200 per week; ▶ *first aid technicians* with EMT or RN certification at $175–$250 per week; ▶ 11 *concessioners/housekeepers/maintenance persons* at $175 per week.

Benefits On-site room and board at no charge, laundry facilities, opportunity to study privately with teaching staff and attend professional concerts at no charge.

Contact Joseph T. Alme, Camp Director, International Music Camp, Department SJ, 1725 11th Street SW, Minot, North Dakota 58701; 701-838-8472, Fax 701-838-8472, E-mail imc@minot.com. Application deadline: February 28.

OHIO

CAMP BUTTERWORTH
8551 BUTTERWORTH ROAD
MAINEVILLE, OHIO 45039

General Information Girls residential camp providing the opportunity to have fun, try new activities, and live in the outdoors with girls from diverse backgrounds. Established in 1930. Owned by Great Rivers Girl Scout Council, Inc. Affiliated with American Camping Association, Girl Scouts of the United States of America. 160-acre facility located 20 miles northeast of Cincinnati. Features: location overlooking the Little Miami River; many hiking trails; wide variety of wildlife found in wooded, rolling hills; location close to Cincinnati and expressway; swimming pool; platform tent units that enable campers and staff to experience the outdoors.

Profile of Summer Employees Total number: 50; average age: 20; 5% male, 95% female; 10% minorities; 1% high school students; 75% college students; 1% retirees; 10% international; 75% local residents. Nonsmokers preferred.

Employment Information Openings are from June 9 to August 14. Year-round positions also offered. Jobs available: ▶ 1 *experienced camp director* (minimum age 25) with college degree at $3910–$4619 per season; ▶ 1 *health supervisor* with RN, EMT, PA, or MD certification at $2800–$4000 per season; ▶ 1 *experienced program director* (minimum age 21) at $1800–$2500 per season; ▶ 1 *experienced business manager* (minimum age 21) at $1800–$2350 per season; ▶ 1 *experienced equestrian director* (minimum age 21) at $1800–$2200 per season; ▶ 2 *experienced horseback riding instructors* (minimum age 18) at $1400–$1650 per season; ▶ 1 *pool director* (minimum age 21) with lifeguard and WSI certification and canoe experience (preferred) at $1800–$2200 per season; ▶ 2 *waterfront assistants* (minimum age 18) with lifeguard certification at $1450–$1800 per season; ▶ 2 *experienced naturalists/crafts consultants* (minimum age 18) at $1380–$1900 per season; ▶ 4 *experienced unit leaders* (minimum age 21) at $1600–$1900 per season; ▶ 10 *unit counselors* (minimum age 18) at $1380–$1600 per season; ▶ 1 *administrative assistant* (minimum age 17) at $1200–$1500 per season; ▶ 6 *kitchen staff members* at $1280–$3910 per season. International students encouraged to apply; must apply through recognized agency.

Benefits On-the-job training, on-site room and board at no charge, laundry facilities, health insurance. Preemployment training of 10 days is required and includes safety and accident prevention, group interaction, first-aid, CPR, leadership, camper-counselor relations. Orientation is paid.

Contact Cyndy Self, Program Services Manager, Camp Butterworth, Department SJ, c/o Great River Girl Scout Council, Inc., 4930 Cornell Road, Cincinnati, Ohio 45242; 513-489-1025, Fax 513-489-1417. Application deadline: May 21.

CAMP ECHOING HILLS
36272 COUNTY ROAD 79
WARSAW, OHIO 43844

General Information Camp experience for 650 mentally and physically disabled campers of all ages. Full camping program with highest standards of care for special population campers. Established in 1966. Owned by Camp Echoing Hills. Affiliated with American Camping Association, National Conference of Lions Camps. 72-acre facility located 15 miles east of Coshooton. Features: swimming pool; basketball gym; fishing pond; multipurpose building (crafts and worship center); full service dining and kitchen area; go-carts.

Profile of Summer Employees Total number: 60; average age: 20; 35% male, 65% female;

10% minorities; 20% high school students; 70% college students; 1% international. Nonsmokers only.

Employment Information Openings are from June 4 to August 19. Christmas break positions also offered. Jobs available: ► 40 *counselors* at $175–$200 per week; ► 20 *support staff members* at $100–$125 per week; ► *nurses* at $200–$225 per week. International students encouraged to apply; must apply through recognized agency.

Benefits College credit, on-the-job training, on-site room and board, laundry facilities, possibility of being sponsored up to $3500 through our student mission support program. Preemployment training of 7 days is required and includes safety and accident prevention, group interaction, first-aid, leadership, camper-counselor relations. Orientation is paid.

Contact Shaker Samuel, Camp Administrator, Camp Echoing Hills, Department SJ, 36272 County Road 79, Warsaw, Ohio 43844; 614-327-2311, Fax 614-327-6371, E-mail campechohl@ aol.com. Application deadline: May 1.

CAMP O'BANNON
9688 BUTLER ROAD, NE
NEWARK, OHIO 43055

General Information Residential camp serving children ages 9–14 with the goal of increasing self-esteem. Established in 1920. Owned by Camp O'Bannon of Licking County, Inc. Operated by United Way. Affiliated with American Camping Association. 169-acre facility located 45 miles east of Columbus. Features: swimming pool; cabins and platform tents; hiking trails; 2 high ropes courses.

Profile of Summer Employees Total number: 20; average age: 21; 40% male, 60% female; 20% high school students; 80% college students. Nonsmokers preferred.

Employment Information Openings are from June 7 to August 15. Jobs available: ► 4 *cabin counselors* (minimum age 19) with one year of college at $1100 per season; ► 3 *outpost counselors* (minimum age 19) with one year of college at $1100 per season; ► 1 *lifeguard* (minimum age 19) with WSI certification (preferred) at $1200 per season; ► 1 *arts and crafts counselor* (minimum age 19) with one year of college at $1100 per season; ► 1 *nature counselor* (minimum age 19) with one year of college at $1100 per season; ► 1 *cook* with ability to cook for 65 or more people at $1500–$1800 per season; ► 1 *nurse* with RN license at $1400 per season; ► 4 *co-counselors* (minimum age 17) at $1000 per season; ► 1 *assistant cook* (minimum age 17) at $900 per season; ► 1 *outpost director* (minimum age 21) with two years of college at $1500 per season; ► 1 *program director* (minimum age 21) with two years of college at $1500 per season; ► 1 *maintenance counselor* (minimum age 18) at $1000 per season; ► *camp director* (minimum age 21) with college degree (preferred) at $1800 per season.

Benefits College credit, on-the-job training, on-site room and board at no charge, laundry facilities, health insurance. Preemployment training of 3 days is required and includes safety and accident prevention, group interaction, first-aid, CPR, leadership. Orientation is unpaid.

Contact Ted Cobb, Camp Director, Camp O'Bannon, 62 West Locust Street, Newark, Ohio 43055; 614-349-9646, Fax 614-349-8618. Application deadline: March 30.

CAMP ROOSEVELT FOR BOYS
4141 DUBLIN ROAD
BOWERSTON, OHIO 44695

General Information Residential camp serving 60 campers per season. Established in 1918. Owned by W.V. Lorimer. Affiliated with National Rifle Association, National Water Ski Association, Camp Archery Association. 150-acre facility located 35 miles south of Akron. Features: 9-mile-long lake; reforested white pines; 2 tennis courts and playing field; 40 boats; 30 horses; rifle and archery ranges.

Profile of Summer Employees Total number: 15; average age: 21; 100% male; 80% college students; 10% international; 10% teachers. Nonsmokers only.

Employment Information Openings are from June 20 to August 18. Jobs available: ► *baseball* *staff members;* ▶ *riflery staff members;* ▶ *tennis staff members;* ▶ *western riding staff members;* ▶ *archery staff members;* ▶ 2 *swimming instructors.* All positions offered at $1600–$2000 per season.

Benefits On-the-job training, on-site room and board at no charge, laundry facilities, travel reimbursement.

Contact W.V. Lorimer, Camp Roosevelt for Boys, Department SJ, 2814 Perry Park Road, Perry, Ohio 44081; 440-259-2901. Application deadline: May 1.

CAMP STONYBROOK
4491 EAST STATE ROUTE 73
WAYNESVILLE, OHIO 45068

General Information Residential camp serving a diverse population of girls providing a rustic outdoor experience emphasizing physical fitness. Established in 1953. Owned by Great Rivers Girl Scout Council, Inc. Affiliated with American Camping Association, Girl Scouts of the United States of America. 315-acre facility located 35 miles north of Cincinnati. Features: many hiking trails; creek running through property; area rich in fossils; pool; par course and other sports facilities; outdoor tennis/volleyball courts.

Profile of Summer Employees Total number: 16; average age: 20; 5% male, 95% female; 12% minorities; 5% high school students; 75% college students; 5% international; 85% local residents. Nonsmokers preferred.

Employment Information Openings are from June 9 to August 14. Jobs available: ▶ 1 *experienced director* (minimum age 25) with college degree at $3910–$4619 per season; ▶ 3 *health supervisors* with RN, EMT, or PA license at $2800–$4000 per season; ▶ 1 *experienced program director* (minimum age 21) at $1800–$2500 per season; ▶ 1 *experienced business manager* (minimum age 21) at $1800–$2350 per season; ▶ 1 *pool director* (minimum age 21) with lifeguard and WSI certification and/or canoe experience (preferred) at $1800–$2200 per season; ▶ 2 *waterfront assistants* (minimum age 18) with lifeguard certification at $1450–$1800 per season; ▶ 1 *experienced naturalist/crafts consultant* (minimum age 18) at $1380–$1900 per season; ▶ 1 *unit leader* (minimum age 21) at $1600–$1900 per season; ▶ 2 *unit counselors* (minimum age 18) at $1380–$1600 per season; ▶ 6 *kitchen staff members* at $1280–$3910 per season. International students encouraged to apply; must apply through recognized agency.

Benefits On-the-job training, on-site room and board at no charge, laundry facilities, health insurance. Preemployment training of 10 days is required and includes safety and accident prevention, group interaction, first-aid, CPR, leadership, camper-counselor relations. Orientation is paid.

Contact Cyndy Self, Program Director, c/o Great Rivers Girl Scout Council, Inc., Camp Stonybrook, Department SJ, 4930 Cornell Road, Cincinnati, Ohio 45242; 513-489-1025, Fax 513-489-1417, E-mail grgsc@mail.iac.net. Application deadline: May 15.

CEDAR POINT
CAUSEWAY DRIVE
SANDUSKY, OHIO 44871

General Information Amusement/theme park with 54 rides, 2 resort hotels, a campground and a water park. Established in 1870. Owned by Cedar Fair, LP. 365-acre facility located 60 miles west of Cleveland. Features: 12 major roller coasters; 2 resort hotels on shores of Lake Erie; various live shows and attractions; major water park.

Profile of Summer Employees Total number: 4,000; average age: 20; 40% male, 60% female; 20% high school students; 60% college students; 20% retirees.

Employment Information Openings are from May 1 to October 15. Jobs available: ▶ *fast food workers* at $5.25 per hour; ▶ *hotel housekeeping staff* at $5.25 per hour; ▶ *ride operators* at $5 per hour; ▶ *games/arcades staff* at $5 per hour; ▶ *gift shop cashiers* at $5 per hour. International students encouraged to apply; must obtain own visa and working papers prior to employment.

Benefits College credit, on-the-job training, on-site room and board at $80 per week, laundry

facilities, free use of amusement park, free nightly activities 6 nights per week, bonus program.
Contact Amanda Rose, Assistant Director of Human Resources, Cedar Point, Department SJ, PO Box 5006, Sandusky, Ohio 44870; 800-668-JOBS, Fax 419-627-2163. Application deadline: September 2.

FIREBIRD FOR GIRLS
4141 DUBLIN ROAD
BOWERSTON, OHIO 44695

General Information Residential camp featuring many outdoor activities including sailing, waterskiing, kneeboarding, hiking, drama, and horsemanship. Established in 1954. Owned by W.V. Lorimer and Robyn Lorimer. Affiliated with National Rifle Association, National Water Ski Association, Camp Archery Association, American Camping Association. 150-acre facility located 35 miles south of Akron. Features: lake frontage; 40 boats; 30 horses, 3 rings, and trails.
Profile of Summer Employees Total number: 30; average age: 21; 10% male, 90% female; 5% minorities; 80% college students; 15% international. Nonsmokers only.
Employment Information Openings are from June 20 to August 20. Jobs available: ▶ 1 *water safety instructor* at $1600–$2000 per season; ▶ 1 *archery staff member* at $1800 per season; ▶ 1 *advanced riding staff member* at $2000 per season; ▶ 1 *nurse* at $2000 per season; ▶ *sailing and canoeing staff members* at $1800 per season; ▶ *crafts staff members* at $1800 per season; ▶ 1 *riflery staff member* at $1600 per season.
Benefits On-site room and board at no charge, laundry facilities, travel reimbursement.
Contact W.V. Lorimer, Firebird for Girls, Department SJ, 2814 Perry Park Road, Perry, Ohio 44081; 440-259-2901. Application deadline: May 15.

FRIENDS MUSIC CAMP
BARNESVILLE, OHIO 43713

General Information Residential camp offering musical instruction to 75 10–18 year olds featuring private music lessons, orchestra, band, jazz, chorus, and musical theater. Established in 1980. Operated by Ohio Valley Yearly Meeting (Friends or Quakers). 30-acre facility located 30 miles west of Wheeling, West Virginia. Features: boarding school campus; 3-acre pond; soccer fields; tennis courts; wooded hilly surroundings; dormitories.
Profile of Summer Employees Total number: 16; average age: 35; 50% male, 50% female; 5% minorities; 50% college students; 10% retirees; 35% teachers. Nonsmokers only.
Employment Information Openings are from July 8 to August 4. Jobs available: ▶ *experienced musical instructors* at $800 per season; ▶ *counselors* at $800 per season. International students encouraged to apply; must obtain own visa and working papers prior to employment.
Benefits On-the-job training, on-site room and board at no charge, laundry facilities, travel reimbursement. Preemployment training of 2 days is required and includes leadership. Orientation is paid.
Contact Peg Champney, Director, Friends Music Camp, PO Box 427, Yellow Springs, Ohio 45387; 937-767-1311. Application deadline: March 31.

GEAUGA LAKE
1060 NORTH AURORA ROAD
AURORA, OHIO 44202

General Information Traditional amusement park with water area serving more than 1 million guests annually. Established in 1888. Owned by Premier Parks, Inc. Affiliated with International Association of Amusement Parks and Attractions, Amusement Industry Manufacturers and Suppliers International, World Waterparks Association. 278-acre facility located 12 miles east of Cleveland. Features: freshwater lake frontage; roller coasters; circular amusement rides; water attractions; picnic areas; Sea World across the lake.
Profile of Summer Employees Total number: 1,784; average age: 18; 40% male, 60% female;

25% minorities; 55% high school students; 25% college students; 5% retirees; 1% international; 95% local residents.

Employment Information Openings are from May 10 to November 2. Spring break positions also offered. Jobs available: ▶ 10 *departmental administrative assistants* with typing, filing, and record keeping experience and/or ability, familiarity with word processors or personal computers, computation and problem-solving skills, and enjoyment of public contact; ▶ 4 *internal auditors* with self-discipline, strong computational, organizational, and interpersonal skills, plus knowledge of public accounting helpful (must be accounting major); ▶ 1 *event coordinator* with organizational, problem-solving, and communication skills; ▶ 30 *gift shop personnel* with sales and inventory control ability plus service, interpersonal relations, and supervisory skills; ▶ 60 *food service personnel* with ability to perform cost containment and inventory control duties, assess product quality, plus service, interpersonal relations, and supervisory skills; ▶ 20 *lifeguards* with certification or ability to be trained in certification requirements plus good interpersonal skills and ability to handle stress. All positions offered at $180–$220 per week. International students encouraged to apply; must obtain own visa and working papers prior to employment.

Benefits College credit, on-the-job training, transportation arranged from off-site housing, merit increases and promotion possibilities, company-sponsored employee events and trips, entertainment, and food discounts at area merchants. Off-site boarding costs are $150 per month. Preemployment training of 2 days is required and includes safety and accident prevention, group interaction, first-aid, CPR, leadership. Orientation is paid.

Contact Employment Coordinator, Geauga Lake, 1060 North Aurora Road, Aurora, Ohio 44202; 216-562-8303, Fax 216-562-7020. Application deadline: March 15.

HIDDEN HOLLOW CAMP
5127 OPPOSSUM RUN ROAD, ROUTE 3
BELLVILLE, OHIO 44813

General Information Traditional residential camp serving boys and girls ages 7–15 with activities such as swimming, nature hikes, trail rides, arts and crafts, archery, tennis, woodworking, dramatics, and pond canoeing. Established in 1940. Owned by Friendly House Community Center. Affiliated with American Camping Association. 620-acre facility located 11 miles north of Mansfield. Features: 10 log cabins and 3 dormitories; swimming pool; tennis court; riding trails; archery range; outdoor theater.

Profile of Summer Employees 50% male, 50% female; 20% minorities; 49% high school students; 51% college students; 85% local residents. Nonsmokers preferred.

Employment Information Openings are from July 4 to August 20. Jobs available: ▶ 15 *camp counselors* at $150–$200 per week.

Benefits On-site room and board at no charge.

Contact Thelda J. Dillon, Director, Hidden Hollow Camp, Department SJ, 380 North Mulberry Street, Mansfield, Ohio 44902; 419-522-0521. Application deadline: January 15.

YMCA CAMP TIPPECANOE
81300 YMCA ROAD
TIPPECANOE, OHIO 44699

General Information Residential camp serving 80–120 campers per week, with an emphasis on horsemanship, waterfront activities, and the natural world. Established in 1957. Operated by Canton Area YMCA. Affiliated with American Camping Association, CHA–The Association for Horsemanship Safety and Education, Ohio Outdoor Educators Association. 1,100-acre facility located 53 miles south of Canton. Features: nature lodge; large freshwater lake; scenic Allegheny Mountains; modern cabins and shower-houses; initiatives course (low challenges); 3 horse barns with 4 riding rings and miles of equestrian trails.

Profile of Summer Employees Total number: 25; average age: 22; 40% male, 60% female; 15% minorities; 5% high school students; 85% college students; 5% retirees; 15% international; 20% local residents. Nonsmokers preferred.

Employment Information Openings are from June 7 to August 15. Spring break, winter break, year-round positions also offered. Jobs available: ► 1 *ranch director* at $150–$200 per week; ► 2 *ranger directors* at $150–$200 per week; ► 1 *health director* at $150–$200 per week; ► 12 *cabin counselors* at $100–$200 per week; ► 2 *foxfire ridge directors* at $150–$200 per week; ► 1 *nature director* at $125–$175 per week; ► 1 *craft director* at $125–$175 per week; ► 3 *lifeguards/waterfront staff members* at $125–$175 per week; ► 4 *riding instructors* at $125–$175 per week. All applicants must have first aid and CPR and riding instructor certification (preferably CHA (The Association for Horsemanship Safety and Education). International students encouraged to apply; must apply through recognized agency.

Benefits On-the-job training, formal ongoing training, on-site room and board at no charge, laundry facilities. Preemployment training of 6 days is required and includes safety and accident prevention, group interaction, first-aid, CPR, leadership, camper-counselor relations. Orientation is paid.

Contact Mr. Jim Glunt, Executive Director, YMCA Camp Tippecanoe, Department SJ, 81300 YMCA Road, Tippecanoe, Ohio 44699; 614-922-0679. Application deadline: April 1.

OKLAHOMA

CAMP RED ROCK
ROUTE 1, BOX 110B
BINGER, OKLAHOMA 73009

General Information Residential camp serving weekly 150 girl scouts ages 6–17. Offers general camping, Western horse riding, swimming, archery, vaulting, crafts, low ropes course, and outdoor skills. Established in 1956. Owned by Red Lands Council of Girl Scouts. Affiliated with Girl Scouts of the United States of America. 300-acre facility located 70 miles west of Oklahoma City. Features: swimming pool; low elements ropes course; several riding trails and 1 large stable facility; activity field for basketball, volleyball, tetherball, and softball; Big Red Rocks, a large sandstone outcropping.

Profile of Summer Employees Total number: 20; average age: 21; 3% male, 97% female; 25% minorities; 25% high school students; 75% college students; 25% international; 75% local residents; 10% teachers.

Employment Information Openings are from June 1 to August 10. Jobs available: ► 6 *unit counselors* (minimum age 17) at $900–$1100 per season; ► 3 *unit leaders* (minimum age 21) with supervisory skills at $1000–$1200 per season; ► 4 *riding staff members* (minimum age 17) with CPR, first aid training, and teaching skills and knowledge of vaulting, Western, and/or English riding at $1000–$1200 per season; ► 1 *riding director* (minimum age 21) with extensive riding experience and supervisory skills and knowledge of vaulting, Western, and/or English riding at $1100–$1300 per season; ► 1 *head cook* (minimum age 21) with food service skills at $1500–$2000 per season; ► 1 *nurse* (minimum age 21) with RN, LPN, or EMT license at $1500–$2000 per season; ► *specialists in archery, ropes, and arts and crafts* (minimum age 18) with teaching skills at $1000–$1200 per season; ► 1 *swimming director (minimum age 21)* with WSI or equivalent certification and ability to teach at $1100–$1300 per season; ► 1 *swimming instructor (minimum age 17)* with current ARC lifeguard certification and ability to teach at $1000–$1200 per season; ► 1 *assistant cook (minimum age 16)* with familiarity of kitchen operation at $1000–$1200 per season; ► 1 *program director (minimum age 21)* with ability to plan and implement all camp activities at $1300–$1500 per season. International students encouraged to apply; must obtain own visa and working papers prior to employment; must apply through recognized agency.

Benefits On-the-job training, on-site room and board at no charge, laundry facilities, health insurance, workmen's compensation.

Contact Linda Marcotte, Program Specialist Red Lands Council of Girl Scouts, Camp Red Rock, Department SJ, 121 Northeast 50th Street, Oklahoma City, Oklahoma 73105; 405-528-3535. Application deadline: April 30.

FRONTIER CITY AND WHITEWATER BAY
GENERAL OFFICE 11501 NORTHEAST EXPRESSWAY
OKLAHOMA CITY, OKLAHOMA 73131

General Information Facility that creates family fun and fond memories. Established in 1958. Owned by Premier Parks, Inc. Affiliated with Chamber of Commerce, Private Industry Council, International Association of Amusement Parks and Attractions. Situated on 75 acres. Features: 5 roller coasters in Frontier City; 12,000-square-foot banquet/entertainment center in Frontier City; wave pool in White Water Bay; water slides in White Water Bay; kids' pool and kids' dry rides in Frontier City and White Water Bay; over 60 rides, shows, and attractions in Frontier City.

Profile of Summer Employees Total number: 1,250; average age: 22; 45% male, 55% female; 25% minorities; 70% high school students; 20% college students; 5% retirees; 5% international; 90% local residents; 20% teachers.

Employment Information Openings are from April 1 to October 31. Jobs available: ▶ *lifeguards (deep water)* at $5.50–$6 per hour; ▶ *lifeguards (shallow water)* at $5–$5.50 per hour; ▶ *team members (rides, games, retail, foods, etc.)* at $4.75–$5.75 per hour; ▶ *security staff* with CLEET certification at $5.50–$6.75 per hour; ▶ *first aid staff* with state and national basic EMT at $5.50–$6.75 per hour. International students encouraged to apply; must obtain own visa and working papers prior to employment.

Benefits On-the-job training, college scholarships, lots of employee parties, free admission to parks. Off-site boarding costs are $300 per month. Preemployment training of 1 day is required and includes safety and accident prevention, group interaction, leadership, guest courtesy. Orientation is paid.

Contact Steve Ball, Human Resource Manager, Frontier City and Whitewater Bay, Department SJ, 11501 NE Expressway, Oklahoma City, Oklahoma 73131; 405-478-2140, Fax 405-478-3104. Application deadline: October 31.

OREGON

CRATER LAKE COMPANY
CRATER LAKE NATIONAL PARK
CRATER LAKE, OREGON 97604

General Information Operates all concession facilities in Crater Lake National Park. Owned by Crater Lake Company. Located 83 miles northeast of Medford. Features: location at the south rim of Crater Lake at a 7,100-foot elevation in the Cascade Range; 40 cabin rooms, service station, 198-site campground, boat tours, food service, gift shop, and grocery store; the nation's deepest lake (1,932 feet).

Profile of Summer Employees Total number: 175; average age: 21; 40% male, 60% female; 2% minorities; 70% college students; 20% retirees; 8% local residents.

Employment Information Openings are from April 10 to October 20. Year-round positions also offered. Jobs available: ▶ 110 *food service workers* at $4.75–$6.50 per hour; ▶ 7 *maintenance/janitorial/registration personnel* with valid driver's license; ▶ 5 *experienced office* *workers* with accounting skills; ▶ 7 *boat tour operators* with Red Cross card; ▶ 27 *gift shop personnel* (retail); ▶ 11 *front desk personnel;* ▶ 16 *housekeeping staff members;* ▶ 4 *laundry staff members;* ▶ 3 *bellhops;* ▶ 9 *convenience store clerks;* ▶ 6 *campground staff members.*

Benefits College credit, on-site room and board at $53 per week, laundry facilities, opportunities for advancement for returning employees.

Contact Personnel, Crater Lake Company, 1211 Avenue C, White City, Oregon 97503; 541-830-4053, Fax 541-830-8514. Application deadline: April 15.

HELLS CANYON ADVENTURES
4200 HC DAM ROAD
OXBOW, OREGON 97840

General Information Outfitter that offers guided recreational opportunities. Established in 1972. Features: jet boat tours on wild section of river; jet boat tours on reservoirs; fishing charters; boat rentals; white water rafting; small store and information center.

Profile of Summer Employees Total number: 10; 50% male, 50% female. Nonsmokers preferred.

Employment Information Openings are from May 1 to September 30. Jobs available: ▶ *customer service and recreation staff* with current first aid and knowledge of motor and non-motor activities; ▶ *kitchen help* with current first aid; ▶ *interpreter and guide* with current first aid and CPR and knowledge of motor and non-motor activities. International students encouraged to apply.

Benefits On-the-job training, on-site room and board, laundry facilities. Off-site boarding costs are $300 per month.

Contact Doris and Bret Armacost, Managers, Hells Canyon Adventures, PO Box 159, Oxbow, Oregon 97840; 541-785-3352, Fax 541-785-3353.

THE INN OF THE SEVENTH MOUNTAIN
18575 SW CENTURY DRIVE
BEND, OREGON 97702

General Information Full-service destination resort. Established in 1971. Owned by Inn of the Seventh Mountain Owner's Association. Operated by Capitol Hotel Group. Located 5 miles southwest of Bend. Features: swimming pool, slide pool, and 2 spas; 8 miles of riding trails and stables; tennis courts; ice/roller rink; cafe and fine dining restaurants; full convention facilities.

Profile of Summer Employees Total number: 100; 50% male, 50% female; 5% minorities; 10% high school students; 30% college students; 5% retirees; 90% local residents; 5% teachers.

Employment Information Openings are from June 1 to October 1. Year-round positions also offered. Jobs available: ▶ *housekeeper* at $5.50 per hour; ▶ *wait staff* with restaurant experience at $5.50 per hour; ▶ *recreation leaders* with first aid/CPR/lifeguard certification at $5.60–$7.50 per hour; ▶ *front desk staff* with computer literacy at $6.25–$9 per hour; ▶ *host/cashier* with cashier/restaurant experience at $6.25 per hour; ▶ *busser* at $5.50 per hour; ▶ *dishwasher* at $5.50–$6.50 per hour.

Benefits On-the-job training, recreation benefits. Off-site boarding costs are $75 per week.

Contact Carol Garrison, Human Resources Director, The Inn of the Seventh Mountain, 18575 SW Century Drive, Bend, Oregon 97702; 541-382-8711, Fax 541-382-3517, E-mail reservations@7thmtn.com.

YWCA CAMP WESTWIND
2353 NORTH THREE ROCKS ROAD
OTIS, OREGON 97368

General Information Coeducational residential camp with traditional activities for children ages 7–18 and adults. Established in 1936. Owned by YWCA. Affiliated with American Camping Association. 500-acre facility located 90 miles west of Portland. Features: location on Pacific Ocean; environmentally rich site (estuary, rainforest, river, oceanfront, beaches, and tidepools);

miles of hiking trails along the Pacific Ocean; hidden ocean coves; natural lakes and ponds (not for swimming).

Profile of Summer Employees Total number: 35; average age: 20; 30% male, 70% female; 4% minorities; 2% high school students; 97% college students; 2% international; 40% local residents. Nonsmokers only.

Employment Information Openings are from June 12 to August 31. Jobs available: ▶ 1 *teen leadership coordinator* (minimum age 21) with challenge course experience (preferred) and CPR/first aid certification at $115–$120 per week; ▶ 1 *assistant horseback riding instructor,* experience preferred, with CPR/first aid certification at $95–$100 per week; ▶ 14 *counselors* with CPR/first aid certification at $95–$100 per week; ▶ 1 *nature/marine science specialist* (minimum age 21) with CPR/first aid certification at $100–$110 per week; ▶ 1 *waterfront director* with lifeguarding and CPR/first aid certification and small craft instructor status at $100–$110 per week; ▶ 1 *head riding instructor* (minimum age 21) with Horsemanship Safety certification and Western riding and instruction experience at $120–$130 per week; ▶ 2 *kitchen aides* at $1200–$1300 per season.

Benefits College credit, on-the-job training, on-site room and board at no charge. Preemployment training of 10 days is required and includes safety and accident prevention, group interaction, leadership, camper-counselor relations, diversity awareness. Orientation is paid.

Contact Miriam Callaghan, Camp Administrator, YWCA Camp Westwind, Department SJ, 1111 Southwest Tenth Avenue, Portland, Oregon 97205; 503-294-7472, Fax 503-294-7473, E-mail miriam.callaghan@ywca.fabrik.com. Application deadline: June 5.

PENNSYLVANIA

BRYN MAWR CAMP
RR 5, BOX 410
HONESDALE, PENNSYLVANIA 18431

General Information Camp serving 350 girls ages 5–15 for eight weeks. Year-round conference center and mountain retreat. Established in 1921. Owned by Herb and Melanie Kutzen. Operated by Bryn Mawr Camp, Inc. Affiliated with American Camping Association, Wayne County Camping Association, Pocono Mountain Vacation Bureau. 135-acre facility located 105 miles northwest of New York, New York. Features: 8 tennis courts; 2 heated swimming pools; 15,000-square-foot theater arts building capable of seating 1,000 people; 12,000-square-foot gymnasium facility; state-of-the-art ropes challenge course; extensive English riding program in 3 rings and trails.

Profile of Summer Employees Total number: 150; average age: 22; 15% male, 85% female; 5% minorities; 2% high school students; 60% college students; 3% retirees; 15% international; 5% local residents; 30% teachers. Nonsmokers only.

Employment Information Openings are from May 15 to September 30. Spring break, year-round positions also offered. Jobs available: ▶ 16 *swimming instructors* with WSI certification at $1100–$2100 per season; ▶ 2 *small craft instructors* with American Red Cross small craft license at $1100–$1700 per season; ▶ 4 *experienced waterskiing instructors* at $1100–$2000 per season; ▶ 20 *tennis instructors* at $950–$2100 per season; ▶ 4 *experienced arts and crafts instructors* at $1000–$2300 per season; ▶ 3 *dance instructors* at $900–$1900 per season; ▶ 5 *English riding instructors* at $900–$1900 per season; ▶ 12 *kitchen assistants* at $1100–$1900 per season; ▶ 5 *laundry/light housekeeping personnel* at $1000–$1500 per season; ▶ 2 *office staff members* at $1100–$2100 per season; ▶ 7 *athletics instructors* at $900–$1900 per season; ▶ 4 *drama instructors* at $900–$1900 per season; ▶ 8 *gymnastics instructors* at $1000–$2100 per season; ▶ 3 *piano/technical theater personnel* at $1000–$2100 per season; ▶ 12 *general counselors* at $900–$1700 per season; ▶ 5 *ropes challenge/outdoors counselors* at $1100–$2100 per season; ▶ 4 *registered nurses* at $1600–$2900 per season; ▶ 2 *nine-month recreation/ marketing/sales interns* at $775–$1300 per month. International students encouraged to apply; must apply through recognized agency.

Benefits College credit, on-the-job training, formal ongoing training, on-site room and board at no charge, laundry facilities, travel reimbursement, staff uniforms, use of staff bicycles, planned staff days, precamp and post-camp work, year-round employment possibility, skill bonuses, and travel allowance.

Contact Herb Kutzen or Brad Finkelstein, Bryn Mawr Camp, Department SJ, 81 Falmouth Street, Short Hills, New Jersey 07078; 973-467-3518, Fax 973-467-3750. Application deadline: May 15.

CAMP AKIBA
REEDERS, PENNSYLVANIA 18352

General Information Private residential brother-sister accredited camp offering four- and eight-week sessions. Established in 1926. Owned by Howard Gordon. Affiliated with American Camping Association, Pocono Mountain Vacation Bureau. 350-acre facility located 90 miles north of Philadelphia. Features: 21 tennis courts; 2 Olympic-size pools; 40-acre lake; climbing tower; ropes course; 8 volleyball courts (4 sand); 2 miniature golf courses; 5 softball fields and 6 basketball courts.

Profile of Summer Employees Total number: 200; average age: 20; 50% male, 50% female; 90% college students. Nonsmokers only.

Employment Information Openings are from June 21 to August 15. Jobs available: ▶ 8 *pool instructors* with LGT and WSI certification at $1200–$1600 per season; ▶ 2 *lakefront personnel* with SCI certification or experience at $1100–$1500 per season; ▶ 10 *experienced tennis instructors* at $1200–$2000 per season; ▶ 150 *general counselors* with desire to work with children at $950–$1700 per season; ▶ 2 *riflery instructors* with experience handling .22 caliber rifles at $950–$1300 per season; ▶ 2 *experienced archery instructors* at $950–$1300 per season; ▶ 2 *experienced minibike/go-cart instructors* at $950–$1400 per season; ▶ 2 *experienced video/ photo instructors* at $950–$1400 per season; ▶ 4 *experienced team sport instructors* at $950– $1500 per season; ▶ 4 *experienced individual sport instructors* at $950–$1500 per season; ▶ 2 *experienced arts and crafts instructors* at $1000–$1500 per season; ▶ 4 *experienced outdoor adventure instructors* with ability to teach ropes course, rappelling, and rafting at $950–$1500 per season; ▶ 2 *experienced jet-skiing instructors* at $950–$1400 per season; ▶ 2 *experienced waterskiing instructors* at $950–$1800 per season; ▶ 2 *experienced horseback riding instructors* at $1000–$1400 per season; ▶ 1 *experienced gymnastics instructor* at $950–$1500 per season. International students encouraged to apply; must apply through recognized agency.

Benefits College credit, on-the-job training, on-site room and board at no charge, laundry facilities, travel reimbursement, internships available. Preemployment training of 3 days is required and includes safety and accident prevention, group interaction, leadership. Orientation is paid.

Contact Debbie Carnochan, Executive Director, Camp Akiba, Box 840, Bala Cynwyd, Pennsylvania 19004; 800-652-5422, Fax 610-660-9556, URL http://www.kidscamps.com/ traditional/akiba. Application deadline: May 1.

CAMP ARCHBALD
RR 2, BOX 123
KINGSLEY, PENNSYLVANIA 18826

General Information Camp for girls ages 6–17 with the purpose of providing an opportunity to make friends, develop an appreciation of nature, learn new skills, and develop self-confidence. Established in 1920. Owned by Scranton Pocono Girl Scout Council. Affiliated with American Camping Association. 288-acre facility located 35 miles north of Scranton. Features: 37-acre natural lake for swimming and boating/canoeing; large open fields; horseback-riding trails and ring; 7 living areas for campers grouped by age levels; arts and crafts building.

Profile of Summer Employees Total number: 40; average age: 20; 2% male, 98% female; 1% minorities; 25% high school students; 75% college students; 3% international. Nonsmokers preferred.

Employment Information Openings are from June 6 to August 18. Spring break positions also offered. Jobs available: ▶ 1 *program director* with ability to supervise and coordinate all phases of camp program at $130–$150 per week; ▶ 1 *office manager* with etiquette and ability to manage camp store and money at $110–$130 per week; ▶ 1 *experienced food service manager* with supervisory skills and ability to manage kitchen, food ordering, and purchasing at $220–$275 per week; ▶ 1 *health care supervisor* with RN or EMT license and CPR certification at $175–$220 per week; ▶ 1 *waterfront director* with WSI, lifeguard, first aid, and CPR certification at $120–$150 per week; ▶ 1 *horseback riding director* with instructor certification or documented experience at $120–$150 per week; ▶ 1 *arts and crafts/nature director* with knowledge of environmental education activities at $100–$125 per week; ▶ 7 *unit leaders* with camp and/or Girl Scout experience at $120–$150 per week; ▶ 2 *waterfront assistants* with WSI, lifeguard, first aid, and CPR certification at $100–$125 per week; ▶ 15 *assistant unit leaders* with camp and/or Girl Scout experience at $90–$110 per week; ▶ 1 *small craft director* with canoe instructor, first aid, and CPR certification and knowledge of rowing and sailing at $100–$125 per week; ▶ 3 *cooks/kitchen staff members* (various positions) with knowledge of food preparation. International students encouraged to apply; must apply through recognized agency.

Benefits College credit, on-the-job training, on-site room and board at no charge, laundry facilities, health insurance, time off as indicated in personnel policies, participate in the State Work Study Program (SWSP) for the Pennsylvania Higher Education Agency (PHEAA). Preemployment training of 5 to 6 days is required and includes safety and accident prevention, group interaction, first-aid, CPR, leadership, camper-counselor relations, OSHA standards. Orientation is paid.

Contact Diane E. Bleam, Camp Director, Camp Archbald, Department SJ, 333 Madison Avenue, Scranton, Pennsylvania 18510; 717-344-1224, Fax 717-346-7259. Application deadline: June 1.

CAMP BALLIBAY FOR THE FINE AND PERFORMING ARTS
BOX 1
CAMPTOWN, PENNSYLVANIA 18815

General Information Coeducational residential camp serving up to 155 children ages 6–16 in two- to nine-week sessions. Established in 1964. Owned by Gerard J. Jannone. Affiliated with American Camping Association. 500-acre facility located 50 miles northwest of Scranton. Features: theater facility; 2 large dance studios; large well-appointed art complex; music building with practice rooms; audio and video studios (high-tech programs); mountain surroundings.

Profile of Summer Employees Total number: 42; average age: 23; 40% male, 60% female; 60% college students; 5% retirees; 15% international; 5% local residents. Nonsmokers preferred.

Employment Information Openings are from June 22 to August 27. Jobs available: ▶ *theater directors;* ▶ *dance instructors* (all phases); ▶ *art instructors* (all areas); ▶ *music instructors* (vocal and instrumental); ▶ *video instructors;* ▶ *technical instructors* (lighting and sound); ▶ *costume instructors;* ▶ *WSI instructors;* ▶ *tennis instructors;* ▶ *golf instructors;* ▶ *riding instructors;* ▶ *supervisory staff members;* ▶ *office staff members.* All positions offered at $750–$2000 per season. International students encouraged to apply; must obtain own visa and working papers prior to employment; must apply through recognized agency.

Benefits On-site room and board at no charge, laundry facilities, travel reimbursement. Preemployment training of 3 to 4 days is required and includes safety and accident prevention, group interaction, first-aid, leadership, camper-counselor relations. Orientation is paid.

Contact Mr. Gerard J. Jannone, Camp Ballibay for the Fine and Performing Arts, Department SJ, Box 1, Camptown, Pennsylvania 18815; 717-746-3223, Fax 717-746-3691, E-mail ballibay@epix.net, URL http://www.ballibay.com.

CAMP CANADENSIS
RR1, BOX 150, LAKE ROAD
CANADENSIS, PENNSYLVANIA 18325

General Information Coeducational residential camp offering an eight-week program for children ages 7–16. Established in 1941. Owned by Saltzman family. Affiliated with American Camping Association. 1,000-acre facility located 90 miles west of New York, New York. Features: 75-acre lake; 2 heated pools; 16 tennis courts; 3 climbing walls; high ropes course; 12 miles of trails for hiking, mountain biking, and motorcycling; 5,000-square-foot fully equipped gymnastics building.
Profile of Summer Employees Total number: 135; average age: 21; 50% male, 50% female; 95% college students; 5% teachers. Nonsmokers only.
Employment Information Openings are from June 21 to August 18. Jobs available: ▶ 7 *swimming instructors* with WSI and lifeguard certification at $1200–$1600 per season; ▶ 30 *athletics instructors* with team experience at $1250–$1500 per season; ▶ 8 *ropes course/climbing instructors* with climbing experience at $1250–$1500 per season; ▶ 5 *drama instructors* at $1250–$1500 per season; ▶ 7 *arts and crafts instructors* at $1250–$1500 per season; ▶ 8 *sailing/waterskiing/windsurfing instructors* with lifeguard certification at $1250–$1600 per season; ▶ 3 *experienced gymnastics instructors* at $1250–$1600 per season; ▶ 7 *experienced rafting/kayaking/scuba instructors* with lifeguard certification at $1250–$1600 per season; ▶ 14 *tennis instructors* with college team/coaching experience at $1200–$2000 per season; ▶ 2 *archery instructors* at $1250–$1400 per season; ▶ 3 *riflery instructors* with NRA certification at $1250–$1400 per season; ▶ 3 *maintenance staff members* with grounds work experience at $1250–$1400 per season; ▶ 3 *nurses* with RN license at $2000–$2500 per season; ▶ 30 *general counselors* at $1250–$1400 per season; ▶ 4 *photography/newspaper instructors* at $1250–$1400 per season; ▶ 2 *nature instructors* at $1250–$1400 per season. International students encouraged to apply; must obtain own visa and working papers prior to employment; must apply through recognized agency.
Benefits College credit, on-site room and board at no charge, laundry facilities, all travel expenses with campers included. Preemployment training of 5 days is required and includes group interaction, leadership. Orientation is unpaid.
Contact Terri or Steve Saltzman, Director, Camp Canadensis, Department SJ, Box 182, Wyncote, Pennsylvania 19095; 215-572-8222, Fax 215-572-8298.

CAMP CAYUGA IN THE POCONOS
POCONO MOUNTAINS, RR 1, BOX 1180 DEPARTMENT PSJ
HONESDALE, PENNSYLVANIA 18431

General Information Private coed nonsectarian residential summer camp for children ages 5–15 specializing in first-time campers. Traditional noncompetitive program offering instruction in over sixty activities. Established in 1957. Owned by Brian and Trish Buynak. Affiliated with American Camping Association, Wayne County Camp Association, United States Tennis Association, American Red Cross, National Rifle Association, American Archery Association. 350-acre facility located 115 miles northwest of New York, New York. Features: 2 swimming pools for instruction and 1 heated pool for special events; private natural stream-fed lake used for sailing, canoeing, fishing, and swimming; Junior/Main campus (ages 5–13) and Teen campus (ages 13–15), each with a special activity program; 45 modern cabins with bathrooms, showers, and electricity; 2 large indoor gymnasiums/recreational centers with stages for theater productions; 25-horse stable on premises, 7 miles of scenic trails, and 2 riding rings.
Profile of Summer Employees Total number: 236; average age: 23; 50% male, 50% female; 9% minorities; 98% college students; 2% retirees; 10% international; 2% local residents; 20% teachers. Nonsmokers preferred.
Employment Information Openings are from June 19 to August 20. Jobs available: ▶ 20 *experienced swimming instructors* with WSI and/or lifeguard certification at $1400–$1800 per season; ▶ 6 *experienced sailing instructors* with lifeguard and/or ARC small craft certification at $1400–$1700 per season; ▶ 10 *gymnastics instructors* with at least one year of college

completed and teaching gymnastics experience preferred at $1300–$1500 per season; ► 10 *experienced ceramics instructors/pottery instructors* with at least one year of college completed and kiln operating experience at $1250–$1500 per season; ► 6 *martial arts instructors* with at least one year of college completed and experience teaching martial arts to children at $1300–$1500 per season; ► 6 *experienced riflery instructors* with NRA certification or equivalent and at least one year of college completed at $1300–$1500 per season; ► 6 *drama instructors* with at least one year of college completed and theater experience required at $1250–$1500 per season; ► 6 *archery instructors* with at least one year of college completed and teaching archery experience preferred at $1300–$1500 per season; ► 12 *experienced tennis instructors* with at least one year of college completed at $1300–$1500 per season; ► 6 *experienced Honda quad-riding instructors* with at least one year of college completed at $1300–$1500 per season; ► 10 *experienced flying trapeze and circus instructors* with at least one year of college completed and experience flying on the trapeze and circus skills at $1250–$2000 per season; ► 6 *ropes course/rock climbing instructors* with at least one year of college completed and certification and/or experience teaching ropes course to children preferred at $1300–$1500 per season; ► 6 *experienced wrestling instructors* with at least one year of college completed at $1300–$1500 per season; ► 6 *windsurfing instructors* with lifeguard certification and at least one year of college completed at $1400–$1700 per season; ► 15 *experienced horseback riding instructors* with at least one year of college completed, stable-care skills, and teaching horsemanship experience preferred at $1300–$1700 per season; ► 10 *team sports instructors* with at least one year of college completed and experience in field sports (baseball, basketball, softball, field hockey) at $1250–$1500 per season; ► 6 *cheerleading instructors* with at least one year of college completed at $1200–$1300 per season; ► 6 *experienced dance instructors* (ballet, jazz, tap, or folk) with at least one year of college completed at $1200–$1400 per season; ► 6 *basketball instructors* with at least one year of college completed at $1250–$1400 per season; ► 3 *waterfront directors* (minimum age 25) with WSI and/or lifeguard certification and pool management experience at $2200–$3500 per season; ► 2 *program directors* (minimum age 25) with coaching experience and supervisory skills at $2000–$3000 per season; ► 2 *experienced athletics directors* (minimum age 25) with coaching experience and supervisory skills at $2000–$3000 per season; ► 5 *experienced head counselors* (minimum age 25) with supervisory skills at $2000–$3000 per season; ► 6 *lacrosse instructors* with at least one year of college completed at $1250–$1400 per season; ► 15 *activity specialists (video camera, model rocketry, radio broadcasting, and roller skating/roller blading)* with at least one year of college completed and experience in activity preferred at $1250–$1500 per season; ► 6 *golf instructors* with at least one year of college completed and experience teaching golf to children preferred at $1250–$1400 per season; ► 6 *experienced nurses* with RN, LPN, or EMT license at $1500–$3000 per season; ► 10 *arts and crafts instructors* with at least one year of college completed and experience teaching art to children preferred at $1200–$1400 per season; ► 4 *experienced office personnel* with good organizational skills, excellent telephone manner, and administration skills at $1200–$1500 per season; ► 6 *experienced volleyball instructors* with at least one year of college completed at $1200–$1400 per season.

Benefits College credit, on-the-job training, formal ongoing training, on-site room and board at no charge, laundry facilities, travel reimbursement, end-of-season bonus, free camp shirt, use of extensive facilities (gymnasiums, tennis courts, weight room, stables, and more), tips and gratuities permitted, free three-day winter camp ski reunion during winter break. Preemployment training of 6 days is required and includes safety and accident prevention, group interaction, first-aid, CPR, leadership, camper-counselor relations. Orientation is paid.

Contact Brian B. Buynak, Camp Director, Camp Cayuga in the Poconos, PO Box 452, Department PSJ, Washington, New Jersey 07882; 908-689-3339, Fax 908-689-8209, E-mail info@campcayuga.com, URL http://www.campcayuga.com. Application deadline: June 10.

CAMP CHEN-A-WANDA
RD 1
THOMPSON, PENNSYLVANIA 18465

General Information Coeducational residential camp serving 350 campers for an eight-week session. Established in 1939. Owned by Caryl and Morey Baldwin. Affiliated with American Camping Association, Wayne County Camping Association. 183-acre facility located 30 miles north of Scranton. Features: heated swimming pool; 7 lighted outdoor tennis courts; 6 large sports fields; 4 outdoor basketball courts and 1 indoor court; indoor fitness center; extensive frontage on Fiddle Lake.

Profile of Summer Employees Total number: 120; average age: 20; 54% male, 46% female; 10% high school students; 65% college students; 20% international. Nonsmokers preferred.

Employment Information Openings are from June 20 to August 24. Jobs available: ▶ 10 *waterfront specialists* (swimming, sailing, or waterskiing) with WSI certification; ▶ 4 *soccer specialists;* ▶ 4 *baseball specialists;* ▶ 4 *basketball specialists;* ▶ 3 *tennis specialists;* ▶ 2 *go-cart/quadrunner specialists;* ▶ 3 *arts and crafts specialists;* ▶ 2 *gymnastics specialists;* ▶ 2 *hockey specialists;* ▶ 2 *stage management/scenery staff members;* ▶ 2 *volleyball specialists;* ▶ 2 *ropes/rock climbing/rappelling specialists.* All positions offered at $600–$1200 per season. International students encouraged to apply; must apply through recognized agency.

Benefits On-site room and board at no charge, travel reimbursement. Preemployment training of 5 days is required and includes safety and accident prevention, group interaction, leadership, camper-counselor relations. Orientation is unpaid.

Contact Morey Baldwin, Director, Camp Chen-A-Wanda, 8 Claverton Court, Dix Hills, New York 11747; 516-643-5878, Fax 516-643-0920. Application deadline: May 31.

CAMP HIDDEN FALLS
RR 2 BOX 720
DINGMAN'S FERRY, PENNSYLVANIA 18328

General Information Eight-week residential camp for girls ages 8–17. Owned by Girl Scouts of Southeastern Pennsylvania. Affiliated with Girl Scouts of the United States of America, American Camping Association. 1,500-acre facility located 60 miles north of Allentown. Features: lake for boating; outdoor pool; riding trails, stable; hiking trails; platform tents and cabins; sports fields.

Profile of Summer Employees Total number: 45; average age: 20; 5% male, 95% female; 15% minorities; 10% high school students; 70% college students; 5% retirees; 100% local residents; 30% teachers. Nonsmokers preferred.

Employment Information Openings are from June 15 to August 15. Jobs available: ▶ *lifeguards* with WSI, lifeguard training, first aid/CPR at $1500–$2000 per season; ▶ *business manager* with experience at $1800–$2000 per season; ▶ *program specialists* with experience in area at $1500–$2000 per season; ▶ *nature counselor* with experience at $1200–$1900 per season; ▶ *counselors* with first aid/CPR at $1200–$1900 per season.

Benefits College credit, on-the-job training. Preemployment training is required and includes safety and accident prevention, group interaction, first-aid, CPR, leadership, camper-counselor relations, program planning. Orientation is paid.

Contact Chris Endres, Camp Administrator, Camp Hidden Falls, Department SJ, Girl Scouts of Southeastern Pennsylvania, 100 North 17th Street, 2nd Floor, Philadelphia, Pennsylvania 19103; 215-564-4657, Fax 215-564-6953. Application deadline: May 15.

CAMP INDIAN RUN
320 INDIAN RUN ROAD
GLENMORE, PENNSYLVANIA 19343

General Information Seven-week residential camp for girls ages 6–17. Established in 1935. Owned by Girl Scouts of Southeastern Pennsylvania. Affiliated with Girl Scouts of the United

States of America, American Camping Association. 150-acre facility located 40 miles west of Philadelphia. Features: large outdoor pool; riding rings, trails, stable; hiking trails; sports field; basketball court; platform tents and cabins.

Profile of Summer Employees Total number: 60; average age: 20; 10% male, 90% female; 40% minorities; 10% high school students; 60% college students; 10% international; 70% local residents; 20% teachers. Nonsmokers preferred.

Employment Information Openings are from June 10 to August 20. Jobs available: ▶ *counselors* with first aid/CPR at $1200–$2000 per season; ▶ *lifeguards* with lifeguard training, WSI, first aid and CPR at $1200–$2000 per season; ▶ *riding instructors* with CHA certification or experience; ▶ *nurses* with RN or EMT; ▶ *cooks;* ▶ *program specialists;* ▶ *business manager.* International students encouraged to apply; must apply through recognized agency.

Benefits College credit, on-the-job training, on-site room and board, laundry facilities. Preemployment training of 7 days is required and includes safety and accident prevention, group interaction, first-aid, CPR, leadership, camper-counselor relations, program planning. Orientation is paid.

Contact Chris Endres, Camp Administrator, Camp Indian Run, Department SJ, Girl Scouts of Southeastern Pennsylvania, 100 North 17th Street, 2nd Floor, Philadelphia, Pennsylvania 19103; 215-564-4657, Fax 215-564-6953. Application deadline: May 15.

CAMP KAUFMANN
12811 OLD ROUTE 16
WAYNESBORO, PENNSYLVANIA 17268

General Information Residential kosher Jewish camp serving young teens. Established in 1987. Owned by UJA Federation of Greater Washington. Affiliated with American Camping Association, Jewish Community Center Association, Association of Jewish Sponsored Camps. 230-acre facility located 90 miles west of Washington, DC. Features: lighted tennis courts; lakefront for boating and waterskiing; Olympic-size pool; location adjacent to the Appalachian Trail in the Catoctin Mountains.

Profile of Summer Employees Total number: 85; average age: 20; 50% male, 50% female; 15% high school students; 75% college students; 10% teachers. Nonsmokers only.

Employment Information Openings are from June 15 to August 15. Jobs available: ▶ *waterfront director* (pool operator preferred) with WSI certification and lifeguard training at $1500–$1800 per season; ▶ *video specialist* with ability to produce camp videos at $1200–$1500 per season; ▶ *arts and crafts director* with art teaching background at $1200–$1500 per season; ▶ *swimming instructors* with lifeguard training and WSI certification at $1100–$1200 per season; ▶ *nature specialist* with ropes course certification and outdoor living skills at $1200–$1500 per season; ▶ *drama specialist* with ability to direct and produce a play at $1200–$1500 per season. International students encouraged to apply; must apply through recognized agency.

Benefits College credit, formal ongoing training, on-site room and board at no charge, laundry facilities, travel reimbursement.

Contact Faye Bousel, Director, Camp Kaufmann, 11710 Hunters Lane, #8, Rockville, Maryland 20852; 301-468-2267, Fax 301-468-1719, E-mail capcamps@aol.com, URL http://members.aol. com/capcamps. We accept applications until positions are filled.

CAMP LAUGHING WATERS
300 HEIDELBEITEL ROAD
GILBERTSVILLE, PENNSYLVANIA 19525

General Information Large camp serving Girl Scout troops, families, and youth groups. Established in 1940. Operated by Girl Scouts of Southeastern Pennsylvania. Affiliated with Girl Scouts of the United States of America, American Camping Association. 533-acre facility located 30 miles northwest of Philadelphia. Features: large outdoor pool; tent and cabin units; dining hall; sports fields; hiking trails; tennis and basketball courts.

Profile of Summer Employees Total number: 15; average age: 21; 100% female; 50% minorities; 90% college students; 90% local residents. Nonsmokers preferred.

Employment Information Openings are from June 15 to August 20. Jobs available: ▶ *lifeguards* with WSI, lifeguard training, first aid/CPR at $1200–$2000 per season; ▶ *business manager* at $1200–$1800 per season.

Benefits College credit, on-the-job training, on-site room and board, laundry facilities. Preemployment training is required and includes safety and accident prevention, group interaction, first-aid, CPR, leadership, camper-counselor relations. Orientation is paid.

Contact Chris Endres, Camp Administrator, Camp Laughing Waters, Girl Scouts of Southeastern Pennsylvania, 100 North 17th Street, 2nd Floor, Philadelphia, Pennsylvania 19103; 215-564-4657, Fax 215-564-6953. Application deadline: May 15.

CAMP LOG-N-TWIG
DINGMAN'S FERRY, PENNSYLVANIA 18328

General Information General coeducational recreation program serving up to 250 campers. Established in 1953. Owned by Morton and Ronne Tener. Affiliated with National Camp Association, American Camping Association. 125-acre facility located 110 miles north of Philadelphia. Features: 5 tennis courts; pool; man-made lake; indoor gymnasium; modern cabins (indoor showers and lavatories); many playing fields.

Profile of Summer Employees Total number: 80; average age: 22; 50% male, 50% female. Nonsmokers preferred.

Employment Information Openings are from June 20 to August 17. Jobs available: ▶ *general counselors* at $900–$1200 per season; ▶ *specialty counselors* at $1000–$1400 per season; ▶ *nurse* at $2000 per season; ▶ *cook* at $400–$500 per week; ▶ *swimming instructors* with WSI certification at $1200–$1400 per season; ▶ *supervising staff counselors (minimum age 21)* with several years of counseling experience and teaching degree at $1400–$1600 per season.

Benefits College credit, on-site room and board at no charge. Preemployment training of 5 days is required and includes safety and accident prevention, group interaction, leadership. Orientation is unpaid.

Contact Dr. Morton Tener, Camp Log-n-Twig, 7700 Doe Lane, Laverock, Pennsylvania 19038; 215-887-9367. Application deadline: May 1.

CAMP NETIMUS
RD 1, BOX 117A
MILFORD, PENNSYLVANIA 18337

General Information Residential girls camp with two-, four-, or eight-week sessions, offering forty activities to help campers develop self-confidence and a positive self image. Established in 1930. Owned by Camp Netimus, Inc. Affiliated with American Camping Association. 400-acre facility located 90 miles west of New York, New York. Features: northeastern Pennsylvania setting; cabins; well-equipped program facilities; ropes course; riding trails; proximity to the Delaware River; waterfalls, lake, and mountains.

Profile of Summer Employees Total number: 75; average age: 24; 10% male, 90% female; 6% minorities; 10% high school students; 70% college students; 15% retirees; 40% international; 10% local residents; 10% teachers. Nonsmokers only.

Employment Information Openings are from June 10 to August 20. Jobs available: ▶ 4 *swimming instructors* with WSI certification and lifeguard training at $1000–$2500 per season; ▶ 2 *sailing instructors* with lifeguard training at $1000–$2000 per season; ▶ 4 *fine arts instructors* at $1000–$2000 per season; ▶ 2 *jewelry/metalcraft instructors* at $1000–$2000 per season; ▶ 2 *waterskiing instructors* (minimum age 21) with lifeguard training at $1500–$2500 per season; ▶ 4 *horseback riding instructors* with first aid/CPR certification at $1200–$2000 per season; ▶ 2 *nurses* with RN license at $2000–$3000 per season; ▶ 1 *fencing instructor* at $1000–$2000 per season; ▶ 1 *rock climbing instructor* at $1000–$2000 per season; ▶ 2 *stained glass instructors* at $1000–$2000 per season; ▶ 2 *woodworking instructors* at $1000–$2000 per season; ▶ 3 *canoeing instructors* with lifeguard training at $1000–$2000 per season; ▶ 3 *outdoor/environmental instructors* at $1000–$2000 per season; ▶ 2 *gymnastics instructors* at $1000–

$2000 per season; ▶ 3 *dance instructors* (jazz, modern, tap, and ballet) at $1000–$2000 per season; ▶ *trip instructors* with first aid, CPR, and lifeguard training at $1000–$2000 per season; ▶ *riflery instructors* with first aid/CPR certification at $1000–$2000 per season; ▶ *archery instructors* with first aid/CPR certification at $1000–$2000 per season. International students encouraged to apply; must apply through recognized agency.

Benefits College credit, on-the-job training, formal ongoing training, on-site room and board at no charge, laundry facilities, transportation on day off, skill development (CPR, first aid, and lifeguard training), salary bonus for certifications and department heads. Preemployment training of 7 to 10 days is required and includes safety and accident prevention, group interaction, first-aid, CPR, leadership, camper-counselor relations. Orientation is paid.

Contact Donna Kistler, Director, Camp Netimus, Department SJ, RD 1, Box 117A, Milford, Pennsylvania 18337; 800-225-0604, Fax 717-296-6128, E-mail netimus@warwick.net. Application deadline: March 31.

CAMP NOCK-A-MIXON
249 TRAUGERS CROSSING ROAD
KINTNERSVILLE, PENNSYLVANIA 18930

General Information All-around residential coeducational camp serving 350 youngsters ages 7–15 during a seven-week session. Established in 1938. Owned by Mark and Bernice Glaser. Affiliated with American Camping Association. 115-acre facility located 48 miles north of Philadelphia. Features: 2 heated pools for instruction and recreation; 2 lakes for boating and sailing; 10 tennis courts; 3 indoor recreation halls; professional 18-hole mini-golf course and driving range; 7 basketball courts.

Profile of Summer Employees Total number: 120; average age: 19; 55% male, 45% female; 10% high school students; 80% college students; 5% teachers. Nonsmokers only.

Employment Information Openings are from June 19 to August 14. Jobs available: ▶ 60 *general counselors* at $900–$1300 per season; ▶ 30 *specialists and counselors* at $900–$1400 per season; ▶ 10 *swimming instructors* with WSI certification and/or lifeguard training at $1000–$2000 per season; ▶ 6 *tennis counselors* at $900–$1400 per season; ▶ 2 *drama directors* at $900–$1300 per season; ▶ 1 *crafts director* at $1200–$1800 per season; ▶ *division leaders* with college degree at $1600–$2400 per season; ▶ 6 *kitchen staff members* at $1500–$1800 per season; ▶ 2 *general cleaning and grounds workers* at $1500–$1800 per season; ▶ *athletic directors* at $1400–$3000 per season; ▶ *nurses* with RN license at $2800–$3200 per season; ▶ *adventure course (ropes and climbing wall) teacher* at $1500–$2200 per season.

Benefits College credit, on-the-job training, formal ongoing training, on-site room and board at no charge, laundry facilities, days off to visit nearby Philadelphia, New York City, and Atlantic City (all within 2 hours). Preemployment training of 5 days is required and includes safety and accident prevention, group interaction, first-aid, CPR, leadership, camper-counselor relations, ropes training.

Contact Mark Glaser, Director, Camp Nock-A-Mixon, Department SJ, 16 Gum Tree Lane, Lafayette Hill, Pennsylvania 19444; 610-941-0128, Fax 610-941-1307, E-mail mglaser851@aol. com. Application deadline: June 1.

CAMP SUNSET HILL
CHADDS FORD, PENNSYLVANIA 19317

General Information Day camp serving 150 girls per two-week session; residential camp serving 100 girls in 3 one-week sessions. Established in 1960. Owned by Girl Scouts of Southeastern Pennsylvania. Affiliated with American Camping Association, Girl Scouts of the United States of America. 188-acre facility located 40 miles southwest of Philadelphia. Features: large outdoor pool; pond for nature exploration; nature trails and activity areas; units of adirondecks, platform tents, and "A" frames.

Profile of Summer Employees Total number: 45; average age: 25; 100% female; 15% minorities; 5% high school students; 80% college students; 10% international; 90% local residents. Nonsmokers preferred.

Employment Information Openings are from June 18 to August 15. Jobs available: ▶ *counselor* at $1200–$1500 per season; ▶ *lifeguard* with lifeguard training, community first aid, and CPR certification at $1200–$1500 per season; ▶ *nurse* with PA, RN, or LPN preferred at $2300–$2500 per season; ▶ *cook* at $1800–$2500 per season; ▶ *crafts/nature specialist* at $1000–$1200 per season.

Benefits College credit, on-the-job training, on-site room and board at no charge, access to all recreational facilities during time off. Preemployment training of 5 days is required and includes safety and accident prevention, group interaction, first-aid, CPR, leadership, camper-counselor relations, program planning. Orientation is paid.

Contact Chris Endres, Girl Scouts of Southeastern Pennsylvania, Camp Sunset Hill, Department SJ, 100 North 17th Street, 2nd Floor, Philadelphia, Pennsylvania 19103; 215-564-4657, Fax 215-564-6953. Application deadline: May 15.

CAMP SUSQUEHANNOCK FOR GIRLS
FRIENDSVILLE, PENNSYLVANIA 18818

General Information Residential camp for 85 girls ages 7–17. Offers three-, four-, or eight-week sessions. Established in 1986. Owned by Edwin and George Shafer. Affiliated with American Camping Association, Camp Directors' Roundtable. 750-acre facility located 15 miles south of Binghamton, New York. Features: lake totally surrounded by camp land; 4 tennis courts; large stone lodge with two fireplaces and stage.

Profile of Summer Employees Total number: 34; average age: 21; 10% male, 90% female; 80% college students; 8% international; 8% local residents. Nonsmokers only.

Employment Information Openings are from June 25 to August 25. Jobs available: ▶ 2 *swimming instructors* with lifeguard certification at $900–$1300 per season; ▶ 2 *arts and crafts instructors* at $950–$1300 per season; ▶ 1 *nurse* with RN license at $1500–$1800 per season; ▶ 2 *horseback riders* at $1000–$1500 per season; ▶ 2 *field sports staff members (hockey, lacrosse, and soccer)* at $950–$1400 per season. International students encouraged to apply; must apply through recognized agency.

Benefits College credit, on-the-job training, on-site room and board at no charge, laundry facilities, travel reimbursement, doctor and nurse on site for attention/evaluation (free). Preemployment training of 7 to 8 days is required and includes safety and accident prevention, group interaction, first-aid, CPR, leadership, camper-counselor relations. Orientation is paid.

Contact Mrs. George C. Shafer, Director, Camp Susquehannock for Girls, Department SJ, 860 Briarwood Road, Newtown Square, Pennsylvania 19073; 610-356-3426, Fax 610-353-1768, E-mail campsusq@zola.trendl.com. Application deadline: May 15.

CAMP TIMBERTOPS
BOX HC, BOX 236
GREELEY, PENNSYLVANIA 18425

General Information Residential camp serving 175 girls ages 7–17 with a wide range of activities. Established in 1963. Owned by Mitchell Black. Affiliated with American Camping Association. Located 100 miles west of New York, New York. Features: 20-station adventure/challenge course; 6 tennis courts; Olympic-size pool; dance pavilion; on-site lake.

Profile of Summer Employees Total number: 75; average age: 20; 2% male, 98% female. Nonsmokers only.

Employment Information Openings are from June 22 to August 17. Jobs available: ▶ *climbing staff members* at $800–$1000 per season; ▶ *WSI staff members* at $800–$1000 per season; ▶ *athletics staff members* at $800–$1000 per season; ▶ *gymnastics staff members* at $800–$1000 per season; ▶ *waterfront staff members* at $800–$1000 per season; ▶ *tennis staff* at $800–$1200 per season; ▶ *dance staff* at $800–$1200 per season. International students encouraged to apply; must obtain own visa and working papers prior to employment; must apply through recognized agency.

Benefits College credit, on-the-job training, on-site room and board, laundry facilities.

Preemployment training of 4 days is required and includes WSI, lifeguard, climbing. Orientation is unpaid.

Contact Camp Timber Tops, Camp Timbertops, 151 Washington Lane, Jenkintown, Pennsylvania 19046; 215-887-9700, E-mail pinetree@pond.com.

CAMP WATONKA
PO BOX 127
HAWLEY, PENNSYLVANIA 18428

General Information Residential science camp for 120 boys offering hands-on experience in all areas of science combined with traditional camp activities. Established in 1963. Owned by Mr. and Mrs. Donald Wacker. Affiliated with American Camping Association, National Rifle Association, American Red Cross. 250-acre facility located 35 miles east of Scranton. Features: modern well-equipped science buildings and laboratories; extensive American Red Cross waterfront program; proximity to town and many well-known tourist areas; several large sports fields; modern, clean, and comfortable cabins.

Profile of Summer Employees Total number: 60; average age: 23; 95% male, 5% female; 10% minorities; 5% high school students; 55% college students; 20% international; 10% local residents; 40% teachers. Nonsmokers only.

Employment Information Openings are from June 16 to August 16. Jobs available: ▶ 15 *cabin counselors* with college junior or senior status at $1100–$1400 per season; ▶ 8 *science instructors* with college or graduate student status at $1100–$2500 per season; ▶ 3 *arts and crafts staff members* at $1100–$1400 per season; ▶ 8 *science supervisors* with teaching certification at $1500–$3000 per season; ▶ 2 *woodworking instructors* with teaching certification at $1500–$3000 per season; ▶ 3 *experienced minibike riding instructors* at $1100–$1800 per season; ▶ 5 *waterfront/water sports instructors* with ARC certification at $1100–$1500 per season; ▶ 1 *waterfront director* with ARC certification at $1500–$3000 per season; ▶ *photography instructor* with college or graduate status at $1100–$2500 per season; ▶ *archery instructor* with college or graduate status at $1100–$2500 per season; ▶ *magic instructor* with college or graduate status at $1100–$2500 per season. International students encouraged to apply; must obtain own visa and working papers prior to employment; must apply through recognized agency.

Benefits On-the-job training, formal ongoing training, on-site room and board at no charge, laundry facilities. Preemployment training of 5 days is required and includes safety and accident prevention, group interaction, first-aid, CPR, leadership. Orientation is paid.

Contact Donald P. Wacker, Director, Camp Watonka, Department SJ, PO Box 127, Hawley, Pennsylvania 18428; 717-857-1401. Application deadline: June 1.

CAMP WESTMONT
POYNTELLE, PENNSYLVANIA 18454

General Information Residential camp offering all land and water sports, individual and team athletics, arts and crafts, drama and dance, woodworking and ceramics, and circus and gymnastics to 350 campers ages 6–16 for eight weeks. Established in 1981. Owned by Jack Pinsky and Fred Moskowitz. Affiliated with American Camping Association, Wayne County Camping Association and Athletic Association, Wayne County Chamber of Commerce. 225-acre facility located 120 miles west of New York, New York. Features: 8 outdoor tennis courts with lights; 4 baseball fields; 3 soccer fields also used for football and lacrosse; gymnastics pavilion with trapeze; indoor gym; stage with woodworking and arts and crafts shops; lake for swimming, sailing, boating, and water skiing.

Profile of Summer Employees Total number: 150; average age: 24; 50% male, 50% female; 5% minorities; 5% high school students; 85% college students; 2% retirees; 10% international; 5% local residents; 20% teachers. Nonsmokers only.

Employment Information Openings are from June 18 to September 1. Jobs available: ▶ 80 *general counselors* at $1200–$1500 per season; ▶ 6 *group leaders* at $1800–$2400 per season;

▶ 6 *waterfront specialists* at $1200–$1500 per season; ▶ 6 *tennis specialists* at $1200–$1500 per season; ▶ 2 *gymnastics specialists* at $1200–$1500 per season; ▶ 12 *sports specialists* at $1200–$1500 per season; ▶ 1 *assistant cook or baker* at $200–$300 per week. International students encouraged to apply; must obtain own visa and working papers prior to employment; must apply through recognized agency.

Benefits On-the-job training, on-site room and board at no charge, laundry facilities. Preemployment training of 5 days is required and includes safety and accident prevention, group interaction, leadership, camper-counselor relations, skill training for sports and activities. Orientation is unpaid.

Contact Jack Pinsky, Owner/Director, Camp Westmont, Department SJ, 14 Squirrel Drive, East Rockaway, New York 11518; 516-599-2963, Fax 516-599-1979, E-mail campwestmt@aol.com. Application deadline: May 30.

COLLEGE SETTLEMENT OF PHILADELPHIA
600 WITMER ROAD
HORSHAM, PENNSYLVANIA 19044

General Information Residential and day camp serving mostly economically disadvantaged youths ages 7–14 from the Philadelphia metropolitan area. Established in 1922. Owned by The College Settlement of Philadelphia. Affiliated with American Camping Association, United Way of Southeastern Pennsylvania. 235-acre facility located 20 miles north of Philadelphia. Features: location in suburbs; outpost facility for trips; large swimming pool; high and low rope courses on site (adventure program for teens); diverse habitat including pond, woods, fields, and meadows; adequate open space for recreation.

Profile of Summer Employees Total number: 60; average age: 21; 50% male, 50% female; 20% minorities; 10% high school students; 80% college students; 20% international; 10% local residents. Nonsmokers preferred.

Employment Information Openings are from June 10 to August 25. Year-round positions also offered. Jobs available: ▶ 12 *cabin counselors* at $1600 per season; ▶ 3 *unit leaders* at $1800 per season; ▶ 3 *trip leaders* with first aid and CPR certification at $1800–$2000 per season; ▶ 2 *environmentalists* at $1600–$1800 per season; ▶ 3 *swimming instructors* with WSI and LGT certification at $1700–$1900 per season; ▶ 1 *provisions coordinator* at $1600–$1800 per season. International students encouraged to apply; must obtain own visa and working papers prior to employment; must apply through recognized agency.

Benefits College credit, on-the-job training, on-site room and board at no charge, laundry facilities. Preemployment training of 7 to 10 days is required and includes safety and accident prevention, group interaction, leadership, archery, ropes course. Orientation is paid.

Contact Wally Grummun, Director of Resident Programs, College Settlement of Philadelphia, Department SJ, 600 Witmer Road, Horsham, Pennsylvania 19044; 215-542-7974, Fax 215-542-7457, E-mail camps2@aol.com. Application deadline: May 1.

DORNEY PARK AND WILDWATER KINGDOM
3830 DORNEY PARK ROAD
ALLENTOWN, PENNSYLVANIA 18104

General Information Amusement park featuring more than 100 rides and attractions including four world-class roller coasters and a premier waterpark. Established in 1860. Owned by Cedar Fair, LP. Affiliated with International Association of Amusement Parks and Attractions, World Water Association. 200-acre facility located 50 miles north of Philadelphia. Features: 5 designated childrens areas; 11 water slides; wave pool; 1921 antique wooden Dentzel carousel; daily live entertainment including "Berenstain Bear Country".

Profile of Summer Employees Total number: 2,500.

Employment Information Openings are from May 1 to October 1. Jobs available: ▶ 350 *ride operators;* ▶ 200 *lifeguards;* ▶ 350 *food hosts and hostesses;* ▶ 100 *game attendants;* ▶ 180 *merchandise clerks;* ▶ *security staff;* ▶ 75 *performers.* International students encouraged to apply; must apply through recognized agency.

Benefits College credit, on-the-job training, scholarships.
Contact Eileen Minninger, Personnel Manager, Dorney Park and Wildwater Kingdom, Department SJ, 3830 Dorney Park Road, Allentown, Pennsylvania 18104; 610-391-7752.

ENSEMBLE THEATRE COMMUNITY SCHOOL
BOX 188
EAGLES MERE, PENNSYLVANIA 17731

General Information Summer theater school serving high school students ages 14–18. Established in 1984. Located 40 miles north of Williamsport. Features: location in the Allegheny Mountains; large residential Victorian housing for faculty and students; community arts facility for performances and classes; swimming, tennis courts, basketball facilities, and hiking trails.
Profile of Summer Employees Total number: 12; average age: 24; 50% male, 50% female; 15% minorities; 33% college students. Nonsmokers preferred.
Employment Information Openings are from June 16 to August 2. Jobs available: ▶ 1 *experienced acting instructor* with extensive training at $1200–$1700 per season; ▶ 1 *experienced acting instructor/director* with extensive training at $1200–$1700 per season; ▶ 1 *experienced movement instructor* with extensive training at $1200–$1700 per season; ▶ 1 *experienced music instructor* with extensive training at $1200–$1700 per season; ▶ 1 *experienced technical director* with extensive training at $1200–$1700 per season; ▶ 4 *college interns* with training and experience in theater and related arts at $400–$450 per season.
Benefits College credit, on-the-job training, on-site room and board at no charge, laundry facilities.
Contact Seth Orbach, Associate Director, Ensemble Theatre Community School, 80 East End Avenue, #4G, New York, New York 10028; 212-794-4696, Fax 212-794-4696, E-mail etc@ compuserve.com, URL http://users.aol.com/etcschool/. Application deadline: February 28.

FORT NECESSITY NATIONAL BATTLEFIELD
1 WASHINGTON WAY
FARMINGTON, PENNSYLVANIA 15437

General Information George Washington's first command and battlefield commemorating the opening battle of the French and Indian War and westward expansion along the National Road. Established in 1931. Owned by United States Government. Operated by National Park Service. 903-acre facility located 60 miles southeast of Pittsburgh. Features: reconstructed log stockade (Fort Necessity); visitor center; Mount Washington Tavern (early nineteenth-century); gravesite of Major General Edward Braddock; Jumonville Glen–site of first skirmishes of French and Indian War (May 28, 1754); picnic area and 3.6 miles of hiking trails.
Profile of Summer Employees Total number: 5; average age: 30; 75% male, 25% female; 10% minorities; 50% college students; 25% retirees.
Employment Information Openings are from June 1 to September 15. Spring break, winter break, Christmas break, year-round positions also offered. Jobs available: ▶ 6 *interpretive park rangers* with public speaking experience and interest in history. All positions offered at $8.31–$9.30 per hour.
Benefits On-the-job training, on-site room and board at $35 per week, laundry facilities.
Contact National Park Service, Fort Necessity National Battlefield, 1 Washington Way, Farmington, Pennsylvania 15437; 412-329-5512. Application deadline: January 15.

HERSHEYPARK
100 WEST HERSHEYPARK DRIVE
HERSHEY, PENNSYLVANIA 17033

General Information Facility producing seven residential shows, song and dance revues, and other types of family entertainment. Established in 1972. Owned by Hershey Entertainment Resort Company. 100-acre facility located 90 miles west of Philadelphia. Features: location in Chocolatetown, USA; 7 residential shows; professional production team; subsidized housing.

Profile of Summer Employees Total number: 75; average age: 21; 50% male, 50% female. Nonsmokers preferred.

Employment Information Openings are from May 1 to September 3. Winter break, Christmas break positions also offered. Jobs available: ► 60 *experienced singing/dancing performers* at $350–$380 per week; ► 5 *experienced stage managers* at $300–$375 per week; ► 3 *experienced sound technicians* at $300–$330 per week; ► 6 *seamstresses/dressers* at $285–$350 per week.

Benefits College credit, on-site room and board at $200 per month, laundry facilities, use of all park facilities, end-of-season bonus, equity eligibility. Preemployment training of 1 day is required. Orientation is paid.

Contact Cherie Lingle, Entertainment Coordinator, Hersheypark, Department SJ, 100 West Hersheypark Drive, Hershey, Pennsylvania 17033; 717-534-3349, Fax 717-534-3336. Application deadline: February 15.

HIDDEN VALLEY CAMP
PO BOX 98, WALLERVILLE ROAD
EQUINUNK, PENNSYLVANIA 18417

General Information Residential camp serving girls ages 7–17. Established in 1971. Owned by Rolling Hills Girl Scout Council. Affiliated with Girl Scouts of the United States of America, American Camping Association. 1,200-acre facility located 10 miles south of Hancock, New York. Features: 40-acre lake; proximity to Delaware River and Pocono Mountains; stables and riding trails on premises; rugged terrain.

Profile of Summer Employees Total number: 30; average age: 20; 2% male, 98% female; 20% minorities; 10% high school students; 70% college students; 10% retirees; 4% international; 20% local residents; 10% teachers.

Employment Information Openings are from June 20 to August 20. Jobs available: ► 1 *business manager* (minimum age 23); ► 1 *program manager* (minimum age 23); ► 15 *unit leaders* (minimum age 21); ► 10 *unit assistants* (minimum age 18); ► 1 *waterfront director* (minimum age 21) with WSI certification; ► 1 *waterfront assistant* (minimum age 18) with lifeguard certification; ► 1 *boating director* (minimum age 21) with WSI and canoe certifications; ► 1 *health supervisor* (minimum age 21) with RN, LPN, or EMT license; ► 1 *cook* (minimum age 21); ► 1 *assistant cook* (minimum age 18); ► 4 *kitchen aides* (minimum age 18); ► 1 *experienced riding instructor* (minimum age 21).

Benefits College credit, on-the-job training, on-site room and board at no charge, laundry facilities, health insurance.

Contact Jane Butts, Director of Camping Services, Hidden Valley Camp, Department SJ, 1171 Highway 28, North Branch, New Jersey 08876; 908-725-1226, Fax 908-725-4933. Application deadline: May 31.

HILL SCHOOL SUMMER PROGRAM/HILL SCHOOL
SUMMER SPORTS PROGRAM
717 EAST HIGH STREET
POTTSTOWN, PENNSYLVANIA 19464

General Information Residential coed academic enrichment camp serving up to 150 students for a five-week extensive studies program. Established in 1901. Operated by The Hill School. 200-acre facility located 35 miles north of Philadelphia. Features: 11 tennis courts; golf course and track field, extensive athletic facilities; highly computerized campus.

Profile of Summer Employees Total number: 30; average age: 30; 50% male, 50% female; 10% minorities; 20% college students; 10% international; 80% teachers. Nonsmokers preferred.

Employment Information Openings are from June 22 to July 25. Jobs available: ► 20 *interns* (junior or senior in college) at $1700–$2000 per season; ► 10 *sports interns* (freshman or sophomore in college) at $500–$800 per season. International students encouraged to apply; must obtain own visa and working papers prior to employment; must apply through recognized agency.

Benefits On-the-job training, on-site room and board at no charge, laundry facilities, travel reimbursement.

Contact Ryckman R. Walbridge, Director of Summer Program, Hill School Summer Program/ Hill School Summer Sports Program, Department SJ, 717 East High Street, Pottstown, Pennsylvania 19464; 610-326-1000, Fax 610-326-3647, E-mail rwalbrid@thehill.org, URL http://www.thehill.org/admissions/summer. Application deadline: February 1.

JKST SUMMER ENRICHMENT CAMP
HAVERFORD COLLEGE
HAVERFORD, PENNSYLVANIA 19041

General Information Residential enrichment camp serving 100 overnight and 25 day campers in two sessions over an eight-week season. Established in 1989. Owned by Julian Krinsky and Adrian Castelli. 250-acre facility located 10 miles west of Philadelphia. Features: 16 tennis courts; large indoor gymnasium; location on Haverford College campus; all-weather track; many ball fields; 6 squash courts.

Profile of Summer Employees Total number: 45; average age: 21; 50% male, 50% female; 20% minorities; 70% college students; 2% retirees; 15% international; 10% local residents; 10% teachers. Nonsmokers only.

Employment Information Openings are from June 16 to August 15. Jobs available: ▶ 18 *resident advisors* at $1100–$1500 per season. International students encouraged to apply; must obtain own visa and working papers prior to employment; must apply through recognized agency.

Benefits On-site room and board at no charge, private room.

Contact Adrian Castelli, Co-Owner, JKST Summer Enrichment Camp, Department SJ, PO Box 333, Haverford, Pennsylvania 19041; 610-265-9401, Fax 610-265-3678, E-mail adrian@jkst. com, URL http://www.jkst.com. Application deadline: May 15.

JKST TENNIS, GOLF, AND SQUASH CAMP
HAVERFORD COLLEGE
HAVERFORD, PENNSYLVANIA 19041

General Information Overnight camp with concentration in tennis, golf, or squash serving 100–150 overnight and 20–40 day campers per week. Established in 1980. Owned by Julian Krinsky and Adrian Castelli. 250-acre facility located 10 miles west of Philadelphia. Features: 40 outdoor tennis courts; 25 indoor tennis courts; 6 squash courts; driving range; practice trap; access to many golf courses.

Profile of Summer Employees Total number: 85; average age: 21; 50% male, 50% female; 20% minorities; 70% college students; 2% retirees; 15% international; 10% local residents; 10% teachers. Nonsmokers only.

Employment Information Openings are from June 15 to August 24. Jobs available: ▶ 2 *tennis counselors;* ▶ 2 *golf counselors;* ▶ 2 *squash counselors;* ▶ 15 *resident counselors;* ▶ 2 *swimming instructors* with WSI certification. International students encouraged to apply; must obtain own visa and working papers prior to employment; must apply through recognized agency.

Benefits On-the-job training, on-site room and board, private room.

Contact Adrian Castelli, Co-Owner, JKST Tennis, Golf, and Squash Camp, Department SJ, PO Box 333, Haverford, Pennsylvania 19041; 610-265-9401, Fax 610-265-3678, E-mail adrian@jkst. com. Application deadline: May 15.

JUMONVILLE
RR 2, BOX 128
HOPWOOD, PENNSYLVANIA 15445

General Information Residential Christian camp serving 250–300 persons of all age levels per week. Established in 1941. Owned by Jumonville, Inc. Operated by United Methodist Church, Western Pennsylvania Conference. Affiliated with Christian Camping International?USA,

American Camping Association, Association of Challenge Course Technology. 281-acre facility located 50 miles south of Pittsburgh. Features: 60-foot cross located on top of mountain; 4 outdoor tennis courts; 4 outdoor volleyball courts; outdoor swimming pool; challenge/ropes course; campus-type setting.

Profile of Summer Employees Total number: 30; average age: 19; 50% male, 50% female; 5% minorities; 10% high school students; 90% college students; 5% international; 10% local residents. Nonsmokers only.

Employment Information Openings are from June 1 to August 25. Jobs available: ▶ 5 *counselors* at $150 per week; ▶ 2 *adventure staff members* at $150 per week; ▶ 1 *office assistant/business manager* at $135 per week; ▶ 1 *business manager/truck driver* at $135 per week; ▶ 2 *certified lifeguards* at $135 per week; ▶ 3 *snack shop workers* at $135 per week; ▶ 4 *dishroom staff members* at $135 per week; ▶ 2 *dining room staff members* at $135 per week; ▶ 1 *kitchen helper* at $135 per week; ▶ 1 *cookout staff member* at $135 per week; ▶ 2 *audio/visual specialists* at $135 per week; ▶ 2 *maintenance/housekeeping helpers* at $135 per week; ▶ 1 *multipurpose floater* at $135 per week; ▶ 1 *health-care staff member* with paramedic, LPN, or RN license at $135 per week; ▶ 1 *assistant program director and arts and crafts instructor* at $135 per week.

Benefits On-the-job training, on-site room and board at no charge, laundry facilities, use of on-site recreational facilities. Preemployment training of 2 to 14 days is required and includes safety and accident prevention, group interaction, first-aid, CPR, leadership, camper-counselor relations, adventure training. Orientation is paid.

Contact Larry Beatty, Executive Director, Jumonville, Department SJ, RR 2, Box 128, Hopwood, Pennsylvania 15445; 412-439-4912, Fax 412-439-1415, URL http://gospelcom.net/cci/jumonville. Application deadline: March 1.

KENNYWOOD PARK
4800 KENNYWOOD BOULEVARD
WEST MIFFLIN, PENNSYLVANIA 15122

General Information Amusement park servicing over one million guests per season. Established in 1898. Affiliated with International Association of Amusement Parks and Attractions. 40-acre facility located 7 miles southeast of Pittsburgh. Features: three wooden roller coasters; five major water rides; large "kiddie ride" area; more than 15 food areas; full-service cafe.

Profile of Summer Employees Total number: 1,450; average age: 18. Nonsmokers preferred.

Employment Information Openings are from April 1 to September 5. Jobs available: ▶ *team members (rides, games, and refreshments)* at $4.90–$5.25 per hour.

Benefits On-the-job training, formal ongoing training. Preemployment training of 1 day is required and includes safety and accident prevention, group interaction. Orientation is paid.

Contact Joseph Barron, Personnel Director-Kennywood, Kennywood Park, 4800 Kennywood Boulevard, West Mifflin, Pennsylvania 15122; 412-461-0500, Fax 412-464-0719.

KEYSTONE TALL TREE SUMMER CAMP PROGRAM
RD 7, BOX 368
KITTANNING, PENNSYLVANIA 16201

General Information A residential camp program with six-day sessions for girls ages 5–17. Serves approximately 400 campers per summer. Established in 1964. 440-acre facility located 50 miles east of Pittsburgh. Features: sports field; horse riding facilities; swimming pool; nature center.

Profile of Summer Employees Total number: 16; average age: 23; 5% male, 95% female; 80% college students; 25% international; 75% local residents; 10% teachers. Nonsmokers preferred.

Employment Information Openings are from June 1 to August 31. Jobs available: ▶ *camp director;* ▶ *assistant camp director;* ▶ *kitchen supervisor;* ▶ *health supervisor;* ▶ *head counselor;* ▶ *assistant counselor;* ▶ *waterfront director;* ▶ *head riding instructor;* ▶ *assistant riding instructor;* ▶ *lifeguard;* ▶ *canoeing instructor;* ▶ *sailing instructor;* ▶ *archery instruc-*

tor; ▶ *ropes course instructor* (usually volunteer). International students encouraged to apply; must apply through recognized agency.

Benefits On-the-job training, on-site room and board at no charge, health insurance.

Contact Sheila Thompson-Moore, Program Director, Keystone Tall Tree Summer Camp Program, RD 7, Box 368, Kittanning, Pennsylvania 16201; 800-221-2995, Fax 412-543-6313. Application deadline: April 15.

LAKE OWEGO
GREELEY, PENNSYLVANIA 18425

General Information Residential camp serving boys for four or eight weeks. Established in 1931. Owned by Marvin and Mickey Black. Affiliated with American Camping Association. 400-acre facility located 88 miles north of New York, New York. Features: Olympic-size swimming pool; 75-acre lake; covered hockey rink; 6 all-weather tennis courts; 100-acre riding ranch with 24 horses (English and Western riding).

Profile of Summer Employees Total number: 100; average age: 20; 90% male, 10% female; 5% minorities; 90% college students; 1% retirees; 25% international. Nonsmokers only.

Employment Information Openings are from June 22 to August 17. Jobs available: ▶ 16 *athletics staff members* with high school or college varsity team experience at $1000–$1500 per season; ▶ 5 *swimming instructors* with WSI and ARC lifeguard certification at $600–$2000 per season; ▶ 2 *arts and crafts staff members* with a major in art at $800–$1500 per season; ▶ 2 *drama/theater instructors* with a major in theater at $800–$1500 per season; ▶ 8 *tennis instructors* with USPTA or team experience at $1000–$2000 per season; ▶ *waterfront staff* with lifeguard or WSI certification at $800–$1500 per season; ▶ 6 *head counselors* with college degree at $1500–$2400 per season; ▶ 2 *athletics directors* with college degree in physical education at $1500–$2500 per season; ▶ 3 *drivers* (minimum age 21) with good driving record at $1000–$1200 per season; ▶ 1 *nature director* with a major in nature studies/conservation or nature study experience at $1000–$1200 per season; ▶ 1 *experienced archery instructor (minimum age 21)* at $800–$1200 per season; ▶ 2 *lake directors (minimum age 21)* with college degree and WSI certification at $2000–$2500 per season; ▶ 1 *pool director (minimum age 21)* with college degree and WSI certification at $2000–$2500 per season; ▶ 8 *certified boating/canoeing instructors* at $800–$2000 per season; ▶ 4 *overnight hikers* with scouting experience at $1000–$1200 per season; ▶ 4 *certified sailing/windsurfing instructors* at $800–$2000 per season.

Benefits College credit, on-the-job training, formal ongoing training, on-site room and board at no charge, laundry facilities, five days off per summer, partial travel reimbursement.

Contact Mickey Black, Director, Lake Owego, Department SJ, 151 Washington Lane, Jenkintown, Pennsylvania 19046; 215-887-9700, Fax 215-887-3901. Application deadline: May 15.

LONGACRE EXPEDITIONS
RD 3, BOX 106
NEWPORT, PENNSYLVANIA 17074

General Information Adventure travel program in Pennsylvania for teenagers, emphasizing group living skills and physical challenges. Using base camp as a staging area, 2–3 staffers and 10–16 campers participate in novice and intermediate expeditions on which they engage in human-powered sports. Established in 1981. Owned by Longacre Expeditions. Affiliated with American Camping Association. 35-acre facility located 32 miles northwest of Harrisburg. Features: ropes course; climbing wall.

Profile of Summer Employees Total number: 50; average age: 25; 50% male, 50% female; 10% minorities; 40% college students; 10% local residents. Nonsmokers only.

Employment Information Openings are from May 15 to August 15. Jobs available: ▶ 2 *rock climbing instructors* (minimum age 21) with American Red Cross first aid, CPR, and completion of water safety course at $360–$450 per week; ▶ 2 *caving instructors* (minimum age 21) at $360–$450 per week; ▶ 8 *support and logistics staff members* (minimum age 21) at $150–$175 per week; ► 1 *equipment manager* (minimum age 21) at $175–$225 per week; ► 24 *assistant trip leaders* (minimum age 21) at $150–$175 per week.

Benefits On-the-job training, on-site room and board at no charge, Pro-Deal package. Preemployment training of 9 days is required and includes safety and accident prevention, group interaction, first-aid, CPR, leadership, camper-counselor relations. Orientation is unpaid.

Contact Roger Smith, Longacre Expeditions, RD 3, Box 106, Newport, Pennsylvania 17074; 717-567-6790, Fax 717-567-3955, URL http://www.longex.com.

NEW JERSEY CAMP JAYCEE
ZIEGLER ROAD
EFFORT, PENNSYLVANIA 18330

General Information Residential camp serving 135 developmentally disabled campers per week. Established in 1975. Owned by New Jersey Camp Jaycee. Operated by Association for Retarded Citizens of New Jersey. Affiliated with Association for Retarded Citizens of New Jersey, American Camping Association, New Jersey Jaycees. 185-acre facility located 18 miles southwest of Stroudsburg. Features: 2-acre lake; natural setting near Pocono Mountains; proximity to New York City (1 hour); location near resort areas; extensive recreation areas; nature trail.

Profile of Summer Employees Total number: 78; average age: 24; 50% male, 50% female; 15% minorities; 95% college students; 50% international; 50% local residents.

Employment Information Openings are from June 16 to August 20. Jobs available: ► 2 *swimming instructors* with WSI certification at $160–$190 per week; ► 2 *lifeguards* with Red Cross certification at $150–$180 per week; ► 6 *specialists* with experience in planning and implementing activities in music, arts and crafts, nature, or recreation for special needs campers at $150–$180 per week; ► 2 *nurses* with RN license at $450–$600 per week; ► 1 *licensed EMT* at $170–$220 per week; ► 1 *maintenance assistant* with driver's license and light maintenance experience at $160–$170 per week; ► 15 *counselors* with experience pertaining to developmental disabilities at $140–$160 per week. International students encouraged to apply; must apply through recognized agency.

Benefits On-the-job training, formal ongoing training, on-site room and board at no charge, laundry facilities, days off with transportation, beautiful staff hall. Preemployment training of 5 to 7 days is required and includes safety and accident prevention, group interaction, first-aid, CPR, leadership, camper-counselor relations. Orientation is paid.

Contact Jim Worrall, Executive Director, New Jersey Camp Jaycee, Department SJ, 33 Lake Drive, Hightstown, New Jersey 08520-5395; 609-443-1200, Fax 609-443-1202. Application deadline: May 15.

ONEKA
TAFTON, PENNSYLVANIA 18464

General Information Residential girls camp serving 100 campers in 2-, 3½-, and 7-week sessions. Established in 1908. Owned by Dale and Barbara Dohner. Affiliated with American Camping Association, Camp Alert Network, National Camp Association, American Canoe Association. 7-acre facility located 30 miles east of Scranton. Features: extensive freshwater lake frontage with waterfront area; picturesque, woodsy environment with 400 acres for hiking; courts for tennis and volleyball; rooms for ceramics and jewelry-making; darkroom.

Profile of Summer Employees Total number: 28; average age: 21; 5% male, 95% female; 5% high school students; 95% college students; 40% international; 15% local residents; 10% teachers. Nonsmokers preferred.

Employment Information Openings are from June 20 to August 23. Jobs available: ► 5 *swimming instructors/lifeguards* with LT, CPR, first aid, and WSI certification at $900–$1200 per season; ► 3 *canoeing/kayaking/boating/sailing instructors* with LT, CPR, first aid, and WSI certification (preferred) at $900–$1200 per season; ► 2 *experienced arts and crafts instructors* at $900–$1200 per season; ► 2 *experienced tennis instructors* at $900–$1200 per season; ► 1 *experienced volleyball instructor* at $900–$1200 per season; ► 3 *experienced field sports/ hockey/*

soccer/softball instructors at $900–$1200 per season; ▶ 1 *experienced campcraft instructor* at $900–$1200 per season; ▶ 1 *archery instructor* with good personal shooting skills (employee may be sent for further training) at $900–$1200 per season; ▶ 1 *music instructor* with piano-playing ability and knowledge of show tunes at $900–$1200 per season; ▶ 1 *drama instructor* with experience in directing and set design at $900–$1200 per season; ▶ 1 *assistant program director* with two years of camp experience at $1500–$2000 per season; ▶ 1 *program director* with three years of camp experience and good management and people skills at $1800–$2500 per season; ▶ 1 *aquatic director* with WSI and LTI certification at $1600–$2000 per season; ▶ 1 *nurse* with RN license at $1800–$2500 per season; ▶ 2 *maintenance helpers* (14–16 years old) at $600–$750 per season.

Benefits On-the-job training, on-site room and board at no charge, laundry facilities. Preemployment training of 5 days is required and includes safety and accident prevention, group interaction, leadership, camper-counselor relations.

Contact Dale H. Dohner, Camp Director, ONEKA, Department SJ, 10 Oakford Road, Wayne, Pennsylvania 19087; 610-687-6260, URL http://www.oneka.com/. Application deadline: March 1.

PENNSYLVANIA DEPARTMENT OF TRANSPORTATION BUREAU OF PERSONNEL, 555 WALNUT STREET 9TH FLOOR, FORUM PLACE
HARRISBURG, PENNSYLVANIA 17101-1900

General Information State government agency responsible for the planning, design, construction, and maintenance of Pennsylvania's transportation systems. Established in 1970.

Profile of Summer Employees Total number: 500; 10% minorities; 75% college students.

Employment Information Openings are from March 1 to October 1. Jobs available: ▶ *engineering/scientific/technical interns* with current enrollment as a college student majoring in engineering, math, science, or architecture at $7.83 per hour; ▶ *highway maintenance workers* at $7.45 per hour; ▶ *government service interns* with current enrollment as a college student in any major at $5.50 per hour; ▶ *transportation/construction inspectors* with two years of construction inspection experience at $7.83 per hour.

Benefits College credit, on-the-job training, travel reimbursement.

Contact Diana Hershey, College Relations Coordinator, Pennsylvania Department of Transportation, 555 Walnut Street, 9th Floor, Forum Place, Harrisburg, Pennsylvania 17101-1900; 717-783-2680.

PINE FOREST CAMPS
BOX 242
GREELEY, PENNSYLVANIA 18425

General Information Residential camps serving children ages 6–16, offering four- and eight-week sessions. Established in 1931. Owned by the Black Family. Affiliated with American Camping Association. 1,000-acre facility located 88 miles north of New York, New York. Features: private lakes and Olympic-size, heated pools; location 1,800 feet above sea level in the forests of the Pocono Mountains; indoor gym; 12 all-weather tennis courts; theater.

Profile of Summer Employees Total number: 175; average age: 20; 50% male, 50% female; 2% minorities; 90% college students; 1% retirees; 10% international; 25% local residents. Nonsmokers only.

Employment Information Openings are from June 22 to August 17. Year-round positions also offered. Jobs available: ▶ 16 *tennis instructors* with high school or college varsity status at $1000–$2000 per season; ▶ 16 *general athletics instructors* with high school or college varsity status at $1000–$1500 per season; ▶ 6 *arts and crafts instructors* with a major in art at $800–$1500 per season; ▶ 4 *drama/theater instructors* with a major in theater at $800–$1500 per season; ▶ 8 *certified canoeing/boating instructors* at $800–$2000 per season; ▶ 4 *certified sailing/windsurfing instructors* at $800–$2000 per season; ▶ 1 *experienced archery instructor* *(minimum age 21)* at $800–$1200 per season; ► 3 *drivers* (minimum age 21) with good driving record at $1000–$1200 per season; ► *overnight hikers* with scouting experience at $1000–$1200 per season; ► 2 *athletics directors* with college degree in physical education at $1500–$2500 per season; ► 6 *head counselors* with college degree at $1500–$2400 per season; ► 2 *lake directors* with college degree and WSI certification at $2000–$2500 per season; ► 2 *pool directors (minimum age 21)* with WSI and ARC certification at $2000–$2500 per season; ► 12 *swimming instructors* with WSI certification at $600–$2000 per season; ► 1 *nature director* with a major in nature studies/conservation or nature study experience at $1000–$1200 per season; ► *waterfront staff* with lifeguard or WSI certification at $800–$1500 per season. International students encouraged to apply; must obtain own visa and working papers prior to employment; must apply through recognized agency.

Benefits College credit, on-the-job training, formal ongoing training, on-site room and board at no charge, laundry facilities, travel reimbursement.

Contact Mickey Black, Director, Pine Forest Camps, 151 Washington Lane, Jenkintown, Pennsylvania 19046; 215-887-9700, Fax 215-887-3901. Application deadline: May 15.

POCONO HIGHLAND CAMP
MARSHALLS CREEK, PENNSYLVANIA 18335

General Information Coed residential camp serving 250 campers ages 5–16. Established in 1935. Owned by Marian and Louis Weinberg. 325-acre facility located 80 miles north of Philadelphia. Features: 13 lighted tennis courts; 4 large sports fields; extensive freshwater lake for sailing, windsurfing, rafting, and canoe trips; riding trails (for English riding); drama and dance facilities; mountain climbing; gymnastics; golf; waterskiing.

Profile of Summer Employees Total number: 80; average age: 21; 50% male, 50% female; 75% college students; 5% international; 5% local residents; 5% teachers. Nonsmokers preferred.

Employment Information Openings are from June 19 to August 17. Jobs available: ► 40 *counselors* with one year of college; ► 8 *athletics instructors* (for all field sports)*;* ► 16 *tennis instructors* with high school or college varsity status; ► 4 *arts and crafts instructors* with major in arts and crafts; ► 4 *drama instructors* with major in theater; ► 8 *certified canoeing and boating instructors;* ► 8 *certified waterskiing and windsurfing instructors;* ► 4 *certified archery instructors;* ► 4 *drivers* (minimum age 24) with good driving record; ► 8 *swimming instructors* with WSI certification. International students encouraged to apply; must obtain own visa and working papers prior to employment; must apply through recognized agency.

Benefits College credit, on-the-job training, formal ongoing training, on-site room and board at no charge, laundry facilities, travel reimbursement, health insurance.

Contact Louis P. Weinberg, Owner, Pocono Highland Camp, 6528 Castor Avenue, Philadelphia, Pennsylvania 19149; 215-533-1557, Fax 215-289-8884. Application deadline: March 1.

SALVATION ARMY OF LOWER BUCKS
APPLETREE DRIVE AND AUTUMN LANE
LEVITTOWN, PENNSYLVANIA 19055

General Information Non-residential summer camp serving 30–35 school children ages 6–12 for all day care (7 a.m. to 6 p.m.) and 30–35 children for half-day care (10 a.m. to 3 p.m.). Camp also hosts other multi-generational programs throughout the year. Established in 1955. Owned by The Salvation Army, Inc. Affiliated with United Way. 4-acre facility located 20 miles north of Philadelphia. Features: residential suburban location; athletic field; fully equipped gymnasium; chapel; craft and recreation rooms; conference rooms.

Profile of Summer Employees Total number: 12; average age: 20; 20% male, 80% female; 10% minorities; 10% high school students; 80% college students; 10% retirees; 90% local residents; 40% teachers. Nonsmokers preferred.

Employment Information Openings are from June 12 to September 1. Christmas break, year-round positions also offered. Jobs available: ► *summer camp counselors* at $6–$7 per hour. International students encouraged to apply; must apply through recognized agency.

Benefits College credit, valuable child care and curriculum experience for education majors, flexible hours, pre-camp training. Preemployment training of 3 days is required and includes safety and accident prevention, group interaction, first-aid, CPR, leadership, camper-counselor relations. Orientation is paid.

Contact Maureen C. Carson, Community Programs Coordinator, Salvation Army of Lower Bucks, Department SJ, Appletree Drive and Autumn Lane, Levittown, Pennsylvania 19055; 215-945-0718, Fax 215-945-0607. Application deadline: May 12.

SHAVER'S CREEK ENVIRONMENTAL CENTER, PENNSYLVANIA STATE UNIVERSITY
508A KELLER BUILDING
UNIVERSITY PARK, PENNSYLVANIA 16802

General Information Environmental education day camp for children ages 6–11, adventure program for children ages 12–17, on-site programs for the general public, outreach within the community, and visitor center which is open daily. Established in 1972. Owned by Pennsylvania State University. Affiliated with Global Network of Environmental Education Centers, Alliance for Environmental Education, Pennsylvania Alliance for Environmental Education. 750-acre facility located 13 miles south of State College. Features: 72-acre lake for boating and aquatic study; Bird of Prey Center with 25 hawks, eagles, and owls; hands-on environmental museum/exhibit room and bookstore; herb gardens and beehive; 25 miles of hiking trails; team building and low ropes course.

Profile of Summer Employees Total number: 6; average age: 20; 50% male, 50% female; 10% minorities; 90% college students; 25% international; 5% local residents; 25% teachers. Nonsmokers preferred.

Employment Information Openings are from June 1 to August 25. Year-round positions also offered. Jobs available: ▶ 6 *environmental education interns* with first aid and CPR certification (preferred) at $125 per week. International students encouraged to apply.

Benefits College credit, on-the-job training, formal ongoing training, on-site room and board at no charge, Macintosh computers on site and access to Internet, use of Pennsylvania State University recreational facilities and health clinic, one- to three-day staff development trips.

Contact Doug Wentzel, Intern Coordinator, Shaver's Creek Environmental Center, Pennsylvania State University, Department SJ, 508A Keller Building, University Park, Pennsylvania 16802; 814-863-2000, Fax 814-865-2706, E-mail djwi05@psu.edu, URL http://www.cde.psu.edu/shaverscreek/. Application deadline: March 1.

SHELLY RIDGE DAY CAMP
330 MANOR ROAD
MIQUON, PENNSYLVANIA 19444

General Information Eight-week day camp for 200 girls ages 6–14. Established in 1975. Owned by Girl Scouts of Southeastern Pennsylvania. Affiliated with Girl Scouts of the United States of America, American Camping Association. 125-acre facility located 5 miles northwest of Philadelphia. Features: large outdoor pool; hiking trails; field; program center; picnic shelters for day use.

Profile of Summer Employees Total number: 60; average age: 25; 5% male, 95% female; 60% minorities; 10% high school students; 70% college students; 5% retirees; 100% local residents; 50% teachers. Nonsmokers preferred.

Employment Information Openings are from June 15 to August 15. Jobs available: ▶ *counselors* with first aid/CPR at $1200–$2000 per season; ▶ *nurse* with RN or EMT at $2000–$2300 per season; ▶ *business manager* with experience at $1800–$2400 per season; ▶ *lifeguards/swim instructors* with WSI or lifeguard training, first aid/CPR at $1200–$2000 per season; ▶ *nature specialist* with experience at $1200–$2000 per season.

Benefits College credit, on-the-job training. Preemployment training is required and includes safety and accident prevention, group interaction, first-aid, CPR, leadership, camper-counselor relations, program planning. Orientation is paid.

Contact Chris Endres, Camp Administrator, Shelly Ridge Day Camp, Department SJ, Girl Scouts of Southeastern Pennsylvania, 100 North 17th Street, 2nd Floor, Philadelphia, Pennsylvania 19103; 215-564-4657, Fax 215-564-6953. Application deadline: May 15.

SPORTS AND ARTS CENTER AT ISLAND LAKE
ISLAND LAKE ROAD
STARRUCCA, PENNSYLVANIA 18462

General Information Residential camp serving 500 campers ages 7–17, with emphasis on individualized programming and a well-rounded program in all sports and performing and visual arts. Established in 1985. Owned by Michael and Beverly Stoltz. Affiliated with American Camping Association, Wayne County Camping Association, Association of Independent Camps. 325-acre facility located 150 miles northwest of New York, New York. Features: 13 outdoor tennis courts; full athletics fields and gymnasium; full-size hockey rink; beach volleyball courts; indoor horseback-riding arena; miles of trails; outdoor pasture; fully equipped theater; 3 rehearsal studios; 3 fully equipped music studios; 2 modern dance studios.

Profile of Summer Employees Total number: 225; average age: 21; 50% male, 50% female; 10% minorities; 85% college students; 1% retirees; 20% international; 1% local residents; 5% teachers. Nonsmokers only.

Employment Information Openings are from June 18 to August 19. Jobs available: ▶ *experienced specialists* (in all areas) at $1300–$1700 per season; ▶ *experienced nurses* at $200–$500 per week; ▶ *doctors* at $700–$1000 per week; ▶ *experienced department heads* at $2500–$8000 per season; ▶ *experienced head counselors* at $3500–$6000 per season; ▶ *swimming instructors* with WSI certification at $1300–$1700 per season.

Benefits College credit, on-the-job training, on-site room and board at no charge, laundry facilities, travel reimbursement, generous time off and no curfew. Preemployment training of 5 days is required and includes safety and accident prevention, group interaction, leadership, camper-counselor relations. Orientation is unpaid.

Contact Matt or Mike Stoltz, Directors, Sports and Arts Center at Island Lake, Department SJ, PO Box 800, Pomona, New York 10970; 914-354-5517, Fax 914-362-3039. Application deadline: May 15.

STREAMSIDE CAMP AND CONFERENCE CENTER
RURAL ROUTE 3 BOX 3307
STROUDSBURG, PENNSYLVANIA 18360

General Information Residential Christian camp with a focus on providing a quality camping experience for inner-city children, youth, and families. Established in 1942. Owned by BCM International, Inc. Operated by Streamside Foundation, Inc. Affiliated with Christian Camping International/USA, American Camping Association, BCM International, Inc. 137-acre facility located 90 miles north of Philadelphia. Features: watersport activities including pool, canoeing, and paddle boating; hiking trails through forest areas; sports fields for soccer, volleyball, baseball, and football; outdoor basketball courts; 300-foot waterslide.

Profile of Summer Employees Total number: 65; average age: 20; 50% male, 50% female; 15% minorities; 25% high school students; 60% college students; 5% retirees; 10% international; 60% local residents; 20% teachers. Nonsmokers only.

Employment Information Openings are from June 15 to August 23. Year-round positions also offered. Jobs available: ▶ *cabin counselor;* ▶ *water safety instructor* with WSI certification; ▶ *kitchen aide* with desire to learn; ▶ *maintenance team worker;* ▶ *dining room worker;* ▶ *program specialist* with ability to teach and relate a specific area of expertise to the Christian daily life; ▶ *lifeguard* with lifeguard certification. All positions offered at $100–$250 per week. International students encouraged to apply; must obtain own visa and working papers prior to employment; must apply through recognized agency.

Benefits On-the-job training, formal ongoing training, on-site room and board at no charge, laundry facilities, travel reimbursement, health insurance, tuition reimbursement, opportunity for service to God and fellow man, multicultural appreciation, leadership development training.

Contact Scott Widman, Streamside Program Director, Streamside Camp and Conference Center, RR #3, Box 3307, Stroudsburg, Pennsylvania 18360; 717-629-1902, Fax 717-629-1902 Ext. 23, E-mail streamsidecamp@juno.com.

SWARTHMORE TENNIS CAMP
SWARTHMORE COLLEGE
SWARTHMORE, PENNSYLVANIA 19081

General Information Tennis instruction for all levels of play for juniors ages 9–17. Additional special programs include high school training, tournament training, and counselor-in-training. Established in 1981. Owned by Lois Broderick. Affiliated with National Camp Association. 325-acre facility located 12 miles southwest of Philadelphia. Features: 6 outdoor tennis courts; fully equipped gym; swimming pool; 3 large sports fields.

Profile of Summer Employees Total number: 6; 70% male, 30% female; 90% college students; 10% teachers. Nonsmokers preferred.

Employment Information Openings are from June 20 to August 12. International students encouraged to apply; must obtain own visa and working papers prior to employment.

Benefits On-site room and board at no charge.

Contact Joe Oyco, Camp Director, Swarthmore Tennis Camp, Department SJ, 1224 Van Woorhis, Townhouse #1, Morgantown, West Virginia 26505; 304-598-2689, E-mail ski10s@imagixx.net.

SWARTHMORE TENNIS CAMP
500 COLLEGE AVENUE
SWARTHMORE, PENNSYLVANIA 19081

General Information Operates both a junior and adult camp from mid-June to mid-August, resident and day campers. 5 hours daily. Adults 3-day, 5-day and weekend programs. Juniors 9–17, coed weekly and multi-week sessions. Established in 1981. Owned by Lois Broderick. Affiliated with National Camp Association. 325-acre facility located 12 miles west of Philadelphia. Features: 12 outdoor tennis courts; fully equipped gym; Olympic-size pool; Nautilus equipment; 3 large sports fields; walking trails.

Profile of Summer Employees 80% male, 20% female; 70% college students. Nonsmokers preferred.

Employment Information Openings are from June 20 to August 10. Jobs available: ▶ 10 *tennis instructors* at $225–$250 per week. International students encouraged to apply; must obtain own visa and working papers prior to employment.

Benefits On-site room and board at no charge. Preemployment training of 3 days is required and includes leadership, tennis instructional program. Orientation is unpaid.

Contact Joe Oyco, Camp Director, Swarthmore Tennis Camp, 1224 Van Woorhis, Townhouse #1, Morgantown, West Virginia 26505; 304-598-2689, E-mail ski10s@imagixx.net. Application deadline: May 1.

YMCA CAMP FITCH
NORTH SPRINGFIELD, PENNSYLVANIA 16430

General Information Traditional residential camp serving 210 campers; special population camp serving 30–70 campers with special needs; specialty camps such as computer, running, and swimming camps serving 30 campers. Established in 1914. Owned by Youngstown, Ohio YMCA. Affiliated with American Camping Association. 450-acre facility located 25 miles west of Erie. Features: 1 mile of lakefront on Lake Erie; swimming pool; large forested areas; extensive sports playing fields; three-acre lake.

Profile of Summer Employees Total number: 100; average age: 18; 50% male, 50% female;

15% minorities; 35% high school students; 65% college students; 10% international; 60% local residents; 5% teachers. Nonsmokers preferred.

Employment Information Openings are from June 10 to September 1. Year-round positions also offered. Jobs available: ▶ *summer camp counselors* at $100–$130 per week; ▶ *special population counselor* at $110–$150 per week; ▶ *kitchen steward* at $150–$175 per week. International students encouraged to apply; must apply through recognized agency.

Benefits On-the-job training, formal ongoing training, on-site room and board at no charge, laundry facilities. Preemployment training of 4 days is required and includes safety and accident prevention, group interaction, first-aid, CPR, leadership, camper-counselor relations. Orientation is unpaid.

Contact Bill Lyder, Executive Camp Director, YMCA Camp Fitch, 17 North Champion Street, Youngstown, Ohio 44501-1287; 330-744-8411, Fax 330-744-8416. Application deadline: May 1.

RHODE ISLAND

UNIVERSITY OF RHODE ISLAND SUMMER PROGRAMS
W. ALTON JONES CAMPUS, 401 VICTORY HIGHWAY
WEST GREENWICH, RHODE ISLAND 02817-2158

General Information Residential facility serving 100 campers for 7 weeks in nature awareness and conservation programs; expedition program for 30 campers for 8 weeks, leading backpacking, kayaking, canoeing, and rock-climbing activities. Established in 1965. Owned by University of Rhode Island. Affiliated with American Camping Association. 2,300-acre facility located 25 miles west of Providence. Features: 2,300 acres of wooded land; 75-acre freshwater lake; organic historical working farm; miles of trails for hiking and mountain biking; housing on site; location surrounded by 40,000 acres of state forests and parks.

Profile of Summer Employees Total number: 40; average age: 21; 50% male, 50% female; 5% minorities; 10% high school students; 90% college students; 15% international; 50% local residents; 5% teachers. Nonsmokers preferred.

Employment Information Openings are from June 15 to August 21. Year-round positions also offered. Jobs available: ▶ *lifeguards* at $160–$180 per week; ▶ *camp EMT or nurse* at $180–$200 per week; ▶ *counselors* at $150–$180 per week; ▶ *expedition leaders* at $180–$200 per week; ▶ *day camp teachers* at $180–$200 per week. International students encouraged to apply; must apply through recognized agency.

Benefits On-the-job training, on-site room and board at no charge, laundry facilities. Preemployment training of 14 days is required and includes safety and accident prevention, group interaction, first-aid, CPR, leadership, camper-counselor relations. Orientation is paid.

Contact John Jacques, Manager, Environmental Education Center, University of Rhode Island Summer Programs, Department SJ, 401 Victory Highway, West Greenwich, Rhode Island 02817; 401-397-3304 Ext. 6043, Fax 401-397-3293, E-mail urieec@uriacc.uri.edu, URL http://www.uri.edu/ajc.

YMCA CAMP FULLER
PO BOX 432
WAKEFIELD, RHODE ISLAND 02880-0432

General Information Residential camp serving 200 campers each session with a focus on saltwater sailing and other aquatic activities. General programs offered to campers ages 7–16. Established in 1887. Owned by Greater Providence YMCA. Affiliated with American Camping Association, YMCA. 40-acre facility located 40 miles south of Providence. Features: extensive saltwater pond frontage for sailing and windsurfing; fourteen 15-foot Gallilees; ten Lasers; rock-climbing tower; two sports fields; high ropes program.

Profile of Summer Employees Total number: 70; average age: 20; 50% male, 50% female; 5% minorities; 20% high school students; 75% college students; 1% international; 50% local residents. Nonsmokers preferred.

Employment Information Openings are from June 15 to August 28. Jobs available: ▶ 10 *senior counselors* (minimum age 19) at $100–$140 per week; ▶ 1 *camp nurse* with RN license at $300–$350 per week; ▶ 2 *experienced division leaders* (minimum age 21) at $150–$200 per week.

Benefits On-the-job training, on-site room and board at no charge, laundry facilities, strengthening of self-confidence and reliability. Preemployment training of 6 days is required and includes safety and accident prevention, group interaction, first-aid, CPR, leadership. Orientation is paid.

Contact Jerry Huncosky, Executive Director, YMCA Camp Fuller, Department SJ, 166 Broad Street, Providence, Rhode Island 02903; 401-521-1470, Fax 401-421-6431. Application deadline: April 30.

SOUTH CAROLINA

CAMP CHATUGA
291 CAMP CHATUGA ROAD
MOUNTAIN REST, SOUTH CAROLINA 29664

General Information Residential coeducational camp serving 155 campers for six weeks. Established in 1956. Owned by Kelly Gordon Moxley. Affiliated with American Camping Association, Association of Independent Camps. 60-acre facility located 100 miles north of Atlanta, Georgia. Features: private 18-acre lake; 20 cabins; 2 large playing fields; horseback-riding ring and stables; indoor recreational facilities; location near the Chattooga River.

Profile of Summer Employees Total number: 45; average age: 21; 50% male, 50% female; 5% minorities; 10% high school students; 75% college students; 5% retirees; 5% international; 50% local residents. Nonsmokers only.

Employment Information Openings are from June 6 to August 4. Jobs available: ▶ *counselor* at $800–$1100 per season; ▶ *junior counselor;* ▶ *waterfront director* with WSI certification at $875–$1200 per season; ▶ *Western horseback riding director* at $875–$1200 per season; ▶ *health supervisor* with CPR/first aid certification (RN preferred) at $1000–$1600 per season; ▶ *nanny* at $1000–$1500 per season; ▶ *program director* at $1000–$1500 per season. International students encouraged to apply; must obtain own visa and working papers prior to employment; must apply through recognized agency.

Benefits College credit, on-the-job training, formal ongoing training, on-site room and board at no charge, laundry facilities, workmen's compensation insurance, off-camp trip. Preemployment training of 7 days is required and includes safety and accident prevention, group interaction, first-aid, CPR, leadership, camper-counselor relations. Orientation is unpaid.

Contact Kelly Moxley, Director/Personnel, Camp Chatuga, 291 Camp Chatuga Road, Mountain Rest, South Carolina 29664; 864-638-3728, Fax 864-638-0898. Application deadline: May 15.

FAIRFIELD OCEAN RIDGE RESORT
101 KING COTTON ROAD
EDISTO ISLAND, SOUTH CAROLINA 29438

General Information Resort offering recreational activities such as fitness walking, biking, line dancing, and water aerobics. Established in 1983. 303-acre facility located 45 miles south of

Charleston. Features: 2 pools; 4 tennis courts; 1 golf course; 7-mile bike trail; beach combing and shelling; state park.

Profile of Summer Employees Total number: 20; average age: 20; 100% college students. Nonsmokers preferred.

Employment Information Openings are from May 1 to September 1. Christmas break, year-round positions also offered. Jobs available: ▶ 20 *recreation attendants* at $4.75–$5.15 per hour.

Benefits . Off-site boarding costs are $350 per month.

Contact Lesa Albright, Recreation Director, Fairfield Ocean Ridge Resort, 1 King Cotton Road, Edisto, South Carolina 29438; 803-869-4533, Fax 803-869-4283. Application deadline: April 1.

KIAWAH ISLAND RESORT
12 KIAWAH BEACH DRIVE
KIAWAH, SOUTH CAROLINA 29455

General Information Resort which offers golf and tennis, accommodations, world-class cuisine, miles of bike trails, pools and parks, children's programs, and nature outings. Established in 1974. Owned by Virginia Investment Trust. 10,000-acre facility located 21 miles west of Charleston. Features: 4 championship golf courses; 28 tennis courts (4 lighted, 23 clay, and 5 hard); 10.6 miles of beach; villa/inn accommodations; 18 miles of paved bicycling and jogging paths; 5 swimming pools.

Profile of Summer Employees Total number: 800; average age: 20; 40% male, 60% female; 40% minorities; 10% high school students; 30% college students; 2% retirees; 70% local residents; 2% teachers. Nonsmokers preferred.

Employment Information Openings are from March 1 to October 31. Spring break, year-round positions also offered. Jobs available: ▶ 40 *servers/bartenders* at $2.50 per hour; ▶ 15 *guest service agents/reservations* at $7–$7.50 per hour; ▶ 10 *tennis/golf shop attendants* at $5.50–$6.50 per hour; ▶ 30 *camp counselors/pool and bike shop attendants* at $5.50–$6.50 per hour; ▶ 40 *room attendants-housekeeping* at $700–$900; ▶ 10 *cooks* at $6–$8 per hour. International students encouraged to apply; must obtain own visa and working papers prior to employment.

Benefits College credit, on-the-job training, formal ongoing training. Off-site boarding costs are $550 per month.

Contact Human Resources Department, Kiawah Island Resort, Department SJ, 12 Kiawah Beach Drive, Kiawah Island, South Carolina 29455; 803-768-6000, Fax 803-768-6061, URL http://www.coolworks.com.

MYRTLE BEACH PAVILION
921 NORTH KINGS HIGHWAY
MYRTLE BEACH, SOUTH CAROLINA 29577

General Information Amusement park with more than forty rides and twenty concession stands. Established in 1948. Owned by Burroughs & Chapin Company, Inc. Affiliated with International Association of Amusement Parks and Attractions, Chamber of Commerce. 12-acre facility located 140 miles east of Columbia. Features: location next to the Atlantic Ocean; The Attic (teenage nightclub); fishing piers; boardwalk along the ocean; gift shops; arcades.

Profile of Summer Employees Total number: 500; average age: 16; 50% male, 50% female; 60% minorities; 70% high school students; 25% college students; 5% retirees; 10% international; 75% local residents; 1% teachers. Nonsmokers preferred.

Employment Information Openings are from February 28 to October 15. Spring break positions also offered. Jobs available: ▶ *ride operators* at $5.55 per hour; ▶ *arcade attendants* at $5.55 per hour; ▶ *games attendants* at $5.55 per hour; ▶ *food service staff (cooks and cashiers)* at $5.75 per hour; ▶ *ride admissions staff* at $5.55 per hour; ▶ *Attic staff (doorman and concessions)* at $5.55 per hour; ▶ *general service staff (custodians)* at $5.55 per hour. International students encouraged to apply; must obtain own visa and working papers prior to employment; must apply through recognized agency.

Benefits On-the-job training, formal ongoing training, on-site room and board, laundry facilities, health insurance, weekly room/board at Oceanic Hotel: quadruple-$35, double-$45.50, single-$45.50, scholarship program.

Contact Scott Radwick, Human Resources Associate, Myrtle Beach Pavilion, PO Box 2095, Myrtle Beach, South Carolina 29578-2095; 803-626-6623, Fax 803-626-8461, E-mail scott. radwick@burroughs-chapin.com.

CAMP THUNDERBIRD
1 THUNDERBIRD LANE
LAKE WYLIE, SOUTH CAROLINA 29710-8811

General Information Coeducational residential camp serving children ages 7–16 during one- and two-week sessions. Established in 1937. Owned by YMCA of Greater Charlotte. Affiliated with American Camping Association, YMCA. 110-acre facility located 12 miles south of Charlotte. Features: 1 mile of shoreline; nature preserve on 110 acres; extensive land and water programs.

Profile of Summer Employees Total number: 130; average age: 20; 55% male, 45% female; 10% minorities; 25% high school students; 75% college students; 5% international; 15% local residents. Nonsmokers preferred.

Employment Information Openings are from June 4 to August 20. Year-round positions also offered. Jobs available: ▶ 2 *outpost instructors* with CPR or first aid training at $160–$200 per week; ▶ 3 *outdoor living skills personnel* at $120–$160 per week; ▶ 4 *experienced waterskiing instructors* with CPR or first aid training at $120–$160 per week; ▶ 4 *challenge course instructors* with CPR or first aid training at $120–$160 per week; ▶ 5 *experienced English-style riding instructors* at $120–$160 per week; ▶ 1 *experienced horseback riding chief* with CHA certification at $180–$210 per week; ▶ 2 *riflery instructors* at $120–$160 per week; ▶ 2 *archery instructors* at $120–$160 per week; ▶ 4 *swimming instructors* with lifeguard training (YMCA or ARC) and YMCA progressive instructor or WSI certification at $120–$160 per week; ▶ 4 *experienced canoeing instructors* with American Red Cross certification at $120–$160 per week; ▶ 5 *experienced sailing instructors* at $120–$160 per week; ▶ 2 *golf instructors* at $120–$160 per week; ▶ 4 *experienced gymnastics instructors* at $120–$160 per week; ▶ 3 *dance/aerobics/ cheerleading/in-line skating instructors* at $120–$160 per week; ▶ 6 *general athletics instructors* at $120–$160 per week; ▶ *roller hockey instructors* at $120–$160 per week.

Benefits On-the-job training, on-site room and board at no charge. Preemployment training of 7 days is required and includes safety and accident prevention, group interaction, leadership, camper-counselor relations, diversity awareness. Orientation is paid.

Contact Sloane Frantz, Associate Camp Director, Camp Thunderbird, Department SJ, 1 Thunderbird Lane, Lake Wylie, South Carolina 29710-8811; 803-831-2121, Fax 803-831-2977, URL http://campthunderbird.com. Application deadline: February 28.

WILD DUNES
5757 PALM BOULEVARD
ISLE OF PALMS, SOUTH CAROLINA 29451

General Information Resort offering summer recreational programs for all age groups who are guests at the resort. Established in 1976. Owned by Lowe Enterprises. 1,700-acre facility located 26 miles north of Charleston. Features: 2.5 miles of pristine beaches; two 18-hole golf courses; 17 tennis courts; conference center for up to 350; full children's recreation program.

Profile of Summer Employees Total number: 25; average age: 19; 100% college students.

Employment Information Openings are from May 16 to September 3. Year-round positions also offered. Jobs available: ▶ 25 *recreational interns* with CPR certification at $150 per month. International students encouraged to apply; must obtain own visa and working papers prior to employment; must apply through recognized agency.

Benefits College credit, on-the-job training, formal ongoing training, laundry facilities, free off-site room and board.

Contact Eric Carlson, Recreation Manager, Wild Dunes, Department SJ, 5757 Palm Boulevard, Isle of Palms, South Carolina 29451; 803-886-2300, Fax 803-886-2171, URL http://www. wilddunes.com.

SOUTH DAKOTA

AMERICAN PRESIDENTS RESORT
HIGHWAY 16A
CUSTER, SOUTH DAKOTA 57730

General Information Resort consisting of cabins, campground, and motel units rented nightly from mid-May to mid-September. Established in 1950. Owned by Jan Charles Gray. Affiliated with South Dakota Campground Owners' Association, Black Hills Badlands and Lakes Association, South Dakota Innkeepers' Association. 12-acre facility located 40 miles south of Rapid City. Features: large outdoor heated swimming pool; 10-person Jacuzzi spa; 12-hole miniature golf course; playground; arcade and game room; horseshoes, volleyball, and basketball facilities.
Profile of Summer Employees Total number: 50; average age: 25; 20% male, 80% female; 35% high school students; 35% college students; 10% retirees; 50% local residents; 20% teachers.
Employment Information Openings are from May 1 to September 8. Jobs available: ▶ 10 *desk clerks* at $5–$6 per hour; ▶ 20 *maids* at $5–$6 per hour; ▶ 5 *laundry workers* at $5–$6 per hour.
Benefits On-the-job training, on-site room and board at $125 per month, laundry facilities, free pass to many tourist attractions, access to all resort facilities. Preemployment training of 1 day is required and includes visitor relations. Orientation is paid.
Contact Ione Fejfar, Manager, American Presidents Resort, Department SJ, PO Box 446, Custer, South Dakota 57730; 605-673-3373, Fax 605-673-3449. Application deadline: April 1.

CUSTER STATE PARK RESORT COMPANY
HC 83, BOX 74
CUSTER, SOUTH DAKOTA 57730

General Information Operator of four resorts offering services such as lodging, dining, groceries, gas, and souvenirs and gifts as well as activities that include trail rides, jeep tours, and cookouts. Established in 1919. Owned by Wild Phil's, Inc. Affiliated with South Dakota Restaurant Association, South Dakota Retailers Association, South Dakota Innkeepers' Association, Industry and Commerce Association of South Dakota, National Tour Association, American Bus Association. 73,000-acre facility located 30 miles south of Rapid City. Features: world's largest public buffalo herd; scenic mountain and plains area site; proximity to Mount Rushmore National Memorial (20 miles); location in the Black Hills; buffalo safari jeep tours to observe wildlife and scenery; buffalo round-up, sorting, and branding every October.
Profile of Summer Employees Total number: 300; average age: 20; 35% male, 65% female; 15% minorities; 10% high school students; 50% college students; 20% retirees; 1% international; 20% local residents. Nonsmokers preferred.
Employment Information Openings are from April 15 to October 30. Jobs available: ▶ 35 *sales clerks* at $750–$800 per month; ▶ 45 *waitpersons* at $600–$750 per month; ▶ 10 *cooks/ chefs* at $800–$1400 per month; ▶ 15 *cook's assistants* at $750–$950 per month; ▶ 8 *kitchen/ food preparation personnel* at $750–$950 per month; ▶ 50 *housekeeping personnel* at $750– $950 per month; ▶ 17 *front desk/reservations personnel* at $800–$1000 per month; ▶ 5 *hosts/ hostesses* at $800–$900 per month; ▶ 6 *maintenance personnel* at $800–$1000 per month; ▶ 5 *jeep drivers* (minimum age 21) with clean driving record at $750–$900 per month; ▶ 8 *wranglers* at $800–$1000 per month; ▶ 4 *bookkeepers* at $800–$1000 per month; ▶ 5 *bartenders* (minimum age 21) at $650–$800 per month; ▶ 3 *manager trainees* with desire to learn the resort business at $1000–$1200 per month; ▶ 18 *dishwashers/buspersons* at $750–$800 per month.
Benefits College credit, on-the-job training, formal ongoing training, on-site room and board, laundry facilities, tuition reimbursement, internships, scholarship bonuses, room/board costs $450 per month and is part of compensation. Off-site boarding costs are $750 per month.

Preemployment training of 1 to 3 days is required and includes safety and accident prevention, group interaction, first-aid, CPR. Orientation is paid.

Contact Phil Lampert, President, Custer State Park Resort Company, Department SJ, HC 83, Box 74, Custer, South Dakota 57730; 605-255-4541, Fax 605-255-4706, URL http://www.coolworks.com/showme/custer/. Application deadline: June 1.

PALMER GULCH RESORT/MT. RUSHMORE KOA
HILL CITY, SOUTH DAKOTA 57745

General Information Full-service resort located 5 miles west of Mount Rushmore. Established in 1972. Owned by Satellite Cable Services, Inc. Affiliated with South Dakota Campground Owners' Association, South Dakota Innkeepers' Association, Black Hills, Badlands, and Lakes Association. 150-acre facility located 25 miles south of Rapid City. Features: campsites, cabins, and lodge motel; cafe; horses; 2 large heated pools and waterslide; shuttle buses; proximity to Mount Rushmore National Memorial, Elk Wilderness Area, Crazy Horse Memorial, and Custer State Park.

Profile of Summer Employees Total number: 85; average age: 22; 50% male, 50% female; 5% minorities; 30% high school students; 40% college students; 30% retirees; 40% local residents; 5% teachers. Nonsmokers preferred.

Employment Information Openings are from April 1 to October 1. Jobs available: ▶ 10 *campground registration office/store personnel* at $210–$235 per week; ▶ 10 *maintenance personnel* at $210–$235 per week; ▶ 3 *reservations staff members* at $210–$235 per week; ▶ 10 *housekeeping staff members* at $210–$235 per week; ▶ 4 *waterslide staff members* with lifesaving, CPR, or first aid certification at $210–$235 per week; ▶ *motel reservations and registration staff members* at $220–$240 per week.

Benefits On-the-job training, formal ongoing training, on-site room and board at $25 per week, laundry facilities, free admission to Black Hills attractions, free use of resort recreation facilities, bonus given to employees who stay through Labor Day and special employee activities. Preemployment training of 1 day is optional and includes first-aid, CPR, hospitality/customer service. Orientation is paid.

Contact Mr. Al Johnson, General Manager, Palmer Gulch Resort/Mt. Rushmore KOA, Department SJ, Box 295, Hill City, South Dakota 57745; 605-574-2525, Fax 605-574-2574, E-mail mtrushal@aol.com.

TENNESSEE

CAMP TANNASSIE
ROUTE 4, BOX 4174
TULLAHOMA, TENNESSEE 37388

General Information Residential summer camp where girls enjoy swimming, canoeing, sailing, waterskiing, snorkeling, arts and crafts, and traditional Girl Scout programs. Established in 1960. Operated by Girl Scouts of Cumberland Valley. Affiliated with American Camping Association, Girls Scouts of the United States of America. 37-acre facility located 10 miles southeast of Nashville. Features: located on non-residential, non-commercial lake; fully equipped lodge; 4 pavilions; Sunfish, canoes, and other waterfront equipment.

Profile of Summer Employees Total number: 10; average age: 22; 2% male, 98% female; 25% minorities; 99% college students; 1% retirees; 5% international; 10% local residents; 10% teachers. Nonsmokers preferred.

Employment Information Openings are from May 1 to August 1. Jobs available: ▶ *swimming* *instructors* at $600 per month; ▶ *lifeguards* at $600 per month; ▶ *canoeing instructors* at $600 per month; ▶ *sailing instructors* at $600 per month; ▶ *waterskiing instructors* at $600 per month; ▶ *administrative staff* at $800 per month. International students encouraged to apply; must obtain own visa and working papers prior to employment.

Benefits   College credit, on-the-job training, on-site room and board at no charge, health insurance, during optional, unpaid, preseason program, the opportunity to acquire national certification in the following: lifeguarding, ropes, archery, equestrian, canoeing, and community first aid and safety. Preemployment training of 6 days is required and includes safety and accident prevention, group interaction, first-aid, CPR, leadership, camper-counselor relations. Orientation is paid.

Contact   Nancy Simms Caukin, Outdoor Program Director, Camp Tannassie, Department SJ, PO Box 40466, Nashville, Tennessee 37204; 800-395-5318 Ext. 252, Fax 615-383-2288. Application deadline: May 1.

CHEROKEE ADVENTURES WHITEWATER RAFTING
2000 JONESBOROUGH ROAD
ERWIN, TENNESSEE 37650-9524

General Information   Guided rafting and mountain-biking trips; also ropes course emphasizing team building and camping. Established in 1979. Owned by Dennis I. Nedelman. Affiliated with America Outdoors. 50-acre facility located 18 miles south of Johnson City. Features: location 1.25 hours from Asheville, North Carolina; proximity to Cherokee National Forest; proximity to the Nolichucky River; sand volleyball court.

Profile of Summer Employees   Total number: 20; average age: 25; 60% male, 40% female; 40% college students; 2% international; 58% local residents. Nonsmokers preferred.

Employment Information   Openings are from May 15 to September 16. Spring break positions also offered. Jobs available: ▶ 6 *raft guides* with responsible, outgoing personalities and Red Cross first aid/CPR certification (salary begins after training completed) at $400–$600 per month; ▶ 1 *grounds/maintenance person* at $4.25–$5 per hour; ▶ 2 *cooks/cleaning staff members* with ability to prepare lunches and perform general cleaning at $4.25–$5 per hour; ▶ 1 *reservationist/general office person* with good phone manner and the ability to type 50 wpm at $4.25–$5.50 per hour. International students encouraged to apply; must obtain own visa and working papers prior to employment.

Benefits   On-the-job training, white-water training provided to guides, including safety, rescue, water-craft guiding, and first aid, white-water trips, camping on the property available with common room and cooking area at $25 per month, bunkhouses at $35 per month. Off-site boarding costs are $300 per month.

Contact   Dennis I. Nedelman, President, Cherokee Adventures Whitewater Rafting, Department SJ, 2000 Jonesborough Road, Erwin, Tennessee 37650-9524; 423-743-7733, Fax 423-743-5400. Application deadline: April 30.

GIRL SCOUT CAMP SYCAMORE HILLS
BOX 40466
NASHVILLE, TENNESSEE 37204

General Information   ACA-accredited residential camp serving 200 girls per session with swimming, canoeing, archery, arts and crafts, ropes and rappelling, horseback programs, and trip and travel programs. Established in 1959. Owned by Cumberland Valley Girl Scout Council. Affiliated with American Camping Association. 742-acre facility located 35 miles northwest of Nashville. Features: wooded rolling hills; covered riding arena; unique dining barn; rappelling cliffs and hiking trails; team challenge course with high and low elements; creek for canoeing through camp.

Profile of Summer Employees   Total number: 60; average age: 20; 1% male, 99% female; 2% minorities; 90% college students; 10% local residents. Nonsmokers preferred.

Employment Information   Openings are from June 1 to July 31. Jobs available: ▶ 1 *assistant* *camp director* with Girl Scout residential camp experience at $700–$1100 per month; ▶ 1 *unit coordinator* with Girl Scout residential camp experience at $600–$1000 per month; ▶ 1 *business manager* with accounting training at $600–$1000 per month; ▶ 1 *health supervisor* with RN or paramedic certification at $600–$1000 per month; ▶ *ropes and rappelling director* at $600–$1000 per month; ▶ 8 *experienced equestrian counselors* at $480–$640 per month; ▶ 2 *waterfront directors* with lifeguard and WSI certification at $520–$800 per month; ▶ 2 *waterfront counselors* with lifeguard training at $480–$640 per month; ▶ 2 *rappelling and ropes staff members* with at least two years of experience at $480–$640 per month; ▶ 2 *experienced arts and crafts staff members* at $480–$640 per month; ▶ 1 *certified canoeing director* at $520–$800 per month; ▶ 1 *nature director* with background in the field at $480–$640 per month; ▶ 9 *unit leaders* at $520–$800 per month; ▶ 18 *unit counselors* at $440–$560 per month; ▶ 1 *counselor-in-training director* with Girl Scout residential camp experience at $520–$800 per month. International students encouraged to apply; must apply through recognized agency.

Benefits On-the-job training, on-site room and board at no charge, laundry facilities, health insurance, free certification in some areas. Preemployment training of 7 days is required and includes safety and accident prevention, group interaction, first-aid, CPR, leadership, camper-counselor relations, psychology, Girl Scout programs, child abuse prevention. Orientation is paid.

Contact Outdoor Program Manager, Girl Scout Camp Sycamore Hills, Department SJ, Box 40466, Nashville, Tennessee 37204; 800-395-5318, Fax 615-383-2288. Application deadline: May 27.

OPRYLAND
2802 OPRYLAND DRIVE
NASHVILLE, TENNESSEE 37214

General Information Convention hotel, 120-acre theme park, 18-hole championship golf course, river showboat, tour company, concert hall and theater, The Grand Ole Opry, river taxis, and campground. Established in 1971. Owned by Gaylord Entertainment Company. Features: Opryland Hotel–3000 guest rooms, 8 acres of indoor gardens, 600,000 square-foot convention/meeting space; 30 retail shops; Opryland Theme Park–120 acre musical theme park with rides and musical shows/entertainment; Springhouse Golf Club at Opryland–18 hole links-style course, home of BellSouth Senior Classic; General Jackson Showboat–capacity of 600+ guests, year-round day and evening dinner cruise with musical show; Grand Ole Opry Tours–daily tour packages of Nashville and surrounding areas; Opryland River Taxis to downtown Nashville area.

Profile of Summer Employees Total number: 3,000; average age: 18.

Employment Information Openings are from February 24 to December 31. Spring break, winter break, Christmas break, year-round positions also offered. Jobs available: ▶ *various positions*. International students encouraged to apply; must obtain own visa and working papers prior to employment.

Benefits On-the-job training, on-site room and board at $50 per week, laundry facilities, discounts, free passes, uniforms provided and cleaned free of charge, advancement opportunities. Off-site boarding costs are $50 per week. Preemployment training of 1 day is required and includes safety and accident prevention, group interaction. Orientation is paid.

Contact Employment Manager, Opryland USA, Opryland, Department SJ, 2802 Opryland Drive, Nashville, Tennessee 37214; 615-871-7831, Fax 615-871-7638.

TEXAS

CAMP BALCONES SPRINGS
HCO4, BOX 349
MARBLE FALLS, TEXAS 78654

General Information Christian residential camp offering sports, ropes course, outdoor, fine arts, and water sports to 230 young boys and girls ages 8–15 every week in the Texas hill country. Established in 1993. Owned by Bo and Steve Baskin. 300-acre facility located 40 miles northwest of Austin. Features: 8-acre private spring fed lake; extensive waterfront on Texas' Lake Travis; ropes course; 4 outdoor lighted tennis courts; 200 acres wooded hill country; 2 large sports fields.

Profile of Summer Employees Total number: 80; average age: 21; 50% male, 50% female; 20% minorities; 2% high school students; 75% college students; 10% international; 40% local residents; 5% teachers. Nonsmokers only.

Employment Information Openings are from May 20 to August 15. Jobs available: ► 6 *experienced swimming instructors* with WSI and lifeguard certification; ► 7 *horseback instructors* with English riding experience; ► 1 *arts and crafts instructor* with art background; ► 3 *experienced sailing/windsurfing instructors;* ► 3 *experienced archery/riflery instructors* with NRA and NAA certification; ► *sports instructors* with strong experience in particular specialty sport required; ► 26 *cabin leaders;* ► *backpacking staff* with strong wilderness experience; ► *mountain climbing staff* with climbing experience; free or sport. All positions offered at $1450–$1500 per season. International students encouraged to apply; must obtain own visa and working papers prior to employment.

Benefits On-the-job training, formal ongoing training, on-site room and board at no charge, health insurance, leadership skills, social skills, Christian environment. Preemployment training of 7 days is required and includes safety and accident prevention, group interaction, first-aid, CPR, leadership, camper-counselor relations. Orientation is unpaid.

Contact Mike Burk, Personnel/Head Counselor, Camp Balcones Springs, Department SJ, HCO 4, Box 349, Marble Falls, Texas 70654; 800-775-9785, Fax 210-693-6478, E-mail balcones@tstar.net. Application deadline: April 1.

CAMP CABO RIO FOR BOYS
MO RANCH
HUNT, TEXAS 78024

General Information Residential camp and conference center serving boys ages 10–15 in two 3-week sessions. Established in 1949. Owned by Presbyterian Mo Ranch Assembly. 434-acre facility located 90 miles west of San Antonio. Features: 1 mile of riverfront; 3 tennis courts; Mexican-tile swimming pool; riding trails; river slide; historic ranch buildings.

Profile of Summer Employees Total number: 8; average age: 21; 99% male, 1% female; 20% minorities; 70% college students. Nonsmokers preferred.

Employment Information Openings are from June 3 to July 27. Year-round positions also offered. Jobs available: ► 4 *counselors/instructors* at $1000–$1200 per season; ► 1 *swimming instructor* at $1200 per season; ► *horseback instructor* at $1200 per season. International students encouraged to apply; must obtain own visa and working papers prior to employment; must apply through recognized agency.

Benefits On-the-job training, on-site room and board at no charge, laundry facilities.

Contact Jerri Petmecky, Assistant Program Director, Camp Cabo Rio for Boys, Department SJ, Route 1, Box 158, Hunt, Texas 78024; 800-460-4401, Fax 830-238-4202. Application deadline: April 1.

CAMP EL TESORO
2700 MEACHAM BOULEVARD
FORT WORTH, TEXAS 76137

General Information Residential camp for boys and girls ages 6–16. Established in 1934. Owned by First Texas Council of Camp Fire. Affiliated with American Camping Association, Camping Association for Mutual Progress, Granbury Chamber of Commerce. 228-acre facility located 45 miles southwest of Fort Worth. Features: 2 swimming pools; 20 horses with barn and arena; location on Brazos River; creek with suspension bridge; extensive hiking trails; screened and enclosed cabins.

Profile of Summer Employees Total number: 50; average age: 21; 40% male, 60% female; 12% minorities; 8% high school students; 86% college students; 50% local residents. Nonsmokers preferred.

Employment Information Openings are from May 28 to August 15. Jobs available: ▶ 20 *cabin counselors* with one year of college at $75–$150 per week; ▶ 4 *horseback staff members* with CHA certification (preferred) at $80–$150 per week; ▶ 4 *waterfront staff members* with lifeguard, CPR, and first aid certification at $80–$150 per week; ▶ 4 *kitchen staff members* at $135–$200 per week; ▶ 1 *experienced program director* at $100–$225 per week; ▶ 3 *unit coordinators* with supervisory experience at $100–$225 per week; ▶ 1 *arts and crafts director* at $75–$200 per week; ▶ 4 *special needs staff members* with one year of college at $75–$150 per week. International students encouraged to apply; must obtain own visa and working papers prior to employment.

Benefits On-the-job training, on-site room and board at no charge, laundry facilities, health insurance. Preemployment training of 6 days is required and includes safety and accident prevention, group interaction, first-aid, CPR, leadership, camper-counselor relations, activity instruction. Orientation is paid.

Contact Laurie Johnston, Camp Director, Camp El Tesoro, Department SJ, 2700 Meacham Boulevard, Fort Worth, Texas 76137; 817-831-2111, Fax 817-831-5070. Application deadline: May 1.

CAMP FERN
ROUTE 4, BOX 584
MARSHALL, TEXAS 75670-9441

General Information Residential camp providing fun, adventure, learning, self-esteem development, and lasting friendships. Established in 1934. Owned by Mrs. Peggy Rotzler. Affiliated with State of Texas Department of Health Resources, Camping Association for Mutual Progress, National Rifle Association, Camp Archery Association. 100-acre facility located 8 miles north of Marshall. Features: 100-acre private lake for swimming; ropes course with 15 low and 10 high elements; specialized clinics in basketball and skeet shooting; nature and campcraft with outpost camp in wilderness for backpacking and overnight camping; boxing and weight-training facilities; 30-horse stable, jump course, 400 acres of trails, and English horseback-riding program.

Profile of Summer Employees Total number: 60; average age: 21; 100% college students. Nonsmokers preferred.

Employment Information Openings are from June 1 to August 15. Jobs available: ▶ *waterfront staff members* with WSI, lifeguard, and CPR certification; ▶ *certified ropes course staff members;* ▶ *English horseback riding staff members;* ▶ *riflery staff members;* ▶ *crafts staff members;* ▶ *tennis staff members.* All positions offered at $500 per month.

Benefits On-the-job training, on-site room and board at no charge, laundry facilities, preemployment training.

Contact Margaret R. Thompson, Director, Camp Fern, Route 4, Box 584, Marshall, Texas 75670-9441; 903-935-5420, Fax 903-935-6372. Application deadline: April 5.

CAMP LA JUNTA
PO BOX 136
HUNT, TEXAS 78024

General Information Private residential camp with a focus on individual lifetime activities serving 200 boys in two- or four-week terms. Established in 1928. Owned by Lawrence L. Graham. Affiliated with Camping Association for Mutual Progress. 150-acre facility located 75 miles northwest of San Antonio. Features: 1 mile of riverfront; traditional stone and wood floors in cabins; adjacent 500-acre game ranch; 6 athletics fields; 4 tennis courts.

Profile of Summer Employees Total number: 50; average age: 21; 90% male, 10% female; 5% minorities; 100% college students; 5% international; 25% local residents. Nonsmokers only.

Employment Information Openings are from June 1 to August 15. Jobs available: ▶ *junior counselors* (age 18 and up) at $500–$600 per month; ▶ *senior counselors* (age 21 and up) at $600–$700 per month.

Benefits On-the-job training, formal ongoing training, on-site room and board at no charge, laundry facilities. Preemployment training of 5 days is required and includes safety and accident prevention, group interaction, first-aid, CPR, leadership, camper-çounselor relations, teaching skills. Orientation is paid.

Contact Blake W. Smith, Director, Camp La Junta, Department SJ, PO Box 136, Hunt, Texas 78024; 210-238-4621, Fax 210-238-4888, E-mail lajunta@ktc.com, URL http://www.umr.edu/guadagno/lajunta/. Application deadline: May 1.

CAMP RIO VISTA FOR BOYS
HCR 78, BOX 215
INGRAM, TEXAS 78025

General Information Private residential camp providing 100–150 boys, ages 6–16, with a fun-filled learning experience in a safe, wholesome environment. Established in 1921. Owned by The Hawkins Family. Affiliated with Camping Association for Mutual Progress, Chamber of Commerce, National Federation of Independent Businesses. 120-acre facility located 70 miles north of San Antonio. Features: over 1 mile of Guadalupe River frontage in the Texas hill country; 6 tennis courts (2 lighted); 3 hole chip and putt golf course; rock buildings and cabins with electricity; ropes course and climbing wall; large rock gymnasium.

Profile of Summer Employees Total number: 45; average age: 25; 100% male; 5% minorities; 10% high school students; 85% college students; 5% international; 2% local residents; 5% teachers. Nonsmokers preferred.

Employment Information Openings are from May 30 to August 15. Jobs available: ▶ 2 *swimming instructors* with WSI certification; ▶ 40 *cabin/activity counselors*. All positions offered at $120–$150 per week. International students encouraged to apply; must obtain own visa and working papers prior to employment; must apply through recognized agency.

Benefits On-site room and board at no charge, health insurance.

Contact Freddie Hawkins, Director, Camp Rio Vista for Boys, Department SJ, HCR 78, Box 215, Ingram, Texas 78025; 210-367-5353, Fax 210-367-4044. Application deadline: March 15.

CAMP SIERRA VISTA FOR GIRLS
HCR 78, BOX 215
INGRAM, TEXAS 78025

General Information Private residential camp for girls ages 6–16. Provides a safe, wholesome, fun-filled, learning experience to 75–90 girls per term. Established in 1982. Owned by The Hawkins Family. Affiliated with Camping Association for Mutual Progress, Chamber of Commerce, National Federation of Independent Businesses. 120-acre facility located 70 miles north of San Antonio. Features: 1 mile of Guadalupe River frontage; 6 outdoor tennis courts (2 lighted); extensive acreage for sports and activities; rock cabins with electricity and connected bathrooms; three-hole chip and putt golf course; wooded Texas hill country.

Profile of Summer Employees Total number: 30; average age: 22; 100% female; 5% minorities; 10% high school students; 85% college students; 10% international; 5% local residents; 5% teachers. Nonsmokers preferred.

Employment Information Openings are from May 30 to August 1. Jobs available: ▶ 25 *cabin/activity counselors* with enjoyment of children; wholesomeness as role models at $120–$150 per week; ▶ 2 *office staff members* at $100–$125 per week; ▶ 2 *nurses* with LVN, RN, or EMT certification at $200–$250 per week; ▶ 2 *swimming instructors* with WSI certification at $120–$150 per week. International students encouraged to apply; must obtain own visa and working papers prior to employment; must apply through recognized agency.

Benefits On-site room and board at no charge, health insurance. Preemployment training of 5 to 6 days is required and includes safety and accident prevention, group interaction, first-aid, CPR, leadership, camper-counselor relations, WSI and lifesaving training. Orientation is unpaid.

Contact Freddie Hawkins, Director, Camp Sierra Vista for Girls, Department SJ, Vista Camps, HCR 78, Box 215, Ingram, Texas 78025; 830-367-5353, Fax 830-367-4044, E-mail fhawkins@ktc.com, URL http://www.ktc.net/vistacamps. Application deadline: March 15.

CAMP STEWART FOR BOYS
ROUTE 1, BOX 110
HUNT, TEXAS 78024-9714

General Information Traditional camp offering a fun, challenging program to 250 boys for fourteen- to twenty-eight-day programs. Established in 1924. Owned by Mr. and Mrs. Silas B. Ragsdale, Jr. Affiliated with Christian Camping International/USA, Camping Association for Mutual Progress, American Horse Show Association, American Tennis Association. 522-acre facility located 80 miles northwest of San Antonio. Features: 1-mile frontage on headwaters of Guadalupe River for all aquatic activities; 7 tennis courts; hardwood floor gymnasium; weight room; extensive riding trails and jump fields; climbing wall; challenge course; 7 baseball fields, 4 soccer fields, and 1 football field.

Profile of Summer Employees Total number: 80; average age: 24; 90% male, 10% female; 10% minorities; 86% college students; 10% international; 2% local residents; 2% teachers. Nonsmokers only.

Employment Information Openings are from May 25 to August 15. Jobs available: ▶ 10 *riding instructors* with ability to take clinic at Stewart (required) at $1000–$2000 per season; ▶ 8 *swimming instructors* with WSI certification at $1000–$2000 per season; ▶ 2 *tennis instructors* at $1000–$2000 per season; ▶ 2 *crafts instructors* at $1000–$2000 per season; ▶ 4 *sports personnel* at $1000–$2000 per season; ▶ 2 *riflery instructors* with NRA certification at $1000–$2000 per season; ▶ 2 *archery instructors* at $1000–$2000 per season; ▶ 3 *certified rock climbing instructors* at $1000–$2000 per season; ▶ 2 *certified challenge course instructors* at $1000–$2000 per season; ▶ 1 *band leader* at $1000–$2000 per season; ▶ 2 *secretaries* at $1000–$2000 per season; ▶ 12 *kitchen personnel* at $1000–$3000 per season; ▶ 24 *general counselors* with leadership ability and good moral character at $1000–$2000 per season. International students encouraged to apply; must apply through recognized agency.

Benefits College credit, on-the-job training, on-site room and board at no charge, health insurance, clothing (shirts and shorts), accident insurance.

Contact Kathy C. Ragsdale, Co-Director, Camp Stewart for Boys, Department SJ, Route 1, Box 110, Hunt, Texas 78024-9714; 830-238-4670, Fax 830-238-4737, E-mail info@campstewart.com, URL http://www.campstewart.com.

CAMP VAL VERDE
BOX 25, ROUTE 2
MCGREGOR, TEXAS 76657

General Information Residential camp serving 75–100 campers, some economically disadvantaged and others from foster homes, for one-week sessions. Established in 1948. Owned by Tejas Council of Camp Fire, Inc. Affiliated with American Camping Association. 397-acre facility located 12 miles west of Waco. Features: 1 mile of riverfront; small lake; swimming pool; 20 horses; abundant wildlife; ropes course.

Profile of Summer Employees Total number: 30; average age: 20; 34% male, 66% female; 2% minorities; 1% high school students; 97% college students; 20% local residents. Nonsmokers preferred.

Employment Information Openings are from May 28 to July 13. Jobs available: ▶ 25 *counselors* at $650–$800 per season; ▶ 4 *lifeguards* with lifeguard certification at $650–$800 per season; ▶ 2 *horseback instructors* at $650–$800 per season; ▶ 1 *nurse* with nursing degree at $800–$1000 per season.

Benefits On-site room and board at no charge.

Contact Matt Meares, Camp Coordinator, Camp Val Verde, Department SJ, 1826 Morrow, Waco, Texas 76657; 817-752-5515, Fax 817-752-0088. Application deadline: May 15.

CAMP WALDEMAR
ROUTE 1, BOX 120
HUNT, TEXAS 78024

General Information Private residential girls camp offering sports, arts, and drama activities. Established in 1926. Owned by Marsha Elmore. Affiliated with National Rifle Association, C.A.M.P. (Texas Camp Association), Association for Horsemanship Safety and Education. 560-acre facility located 80 miles north of San Antonio. Features: 8 outdoor tennis courts (4 lighted); 2 large sports fields; 8-10 miles of riding trails; 1 mile of frontage on a river which is spring-fed, clear, and cool; location in Texas hill country with rivers, hills, and trees.

Profile of Summer Employees Total number: 220; average age: 30; 30% male, 70% female; 20% minorities; 10% high school students; 50% college students; 5% retirees; 12% international; 3% local residents; 20% teachers. Nonsmokers preferred.

Employment Information Openings are from May 31 to July 15. Jobs available: ▶ 10 *riding teachers or wranglers* with English or Western equitation horsemanship; ▶ *tennis staff members* with varsity high school or college experience; ▶ *rifle staff members* with NRA certification; ▶ *gymnastics/trampoline staff members;* ▶ *fencing staff members* with college team playing experience; ▶ *arts and crafts* (ceramics, jewelry, and weaving) *staff members* with college or teaching experience; ▶ 16 *swimming/diving instructors* with WSI certification. All positions offered at $450–$700 per month. International students encouraged to apply; must obtain own visa and working papers prior to employment; must apply through recognized agency.

Benefits College credit, on-the-job training, on-site room and board at no charge, laundry facilities, travel reimbursement, health insurance, job references. Preemployment training of 2 to 4 days is required and includes safety and accident prevention, group interaction, first-aid, CPR, leadership, camper-counselor relations, W.S.I., lifeguard, rifle, horsemanship, canoe. Orientation is unpaid.

Contact Marsha Elmore, Owner/Director, Camp Waldemar, Department SJ, Route 1, Box 120, Hunt, Texas 78024; 830-238-4821, Fax 830-238-4051. Application deadline: March 15.

LAZY HILLS GUEST RANCH
INGRAM, TEXAS 78025

General Information Resort ranch catering to families and groups. Established in 1960. Owned by Bob and Carol Steinruck. Affiliated with Texas Hotel and Motel Association, Texas Restaurant Association, Kerrville Chamber of Commerce. 750-acre facility located 75 miles northwest of San Antonio. Features: junior Olympic swimming pool; 2 lighted tennis courts; hot tub; 3 large, spring-fed fishing ponds; game room with pool tables, Ping-Pong tables, and video games; children's playground; wading pool.

Profile of Summer Employees Total number: 10; average age: 20; 20% male, 80% female; 10% minorities; 25% high school students; 75% college students. Nonsmokers preferred.

Employment Information Openings are from May 1 to August 1. Year-round positions also offered. Jobs available: ▶ 1 *activities director* with enthusiasm and ability to work well with children and adults; ▶ 5 *waiters/waitresses;* ▶ 2 *wranglers* with Red Cross certification; ▶ 1 *office worker* with computer experience. All positions offered at $500–$600 per month.

Benefits College credit, on-the-job training, on-site room and board at no charge, laundry facilities, tips.

Contact Mindy Ferguson, Office Manager, Lazy Hills Guest Ranch, Department SJ, Box G, Ingram, Texas 78025; 210-367-5600, Fax 210-367-5667. Application deadline: March 1.

LONGHORN TENNIS CAMP
IAW BELLMONT 718
AUSTIN, TEXAS 78712-1286

General Information Coed tennis camp for juniors ages 10–17. Provides group instruction, video tape analysis of strokes, mental and physical conditioning, private lessons, and team competition. Established in 1986. Owned by University of Texas. Affiliated with United States Tennis Association, Texas Tennis Association. Features: use of facilities at the University of Texas; location in Austin, the capital of Texas; 12 courts at the Penick-Allison Tennis Center.

Profile of Summer Employees Total number: 20; average age: 28; 60% male, 40% female; 50% college students; 50% teachers. Nonsmokers only.

Employment Information Openings are from May 30 to July 4. Jobs available: ▶ *tennis instructors/counselors* with collegiate tennis and tennis teaching experience (physical education background, CPR, and first aid helpful) at $250–$300 per week.

Benefits On-the-job training, on-site room and board at no charge, opportunity to work with two top collegiate coaches.

Contact Bob Haugen, Coordinator, Longhorn Tennis Camp, IAW Bellmont 718, Austin, Texas 78712-1286; 512-471-4404, Fax 512-471-0794, URL http://www.utexas.edu/athletics/camps/tennis.

Y. O. ADVENTURE CAMP
HC 01 BOX 555
MOUNTAIN HOME, TEXAS 78058-9705

General Information Residential coeducational camp serving 80 campers per session. Established in 1976. Owned by Y. O. Ranch. Affiliated with American Camping Association, Camping Association for Mutual Progress, National Association of Experiential Education. 40,000-acre facility located 90 miles north of San Antonio. Features: high ropes course; horseback riding on 40,000 private acres; pool; 7 wilderness campsites; exotic wildlife, including giraffes and zebra; climbing tower.

Profile of Summer Employees Total number: 28; average age: 20; 50% male, 50% female; 10% high school students; 20% college students. Nonsmokers preferred.

Employment Information Openings are from May 19 to August 18. Year-round positions also offered. Jobs available: ▶ 8 *counselors* with CPR, first aid, and lifeguard training at $425 per month; ▶ *seasonal instructors* with CPR, first aid, and lifeguard training at $500 per month; ▶ *assistant wrangler* with CPR, first aid, lifeguard training, and CHA certification preferred at $500 per month; ▶ *health officer* with EMT, RN, or First Aid Responder at $800 per month; ▶ *corral assistant* with experience with horses and children at $550 per month. International students encouraged to apply; must obtain own visa and working papers prior to employment.

Benefits College credit, on-the-job training, on-site room and board at no charge, laundry facilities. Preemployment training of 15 days is required and includes safety and accident prevention, group interaction, leadership, camper-counselor relations, ropes training. Orientation is paid.

Contact Dan W. Reynolds, Director, Y. O. Adventure Camp, Department SJ, HC 01, Box 555, Mountain Home, Texas 78058-9705; 210-640-3220, Fax 210-640-3348, E-mail dreynold@ktc. com, URL http://www.kidscamps.com/raditional/yo-adventure. Application deadline: May 1.

UTAH

FLAMING GORGE LODGE
155 GREENDALE U.S. 191
DUTCH JOHN, UTAH 84023

General Information   Public lodging, restaurant, flying tackle shop, river raft rentals, and fishing guide trips on the Green River. Established in 1971. Owned by Collett's Recreation Service, Inc. 40-acre facility located 40 miles north of Vernal. Features: Flaming Gorge Reservoir; Green River; boating; rafting; fishing; hiking.

Profile of Summer Employees   Total number: 100; average age: 21; 40% male, 60% female; 20% college students; 5% retirees. Nonsmokers preferred.

Employment Information   Openings are from March 1 to October 31. Jobs available: ▶ *shuttle driver and raft rental staff* with WSI certification at $6.50 per hour; ▶ *housekeeping staff* at $5.25–$6.50 per hour; ▶ *fly shop clerk* at $5.25–$6.50 per hour; ▶ *cook* at $6.50–$8.50 per hour; ▶ *kitchen help* at $5.25–$6.50 per hour; ▶ *yard person* at $5.25–$6.50 per hour; ▶ *waitstaff* at $3.25–$3.75 per hour.

Benefits   On-the-job training, on-site room costs $25 per week, discounts on meals.

Contact   Craig W. Collett, General Manager, Flaming Gorge Lodge, 151 Greendale U.S. 191, Dutch John, Utah 84023; 801-889-3773, Fax 801-889-3788. Application deadline: March 1.

FOUR CORNERS SCHOOL OF OUTDOOR EDUCATION
PO BOX 1029
MONTICELLO, UTAH 84535

General Information   Program offering educational adventures using the spectacular Colorado Plateau as an outdoor classroom. Three-day to two-week programs are available on natural and human history via raft, backpack, van, or skis. Established in 1985. 7-acre facility located 250 miles south of Salt Lake City. Features: rustic 1930's Mormon Homestead used for basecamp; location in the heart of the Colorado Plateau near the Four Corners; archaeology, geology, and native culture sites nearby; major outdoor destinations such as Mesa Verde, Canyonlands, and the San Juan River (within 1 hour); 160,000-acre wonderland of high mesas, deep canyons, and winding rivers.

Profile of Summer Employees   Total number: 6; average age: 25; 70% male, 30% female; 5% minorities; 5% high school students; 95% college students; 5% local residents. Nonsmokers preferred.

Employment Information   Openings are from March 15 to October 30. Jobs available: ▶ *outdoor education interns* with interest in a career in outdoor education, knowledge of the Southwest, and First Responder and CPR certification preferred at $75 per week. International students encouraged to apply.

Benefits   College credit, on-the-job training, on-site room and board at no charge, laundry facilities, intern stipend of $75 per week, workmen's compensation insurance, opportunities for hands-on outdoor education, paid opportunities to hike, backpack, and run rivers.

Contact   Janet Ross, Director, Four Corners School of Outdoor Education, Department SJ, PO Box 1029, Monticello, Utah 84535; 801-587-2156, Fax 801-587-2193, E-mail fcs@igc.apc.org.

WORLD HOST BRYCE VALLEY INN
200 NORTH MAIN STREET
TROPIC, UTAH 84776

General Information   Room and board for European tourists traveling independently or on an excursion bus. Established in 1987. Owned by Tropic Realty L.L.C., World Host Bryce Valley

Inn. 1-acre facility located 95 miles west of Cedar City. Features: location in Bryce Valley next to Bryce Canyon National Park; backpacking in National and State Parks; mountain bike trails; horseback riding; adjacent to Grand Staircase National Monument; proximity to Lake Powell (150 miles away); proximity to Grand Canyon (160 miles away).

Profile of Summer Employees Total number: 40; average age: 20; 50% male, 50% female; 5% minorities; 20% high school students; 40% college students; 10% retirees; 50% local residents. Nonsmokers preferred.

Employment Information Openings are from March 15 to October 14. Jobs available: ▶ 10 *maids* at $5–$7 per hour; ▶ 4 *hosts/hostesses* at $5 per hour; ▶ 10 *waiters/waitresses* at $4.25 per hour; ▶ 2 *prep cooks* at $6 per hour; ▶ 3 *cooks* at $6.75 per hour; ▶ 4 *dishwashers* at $5 per hour; ▶ 3 *gift shop sales staff members* at $5 per hour. International students encouraged to apply; must obtain own visa and working papers prior to employment.

Benefits On-the-job training, laundry facilities, limited on-site room and board at $250 per month.

Contact Joe Decker, Operations Manager, World Host Bryce Valley Inn, Department SJ, PO Box A, Tropic, Utah 84776; 801-679-8811, Fax 801-679-8846. Application deadline: March 10.

VERMONT

BRIDGES RESORT AND RACQUET CLUB
SUGARBUSH ACCESS ROAD
WARREN, VERMONT 05674

General Information Tennis and condominium facility at major ski area in Vermont's Green Mountains. Established in 1975. Owned by Bridges Owners Association. Affiliated with Vermont Lodging and Restaurant Association, Association of Vacation Home Managers, New England Lawn Tennis Association. 45-acre facility located 40 miles south of Burlington. Features: health club; 12 tennis courts (10 Har-Tru clay and 2 indoor); 3 swimming pools (one indoor); children's camp programs; competititive tennis camp for juniors; Green Mountains.

Profile of Summer Employees Total number: 35; average age: 25; 60% male, 40% female; 10% minorities; 10% high school students; 20% college students; 10% international; 80% local residents. Nonsmokers preferred.

Employment Information Openings are from June 1 to September 1. Jobs available: ▶ *tennis desk/front desk staff* at $6.25–$6.50 per hour; ▶ *tennis staff* at $200–$400 per week; ▶ *swimming instructors* with WSI and Red Cross certification at $6.25–$6.50 per hour. International students encouraged to apply; must obtain own visa and working papers prior to employment.

Benefits On-the-job training. Off-site boarding costs are $500 per month.

Contact Holly Hodgkins, General Manager, Bridges Resort and Racquet Club, Department SJ, Sugarbush Access Road, Warren, Vermont 05674; 802-583-2922, Fax 802-583-1018, E-mail bridges@madriver.com, URL http://www.bridgesresort.com. Application deadline: March 1.

BURKLYN BALLET THEATRE
JOHNSON STATE COLLEGE
JOHNSON, VERMONT 05656

General Information Classical ballet workshop offers weekly performance opportunity to 136 boys and girls ages 12–20 in one 6-week program. Established in 1977. Owned by Angela Whitehill. Features: college dormitory; 600-seat theater; professional studios.

Profile of Summer Employees Total number: 16. Nonsmokers only.

Employment Information Jobs available: ▶ 14 *counselors (minimum age 20)* with current professional dance contract or college dance major; ▶ 1 *technical director (minimum age 20)* with professional experience or college technical theater major; ▶ *registered nurse.*
Benefits On-site room and board.
Contact Angela Whitehill, Artistic Director, Burklyn Ballet Theatre, PO Box 907, Island Heights, New Jersey 08732; 908-288-2660, Fax 908-288-2663.

BURKLYN BALLET THEATRE II
JOHNSON STATE COLLEGE
JOHNSON, VERMONT 05656

General Information Classical ballet workshop for 18 girls ages 8–11 in one three-week session. Established in 1995. Owned by Angela Whitehill. Features: college dormitory; 600-seat theater; professional studios.
Profile of Summer Employees Total number: 4. Nonsmokers only.
Employment Information Openings are from June 28 to July 19. Jobs available: ▶ 4 *certified teachers;* ▶ *registered nurse.*
Benefits On-site room and board.
Contact Angela Whitehill, Artistic Director, Burklyn Ballet Theatre II, PO Box 907, Island Heights, New Jersey 08732; 908-288-2660, Fax 908-288-2663.

CAMP FARNSWORTH
ROUTE 113
THETFORD, VERMONT 05074

General Information Residential Girl Scout camp for girls ages 6–16 offering four 2-week sessions. Established in 1909. Owned by Swift Water Girl Scout Council. Affiliated with American Camping Association, Vermont Camping Association, Association for Horsemanship Safety and Education. 300-acre facility located 150 miles northwest of Boston, Massachusetts. Features: location in the Green Mountains of Vermont; private 50-acre lake; 50-foot waterslide; low and high ropes courses; 2 riding rings.
Profile of Summer Employees Total number: 100; average age: 22; 1% male, 99% female; 5% minorities; 50% college students; 30% international; 20% local residents. Nonsmokers preferred.
Employment Information Openings are from June 13 to August 22. Jobs available: ▶ 2 *health directors* with RN, LPN, or EMT license at $1600–$3800 per season; ▶ 1 *experienced waterfront director* with WSI and LGT certification at $1600–$2900 per season; ▶ 8 *waterfront assistants* with WSI and LGT certification at $1200–$2100 per season; ▶ 12 *experienced unit leaders* with experience supervising adults and working with groups of children at $1600–$2100 per season; ▶ 30 *unit assistants* with child supervisory experience at $1200–$1600 per season; ▶ 1 *counselor-in-training director* with camp supervisory experience at $1700–$2100 per season; ▶ 1 *horseback riding director* with experience supervising English riding program at $2000–$2900 per season; ▶ 4 *riding assistants* with instructor experience at $1200–$2000 per season; ▶ 1 *adventure director* with experience instructing ropes course at $1600–$2700 per season; ▶ 1 *experienced ecology director* at $1600–$2700 per season; ▶ 1 *experienced arts director* at $1600–$2700 per season; ▶ 3 *experienced arts assistants* at $1200–$1600 per season; ▶ 1 *food supervisor* with experience in menu planning and quantity cooking at $2300–$3850 per season.
Benefits On-the-job training, formal ongoing training, on-site room and board at no charge, laundry facilities, health insurance. Preemployment training of 7 days is required and includes safety and accident prevention, group interaction, first-aid, CPR, leadership, camper-counselor relations, child development. Orientation is paid.
Contact Nancy Frankel, Director of Outdoor Education, Camp Farnsworth, Department SJ, 88 Harvey Road, #4, Manchester, New Hampshire 03103; 603-627-4158, Fax 603-627-4169, E-mail camping@swgirlscouts.org, URL http://www.swgirlscouts.org.

CAMP THOREAU-IN-VERMONT
RR 1, BOX 88, MILLER POND ROAD
THETFORD CENTER, VERMONT 05075-9601

General Information Interracial coeducational democratic community living for 140 campers and 64 staff members. Established in 1962. Owned by An Experience In People, Inc. Affiliated with American Camping Association, Vermont Camping Association, Association for Horsemanship Safety and Education. 280-acre facility located 30 miles north of White River Junction. Features: rural environment; campsite on a 64-acre lake; hiking in nearby White and Green Mountains; on-site riding facility and stables; fully-equipped darkroom; video studio; 4 clay tennis courts.

Profile of Summer Employees Total number: 65; average age: 25; 50% male, 50% female; 15% minorities; 8% high school students; 60% college students; 20% international; 10% local residents; 15% teachers. Nonsmokers preferred.

Employment Information Openings are from June 15 to August 22. Jobs available: ▶ 8 *counselors/swimming instructors* with WSI, LGT, first aid, and CPR/FPR certification at $1400–$2200 per season; ▶ 12 *counselors/lifeguards* with LGT, CPR/FPR, and first aid certification at $1400–$2200 per season; ▶ 6 *counselors/small craft instructors* with LGT and canoeing/sailing/kayaking instructor certification at $1400–$2200 per season; ▶ 4 *counselors/riding instructors* with CHA and CPR/first aid certification at $1400–$2200 per season; ▶ 2 *experienced counselors/woodshop instructors* with CPR/first aid certification at $1200–$2000 per season; ▶ 3 *experienced counselors/arts and crafts instructors* with CPR/first aid certification at $1200–$2000 per season; ▶ 2 *experienced counselors/photography instructors* with CPR/first aid certification at $1200–$2000 per season; ▶ 4 *experienced counselors/sports instructors* with CPR/first aid certification at $1400–$2200 per season; ▶ 2 *experienced counselors/martial arts and fencing instructors* with belt and CPR/first aid certification at $1400–$2200 per season; ▶ 1 *experienced counselor/newspaper person* at $1400–$2200 per season; ▶ 2 *experienced counselors/drama instructors* at $1400–$2200 per season; ▶ 2 *experienced counselors/nature* (small animals) *instructors* with CPR/first aid certification at $1400–$2200 per season; ▶ 2 *experienced counselors/hiking and outdoor living instructors* with familiarity with area and CPR/first aid certification and Wilderness First Responder or Wilderness EMT (preferred) at $1400–$2200 per season; ▶ 2 *experienced counselors/low-ropes instructors* with CPR/first aid certification at $1400–$2200 per season; ▶ 2 *experienced counselors/evening programs instructors* with creativity to design activities for the entire camp at $1400–$2200 per season; ▶ *nurses* with RN license, ability to obtain Vermont RN license, and CPR certification at $3300–$3600 per season; ▶ *experienced maintenance staff* at $1400–$2800 per season; ▶ *office manager* with filing, simple bookkeeping, and telephone skills at $1300–$2500 per season; ▶ 2 *experienced counselors/high-ropes instructors* at $1400–$2200 per season; ▶ 2 *experienced counselors/top-rope rock climbing instructors* at $1400–$2200 per season.

Benefits College credit, on-the-job training, on-site room and board at no charge, laundry facilities, travel reimbursement, health insurance, opportunity to work with diverse, multicultural staff in several different program areas. Preemployment training of 6 to 7 days is required and includes safety and accident prevention, group interaction, leadership, camper-counselor relations, program specific skill development. Orientation is paid.

Contact Gregory H. Finger, Director, Camp Thoreau-In-Vermont, Department SJ, 157 Tillson Lake Road, Wallkill, New York 12589-3213; 914-895-2974, Fax 914-895-1281. Application deadline: February 15.

CAMP THORPE, INC.
RR 3, BOX 3314
GOSHEN, VERMONT 05733

General Information Summer recreational camp that serves children and adults with special needs. Established in 1927. Owned by Camp Thorpe, Inc. Affiliated with Vermont Camping Association. 200-acre facility located 60 miles south of Burlington. Features: location in the

Green Mountains; trout pond; playground; modern cabins; 43 camp buildings; overnight sites; 100' x 50' pool; multipurpose tennis court.

Profile of Summer Employees Total number: 25; average age: 21; 40% male, 60% female; 90% college students; 25% international; 75% local residents. Nonsmokers preferred.

Employment Information Openings are from June 20 to August 20. Jobs available: ▶ *cook* at $2500–$3000 per season; ▶ 2 *head counselors* with two years of college completed at $1500–$2000 per season; ▶ 5 *specialists* (art, nature, music, pool, and sports) with one year of college completed at $1200–$1500 per season; ▶ 12 *general counselors* (minimum age 18) at $1000–$1200 per season; ▶ 1 *camp nurse* with RN, LPN, or EMT license at $2000–$2500 per season. International students encouraged to apply; must apply through recognized agency.

Benefits College credit, on-the-job training, on-site room and board at no charge, laundry facilities. Preemployment training of 4 days is required and includes safety and accident prevention, group interaction, first-aid, CPR, leadership, camper-counselor relations. Orientation is paid.

Contact Lyle P. Jepson, Director, Camp Thorpe, Inc., RR 3, Box 3314, Goshen, Vermont 05733; 802-247-6611. Application deadline: April 30.

CHALLENGE WILDERNESS CAMP
BRADFORD, VERMONT 05033

General Information Residential camp serving 45 boys ages 9–16 with outdoor skills and wilderness trips. Established in 1965. Owned by Drs. J. Thayer and Candice L. Raines. Affiliated with American Camping Association. 650-acre facility located 26 miles north of Hanover, New Hampshire. Features: backpacking and canoe trips; 15-acre private lake; 650-acre forest preserve.

Profile of Summer Employees Total number: 12; average age: 24; 100% male; 60% college students; 40% international. Nonsmokers only.

Employment Information Openings are from June 18 to August 24. Jobs available: ▶ 1 *waterfront director* with WSI certification/lifeguard training; ▶ 1 *kayak instructor* with ACA or BCU certification; ▶ 3 *rock climbing instructors* with one 5.10 lead plus two 5.9 seconds; ▶ 1 *woodworking instructor;* ▶ 1 *marksmanship instructor* with.22-caliber and military experience; ▶ 1 *blacksmithing instructor* with ability to be trained; ▶ 1 *food services director* with outdoorsman and cooking skills; ▶ 1 *kitchen assistant* with outdoorsman skills. All positions offered at $1200–$2000 per season. International students encouraged to apply; must apply through recognized agency.

Benefits On-the-job training, on-site room and board at no charge, laundry facilities. Preemployment training of 8 days is required and includes safety and accident prevention, group interaction, first-aid, CPR, leadership, camper-counselor relations. Orientation is paid.

Contact Drs. J. Thayer and Candice L. Raines, Directors, Challenge Wilderness Camp, 300 North Grove Street, #4, Rutland, Vermont 05701; 800-832-HAWK, E-mail rainest@sover.net.

FARM AND WILDERNESS CAMPS
HCR 70, BOX 27
PLYMOUTH, VERMONT 05056

General Information Five separate individual residential programs for boys/girls ages 9–17 offering diverse outdoor wilderness activities within Quaker-based communities. Also day camp for boys and girls ages 3–10. Established in 1939. Affiliated with American Camping Association. 3,000-acre facility located 23 miles east of Rutland. Features: ten-acre secluded freshwater lake; location on the southern edge of Green Mountain National Forest; rustic wilderness lifestyle; access to Adirondacks, Green Mountains, White Mountains, and northern Maine; access to over 3000 acres of wooded mountain terrain.

Profile of Summer Employees Total number: 150; average age: 21; 50% male, 50% female; 5% minorities; 5% high school students; 90% college students; 4% international; 10% local residents; 20% teachers. Nonsmokers only.

Employment Information Openings are from June 13 to August 18. Jobs available: ▶ 120

counselors at $1500–$2250 per season; ▶ 5 *nurses* with RN license or graduate nursing student status at $1500–$2500 per season; ▶ 5 *maintenance staff members* at $1350–$2250 per season; ▶ 16 *cooks* at $1400–$2300 per season; ▶ *swimming instructors* with WSI certification at $1350–$2250 per season. International students encouraged to apply; must apply through recognized agency.

Benefits On-the-job training, on-site room and board at no charge, laundry facilities, health insurance, workmen's compensation. Preemployment training of 8 days is required and includes safety and accident prevention, group interaction, first-aid, CPR, leadership, camper-counselor relations, child development. Orientation is paid.

Contact Philip Tobin, Administrator, Farm and Wilderness Camps, HCR 70, Box 27, Plymouth, Vermont 05056; 802-422-3761, Fax 802-422-8660, E-mail fandw@sover.net. Application deadline: May 15.

KILLOOLEET
ROUTE 100
HANCOCK, VERMONT 05748-0070

General Information Full-season, noncompetitive, coeducational camp serving 100 campers ages 9–14 for seven or more weeks. Emphasis is on developing techniques in group leadership and individual counseling. Children specialize in a variety of sports and arts activities. Established in 1927. Owned by John, Eleanor, and Katherine Seeger. Affiliated with American Camping Association, Association for Horsemanship Safety and Education, Vermont Camping Association. 300-acre facility located 35 miles north of Rutland. Features: small private lake; 2 tennis courts; 3 sports fields; flat campus for bike trips (bring your own or rent bikes); 12 horses with ring and trails; video studio.

Profile of Summer Employees Total number: 40; average age: 22; 52% male, 48% female; 7% minorities; 6% high school students; 65% college students; 15% international; 15% local residents; 8% teachers. Nonsmokers preferred.

Employment Information Openings are from June 20 to August 24. Jobs available: ▶ 2 *group horseback riding* (English) *instructors* with Pony Club or equivalent group teaching experience at $1200–$2000 per season; ▶ 1 *electronics instructor* at $1200–$1700 per season; ▶ 1 *secretary* at $1200–$1700 per season; ▶ 1 *nature instructor* with teaching ideas using pond, fields, stream, and woods at $1200–$1700 per season; ▶ 1 *video, control room, and editing instructor* at $1200–$2000 per season; ▶ 1 *boating* (canoeing, windsurfing) *instructor* at $1200–$1700 per season; ▶ 1 *music* (folk, rhythm and blues/funk) *instructor* at $1200–$1700 per season; ▶ 2 *sports* (individual and team) *instructors* at $1200–$1700 per season; ▶ 1 *drama counselor* with ability to direct a musical as well as teach improvisation/creative dramatics at $1200–$1700 per season; ▶ 1 *music counselor* with ability to play piano for the camp musical and help campers with learning their songs (other activity skills desirable, too) at $1200–$1700 per season; ▶ *swimming instructor* with current WSI and lifeguard certification at $1400–$2000 per season; ▶ *shop counselor (woodworking or crafts)* at $1200–$1700 per season. International students encouraged to apply; must apply through recognized agency.

Benefits College credit, on-the-job training, formal ongoing training, on-site room and board at no charge, laundry facilities, health insurance, reimbursement for half of travel costs. Preemployment training of 6 to 8 days is required and includes safety and accident prevention, group interaction, first-aid, CPR, leadership, camper-counselor relations. Orientation is paid.

Contact Kate Spencer-Seeger, Director, Killooleet, Department SJ, 70 Trull Street, Somerville, Massachusetts 02145; 617-666-1484, Fax 617-666-0378, URL http://www.tiac.net/users/ccarter/killooleet/killooleet.html. Application deadline: May 10.

LOCHEARN CAMP FOR GIRLS
LAKE FAIRLEE, PO BOX 400
POST MILLS, VERMONT 05058

General Information Private residential camp for girls ages 7–16 offering a comprehensive activity program with special emphasis on positive character development of children. Established in 1916. Owned by Rich and Ginny Maxson. Affiliated with American Camping Association, Vermont Camping Association, Association of Independent Camps. 51-acre facility located 150 miles north of Boston, Massachusetts. Features: 5 outdoor tennis courts (2 clay, 3 all-season); all-purpose gamefield with regulation-size basketball court; lakeside cabins; recreation hall, including 4 art studios, dance studio, and lakeside dining room; gymnastics center; 16 horses and riding complex with 2 riding rings.

Profile of Summer Employees Total number: 70; average age: 22; 10% male, 90% female; 10% high school students; 80% college students; 10% retirees; 15% international; 15% teachers. Nonsmokers only.

Employment Information Openings are from June 10 to August 16. Jobs available: ▶ 5 *field sports instructors* at $1200–$1400 per season; ▶ 3 *gymnastics instructors* with floor and full apparatus experience at $1200–$1400 per season; ▶ 4 *tennis instructors* at $1200–$1400 per season; ▶ 4 *studio arts instructors* at $1200–$1400 per season; ▶ 2 *performing arts instructors* at $1200–$1400 per season; ▶ 2 *sailing instructors* with LGT certification at $1200–$1400 per season; ▶ 2 *leadership trainers* at $1400–$1600 per season; ▶ 2 *swimming instructors* with WSI certification at $1200–$1400 per season; ▶ 2 *canoeing instructors* with LGT certification at $1200–$1400 per season; ▶ 1 *diving instructor* with LGT certification at $1200–$1400 per season; ▶ 2 *English-style riding instructors* at $1300–$1500 per season; ▶ 2 *waterskiing instructors/boat drivers* with LGT certification at $1300–$1500 per season; ▶ 3 *kitchen assistants* at $1600–$1800 per season. International students encouraged to apply; must apply through recognized agency.

Benefits College credit, on-the-job training, formal ongoing training, on-site room and board at no charge, laundry facilities, travel reimbursement. Preemployment training of 10 days is required and includes safety and accident prevention, group interaction, first-aid, CPR, leadership, camper-counselor relations. Orientation is paid.

Contact Rich Maxson, Owner/Director, Lochearn Camp for Girls, Department SJ, Camp Lochearn on Lake Fairlee, Post Mills, Vermont 05058; 800-235-6659, Fax 802-333-4856. Application deadline: May 1.

POINT COUNTER POINT CHAMBER MUSIC CAMP
LAKE DUNEMORE, VERMONT 05733

General Information Residential camp serving 50 string players and pianists for three-, four-, or seven-week sessions. Established in 1963. Owned by Paul and Margaret Roby. 2-acre facility located 55 miles south of Burlington. Features: lake; waterskiing; mountains; hiking trails.

Profile of Summer Employees Total number: 6; average age: 25; 34% male, 66% female; 16% minorities; 33% college students; 16% international; 27% local residents; 50% teachers. Nonsmokers preferred.

Employment Information Openings are from June 18 to August 12. Jobs available: ▶ 6 *activity counselors* with WSI, first aid, and CPR certification (preferred) at $1500–$1700 per season; ▶ 8 *music staff members* (4 violinists, 1 violist, 2 cellists, and 1 pianist) with performing and teaching experience at $2400–$2800 per season; ▶ *experienced cooks* at $2200–$3500 per season.

Benefits On-site room and board at no charge. Preemployment training is required.

Contact Paul Roby, Director, Point Counter Point Chamber Music Camp, PO Box 3181, Terre Haute, Indiana 47803; 812-877-3745, Fax 812-877-2174, E-mail pointcp@aol.com. Application deadline: March 15.

PUTNEY SUMMER PROGRAMS
ELM LEA FARM
PUTNEY, VERMONT 05346

General Information Residential program in visual and performing arts, field ecology, writing, English as a second language for 80 students, and a Galapagos field ecology trip. Established in 1987. Operated by The Putney School. Affiliated with National Camp Association. 500-acre facility located 10 miles north of Brattleboro. Features: 75-acre nature preserve; working dairy farm and produce garden; extensive arts facilities; summer music festival in residence on campus; small, cottage-like dormitories; rural setting.

Profile of Summer Employees Total number: 30; average age: 25; 40% male, 60% female; 20% minorities; 30% college students; 10% international; 40% local residents; 70% teachers. Nonsmokers only.

Employment Information Openings are from June 24 to August 9. Jobs available: ▶ 12 *residential assistants* (minimum age 21) with experience in arts, ecology, writing, or English as a Second Language preferred; also residential and outdoor experience and first aid training at $1500 per season. International students encouraged to apply; must obtain own visa and working papers prior to employment.

Benefits On-the-job training, formal ongoing training, on-site room and board at no charge, laundry facilities, travel reimbursement, assistant teaching experience. Preemployment training of 4 days is required and includes safety and accident prevention, group interaction, first-aid, CPR, leadership, camper-counselor relations. Orientation is paid.

Contact Brian D. Cohen, Director, Summer Programs, Putney Summer Programs, The Putney School, Putney, Vermont 05346; 802-387-6216, Fax 802-387-6216, E-mail summer_programs@ pegasus.putney.com. Application deadline: March 1.

TOPNOTCH AT STOWE
4000 MOUNTAIN ROAD
STOWE, VERMONT 05672

General Information Destination resort offering fine dining, tennis, equestrian center, individually decorated rooms, town houses, condos, a world-class spa, and a conference center. Established in 1973. Affiliated with Stowe Area Association, Preferred Hotels and Resorts Worldwide, American Hotel and Motel Association. 120-acre facility located 30 miles northwest of Burlington. Features: 10 outdoor tennis courts; European-style spa; outdoor pool; location in the Green Mountains of Vermont; four boutiques on property.

Profile of Summer Employees Total number: 10; average age: 20; 40% male, 60% female; 50% high school students; 50% college students; 100% local residents.

Employment Information Year-round positions offered. Jobs available: ▶ *housekeeping staff* at $6–$6.50 per hour; ▶ *waitstaff;* ▶ *bell staff/door staff;* ▶ *locker room attendants* at $6–$6.50 per hour. International students encouraged to apply; must obtain own visa and working papers prior to employment.

Benefits On-the-job training, health club access, duty meals. Off-site boarding costs are $500 per month. Preemployment training of 1 day is required. Orientation is paid.

Contact Judy Ruggles, Human Resources Director, Topnotch at Stowe, PO Box 1458, Stowe, Vermont 05672; 802-253-8585, Fax 802-253-9263.

WAPANACKI PROGRAM CENTER
RR 1, BOX 1086 WEST HILL ROAD
HARDWICK, VERMONT 05843

General Information Residential summer camp with one-, two-, or three-week sessions for girls ages 6–17. Girl-adult partnership is emphasized in small group activities based on Girl Scout principles. Established in 1992. Owned by Vermont Girl Scout Council. Affiliated with American Camping Association, Girl Scouts of the United States of America, Vermont Camping Association. 220-acre facility located 50 miles east of Burlington. Features: rolling meadows, coniferous and hardwood forests; brooks and wetland areas; arts and crafts and recreational buildings; 10-person cabins with running water and bathrooms; location with 1700-foot elevation; 22-acre swimming and boating lake; athletic fields.

Profile of Summer Employees Total number: 40; average age: 21; 5% male, 95% female; 4% minorities; 4% high school students; 95% college students; 1% retirees; 15% international; 3% local residents.

Employment Information Openings are from June 28 to August 14. Jobs available: ▶ 1 *camp director* (minimum age 25) with administration/supervision abilities and resident camp experience (knowledge of Girl Scout program preferred) at $2500–$4000 per season; ▶ 1 *assistant camp director* (minimum age 21) with administration, supervision, and Girl Scout program abilities (camp experience preferred) at $1500–$2500 per season; ▶ 1 *business manager* (minimum age 21) with business training (typing, bookkeeping, and office practices), attention to detail, and a current driver's license at $900–$1400 per season; ▶ 1 *health supervisor* (minimum age 21) with RN, LPN, EMT, or physician's license and recent first aid training at $1500–$2500 per season; ▶ 1 *waterfront/boating director* (minimum age 21) with current WSI certification, CPR training, and experience as an aquatics instructor at $1500–$2500 per season; ▶ 2 *waterfront counselors* (minimum age 18) with current ALS or WSI certification and/or SCI certification at $900–$1400 per season; ▶ 4 *unit leaders* (minimum age 21) with experience with children in groups, supervisory background, and experience with Girl Scout and outdoor programs at $1000–$1600 per season; ▶ 12 *unit counselors* (minimum age 18) with ability to work with children, experience in Girl Scout programs, and outdoor skills at $700–$1100 per season; ▶ 1 *trip leader/director of counselors-in-training* (minimum age 21) with experience with children in groups, current ALS and SCI certifications, and canoe trip experience at $1000–$1600 per season; ▶ 1 *program director* (minimum age 21) with experience in camp supervising, working with groups, and teaching in specialized program areas at $1000–$1600 per season; ▶ *cook* (minimum age 21) with menu-planning, purchasing, and quantity food preparation experience and ability to supervise kitchen personnel at $2200–$3500 per season; ▶ *assistant cook* (minimum age 18) with ability to assist quantity food preparation and experience in camp or school cooking at $1000–$1600 per season; ▶ *kitchen helpers* (minimum age 16) with ability to work with people and a willingness to fulfill responsibilities as directed at $600–$1000 per season; ▶ *maintenance person* (minimum age 18) with experience in minor building, grounds, and equipment repair at $1100–$1700 per season; ▶ *program specialists* (minimum age 18) with training and teaching experience in specialized program areas and experience working with groups and/or previous camp experience at $900–$1400 per season. International students encouraged to apply; must apply through recognized agency.

Benefits College credit, on-the-job training, formal ongoing training, on-site room and board at no charge, laundry facilities, health insurance, first-aid, CPR, and lifeguard training. Preemployment training of 7 days is required and includes safety and accident prevention, group interaction, first-aid, CPR, leadership, camper-counselor relations. Orientation is paid.

Contact Kathy Reise, Director of Program and Training, Wapanacki Program Center, Department SJ, 79 Allen Martin Drive, Essex Junction, Vermont 05452; 802-878-7131, Fax 802-878-3943, E-mail vtgsc@aol.com. Application deadline: May 1.

WINDRIDGE TENNIS CAMP AT CRAFTSBURY COMMON
PO BOX 27
CRAFTSBURY COMMON, VERMONT 05827

General Information Residential coeducational camp serving 110 campers with an emphasis on tennis along with traditional camp activities. Established in 1973. Owned by Ted Hoehn. Affiliated with Vermont Camping Association, American Camping Association. 50-acre facility located 40 miles north of Montpelier. Features: 16 tennis courts (14 clay, 2 hard surface); fully equipped waterfront on 2-mile lake; soccer field; outdoor basketball court; Sunfish sailing program; wilderness setting.

Profile of Summer Employees Total number: 35; average age: 20; 50% male, 50% female; 10% minorities; 80% college students; 20% international; 10% local residents. Nonsmokers only.

Employment Information Openings are from June 6 to August 24. Jobs available: ▶ 12 *tennis instructors* at $1500–$2500 per season; ▶ 3 *soccer instructors* at $1500–$2500 per season; ▶ 1 *waterfront director* with LGT at $2000–$3000 per season; ▶ 1 *lifeguard* with LGT at $1500–$2000 per season; ▶ 1 *photography instructor* at $1500–$2000 per season; ▶ 1 *registered nurse* at $400–$425 per week; ▶ 2 *sailing instructors* with LGT at $1500–$2000 per season. International students encouraged to apply; must apply through recognized agency.

Benefits On-site room and board at no charge, laundry facilities, exposure to first-class tennis coaching, opportunity for self-directed teaching and creation of programs in elective areas. Preemployment training of 6 days is required and includes safety and accident prevention, group interaction, first-aid, CPR, leadership, camper-counselor relations, tennis teaching guidelines. Orientation is paid.

Contact Charles Witherell, Director, Windridge Tennis Camp at Craftsbury Common, Department SJ, PO Box 4518, Burlington, Vermont 05406; 802-586-9646, Fax 802-658-0288. Application deadline: February 15.

WINDRIDGE TENNIS CAMP AT TEELA-WOOKET, VERMONT
BOX 88, ROUTE 12A
ROXBURY, VERMONT 05669

General Information Residential camp for boys and girls ages 9–15 specializing in tennis, riding, and soccer. Established in 1986. Owned by Ted Hoehn and Alden Bryan. 235-acre facility located 50 miles south of Burlington. Features: 21 clay and Har-Tru tennis courts; 2 soccer fields; 5 riding rings; 30′ x 60′ swimming pool; hockey rink; miles of trails for riding and biking.

Profile of Summer Employees Total number: 70; average age: 23; 50% male, 50% female; 5% minorities; 5% high school students; 65% college students; 20% international; 10% teachers. Nonsmokers only.

Employment Information Openings are from June 5 to August 23. Jobs available: ▶ *tennis instructors;* ▶ *riding instructors;* ▶ *soccer instructors;* ▶ *archery instructors.* All positions offered at $1155–$2000 per season. International students encouraged to apply; must apply through recognized agency.

Benefits On-the-job training, on-site room and board at no charge, laundry facilities, travel reimbursement for some applicants. Preemployment training of 6 days is required and includes safety and accident prevention, group interaction, leadership, camper-counselor relations. Orientation is paid.

Contact Ms. Cub Momsen, Director, Windridge Tennis Camp at Teela-Wooket, Vermont, Department SJ, PO Box 4518, Burlington, Vermont 05406-4518; 802-658-0313, Fax 802-658-0288; E-mail wcamps@aol.com. Application deadline: June 1.

VIRGINIA

BUSCH GARDENS/WHITEWATER COUNTRY U.S.A.
ONE BUSCH GARDENS BOULEVARD
WILLIAMSBURG, VIRGINIA 23187

General Information Theme park offering family entertainment. Established in 1975. Owned by Anheuser Busch, Inc. 360-acre facility located 50 miles southeast of Richmond. Features: water elements for swimming.

Profile of Summer Employees Total number: 4,000.

Employment Information Openings are from January 1 to December 1. Jobs available: ▶ *retail sales staff* at $4.75–$9.65 per hour; ▶ *games staff;* ▶ *entertainment staff;* ▶ *food and beverage staff;* ▶ *park operations staff;* ▶ *warehouse staff;* ▶ *grounds staff;* ▶ *maintenance staff;* ▶ *safety staff;* ▶ *cash control staff;* ▶ *finance staff;* ▶ *clerical staff;* ▶ *lifeguards;* ▶ *security staff.*

International students encouraged to apply; must apply through recognized agency.

Benefits On-the-job training. Preemployment training of 1 day is required and includes safety and accident prevention, group interaction, hospitality training. Orientation is paid.

Contact Busch Gardens/Water Country USA Employment Office, Busch Gardens/Whitewater Country U.S.A., One Busch Gardens Boulevard, Williamsburg, Virginia 23187-8785; 757-253-3020, Fax 757-253-3013.

CAMP CARYSBROOK/CAMP CARYSBROOK DAY CAMP
3500 CAMP CARYSBROOK ROAD
RINER, VIRGINIA 24149

General Information Traditional residential camp for girls ages 6–16 in two-, four-, six-, and eight-week sessions; two-week day camp in late August. Established in 1923. Owned by Toni M. Baughman. Affiliated with American Camping Association, Association of Independent Camps, National Archery Association, Association for Horsemanship Safety and Education. 200-acre facility located 30 miles west of Roanoke. Features: 200 forested acres; spring-fed lake; 2 tennis courts; stable and riding rings with 5 miles of trails; archery range; rifle range.

Profile of Summer Employees Total number: 25; average age: 21; 2% male, 98% female; 10% minorities; 90% college students; 10% international; 5% local residents. Nonsmokers preferred.

Employment Information Openings are from June 15 to August 18. Jobs available: ► 2 *experienced riding instructors* with CHA certification at $550–$1200 per season; ► 3 *swimming instructors* with WSI or lifesaving certification and Bronze Medallion at $550–$1200 per season; ► 1 *canoeing instructor* with Red Cross canoe and lifesaving certification at $550–$1000 per season; ► 1 *experienced tennis instructor* at $550–$1000 per season; ► 2 *experienced team sports staff members* at $550–$1000 per season; ► 1 *experienced recreational sports staff member* at $550–$1000 per season; ► 1 *experienced fencing instructor* at $500–$1000 per season; ► 1 *experienced dance instructor* at $550–$1000 per season; ► 1 *experienced drama instructor* at $550–$1000 per season; ► 1 *experienced arts and crafts instructor* at $550–$1000 per season; ► 1 *experienced riflery instructor* at $550–$1000 per season; ► 1 *experienced archery instructor* at $550–$1000 per season; ► 1 *experienced climbing, rappelling, and caving instructor* at $550–$1200 per season; ► 1 *experienced ecology instructor* at $550–$1000 per season; ► 1 *experienced outdoor living skills instructor* at $550–$1000 per season. International students encouraged to apply; must obtain own visa and working papers prior to employment; must apply through recognized agency.

Benefits On-the-job training, on-site room and board at no charge, chance to receive letters of recommendation. Preemployment training of 7 days is required and includes safety and accident prevention, group interaction, first-aid, CPR, leadership, camper-counselor relations, child development. Orientation is paid.

Contact Toni M. Baughman, Director, Camp Carysbrook/Camp Carysbrook Day Camp, Department SJ, 2705 King Street, Alexandria, Virginia 22302; 703-836-7548, Fax 703-836-0725, E-mail tmoose@aol.com. Application deadline: June 1.

CAMP CHEERIO ADVENTURE CAMP
754 FOX KNOB ROAD
MOUTH OF WILSON, VIRGINIA 24363

General Information Program in adventure tripping and wilderness travel serving campers ages 10–17. Established in 1982. Owned by YMCA of High Point. Affiliated with American Camping Association. 60-acre facility located 90 miles north of Charlotte, North Carolina. Features: ¾ mile river front on New River; large open fields; hiking trails.

Profile of Summer Employees Total number: 14; average age: 20; 50% male, 50% female; 20% minorities; 90% college students. Nonsmokers preferred.

Employment Information Openings are from June 1 to August 20. Spring break positions also offered. Jobs available: ► 8 *counselors* at $135–$175 per week; ► 2 *trip leaders* at $160–$210 per week; ► 1 *logistics director* at $175–$230 per week; ► 1 *assistant logistics director* at

$140–$200 per week; ▶ 1 *program director* at $190&–$250 per week. International students encouraged to apply; must obtain own visa and working papers prior to employment; must apply through recognized agency.

Benefits On-the-job training, on-site room and board at no charge, laundry facilities, health insurance, internships.

Contact Keith Russell, Director, Camp Cheerio Adventure Camp, PO Box 6258, High Point, North Carolina 27262; 910-869-0195, Fax 910-869-0118. Application deadline: May 15.

CAMP FRIENDSHIP
PO BOX 145
PALMYRA, VIRGINIA 22963

General Information Residential camp with a traditional program, specialized equestrian program, and adventure trips for teens in one- and two-week sessions. Established in 1967. Owned by Charles R. Ackenbom. Affiliated with American Camping Association, National Rifle Association, National Archery Association. 730-acre facility located 25 miles southeast of Charlottesville. Features: 4 tennis courts; 60-event ropes course; stables for 80 horses and indoor arena; gymnasium; location in Blue Ridge foothills; lake, river, and swimming pool.

Profile of Summer Employees Total number: 130; average age: 25; 50% male, 50% female; 5% minorities; 10% high school students; 50% college students; 10% international; 10% local residents. Nonsmokers only.

Employment Information Openings are from June 5 to August 20. Year-round positions also offered. Jobs available: ▶ 55 *cabin counselors/trip leaders* with teaching skills at $1050–$1350 per season; ▶ 1 *waterfront director* with WSI certification at $1200–$1400 per season; ▶ 1 *experienced tennis instructor* at $1200–$1400 per season; ▶ 1 *experienced ropes course director* at $1200–$1400 per season; ▶ 1 *creative arts director* with crafts and drama skills at $1200–$1400 per season; ▶ 8 *experienced riding counselors/instructors* at $1100–$1500 per season; ▶ 4 *village directors* with college degree and supervisory experience at $1600–$2000 per season; ▶ 11 *kitchen staff members* at $1000–$2000 per season; ▶ 3 *drivers/maintenance personnel* (minimum age 21) with driver's license at $1200–$1400 per season; ▶ 2 *nurses* with RN license; ▶ 2 *laundry staff members* with willingness to perform night work at $1200–$1400 per season. International students encouraged to apply; must apply through recognized agency.

Benefits On-the-job training, on-site room and board at no charge. Preemployment training of 7 to 14 days is required and includes safety and accident prevention, group interaction, first-aid, CPR, leadership, camper-counselor relations, specific program skill training. Orientation is paid.

Contact Linda Grier and Ray Ackenbom, Directors, Camp Friendship, Department SJ, PO Box 145, Palmyra, Virginia 22963; 804-589-8950, Fax 804-589-3925, URL http://www.campfriendship.com. Application deadline: April 1.

CAMP HORIZONS
ROUTE 3, BOX 374
HARRISONBURG, VIRGINIA 22801

General Information Summer residential camp for children ages 7–16. Corporate training center and retreat center for schools, churches, and universities in the spring and fall. Teen adventure and traditional camp programs. Established in 1983. Owned by John Hall. Affiliated with American Camping Association, Virginia Council of Outdoor Adventure Education, International Camping Fellowship. 240-acre facility located 10 miles north of Harrisonburg. Features: meeting rooms; outdoor swimming pool and private lake; riding trails; extensive high and low adventure initiative ropes course; beach volleyball court; 2 tennis courts.

Profile of Summer Employees Total number: 60; average age: 21; 50% male, 50% female; 10% minorities; 100% college students; 50% international; 30% local residents; 5% teachers. Nonsmokers only.

Employment Information Openings are from April 1 to November 30. Year-round positions also offered. Jobs available: ▶ 4 *waterfront counselors* with lifeguard, first aid, and CPR certification at $1050–$1400 per season; ► 20 *general activities counselors* with first aid, CPR certification, and experience in any combination of the following: swimming, French, Spanish, Japanese, ESL, drama, model rocketry, caving, or rock climbing at $1050–$1400 per season; ► 3 *riding counselors* with first aid, CPR certification, and knowledge of Western-style horseback riding at $1050–$1400 per season; ► 2 *experienced program directors* with bachelor's degree and skills in education, administration, international education, and counseling at $1400–$2000 per season; ► 14 *adventure counselors* with skills in caving, rock climbing, canoeing, ropes course, and backpacking at $1050–$1400 per season; ► *general counselors/kitchen staff* at $1000–$1050 per season. International students encouraged to apply; must apply through recognized agency.

Benefits College credit, on-the-job training, on-site room and board at no charge. Preemployment training of 7 days is required and includes safety and accident prevention, group interaction, first-aid, CPR, leadership, camper-counselor relations, ropes, adventure skills. Orientation is paid.

Contact Rajan M. Bajumpaa, Camp Director, Camp Horizons, Department SJ, Route 3, Box 374, Harrisonburg, Virginia 22801; 540-896-7600, Fax 540-896-5455, E-mail camphorizons@ rica.net, URL http://www.kidscamps.com/traditional/horizons. Application deadline: March 1.

CAT'S CAP & ST. CATHERINE'S CREATIVE ARTS PROGRAM

General Information Day camp concentrating on exploration of the visual and performing arts, as well as offering sports, horseback riding, and river exploration. Established in 1976. Owned by St. Catherine's School. Affiliated with Virginia Association of Independent Schools (VAIS), Episcopalian Diocesan Church School Association. 16-acre facility located 110 miles south of Washington, DC. Features: 6 outdoor tennis courts; theater; large sports fields; dance studio; gymnasium; photography lab; extensive art studios.

Profile of Summer Employees Total number: 130; average age: 29; 50% male, 50% female; 25% high school students; 15% college students; 1% international; 98% local residents; 60% teachers. Nonsmokers preferred.

Employment Information Openings are from June 20 to July 30. Jobs available: ► *instructors* with certification in dance, music, art, theater, physical education, or other visual or performing arts at $11–$13 per hour; ► *assistants* with training or degree in education at $6–$8 per hour; ► *junior counselors* at $3.80–$4.25 per hour; ► *counselors* at $4.25–$5.25 per hour; ► *canoeing instructors* at $11 per hour; ► *rappelling instructors* at $11 per hour; ► *nurse/clerk* with RN license at $11 per hour; ► *senior counselors* at $6–$6.75 per hour. International students encouraged to apply; must obtain own visa and working papers prior to employment.

Benefits On-the-job training, tuition reimbursement, lunch provided for full-day staff, 35% tuition discount for staff children. Off-site boarding costs are $250 per month.

Contact Jan Holland, Director, Cat's Cap & St. Catherine's Creative Arts Program, 6001 Grove Avenue, Richmond, Virginia 23226; 804-288-2804 Ext. 45, Fax 804-285-8169. Application deadline: December 1.

4 STAR TENNIS & ENRICHMENT CAMP AT THE UNIVERSITY OF VIRGINIA
CHARLOTTESVILLE, VIRGINIA 22901

General Information Residential tennis camp serving 90 students per week with private lessons and match play daily and other sporting events in the evenings. Also an enrichment camp to be taken alone or as ½ day of tennis and ½ day of enrichment camp. Established in 1974. Owned by Mike Eikenberry. Affiliated with United States Tennis Association, United States Professional Tennis Association. Located 100 miles south of Washington, DC. Features: 13 outdoor hard surface tennis courts and 3 indoor synthetic tennis courts; indoor swimming pool and numerous athletics fields; location 2 hours from Washington, DC; location at the University of Virginia in historic Charlottesville; housing in apartment-style air-conditioned dormitories; 40 courses in enrichment camp including PSAT & SAT.

Profile of Summer Employees Total number: 30; average age: 22; 60% male, 40% female; 10% minorities; 70% college students; 10% local residents; 15% teachers. Nonsmokers only.

Employment Information Openings are from June 15 to August 10. Jobs available: ▶ 25 *tennis instructors/camp counselors* (college student or older) with advanced-level tennis player status and some competitive experience at $900–$1400 per season; ▶ 1 *evening activities director/ recreation director* with good organization and planning skills at $1800–$2250 per season; ▶ 1 *dormitory supervisor* with good organization and problem-solving skills at $1575–$2025 per season; ▶ 10 *academic instructors* with teaching background.

Benefits On-the-job training, on-site room and board at no charge, laundry facilities, training in teaching tennis, work with children as well as program and activity planning.

Contact Ann Grubbs, Assistant Director, 4 Star Tennis & Enrichment Camp at the University of Virginia, Department SJ, PO Box 3387, Falls Church, Virginia 22043; 703-573-0890, Fax 703-573-0297. Application deadline: May 1.

FREDERICKSBURG AND SPOTSYLVANIA NATIONAL MILITARY PARK
120 CHATHAM LANE
FREDERICKSBURG, VIRGINIA 22405

General Information Historic park preserving and interpreting four Civil War battlefields in the Fredericksburg area. Established in 1927. Operated by United States Department of the Interior, National Park Service. 7,000-acre facility located 50 miles south of Washington, DC. Features: Fredericksburg Battlefield with visitor center and guided walking tour along Confederate battleline; Chancellorsville Battlefield with visitor center and guided walking tour at site of "Stonewall" Jackson's wounding; "Stonewall" Jackson shrine with tours; historic structure (Chatham) with exhibits; Wilderness Battlefield with guided tour; Spotsylvania Battlefield with tour.

Profile of Summer Employees Total number: 8; average age: 27; 50% male, 50% female; 20% minorities; 40% college students; 30% local residents.

Employment Information Openings are from June 1 to September 1. Spring break, Christmas break, year-round positions also offered. Jobs available: ▶ 8 *seasonal park historians;* ▶ 1 *seasonal cultural resource assistant;* ▶ 1 *seasonal natural resource assistant.* All positions offered at $9.46–$10.34 per hour.

Benefits On-the-job training, on-site room and board at $30 per week, opportunity to meet and work with top Civil War scholars in the nation (several staff members have been published). Preemployment training of 4 days is required and includes interpretation, history. Orientation is paid.

Contact Gregory A. Mertz, Supervisory Historian, Fredericksburg and Spotsylvania National Military Park, 120 Chatham Lane, Fredericksburg, Virginia 22405; 540-373-6124, Fax 540-371-1907. Application deadline: January 15.

LEGACY INTERNATIONAL'S GLOBAL YOUTH VILLAGE
ROUTE 4, BOX 265-D
BEDFORD, VIRGINIA 24523

General Information Residential coeducational leadership-training program for youths from all over the world offering training and workshops in conflict resolution, environmental leadership, global issues, cross-cultural relations, English as a second language, and issue-oriented theater. Established in 1979. Operated by Legacy International. Affiliated with American Camping Association. 86-acre facility located 15 miles northeast of Lynchburg. Features: rural setting; location in the foothills of the Blue Ridge Mountains (close to lakes and hiking trails); ropes course, swimming pool, basektball, and volleyball courts; soccer field; hiking trail; small rock face for beginning climbers.

Profile of Summer Employees Total number: 40; average age: 25; 40% male, 60% female; 15% minorities; 10% college students; 30% international; 1% local residents; 15% teachers. Nonsmokers preferred.

Employment Information Openings are from June 16 to August 20. Jobs available: ▶ 1 *experienced pool director* with first aid, CPR, and lifeguarding experience; ▶ 4 *experienced lead counselors* (male); ▶ 6 *experienced lead counselors* (female); ▶ 3 *experienced art instructors;* ▶ 1 *evening and special program coordinator* with performing arts background (preferred) and very good organizational and motivational skills; ▶ 1 *summer office manager* with orientation to detail, bookkeeping and organizational skills, and an interest in working with people; ▶ 1 *program assistant* with organizational and word-processing skills; ▶ 7 *kitchen staff members;* ▶ 1 *maintenance person* with valid driver's license; ▶ 1 *program support/set-up person* with valid driver's license; ▶ 2 *experienced adventure/outdoor skills instructors* with first aid and CPR certification and rock-climbing experience (preferred); ▶ 3 *experienced leadership instructors* with ability to teach skills such as event planning, setting priorities, and running meetings; ▶ 2 *experienced environmental educators;* ▶ 1 *experienced bookkeeper* with knowledge of LOTUS and Excel; ▶ 2 *experienced or certified English as a second language instructors;* ▶ 2 *theater arts instructors* with improvisational theater experience and experience teaching youths; ▶ 2 *experienced ropes course instructors* with certification or documentation of training in high and low ropes; ▶ 1 *housekeeper* with valid driver's license and motivational and organizational skills; ▶ 1 *sports and games coordinator* with ability to lead and guide large groups in various games and sports and familiarity with new games and noncompetitive sports; ▶ 1 *experienced global issues instructor* with background and knowledge in international relations and teaching experience. International students encouraged to apply; must obtain own visa and working papers prior to employment; must apply through recognized agency.

Benefits College credit, on-the-job training, on-site room and board at no charge, laundry facilities, health insurance, travel reimbursement for international staff, negotiable stipend for non-interns, internships for college-level applicants (work-exchange program). Preemployment training of 13 to 14 days is required and includes safety and accident prevention, group interaction, first-aid, CPR, leadership, camper-counselor relations, cross-cultural communication.

Contact Leila Baz, Co-Director, Legacy International's Global Youth Village, Route 4, Box 265–D, Bedford, Virginia 24523; 540-297-5982, Fax 540-297-1860, E-mail mail@legacyintl. org, URL http://www.legacyintl.org. Application deadline: May 15.

OAKLAND SCHOOL AND CAMP
BOYD TAVERN
KESWICK, VIRGINIA 22947

General Information Coed residential and day camp for 130 students ages 8-14 with learning disabilities or other academic difficulties. Established in 1950. Owned by Joanne Dondero. Affiliated with Virginia Association for Independent Specialized Education Facilities, Orton Dyslexia Society. 450-acre facility located 11 miles east of Charlottesville. Features: riding stable, ring, and trails; swimming pool; large gymnasium/recreation building; creek with fishing; tennis courts; playing fields.

Profile of Summer Employees Total number: 15; average age: 21; 50% male, 50% female; 75% college students; 25% teachers. Nonsmokers preferred.

Employment Information Openings are from June 9 to August 9. Year-round positions also offered. Jobs available: ▶ 2 *swimming instructors* with lifesaving certification at $1800–$2400 per season; ▶ 12 *camp counselors* at $1800–$2200 per season; ▶ 1 *pool director* with WSI certification at $2300–$2700 per season; ▶ *teachers* with special education certification at $3200–$3600 per season. International students encouraged to apply; must obtain own visa and working papers prior to employment.

Benefits On-the-job training, on-site room and board at no charge, laundry facilities, teaching positions do not offer on-site room/board.

Contact Judith Edwards, Director, Oakland School, Oakland School and Camp, Boyd Tavern, Keswick, Virginia 22947; 804-293-9059, Fax 804-296-8930. Application deadline: June 1.

WOODBERRY FOREST SUMMER SCHOOL
PO BOX 354
WOODBERRY FOREST, VIRGINIA 22989

General Information Coeducational boarding school for approximately 200 students grades 8–12. Established in 1888. Operated by Woodberry Forest School. Affiliated with Virginia Association of Independent Schools, Southern Association of Independent Schools. 1,400-acre facility located 35 miles north of Charlottesville. Features: modern science facility with greenhouses, aquariums, and computers; air-conditioned classrooms; 9-hole golf course; 7 tennis courts; 3 squash courts; fully equipped field house; 2 swimming pools.

Profile of Summer Employees Total number: 60; 66% male, 34% female; 36% college students; 64% teachers. Nonsmokers preferred.

Employment Information Openings are from June 20 to August 4. Jobs available: ▶ 21 *interns (all subjects)* with three or four years of college (or recent graduate) at $1300 per season; ▶ 30 *teachers (all subjects)* at $2500 per season.

Benefits On-the-job training, on-site room and board at no charge, laundry facilities, use of school facilities.

Contact Jeffrey J. Davidsson, Director, Woodberry Forest Summer School, Department SJ, PO Box 354, Woodberry Forest, Virginia 22989; 540-672-6047, Fax 540-672-9076, E-mail wfssummer@woodberry.org. Application deadline: March 1.

WASHINGTON

CAMP BERACHAH
19830 SOUTHEAST 328TH PLACE
AUBURN, WASHINGTON 98002

General Information Offers eleven day (150 campers each), ten horse (24 campers each), junior and teen (300 campers each), gymnastics (200 campers each), and soccer (200 campers) camps. Established in 1975. Owned by Multi-Church Board. Affiliated with Christian Camping International. 160-acre facility located 30 miles south of Seattle. Features: indoor Olympic-size pool; gymnasium; woods with 6 miles of riding trails; mountain bikes; obstacle course; low challenge course; 440 cinder track; horses, indoor riding arena.

Profile of Summer Employees Total number: 60; average age: 20; 40% male, 60% female; 5% minorities; 30% high school students; 70% college students; 25% local residents. Nonsmokers only.

Employment Information Openings are from June 1 to August 30. Year-round positions also offered. Jobs available: ▶ *counselors* at $100–$135 per week; ▶ 1 *recreation director* at $125–$135 per week; ▶ 1 *nurse* at $125–$150 per week; ▶ 1 *crafts director* at $125–$135 per week; ▶ *lifeguard* at $500–$600 per month; ▶ *horsemanship wrangler/instructor* at $900–$1500 per season; ▶ *mountain bike leader* at $125–$150 per week. International students encouraged to apply; must obtain own visa and working papers prior to employment; must apply through recognized agency.

Benefits College credit, on-the-job training, on-site room and board at no charge, laundry facilities. Preemployment training of 3 to 7 days is required and includes safety and accident prevention, group interaction, first-aid, CPR, leadership, camper-counselor relations.

Contact James Richey, Program Director, Camp Berachah, Department SJ, 19830 Southeast 328th Place, Auburn, Washington 98002; 253-939-0488, Fax 253-833-7027, E-mail berachah@tcm.com, URL http://tcmnet.com/~berachah/. Application deadline: May 15.

LONGACRE EXPEDITIONS
GLACIER, WASHINGTON

General Information Adventure travel program emphasizing group living skills and physical challenges. Using base camp as a staging area, 2–3 staffers and 10–16 campers participate in intermediate and advanced expeditions on which they engage in human-powered sports. Established in 1981. Owned by Longacre Expeditions. Affiliated with American Camping Association. Located 30 miles west of Bellingham.

Profile of Summer Employees Total number: 15; average age: 25; 50% male, 50% female; 10% minorities; 40% college students; 30% local residents. Nonsmokers only.

Employment Information Openings are from June 14 to August 4. Jobs available: ▶ 1 *mountaineering instructor* (minimum age 21) with advanced first aid or advanced wilderness first aid, CPR, and completion of water safety course at $300–$400 per week; ▶ 1 *rock climbing instructor* (minimum age 21) at $300–$400 per week; ▶ 3 *support and logistics staff members* (minimum age 21) at $150–$175 per week; ▶ 8 *assistant trip leaders* (minimum age 21) at $150–$175 per week; ▶ *sea kayaking instructor* (minimum age 21) at $300–$400 per week.

Benefits On-the-job training, on-site room and board at no charge, Pro-Deal package. Preemployment training of 9 days is required and includes safety and accident prevention, group interaction, first-aid, CPR, leadership, camper-counselor relations. Orientation is unpaid.

Contact Roger Smith, Longacre Expeditions, RD 3, Box 106, Newport, Pennsylvania 17074; 717-567-6790, Fax 717-567-3955, E-mail longacre@pa.net, URL http://www.longex.com.

MT. RAINIER GUEST SERVICES
PO BOX 108
ASHFORD, WASHINGTON 98304

General Information Operates hotels, food services, and gift shops in Mt. Rainier National Park. Established in 1917. Located 90 miles south of Tacoma. Features: location in central Washington State; the historic, 126-room Paradise Inn (elevation of 5,400 feet); The National Park Inn at Longmire (newly renovated with 26 rooms and location at an elevation of 2,700 feet); rustic atmosphere (rooms do not have televisions or telephones); a pristine environment with Alpine meadows, streams, canyons, lakes, rivers, old-growth forests, and glaciers.

Profile of Summer Employees Total number: 240; average age: 25; 50% male, 50% female; 10% minorities; 75% college students; 25% retirees; 10% local residents. Nonsmokers preferred.

Employment Information Openings are from May 1 to October 10. Jobs available: ▶ 20 *housekeeping staff members* with ability to clean guest rooms and hotel at $216 per week; ▶ 10 *desk clerks* with ability to register guests and handle cash at $220 per week; ▶ 20 *cook's helpers/pantry persons* with ability to perform prep work plus make salads and sandwiches at $216 per week; ▶ 30 *kitchen/utility personnel* at $216 per week; ▶ 30 *fast food attendants* with ability to take/fill orders, bus tables, and operate cash register at $216 per week; ▶ 5 *janitors* (night and day) with ability to clean halls, restrooms, windows, and carpets and empty garbage at $220–$280 per week; ▶ 5 *kitchen porters* (night and day) with ability to clean hoods, ovens, and floors and assist in dishwashing at $216–$240 per week; ▶ 20 *retail clerks* with ability to perform retail sales, stocking, and cleaning duties at $220 per week; ▶ 10 *cooks* with ability to work in casual and fine dining restaurants at $280–$400 per week. International students encouraged to apply; must apply through recognized agency.

Benefits On-the-job training, on-site room and board at $50 per week, laundry facilities, bonuses available to those who finish employment agreement, discounts in dining room and gift shops.

Contact Sandra Miller, Personnel Department, Mt. Rainier Guest Services, Department SJ, PO Box 108, Ashford, Washington 98304; 360-569-2440 EXT 119, Fax 360-569-2770, URL http://www.coolworks.com/showme/rainier.

YMCA CAMP SEYMOUR
9725 CRAMER ROAD KPN
GIG HARBOR, WASHINGTON 98329

General Information Residential camp serving 140 campers weekly and biweekly. Shorter minicamps of four days are also available. Camp provides "in camp" and outpost adventure travel for teenagers. Established in 1906. Owned by YMCA of Tacoma–Pierce County. Affiliated with YMCA, American Camping Association. 150-acre facility located 18 miles northwest of Tacoma. Features: one-half mile of shoreline on Puget Sound; outdoor swimming pool; building with touch tanks for hands-on marine study; outpost trips for individuals of middle school age; leadership program for high school age participants; low ropes initiative and group building cooperation course.

Profile of Summer Employees Total number: 50; average age: 21; 55% male, 45% female; 10% minorities; 10% high school students; 50% college students; 10% international; 50% local residents. Nonsmokers preferred.

Employment Information Openings are from June 11 to August 15. Jobs available: ▶ 12 *cabin leaders* at $100–$130 per week; ▶ 1 *experienced pool manager* with WSI, American Red Cross advanced lifesaving, and American Red Cross lifeguarding certification at $150–$190 per week; ▶ 1 *experienced waterfront manager* with American Red Cross advanced lifesaving and American Red Cross lifeguarding certification at $160–$200 per week; ▶ 2 *program specialists* (arts and crafts, outdoor education) at $130–$170 per week; ▶ 4 *experienced trip leaders* with ability to lead bike, backpack, canoe, and kayak trips at $130–$180 per week; ▶ 2 *outpost coordinators* with ability to outfit all extended trips and overnights, oversee pretrip meetings and menu planning, and share driving responsibilities at $140–$170 per week; ▶ 3 *unit leaders* at $150–$190 per week.

Benefits College credit, on-the-job training, formal ongoing training, on-site room and board at no charge, laundry facilities, possible internships. Preemployment training of 7 to 10 days is required and includes safety and accident prevention, group interaction, first-aid, CPR, leadership, camper-counselor relations. Orientation is paid.

Contact Dan Martin, Director of Camping and Conference Services, YMCA Camp Seymour, Department SJ, 1002 South Pearl Street, Tacoma, Washington 98465; 206-564-9622, Fax 206-566-1211. Application deadline: April 15.

WEST VIRGINIA

CAMP RIM ROCK
BOX 69
YELLOW SPRING, WEST VIRGINIA 26865

General Information Residential camp serving 180 girls offering a strong general program and horseback riding, aquatics, and performing arts programs. Established in 1952. Owned by James L. Matheson. Affiliated with American Camping Association, Association for Horsemanship Safety and Education. 600-acre facility located 100 miles west of Washington, D.C. Features: 2 pools; canoeing on the Cacapun River; 5 riding rings and 55 horses; 5 miles of riding trails; dance and drama facilities with outdoor theater; scenic mountain setting with mild climate; 2 large sports fields.

Profile of Summer Employees Total number: 70; average age: 25; 5% male, 95% female; 10% minorities; 75% college students; 40% international; 40% teachers. Nonsmokers only.

Employment Information Openings are from June 7 to September 2. Jobs available: ▶ 5 *swimming counselors* with WSI certification and ability to teach at $1800–$2400 per season; ▶ 2 *experienced tennis counselors* at $1600–$2000 per season; ▶ 7 *riding staff members* with teacher certification at $1800–$2500 per season; ▶ 20 *sports and general counselors* with ability to work with children and skill in sports at $1600–$2200 per season; ▶ 2 *certified archery instructors* at $1600–$2000 per season; ▶ 2 *certified canoeing instructors* at $1600–$2000 per season; ▶ *dance instructor* at $1600–$2000 per season; ▶ *drama instructor* at $1600–$2000 per season. International students encouraged to apply; must apply through recognized agency.

Benefits College credit, on-the-job training, formal ongoing training, on-site room and board at no charge, laundry facilities, travel reimbursement, workmen's compensation, use of camp recreational materials, liberal time off policy. Preemployment training of 10 days is required and includes safety and accident prevention, group interaction, first-aid, CPR, leadership, camper-counselor relations, lifeguard training. Orientation is paid.

Contact Jim Matheson, Director, Camp Rim Rock, Department SJ, Box 69, Yellow Spring, West Virginia 26865; 800-662-4650, Fax 304-856-3201, E-mail rimrock@naven-villages.net. Application deadline: May 1.

GREENBRIER RIVER OUTDOOR ADVENTURES
PO BOX 160
BARTOW, WEST VIRGINIA 24920

General Information Coed outdoor adventure program with variety of itineraries and focuses including backpacking, rock climbing, mountain biking, caving, whitewater rafting, farming, community service, canoeing, and kayaking. One-, two-, three-, and four-week sessions in West Virginia and New England. Established in 1992. Owned by Tom and Rachel Bryant. Affiliated with Greenbrier River Learning Center. 250-acre facility located 150 miles west of Richmond, Virginia. Features: location near the 900,000-acre Monogahela National Forest; 250-acre mountain farm basecamp; 350 miles of mountain bike trails; rock climbing at Seneca Rocks and other areas; countless number of caves and whitewater opportunities; indoor climbing wall.

Profile of Summer Employees Total number: 20; average age: 25; 50% male, 50% female; 60% college students; 20% teachers. Nonsmokers preferred.

Employment Information Openings are from June 20 to August 16. Jobs available: ▶ *group leaders* with CPR and first aid training and safe driving record at $200–$250 per week; ▶ *support staff members* at $130 per week; ▶ *assistant director* at $200–$300 per week; ▶ *climbing specialist* at $200–$250 per week; ▶ *caving specialist* at $200–$250 per week; ▶ *summer interns* at $100 per week; ▶ *assistant leaders* at $175 per week; ▶ *canoeing/kayaking specialist* at $200–$250 per week. International students encouraged to apply; must obtain own visa and working papers prior to employment; must apply through recognized agency.

Benefits On-the-job training, on-site room and board at no charge, opportunity to work with youth in outdoor setting, small group experience (maximum 12 students per group).

Contact Tom and Rachel Bryant, Directors/Owners, Greenbrier River Outdoor Adventures, Department SJ, PO Box 160, Bartow, West Virginia 24920; 304-456-5191, Fax 304-456-3121.

TIMBER RIDGE CAMPS
HIGH VIEW, WEST VIRGINIA 26808

General Information Two residential coeducational camps serving 500 children over nine weeks. Established in 1954. Owned by Fred Greenberg. 685-acre facility located 90 miles west of Washington, DC. Features: 14 tennis courts with lights; indoor theater with professional sound and light systems; complete horseback riding facilities; 12-acre lake; 18-hole golf course; 2 flying trapezes.

Profile of Summer Employees Total number: 200; average age: 21; 50% male, 50% female; 30% minorities; 2% high school students; 90% college students; 8% retirees; 2% international; 4% local residents. Nonsmokers only.

Employment Information Openings are from June 16 to August 18. Jobs available: ▶ 20

tennis instructors at $1200–$1500 per season; ▶ 10 *swimming instructors* with WSI certification at $1200–$1500 per season; ▶ *horseback riding instructors* at $1200–$1500 per season; ▶ *athletics staff members* at $1200–$1500 per season; ▶ *woodshop staff* at $1200–$1500 per season; ▶ *computer instructors* at $1200–$1500 per season; ▶ *archery/riflery instructors* at $1200–$1500 per season; ▶ *performing arts/dance instructors* at $1000–$1400 per season.

Benefits College credit, on-the-job training, on-site room and board at no charge, laundry facilities, travel reimbursement. Preemployment training of 4 days is required and includes safety and accident prevention, group interaction, leadership, camper-counselor relations. Orientation is paid.

Contact Jerry Shoemake, Personnel Director, Timber Ridge Camps, Department SJ, 10 Old Court Road, Baltimore, Maryland 21208; 410-484-2233, Fax 410-484-2292, E-mail trcamps@aol.com. Application deadline: April 1.

USA RAFT
PO BOX 277
ROWLESBURG, WEST VIRGINIA 26425

General Information Guided whitewater raft trips on the Ocoee, Nantahala, Pigeon, French Broad, Nolichucky, New and Gauley, Cheat, and Potomac Rivers. Established in 1972. Affiliated with America Outdoors.

Profile of Summer Employees Total number: 200. Nonsmokers preferred.

Employment Information Jobs available: ▶ *raft guides (minimum age 18)* with basic first aid and CPR certification at $1000–$4000 per season; ▶ *receptionists/store clerks* at $5.15 per hour.

Benefits On-site room and board at some locations costing about $20–$25 per week.

Contact Summer Jobs Director, USA Raft, Department SJ, PO Box 277, Rowlesburg, West Virginia 26425; 304-454-2475, Fax 304-454-2472. Application deadline: February 28.

WISCONSIN

BACHMAN-LAING TENNIS CAMP
6040 NORTH LYDELL AVENUE
WHITEFISH BAY, WISCONSIN 53217

General Information Camp for teaching tennis to boys and girls ages 7–17 in four junior sessions. Established in 1960. Owned by J. Cary Bachman and James M. Laing. Situated on 100 acres. Features: 9 outdoor tennis courts; 5 indoor tennis courts; 10 indoor courts at nearby private clubs used during periods of extended rain; indoor pool; recreation hall; golf course.

Profile of Summer Employees Total number: 16; average age: 35; 60% male, 40% female; 10% minorities; 20% high school students; 30% college students; 2% retirees; 20% teachers. Nonsmokers preferred.

Employment Information Openings are from June 12 to July 20. Jobs available: ▶ *supervisory tennis instructors* at $200–$340 per week; ▶ *tennis instructors* at $140–$190 per week. International students encouraged to apply; must obtain own visa and working papers prior to employment.

Benefits On-the-job training, on-site room and board at no charge.

Contact J. Cary Bachman, Director, Bachman-Laing Tennis Camp, 6040 North Lydell Avenue, Milwaukee, Wisconsin 53217; 414-962-3306. Application deadline: March 1.

BIRCH TRAIL CAMP FOR GIRLS
PO BOX 527
MINONG, WISCONSIN 54859

General Information Residential camp serving 185 girls ages 8–15 in two- to four-week sessions including extensive wilderness trips. Established in 1959. Owned by Richard and Barbara Chernov. Affiliated with American Camping Association, Association for Experiential Education, Wilderness Education Association. 310-acre facility located 50 miles south of Duluth, Minnesota. Features: 2 climbing walls; low and high ropes course; 4,000-foot freshwater shoreline; 6 miles of mountain biking trails; 2,200-foot long athletic field; full water ski program (barefoot, tricks, and slalom course).

Profile of Summer Employees Total number: 90; average age: 21; 5% male, 95% female; 10% minorities; 10% high school students; 80% college students; 15% international; 5% local residents. Nonsmokers preferred.

Employment Information Openings are from June 8 to August 12. Jobs available: ▶ *swimming instructors* with WSI certification at $1000–$1500 per season; ▶ *wilderness trip leaders* (minimum age 21) with LGT certification at $1700–$1900 per season; ▶ *cabin counselors* (minimum age 17) at $1100–$1400 per season; ▶ *kitchen helpers* (minimum age 17) at $1350–$1750 per season; ▶ *housekeepers* (minimum age 17) at $1350–$1750 per season; ▶ *caretaker's assistant* (minimum age 17) at $1350–$1750 per season; ▶ *nurse* at $2150–$2550 per season. International students encouraged to apply; must apply through recognized agency.

Benefits Formal ongoing training, on-site room and board at no charge, laundry facilities, travel reimbursement, health insurance, internships. Preemployment training of 8 days is required and includes safety and accident prevention, group interaction, first-aid, CPR, leadership, camper-counselor relations. Orientation is unpaid.

Contact Richard Chernov, Owner/Director, Birch Trail Camp for Girls, Department SJ, 6570 Regal Manor Drive, Tucson, Arizona 85750; 520-529-9358, Fax 520-529-9357, E-mail brchtrail@ aol.com. Application deadline: February 1.

BOYD'S MASON LAKE RESORT
PO BOX 57
FIFIELD, WISCONSIN 54524

General Information American-plan family resort that rents eighteen cabins, serves three meals daily, and performs daily maid service for up to 100 guests. Established in 1895. Owned by Richard Simon. Affiliated with Park Falls Area Chamber of Commerce, Wisconsin Innkeepers' Association. 2,600-acre facility located 400 miles north of Chicago, Illinois. Features: 4 private lakes; secluded Northwoods environment; miles of maintained hiking trails; swimming beach; playgrounds and supervised children's activities; extensive water sports (fishing, canoeing, boating, and sailing).

Profile of Summer Employees Total number: 22; average age: 26; 30% male, 70% female; 15% college students; 25% local residents. Nonsmokers preferred.

Employment Information Openings are from May 10 to October 10. Jobs available: ▶ 5 *dining room attendants* at $210–$260 per week; ▶ 1 *children's recreation supervisor* with background in elementary education at $210 per week; ▶ 1 *dishwasher* at $210–$260 per week; ▶ 1 *pots and pans washer* at $210–$260 per week; ▶ 1 *swing cook* at $210–$260 per week; ▶ *receptionist* at $210 per week.

Benefits On-the-job training, on-site room and board at no charge, laundry facilities.

Contact Richard Simon, Manager/Owner, Boyd's Mason Lake Resort, Department SJ, PO Box 57, Fifield, Wisconsin 54524; 715-762-3469. Application deadline: May 1.

CAMP BIRCH KNOLL FOR GIRLS
EAGLE RIVER, WISCONSIN 54554

General Information Residential camp with 40 instructed activities for girls ages 8–16. Established in 1944. Owned by Gary Baier. 400-acre facility located 200 miles north of Milwaukee.

Features: lakefront with extensive waterskiing, swimming, and boating facilities; 7 tennis courts; sports complex for soccer, softball, volleyball, and basketball; indoor gymnastics and dance complex; two art buildings for pottery, jewelry, graphics, and painting; dual horseback arena and 10 groomed trails.

Profile of Summer Employees Total number: 60; average age: 22; 20% male, 80% female; 5% high school students; 70% college students; 5% local residents; 5% teachers. Nonsmokers only.

Employment Information Openings are from June 1 to August 10. Jobs available: ▶ *counselors/ instructors* at $1500–$1800 per season; ▶ *tennis director* at $2000–$2500 per season; ▶ *gymnastics director* at $1500–$2000 per season; ▶ *registered nurse* at $3000–$3500 per season; ▶ *riding director* at $2500–$3500 per season; ▶ *swimming director* at $1500–$2500 per season; ▶ *cook* at $200–$300 per week. International students encouraged to apply; must obtain own visa and working papers prior to employment.

Benefits On-the-job training, on-site room and board at no charge.

Contact Gary Baier, Director, Camp Birch Knoll for Girls, Department SJ, PO Box 13, Stevens Point, Wisconsin 54481; 800-843-2904, Fax 715-341-4261, E-mail cbkfun@aol.com, URL http://www.campchannel.com/cbkfun. Application deadline: May 1.

CAMP EDWARDS
PO BOX 16
EAST TROY, WISCONSIN 53120

General Information Residential camp serving youth and families with six- and eleven-day sessions. Established in 1929. Owned by Greater Elgin Area YMCA. 132-acre facility located 45 miles west of Milwaukee. Features: extensive freshwater lake frontage; ½ mile elevated marsh boardwalk; 2 low ropes courses.

Profile of Summer Employees Total number: 40; average age: 20; 50% male, 50% female; 2% minorities; 10% high school students; 90% college students; 1% retirees; 1% local residents; 1% teachers. Nonsmokers only.

Employment Information Openings are from June 7 to August 14. Jobs available: ▶ *cabin counselors* at $125–$135 per week; ▶ *support staff positions* at $165–$250 per week; ▶ *aquatic directors* at $165–$250 per week; ▶ *nurse* at $250–$300 per week.

Benefits On-the-job training, on-site room and board at no charge, laundry facilities.

Contact Mr. Kim Harron, Executive Director, Camp Edwards, Department SJ, PO Box 16, East Troy, Wisconsin 53120; 414-642-7466, Fax 414-642-5108.

CAMP INTERLAKEN JCC
7050 OLD HIGHWAY 70
EAGLE RIVER, WISCONSIN 54521

General Information Residential Jewish coeducational camp serving 400 campers ages 8–16. Established in 1966. Owned by Jewish Community Center of Milwaukee. Affiliated with Jewish Community Centers of America, American Camping Association. 110-acre facility located 250 miles north of Milwaukee. Features: spring-fed lake; location in the Northwoods; family accommodations for August family camp; complete waterfront program; 5 outdoor tennis courts.

Profile of Summer Employees Total number: 60; average age: 20; 50% male, 50% female; 5% minorities; 90% college students; 5% international. Nonsmokers preferred.

Employment Information Openings are from June 1 to August 25. Jobs available: ▶ 4 *experienced kitchen stewards* at $1500 per season; ▶ 1 *experienced gymnastics instructor* with instructor-level expertise at $1000–$1500 per season; ▶ 1 *trip director* with LGT, CPR, and first aid certification at $1700–$2200 per season; ▶ 1 *experienced sailing instructor* with LGT certification at $1200–$1800 per season; ▶ 2 *crafts instructors* with knowledge of ceramics, tie-dyeing, crafts, and painting preferred at $1200–$2000 per season; ▶ 1 *tennis instructor* with USTA certification at $1200–$2000 per season; ▶ *nurse* with LPN or RN license at $2000–$3000 per season.

Benefits On-the-job training, on-site room and board at no charge, travel reimbursement.

Preemployment training of 5 days is required and includes safety and accident prevention, group interaction, first-aid, CPR, leadership, camper-counselor relations. Orientation is paid.
Contact Judy Young, Director, Camp Interlaken JCC, Department SJ, 6255 North Santa Monica, Milwaukee, Wisconsin 53217; 414-964-4444, Fax 414-964-0922. Application deadline: March 1.

CAMP LUCERNE
ROUTE 1, BOX 3150, COUNTY YY
NESHKORO, WISCONSIN 54960-9329

General Information Residential camp serving 150 campers weekly. Established in 1947. Owned by United Methodist Church. Affiliated with American Camping Association, Christian Camping International/USA, International Association of Conference Center Administrators. 530-acre facility located 40 miles west of Oshkosh. Features: clear 50-acre lake; woods; meadow; climate conducive to traditional camp activity; comfortable sleeping cabins; serene wooded area.
Profile of Summer Employees Total number: 50; average age: 20; 50% male, 50% female; 10% minorities; 70% college students; 30% international; 10% local residents. Nonsmokers only.
Employment Information Openings are from June 4 to August 17. Jobs available: ▶ 12 *counselors* at $110–$120 per week; ▶ 1 *relief worker* with ability to assist in kitchen (primary responsibility) at $120 per week; ▶ 1 *maintenance person* with valid driver's license at $120–$140 per week; ▶ 1 *truck driver* with valid driver's license at $110–$125 per week; ▶ 2 *waterfront personnel* with lifeguard training at $115–$140 per week; ▶ 1 *waterfront director* with lifeguard training and WSI certification at $125–$140 per week; ▶ 1 *dishwasher* at $110–$120 per week; ▶ 1 *health supervisor* with first aid/CPR certification or RN license (preferred) at $160–$185 per week; ▶ 1 *dining room coordinator* at $110–$125 per week; ▶ 1 *assistant cook* at $115–$130 per week. International students encouraged to apply; must apply through recognized agency.
Benefits On-site room and board at no charge, laundry facilities.
Contact Joel Jarvis, Director, Camp Lucerne, Department SJ, Route 1, Box 3150, County YY, Neshkoro, Wisconsin 54960-9329; 414-293-4488, Fax 414-293-4361. Application deadline: May 1.

CAMP MANITO-WISH YMCA
BOULDER JUNCTION, WISCONSIN 54512

General Information Facility offering wilderness tripping, canoeing, kayaking, and backpacking for 220 campers ages 11–15 in a 3-week session. Traditional camp programs offer variety when campers are not on the trail. Established in 1919. Operated by YMCA. Affiliated with American Camping Association, Association for Experiential Education. 300-acre facility located 250 miles north of Milwaukee. Features: high and low ropes course; lake frontage with access to various lakes and rivers; old log dining hall dating from 1925; over 70 buildings on site; enclosed cabins housing 10 campers and 2 staff; leadership center.
Profile of Summer Employees Total number: 150; average age: 21; 50% male, 50% female; 10% high school students; 90% college students; 1% international; 1% local residents. Nonsmokers preferred.
Employment Information Openings are from June 3 to August 10. Jobs available: ▶ 5 *wilderness adventure teachers* with Wilderness First Responder certification (training available), CPR, and LGT at $500–$550 per month; ▶ 1 *experienced ropes course lead instructor* with ropes course certified training at $170 per week; ▶ 2 *ropes course instructors/logistical assistants* with first aid/CPR certification at $500–$550 per month; ▶ 20 *cabin counselors* with LGT and first aid/CPR certification at $118–$124 per week; ▶ 10 *program area staff* with first aid/CPR certification at $118 per week; ▶ 10 *tripping assistants* with LGT and first aid/CPR certification at $106–$111 per week; ▶ *swimming instructors* with WSI certification at $600–$700 per month. International students encouraged to apply; must apply through recognized agency.
Benefits On-the-job training, formal ongoing training, on-site room and board at no charge, laundry facilities, health insurance, staff grant opportunities. Preemployment training of 3 to 9

days is optional and includes safety and accident prevention, group interaction, first-aid, leadership, wilderness skills, navigation, canoe instruction. Orientation is unpaid.

Contact Anne Derber, Assistant Director, Camp Manito-Wish YMCA, Department SJ, N14 W24200 Tower Place 205, Waukesha, Wisconsin 53188; 414-523-1623, Fax 414-523-1626, E-mail expmwish@ekecpc.com. Application deadline: May 1.

CAMP NEBAGAMON FOR BOYS
PO BOX 429
LAKE NEBAGAMON, WISCONSIN 54849

General Information Residential boys camp for 220 campers from forty different communities and several countries. Established in 1929. Owned by Roger and Judy Wallenstein. Affiliated with American Camping Association, Midwest Association of Independent Camps, American Camping Association–Illinois Section. 70-acre facility located 35 miles southeast of Duluth, Minnesota. Features: setting in heart of the Northwoods; complete waterfront; 7 tennis courts; log cabin art building; well-equipped darkroom; spacious playing fields.

Profile of Summer Employees Total number: 125; average age: 20; 80% male, 20% female; 5% minorities; 27% high school students; 40% college students; 10% international; 18% local residents.

Employment Information Openings are from June 18 to August 18. Jobs available: ▶ 2 *waterfront directors* with WSI or Red Cross lifeguard certification at $1400–$2200 per season; ▶ 25 *senior cabin counselors* (college age) with skills in water and land sports, tennis, target skills, art, campcraft, and photography at $1050–$1200 per season; ▶ 1 *nurse* with RN license at $200–$250 per week; ▶ 2 *cooks* with experience cooking for large groups at $200–$250 per week; ▶ 2 *drivers* (minimum age 21) with clean driving record at $1400–$1700 per season; ▶ 25 *junior cabin counselors* (11th and 12th graders) with skills in water and land sports, tennis, target skills, art, campcraft, and photography at $900–$950 per season; ▶ 2 *swimming instructors* with WSI or lifeguard certification at $800–$1200 per season. International students encouraged to apply; must apply through recognized agency.

Benefits On-the-job training, formal ongoing training, on-site room and board at no charge, laundry facilities, travel reimbursement, health insurance, many options for time off, excellent opportunity to work with professional staff. Preemployment training of 7 days is required and includes safety and accident prevention, group interaction, first-aid, CPR, leadership, camper-counselor relations, skill instruction. Orientation is unpaid.

Contact Roger and Judy Wallenstein, Directors, Camp Nebagamon for Boys, 5237 North Lakewood, Chicago, Illinois 60640; 773-271-9500, Fax 773-271-9816, E-mail cnebagamon@aol.com. Application deadline: April 1.

CAMP SHEWAHMEGON
DRUMMOND, WISCONSIN 54832

General Information Non-competitive residential camp for 80 boys ages 8–14 offering daily choice of activities; emphasizing growth in skills, confidence, and independence. Established in 1934. Owned by Bill and Gerry Will. Affiliated with American Camping Association. 45-acre facility located 70 miles southeast of Duluth, Minnesota. Features: Lake Owen with natural sand beach; 3 tennis courts; nearby golf course; location surrounded by Chequamegon National Forest; athletic field; basketball court; recreation lodge.

Profile of Summer Employees Total number: 30; average age: 20; 90% male, 10% female; 5% minorities; 20% high school students; 40% college students; 12% international; 10% local residents; 5% teachers. Nonsmokers preferred.

Employment Information Openings are from June 14 to August 14. Jobs available: ▶ 8 *general staff members* at $1000–$2000 per season; ▶ 2 *lifeguards* with ARC certification at $1200–$1800 per season; ▶ 2 *campout trip leaders* with campcraft experience and first aid certification at $1000–$1800 per season; ▶ 2 *swimming instructors* with WSI certification at $1000–$2000 per season; ▶ 1 *assistant cook* at $1800–$2100 per season; ▶ 3 *dishwashers* at $1100–$1400 per season. International students encouraged to apply; must apply through recognized agency.

Benefits College credit, on-the-job training, on-site room and board at no charge, laundry facilities. Preemployment training is required and includes safety and accident prevention, group interaction, leadership, camper-counselor relations.

Contact Bill Will, Director, Camp Shewahmegon, Department SJ, 1208 East Miner Street, Arlington Heights, Illinois 60004; 847-255-9710, E-mail wwill57321@aol.com. Application deadline: June 1.

CAMPS WOODLAND AND TOWERING PINES
EAGLE RIVER, WISCONSIN 54521

General Information Residential camps on separate sites having four- or six-week seasons. Established in 1946. Owned by John and Anne Jordan. Affiliated with American Camping Association, Association of Independent Camps. 400-acre facility located 20 miles north of Rhinelander. Features: extensive lake frontage; private settings in state forests; acclimatization ecology center; Lake Superior sailing outpost; river canoe trips.

Profile of Summer Employees Total number: 50; average age: 20; 60% male, 40% female; 80% college students; 5% retirees; 5% international; 5% local residents; 5% teachers. Nonsmokers only.

Employment Information Openings are from June 23 to August 14. Jobs available: ► *swimming/ small craft staff members* with WSI certification at $200 per week; ► *crafts/Indian lore staff members* at $150 per week; ► *riflery/archery staff members* with NRA training at $150 per week; ► *tennis/gymnastics staff members* at $150 per week; ► *experienced cooks/assistant cooks* at $200 per week; ► *dishwashers* at $150 per week; ► *nurse* with RN license at $250 per week. International students encouraged to apply; must obtain own visa and working papers prior to employment; must apply through recognized agency.

Benefits College credit, on-the-job training, on-site room and board at no charge, laundry facilities, travel reimbursement, accident insurance. Preemployment training of 6 days is required and includes safety and accident prevention, group interaction, first-aid, CPR, leadership, camper-counselor relations. Orientation is paid.

Contact John and Anne Jordan, Camps Woodland and Towering Pines, Department SJ, 242 Bristol Street, Northfield, Illinois 60093; 847-446-7311, Fax 847-446-7710, E-mail towpines@ aol.com.

CAMP TIMBERLANE FOR BOYS
AV 11400 AIRPORT ROAD
WOODRUFF, WISCONSIN 54568

General Information Noncompetitive residential camp offering four- and eight-week sessions serving 150 boys from across the country. Established in 1960. Owned by Leslie and Mike Cohen. Affiliated with American Camping Association, Midwest Association of Independent Camps, International Camping Fellowship. 250-acre facility located 250 miles north of Milwaukee. Features: 2,000 feet of secluded lake shoreline; location 5 miles from small but active town; 250 acres of secluded forest land; 4 tennis courts; 2 basketball courts; 50-foot tall rock climbing wall.

Profile of Summer Employees Total number: 70; average age: 22; 80% male, 20% female; 10% minorities; 25% high school students; 60% college students; 5% local residents. Nonsmokers preferred.

Employment Information Openings are from June 15 to August 15. Jobs available: ► 2 *counselors/swimming instructors* with lifeguard or WSI certification at $1000–$1200 per season; ► 1 *counselor/sailing instructor* at $1000–$1200 per season; ► 2 *counselors/scuba diving instructors* with PADI advanced open water or divemaster certification at $1000–$1500 per season; ► 2 *counselors/waterskiing instructors* with teaching and boat driving experience at $1000–$1500 per season; ► 2 *counselors/tennis instructors* at $1000–$1500 per season; ► 1 *counselor/ photography instructor* with experience developing black-and-white film at $1000–$1500 per season; ► 1 *counselor/pottery instructor* with experience in wheel and kiln use at $1000–$1200 per season; ▶ 2 *counselors/horseback riding instructors* with significant English saddle experience at $1000–$1500 per season; ▶ 1 *counselor/guitar instructor* at $1000–$1500 per season; ▶ 1 *counselor/golf instructor* at $1000–$1500 per season; ▶ 6 *trip leaders* with canoeing and/or rock climbing background and lifeguard certification at $1200–$1600 per season; ▶ 2 *nurses* with RN, GN, or LPN license at $2000–$2500 per season; ▶ 1 *experienced assistant cook* at $1000–$3000 per season; ▶ 2 *maintenance persons* with carpentry skill at $1000–$2000 per season; ▶ 1 *driver* with good driving record at $1000–$1500 per season.

Benefits College credit, on-the-job training, formal ongoing training, on-site room and board at no charge, travel reimbursement, accommodation of special dietary needs. Preemployment training of 1 to 14 days is required and includes safety and accident prevention, group interaction, first-aid, CPR, leadership, camper-counselor relations, lifeguard training. Orientation is paid.

Contact Mike Cohen, Director, Camp Timberlane for Boys, Department SJ, 802 East Placita De Roberta, Tucson, Arizona 85718; 520-544-7801, Fax 520-544-3919. Application deadline: May 31.

CENTRAL WISCONSIN ENVIRONMENTAL STATION
7290 COUNTY MM
AMHERST JUNCTION, WISCONSIN 54407

General Information Residential camp serving 50–60 campers a week. Campers range in age from 7–18 years old. All programs have an environmental focus. Established in 1975. Operated by University of Wisconsin- Stevens Point. 80-acre facility located 15 miles east of Stevens Point. Features: lakefront beach with swimming area; canoes, sailboard, and sail boat; challenge course; forests; pond; log cabins and dormitory.

Profile of Summer Employees Total number: 10; average age: 22; 50% male, 50% female; 10% minorities; 95% college students; 10% international; 60% local residents. Nonsmokers preferred.

Employment Information Openings are from May 23 to August 24. Year-round positions also offered. Jobs available: ▶ *summer program director* at $200–$225 per week; ▶ *waterfront director* with WSI and lifeguard certification at $150–$170 per week; ▶ *counselors/naturalists* at $120–$140 per week; ▶ *health lodge supervisor* with EMT, RN, and advanced first aid training at $150–$170 per week; ▶ *tripping leaders* at $130–$145 per week. International students encouraged to apply; must apply through recognized agency.

Benefits College credit, on-the-job training, formal ongoing training, on-site room and board at no charge. Preemployment training of 8 days is required and includes safety and accident prevention, group interaction, leadership, camper-counselor relations. Orientation is paid.

Contact Peter Matthai, Summer Camp Director, Central Wisconsin Environmental Station, Department SJ, 7290 County MM, Amherst Junction, Wisconsin 54407; 715-824-2428, Fax 715-824-3201. Application deadline: May 1.

CLEARWATER CAMP FOR GIRLS
7490 CLEARWATER ROAD
MINOCQUA, WISCONSIN 54548

General Information Traditional residential camp providing caring staff and high-quality camping experiences for girls ages 8–16. Established in 1933. Owned by Clearwater Camp, Inc. Affiliated with American Camping Association. 80-acre facility located 25 miles southeast of Rhinelander. Features: 3,600-acre Headwaters Lake; 5-acre island with 25 cabins for campers and staff; location surrounded by nature conservancy; sailing and waterfront area; location within 5 miles of a resort community.

Profile of Summer Employees Total number: 40; average age: 20; 2% male, 98% female; 5% high school students; 90% college students; 2% international; 1% local residents; 2% teachers. Nonsmokers preferred.

Employment Information Openings are from June 10 to August 15. Jobs available: ▶ 6 *sailing instructors* with experience handling C scows, Red Cross sailing USRA rating, and CPR certification at $1200–$2500 per season; ▶ 5 *swimming instructors* with CPR, WSI, and lifeguard certification at $1200–$2400 per season; ▶ 1 *experienced archery instructor* at $1200–$1500 per season; ▶ 2 *crafts instructors* with creativity and varied skills in weaving, pottery, and leather at $1200–$1600 per season; ▶ 2 *tennis instructors* with CPR certification and the ability to teach with enthusiasm at $1200–$1600 per season; ▶ 2 *experienced English-style riding instructors* with first aid, CPR, CHA, and HSA certification at $1200–$4000 per season; ▶ 4 *experienced canoeing instructors* with lifeguard or emergency water safety, CPR, and canoe certification (preferred) at $1200–$1600 per season; ▶ 2 *trip leaders* with campcraft, canoeing, and backpacking experience and first aid, CPR, and lifeguard or wilderness first aid/safety and Wilderness Water Safety at $1200–$4000 per season; ▶ 2 *drama instructors* with talent, ability to direct, and creativity at $1200–$1500 per season; ▶ 1 *windsurfing instructor* with lifeguard and windsurfing instructor rating (preferred) at $1200–$1400 per season; ▶ 2 *waterskiing instructors* with boat-driving experience and WSI, or lifeguard certification and waterski instructor course preferred at $1200–$2000 per season; ▶ *experienced cook and assistant cook* at $1500–$4000 per season; ▶ 6 *kitchen staff members* at $900–$1200 per season; ▶ 5 *general counselors* with love for children, willingness and ability to assist youngsters, lifeguard, first aid, CPR certification, and good role modeling at $1200–$1600 per season; ▶ 2 *skilled tripping leaders* with Wilderness Water Safety certification and first aid, CPR, and LGT at $1200–$1400 per season. International students encouraged to apply; must obtain own visa and working papers prior to employment; must apply through recognized agency.

Benefits College credit, on-the-job training, on-site room and board at no charge, health insurance, tuition reimbursement, positive reference on résumé, added skill and confidence working with children, increased communications skills and confidence.

Contact Sunny Moore, Director, Clearwater Camp for Girls, Department SJ, 7490 Clearwater Road, Minocqua, Wisconsin 54548; 800-399-5030, Fax 715-356-3124. Application deadline: April 15.

HONEY ROCK CAMP
8660 HONEY ROCK ROAD
THREE LAKES, WISCONSIN 54562

General Information Northwoods campus of Wheaton College providing year-round leadership training and wilderness experiences for college students and young people. Established in 1951. Owned by Wheaton College. Affiliated with Christian Camping International/USA, American Camping Association. 600-acre facility located 250 miles north of Milwaukee. Features: rustic wilderness setting including Nicolet National Forest; 50 horses, 2 rings, and miles of trails; climbing tower and indoor climbing gym; 1½ miles of lakefront; 13 camp activities including waterskiing, riflery, archery, and kayaking.

Profile of Summer Employees Total number: 150; average age: 20; 50% male, 50% female; 5% minorities; 20% high school students; 80% college students; 5% international; 1% local residents; 3% teachers. Nonsmokers only.

Employment Information Openings are from May 12 to August 22. Year-round positions also offered. Jobs available: ▶ *waterfront staff members;* ▶ *kitchen staff members;* ▶ *barn staff members;* ▶ *operational staff members;* ▶ *activity area supervisors.* All positions offered at $91–$110 per week. International students encouraged to apply; must obtain own visa and working papers prior to employment.

Benefits College credit, on-the-job training, on-site room and board at no charge.

Contact Shannon Crowder, Office Manager, Honey Rock Camp, Wheaton College, Wheaton, Illinois 60187; 630-752-5124, Fax 630-752-5555.

LAKE GENEVA CAMPUS, GEORGE WILLIAMS COLLEGE EDUCATION CENTERS
PO BOX 210
WILLIAMS BAY, WISCONSIN 53191

General Information Educational conference center serving families, nonprofit organizations, and groups. Established in 1886. Owned by George Williams College Educational Centers. Affiliated with International Association of Conference Center Administrators, American Camping Association, Association for Experiential Education. 200-acre facility located 50 miles east of Milwaukee. Features: 1,200 feet of lake frontage; 18-hole golf course; 4 tennis courts; nature trails; sports fields.

Profile of Summer Employees Total number: 75; average age: 17; 40% male, 60% female; 60% high school students; 40% college students; 10% international. Nonsmokers preferred.

Employment Information Openings are from May 15 to October 15. Jobs available: ▶ 6 *lifeguards* (minimum age 18) with WSI certification, CPR, and advanced first aid at $5.50–$6 per hour; ▶ 3 *sailing instructors* (minimum age 18) with Red Cross sailing instructor certification and CPR training at $6–$7 per hour; ▶ 12 *housekeepers* at $5.15–$6 per hour; ▶ 30 *food service workers* at $5.15–$6 per hour; ▶ 2 *painters* at $7–$8 per hour; ▶ 5 *grounds crew* at $5.15–$6 per hour; ▶ 2 *front desk workers* (minimum age 18) at $5.40–$6.50 per hour; ▶ 2 *arts and crafts staff members* (minimum age 18) at $5.50–$6.50 per hour; ▶ 4 *preschool/day care staff members* (minimum age 18) at $5.15–$6.15 per hour; ▶ 10 *golf course staff members* (minimum age 18) at $5.15–$6.15 per hour; ▶ 2 *swimming instructors* with WSI, CPR, and first aid certification at $5.50–$6.50 per hour; ▶ 7 *snack shop clerks* at $5.15–$6.15 per hour; ▶ 4 *conference center set-up crew* at $5.50–$6.50 per hour. International students encouraged to apply; must obtain own visa and working papers prior to employment.

Benefits On-the-job training, formal ongoing training, on-site room and board at $75 per week, laundry facilities, health insurance.

Contact Richard Miller, Director of Personnel, Lake Geneva Campus, George Williams College Education Centers, Department SJ, PO Box 210, Williams Bay, Wisconsin 53191-0210; 414-245-5531, Fax 414-245-5652.

MENOMINEE FOR THE BOYS
OLD COUNSELORS ROAD
EAGLE RIVER, WISCONSIN 54521

General Information Residential boys camp serving 160 boys per program from all over the world. Established in 1928. Owned by Glenn and Dawn Klein. Affiliated with American Camping Association, Midwest Association of Independent Camps. 80-acre facility located 90 miles north of Wausau. Features: 8 baseball/softball fields; 5 tennis courts; 4 basketball courts; 5-hole golf course; 2 soccer/football fields; complete waterfront on Sand Lake.

Profile of Summer Employees Total number: 60; average age: 21; 90% male, 10% female; 5% minorities; 10% high school students; 80% college students; 1% retirees; 10% international; 5% local residents; 5% teachers. Nonsmokers only.

Employment Information Openings are from June 10 to August 16. Jobs available: ▶ *team sports instructors* at $1100–$1350 per season; ▶ *tennis instructors;* ▶ *golf instructors;* ▶ *swimming instructors;* ▶ *waterskiing instructors;* ▶ *sailing instructors;* ▶ *soccer instructors.* International students encouraged to apply; must apply through recognized agency.

Benefits College credit, on-the-job training, formal ongoing training, on-site room and board at no charge, travel reimbursement, use of all facilities/staff intramural teams, summer-long membership in local health club.

Contact Glenn Klein, Owner/Director, Menominee for the Boys, Department SJ, 805 Centerbrook Drive, Brandon, Florida 33511; 800-236-2267, Fax 813-662-5512, E-mail menominee@theramp. net, URL http://www.campchannel.com/menominee. Application deadline: May 1.

RED PINE CAMP FOR GIRLS
CLEAR LAKE, 8531 RED PINE ROAD COUNTY J, PO BOX 69 MINOCQUA, WISCONSIN 54548

General Information Private traditional camp providing individual attention for girls ages 6–16, enrolling 115 campers for two-, four-, and eight-week sessions. Established in 1937. Owned by Sarah Wittenkamp Rolley. Affiliated with American Camping Association, Midwest Association of Independent Camps, National Water Ski Association, Camp Archery Association, United States Tennis Association. 40-acre facility located 70 miles north of Wausau. Features: 1200-acre spring fed land-locked lake; 16 sleeping cabins; large recreation hall; infirmary; arts and crafts cabin; staff lounge and office; large riding ring and stable; tennis courts surrounded by storm fences; practice boards; ball machine; all cabins pine-paneled and with view of lake; dining room overlooking lake.

Profile of Summer Employees Total number: 48; average age: 21; 10% male, 90% female; 80% college students; 10% international; 8% local residents; 8% teachers. Nonsmokers preferred.

Employment Information Openings are from June 17 to August 17. Jobs available: ▶ *swimming instructors* with WSI, LGT, CPR, and first aid certification at $1200–$1800 per season; ▶ *English-style riding instructors or stable managers* with experience, skill, and love of horses at $1300–$2000 per season; ▶ *tennis staff members* with high degree of skill, teaching experience, and professional training preferred at $1200–$1800 per season; ▶ *sailing staff members* with swimming, LGT, and small craft certification preferred and skill in sailing Sunfish, Puffers, and Zumas at $1200–$1800 per season; ▶ *canoeing staff members* with emergency and basic water safety (Red Cross) certification, skill and experience in still waters, and knowledge of campcraft at $1200–$1800 per season; ▶ *sail boarding staff members* with skill and experience at $1200–$1800 per season; ▶ *arts and crafts, gymnastics, aerobic jazz, cheerleading, and archery staff members* with skill and experience in combination of areas at $1200–$1500 per season; ▶ *experienced food service staff members* with cook, assistant to cook, and general kitchen and dining room help experience at $1350–$2000 per season; ▶ *nurses* with RN, LPN, or GN license at $1500–$2200 per season. International students encouraged to apply; must apply through recognized agency.

Benefits College credit, on-the-job training, on-site room and board at no charge, use of camp transportation into Minocqua once a week, $50 laundry allowance. Preemployment training of 6 days is required and includes safety and accident prevention, group interaction, first-aid, CPR, leadership, lifeguard training. Orientation is paid.

Contact A. Irene Boudreaux, Co-Director, Red Pine Camp for Girls, PO Box 69, Minocqua, Wisconsin 54548; 715-356-6231, Fax 715-356-1077. Application deadline: April 1.

SALVATION ARMY WONDERLAND CAMP AND CONFERENCE CENTER
CAMP LAKE, WISCONSIN 53109

General Information Residential Evangelical Christian camping program for Chicago-area Salvation Army, including camps for 120 low-income and at-risk young people for six 8-day sessions. Established in 1924. Owned by The Salvation Army Metro Division. Affiliated with American Camping Association, Christian Camping International/USA. 140-acre facility located 45 miles south of Milwaukee. Features: low-ropes course; rural area with 60 wooded acres for primitive camping and hiking; lake with boating and fishing; swimming pool with dive tank and children's pool with slide; nature center; 2 large sports fields, 6 tennis courts, gymnasium, and 2 sand volleyball courts.

Profile of Summer Employees Total number: 54; average age: 20; 50% male, 50% female; 5% minorities; 8% high school students; 90% college students; 2% retirees; 5% international; 10% local residents; 5% teachers. Nonsmokers only.

Employment Information Openings are from May 21 to August 31. Christmas break positions also offered. Jobs available: ▶ 1 *aquatics director* with WSI and LTI certification (preferred) at $160 per week; ▶ 1 *aquatics assistant* with WSI and LTI certification (preferred) at $155 per week; ▶ 6 *boys counselors* (minimum age 19) with one year of college completed at $150 per week; ▶ 6 *girls counselors* (minimum age 19) with one year of college completed at $150 per week; ▶ 4 *program unit directors* (minimum age 21) with two years of college completed at $160 per week; ▶ 1 *nature director* (minimum age 21) with two years of college completed at $160 per week; ▶ 1 *pioneer director* (minimum age 21) with two years of college completed at $160 per week; ▶ 1 *arts and crafts director* (minimum age 21) with two years of college completed at $160 per week; ▶ 1 *nurse* with BSN or RN license with CPR training (U.S.A. certification) at $400 per week; ▶ 1 *nurse's assistant* with student nurse status or experience in nursing at $160 per week; ▶ 2 *experienced cooks* at $200 per week; ▶ 6 *support counselors* with one year of college (preferred) at $150 per week. International students encouraged to apply; must apply through recognized agency.

Benefits College credit, on-the-job training, formal ongoing training, on-site room and board at no charge, laundry facilities, Christian staff fellowship and discipleship, Christian leadership training. Preemployment training of 6 days is required and includes safety and accident prevention, group interaction, first-aid, CPR, leadership, camper-counselor relations, lifeguard training. Orientation is paid.

Contact David Ditzler, Director of Camping Services, Salvation Army Wonderland Camp and Conference Center, Department SJ, 9241 Camp Lake Road, PO Box 222, Camp Lake, Wisconsin 53109-0222; 414-889-4305 Ext. 304, Fax 414-889-4307, E-mail wonderland@techheadnet.com, URL http://www.techhead.com/wonderland. Application deadline: April 15.

SILVER SANDS GOLF ACADEMY
563 UPPER GARDENS
FONTANA, WISCONSIN 53125

General Information Residential golf school featuring clinics and tournaments for junior golfers (ages 9–18) of all abilities at 3 locations: two resort locations and one camp facility. Established in 1975. Owned by Wayne Rolfs. 600-acre facility located 85 miles north of Chicago, Illinois. Features: 18-hole golf course; driving range; lake frontage; two tennis courts; other sports fields; swimming pool.

Profile of Summer Employees Total number: 4; average age: 20; 90% male, 10% female; 80% college students. Nonsmokers only.

Employment Information Openings are from June 10 to August 10. Jobs available: ▶ 3 *counselors/instructors* at $150–$200 per week; ▶ 2 *swimming instructors* at $600–$800 per month.

Benefits On-the-job training, on-site room and board. Preemployment training of 1 to 2 days is required and includes safety and accident prevention, group interaction, leadership, camper-counselor relations. Orientation is paid.

Contact Wayne Rolfs, Silver Sands Golf Academy, Department SJ, 563 Upper Gardens Road, Fontana, Wisconsin 53125; 800-232-1834. Application deadline: May 1.

THUMB FUN PARK
PO BOX 128 3851 HIGHWAY 42
FISH CREEK, WISCONSIN 54212

General Information Outdoor family fun park with rides, waterslides, and games. Established in 1965. Owned by Thumb Fun, Inc. Affiliated with International Association of Amusement Parks and Attractions, World Waterpark Association, Fish Creek Civic Association. 10-acre facility located 65 miles northeast of Green Bay. Features: 5 waterslides; go-carts; bumper boats; miniature golf; haunted mansion; 6 children's rides.

Profile of Summer Employees Total number: 65; average age: 19; 40% male, 60% female; 10% minorities; 15% high school students; 70% college students; 1% retirees; 5% international; 35% local residents; 1% teachers.

Employment Information Openings are from May 20 to September 5. Jobs available: ▶ 16 *ride operators (minimum age 18)* at $5–$5.40 per hour; ▶ 10 *lifeguards* with lifeguard certification at $5–$5.40 per hour; ▶ 10 *cashiers* at $5–$5.40 per hour; ▶ 6 *games operators* at $5–$5.40 per hour; ▶ 7 *food service staff* at $5–$5.40 per hour; ▶ 6 *haunted mansion actors* at $5–$5.40 per hour; ▶ 5 *maintenance staff (minimum age 18)* at $5–$5.40 per hour. International students encouraged to apply; must obtain own visa and working papers prior to employment; must apply through recognized agency.

Benefits College credit, on-the-job training, employee appreciation parties every two weeks, free passes, on-site housing costs $28 per week, discounts on food and merchandise. Preemployment training of 1 day is optional and includes safety and accident prevention, first-aid, CPR, lifeguarding. Orientation is paid.

Contact Peg Butchart, General Manager, Thumb Fun Park, Department SJ, PO Box 128, Fish Creek, Wisconsin 54212; 414-868-3418, Fax 414-868-3418. Application deadline: May 15.

WOODSIDE RANCH RESORT
W4015 HIGHWAY 82
MAUSTON, WISCONSIN 53948

General Information Full-service American-plan dude ranch offering log cabins with fireplaces. Established in 1926. Owned by Feldmann family. Affiliated with Wisconsin Innkeepers' Association, Central Wisconsin River Country, Mauston Chamber of Commerce. 1,200-acre facility located 65 miles northwest of Madison. Features: pool; pond for paddle boats and row boats; 12 miles of marked hiking trails; buffalo herd; pony ring and play school for kids; weekly professional horse show (gymkhana).

Profile of Summer Employees Total number: 60; average age: 19; 40% male, 60% female; 5% minorities; 25% high school students; 25% college students; 5% international; 50% local residents.

Employment Information Openings are from June 1 to September 7. Christmas break positions also offered. Jobs available: ▶ 6 *horse-trail guides, experience preferred,* at $190&–$200 per week; ▶ 6 *food service personnel* at $190&–$200 per week; ▶ 6 *bartenders/country store clerks, experience preferred,* at $200–$220 per week; ▶ 1 *recreation director* at $250 per week; ▶ 1 *yard and pool maintenance person* at $200–$250 per week; ▶ 2 *housekeepers* at $190&–$200 per week; ▶ 1 *experienced horse-drawn wagon teamster* at $200–$250 per week. International students encouraged to apply; must apply through recognized agency.

Benefits On-the-job training, on-site room and board at no charge, laundry facilities, free use of most resort facilities: pool, tennis, and mini-golf (if use does not conflict with guest use).

Contact Rick Feldmann, Woodside Ranch Resort, Department SJ, W4015 Highway 82, Mauston, Wisconsin 53948; 608-847-4275.

YMCA CAMP U-NAH-LI-YA
13654 SOUTH SHORE DRIVE
SURING, WISCONSIN 54174

General Information YMCA camp offering outdoor environmental education and retreats for children grades 5–8. Established in 1942. Owned by Green Bay YMCA. Affiliated with American Camping Association, Young Men's Christian Association. Situated on 140 acres. Features: 700-acre lake; hiking trails; dining hall; lodge; 15 sleeping cabins with 200 beds.

Profile of Summer Employees Total number: 40; average age: 20; 40% male, 60% female; 1% minorities; 70% college students; 1% international. Nonsmokers preferred.

Employment Information Openings are from June 1 to August 30. Christmas break, year-round positions also offered. Jobs available: ▶ *resident counselors;* ▶ *tripping counselors;* ▶ *waterfront director;* ▶ *sailing director;* ▶ *trail director;* ▶ *health supervisor;* ▶ *CIT director;* ▶ *assistant camp director.* International students encouraged to apply; must obtain own visa and working papers prior to employment; must apply through recognized agency.

Benefits On-the-job training, on-site room and board at no charge, laundry facilities.

Contact Ken Losinski, Camp Director, YMCA Camp U-Nah-Li-Ya, 13654 South Shore Drive, Suring, Wisconsin 54174; 715-276-7116, Fax 715-276-1701.

YMCA CAMP ICAGHOWAN
899-A 115TH STREET
AMERY, WISCONSIN 54001

General Information Coed residential camp providing opportunities for building self-esteem, confidence, fun, leadership, respect, and appreciation for the environment, self, and others. Serves 120–150 campers weekly. Established in 1909. Owned by YMCA of Metropolitan Minneapolis. Affiliated with American Camping Association, YMCA. 120-acre facility located 65 miles northeast of Minneapolis, Minnesota. Features: sailing camp; rustic base camp facility with "back-to-basics" amenities; full waterfront facility on island-peninsula of 120 acres; horseback riding program; backpacking/canoe trips in northern Minnesota and north central Wisconsin; Youth Leadership Development Program.

Profile of Summer Employees 50% male, 50% female; 5% minorities; 20% high school students; 80% college students; 5% international; 75% local residents. Nonsmokers only.

Employment Information Openings are from June 11 to August 28. Christmas break, year-round positions also offered. Jobs available: ▶ 24 *trail counselors/cabin counselors* with CPR, first aid, and lifeguard training at $115–$145 per week; ▶ 1 *waterfront director* with CPR, first aid, lifeguard training, and WSI certification at $125–$160 per week; ▶ 1 *program coordinator* with CPR, first aid, and lifeguard training at $130–$180 per week; ▶ 3 *ropes course directors* with CPR, first aid, and lifeguard training at $120–$150 per week; ▶ 1 *nurse* with current license at $150–$200 per week; ▶ 1 *horseback riding director* with CPR, first aid, and horsemanship safety instructor certification at $130–$160 per week; ▶ *sailing/boating director* at $120–$150 per week.

Benefits College credit, on-the-job training, formal ongoing training, on-site room and board at no charge, laundry facilities, possible scholarship, pre-employment training.

Contact Nancy Hoppe, Executive Director, YMCA Camp Icaghowan, Department SJ, 4 West Rustic Lodge Avenue, Minneapolis, Minnesota 55409; 612-823-5283, Fax 612-823-2482. Application deadline: March 15.

WYOMING

ABSAROKA MOUNTAIN LODGE
1231 EAST YELLOWSTONE HIGHWAY
WAPITI, WYOMING 82450

General Information Guest ranch on the eastern edge of Yellowstone National Park with lodging, meals, horseback riding, fishing, and other activities. Established in 1910. Owned by Bob and France Kudelski. Affiliated with American Automobile Association, Mobil Travel Guide, Cody Chamber of Commerce. 7-acre facility located 40 miles west of Cody. Features: location 12 miles east of Yellowstone National Park; historical mountain lodge; 16 log cabins; horseback rides in Shoshone National Forest; mountain stream; abundant wildlife.

Profile of Summer Employees Total number: 12; average age: 22; 50% male, 50% female; 10% high school students; 80% college students; 10% retirees; 25% local residents.

Employment Information Openings are from May 1 to November 1. Jobs available: ▶ 2 *cooks, experience preferred,* at $500 per month; ▶ 4 *waitstaff/cabin staff members* at $400 per month; ▶ 2 *experienced wranglers* at $400 per month; ▶ 1 *maintenance person, experience preferred,* at $400 per month; ▶ 1 *front desk person* at $400 per month. International students encouraged to apply; must obtain own visa and working papers prior to employment; must apply through recognized agency.

Benefits On-the-job training, on-site room and board at no charge, laundry facilities, salaries supplemented by gratuities, possible end-of-season bonus.
Contact Bob Kudelski, Owner, Absaroka Mountain Lodge, 1231 East Yellowstone Highway, Wapiti, Wyoming 82450; 307-587-3963, Fax 307-527-9628, E-mail bkudelsk@wyoming.com. Application deadline: April 1.

ALPENHOF LODGE
BOX 288, 3255 WEST McCOLLISTER AVENUE
TETON VILLAGE, WYOMING 83025

General Information Alpine-style resort lodge with 40 rooms providing clientele with personalized service. Established in 1965. Affiliated with Wyoming Restaurant Association. 1-acre facility located 250 miles northeast of Salt Lake City, UT. Features: location at the base of Jackson Hole ski area, 8 miles from Grand Teton National Park, and 45 miles from Yellowstone National Park; easy access to rafting, fishing, and hiking; 100-seat, four-star restaurant; bar and bistro with sundeck; outdoor pool and whirlpool.
Profile of Summer Employees Total number: 90; average age: 22; 50% male, 50% female; 1% high school students; 70% college students; 10% international. Nonsmokers preferred.
Employment Information Openings are from May 20 to October 8. Winter break, year-round positions also offered. Jobs available: ▶ 5 *housekeeping staff members* with ability to clean rooms and willingness to do hard work at $960 per month; ▶ 3 *bellmen* with aptitude for greeting guests in a friendly manner, ability to assist with luggage, run errands, and do light maintenance work at $840 per month; ▶ 3 *dishwashers* with ability to work quickly at $960–$1040 per month; ▶ *prep or line cooks* with ability to cook in line and work quickly at $1120–$1280 per month; ▶ 8 *food waitstaff members* with interest in working with public and the ability to serve at $370 per month; ▶ 8 *dining room staff members* (buspersons and waitstaff) with tableside experience and wine knowledge at $275–$420 per month. International students encouraged to apply; must obtain own visa and working papers prior to employment; must apply through recognized agency.
Benefits On-the-job training, formal ongoing training, employee rewards/special recognition, some jobs have housing at a nominal charge, excellent working conditions with a five-day work week. Off-site boarding costs are $400 per month. Preemployment training of 1 day is required and includes safety and accident prevention, group interaction. Orientation is paid.
Contact Personnel Manager, Alpenhof Lodge, Box 288, Teton Village, Wyoming 83025; 307-733-3242, Fax 307-739-1516.

BILL CODY RANCH
2604 YELLOWSTONE HIGHWAY
CODY, WYOMING 82414

General Information Guest ranch catering to families with 14 cabins, cookouts, entertainment, daily horseback rides. Established in 1925. Owned by John and Jamie Parsons. Affiliated with American Automobile Association, United States Chamber of Commerce, Cody Country Chamber of Commerce. Located 100 miles south of Billings, Montana. Features: proximity to Yellowstone and Teton National Parks; 70 riding horses; 17 different trails, all located in Shoshone National Forest east of Yellowstone National Park.
Profile of Summer Employees Total number: 20; average age: 21; 40% male, 60% female; 90% college students; 2% local residents. Nonsmokers preferred.
Employment Information Openings are from May 1 to September 30. Jobs available: ▶ 5 *horse wranglers* with physical ability to perform required duties, valid driver's license, and a clean driving record at $400–$600 per month; ▶ 2 *cooks* with some culinary experience at $500–$800 per month; ▶ 6 *housekeepers/waitstafff* at $400–$500 per month; ▶ 1 *prep cook* at $400–$600 per month; ▶ 2 *office assistants* at $400–$500 per month.
Benefits On-the-job training, on-site room and board at no charge, laundry facilities, free horseback riding, rodeo pass, river rafting.

Contact John and Jamie Parsons, Owners, Bill Cody Ranch, 2604 Yellowstone Highway, Cody, Wyoming 82414; 307-587-6271.

HATCHET MOTEL AND RESTAURANT
PO BOX 316
MORAN, WYOMING 83013

General Information Rustic log motel with twenty-two units, restaurant, gift shop, and gas station. Established in 1953. Owned by Don Albrecht. Operated by Stan and Carlene Barthel, Managers. Affiliated with Jackson Chamber of Commerce, Wyoming Lodging and Restaurant Association, American Automobile Association. 35-acre facility located 35 miles east of Jackson. Features: proximity to the Grand Tetons and Yellowstone Park; referral for float trips; horseback riding; hiking and fishing nearby.

Profile of Summer Employees Total number: 18; average age: 23; 40% male, 60% female; 23% minorities; 15% high school students; 50% college students; 25% retirees; 10% local residents. Nonsmokers preferred.

Employment Information Openings are from May 21 to September 15. Jobs available: ▶ 2 *station attendants* (morning and evening shift) at $500 per month; ▶ 2 *desk attendants* (morning and evening shift) at $500 per month; ▶ 2 *cooks* (morning and evening shift) at $600 per month; ▶ 5 *kitchen helpers* (morning and evening shift) at $500 per month; ▶ 5 *waiters/waitresses* (morning and evening shift) at $600 per month; ▶ 2 *housekeeping staff members* at $500 per month; ▶ 1 *yard maintenance person* at $500 per month; ▶ 2 *relief position personnel* at $500 per month. International students encouraged to apply.

Benefits College credit, on-the-job training, formal ongoing training, on-site room and board at no charge, laundry facilities.

Contact Stan and Carlene Barthel, Managers, Hatchet Motel and Restaurant, Department SJ, PO Box 316, Moran, Wyoming 83013; 208-787-2166, Fax 208-787-2166. Application deadline: May 15.

SIGNAL MOUNTAIN LODGE
GRAND TETON NATIONAL PARK, PO BOX 50
MORAN, WYOMING 83013

General Information Summer resort providing national park visitors with services such as lodging, food, marinas, gifts, guided fishing, groceries, and gasoline. Established in 1940. Owned by Rex Maughan. Affiliated with Jackson Hole Chamber of Commerce. 30-acre facility located 30 miles north of Jackson. Features: location on Jackson Lake at the foot of the Grand Tetons; 30 miles south of the south gate of Yellowstone National Park; new top-rate dormitories with private bath for employees; family environment; hiking, biking, camping, climbing, and water activities in the immediate area.

Profile of Summer Employees Total number: 130; average age: 28; 50% male, 50% female; 5% minorities; 60% college students; 15% retirees; 1% international; 5% local residents. Nonsmokers preferred.

Employment Information Openings are from May 1 to October 20. Jobs available: ▶ 5 *front desk and reservations persons* with typing and interpersonal skills at $5.25 per hour; ▶ 3 *experienced accounting personnel* (day and night audit) at $6 per hour; ▶ 6 *marina attendants* with ability to handle boat rentals, shuttle guests to and from boats, and pump gas at $4.75 per hour; ▶ 20 *lodging helpers* with ability to make beds, clean, and do laundry at $4.75 per hour; ▶ 5 *cooks* with experience planning fine dining and coffee shop menus at $6.50 per hour; ▶ 5 *pantry personnel* with ability to prepare salads and desserts at $5.25 per hour; ▶ 4 *employee dining room staff members* at $5–$6 per hour; ▶ 15 *experienced waiters/waitresses* at $2.25 per hour; ▶ 2 *experienced bartenders* at $4.75 per hour; ▶ 2 *cocktail waitpersons;* ▶ 4 *hosts/hostesses* at $5 per hour; ▶ 7 *buspersons* at $4 per hour; ▶ 5 *experienced gift store sales clerks* at $4.75 per hour; ▶ *experienced convenience store attendants* at $4.75 per hour; ▶ 10 *experienced management and staff positions* with full-season availability; ▶ 7 *dishwashers* at $5.25 per hour.

Benefits College credit, on-the-job training, on-site room and board at $195 per month, laundry facilities, discounts in the restaurants, gift stores, and marinas, free river rafting trips, bonuses for some positions, proximity to religious services.

Contact Paulette Phlipot, Personnel Manager, Signal Mountain Lodge, Department SJ, PO Box 50, Moran, Wyoming 83013; 800-672-6012, Fax 307-543-2569, E-mail 102547.1642@ compuserve.com. Application deadline: April 1.

TETON VALLEY RANCH CAMP
JACKSON HOLE, PO BOX 8
KELLY, WYOMING 83011

General Information Residential summer camp serving 125 campers each five-week session with a strong Western horseback-riding and backpacking program. Program also features multi-day trips into the mountains on foot and horseback. Established in 1939. Affiliated with American Camping Association, Western Association of Independent Camps. 1,200-acre facility located 15 miles from Jackson. Features: warm, spring-fed pond; mountain country of Jackson Hole and Grand Teton National Park; hundreds of miles of riding and hiking trails; located on a longhorn cattle ranch with a herd of 45 horses and two mule stations; horse packtrips, hiking, gymkhana rodeo events, fly fishing, photography, leadership training, crafts and lapidary, ham radio, archery/riflery, outdoor skills, and a nature discovery program.

Profile of Summer Employees Total number: 70; average age: 22; 50% male, 50% female; 5% minorities; 10% high school students; 70% college students; 10% retirees; 2% international; 10% local residents; 10% teachers. Nonsmokers only.

Employment Information Openings are from June 5 to August 23. Jobs available: ► 16 *boys cabin counselors* (first five weeks of summer) with first aid and CPR certification at $500–$800 per season; ► 16 *girls cabin counselors* (second five weeks of summer) with first aid and CPR certification at $500–$800 per season; ► 5 *kitchen staff members* at $1100–$1500 per season; ► 2 *laundry workers* at $1300–$1500 per season; ► *maintenance staff members* at $1200 per season; ► *dishwashers* at $1000 per season; ► *horse wranglers* at $1200–$1800 per season. International students encouraged to apply; must obtain own visa and working papers prior to employment; must apply through recognized agency.

Benefits On-the-job training, on-site room and board at no charge, laundry facilities, travel reimbursement. Preemployment training of 5 to 7 days is required and includes safety and accident prevention, group interaction, leadership, camper-counselor relations. Orientation is paid.

Contact Director of Personnel, Teton Valley Ranch Camp, Department SJ, PO Box 8, Kelly, Wyoming 83011; 307-733-2958, Fax 307-733-2978. Application deadline: May 1.

COWBOY VILLAGE RESORT AT TOGWOTEE
PO BOX 91
MORAN, WYOMING 83013

General Information Mountain lodge serving a varied clientele. Established in 1925. Owned by Bryan Carson. Affiliated with American Hotel and Motel Association, National Federation of Independent Businesses, National Forest Recreation Association. 67-acre facility located 48 miles north of Jackson Hole. Features: remote location; proximity to Yellowstone and Grand Teton National Parks, with hiking and backpacking in wilderness areas; mountain streams for fishing; horses on premises; mountain biking; hot tubs.

Profile of Summer Employees Total number: 60; average age: 25; 60% male, 40% female; 5% high school students; 50% college students; 5% retirees; 5% local residents. Nonsmokers preferred.

Employment Information Openings are from June 1 to October 20. Winter break, Christmas break, year-round positions also offered. Jobs available: ► 3 *front desk/reservations persons* with good math aptitude and an outgoing personality at $5.50–$6.50 per hour; ► 5 *housekeepers/laundry personnel* with neat appearance and efficient work habits at $5–$6 per hour; ► 7 *waitstaff members* (food servers) with an outgoing personality and desire to perform a thorough job at $3.90 per hour; ▶ 2 *experienced bartenders* with an outgoing personality and desire to perform a thorough job at $5 per hour; ▶ 3 *dishwashers* with ability to accomplish tasks neatly and quickly at $5–$6 per hour; ▶ 4 *experienced cooks* with neat and efficient work habits at $5–$6 per hour; ▶ 2 *gas attendants* (minimum age 21) with good math skills and an outgoing personality at $5.50–$6 per hour; ▶ 1 *night auditor* with good math aptitude *(should enjoy working nights)* at $5.50–$6.50 per hour; ▶ 2 *general laborers* with efficient work habits at $6–$8 per hour; ▶ *drivers (minimum age 25)* with an outgoing personality and good driving record at $5–$6 per hour; ▶ *resort naturalist* with biology background; experience with large group and children's presentations at $700 per month.

Benefits On-the-job training, on-site room and board at $300 per month, laundry facilities, health insurance, end-of-season bonus of $25 per week worked, discounts on activities.

Contact Personnel Director, Cowboy Village Resort at Togwotee, Department SJ, PO Box 91, Moran, Wyoming 83013; 307-543-2847, Fax 307-543-2391.

YELLOWSTONE PARK SERVICE STATIONS
YELLOWSTONE NATIONAL PARK
YELLOWSTONE, WYOMING 82190

General Information Automotive service facilities and information service in Yellowstone National Park. Established in 1947. Affiliated with National Park Hospitality, Adopt-A-Highway Program. Located 90 miles south of Bozeman, Montana. Features: proximity to Grand Teton National Park and several national forests; geysers; waterfalls, mountains, and canyons; Yellowstone Lake (the largest Alpine lake in the United States); 1000 miles of hiking trails; camping and fishing opportunities.

Profile of Summer Employees Total number: 95; average age: 23; 68% male, 32% female; 5% minorities; 63% college students; 4% retirees; 1% international; 10% local residents; 2% teachers. Nonsmokers preferred.

Employment Information Openings are from May 1 to October 15. Jobs available: ▶ 50 *service station attendants* with good interpersonal skills and desire to work outdoors at $208 per week; ▶ 18 *automobile mechanics* with ASE certification or current enrollment in an ASE program at $260–$320 per week; ▶ 3 *accounting clerks* with ability to operate 10-key adding machine by touch plus computer and communication skills at $212 per week; ▶ 1 *warehouse helper* with good driving record and communication skills at $212 per week.

Benefits College credit, on-the-job training, on-site room and board at $58 per week, laundry facilities, health insurance, employee assistance program, accident insurance, employee recreation program, and outdoor work, advancement potential. Preemployment training of 2 days is required and includes safety and accident prevention, group interaction, leadership, Yellowstone facts. Orientation is paid.

Contact Hal Broadhead, General Manager, Yellowstone Park Service Stations, PO Box 11–Department WDM, Gardiner, Montana 59030-0011; 406-848-7333, Fax 406-848-7731, E-mail ypss@worldnet.att.net, URL http://coolworks.com/showme/ypss. Application deadline: May 1.

CANADA

BRITISH COLUMBIA

CAMP ARTABAN
1058 RIDGEWOOD DRIVE
NORTH VANCOUVER, BRITISH COLUMBIA V7R 1H8

General Information Residential camp with Anglican Church affiliation offering traditional program to 100 boys and girls entering grades 3 through 11 in 7-day sessions. Established in 1923. Owned by Camp Artaban Society. Operated by Society Members. Affiliated with British Columbia Camping Association. 63-acre facility located 45 miles north of Vancouver. Features: protected views of British Columbia coastline and mountains; 45 buildings including cedar cabins; log gym; native craft building; large waterfront with boating, canoeing, and sailing; large dining hall and lodge.

Profile of Summer Employees Total number: 15; average age: 20; 50% male, 50% female; 30% minorities; 20% high school students; 80% college students; 50% teachers. Nonsmokers only.

Employment Information Openings are from June 15 to August 30. Jobs available: ▶ 5 *kitchen staff members* at $2000–$6000 per season; ▶ 2 *swimming staff members* (minimum age 19) with WSI and NLS certification at $2000–$4000 per season; ▶ 3 *maintenance staff members* at $2000–$4000 per season; ▶ 1 *registrar/expediter* at $2000–$4000 per season; ▶ *theme staff members* at $2000 per season. *International students encouraged to apply; must obtain own visa and working papers prior to employment.*

Benefits On-the-job training, on-site room and board at no charge, laundry facilities.

Contact Vi Calhoun, Office Manager, Camp Artaban, Department SJ, 1058 Ridgewood Drive, North Vancouver, British Columbia, V7R 1H8 Canada; 604-980-0391, Fax 604-980-0395, E-mail artaban@portal.ca, URL http://www.portal.ca/~artaban/. Application deadline: April 30.

EVANS LAKE FORESTRY CENTRE
SQUANISH, BRITISH COLUMBIA VON 3G0

General Information Residential camp offering environmental education for children 8–11 years old (6-day camp) and 10–14 years old (8-day camp) with a capacity of 80 children. Established in 1960. Owned by Evans Lake Forest Education Society. Affiliated with British Columbia Camping Association, Canadian Camping Association. 604-acre facility located 50 miles north of Vancouver. Features: location on small lake; 15 kilometers of forest trails; boating and canoeing; access to nearby lakes for camping; 1½ kilometers of guided nature walks.

Profile of Summer Employees Total number: 30; 50% male, 50% female; 10% minorities; 60% high school students; 35% college students; 5% local residents; 5% teachers.

Employment Information Openings are from July 4 to September 1. Jobs available: ▶ *instructor* with experience working with children and in outdoor education and first aid certification; ▶ *lifeguard* with NLSS certification and outdoor education experience; ▶ *cabin leaders* with counselor training and outdoor experience. International students encouraged to apply; must obtain own visa and working papers prior to employment.

Benefits On-the-job training, on-site room and board at no charge.

Contact Matt Thorn, Director, Evans Lake Forestry Centre, Department SJ, 202-304 Columbia Street, New Westminster, British Columbia, V3L 1A6 Canada; 604-520-7600, Fax 604-520-5450.

PIONEER PACIFIC CAMP
THETIS ISLAND, BRITISH COLUMBIA V0R 2Y0

General Information Residential waterfront camp accommodating 150 campers. Established in 1954. Owned by Inter-Varsity Christian Fellowship of Canada. Affiliated with Christian Camping International, British Columbia, British Columbia Camping Association. 75-acre facility located 25 miles west of Vancouver. Features: ocean frontage in Canadian Gulf Islands; small boat sailing fleet; swimming pool; ski boat; playing field; hiking trails.

Profile of Summer Employees Total number: 9; average age: 21; 50% male, 50% female; 10% high school students; 30% college students; 40% local residents; 20% teachers. Nonsmokers only.

Employment Information Openings are from July 1 to August 31. Jobs available: ▶ 1 *head cook* at $1920 per month; ▶ 3 *lifeguards* with NLS and AquaQuest certification at $1750 per month; ▶ 1 *secretary* at $1750 per month; ▶ 1 *experienced waterfront director* at $1750 per month; ▶ 1 *sailing instructor* with CYA (Canadian Yachting Association) White Sail III instructor's certification at $1750 per month; ▶ 1 *boat maintenance staff member* at $1750 per month.

Benefits On-the-job training, on-site room and board at $325 per month, laundry facilities, Christian community living, pre-employment training.

Contact David Roycroft, Camp Manager, Pioneer Pacific Camp, Box 5-10, Thetis Island, British Columbia, V0R 2Y0 Canada; 250-246-9613, Fax 250-246-1202, E-mail pipac@island. net. Application deadline: February 1.

SILVER LAKE FORESTRY CENTER
2363A SPRINGFIELD ROAD
KELOWNA, BRITISH COLUMBIA V1X 7N7

General Information Coed residential camp serving 70 campers per week teaching forestry, tree identification, and outdoor education. Activities include camp-outs, canoeing, swimming, and archery. Established in 1970. Owned by Forest Education British Columbia. 94-acre facility located 40 miles south of Kelowna. Features: 5 large log bunkhouses; 2 volleyball courts; obstacle course with ropes; logging museum; canoe and swimming docks; 15 miles of hiking trails.

Profile of Summer Employees Total number: 16; average age: 20; 50% male, 50% female; 20% high school students; 80% college students; 85% local residents. Nonsmokers only.

Employment Information Openings are from May 1 to September 1. Year-round positions also offered. Jobs available: ▶ *senior camp instructors* at $1200 per month; ▶ *cabin counselors* at $1040 per month.

Benefits On-the-job training, on-site room and board at $125 per week.

Contact Forest Education British Columbia, Silver Lake Forestry Centre, Silver Lake Forestry Center, Department SJ, 2363 A Springfield Road, Kelowna, British Columbia, V1X 7N7 Canada; 604-860-6410, Fax 604-860-6414. Application deadline: March 15.

ONTARIO

BELWOOD LODGE & CAMP
RR#1
BELWOOD, ONTARIO N0B 1J0

General Information Residential camp for mentally handicapped individuals ranging from ages 8–85. Established in 1948. Operated by Board of Directors, Guelph Kiwanis Group. Affiliated with Ontario Camping Association. 13-acre facility located 15 miles north of Guelph. Features: in-ground heated swimming pool; trampoline; waterfront for pontoons and paddle boats; animal farm; soccer and baseball fields; volleyball court; archery range.

Profile of Summer Employees Total number: 55; average age: 20; 45% male, 55% female; 5% minorities; 40% high school students; 40% college students; 50% local residents.

Employment Information Openings are from June 1 to September 1. Jobs available: ▶ 1 *program director* at $250 per week; ▶ 2 *swimming instructors* with lifeguard qualifications at $200 per week; ▶ 10 *senior counselors* at $180 per week; ▶ 2 *cooks* at $200–$300 per week; ▶ 1 *craft director* at $200 per week; ▶ 10 *junior counselors* at $145 per week; ▶ *nurse* at $350 per week.

Benefits On-the-job training, on-site room and board at no charge, laundry facilities.

Contact Ms. Chris Murdoch, Director, Belwood Lodge & Camp, Department SJ, RR #1, Belwood, Ontario, N0B 1J0 Canada; 519-843-1211.

CAMP HURON
PO BOX 509
BAYFIELD, ONTARIO N0M 1G0

General Information Coeducational residential camp serving 100 persons regardless of race, creed, economic status, and physical or mental abilities. Established in 1939. Operated by The Incorporated Synod of the Diocese of Huron. Affiliated with Ontario Camping Association, The Royal Lifesaving Society Ontario Division. 40-acre facility located 60 miles north of London, Ontario. Features: extensive freshwater lake frontage (Lake Huron); 2 large sports fields; 3 large program buildings; extensive off-site outdoor living; off-site canoe program.

Profile of Summer Employees Total number: 40; average age: 21; 51% male, 49% female; 1% minorities; 51% high school students; 49% college students; 1% international; 1% local residents. Nonsmokers preferred.

Employment Information Openings are from June 1 to August 1. Jobs available: ▶ 1 *experienced waterfront director* (minimum age 21) with NLS and CPR certification and three to five years experience at $1800 per season; ▶ 1 *experienced program director* at $1800 per season; ▶ 1 *experienced outdoor living skills director* with Bronze Cross/Medallion, first aid, and CPR certification at $1800 per season; ▶ 4 *L.I.T. counselors* with senior leadership experience, Bronze Cross/Medallion, first aid, and CPR certification at $1400–$1800 per season; ▶ 20 *cabin counselors* with Bronze Cross/Medallion, first aid, CPR certification, and L.I.T. graduate status or equivalent at $500–$1000 per season; ▶ 1 *skill development manager* with college/university degree, supervisory, teaching, and risk management experience at $2500–$3200 per season; ▶ 1 *program integration manager* with college/university degree, experience supervising, designing, and delivering recreation programs, and working with physical and behavioral disabilities at $2500–$3200 per season; ▶ 1 *support manager* with college/university degree, experience supervising people with physical and behavioral disabilities and with maintenance routines at $2500–$3200 per season. International students encouraged to apply; must obtain own visa and working papers prior to employment.

Benefits College credit, on-the-job training, on-site room and board at $74 per week, laundry

facilities, health coverage is paid by Province for Canadian residents only.
Contact Ms. Gerry Adam, Director, Camp Huron, Department SJ, 397 Springbank Drive, London, Ontario, N6J 1G7 Canada; 519-565-2822. Application deadline: January 31.

CAMP KIAWA GIRL GUIDES
RR#9
DUNNVILLE, ONTARIO N1A 2W8

General Information Residential camp using the Girl Guides of Canada program. Established in 1929. Operated by Girl Guides of Canada, Hamilton Area. 99-acre facility located 40 miles southwest of Hamilton. Features: recreation building; craft building; lakefront beach; playing field; nature trail.
Profile of Summer Employees Total number: 10; average age: 18; 100% female; 90% high school students; 10% college students. Nonsmokers preferred.
Employment Information Openings are from July 7 to August 17. Jobs available: ▶ 1 *waterfront director* at $1200–$1500 per season; ▶ 3 *waterfront staff members* at $900–$1000 per season; ▶ 1 *program director* at $800–$900 per season; ▶ 2 *craft helpers* at $800–$900 per season; ▶ 2 *quartermast assistants* at $800–$900 per season. International students encouraged to apply; must obtain own visa and working papers prior to employment; must apply through recognized agency.
Benefits On-the-job training, on-site room and board at $70 per week, laundry facilities. Preemployment training is required. Orientation is unpaid.
Contact Personnel Director, Camp Kiawa Girl Guides, 918 Main Street East, Hamilton, Ontario, L8M 1M5 Canada; 905-549-2429, Fax 905-549-3396. Application deadline: April 1.

CAMP ROBIN HOOD
158 LIMESTONE CRESCENT
DOWNSVIEW, ONTARIO M3J 2S4

General Information Day camp serving 850 campers daily. Established in 1946. Owned by Larry Bell. Situated on 50 acres. Features: 4 swimming pools; 1 canoe pond; many indoor areas; large barn converted to theater; 4 baseball diamonds; 4 sports fields.
Profile of Summer Employees Total number: 250; average age: 20; 40% male, 60% female; 5% minorities; 50% high school students; 50% college students; 100% local residents; 15% teachers. Nonsmokers only.
Employment Information Openings are from July 2 to August 22. Jobs available: ▶ 32 *section and specialty heads* at $2000–$3000 per month; ▶ 100 *counselors* at $500–$1200 per season; ▶ 100 *specialty counselors* at $500–$1200 per season.
Benefits On-the-job training, formal ongoing training.
Contact Patti Stulberg, Registrar, Camp Robin Hood, 158 Limestone Crescent, Downsview, Ontario, M3J 2S4 Canada; 416-736-4443, Fax 416-736-9971, URL http://www.camprh.com.

CAMP TRILLIUM
PO BOX 359
BLOOMFIELD, ONTARIO K0K 1G0

General Information Program offering support and recreational activities to children with cancer and their families. Established in 1984. Operated by Garratt's Island Farm Retreat. Affiliated with Children's Oncology Camps of America, Ontario Camping Association, Canadian Cancer Society- Ontario Division. 70-acre facility located 50 miles east of Kingston. Features: island location across from Sandbanks Provincial Park; approximately 60 acres of untouched natural land; waterfront area for swimming, canoeing, kayaking, and sailing.
Profile of Summer Employees Total number: 35; average age: 22; 40% male, 60% female; 10% minorities; 10% high school students; 90% college students; 2% local residents. Nonsmokers only.
Employment Information Openings are from June 1 to July 1. Winter break, year-round

positions also offered. Jobs available: ▶ 3 *sailing instructors* (volunteer); ▶ 3 *outtrippers* (volunteer); ▶ 2 *canoe/kayak specialists* (volunteer); ▶ 1 *adventure program staff member* (volunteer); ▶ 4 *waterfront/swimming instructors* (volunteer) with NLS and Red Cross certifications; ▶ 1 *drama instructor* (volunteer); ▶ 3 *arts and crafts/creative writing staff members* (volunteer). International students encouraged to apply.

Benefits On-site room and board at no charge, laundry facilities, camping experience with special children affected by cancer. Preemployment training of 14 days is required and includes safety and accident prevention, group interaction, first-aid, CPR, leadership, camper-counselor relations. Orientation is unpaid.

Contact Marci Shea, Assistant Director of Programs, Camp Trillium, Department SJ, 179 Sydenham Street, Suite 2, Kingston, Ontario, K7K 3M1 Canada; 613-542-1113, Fax 613-542-2499. Application deadline: January 15.

CENTRE CAMP
4588 BATHURST STREET
NORTH YORK, ONTARIO M2R 1W6

General Information Day camp serving 700 campers each summer. Established in 1989. Operated by Jewish Community Centre of Toronto (Bathurst Jewish Centre). Affiliated with Jewish Community Centre Association, Ontario Camping Association, Canadian Camping Association. Situated on 9 acres. Features: 8 outdoor tennis courts; 1 large outdoor swimming pool; 1 large indoor swimming pool; 3 large sport fields; 3 fully equipped gymnasiums; 2 indoor and 1 outdoor running/walking tracks; outdoor basketball and beach volleyball courts.

Profile of Summer Employees Total number: 175; average age: 22; 50% male, 50% female; 40% high school students; 60% college students.

Employment Information Openings are from May 1 to September 1. Spring break, winter break, Christmas break positions also offered. Jobs available: ▶ 45 *junior counselors* with grade 10 completed *(minimum)* at $600–$900 per season; ▶ 30 *senior counselors* with grade 12 completed *(minimum)* at $800–$1600 per season; ▶ 6 *unit heads* with post-secondary education at $1800–$3200 per season; ▶ 8 *specialists* with post-secondary education at $1800–$3000 per season; ▶ 15 *swimming instructors, leaders* with NLS certification at $1800–$3000 per season; ▶ 1 *nurse* with RN license at $2000–$4000 per season.

Benefits On-the-job training, athletic membership at Jewish Community Center, pre-employment training. Off-site boarding costs are $700 per month.

Contact Karen Nusbaum, Director, Centre Camp, Department SJ, 4588 Bathurst Street, North York, Ontario, M2R 1W6 Canada; 416-636-1880, Fax 416-636-5813.

GANADAOWEH
RR#3
AYR, ONTARIO N0B 1E0

General Information Residential, day, and wilderness camping programs offering Christian education to 100 campers weekly. Established in 1959. Owned by United Church Outdoor Ministries Hamilton Conference. Affiliated with Ontario Camping Association, Canadian Camping Association, Christian Camping International- Canada. 174-acre facility located 20 miles west of Kitchener. Features: outdoor sports court; large playing field; swimming pool; lake owned by the camp on camp property; farm owned by the camp on camp property; 3 ponds.

Profile of Summer Employees Total number: 35; average age: 20; 40% male, 60% female; 10% minorities; 60% high school students; 35% college students; 2% retirees; 5% international; 95% local residents; 3% teachers. Nonsmokers only.

Employment Information Openings are from May 1 to June 25. Year-round positions also offered. Jobs available: ▶ 2 *lifeguards* with NLS or Bronze Cross at $100–$150 per week; ▶ 14 *counselors* at $100–$120 per week; ▶ 1 *program leader* at $120–$150 per week; ▶ 2 *wilderness camp leaders* with NLS or Bronze Cross at $120–$150 per week; ▶ 5 *cooks* at $100–$150 per week; ▶ 2 *maintenance staff members* at $100–$150 per week; ▶ 1 *registered nurse* at $120–$150 per week; ▶ 1 *secretarial staff member* at $100–$120 per week.

Benefits On-the-job training, formal ongoing training, on-site room and board at no charge, laundry facilities, religious training and growth. Preemployment training of 7 days is required and includes safety and accident prevention, group interaction, first-aid, leadership, camper-counselor relations, how to lead Christian education. Orientation is paid.

Contact Jennifer Forrest, Director, Ganadaoweh, Department SJ, RR 3, Ayr, Ontario, N0B 1E0 Canada; 519-632-7559, Fax 519-632-7559. Application deadline: March 1.

THE HORSE PEOPLE
RR1
WENDOVER, ONTARIO KOA 3KO

General Information Residential equestrian training center serving 60 coed students biweekly. Program emphasizes keen competition and long-term goals. Established in 1976. Owned by Bev and Wolfgang Schinke. Affiliated with American Camping Association, Canadian Camping Association, Ontario Equestrian Federation. 200-acre facility located 25 miles east of Ottawa. Features: indoor riding arena, 60' x 150', attached to a barn with viewing lounge on upper level; cross-country championship site for training and preliminary level eventing including steeplechase; 2 dressage rings, 20' x 40' and 20' x 60'; permanent hunt course; professional jump course; all cabins have showers and bathrooms; location bordered by 11-acre reserve with unlimited access to trails.

Profile of Summer Employees Total number: 20; average age: 23; 25% male, 75% female; 1% minorities; 1% high school students; 95% college students; 1% retirees; 1% international; 1% local residents. Nonsmokers only.

Employment Information Openings are from June 25 to August 19. Year-round positions also offered. Jobs available: ▶ *child counselors* with St. John's Ambulance first aid training at $75–$175 per week; ▶ *swimming staff members* with Red Cross swimming certification and St. John's Ambulance first aid training at $150–$200 per week; ▶ *extracurricular activities staff members* with St. John's Ambulance first aid training; ▶ *riding instructors* with NCCP Level I and St. John's Ambulance first aid training at $150–$300 per week. International students encouraged to apply; must obtain own visa and working papers prior to employment.

Benefits On-the-job training, formal ongoing training, on-site room and board at no charge, riding lessons for interested staff at no charge, laundry service, health insurance only for Canadians. Preemployment training of 7 days is required and includes safety and accident prevention, group interaction, leadership. Orientation is unpaid.

Contact Bev Schinke, The Horse People, Department SJ, RR 1, Wendover, Ontario, K0A 3K0 Canada; 613-673-5905, Fax 613-673-4787, E-mail horsefun@fox.nstn.ca. Application deadline: April 15.

THE INN AT MANITOU
77 INGRAM DRIVE, SUITE 200
TORONTO, ONTARIO M6M 2L7

General Information Tennis and spa resort. Established in 1974. Owned by Ben Wise. Affiliated with Relais and Chateaux. 500-acre facility located 150 miles north of Toronto. Features: 13 tennis courts (4 clay and 1 indoor); full spa facility (massages, athletics, fitness and exercise classes, and equipped gym); full waterfront facility (sailing, canoeing, windsurfing, and fishing); outdoor heated pool; bar and lounges; golf teaching facility; driving range; putting green.

Profile of Summer Employees Total number: 60; average age: 25; 50% male, 50% female. Nonsmokers preferred.

Employment Information Openings are from May 10 to October 20. Jobs available: ▶ *bartenders* at $4000–$6000 per season; ▶ *waiters;* ▶ *masseuses;* ▶ *estheticians;* ▶ *boat person/porter;* ▶ *grounds person/porter;* ▶ *aerobics instructor;* ▶ *tennis pros.* International students encouraged to apply.

Benefits On-the-job training, formal ongoing training, on-site room and board.

Contact Ben Wise, Owner/Manager, The Inn at Manitou, 77 Ingram Drive, Suite 200, Toronto, Ontario, M6M 2L7 Canada; 416-245-5606, Fax 416-245-2460, URL http://manitou-online.com.

KITCHIKEWANA
HONEY HARBOUR, ONTARIO POE 1E0

General Information YMCA Outdoor Education Center serving more than 750 school-age students during spring and fall sessions. Established in 1919. Owned by YMCA of Midland. Affiliated with Midland Family YMCA, Ontario Camping Association, Canadian Camping Association. 15-acre facility located 50 miles north of Barrie. Features: extensive freshwater lake frontage; expansive beachfront and sandy soil base; large dining hall bordered by 2 spacious lodges; 18 camper cabins (10-14 bunks); located on Beausdeil Island in GBI National Park.

Profile of Summer Employees Total number: 64; average age: 20; 40% male, 60% female; 3% minorities; 60% high school students; 35% college students; 7% local residents; 1% teachers. Nonsmokers only.

Employment Information Openings are from May 1 to August 30. Jobs available: ▶ *counselors* (male) with NLS *(National Lifesaving Award)*, standard first aid (minimum of Red Cross leaders), level C CPR, and instructor certification at $120 per week; ▶ *counselors* (female) with NLS, standard first aid, level C CPR, and instructor certification at $120 per week; ▶ *prep cook* with Level C CPR and standard first aid certification at $200 per week; ▶ *head cook* with Level C CPR and standard first aid certification at $250 per week; ▶ *food service manager* with Level C CPR, standard first aid certification, and chef's papers at $300 per week; ▶ *office administrator* with NLS, standard first aid, Level C CPR, and instructor certification at $220 per week; ▶ *leadership director* with NLS, standard first aid, level C CPR, and instructor certification at $220 per week. International students encouraged to apply; must obtain own visa and working papers prior to employment.

Benefits On-the-job training, on-site room and board at no charge, laundry facilities. Preemployment training of 7 days is required and includes safety and accident prevention, group interaction, CPR, leadership. Orientation is paid.

Contact Greg MacQuarrie, Camp Director, Kitchikewana, Department SJ, Little Lake Park, PO Box 488, Midland, Ontario, L4R 4L3 Canada; 705-527-6649. Application deadline: December 1.

MANITOU-WABING SPORTS AND ARTS CENTRE
MCKELLAR, ONTARIO POG 1CO

General Information Residential camp for boys and girls ages 8 to 17 offering professional instruction and training in sports and arts. Established in 1959. Owned by Ben Wise. Affiliated with Ontario Camping Association. Situated on 500 acres. Features: 14 tennis courts; baseball diamond; golf driving range; indoor and outdoor basketball courts; theater and dance studios; radio station; pottery studio; sculpture studio; printmaking studio; English riding stables and trails; 3 water skiing docks; sailing dock; canoeing.

Profile of Summer Employees Total number: 125; average age: 21; 50% male, 50% female; 75% college students; 5% international; 15% teachers. Nonsmokers only.

Employment Information Openings are from June 15 to August 15. Jobs available: ▶ 100 *staff members* at $800–$3000 per season. International students encouraged to apply; must apply through recognized agency.

Benefits On-the-job training, on-site room and board.

Contact Jordanna Lipson, Camp Director, Manitou-Wabing Sports and Arts Centre, 77 Ingram Drive, Suite 200, Toronto, Ontario, M6M 2L7 Canada; 416-245-0605, Fax 416-245-6844, URL http://www.manitou-online.com. Application deadline: May 1.

NEW FRENDA YOUTH CAMP
SEVENTH-DAY ADVENTIST CHURCH RR #2
PORT CARLING, ONTARIO POB 1JO

General Information Residential camp serving over 100 children ages 8–16. Established in 1946. Affiliated with Ontario Conference Seventh Day Adventist Church. 60-acre facility located

100 miles north of Toronto. Features: 1 basketball court; 1 large soccer field; 5 miles of riding trails; extensive freshwater lake frontage; 1 large assembly hall; 5 miles of hiking trails.

Profile of Summer Employees Total number: 45; average age: 20; 50% male, 50% female; 20% minorities; 80% college students; 1% retirees; 1% teachers. Nonsmokers only.

Employment Information Openings are from June 16 to August 31. Jobs available: ▶ 4 *horsemanship staff members;* ▶ 1 *canoeing staff member;* ▶ 4 *waterskiing staff members;* ▶ 1 *windsurfing staff member;* ▶ 1 *sailing staff member;* ▶ 1 *archery staff member;* ▶ 5 *swimming staff members;* ▶ 1 *rappelling staff member;* ▶ 1 *tumbling staff member;* ▶ 1 *photography staff member;* ▶ 1 *silkscreening staff member;* ▶ 1 *radio broadcasting staff member;* ▶ 1 *glass etching staff member;* ▶ *outdoor living skills staff members;* ▶ *kitchen staff members;* ▶ *maintenance staff members.* International students encouraged to apply; must apply through recognized agency.

Benefits College credit, on-the-job training, on-site room and board at no charge, laundry facilities, tuition reimbursement.

Contact Milton Perkins, Director, New Frenda Youth Camp, 1110 King Street East, Oshawa, Ontario, L1H 7M1 Canada; 905-571-1022, Fax 905-571-5995. Application deadline: March 7.

NEW MOON
BAYSVILLE, ONTARIO P0B 1A0

General Information Residential camp serving boys and girls ages 7–16. Established in 1960. Owned by Jack Goodman. 150-acre facility located 130 miles north of Toronto. Features: 2 professional baseball diamonds; 5 tennis courts; 2 waterski power boats; extensive freshwater lake frontage; 50 canoes, 16 sailboats, 14 windsurfers; high ropes adventure.

Profile of Summer Employees Total number: 80; average age: 19; 50% male, 50% female; 70% high school students; 30% college students. Nonsmokers preferred.

Employment Information Openings are from June 20 to August 15. Jobs available: ▶ *swimming instructors* at $1000–$2500 per season; ▶ *sailing instructors* at $1000–$2500 per season; ▶ *counselors* at $1000–$2000 per season. International students encouraged to apply; must obtain own visa and working papers prior to employment.

Benefits On-the-job training, formal ongoing training, on-site room and board at no charge, laundry facilities.

Contact Personnel Director, New Moon, Department SJ, 57 Elm Ridge Drive, Toronto, Ontario, M6B 1A2 Canada; 416-787-4461, Fax 416-785-7198.

NEW STRIDES DAY CAMP
ETOBICOKE CITY HALL, 399 THE WEST MALL
ETOBICOKE, ONTARIO M9C 2Y2

General Information The Adapted-Integrated service section provides resources and transition support to individuals with disabilities; also day camp serving 105 individuals with varying special needs. Established in 1977. Owned by City of Etobicoke Parks and Recreation Services. Affiliated with Ontario Camping Association, Canadian Parks and Recreation Association, Ontario Recreation Society. 525-acre facility located west of Toronto. Features: 525-acre park; 3 tennis courts; walking trails, greenhouse; 4 sports fields, picnic sites; miniature golf, wading pool, golf center; stadium, 3 baseball diamonds, indoor pool.

Profile of Summer Employees Total number: 10; average age: 20; 20% male, 80% female; 30% high school students; 70% college students; 100% local residents. Nonsmokers preferred.

Employment Information Openings are from May 15 to August 31. Year-round positions also offered. Jobs available: ▶ 1 *community integration coordinator* at $8.95 per hour; ▶ 1 *new strides director* at $8.95 per hour; ▶ 4 *leader positions* at $6.85–$7.15 per hour.

Benefits On-the-job training. Preemployment training of 5 days is required and includes safety and accident prevention, group interaction, first-aid, CPR, leadership, behavior management, disability awareness. Orientation is paid.

Contact Lorene Bodiam, Supervisor, Adapted/Integrated Services, New Strides Day Camp,

Department SJ, 399 The West Mall, Etobicoke, Ontario, M9C 2Y2 Canada; 416-394-8533. Application deadline: March 1.

PEARCE-WILLIAMS CHRISTIAN CENTRE
RR#1
FINGAL, ONTARIO NOL 1KO

General Information Residential camp serving 75 campers per week with general activities. Established in 1960. Owned by United Church of Canada. Affiliated with Ontario Camping Association, National Camping Committee- United Church of Canada. 195-acre facility located 25 miles west of London. Features: 195 acres of rolling hills, woods, and playing fields; well-maintained modest setting; convenient southwestern Ontario location.

Profile of Summer Employees Total number: 40; average age: 17; 30% male, 70% female; 95% high school students; 5% college students; 99% local residents. Nonsmokers only.

Employment Information Openings are from June 25 to August 17. Jobs available: ▶ *counseling staff members* (all positions) at $150–$200 per week.

Benefits On-site room and board at no charge.

Contact Don MacPherson, Coordinator, Pearce-Williams Christian Centre, Department SJ, Pearce-Williams Christian Centre RR 1, Fingal, Ontario, N0L 1K0 Canada; 519-764-2317.

YMCA JOHN ISLAND CAMP
GENERAL DELIVERY
SPANISH, ONTARIO POP 2AO

General Information Residential camp for 150 participants ages 6–16 with spring and fall outdoor center. Established in 1954. Operated by YMCA. Affiliated with Ontario Camping Association, International Camping Fellowship, YMCA. 275-acre facility located 80 miles west of Sudbury. Features: location on island on Lake Huron; site of ghost town; 10 miles of lake frontage.

Profile of Summer Employees Total number: 65; average age: 24; 50% male, 50% female; 50% minorities; 50% high school students; 30% college students; 10% retirees; 5% international; 60% local residents; 20% teachers. Nonsmokers only.

Employment Information Openings are from May 1 to October 31. Year-round positions also offered. Jobs available: ▶ 25 *counselors* with lifeguard training at $200–$300 per week; ▶ 4 *leadership staff members* with lifeguard training at $200–$300 per week; ▶ 5 *maintenance staff members* with CPR certification at $300–$400 per week; ▶ *kitchen staff members* at $300–$400 per week. International students encouraged to apply; must obtain own visa and working papers prior to employment.

Benefits On-the-job training, formal ongoing training, on-site room and board at no charge, laundry facilities.

Contact David R. Ward, Director, YMCA John Island Camp, Department SJ, 185 Lloyd Street, Sudbury, Ontario, P3B 1N1 Canada; 705-674-8315, Fax 705-688-0751, E-mail daveward@mcd.on.ca.

QUEBEC

CAMP NOMININGUE
LAC NOMININGUE, QUEBEC JOW 1RO

General Information Residential camp for 220 boys ages 7–15 providing a place to cultivate friendships, self-confidence, and a sense of achievement. Established in 1925. Owned by Peter F.

Van Wagner. Affiliated with Ontario Camping Association, Quebec Camping Association, Canadian Camping Association. 400-acre facility located 120 miles north of Montreal. Features: 1 mile of extensive freshwater lake frontage; proximity to excellent wilderness canoe-tripping country; 4 outdoor tennis courts; many sports fields and mixed woods for games; extensive and varied equipment for all sports, including a fleet of 100 canoes, kayaks, rowboats, sail boats, and sail boards; fully equipped woodworking shop.

Profile of Summer Employees Total number: 100; average age: 21; 99% male, 1% female; 15% minorities; 10% high school students; 70% college students; 1% retirees; 80% local residents; 10% teachers. Nonsmokers preferred.

Employment Information Openings are from June 24 to August 25. Jobs available: ▶ *windsurfing instructors* at $200 per week; ▶ *sailing instructors* at $200 per week; ▶ *woodworking instructors* at $200 per week; ▶ *nature awareness instructors* at $200 per week.

Benefits On-the-job training, formal ongoing training, on-site room and board at $135 per week, opportunity to learn new skills, use of camp equipment, opportunity to lead wilderness canoe trips. Preemployment training of 5 days is required and includes safety and accident prevention, group interaction, first-aid, leadership, camper-counselor relations, canoe tripping. Orientation is paid.

Contact Shannon Van Wagner, Executive Director, Camp Nominingue, 119 Guy, Vaudreuil, Quebec, J7V 8B1 Canada; 514-455-4447, Fax 514-455-7062, E-mail camp@axess.com, URL http://www.nominigue.com.

OUAREAU
2494 RTE. 125 SOUTH
ST. DONAT, QUEBEC J0T 2C0

General Information Residential camp serving 106 girls, half of whom are French, half English. We run two days in French and then two days in English, on rotation. Activities include language classes, sailing, windsurfing, canoeing, kayaking, swimming, tennis, archery, crafts, drama, and an obstacle course. Established in 1922. Owned by Madeline Allen. Affiliated with Ontario Camping Association, Quebec Camping Association, Canadian Camping Association. Situated on 14 acres. Features: large freshwater lake; log buildings; climbing wall.

Profile of Summer Employees Total number: 40; average age: 21; 2% male, 98% female; 10% minorities; 10% high school students; 90% college students; 5% international; 5% local residents; 25% teachers. Nonsmokers preferred.

Employment Information Openings are from June 22 to August 27. Jobs available: ▶ 8 *general counselors* with Bronze Cross and working knowledge of French at $900–$1100 per season; ▶ 6 *assistant activity heads and counselors* with NLS training for water sports and working knowledge of French for land and water sports at $1100–$1260 per season; ▶ 9 *heads of activity and counselors* with NLS training for water sports and working knowledge of French for land and water sports at $1300–$1800 per season; ▶ 2 *nurses or assistant nurses* with nursing qualifications and working knowledge of French at $1800–$2400 per season. International students encouraged to apply; must obtain own visa and working papers prior to employment; must apply through recognized agency.

Benefits On-the-job training, on-site room and board at no charge, pre-employment training.

Contact Jacqui Raill, Director, Ouareau, Department SJ, 2494 Rte. 125 Sud, St. Donat, Quebec, J0T 2C0 Canada; 819-424-2662, Fax 819-424-4145, E-mail ouareau@login.net./inverc, URL http://www.login.net/inverc. Application deadline: April 1.

CATEGORY INDEX

Camps–Horsemanship

Camps–Learning Disabilities

Camps–Outdoor Adventure and Travel

Camps–Performing and Fine Arts

Camps–Special Needs

Camps–Sports

Camps–Visual Impairments

Conference Centers

Conservation and Environmental Programs

Resorts *(Also see* **State and National Parks** and **Ranches.**)

Sports Touring Program

State and National Parks

(Commercially operated visitor services in State and National Parks including resorts, restaurants, concessions, transportation, etc.)

Theaters/Summer Theaters

*(Includes acting and technical/
auxiliary staff opportunities.)*

**Theme and Amusement Parks/
Attractions** *(Includes local
historic sites and attractions.)*

Volunteer Programs

Yacht Clubs/Sailing

EMPLOYER INDEX

JOB TITLES INDEX